THE ROLLING STONE
JAZZ RECORD GUIDE

THE Rolling Stone® JAZZ RECORD GUIDE

Edited by John Swenson

RollingStone.

A Random House/Rolling Stone Press Book/New York

Copyright © 1979, 1985 by Rolling Stone Press

All rights reserved under International and Pan-American Copyright
Conventions. Published in the United States by Random House, Inc.,
New York, and simultaneously in Canada by Random House of
Canada Limited, Toronto. Parts of this work appeared originally in the
Rolling Stone Record Guide, Random House, Inc., New York, 1979.

Library of Congress Cataloging in Publication Data

Swenson, John.
The Rolling stone jazz record guide.

"A Random House/Rolling Stone Press Book."
1. Jazz music—Discography. 2. Sound recordings—
Reviews. I. Title.
ML156.4.J3S9 1985   789.9′136542   84-42510
ISBN 0-394-72643-X

Manufactured in the United States of America
Typography by J. K. Lambert
4689753

Foreword

The first record I ever bought was a copy of *Body and Soul,* a twelve-inch record by Chu Berry and his Jazz Ensemble. I remember that it had the soon-to-be-familiar red Commodore label and I bought it at the Commodore Music Shop on Forty-second Street. I believe that was before they opened their store on Fifty-second Street; certainly it was before I even owned a phonograph on which to play it.

I don't remember precisely why I bought that particular record, but it was a lucky choice. The trumpet player was Roy Eldridge, who was the perfect bridge from Louis Armstrong to Dizzy Gillespie. In those days records were few and far between and money to buy them extremely limited. Naturally, those records we *did* buy got played—and I mean over and over until they turned gray and the grooves broke down. Anyone who couldn't sing along with the trumpet solos or saxophone section riffs was just not listening hard enough!

But in those days, live jazz was easily available on the radio; in retrospect, I realize how lucky we were. We could hear Don Redman, Erskine Hawkins, Chick Webb and many lesser bands broadcasting on location from nightclubs and hotel ballrooms. The trick was to figure out that George Hall broadcasting from the Taft Hotel in New York or Freddie Martin from any one of a number of hotels around the country were not cut from the same cloth as Cab Calloway or Claude Hopkins or Jimmie Lunceford, all of whom could be heard frequently on radio broadcasts.

More time was needed for the realization to dawn that there were even greater bands out there and that their greatness depended in large part on the men (never women in those days) who actually played instruments.

It was about this time that Hughes Panassie's *Hot Jazz* and Charles Delaunay's *Hot Discography* became available and then, in 1939, *Jazzmen* by Fred Ramsey and Charles Edward Smith. They became as essential to jazz fans as the *Racing Form* is to racing fans. They made available, for the first time, past-performance charts of the great jazz stars. They were the only game in town, and they were essential reading for any jazz fan.

This *Rolling Stone Jazz Record Guide* should serve much the same purpose today for anyone trying to play catch-up while assembling a jazz library of a definitive nature. It saddens me to realize how many great records from the past are out of print. Yet there remain encouraging signs that many may be made available once more. At the same time, there are great records being recorded right now, and it's helpful to have some guidance as to which ones are worth spending hard-earned money on.

I could quarrel with some inclusions herein and, more importantly, some exclusions. But on the whole the truly great innovators all receive the plaudits they so well deserve, and all are well represented on records currently available. Frequently, unavailable records are mentioned in the text so as to alert the reader to the possibility of further search for rare items. This is important if anyone wishes, as I do, for example, to own every record John Coltrane ever played on.

Furthermore, it's obvious that all the contributors to the *Jazz Record Guide* truly love the music. That's the absolutely essential ingredient that makes this a first-rate resource book.

Jean R. Gleason
Spring 1985

Preface

Jazz is a vital piece of American history —*the* indigenous American music—but nowadays it is too often viewed as a rarefied special interest, especially by the recording industry. A musician friend recently shopped around an excellent demo tape to various record companies. One savvy executive liked what he heard but cautioned, "If you want to make the record, don't call this jazz."

But as rock music has moved further into the realm of fashionmongering, shortsightedly attempting to become soundtrack music for video, it has abandoned an audience that once looked to it for qualities of emotional commitment and what generally can be called soul. Now these listeners have turned in even greater numbers to jazz, a music that has championed the essence of soul throughout its existence. It is a music of substance and passion, rewarding creativity, personal vision, and precocious talent, not just the product of a demographically astute entertainment industry process. You probably won't have to worry ten years from now why you ever wanted to listen to the jazz records you buy next week.

Because jazz is an omnibus term, encompassing styles as disparate as Dixieland and the farthest reaches of synthesizer experimentation, it has long been a battleground for critics and fans of various forms. Even musicians themselves have been embroiled in the controversy, one generation pitted against another. By now, with virtually every musical barrier breached, innovation has become a new way of saying something familiar rather than a challenge to existing styles. Enough time has elapsed for the generic jazz rivalries to dissipate and for each style and each era—Dixieland, big band, bop, soul-jazz, cool, Third Stream, electronics, funk, fusion—to be considered on its own merits and as part of a greater whole. The main purpose of this book is to articulate these different interests.

We have resisted the temptation to promote particular styles or to carve out a critical niche to defend. Instead, we have tried to cover the broadest possible range of musicians, appealing to a spectrum of tastes, from a number of different critical perspectives. No doubt there have been omissions, for no compendium can be exhaustive, and there may be some surprises here as well. In reviewing the relative merits of such a large body of recordings, we have discovered more than a few gifted musicians who have been unjustly ignored or underrated. A few other overpromoted talents have been cut down to size. Naturally, many will find cause for disagreement as well as confirmation of long-held beliefs. We may be opinionated but we're not infallible.

Records have been rated from one to five stars, a system carried over from the original *Rolling Stone Record Guide,* which jazz fans may also find familiar from *Downbeat* reviews. (One star is the least favorable rating, and five stars the most enthusiastic.) The ratings inevitably represent the particular bias of each reviewer. In some cases there are apparent inequities: If a John Klemmer album gets a higher rating than a Louis Armstrong album, it certainly doesn't mean that Klemmer's better. The ratings reflect the reviewer's opinion of the relative merits of an artist's work over a career. A three-star record from a marginal player is probably not as good as a three-star record from a genius.

Veteran collectors will find this book a reference point for the delicious pastime of comparing notes and arguing critical points. New listeners will find it an annotated map, to guide them through the morass of records on the market. Those just beginning to assemble jazz collections might begin with the major mail-order catalogues. Now that the landmark Time-Life jazz series has gone out of print, the best two are the Mosaic and Smithsonian collections. The Mosaic sets are particularly good on some elusive Blue Note recordings, collecting in separate volumes the complete work of Clifford Brown, Thelonious Monk and Albert Ammons/Meade Lux Lewis for that label. Write to Mosaic at 197 Strawberry Hill Avenue, Stamford, Connecticut 06902.

The Smithsonian records are some of the best collections ever put together, superbly annotated and with a keen historic overview in the material selected. The Louis Armstrong and Earl Hines, Armstrong and Sidney Bechet, Dizzy Gillespie, Fletcher Henderson, Teddy Wilson, Art Tatum, King Oliver, Red Allen and Coleman Hawkins and the John Kirby sets are all worth having, but can't be bought in stores. They are available by mail only from Smithsonian, Box 10230, Des Moines, Iowa 50336.

In listing the releases, we have tried to concentrate on records generally available in the United States, though we have included a number of import records that do not duplicate material already available domestically. We have relied on a variety of sources: the Schwann and Phonolog catalogues, the invaluable Daybreak Express catalogue, the New Music Distribution Service publication and the lists from a number of individual record companies, as well as our own research. The Daybreak Express catalogue is the most complete and reliable access to jazz records in the United States. It can be obtained by writing to P.O. Box 250, Van Brunt Station, Brooklyn, New York 11215. The New Music Distribution Service catalogue specializes in contemporary jazz and is a particularly useful guide to new and challenging artists. Brief descriptions of the records make your selections that much easier. That address is 500 Broadway, New York, New York 10012.

We've had considerable difficulty with companies changing the catalogue numbers of certain records, and with numerous repackagings and rereleases that sometimes confuse information about the music included. To avoid this difficulty, we've tried to identify records solely by titles. Since release dates are also at great variance to the time when the records were actually made, album dates and chronology are treated in the reviews themselves where that information is appropriate. Consequently the albums are arranged alphabetically.

The most frustrating problem we encountered was the maddeningly transitory nature of jazz releases. Many of the records that were in print as we prepared the book are now cutouts, which can't be ordered but mysteriously flood the record stores at budget prices. The situation with the Blue Note label offers a dramatic example of the difficulties of tracking titles. When we started to assemble the book, Blue Note was involved in an extensive reissue project, but the records were disappearing almost as fast as they were being released. Eventually there were, for all practical purposes, no domestically available Blue Note recordings. There were facsimile copies of original Blue Note LPs available as Japanese imports. Although at first these were difficult to obtain and priced at prohibitively high rates, the fluctuating value of the dollar eventually made them bargains. Major record stores began carrying the Japanese Blue Notes in bulk. Now, however, Blue Note is embarking on another domestic reissue program, so the Japanese facsimile records have lost their impact. It may seem absurd that availability of major jazz records can be tied to the monetary exchange rate, but that's exactly what happened to one of the most important jazz catalogues in history.

One happy exception to this trend is Fantasy/Prestige/Milestone records, a company with tremendous commitment to keeping valuable records in print and reissuing important records from the past. In particular, the Prestige Original Jazz Classics series, budget LPs reissued with original cover artwork and liner notes, is worthy of note.

Still, in some cases we were unable to cover artists of considerable merit because their records are either not in print or simply aren't available. This is especially true of people who recorded before 1950, though some of the most innovative contemporary players also fall into this category. When you take into account the haphazard way major labels keep repackaging their catalogues and the precarious financial position of the smaller companies, the inevitable realization is that jazz and its public are mightily discriminated against. If this project can help to counteract that trend it will have been worthwhile.

A book like this has never been attempted before. We are proud to have produced the first comprehensive jazz record guide. We hope it will be a significant contribution toward the wider appreciation of jazz by the public and the greater respect owed to the music by the recording industry it helped build.

Without some sacrifice and a lot of enthusiasm on a number of people's parts, this book would not have been possible. Dave Marsh, my co-editor on *The Rolling Stone Record Guide,* vigorously promoted the idea of an offshoot jazz volume. Rob Cowley, our editor at Random House, has backed us with unusual support and attention. Rob's guidance and advice have definitely left a distinctive stamp on the project. Nancy Inglis and Sam Flores, our copy editors at Random House, have been stalwart aids throughout. Sarah Lazin at Rolling Stone Press went out of her way to ensure that the idea got off the ground. Steve Futterman offered tireless fact-checking and valuable editorial advice at several crucial stages. Bob Blumenthal has offered generous support since the time when the project was only part of the original *Rolling Stone Record Guide.*

A number of other people helped out in large and small ways. Thanks to Elisa Petrini, Ruth Singleton, Carrie Schneider, Patty Romanowski, Mary Astadourian, Janis Bultman, Sharon Gude, Tom Tintle, Dan Doyle, Tom Cooley, Jimmy Eigo, Andy Doherty, Tom Ligamari, Barbara Mathe, Philippa Rendle, Tower Records, Teri Hinte, Joe Fields, John Koenig, Arthur Levy, Lynn Kellerman, Andy McKaie, Maureen O'Connor, Marguerite Renz, Elliot Horne, radio stations WKCR and WBGO, and finally, to the late Ralph J. Gleason—whose wife has kindly provided a foreword to this book—for his inspiration.

John Swenson
Spring 1985

Ratings

★ ★ ★ ★ ★

Indispensable: a record that must be included in
any comprehensive collection.

★ ★ ★ ★

Excellent: a record of substantial merit, though flawed
in some essential way.

★ ★ ★

Good: a record of average worth, but one that might possess considerable
appeal for fans of a particular style.

★ ★

Mediocre: records that are artistically insubstantial,
though not truly wretched.

★

Poor: records in which even technical competence is at question,
or which are remarkably ill-conceived.

Contributors

EDITOR

John Swenson (J.S.) has written and edited over a dozen books and worked on a variety of magazines and newspapers. Swenson has written about jazz for *Saturday Review, Rolling Stone, Crawdaddy,* the *Village Voice* and other publications.

Bob Blumenthal (B.B.) is a Massachusetts attorney who writes about jazz for the *Boston Phoenix, Rolling Stone, Downbeat* and *Musician.* He was one of six commissioners named by the Record Industry Association of America to select the Carter White House record library.

Jean Charles Costa (J.C.C.) is a guitarist who was editor of the music publication *Gig.*

Steve Futterman (S.F.) has written about jazz for *Rolling Stone,* the *Village Voice, High Fidelity, Musician* and the *Record,* and has contributed to the *Rolling Stone Encyclopedia of Rock & Roll* and the *Rolling Stone Rock Almanac.*

Russell Gersten (R.G.) works in educational research in the Pacific Northwest and has been writing about music for more than a decade.

Mikal Gilmore (M.G.) is a contributing editor at *Rolling Stone* and music editor at *L.A. Weekly.*

Alan E. Goodman (A.E.G.) has written extensively about jazz for *Crawdaddy* and worked as a disc jockey at radio station WKCR.

Fred Goodman (F.G.) is an editor at *Billboard* who's written about jazz for the *New York Post* and *Cashbox.*

Stephen Holden (S.H.) writes for the *New York Times* and *Rolling Stone* and is the author of a novel about the music business, *Triple Platinum.*

Ashley Kahn (A.K.) has written for the *Record* and *Musician* and is currently a disc jockey at Columbia University's radio station WKCR.

Bruce Malamut (B.M.) has written about music for *Rolling Stone, Crawdaddy, Circus* and the *Village Voice.* He is currently reviews editor for *Guitar World.*

Joe McEwen (J.Mc.) was once known to Boston radio listeners as the disc jockey Mr. C. He has written under both names for the *Boston Phoenix, Real Paper,* the *Village Voice* and *Rolling Stone.* McEwen is currently an A&R man at Columbia Records.

Michael Rozek (M.R.) has written for *Rolling Stone, Texas Monthly, Omni, Cosmopolitan* and other publications.

Andy Rowan (A.R.) is a freelance writer who lives in New York City.

Bart Testa (B.T.) teaches film studies at Innis College, University of Toronto. He is the jazz critic for *McLean's* magazine and contributes to the *Globe and Mail, Canadian Forum* and *Toronto Life.*

Charley Walters (C.W.) manages a record store on Nantucket Island, where he lives year round.

Record Label Abbreviations

A&M
ABC
About Time (**About T.**)
Accord (**Acc.**)
Adelphi (**Adel.**)
Advent
Affinity (**Aff.**)
Aircheck (**Air.**)
Alligator (**Alli.**)
American Clave (**Amer. C.**)
Andrew's Music (**Andr.**)
Angelaco
Anima
Antilles (**Ant.**)
Archive of Folk and Jazz
　Music (**Arc. Folk**)
Argo
Arhoolie (**Arhoo.**)
Arista (**Ari.**)
Arista/Freedom (**Ari./**
　Free.)
Arista/GRP (**Ari./GRP**)
Arista/Novus (**Ari./No.**)
Artists House (**Artists H.**)
Ascent
Atco
Atlantic (**Atl.**)
Audio Fidelity (**Audio Fi.**)
Audio Masterworks (**Audio**
　M.)
Audiophile (**Audiop.**)
Au Roar

Bainbridge (**Bain.**)
Barnaby (**Barn.**)
Base
Bee Hive (**Bee**)
Bent
Bet-Car
Bethlehem (**Beth.**)
Big City Records
Bija
Biograph (**Bio.**)
Birdseye (**Bird.**)

Birth
Bisharra
Black Lion (**Black L.**)
Black Saint (**Black S.**)
Bluebird (**Blueb.**)
Blue Goose (**Blue G.**)
Blue Note (**Blue N.**)
Blue Note/PolyGram Spe-
　cial Imports (**Blue N./**
　PSI)
Brunswick (**Bruns.**)
Buddha (**Bud.**)
Buena Vista (**Buena**)

Cadet
Camden (**Camd.**)
Candid
Capitol (**Cap.**)
Capricorn (**Capri.**)
Carousel (**Car.**)
Casablanca (**Casa.**)
Catalyst (**Cata.**)
CBS
CCJ
Century (**Cen.**)
Charlie Parker Records/
　Audio Fidelity (**Charlie**
　Parker Rec./Audio Fi.)
Chess
Chiaroscuro (**Chi.**)
Chi-Sound (**Chi-S.**)
Choice
Classic Jazz (**Class.**)
Columbia (**Col.**)
Columbia Special Products
　(**CSP**)
Commodore (**Commo.**)
Concept
Concept/Sonet
Concord (**Conc.**)
Concord Concerto (**Conc.**
　C.)
Concord Jazz (**Conc. J.**)
Concord Picante (**Conc. P.**)

Contemporary (**Contem.**)
Corn Pride (**Corn P.**)
Crusaders Records (**Crus.**)
Crystal Clear (**Crys. C.**)
CTI

Daagnim
Daffodil (**Daf.**)
Debut/Fantasy (**Debut/**
　Fan.)
Delmark (**Del.**)
Different Drummer (**Dif.**
　Drum.)
Discovery (**Discov.**)
DJM
Dobre
Doctor Jazz (**Doctor J.**)
Dooto (**Doo.**)
Dot
Douglas (**Doug.**)
DRG

East Coasting
Eastworld/PolyGram Spe-
　cial Imports (**East./PSI**)
ECM/Warner Bros.
　(**ECM/War.**)
ECM/PolyGram Special
　Imports (**ECM/PSI**)
Ekapa
Elektra (**Elek.**)
Elektra/Musician (**Elek./**
　Mus.)
E/Leo
Emanem (**Eman.**)
EmArcy (**Em.**)
Embryo
Emily
Empire (**Emp.**)
Enja
Epic
ESP Disk (**ESP**)
Euphonic (**Euphon.**)
Europa (**Eur.**)

Everest (**Ev.**)
Evergreen (**Ever.**)
Excello (**Ex.**)

Famous Door (**Fam. D.**)
Fantasy (**Fan.**)
Fantasy/Original Jazz Classics (**Fan./OJC**)
Finesse (**Fine.**)
Finnadar (**Finn.**)
Flying Dutchman (**Fly. D.**)
Flying Fish (**Fly. Fish**)
Free Music Production (**FMP**)
Folklyric
Folkways (**Folk.**)

Galaxy (**Gal.**)
Gamble (**Gam.**)
Gatemouth (**Gatem.**)
GHB
Glendale (**Glen.**)
GNP Crescendo (**GNP**)
Golden Crest (**Gold. C.**)
Good Time Jazz (**Good T.**)
Gramavision (**Gram.**)
Groove Merchant (**G.M.**)
GRT
Gryphon (**Gry.**)

Halcyon (**Hal.**)
Hall of Fame (**Hall**)
Hat Hut
Headfirst (**Head.**)
Herwin (**Her.**)
Hidden Meaning (**Hidden M.**)
Horizon (**Hori.**)

IAI
Ictus
Improv
Impulse (**Imp.**)
India Navigation (**In. Nav.**)
Inner City (**Inner**)
Institute of Percussive Studies (**IPS**)
Interplay (**Interp.**)
Invictus (**Inv.**)
Island (**Is.**)
ITI Records (**ITI**)

JAM
JAPO Records/PolyGram Special Imports (**JAPO/ PSI**)
Jasmine
Jazz à la Carte
Jazz Anthology
Jazz Classics (**Jazz Cl.**)

Jazzland (**Jazzl.**)
Jazz Man (**Jazz M.**)
Jazzology (**Jazzo.**)
Jazz Records (**Jazz R.**)
Jazz Workshop (**Jazz Work.**)
Jazz Workshop/Fantasy (**Jazz Work./Fan.**)
Jazzz
JCOA
John Hammond Records/ Columbia (**JHR/Col.**)

Kabell Records
Kayvette (**Kayv.**)
Kent
King
Kudu

Labor
Land o' Jazz (**Land**)
Landslide (**Landsl.**)
Legacy (**Leg.**)
Liberty (**Lib.**)
Limelight (**Lime.**)
Little David (**Li. Dav.**)
London (**Lon.**)
Lovely Music (**Lovely M.**)

Magpie (**Mag.**)
Mainstream (**Main.**)
Marlin (**Mar.**)
Master Jazz (**Mas. J.**)
MCA
MCA/Impulse (**MCA/Imp.**)
Mercury (**Mer.**)
Milestone (**Mile.**)
Modern Jazz (**Mod. J.**)
Moers Music (**Moers**)
Monmouth (**Mon.**)
Monmouth-Evergreen (**Mon.-Ev.**)
Mosaic
Motown (**Mo.**)
Muse
Musician (**Mus.**)
Musicraft

Nashboro (**Nashb.**)
Nautilus (**Naut.**)
Nemperor (**Nemp.**)
Nemperor/Atlantic (**Nemp. /Atl.**)
Nessa
New Artists
New World (**New W.**)
Nimbus (**Nim.**)

Oblivion (**Obliv.**)
Ode

Odyssey (**Odys.**)
OJC
Oldie Blues (**Oldie B.**)
Olympic (University of Washington) (**Olym.**)
Omnisound (**Omni.**)
Omnisound Jazz (**Omni. Jazz**)
Onyx
Opus One (**Op. One**)
Original Jazz Library (**Orig. Jazz**)
Osmosis (**Osm.**)
Ovation (**Ova.**)

Pablo
Pablo Live (**Pablo L.**)
Pablo Today (**Pablo T.**)
Pacific Jazz (**Pac. J.**)
Palo Alto Jazz (**Palo Alto**)
Paula
Pausa
PBR International (**PBR**)
Personal Choice (**Pers.**)
Philips (**Phi.**)
Philly Groove (**Philly**)
Philly Jazz
Phoenix (**Phoen.**)
Piccadilly (**Picca.**)
Pickwick (**Pick.**)
Plainisphere (**Plain.**)
PM
Polydor (**Poly.**)
PolyGram (**Polygr.**)
PolyGram Special Imports (**PSI**)
Press Prestige (**Prest.**)
Prestige Original Jazz Classics (**Prest. OJC**)
Progressive (**Prog.**)
P.T.

QED
Quintessence (**Quin.**)
Qwest/Warner Bros. (**Qwest/War.**)

Ra Records (**Ra**)
Ranwood (**Ran.**)
RCA
RCA International
RealTime (**Real.**)
Red Records (**Red R.**)
Reprise (**Rep.**)
Revelation (**Rev.**)
Riverside (**Riv.**)
Roulette (**Rou.**)
Rounder (**Roun.**)

Sackville (**Sack.**)
Saga
Sandra
Sandy Hook
Savoy
1750 Arch
Silveto
Smithsonian
Solid State (**Solid St.**)
Sonet
Soul Note (**Soul N.**)
Spotlite (**Spot.**)
Springboard (**Sp.**)
Stanyan (**Stan.**)
Starday (**Star.**)
Stash
SteepleChase (**Steep.**)
Stinson (**Stin.**)
Storyville (**Story.**)
Strata-East
Studio 7

Swaggie (**Swag.**)
Sweet Earth

Tappan Zee (**Tap.**)
Telarc
Theresa (**Ther.**)
360 Records (**360 Rec.**)
Tico
Timeless (**Timel.**)
Tomato (**Toma.**)
Tradition (**Trad.**)
Trend
Trip
Twentieth Century-Fox
 (**Twentieth C.**)
Two Flats Disc (**Two Fl.**)

Umbrella (**Umb.**)
Unit Core
United Artists (**UA**)

Up Front (**Up Fr.**)
Uptown

Vanguard (**Van.**)
Verve
Vocalion (**Voc.**)
Vogue

Warner Bros. (**War.**)
Watt
Watt/ECM
West
West 54
Who's Who in Jazz (**Who**)
Windham Hill (**Wind. H.**)
World Jazz (**World**)

Xanadu (**Xan.**)

Ze/Island
Zim

THE ROLLING STONE
JAZZ RECORD GUIDE

JOHN ABERCROMBIE

★ ★ ★ **Abercrombie Quartet / ECM/War.**
★ ★ ★ **Arcade / ECM/War.**
★ ★ ★ ★ **Characters / ECM/War.**
★ ★ ★ ★ **Five Years Later (with Ralph Towner) / ECM/War.**
★ ★ ★ **Friends / Obliv.**
★ ★ ★ **Gateway / ECM/War.**
★ ★ ★ **M / ECM/War.**
★ ★ ★ **Night / ECM/War.**
★ ★ ★ ★ **Sargasso Sea (with Ralph Towner) / ECM/War.**
★ ★ ★ ★ **Timeless / ECM/War.**

The incredible range and technique of John Abercrombie (b. 1944) make him one of the finest electric guitarists currently recording and one of the most sought-after session players for challenging new material. A founding member of Dreams, he worked as a sideman with Chico Hamilton, Barry Miles, Gil Evans and Jack DeJohnette, and in 1972 he collaborated on a remarkable quartet record, *Friends,* with saxophonist Mark Cohen, bassist Clint Houston and drummer Jeff Williams. Abercrombie's playing on that session is a perfect illustration of the bridge between jazz and rock guitar technique.

Timeless, Abercrombie's first solo effort for ECM, was recorded in 1974 with DeJohnette on drums and Jan Hammer on organ, synthesizer and piano. Hammer, especially, plays with astounding fire and grace on this session, some of the finest organ playing he's recorded. *Gateway,* recorded in 1975 with DeJohnette and bassist David Holland, is more serene and uses subtler electronic effects from Abercrombie's guitar. *Sargasso Sea* is a 1976 duet with Oregon's virtuoso guitarist Ralph Towner. The alternately pensive and vibrant electric/acoustic interplay between these two master guitarists makes this a classic album of guitar duets.

Abercrombie Quartet and *Arcade* feature his late-Seventies unit of pianist Richard Beirach, bassist George Mraz and drummer Peter Donald. *Characters* is a tremendous solo display of Abercrombie's acoustic/ electric guitar and mandolin playing. *Five Years Later* reunites Abercrombie and Towner for another album of spectacular duets. — J.S.

MUHAL RICHARD ABRAMS

★ ★ ★ **Levels and Degrees of Light / Del.**
★ ★ ★ ★ **Sightsong / Black S.**
★ ★ ★ **Things to Come from Those Now Gone / Del.**
★ ★ ★ ★ **Young at Heart/Wise in Time / Del.**

Throughout the Fifties, Richard Abrams (b. 1930) was one of Chicago's most sought-after local pianists when visiting jazz stars needed support. With the formation of his Experimental Band in 1961 and the Association for the Advancement of Creative Musicians (AACM) in 1965, Abrams (who began calling himself Muhal at the decade's end) led many young Chicago players into a new phase of avant-garde expression that stressed a thorough knowledge of black music tradition and an endless series of new formats.

Abrams' albums all have powerful and exciting moments, but leave the overriding impression that we have only heard a portion of the man's musical universe. *Levels and Degrees of Light* features an intriguing first side with wordless vocal and several AACM mainstays (Anthony Braxton, Maurice McIntyre), but falls apart in the poorly recorded wall of sound that covers side two. *Young at Heart/Wise in Time* is better, with a long example of Abrams' reflective piano and a tighter group performance by an excellent AACM quintet (Leo Smith, Henry Threadgill, Abrams, Lester Lashley, Thurman Barker).

Things to Come from Those Now Gone captures Abrams and the AACM in the middle of this decade running the gamut between chamber ballads, hard bop, electronics, mock opera and high energy. Fascinating, but too many bits and pieces. *Sightsong* is a more successful survey from 1975, with Art Ensemble bassist Malachi Favors along to help Abrams explore the AACM's roots.

★ ★ ★ ★ **Afrisong** / **In. Nav.**
★ ★ ★ ★ ★ **Blues Forever** / **Black S.**
★ ★ ★ ★ **Duet (with Amina Claudine Myers)** / **Black S.**
★ ★ ★ ★ ★ **Mama and Daddy** / **Black S.**
★ ★ ★ ★ **1-OQA + 19** / **Black S.**
★ ★ **Spihumonesty** / **Black S.**

Abrams' recording activity picked up noticeably from the end of 1977, which is not to say that his albums will be easy to find. The two 1978 sessions on Arista/Novus are already out of print, and the Black Saints are Italian imports. By all means look for the Black Saints, for this inconsistent musician has made his best records for that label.

The constant shifting of instrumental situations and emotional attitudes haven't always worked in Abrams' music; sometimes, as on the synthesizer- and voice-laden *Spihumonesty,* what should be a good band doesn't come up with much. But Abrams the small-group leader has never sounded better than on the numerologically titled *1-OQA + 19,* where Anthony Braxton and Henry Threadgill are the saxophonists and Steve McCall is on drums. His finest achievement in any format may be *Mama and Daddy;* this ambitious set of compositions for a ten-piece group, with its masterful blends of brass, strings and percussion, has a balance in its glowing execution that suggests black chamber music.

The year 1982 was Abrams' most successful, at least in terms of recordings. *Duet* is a surprisingly lyrical and diverse encounter with pianist Myers while *Afrisong* contains the best of his early solo work recorded for Japanese release in 1975. Abrams' crowning achievement, however, was *Blues Forever,* a set of orchestral performances expanding on the ideas heard on *Mama and Daddy.*
— B.B.

WILLIAM ACKERMAN

★ ★ ★ **Childhood and Memory** / **Wind. H.**
★ ★ ★ **It Takes a Year** / **Wind. H.**
★ ★ ★ **Passage** / **Wind. H.**
★ ★ ★ **Past Light** / **Wind. H.**
★ ★ ★ **Search for the Turtle's Navel** / **Wind. H.**

Guitarist William Ackerman (b. 1949) formed the Windham Hill label in the Seventies after getting positive response to his solo

acoustic guitar experiments, first heard on *Turtle's Navel.* The increasingly glossy and atmospheric productions subsequently produced by Ackerman are of primary interest only to other guitarists or lovers of electronically manicured sound. On *Passage* Ackerman expanded his format to include several duet pieces, while *Past Light* employed even more elaborate settings, including a string quartet. — J.S.

GEORGE ADAMS

★ ★ ★ **Earth Beams** / **Timel.**
★ ★ ★ ★ **Life Line** / **Timel.**
★ ★ ★ ★ **Melodic Excursions** / **Timel.**
★ ★ ★ ★ **Paradise Space Shuttle** / **Timel.**
★ ★ ★ ★ **Sound Suggestions** / **ECM**

George Adams (b. 1940) has worked in various contexts from Howling Wolf and other blues players to jazz bands led by Charles Mingus, Gil Evans, Art Blakey and Roy Haynes. Though obviously influenced by John Coltrane's soul and energy as a saxophonist, Adams never makes the mistake of recycling entire phrases borrowed from Coltrane. His phrasing and timing are his own. *Sound Suggestions* is a high-powered '79 sextet session prompted by the Dave Holland (bass)/Jack DeJohnette (drums)/Richard Beirach (piano) rhythm section. The Timeless albums are collaborations with pianist Don Pullen in which Adams and Pullen contrast jumping, bluesy numbers with more experimental sounds. *Melodic Excursions* is a duet, the others are quartet (*Earth Beams, Life Line*) and quintet (*Shuttle*) sessions.
— J.S.

PEPPER ADAMS

★ ★ ★ ★ **Encounter! (with Zoot Sims)** / **Prest.**
★ ★ ★ ★ **Ephemera** / **Zim**
★ ★ ★ ★ **Julian** / **Enja**
★ ★ ★ ★ **Live at Fat Tuesdays** / **Uptown**
★ ★ ★ ★ **Pure Pepper** / **Savoy**
★ ★ ★ ★ **The Master** / **Muse**
★ ★ ★ ★ **Mean What You Say (with Thad Jones)** / **Mile.**
★ ★ ★ ★ ★ **Reflectory** / **Muse**
★ ★ ★ ★ **Urban Dreams** / **Palo Alto**
★ ★ ★ ★ **10–4 at the Five Spot** / **Prest.**

Like Harry Carney and Serge Chaloff before him, Pepper Adams is the boss of the baritone sax. More so than Chaloff, whose style matured in the late Forties but remained under the sway of Lester Young, Adams (b. 1930) fully applied Charlie Parker's swift bop conception to the instrument.

Springing out of Detroit in the mid-Fifties, Adams quickly established himself on the

New York scene through his gutsy work with a quintet he coled with Donald Byrd (*10-4*) and numerous sideman dates for Blue Note and Prestige. In an era dominated by the cool, even-tempered melodiousness of Gerry Mulligan, Adams' baritone was heard as the fiery alternative. His incredible up-tempo work on Lee Morgan's *The Cooker* on Blue Note is a typical example of the massive bop chops that made him so popular among his contemporaries.

By the mid-Sixties Adams was an important mainstay of the classic first edition of the Thad Jones–Mel Lewis big band. After worthy small-group collaborations with second horns—Thad Jones on *Mean What You Say*; Zoot Sims on *Encounter!*—Adams began cutting a series of baritone-plus-rhythm-section solo albums that have all been of consistently high quality. Each is marked by a thoughtful and intriguing approach to song selection, arrangement and soloist ensemble interaction.

Adams always surrounds himself with the best players; the impending monotony of the group setting is avoided by varying pianists—Roland Hanna (*Ephemera* and *Reflectory*), Walter Norris (*Julian*), Tommy Flanagan (*The Master*) and Jimmy Rowles (*Urban Dreams*)—and drummers including Mel Lewis, Leroy Williams and Billy Hart. The one constant is super bassist George Mraz, who is deservedly given much solo, and often with Adams, duo space.

Both *Julian,* a live date, and *Ephemera* have their share of remarkable moments but are a bit long-winded; from *Reflectory* on, each LP has been exquisitely balanced between hard-bop cooking and Adams' muscular introspection on well-chosen ballads. Despite the threats of young contenders Hamiet Bluiett and Nick Brignola, these albums prove Adams is still the master of the big horn. — s.f.

CANNONBALL ADDERLEY
★ ★ ★ ★ **Alabama/Africa** / Mile.
★ ★ ★ ★ **Beginnings** / Em.
★ ★ ★ **Best** / Cap.
★ ★ **Big Man** / Fan.
★ ★ ★ **Cannonball Adderley and 8 Giants** / Mile.
★ ★ ★ **Cannonball Adderley and Friends** / Cap.
★ ★ **Cannonball Adderley and Nancy Wilson** / Cap.
★ **Cannonball Adderley and Strings** / Trip
★ ★ ★ **Cannonball in the Land of Hi-Fi** / Trip
★ ★ **Cannonball, Vol. 1** / Dobre

★ ★ ★ **Coast to Coast** / Mile.
★ ★ ★ ★ **In Chicago** / Mer.
★ ★ **In New Orleans** / Mile.
★ ★ ★ **In New York** / Fan./OJC
★ ★ **Inside Straight** / Fan.
★ ★ ★ **Japanese Concerts** / Mile.
★ ★ ★ **Live!** / Cap.
★ ★ **Lovers** / Fan.
★ **Love, Sex, and the Zodiac** / Fan.
★ ★ ★ ★ ★ **Mercy, Mercy, Mercy!** / Cap.
★ ★ ★ **Music, You All** / Cap.
★ **Phenix** / Fan.
★ **Pyramid** / Fan.
★ ★ ★ ★ **The Sextet** / Mile.
★ ★ ★ **Somethin' Else** / Blue N.
★ **Soul Zodiac** / Cap.
★ ★ ★ **Spontaneous Combustion** / Savoy
★ ★ ★ **What I Mean** / Mile.
★ ★ ★ ★ **What Is This Thing Called Soul** / Mile.

Cannonball Adderley (1928–1978) first began to attract attention when he played in the late Fifties with Miles Davis' first supergroup, which included John Coltrane, Philly Joe Jones, Red Garland (later Bill Evans) and Paul Chambers. But Adderley began recording in 1955, just days after he arrived in New York. He had learned from Charlie Parker how to sail comfortably against the rhythm, how to swing sixteenth notes through scales arranged like mine fields, and how to bend his lip around the blues until he'd squeezed them dry. In fact, Adderley is partly responsible for institutionalizing Parker, by playing Parker-like lines that were easier for listeners to follow.

The recordings on Savoy and EmArcy (some of whose sessions were reissued by the now-defunct Trip label) chronicle the period before he joined Davis. Later he found a more soulful groove, with compositions that relied heavily on the blues and a driving beat. While dedicated jazz listeners were turning to the power saxophonists such as Ornette Coleman and John Coltrane, Adderley was finding funky piano players such as Bobby Timmons, Joe Zawinul and George Duke more to his liking. Zawinul, who later recorded with Miles' late-Sixties band, then formed Weather Report, brought Adderley to his most popular point in the late Sixties with "Mercy, Mercy, Mercy!" (a pop hit) and "Country Preacher," songs with their roots in Memphis soil. And all along the way, brother Nat Adderley was always to be relied upon for a few new themes and darting cornet choruses.

As tastes changed, so did Adderley, and although he never left the blues behind, a few projects in search of an audience were less than artistic successes. But for session players Dave Sanborn, Tom Scott and many lesser-known musicians, there's nothing quite as righteous as the sound of Cannonball preachin'. They've emulated his deep-fried attack and fancy-free howl. And so traditions are born. — A.E.G.

NAT ADDERLEY
★ ★ ★ **Double Exposure / Prest.**
★ ★ ★ **Little New York Midtown Music / Gal.**
★ ★ ★ **Natural Soul / Mile.**
★ ★ ★ **On the Move / Ther.**
★ ★ ★ **Scavenger / Mile.**
★ ★ ★ **Work Song / Riv.**
★ ★ ★ ★ **Work Songs / Mile.**
As part of the group led by his brother Cannonball, cornet/trumpet player Nat Adderley (b. 1931) spearheaded the bluesy soul/jazz movement of the early Sixties. In 1960, using Adderley associates Bobby Timmons (piano), Louis Hayes (drums) and Sam Jones (cello), as well as Wes Montgomery on guitar and Percy Heath on bass, Nat recorded the soul classic "Work Song," which has subsequently been popularized in cover versions. *Work Songs* is a good collection of Adderley's material. *Scavenger* and *Natural Soul* are late-Sixties sets, the former featuring Cannonball's keyboardist Joe Zawinul, Joe Henderson on sax and Jeremy Steig on flute. *Double Exposure* and *Midtown Music* are mid-Seventies sessions, the latter featuring Johnny Griffin on sax. The 1983 *On the Move* release features Sonny Fortune on alto sax, Larry Willis on piano, Walter Booker on bass and Jimmy Cobb on drums. — J.S.

AIR
★ ★ ★ ★ ★ **Air Lore / Ari./No.**
★ ★ ★ ★ **Air Mail / Black S.**
★ ★ ★ ★ **Air Song / In. Nav.**
★ ★ ★ ★ ★ **Air Time / Nessa**
★ ★ ★ ★ **80 Below '82 / Ant.**
★ ★ ★ ★ **Live Air / Black S.**
Saxophonist Henry Threadgill, bassist Fred Hopkins and drummer Steve McCall formed Air in Chicago in 1971. Until 1976, when they began appearing regularly in New York, Air quietly developed their strengths, recording two stunning albums for the Japanese Whynot label that were never readily available in the U.S. *Air Song,* the first of these two records, finally appeared domestically in 1982. From the time their American recording activity began in earnest in 1978 (two Arista/Novus titles of that period have already been deleted), Air was elevated to the ranks of those permanent bands that had developed something special.

Among Air's virtues are their classic sax/bass/drums lineup, a willingness to explore all manner of material, attention to detail at even the most collectively heated junctures, and the earth-moving Hopkins/McCall rhythm section. This trio doesn't make bad records, but they have tended to be most impressive when avoiding side-long performances. *Air Time* is probably the best single-album indication of the band's range, which encompasses the heroic ("Keep Right On Playing . . .") and the whimsical ("G.v.E.," where Threadgill plays his array of hubcaps, the hubkaphone). Still, if one Air album belongs in every collection, it is *Air Lore,* a 1979 performance of Scott Joplin rags and Jelly Roll Morton tunes that is currently unsurpassed as a statement of historical homage from the perspective of the frontiers. A word to the wise: buy it now, for the fate of most of the Arista/Novus catalogue looms precariously.

One of the best jazz albums of 1982, *80 Below '82,* captures the telepathic agreement of Air's members in full glory. Unfortunately, it may prove the swan song of at least this edition of Air. Steve McCall left the trio in early 1983; and while Threadgill and Hopkins continue to perform with various drummers, the strong critical reaction to Threadgill's sextet (heard on the About Time *When Was That?* album) raises the possibility that the saxophonist will place greater emphasis on a larger ensemble in the future. — B.B.

AIRTO
★ ★ ★ ★ **The Essential Airto / Bud.**
★ ★ ★ ★ **Fingers / CTI**
★ ★ ★ ★ **Free / CTI**
★ ★ ★ **In Concert / CTI**
★ ★ ★ **Promises of the Sun / Ari.**
★ ★ ★ **Virgin Land / CTI**
Airto Moreira (b. 1941) arrived in the U.S. in time to lead a small explosion of interest in Seventies-style Brazilian rhythms. His first recordings in the States with Miles Davis and Chick Corea's original Return to Forever displayed a taste for extraordinary percussion work. *Essential* is decidedly cooler than his later work, with more folk melodies than jazz rhythms, but the contributions of his fellow Brazilian musicians, wife Flora Purim's clear, unadorned vocals and Ron Carter on bass make for some compelling music.

Free joins the CTI all-stars with ringers Keith Jarrett and Return to Forever members Stanley Clarke, Chick, Flora and Joe Farrell, who provide most of the excitement on this set. *Fingers* is less distinctive. Several of the tunes are more bossa nova pop than progressive jazz and the sound is a little thin until David Amaro's guitar sparkles through. *Promises of the Sun* lacks intensity, but Airto still displays his talent for creating musical hooks, and the inventiveness on many of his instruments that has made him perennially *Downbeat* magazine's number one percussionist. — A.E.G.

TOSHIKO AKIYOSHI
★ ★ ★ **Dedications / Inner**
★ ★ ★ **Farewell / JAM**
★ ★ ★ **Finesse / Conc. J.**
★ ★ ★ ★ ★ **Insights / RCA**
★ ★ ★ ★ ★ **Long Yellow Road / RCA**
★ ★ ★ **Notorious Tourist from the East /**
Inner
★ ★ ★ ★ **Road Time / RCA**
★ ★ ★ ★ **Salted Gingko Nuts / Ascent**
★ ★ ★ ★ **Tanuki's Night Out / JAM**
Toshiko Akiyoshi (b. 1929) was something of a curiosity when she arrived in the United States in 1956—Japan's leading jazz musician and a female Bud Powell disciple. Her combo albums from the late Fifties are long out of print, and after a 1962 spell with the Charles Mingus Jazz Workshop she was primarily heard from only in her native Japan until the mid-Seventies, when she emerged as the exclusive composer and arranger for a big band of Los Angeles studio aces. Lew Tabackin, Akiyoshi's husband and the band's primary soloist (on tenor sax and flute), is the coleader.

The band was recorded by RCA, initially for Japanese release, between 1974 and '76. In relatively little time, it was recognized as outstanding due to the extremely personal orchestral colors Akiyoshi attains (particularly a trademark flutes-and-clarinets blend) and the consistently strong contributions by the authoritative Tabackin and other soloists. Three albums from this period are still in print: *Long Yellow Road* (from the beginning of the period) and *Insights* (from the end) are superb programs of what came to be a standard mix of swinging, fresh writing and a touch of oriental shading; *Road Time,* a live double-album from a Japanese tour, has the requisite spirit, but when the main business remains the writer the opportunity for stretched-out solos isn't necessarily a benefit.

After an American hiatus, the band started recording again in 1980 on JAM. While Akiyoshi remains one of the few jazz orchestrators to grapple seriously with big

bands in the Ellington spirit, the substantial shift in personnel is noticeable on *Farewell* (her dedication to Mingus). *Tanuki's Night Out,* where Akiyoshi has arranged a set of Tabackin's blowing tunes, sounds better and affords a nice change of pace for the band.

With her profile restored, Akiyoshi recorded trio and quartet sessions for Inner City and Concord Jazz during the period when the band was without an American record contract. Her boppish fleetness has since been tempered by a focus on harmonic shading that marks arrangers who also play piano. *Dedications,* where Akiyoshi plays jazz standards that predate her U.S. arrival, is a winning session, but small-band versions of her recent music only leave one with a taste for the full-sized editions.

Further dissatisfaction with American record companies led Akiyoshi/Tabackin to revive their Ascent label (38 West 94th St., New York, New York 10025) in order to release their 1978 *Salted Gingko Nuts,* previously available only in Japan. The couple also relocated from Los Angeles to New York and completely reorganized their band; the new ensemble debuted in June 1983. — B.B.

JOE ALBANY
★ ★ ★ ★ **Bird Lives! / Interp.**
★ ★ ★ ★ **Portrait of an Artist / Elek./Mus.**
★ ★ ★ **Proto-Bopper / Rev.**
★ ★ ★ ★ **The Right Combination / Prest.**
★ ★ ★ **Two's Company . . . / Steep.**
Much heralded yet oft overlooked pianist. Like Thelonious Monk, Joe Albany (b. 1924) is something of an enigma in that he is invariably lumped with the bebop pianists yet possesses a style equally suited to the post-bop modernists. Among his available recordings, *Portrait of an Artist* is strongly recommended, demonstrating both a soulful bent and an awesome intelligence. *Bird Lives!* is a collection of Parker compositions that recalls the pianist's professional and artistic link with the altoist, while *Proto-Bopper* was cut in Europe during Albany's period as an expatriate. Albany also worked with tenorman Warne Marsh. *The Right Combination* is a fine session with Marsh. *Two's Company* is a duet LP with bassist Niels-Henning Orsted Pedersen. — F.G.

LOREZ ALEXANDRIA
★ ★ ★ **How Will I Remember You? /**
Discov.
★ ★ ★ ★ **Lorez Alexandria Sings the Songs**
of Johnny Mercer, Vol. 1 / Discov.

★ ★ **Lorez Alexandria the Great** / MCA
★ ★ ★ **A Woman Knows** / Discov.
Lorez Alexandria's cool, billowing vocal
style is a trademark sound with mixed bless-
ings. Especially during the earlier part of her
career the approach was *too* cool. The MCA
set suffers from the tendency she once had to
approach songs too passively. Happily, Alexandria developed into a more confident, aggressive singer in the Seventies, as the Discovery sides demonstrate. The Johnny
Mercer set is the best of her performances
listed here, but Alexandria's finest album,
Deep Roots (Argo) is worth seeking out although it is out of print and hard to come
by. — A.R.

MOSE ALLISON
★ ★ ★ ★ **Best of** / Atl.
★ ★ ★ **Creek Bank** / Prest.
★ ★ ★ **Down Home Piano** / Prest.
★ ★ ★ **I've Been Doin' Some Thinkin'** / Atl.
★ ★ ★ **Jazz Years** / Atl.
★ ★ ★ ★ **Lessons in Living** / Elek./Mus.
★ ★ ★ **Middle Class White Boy** / Elek./
Mus.
★ ★ ★ **Mose Alive** / Atl.
★ ★ ★ **Mose Allison** / Prest.
★ ★ **Mose Allison Plays for Lovers** / Prest.
★ ★ ★ **Mose in Your Ear** / Atl.
★ ★ ★ **Ol' Devil Mose** / Prest.
★ ★ ★ **Retrospective** / Col.
★ ★ ★ **Seventh Son** / Prest.
★ ★ ★ ★ **Your Mind Is on Vacation** / Atl.
Mose Allison (b. 1927) is the embodiment of
the cool jazzman. His blues-based, boogying
yet laid-back piano noodlings and laconic,
semidetached vocal style made him patron
saint of the beatnik lounge buffs (he'll cram
all the syllables from a line into the beginning of a measure, then sustain the last note
over a cascading piano response). Gnossos
Papadoupolis, hero of Richard Farina's *Been
Down So Long It Looks Like Up to Me,*
played an Allison record as the selected
soundtrack throughout his constant Kerouac
hustle. Later, Allison's "Young Man Blues"
became a hard-rock remake for the Who.
His playing, attitude, song selection and instrumentation have been fairly standard over
his long career. Allison suffered a drop in
popularity in the mid-Seventies until the extraordinary 1976 Atlantic release, *Your Mind
Is on Vacation,* on which he steamed
through a variety of new and old tunes at
comparatively breakneck speed, augmented
by a horn section featuring Joe Farrell (tenor
sax), Dave Sanborn (alto sax), Al Porcino
(trumpet) and Al Cohn (tenor sax).
Allison has continued on sturdily into the
Eighties, recording solid records for Elektra/

Musician. *Middle Class White Boy* is an '82
studio set with a commercial blues/pop slant
and a fine band led by Joe Farrell on tenor
and flute and Phil Upchurch on guitar. *Lessons in Living* is a live set from the 1982
Montreux Jazz Festival with a rocking fusion quintet featuring Jack Bruce on bass,
Billy Cobham on drums, Eric Gale on guitar, Lou Donaldson on alto sax and Allison
on piano. — J.S.

LAURINDO ALMEIDA
★ ★ ★ **Brazilian Soul (with Charlie Byrd)** /
Conc. P.
★ ★ ★ **Chamber Jazz** / Conc. J.
★ ★ ★ **Collaboration (with The Modern Jazz
Quartet)** / Atl.
★ ★ ★ **First Concerto for Guitar &
Orchestra** / Conc. C.
Brazilian acoustic guitarist who entered the
jazz world via an association with Stan Ken-
ton. Though not as accomplished an impro-
viser as Charlie Byrd, whom he shares *Bra-
zilian Soul* with, Almeida (b. 1917) makes
consistently listenable music. — F.G.

GREG ALPER
★ ★ **Fat Doggie** / Adel.
Earnest, listenable 1978 funk/fusion set led
by Alper (b. 1953) on tenor and soprano sax
and flute. But that's about all. — J.S.

HERB ALPERT
★ ★ **Bullish** / A&M
★ **Fandango** / A&M
★ ★ **Greatest Hits, Vol. 2 (with Tijuana
Brass)** / A&M
★ **Magic Man** / A&M
★ ★ **Rise** / A&M
The thin, singsong trumpet tones of Herb
Alpert (b. 1937) have made for the most
successful pop/jazz formulae over the past
quarter of a century. Alpert's genius for
commercial hooks was so keen that he
started out with his own record company
(Alpert & Moss = A&M) in the early sixties
to release his records, the first of which,
"The Lonely Bull," became a huge hit, soon
to be followed by "Spanish Flea," the *Casino
Royale* theme, "This Guy's in Love with
You," etc. When Alpert returned to recording in the late Seventies under his own
name, the trumpet tone was richer and the
arrangements far more sophisticated. "Rise,"
the massive disco/funk hit recorded in 1979,
owes a stylistic debt to Chuck Mangione's
"Feel So Good" and is probably the most
hated tune by working jazz trumpeters, who
are constantly asked to play it at less than
desirable gigs. — J.S.

BARRY ALTSCHUL
★ ★ ★ ★ ★ Another Time/Another Place /
  Muse
★ ★ ★ Irina / Soul N.
★ ★ ★ ★ You Can't Name Your Own Tune /
  Muse
Percussionist/drummer Barry Altschul (b.
1943) is a player of awesome technique and
versatility who teamed with Dave Holland to
form one of the strongest rhythm sections
playing experimental jazz during the Seventies. They were part of Circle, with Chick
Corea and Anthony Braxton, as well as the
section on records by Braxton, Sam Rivers
and Paul Bley. Perhaps their finest work together, though, was on Holland's wonderful
Conference of the Birds LP. Holland was
around once again for Altschul's 1977 debut,
You Can't Name Your Own Tune, along
with Sam Rivers on flute, tenor and soprano
saxophone, Muhal Richard Abrams on piano
and George Lewis on trombone. *Another
Time* is an even more impressive record
sparked by the performances of Arthur
Blythe on alto sax, Ray Anderson on trombone, Anthony Davis on piano and Abdul
Wadud on cello. "Crépuscule: Suite for
Monk" is a stunning tribute to that master
composer that climaxes with a stirring version of "Epistrophy." *Irina* is a quartet with
Enrico Rava on trumpet and fluegelhorn,
John Surman on baritone and soprano sax
and Mark Helias on bass. — J.S.

ALBERT AMMONS
★ ★ ★ ★ ★ The Complete Blue Note
  Recordings of Albert Ammons and Meade
  Lux Lewis / Mosaic, 197 Strawberry Hill
  Avenue, Stamford, CT 06902
★ ★ ★ ★ ★ King of Blues and Boogie
  Woogie / Oldie B.
Chicago-born boogie-woogie pianist learned
from Pinetop Smith and Meade Lux Lewis
before coming to New York to establish his
name at Café Society, where he worked as a
team with pianist Pete Johnson. Ammons
was one of the best practitioners of the
genre. — J.S.

GENE AMMONS
★ ★ ★ ★ Gene Ammons and Friends at
  Montreux / Prest.
★ ★ ★ ★ ★ Gene Ammons All-Star Sessions
  / Prest. OJC
★ ★ ★ ★ The Gene Ammons Story: Gentle
  Jug / Prest.
★ ★ ★ ★ The Gene Ammons Story: Organ
  Combos / Prest.
★ ★ ★ ★ ★ The Gene Ammons Story: The 78
  Era / Prest.
★ ★ ★ Angel Eyes / Prest.

★ ★ ★ The Best of Gene Ammons / Prest.
★ ★ ★ ★ The Big Sound / Prest.
★ ★ ★ The Black Cat / Prest.
★ ★ ★ Blue Groove / Prest.
★ ★ ★ ★ ★ Blues Up and Down, Vol. 1 /
  Prest.
★ ★ ★ The Boss Is Back / Prest.
★ ★ ★ Boss Soul! / Prest.
★ ★ ★ ★ Boss Tenor / Prest.
★ ★ ★ Brother Jug! / Prest.
★ ★ ★ ★ The Chase! / Prest.
★ ★ ★ Free Again / Prest.
★ ★ ★ Goodbye / Prest.
★ ★ Got My Own / Prest.
★ ★ ★ Greatest Hits / Prest.
★ ★ ★ ★ ★ The Happy Blues / Prest. OJC
★ ★ ★ ★ ★ The Happy Blues / Prest.
★ ★ ★ ★ Jammin' with Gene / Prest.
★ ★ ★ ★ Jammin' in Hi-Fi with Gene
  Ammons / Fan./OJC
★ ★ ★ Jug / Prest.
★ ★ ★ ★ Jug and Dodo / Prest.
★ ★ ★ ★ Juganthology / Prest.
★ ★ ★ Jungle Soul / Prest.
★ ★ ★ Live! In Chicago / Prest.
★ ★ ★ My Way / Prest.
★ ★ ★ ★ Sock! / Prest.
★ ★ ★ Soul Summit / Prest.
★ ★ ★ Together Again for the Last Time /
  Prest.
★ ★ ★ Velvet Soul / Prest.
★ ★ ★ ★ We'll Be Together Again / Prest.
★ ★ ★ ★ You Talk That Talk / Prest.
Tenor saxophonist Gene Ammons (1925–
1974) was the son of boogie-woogie piano
player Albert Ammons, and the blues tradi-
tion that his father represented can be heard
throughout Gene Ammons' recording career.
A warm, big-toned player, Ammons comes
out of the Coleman Hawkins/Herschel
Evans tenor tradition although many critics
have pointed out that his phrasing and melodic sense derive from the seemingly anti-
thetical influence of Lester Young.
  While he was still a teenager in Chicago
during the early Forties Ammons began
playing with a local band led by King
Kolax. Between 1944–47 Ammons was part
of Billy Eckstine's legendary big band, which
included at various points during Ammons'
tenure such players as Charlie Parker, Sonny
Stitt, Dexter Gordon, Dizzy Gillespie, Fats
Navarro, Miles Davis, Lucky Thompson and
Art Blakey. Ammons was the featured solo-
ist in Eckstine's band, and his tradeoffs with
Dexter Gordon were memorable. It was
Stitt, however, who would go on to become
Ammons' partner after the two left Eckstine.
In the meantime Ammons replaced Stan
Getz in Woody Herman's big band at the
end of the Forties.

Between 1950 and 1952 Ammons and Stitt coled a fantastic group notable for its "tenor battles." This music still sounds fresh and exciting today and can be heard on *Blues Up and Down, Vol. 1, The Gene Ammons Story: The 78 Era* and one side of *All-Star Sessions.* Stitt left in 1952 and Ammons continued the group on his own, scoring a popular hit in 1953 with "Red Top," which you can hear on the out-of-print but not impossible to find Savoy session, *Red Top.*

Throughout the Fifties Ammons led a number of blowing jam sessions with consistently great musicians. Excellent selections from this era can be heard on *The Big Sound,* sessions featuring John Coltrane playing alto sax, Pepper Adams, Paul Quinichette, Jerome Richardson, George Joyner a.k.a. Jamil Nasser, Art Taylor and Mal Maldron. *The Happy Blues,* which is available both as Volume 1 of the Gene Ammons Jam Sessions series and as part of the Original Jazz Classics series with its original cover art, is a '56 set featuring Jackie McLean on alto sax, Art Farmer on trumpet, Duke Jordan on piano, Addison Farmer on bass, Art Taylor on drums and Candido playing congas. *Jammin' with Gene,* another '56 classic, adds Donald Byrd's trumpet and replaces Jordan with Waldron and Addison Farmer with Doug Watkins. *Angel Eyes* includes a couple of tracks from part of that latter unit. *Juganthology* is selections from sessions from '55 to '57.

In the early Sixties Ammons recorded frequently in an impressive variety of musical contexts with generally favorable results. There were a couple of reunions with Stitt (*Soul Summit, We'll Be Together Again*), a lot of small organ combos, including *Live! In Chicago, Soul Summit* (Ammons and Stitt with Brother Jack McDuff), *Velvet Soul, The Gene Ammons Story: Organ Combos,* and *Best of* (with McDuff). *Jug and Dodo* is a two-record set of 1962 quartets led by Ammons and Dodo Marmarosa. *Blue Groove* is another '62 session with a group including Clarence "Sleepy" Anderson on piano and organ. Other early-Sixties sets include the quartet ballads on *The Gene Ammons Story: Gentle Jug* and the quartets and quintets augmented by conga drums or bongos, *Boss Tenor, Jug, Boss Soul!* and *Jungle Soul. Sock!* collects some early-Sixties material with Fifties sides; *Greatest Hits* matches early-Sixties material with early-Seventies cuts.

From late 1962 until the very end of the decade Ammons was off the scene serving a prison term on a narcotics charge. In the last five years of his life he went back into the studio for a number of sessions and was also caught live on several recordings. *The Boss Is Back,* his triumphant return, introduces an even funkier sound than Ammons had been playing during his early-Sixties soul groove. *Brother Jug!* and *The Black Cat* are similar forays. *Free Again* and *My Way* are orchestrated big-band sessions, *Got My Own* uses a sextet with strings. *The Chase!* is a tenor battle with Dexter Gordon from 1970; *You Talk That Talk* and *Together Again for the Last Time* are Ammons' final pair of collaborations with Sonny Stitt. Ammons recorded *Goodbye,* with Nat Adderley on cornet, Kenny Drew on piano, Sam Jones on bass, Louis Hayes on drums, Ray Barretto on congas and Gary Bartz on alto sax, five months before his death. — J.S.

DAVID AMRAM
★ ★ **David Amram's Latin-Jazz Celebration / Mus.**
★ ★ **Friends, at Home/Around the World / Fly. Fish**
★ ★ **Havana/New York / Fly. Fish**
Versatile instrumentalist/composer David Amram (b. 1930) is one of the few jazz French horn players. In the Fifties he played with Lionel Hampton, Sonny Rollins, Charlie Mingus, Oscar Pettiford and Kenny Dorham. In 1966 he became the first composer-in-residence at the New York Philharmonic. His best and most ambitious recording, *No More Walls,* mixed classical, jazz and folk elements deftly and is definitely worth seeking out. The records listed here are recent sessions typical of Amram's wide-ranging musical interests. The *Latin-Jazz* set, with Paquito d'Rivera (alto sax, flute), David Newman (tenor sax), Pepper Adams (baritone sax), percussionists Machito and Candido, gets a narrow preference over the Flying Fish records. — J.S.

CAT ANDERSON
★ ★ **Cat Anderson / Inner**
★ ★ **Cat Speaks / Class.**
Trumpeter Cat Anderson (1916–1981) plied his growling, high-intensity style to good effect with the Duke Ellington orchestra over the space of several decades, but simply doesn't come off as well on his solo outings, which are stilted and directionless. — J.S.

ERNESTINE ANDERSON
★ ★ ★ ★ **Big City / Conc. J.**
★ ★ ★ ★ **Hello Like Before / Conc. J.**
★ ★ ★ **Live at the Concord Jazz Festival— 1979 (with Ray Brown) / Conc. J.**

★ ★ Live from Concord to London / Conc.
J.
★ ★ ★ ★ Never Make Your Move Too Soon
/ Conc. J.
★ ★ ★ Sunshine / Conc. J.

Ernestine Anderson (b. 1928) can sound sophisticated and down-home at the same
time. She can (and will) sing the blues, too.
Her return to performance and recording,
fostered by bassist Ray Brown in 1976,
marks the revivification of one of the Fifties'
brightest singing careers.

It is true that Anderson's essential funki-
ness can, at times, get out of hand, replacing
back-in-the-alley soul with near parody; but
albums such as *Hello Like Before, Never
Make Your Move Too Soon* and *Big City*
successfully balance the hand-on-the-hip with
elegance. Concerning these three dates, it
should also be noted that the repertoire (not
a strong point with Anderson) is far above
average. Ray Brown, Hank Jones, Monty Alexander, Frank Gant, Monty Budwig and
Jeff Hamilton take turns providing ballast
for Anderson's magic on choice songs like
"Just One More Chance" (*Never Make Your
Move*)" and "Welcome to the Club" (*Big
City*). — A.R.

LOUIS ARMSTRONG
★ ★ ★ ★ Early Portrait / Mile.
★ ★ ★ ★ ★ The Genius of Louis Armstrong
/ Col.
★ ★ ★ ★ The Great Soloists featuring Louis
Armstrong / Bio.
★ ★ ★ ★ The King Oliver Creole Jazz Band
/ Olym.
★ ★ ★ ★ ★ King Oliver's Jazz Band 1923 /
Smithsonian
★ ★ ★ ★ ★ Louis Armstrong and Earl Hines
1928 / Smithsonian
★ ★ ★ ★ ★ Louis Armstrong and His Hot
Four with Lillie Delk Christian; with
Bertha Chippie Hill / CBS (France)
★ ★ ★ ★ ★ Louis Armstrong and King
Oliver / Mile.
★ ★ ★ ★ ★ Louis Armstrong/Sidney Bechet
with the Clarence Williams Blue Five /
CBS (France)
★ ★ ★ ★ Louis Armstrong Special / CBS
(France)
★ ★ ★ ★ ★ The Louis Armstrong Story,
Vols. 1–3 / Col.
★ ★ ★ ★ ★ Louis Armstrong with Blanche
Calloway, Baby Mack, Hociel Thomas,
Bertha "Chippie" Hill, Sippie Wallace,
Victoria Spivey / CBS (France)
★ ★ ★ ★ Louis Armstrong with Maggie
Jones, Nolan Welsh, Clara Smith, Sippie
Wallace / CBS (France)
★ ★ ★ ★ Louis Armstrong with V. Liston,
M. Johnson, S. Wallace, E. Taylor, H.
Thomas / CBS (France)
★ ★ ★ ★ Mr. Armstrong Plays the Blues /
Bio.
★ ★ ★ ★ Young Louis Armstrong: The
Sideman / MCA (Jazz Heritage)

It was the loudest sound they ever heard.
The recording engineers at the Gennett
Company in Richmond, Indiana, had sched-
uled a session with the King Oliver band, a
hot group out of Chicago that had been on
tour through Illinois, Ohio and Indiana in
April 1923. When the band started to play
in the studio, however, it wasn't Oliver who
stood out but his second cornetist, Louis
Armstrong (1900–1971). Armstrong played
with so much force that he had to be placed
twenty feet behind the rest of the band in
order to keep the sound balanced.

It was during that legendary recording
debut that Armstrong played his first solo
with Oliver, "Chime Blues." Oliver had been
careful to keep Armstrong in the background during live performances, because the
precocious young player could upstage anyone. That explosive personality breaks
through in his solo as Louis develops round-
toned, viscous notes that suddenly disappear
in shimmering implosions.

Armstrong's performances in both solo
and ensemble settings with Oliver can be
heard on *The King Oliver Creole Jazz Band,
King Oliver's Jazz Band 1923* and *Louis
Armstrong and King Oliver.* The Smithsonian
set is accompanied by excellent, extensive
liner notes; the Milestone set also includes
some 1924 Armstrong sessions with the Red
Onion Jazz Babies, including Sidney Bechet
on some tracks.

Within a year of his recording debut,
Armstrong had changed the face of American music permanently. Arriving in Harlem
in the fall of 1924 to join Fletcher Henderson's orchestra, Armstrong created an immediate sensation. With a brilliant blues sense,
he went beyond the strictures of the New
Orleans ensemble tradition to develop a radical solo voice on the cornet and a rhythmic
blueprint for the small jazz group that laid
the cornerstone for later developments in all
phases of popular music. His approach to
solo improvisation and impressionistic scat
singing have influenced countless players and
singers.

Armstrong recorded prolifically in a variety of contexts during the Twenties, and fortunately a lot of this material is still around.
His accompaniments of the classic blues
singer Bessie Smith are amazingly sensitive—

Armstrong would later sing some of the same material himself. If you can find Smith's *The Empress* and *Nobody's Blues But Mine* you can hear Armstrong's work with her. Louis also recorded with a number of other female singers of varying skills for Okeh records, and much of this material is collected on the French CBS records and *Mr. Armstrong Plays the Blues* (Biograph).

After a year with Henderson's band, documented best on *Fletcher Henderson's Orchestra* (Biograph), Armstrong returned to Chicago to front a band led by his wife, pianist Lil Hardin. Throughout the rest of the decade Armstrong, a brilliant soloist and improviser, was the king of the flourishing Chicago jazz scene. Early in 1927 he made his first recording sessions as a leader with the legendary Hot Five band—himself, Lil, clarinetist Johnny Dodds, trombonist Kid Ory and banjo player Johnny St. Cyr. During a two-year period the Hot Five and its augmented offshoot, the Hot Seven, recorded forty-five sides for Okeh that are without a doubt some of the best jazz records ever made. Such classics as "Cornet Chop Suey," "Fireworks," "A Monday Date," "West End Blues," "Sugar Foot Strut," "Chicago Breakdown" and others date from this era. The greatest combos from this period featured Earl Hines taking over Hardin's place on the piano. The Armstrong/Hines duet, "Weather Bird," is a sublime moment. The Hot Five/Hot Seven sessions appear on the first three volumes of *The Louis Armstrong Story, The Genius of Louis Armstrong* and the superbly annotated *Louis Armstrong and Earl Hines 1928*, which also includes other valuable material. The Smithsonian albums are only available by mail order from Smithsonian Recordings, P.O. Box 10230, Des Moines, Iowa 50336.

The best of the CBS French imports listed is the album Armstrong recorded with Sidney Bechet and the Clarence Williams Blue Five. Armstrong's cornet and Bechet's soprano saxophone playing intermesh in a breathtaking exchange on these sides. A couple of Clarence Williams tracks also appear on *The Great Soloists featuring Louis Armstrong. Early Portrait* combines Red Onion Jazz Babies tracks with vocal tracks by Trixie Smith and Ma Rainey that feature Armstrong cornet accompaniments. *Young Louis The Sideman* collects Armstrong session performances with Fletcher Henderson, Perry Bradford's Jazz Phools, Lil's Hot Shots, Erskine Tate's Vendome Orchestra, Jimmy Bertrand's Washboard Wizards, and Johnny Dodds' Black Bottom Stompers.

★ ★ ★ ★ **Ambassador Satch** / CSP
★ ★ ★ **Best of** / Audio Fi.
★ ★ ★ ★ **Best of** / MCA
★ ★ ★ **Chicago Concert** / Col.
★ ★ **Definitive Album** / Audio Fi.
★ **Disney Songs the Satchmo Way** / Buena
★ ★ ★ ★ **Ella and Louis** / Verve
★ ★ ★ **The Essential** / Van.
★ ★ ★ **An Evening with Louis Armstrong and His All-Stars** / GNP
★ ★ ★ **Great Alternatives** / Chi.
★ ★ ★ **The Greatest of Louis Armstrong** / Pausa
★ ★ ★ ★ **Great Jazz Composers—Louis Armstrong Plays W. C. Handy** / CSP
★ ★ ★ **Hello Dolly** / MCA
★ ★ ★ **Here's Louis Armstrong** / Voc.
★ ★ ★ **High Society** / Cap.
★ ★ ★ **July 4, 1900/July 6, 1971** / RCA
★ ★ ★ **Louis and the Good Book** / MCA (Jazz Heritage)
★ ★ ★ **Louis Armstrong** / Audio Fi.
★ ★ ★ ★ **Louis Armstrong and Duke Ellington** / Col.
★ ★ ★ **Louis Armstrong and His All-Stars** / Story.
★ ★ ★ ★ **Louis Armstrong and His Orchestra, Vols. 1–7** / Swag.
★ ★ ★ **Louis Armstrong and the Dukes of Dixieland** / Audio Fi.
★ ★ ★ ★ **Louis Armstrong at the Crescendo** / MCA
★ ★ ★ ★ **Louis Armstrong: First Recorded Concerts** / Jazz Anth.
★ ★ ★ **Louis Armstrong Greatest Hits** / Col.
★ ★ ★ **Louis Armstrong Greatest Hits Recorded Live** / Bruns.
★ ★ ★ ★ ★ **The Louis Armstrong Story, Vol. 4** / Col.
★ ★ ★ **Louis "Satchmo" Armstrong** / Arc. Folk
★ ★ ★ **Mame** / Pick.
★ ★ **Meets Oscar Peterson** / Verve
★ ★ ★ **Mister Music** / Acc.
★ ★ ★ ★ **Mostly Blues** / Olym.
★ ★ ★ ★ **Old Favorites** / MCA (Jazz Heritage)
★ ★ ★ **One and Only Louis Armstrong** / Voc.
★ ★ ★ **On the Sunny Side of the Street** / CBS (France)
★ ★ ★ ★ **Pops** / Audio Fi.
★ ★ ★ **Porgy and Bess** / Verve
★ ★ ★ ★ **Rare Items** / MCA (Jazz Heritage)
★ ★ ★ ★ **Rare Louis Armstrong** / Jazz Anth.
★ ★ ★ ★ **Satchmo** / MCA
★ ★ ★ ★ **Satchmo at Symphony Hall** / MCA
★ ★ ★ **Satchmo Serenades** / MCA (Jazz Heritage)

★ ★ ★ Satchmo the Great / CSP
★ ★ ★ ★ Satch Plays Fats / CSP
★ ★ ★ ★ Snake Rag / Chi.
★ ★ Sweetheart / Chi.
★ ★ ★ ★ Swing That Music / MCA (Jazz Heritage)
★ ★ ★ ★ Town Hall Concert Plus / RCA International
★ ★ ★ Young Louis Armstrong / RCA

The Armstrong of the Twenties made his mark as a brilliant soloist and improviser. By 1930 Armstrong's singing had become just as popular as his playing and nearly as revolutionary. His live performances were galvanized by his mugging, comic antics and vibrant, growling vocals. Almost magically, he managed to transfer this wit and sheer joy into his recordings as well.

During the early Thirties Armstrong toured incessantly, both in the United States and Europe, where he became one of the first jazz players to capture European audiences. His reputation grew, not only on both continents but also in the media—Broadway plays and Hollywood musicals. Between 1932, when he made his last Okeh recordings, and 1935, when he began his long-term relationship with Decca, Armstrong's domestic recordings were a handful of uneven sides for RCA/Bluebird, collected on the RCA *Young Louis Armstrong* set. He did, however, record six tracks in 1934 in a Paris studio for French Brunswick. These included the haunting, beautiful "On the Sunny Side of the Street" and a toe-tapping instrumental marijuana tribute, "Song of the Vipers," which was immediately yanked off the market when the embarrassed record company discovered that a "viper" was a pot smoker. The six tracks made for French Brunswick are reissued on *Rare Louis Armstrong,* while some live performances and soundtrack pieces from 1932–33 make up *Louis Armstrong: First Recorded Concerts.*

From the Thirties onward Armstrong suffered terrible problems with his lip, which became so scarred and stiff that it sometimes perceptibly affected his playing. Even so, he adapted well enough to keep his playing rich and exciting, if not always as spectacular as on the Twenties recordings. Even in the worst of settings—his accompaniment was not always that good—Armstrong usually managed to make virtually every track he played on sparkle with some aspect of his fertile musical imagination.

Armstrong continued to grow as a vocalist as well. His warmth and his ability to charge even the sappiest of tunes with sincere feeling made simple melodies yield every nuance of beauty. He recorded over one hundred

sides for Decca between 1935 and 1945 in front of various orchestras, and his singing alone was almost always enough to make the performances memorable. The Swaggie set and the MCA Jazz Heritage sides collect this material.

By 1947 the big-band era had ended. Although he would continue to use orchestras for some recording sessions, Armstrong returned to playing with small groups, known as the Louis Armstrong All-Stars, until his death. This small ensemble work was Armstrong's most comfortable context, playing with such gifted collaborators as trombonist Jack Teagarden and, until 1952, pianist Earl Hines.

In the late Fifties and Sixties Armstrong freelanced for a number of labels, especially Decca, where he played large-band arrangements as well as accompaniments for the Mills Brothers, and Columbia, where he recorded more adventurous sides. He also released a number of live records. The later sets reflect the fact that Armstrong's shows varied very little from night to night over the last twenty years of his life. Even on the weakest sounding of these sets, such as the late-Fifties shows captured on Vanguard's *Essential,* Armstrong's presence is clear and strong, making the records more enjoyable and dramatic than studio recordings. But the best of the live records capture the quintessence of his art. *Ambassador Satch,* a 1955 European set featuring the All-Stars lineup of Trummy Young on trombone, Edmond Hall on clarinet, Billy Kyle on piano, Arvell Shaw on bass and Barrett Deems on drums, smokes with maddening intensity—"Muskrat Ramble," "Royal Garden Blues" and the perennial hard-rocking showstopper, "Tiger Rag," are fueled by the ecstatic cries of an audience gone berserk. Other superior live sets are the hard-to-find 1947 *Louis Armstrong at Carnegie Hall* (Archive of Folk & Jazz Music) and *Satchmo at Symphony Hall,* the November 1947 Boston show.

You can hear Armstrong rediscovering his small-band roots on the excellent 1957 retrospective *Satchmo* set, which has now been broken down by MCA into a pair of twodisc volumes. The record features Armstrong's spoken observations on material dating back through his career with updated versions of songs from "Dippermouth Blues" to "On the Sunny Side of the Street." There are several live tracks, small-band studio recordings with the All-Stars and larger group sessions arranged by Sy Oliver.

Armstrong's records with the Dukes of Dixieland (*Great Alternatives, Definitive Album, Sweetheart*) were unsuccessful, some of the very few instances where Armstrong's talent was unable to overcome uninspired accompaniment. These records should be avoided. But his work with Ella Fitzgerald—*Ella and Louis* and *Porgy and Bess*—is superb, as is his '60–'61 meeting with Duke Ellington. The Oscar Peterson set is less interesting.

Armstrong's Fifties album of W. C. Handy songs played by the All-Stars was successful enough to prompt a similar cover set of Fats Waller tunes, *Satch Plays Fats,* which is one of the high points of Armstrong's later work. Louis had collaborated merrily with Waller in the Thirties (*Mostly Blues* and *Pops*) and once again showed his affinity for Waller material.

Though his playing powers were waning toward the end of his life, Armstrong remained one of America's greatest vocalists. He scored hit singles with his gruff covers of "Blueberry Hill" and "Mack the Knife." But his final moment of triumph came with his greatest hit, "Hello Dolly," in 1964.

Armstrong left behind a large and varied body of work, and critics have continued to quarrel about the relative quality of his material from the Thirties onward. Certainly the best of his New Orleans-style Hot Fives and Hot Sevens are more compelling than his later work, although comparisons of such different styles miss the point—Armstrong towers over twentieth-century music and his entire career was of priceless value. Armstrong influenced an entire generation of younger trumpet players through the supposedly inferior work he was doing in the Thirties at a time when the legendary Twenties recordings simply weren't available. Armstrong went on from there to international stardom, becoming the principal exponent of jazz around the world. It seems ridiculous to suggest that all his work during these years is negligible. If you can only listen to one Armstrong album, the Smithsonian Armstrong/Hines collection or *Genius* would probably be it, but after that you can ignore whole sections of his career only at your own peril. — J.S.

HORACEE ARNOLD
★ ★ ★ ★ **Tales of the Exonerated Flea /
   Col.**
★ ★ ★ ★ **Tribe / Col.**
Drummer Horacee Arnold (b. 1937) apprenticed with Bud Powell, Charles Mingus, Stan Getz and Chick Corea before recording his first LP. *Tribe,* as a leader in 1973. It is a beautiful record offering superb Afro-Latin accompaniment from percussionists David

Friedman and Ralph McDonald, reedmen Joe Farrell and Billy Harper, bassist George Mraz and acoustic-guitar virtuoso Ralph Towner. The 1974 set, *Flea,* featuring excellent performances from Jan Hammer (synthesizer), John Abercrombie and Towner (guitars), Dom Um Romao (percussion) and Sonny Fortune (soprano sax and flute), remains an exemplar of fusion music. — J.S.

ART ENSEMBLE OF CHICAGO
★ ★ ★ ★ ★ **Art Ensemble of Chicago with
   Fontella Bass / Prest.**
★ ★ **Certain Blacks / Inner**
★ ★ ★ **Chi-Conga / Paula**
★ ★ ★ **The Paris Session / Ari./Free.**
★ ★ ★ ★ ★ **People in Sorrow / Nessa**
★ ★ ★ ★ **Phase One / Prest.**
★ ★ ★ ★ ★ **Les Stances à Sophie / Nessa**
If asked to name the most innovative jazz group of the past decade, I would probably choose the Art Ensemble of Chicago. Growing out of the Association for the Advancement of Creative Musicians, the AEC first appeared as Roscoe Mitchell's Art Ensemble in 1967, with Mitchell (b. 1940) on alto sax, Lester Bowie (b. 1941) on trumpet and Malachi Favors (b. 1937) on bass—everyone also plays numerous "little instruments." Reedman Joseph Jarman (b. 1937) joined in April 1969, making the band the Art Ensemble, and drummer Don Moye was also added.

All of the above albums are from the AEC's European years (1969–71). The best of these is their masterpiece, *People in Sorrow,* a forty-minute example of how the group's menagerie of instruments and spontaneous approach to structure can create clearly delineated, precisely shaded and starkly emotional music. Nearly as impressive are *Art Ensemble of Chicago with Fontella Bass* and *Les Stances à Sophie,* both of which feature the singing of former soul star Bass. *Les Stances* has some of the group's most varied playing. *Phase One* is important for "Ohnedaruth," a rare piece using the familiar series-of-soloists format, but the other side is a shrill free form made shriller by bad recording. The *Paris Session* double album has good duets and one successful extended work, but also contains tiresome theatrics. *Chi-Conga* is simply the band on one of its lesser sessions, while *Certain Blacks* adds Chicago bluesmen to no one's benefit.
★ ★ ★ ★ ★ **Full Force / ECM/War.**
★ ★ ★ **Live at Mandel Hall / Del.**
★ ★ ★ ★ **Nice Guys / ECM/War.**
★ ★ ★ ★ **Urban Bushmen / ECM/War.**
Live at Mandel Hall is a double-album recording of a 1972 Chicago concert, right

after the Art Ensemble returned from living and touring in Europe. Work didn't pick up significantly in the U.S., though, until the end of the decade, around 1978 when they ended a long recording silence and signed with ECM. The "we're not really out to assault you" joke in the *Nice Guys* title is mirrored by a bunch of compositions and moods, including reggae vocals, a collectively improvised percussion piece, deliberate corn, the usual energy bursts, and a vision of Coltrane's modal period. Sort of a Whitman's Sampler of Art Ensemble attitudes.

Full Force is something of a blend of *Nice Guys* eclecticism and the more extended creations of earlier albums. The side-long "Magg Zelma" builds through several effective moods, and among the shorter pieces is Bowie's "Charlie M," a Mingus tribute that also calls up Duke.

The live two-record *Urban Bushmen* offers a fine summary of the Art Ensemble's attack in several of its preferred tunes and styles. That their approach has become familiar over time explains the slight predictability of this once unpredictable band.

The British Affinity label, which can be found in some areas of the United States, has salvaged the important 1969 European sessions made shortly after the Art Ensemble's arrival there (and prior to the advent of Moye). Try to find, if you're a fan. — B.B.

DOROTHY ASHBY
★ ★ The Best of Dorothy Ashby / Prest.
★ ★ Dorothy Ashby Plays for Beautiful
   People / Prest.
The jazz harp of Dorothy Ashby (b. 1932) is not a novelty sound; she just swings. Frank Wess joins the proceedings on flute on both dates.

Sameness in mood and tempo plagues both albums, though. Neither drummer (Roy Haynes or Art Taylor) is ever unleashed with the sticks to bring up the intensity of the tracks. Perhaps the harp itself poses limitations on dynamics. These recordings, while proficient and professional, are not very compelling. — A.R.

HAROLD ASHBY
★ ★ ★ Presenting / Prog.
Presenting, a 1978 rediscovery date for Harold Ashby (b. 1925), an Ellington stablemate of the Sixties and Seventies, will not warrant the rewriting of jazz history but it's still a modestly lovely record. Ashby employs the patented breathy sound of Ben Webster,

Duke's first great tenorman, on some well-chosen ballads and swinging standards.

Progressive's practice of using a contemporary rhythm section to back older musicians pays off well here. Bassist George Mraz and pianist Don Friedman fit in perfectly while keeping the feel fresh. — S.F.

ROY AYERS
★ ★ ★ Africa, Center of the World / Poly.
★ ★ ★ ★ Daddy Bug and Friends / Atco
★ Everybody Loves the Sunshine / Poly.
★ Feeling Good / Poly.
★ Fever / Poly.
★ ★ ★ In the Dark / Col.
★ Let's Do It Again / Poly.
★ Lifeline / Poly.
★ Love Fantasy / Poly.
★ ★ Mystic Voyage / Poly.
★ No Stranger to Love / Poly.
★ Prime Time / Poly.
★ ★ ★ Red, Black and Green / Poly.
★ Starbooty / Elek.
★ Step into Our Life / Poly.
★ ★ ★ Tear to a Smile / Poly.
★ You Send Me / Poly.
Vibraphonist Roy Ayers (b. 1940) built a reputation out of his playing on Herbie Mann's albums from *Impressions of the Middle East* (1967) to *Memphis Two Step* (1971). Mann produced two solo albums for Ayers during that time, the best tracks of which are now condensed into *Daddy Bug and Friends,* Ayers' best record. *Red, Black and Green* also comes close, matching Ayers' speed to a tensile front line of Sonny Fortune's soprano sax, Charles Tolliver's trumpet and Garnett Brown's trombone. Subsequently Ayers found commercial success with disco by minimizing soloing and composition in favor of urgent, bass-dominated rhythm patterns, but the price he paid for fame is our boredom.

After a 1980 African tour during which he came under the influence of Fela Anikulapo Kuti, Ayers made the fine *Africa, Center of the World* album. The 1984 collaboration with Stanley Clarke, *In the Dark,* saw Ayers move comfortably into the mid-Eighties dance-mix style. — J.S.

ALBERT AYLER
★ ★ ★ ★ Albert Ayler in Greenwich Village
   / Imp.
★ ★ ★ ★ Bells / Base
★ ★ ★ First Recordings / GNP
★ ★ ★ ★ ★ Hilversum Session / Osm.
★ ★ ★ ★ ★ Lörrach/Paris 1966 / Hat Hut
★ ★ ★ ★ Love Cry / Imp.

★ ★ **Music Is the Healing Force of the Universe / Imp.**
★ ★ ★ ★ **My Name Is Albert Ayler / Fan.**
★ ★ **New Grass / Imp.**
★ ★ ★ ★ ★ **New Wave in Jazz / Imp.**
★ ★ ★ **New York Eye and Ear Control / Base**
★ ★ ★ ★ ★ **Prophecy / Base**
★ ★ ★ ★ ★ **Spirits Rejoice / Base**
★ ★ ★ ★ ★ **Spiritual Unity / Base**
★ ★ **Swing Low, Sweet Spiritual / Osm.**
★ ★ ★ ★ ★ **Vibrations / Ari./Free.**
★ ★ ★ ★ **Village / Impulse**
★ ★ ★ ★ ★ **Witches and Devils / Ari./Free.**

Albert Ayler (1936–1970) shot like a comet through jazz—from unknown to avant-garde extreme, then early jazz-R&B fusion and (possibly) suicide in a mere eight years. As *First Recordings* and *My Name Is Albert Ayler* (both made during his early-Sixties European period) show, post-bop formalities were not totally alien to his muse, but the oversized vibrato and expansive emotion of his tenor-sax work demanded the freer situation he found in a brief stay with Cecil Taylor (unfortunately not recorded).

Ayler's style came together on several brilliant 1964 recordings that offer the best view of his stark and extreme conception. *Prophecy* and *Spiritual Unity* involve one of the few perfect bands in jazz history—Ayler, Gary Peacock and Sunny Murray. The primal explorations of tone, texture and rhythm from each player, magnified in the overlapping rush of all three, unleashed a force beyond what even Coleman, Coltrane and Taylor seemed to have prepared jazz for. *Spiritual Unity,* with its short and long versions of "Ghosts," helped define, and still defines, "energy music."

Trumpeter Don Cherry and his more intimate sensitivities joins the trio for the *Hilversum Session,* and as usual he brings additional qualities out of Ayler's naively beautiful tunes. *New York Eye and Ear,* which swells the band further to a sextet, is an all-star free jam session that didn't work. Ayler knew the value of additional horns as far as his own compositions went, and the folk qualities emerged strongly on the 1965 *Bells* and *Spirits Rejoice,* each of which features a front line of Albert's tenor, brother Donald's trumpet and Charles Tyler's alto. More horns also provided contrast in the din, though not that much (Tyler is often indistinguishable from Albert). *Spirits Rejoice* may be the best Ayler album if you only want one, with the Salvation Army march groove of the title track, the stomping "Holy Family" and the lurid ballad "Angels" (with

Call Cobbs on harpsichord for the last). *Bells* is a one-sided album of a major Ayler concert.

Witches and Devils has the tenor/trumpet/bass/drum format, themes that are simple to the point of naiveté, the unfettered tonal and rhythmic energy of Ayler's tenor, and the perfectly supportive cataclysmic drumming of Sunny Murray. *Vibrations* unites Ayler and Murray with bassist Gary Peacock—these three are the quintessential Ayler trio—and trumpeter Don Cherry, who adds some contrasting reserve. The empathy among the players, and two takes of Ayler's anthem "Ghosts," make this one of his finest works. *Swing Low* is a collection of spirituals recorded in 1964. Fascinating concept, mawkish and surprisingly cautious execution. *Lörrach/Paris 1966,* on the other hand, contains two exultant live performances from a successful European tour. In its typically eccentric fashion, Hat Hut pressed one of the two 12-inch LPs at 45 rpm.

Ayler's affiliation with Impulse in the final years of his life saw a strange decline, from the collective exorcism of his 1965 "Holy Ghost" performance in the *New Wave in Jazz* anthology (also featuring John Coltrane, Archie Shepp and others) to the tedious blues-rock-energy-message muddle of 1969's *Music Is the Healing Force of the Universe,* where Ayler collaborates with lyricist Mary Maria. In between are two notable collections, a cut below the Freedom-ESP sessions, and one grand change of direction that might be simply ludicrous if it weren't so prophetic of jazz-rock trends. *Albert Ayler in Greenwich Village* adds violin and cello for a touch of the European, with stunning effect on the brooding "For John Coltrane" (where Ayler plays alto); "Change Has Come" is more characteristically incendiary. *Love Cry* is a studio date with the old format—an excellent free-rhythm section (Alan Silva, bass; Milford Graves, drums), Albert's brother and frequent collaborator Donald on trumpet, and the bizarrely baroque harpsichord of Call Cobbs—but the energy sounds as if it has already begun to be depleted.

New Grass has to be the greatest turnaround in new music history, with Ayler verbally denouncing his past excesses in favor of a raunchy R&B approach that could easily pass for Maceo Parker among the JBs. The skeptics had to admit that Ayler could play the tenor, and numerous less esoteric jazz artists would take a similar course in the Seventies and Eighties, but the musical results are disturbing. Ayler's true motivation regarding this and his last Impulse recordings are as clouded as the circumstances that led to his being found in the East River (tied, according to some accounts, to a jukebox).   — B.B.

AZYMUTH
★ ★ ★ **Cascades** / **Mile.**
★ ★ ★ **Flame** / **Mile.**
★ ★ ★ **Light as a Feather** / **Mile.**
★ ★ ★ **Outubro** / **Mile.**

★ ★ ★ **Rapid Transit** / **Mile.**
★ ★ ★ **Telecommunication** / **Mile.**
Azymuth is a very popular Brazilian trio made up of keyboardist/producer Jose Roberto Bertrami (b. 1946), bassist Alex Malheiros (b. 1946) and drummer Ivan Conti (b. 1946). Coming out of an admitted bossa nova/jazz background, the group's late-Seventies to Eighties sound very effectively incorporates popular funk conceptions as well as samba and jazz.   — J.S.

CHET BAKER

★ ★ ★ **Albert's House / Bain.**
★ ★ ★ **Broken Wing / Inner**
★ ★ ★ **Chet / Prest. OJC**
★ ★ ★ **Daybreak / Steep.**
★ ★ ★ **Once upon a Summertime / Gal.**
★ ★ ★ **Plays the Best of Lerner and Loewe / Fan./OJC**
★ ★ ★ **Rendez-Vouz / Eur.**
★ ★ ★ **Touch of Your Lips / Steep.**
★ ★ ★ **You Can't Go Home Again / Hori.**

Chet Baker (b. 1929) has always been a controversial figure, especially during the height of his popularity in the Fifties. A delicate, fluffy-toned trumpet stylist, Baker was deeply influenced by the cool Miles Davis. A subsequent spot in Gerry Mulligan's band launched Baker to an over-hyped popularity during the mid-Fifties when he became a cult idol as revered for his singing as playing. A bout with drugs led to the inevitable hard times, and Baker returned to the scene with a mellowed, mature style that can be heard on the above records. — J.S.

BILLY BANG

★ ★ **Bangception (with Dennis Charles) / Hat Hut**
★ ★ ★ **Billy Bang and Charles Tyler / Anima**
★ ★ **Billy Bang/John Lindberg / Anima**
★ ★ ★ **Distinction without a Difference / Hat Hut**
★ ★ ★ **Invitation / Soul N.**
★ ★ ★ **Rainbow Gladiator / Soul N.**
★ ★ ★ ★ **Outline No. 12 / OAO**

Aside from his work with bassist John Lindberg and guitarist James Emery in an ongoing experimental group, the String Trio of New York, violinist Billy Bang has pursued his progressive yet melodic approach to violin as a leader in a wide range of settings. *Distinction without a Difference* is a solo recording that demonstrates an innocence free from dogma and quite at odds with the Leroy Jenkins scratch-'n-sniff style of experimental violin music despite Bang's having studied with Jenkins. Three duet albums do little to elaborate on Bang's abilities as a soloist, although he proves himself an adept and sensitive partner, especially on the live disc with baritone saxophonist Tyler, which is the most satisfying of the three recordings. On *Rainbow Gladiator* and *Invitation* Bang is fronting his own quintet, and it's on these that his depth as a composer, leader and instrumentalist are most in evidence. Both are characterized by an unorthodox swing and will appeal to more traditionally minded listeners through their strong dedication to melody and rhythm. *Outline No. 12* is a challenging set featuring extraordinary instrumentation—three violins, three clarinets, saxophone, vibraphone, bass and two percussionists—which creates an unusual and impressive effect. — F.G.

AMIRI BARAKA (LEROI JONES)

★ **New Music—New Poetry / In. Nav.**

Amiri Baraka (b. 1934) recites poetry while tenor saxophonist David Murray and drummer Steve McCall improvise behind him. Meant to celebrate and expand the political and social revolution inherent in creative music, it succeeds only in trivializing it. As Baraka says on the LP's "Against Bourgeois Art": "They think they shit is profound, and complex but the people think it's / as profound and complex as monkey farts." Nothing new here and not even done well.
— F.G.

GATO BARBIERI

★ ★ ★ **Confluence / Ari.**
★ **Gato Barbieri Quartet / ESP**
★ ★ ★ **The Third World / Fly. D.**

Gato Barbieri's (b. 1934) throaty, lyrical tenor-saxophone style owes as much to the experimental jazz albums that reached his ears as to the cultural environment of his Argentinian homeland. His first notable work was on Don Cherry's decidedly avant-garde *Complete Communion.* Two years later he recorded his first album as a leader, *Gato Barbieri,* for ESP Disk, and though his performance is erratic, he is still an emotionally hard-hitting soloist in the tradition of others on that label, Albert Ayler and Frank Wright. *Confluence,* the 1968 duet recorded in Milan with South African pianist Dollar Brand, continues his exploration into the free-jazz vocabulary. Barbieri returned to America to record the last of his new music experiments, *The Third World.* The album's Afro-Latin theme indicated Barbieri's future direction.

★ ★ ★ **Bolivia** / Fly. D.
★ ★ ★ **Fenix** / Fly. D.
★ ★ ★ **Last Tango in Paris** / UA
★ ★ ★ **The Legend of Gato Barbieri** / Fly. D.
★ ★ ★ **El Pampero** / Fly. D.
★ ★ ★ ★ **Under Fire** / Fly. D.
★ ★ ★ **Yesterdays** / Fly. D.

When Barbieri dropped his free-jazz experiments in 1971 for a completely Afro-Latin style, he didn't so much change his playing as its context. Only keyboardist Lonnie Liston Smith remained, and the accent was now completely on native Latin American rhythms. *Fenix* successfully employs two percussionists, drummer Lenny White, bassist Ron Carter and guitarist Joe Beck to evoke a lush atmosphere. *El Pampero* is a live set recorded at the Montreux Jazz Festival with Barbieri soloing fiercely throughout. *The Legend of Gato Barbieri* collects essential cuts from *The Third World, Fenix* and *El Pampero.*

Under Fire is Barbieri's crowning achievement in this phase, a verdant rain forest of rhythmic ideas. Bassist Stanley Clarke delivers a memorable performance that links the support function of the rhythmic foundation with the melodic responsibilities of the solo improvisers.

Under Fire and its follow-up with the same band, *Bolivia,* were overshadowed by Barbieri's soundtrack for Bernardo Bertolucci's *Last Tango in Paris,* which attempted to match a groaning Brando's mute screaming to Barbieri's stifled cries. *Yesterdays,* an almost traditional set of improvisations, is a tribute to John Coltrane's hymnal ballad style.

★ ★ ★ **Caliente!** / A&M
★ ★ ★ ★ **Chapter One: Latin America** / Imp.
★ ★ ★ **Chapter Two: Hasta Siempre** / Imp.
★ ★ ★ ★ **Chapter Three: Viva Emiliano Zapata** / Imp.
★ ★ ★ **Chapter Four: Alive in New York** / Imp.
★ ★ ★ **Euphoria** / A&M
★ ★ ★ **El Gato** / Fly. D.
★ ★ ★ **Ruby, Ruby** / A&M
★ ★ ★ ★ **Para Los Amigos** / Doctor J.
★ ★ ★ **Tropico** / A&M

Recorded in Buenos Aires with an excellent band of South American musicians, *Chapter One: Latin America* burns with exotic rhythms and passionate playing. *Chapter Two,* recorded in Los Angeles with roughly the same musicians, is not quite as successful, but Barbieri's collaboration with the brilliant arranger Chico O'Farrill, *Chapter Three,* is a remarkable set of orchestrated Latin American songs. The *Chapter Four* Bottom Line recording is notable just for Barbieri's interplay with Howard Johnson's tuba. *El Gato* is a Flying Dutchman collection from *Under Fire* and *Bolivia* with one previously unreleased track.

Herb Alpert helped popularize Latin American music in the United States in the Sixties with his MOR hits, but he didn't have to ask Barbieri to recut "Spanish Flea" to make *Caliente!* commercial. Producer Alpert assembled a studio orchestra of staggering proportions for Barbieri's A&M debut, and though it's far from Barbieri's most challenging work, the album is, like its successors on that label, certainly accessible. Barbieri's fiery style continues to be well suited to live performance as the fine 1983 *Para Los Amigos* set proves.   — J.S.

RAY BARRETTO
★ ★ **The Big Hits Latin Style** / Tico
★ ★ ★ ★ **Charanga Moderna** / Tico
★ ★ ★ **Guajira y Guaguanco** / Tico
★ ★ ★ **La Moderna de Siempre** / Tico
★ ★ ★ **On Fire Again** / Tico
★ ★ ★ ★ **Tomorrow** / Atl.

Ray Barretto was already a highly respected jazz percussionist when he clicked in the Sixties with the spicy AM hit "El Watusi." The nonsense chanting made it a novelty song, which is undoubtedly what most people thought of it, but the totally irresistible rhythm and those stirring flute melodies made it a masterpiece of pop simplicity.

Barretto's charanga band made several joyful records during these years with Ray's fierce conga attack earning him the nickname Mr. Hard Hands. Barretto has gone on to be one of the kings of salsa, and his orchestra has provided some of salsa's liveliest moments. *Tomorrow: Barretto Live* is a consummate recording of some of his finest music in a superb orchestral context, with Tito Puente joining the band for a side-long finale, "Que Viva La Musica." — J.S.

GARY BARTZ

★ ★ Another Earth / Mile.
★ ★ Bartz / Ari.
★ ★ ★ Follow, the Medicine Man / Prest.
★ ★ ★ Harlem Bush Music—Taifa / Mile.
★ ★ ★ Harlem Bush Music—Uhuru / Mile.
★ ★ ★ ★ Home / Mile.
★ ★ ★ ★ I've Known Rivers / Prest.
★ ★ Juju Street Song / Prest.
★ ★ ★ Libra / Mile.
★ ★ Love Affair / Cap.
★ ★ ★ Music Is My Sanctuary / Cap.
★ Singerella—A Ghetto Fairy Tale / Prest.
★ ★ The Shadow Do / Prest.

Gary Bartz (b. 1940) is one of the many young jazz musicians nurtured in the late Sixties and Seventies who came up through the traditional musicians' hierarchy, mastering their instruments in post-bop combos, yet saw their rock and R&B contemporaries making money with commercial music and decided to have a go at it themselves. His best work as an apprentice was with McCoy Tyner on *Expansions.* Some of the Bartz albums that feature him playing solo (*I've Known Rivers, Home*) indicate that he is a better-than-average contemporary saxophonist. Yet Bartz tried to come up with a hook, and chose the political-commentary route on other Milestone and Prestige albums with little success. He also started singing, a major mistake. Bartz reached a low point with *The Shadow Do,* sinking into self-parody.

The two Capitol records are still attempts at crossover, but at least they are done without image gimmicks; Bartz even sneaks a few hot sax licks in between the funk ensemble singing and disco-R&B rhythm section. — J.S.

COUNT BASIE

★ ★ ★ ★ Afrique / Doctor J.
★ ★ ★ ★ April In Paris / Verve
★ ★ ★ Basie-Eckstine Inc. / Rou.
★ ★ ★ ★ Basie and Zoot / Pablo
★ ★ ★ ★ Basie Jam / Pablo
★ ★ ★ ★ Basie Live! / Trip
★ ★ ★ ★ Basie's Best / Olym.
★ ★ ★ ★ ★ Best of / MCA
★ ★ ★ ★ Best of / Pablo
★ ★ ★ ★ Blues By Basie / Col.
★ ★ ★ The Bosses / Pablo
★ ★ Broadway—Basie's Way / Camd.
★ ★ ★ ★ ★ Count Basie / RCA (France)

★ ★ ★ Count Basie and His Kansas City 7 / Imp.
★ ★ ★ Count Basie and Sarah Vaughan / Rou.
★ ★ ★ Count Basie and Zoot / Pablo
★ ★ ★ ★ ★ Count Basie at the Savoy Ballroom / Ev.
★ ★ ★ ★ Count Basie Big Band / Pablo
★ Count Basie Meets Bond / Solid St.
★ ★ ★ Count Basie Meets Oscar Peterson / Pablo
★ ★ ★ Count Basie's in the Bag / Bruns.
★ ★ Count Basie Straight Ahead / Dot
★ ★ ★ Count Basie Swings and Joe Williams Sings / Verve
★ ★ ★ Echoes of an Era—Basie, Getz and Vaughan Live at Birdland / Rou.
★ ★ ★ ★ Echoes of an Era—Best of Count Basie / Rou.
★ ★ ★ Echoes of an Era—Count Basie Vocal Years / Rou.
★ ★ ★ ★ Echoes of an Era—Count Basie Years / Rou.
★ ★ ★ 88 Basie Street / Pablo
★ ★ ★ Fantail / Rou.
★ ★ ★ First Time / Col.
★ ★ ★ ★ For the First Time / Pablo
★ ★ ★ From Broadway to Paris / ABC
★ ★ ★ Gifted Ones / Pablo
★ ★ ★ ★ ★ Good Morning Blues / MCA
★ ★ ★ ★ ★ Indispensable / RCA (France)
★ ★ ★ ★ I Told You So / Pablo
★ ★ It Might as Well Be Swing / Rep.
★ ★ ★ Jazz at the Santa Monica Civic '72 / Pablo
★ ★ ★ Kansas City Shout / Pablo
★ ★ ★ ★ ★ Kansas City Style / RCA
★ ★ ★ ★ Kansas City Suite/Easin' It / Rou.
★ ★ ★ Kid from Red Bank / Rou.
★ ★ ★ Master's Touch / Savoy
★ ★ ★ Me and You / Pablo
★ ★ ★ ★ Montreux Collection / Pablo
★ ★ ★ ★ Montreux-Count Basie Jam / Pablo
★ ★ ★ ★ One O'Clock Jump / CSP
★ ★ ★ Perfect Match / Pablo
★ ★ ★ Prime Time / Pablo
★ ★ ★ ★ Satch and Josh / Pablo
★ ★ ★ ★ Satch and Josh Again / Pablo
★ ★ ★ ★ Sixteen Men Swinging / Verve
★ ★ ★ ★ ★ Super Chief / Col.

William "Count" Basie (1904–1984) was one of the most important jazz figures because of his understanding of the use of the rhythm section in big-band arrangements, his perfection of the concept of riffing (repeating an insistent melodic statement, usually voiced by the horns in Basie's group, against a strong basic rhythm) and his adaptation of the blues to large-band formats. Basie's key-

board playing set up the architecture of his
band's sound by stripping all melodic ideas
down to their essential elements, a practice
that did much to loosen the idea of jazz arrangements and has also filtered down
through the years into pop song structures.

After studying organ under Fats Waller
and learning to play stride piano at New
York nightspots, Basie took off to Kansas
City, where he hooked up with one of the
more raucous examples of the big beat coming out of the Southwest, Bennie Moten's
band. Basie performances with Moten from
1929 to 1932 can be heard on *Kansas City
Style.* After gigging with that group for a
while, Basie formed his own organization out
of elements of the Moten band and other
musicians in the Kansas City area. In 1936
Basie brought this group to New York at
John Hammond's suggestion after Hammond
heard a radio broadcast of the band from
Kansas City. Within a year Basie's organization won international acclaim. The personnel was one of the greatest collections of
twentieth-century musicians: vocalists Billie
Holiday and Jimmy Rushing (Holiday was
replaced by Helen Humes); saxophonists
Lester Young, Herschel Evans and Earl
Warren; trumpeters Buck Clayton and Harry
Edison; trombonists Benny Morton and
Dicky Wells; and the most astounding
rhythm section of Basie at keyboards, drummer Jo Jones, guitarist Freddie Green and
bassist Walter Page.

With certain alterations, that's the band
assembled on the live radio broadcast from
1937, *Count Basie at the Savoy Ballroom.* Introduced as "ultra-modern rhythm," this set
gives good indication of the impact this
music had on the jazz world. Billie Holiday
is also on the mixed bag of sessions from the
late Thirties assembled on *Super Chief,* but
is not on the full-scale sessions Basie's band
recorded for Decca. These sides, collected on
Best of and *Good Morning Blues,* show Basie
and Co. in full swing, and include standards
like "One O'Clock Jump," "Jumpin' at the
Woodside," "Good Morning Blues" and
"Hey Lawdy Mama."

Basie's Best and *Basie Live!* are also radio
broadcasts. *Basie's Best* is from a date at the
Meadowbrook in Cedar Grove, New Jersey,
in November 1937, while the Trip *Live!* set
combines tracks from the Meadowbrook and
Savoy recordings with a 1940 set from Boston.

Basie's postwar bands introduced trombonist J. J. Johnson and a series of tremendous saxophonists, including Illinois Jacquet,
Don Byas, Lucky Thompson, Paul Gons-

alves and Frank Foster. While these groups
still met high standards, they naturally suffered in comparison with the brilliant, free-
swinging late-Thirties outfit. The Verve and
Roulette sides from the Fifties and Sixties
feature the great "two Franks" saxophone
combo of Frank Foster and Frank Wess.
Wess doubled on flute, yielding some fascinating tunes on *Sixteen Men Swinging. April
in Paris,* the 1955 album with its hit single
of a title track, was a commercial high point
for this outfit. Frank Foster's "Shiny Stock-
ings" was another popular high-water mark
for the organization. Vocalist Joe Williams
fronted this band and popularized the song
"Every Day I Have the Blues."

Basie's outstanding taste and musical
chops can never be called into question, and
he released a series of excellent records for
Flying Dutchman and Pablo in the Seventies. *Afrique* is an engaging conceptual
album in an Afro-Cuban style arranged and
conducted by Oliver Nelson and therefore
not identified with Basie's own rhythmic experiments. Oliver Nelson's arrangements for
that set are quite nice. The Pablo series features Basie in small- and large-group contexts and includes much excellent playing. *88
Basie Street* was the last album Basie made
before his death. — J.S.

SIDNEY BECHET
★ ★ ★ ★ ★ **Jazz Classics, Vol. 1 / Blue N.**
★ ★ ★ ★ ★ **Jazz Classics, Vol. 2 / Blue N.**
★ ★ ★ ★ ★ **Master Musician / RCA**
★ ★ ★ ★ ★ **Sidney Bechet / RCA (France)**
★ ★ ★ ★ **Sidney Bechet and Mezz Mezzrow
/ Class.**

New Orleans native Bechet (1897–1959) is
one of jazz's true originators. A broad-toned,
florid improviser, he worked often on clarinet but spent most of his time on soprano
sax, creating the definitive approach to the
straight saxophone until the arrival of Steve
Lacy and John Coltrane. After early fame
and an eclipse, which most of his contemporaries also met during the Depression, Bechet had a resurgence during the traditional
revival of the Forties and spent his last years
in Europe as a revered celebrity.

The Bechet albums above also make room
for numerous exceptional contributors. *Master Musician,* covering 1932–41, features the
New Orleans Feetwarmers with trumpeter
Tommy Ladnier; Earl Hines, Red Allen,
Willie "The Lion" Smith, Rex Stewart,
Kenny Clarke and others; plus early examples of studio overdubbing as Bechet becomes a six-piece one-man band. The
three-LP set *Sidney Bechet* includes more

material from the same period. *Jazz Classics* spans 1939–51, has Bunk Johnson, Meade Lux Lewis, Sid Catlett and Frankie Newton among the greats, and includes classic Bechet solos on "Summertime" and "Blue Horizon." More of this material can be found on the Port of Harlem Jazzmen set on Mosaic. Mezzrow's featured presence brings down the level of the Classic Jazz double album, recorded between 1945 and 1947.

★ ★ ★ ★ ★ **Bechet of New Orleans / Quin.**
★ ★ ★ **Blackstick / MCA**
★ ★ ★ **Giants of Traditional Jazz / Savoy**
★ ★ ★ ★ ★ **Louis Armstrong and Sidney Bechet in New York 1923–1925 / Smithsonian (available by mail only from Smithsonian Recordings, P.O. Box 10230, Des Moines, Iowa 50336)**
★ ★ ★ ★ **New Orleans Style Old and New / Commo.**
★ ★ ★ ★ **Sidney Bechet, Vol. 2, with Mezz Mezzrow / Arc. Folk**
★ ★ ★ ★ ★ **When a Soprano Meets a Piano / Inner**

The Quintessence album is a sampler from *Master Musician,* while the sessions with Mezzrow (*Bechet, Vol. 2*) are those also available on the earlier Classic Jazz double album.

The Smithsonian double album is an invaluable sampler of the first two great solo voices in jazz history, both together (in the Clarence Williams Blue Five) and apart. Bechet's first record session is included, plus Armstrong with Fletcher Henderson and blues singers Alberta Hunter and Trixie Smith. In *Blackstick,* from the Thirties, Bechet is featured with the orchestra of Eubie Blake's lyricist, Noble Sissle. Both the Savoy and Commodore albums are anthologies that include Bechet's work from the late Forties; the Commodore, with a side by Bechet's young New York disciples of the time (led by Bob Wilber), is a good pairing. *When a Soprano,* from 1956, puts Bechet in front of a modern trio led by pianist Martial Solal, and the "trad" giant shines. — B.B.

JOE BECK

★ ★ ★ **Beck / Kudu**
★ **Watch the Time / Poly.**

A longtime studio guitarist and arranger, Joe Beck (b. 1945) can probably play anything. But he's a surprisingly run-of-the-mill solo artist. True, *Beck,* with a dynamic, pressurized feel, features clean but raw jazz-rock guitar, engagingly melodic charts and powerful Dave Sanborn alto solos. But there is nothing distinctive about the pop R&B-rock

of *Watch.* Beck's guitar is not prominent or unusual enough, and most of the tunes are fronted by Tom Flynn's irritating vocals.

Most of Beck's LPs are out of print. Best is the 1969 *Nature Boy* (Verve-Forecast), a virtual one-man show that's a bit dated now. With his vocals multitracked, Beck sounds like the Mamas and the Papas. Still, *Boy* is strangely pleasant listening; parts of it, obviously conceptually progressive for their time, hold up nicely. Despite his omnipresence during the fusion era of the Seventies, Beck has all but disappeared—along with his records—in the Eighties. — M.R.

LEON BIX BEIDERBECKE

★ ★ ★ ★ ★ **Bix Beiderbecke / Time–Life**
★ ★ ★ ★ ★ **Bix Beiderbecke and the Chicago Cornets / Mile.**
★ ★ ★ ★ **Story, Vol. 1: Bix and His Gang / Col.**
★ ★ ★ ★ ★ **Story, Vol. 2: Bix and Tram / Col.**
★ ★ ★ ★ **Story, Vol. 3: Whiteman Days / Col.**

Among other things, Bix Beiderbecke (1903–1931) is a fount of clichés concerning musicians. Beiderbecke was the original sensitive white student who sought his own voice through the example of black masters, the prototype serious artist hemmed in by commercial mediocrity, the grand alcoholic wipeout. If Scott Fitzgerald might have invented the trumpeter's life as a Jazz Age parable, Beiderbecke's music has a moody and fragile existence of its own, one that provided a complement to Louis Armstrong's bravura and first hinted at less blues-centered implications for jazz.

Of the available Beiderbecke albums, the Milestone has the earliest recordings (1924) by the rambunctious Wolverines, a Midwest combo in love with the sound of the early white bands from New Orleans. Part of this two-record set offers the contrasting example of other young white trumpets, Jimmy McPartland and Muggsy Spanier. The key volume in Columbia's *Beiderbecke Story,* covering 1927–28, is the second, where the trumpeter is teamed with his good friend and perfect partner, C-melody saxophonist Frank Trumbauer, plus assorted other greats. Volume 3, despite the overblown pop music of Paul Whiteman's orchestra (where Beiderbecke finished his career as a featured soloist), warrants a place of honor for Beiderbecke's impressionistic piano solo, "In a Mist." The anthology in the Time–Life Giants of Jazz series is the most comprehensive look at his work. — B.B.

RICHARD BEIRACH
★ ★ ★ Elegy for Bill Evans / Palo Alto
★ ★ Eon / ECM/War.
★ ★ ★ Hubris / ECM/War.
Richard Beirach (b. 1947) came to prominence as part of Dave Liebman's Lookout
Farm group in the mid-Seventies. He went
on to make several piano records in solo and
group contexts. *Hubris,* a solo piano record,
shows Beirach's richly melodic playing at its
best. — J.S.

SATHIMA BEA BENJAMIN
★ ★ ★ Dedications / Ekapa
★ ★ ★ Sathima Sings Ellington / Ekapa
South African vocalist married to pianist
Abdullah Ibrahim (Dollar Brand). While
Ibrahim has concentrated on developing a
style that incorporates the music of his native Cape Town into the American jazz tradition, Benjamin has opted for a more traditional path: the title of her first album (*Sings
Ellington*) describes the selection as suc-
cinctly as possible; *Dedications* is a collection
of American pop standards. As a vocalist,
Benjamin is warm and mature, capable of
personalizing well-known compositions without resorting to gimmicks or pyrotechnics.
— F.G.

GEORGE BENSON
★ ★ Bad Benson / CTI
★ ★ ★ Benson and Farrell / CTI
★ ★ ★ ★ Benson Burner / Col.
★ ★ ★ Best / A&M
★ ★ ★ Beyond the Blue Horizon / CTI
★ ★ Blue Benson / Poly.
★ ★ ★ ★ Body Talk / CTI
★ ★ ★ Breezin' / War.
★ ★ Cast Your Fate to the Wind / CTI
★ ★ ★ Collection / War.
★ ★ ★ The George Benson Cookbook / Col.
★ ★ ★ George Benson/Jack McDuff / Prest.
★ ★ ★ ★ Good King Bad / CTI
★ ★ ★ Give Me the Night / Qwest/War.
★ ★ ★ The Greatest / Ari.
★ ★ ★ In Flight / War.
★ ★ ★ ★ ★ It's Uptown / Col.
★ ★ ★ Livin' Inside Your Love / War.
★ ★ ★ New Boss Guitar of George Benson /
   Prest.
★ ★ ★ The Other Side of Abbey Road /
   A&M
★ ★ Shape of Things to Come / A&M
★ ★ Space / CTI
★ ★ ★ Summertime: In Concert / CTI
★ ★ Take Five / CTI
★ ★ ★ Weekend in L.A. / War.
★ ★ White Rabbit / CTI

Breezin' was the first jazz album ever to "go
platinum"—sell more than a million copies—and that event released a flood of criticism. "Why Benson," some have asked, "and
not a hundred others before him? After tons
of lame numbers, cushioned in fluffy pillows
of strings and horns, and a philosophy seemingly based on personal mercantilism rather
than musical value, why should he get the
honor?"
   Well, why not? First of all, platinum is
sales, not honor, and besides, Benson (b.
1943) happens to be one of the best jazz guitarists alive. He is a consistent player: most
of the more recent albums feature some of
the best funk and jazz session players in the
business. His predilection for pop-sounding
material is as much a result of having served
Brother Jack McDuff for years before going
solo (Lonnie Smith carried the organ tradition onto Benson's early Columbia albums),
as well as Benson's genuine comfort in a
rhythmic rock & roller role, as it is commercial design.
   What made Benson a big hit, finally, was
his singing voice, not his guitar playing. Too
bad, for Benson knows how to use solo
space—he organizes his featured spots with a
beginning, middle and end, building plunks
of notes into octave strums in the manner of
Wes Montgomery, with infallible rhythm. If
the pop thing stops clicking, he can always
fall back on his talent. — A.E.G.

BUNNY BERIGAN
★ ★ ★ ★ The Best Vol. 1 / RCA (France)
★ ★ ★ ★ Indispensable / RCA (France)
★ ★ ★ Take It Bunny / CSP
A big-band trumpeter who made a name for
himself in the Thirties with the Dorsey
Brothers, Benny Goodman and Tommy Dorsey before forming his own group, Bunny
Berigan (1908–1942) popularized the jazz
standard, "I Can't Get Started." A legendary drinker, Berigan (like Bix Beiderbecke)
epitomized the myth of the self-destructive
musical genius. The RCA Black and White
imports cover Berigan's most important
sides. — J.S.

TIM BERNE
★ ★ ★ The Ancestors / Soul N.
★ ★ ★ The Five-Year Plan / Emp.
★ ★ ★ Mutant Variations / Soul N.
★ ★ ★ 7X / Emp.
★ ★ ★ Spectres / Emp.
★ ★ ★ Songs and Rituals in Real Time /
   Emp.
A Brooklyn-based alto saxophonist, Tim
Berne (b. 1954) has good chops, strong side-

men and better-than-average compositions. He also has a sense of humor, something of a rarity among experimentalists. *Songs and Rituals In Real Time* and *The Ancestors* show a growing sophistication in terms of melody and structure, although they are no more conservative than the earlier recordings. — F.G.

CHU BERRY
★ ★ ★ ★ ★ "Chu" / CSP
★ ★ ★ ★ Dentistry in Rhythm (Fillin' Chu Gaps) / Two Fl.

Leon "Chu" Berry (1910–1941) is perhaps the greatest Coleman Hawkins disciple of the swing era. On *Chu* the tenor saxophonist is heard with small groups and the Cab Calloway orchestra, where he was featured from 1937 until his death. The Italian reissue *Dentistry in Rhythm* is not exactly commonplace, but even if it were, how could this title go unremarked? Even under a more mundane name it would still contain those valuable Berry solos with Fletcher Henderson, Wingy Manone, etc. See also Fletcher Henderson and especially the Lionel Hampton boxed set on Bluebird. — B.B.

GENE BERTONCINI
★ ★ ★ ★ ★ Bridges / GHB
★ ★ ★ ★ ★ Close Ties / Omni.

Known primarily for his refined session work on albums by Paul Desmond, Hubert Laws, Paul Winter and Wayne Shorter, guitarist Gene Bertoncini (b. 1937) in his current stint with bassist Mike Moore is making some of the loveliest chamber jazz since the early-Sixties collaborations of Bill Evans and Jim Hall. Bertoncini's conception incorporates both the jazz and classical repertoires, but his success has nothing to do with the overblown ambitions of any Third Stream or modernist movements. By simply interpreting classical pieces along with jazz and popular standards, the Bertoncini/Moore duo produce an unpretentious synthesis that exposes the organic connections between these worlds of music.

Where *Bridges* does include a few cuts using electric guitar, the majority of *Close Ties* features Bertoncini's preferred instrument, the classical guitar. For all his obvious technical skills he remains a subtle, understated player whose gifts lie in his exemplary tone and melodic ideas rather than his speed. Moore is his bass counterpart, a phenomenal improviser and support player whose added virtues are his taste and restraint. Bertoncini's intriguing arrangements leave plenty of room for personal expression.

The programing is often illuminating, such as the juxtapositions of classical and popular tunes that share similar chord progressions (Chopin's Prelude in A Minor and Jobim's "How Insensitive") or ingenious reworkings of unexpected material (funky workout on Gershwin's Piano Concerto in F). The classic bent notwithstanding, these albums have nothing to do with the Claude Bolling-esque drivel that remains so popular. One listen to the flowing virtuosity and sheer inventiveness of these two will convince any knowledgeable listener that they are first-class jazzmen. — S.F.

JOSE ROBERTO BERTRAMI
★ ★ ★ Blue Wave / Mile.

Engaging debut LP from the keyboardist/producer of the Brazilian group Azymuth. Bertrami (b. 1946) surrounds himself here with some of Brazil's better (though not necessarily better-known) players. — J.S.

BLACKBYRDS
★ Action / Fan.
★ Better Days / Fan.
★ ★ ★ ★ The Blackbyrds / Fan.
★ ★ City Life / Fan.
★ ★ ★ ★ Flying Start / Fan.
★ Night Groove / Fan.
★ Unfinished Business / Fan.

After working as Donald Byrd's backup band, the Blackbyrds recorded under their own name as a jazz-funk fusion group and struck gold with the hit single, "Walking in Rhythm." *Blackbyrds* and *Flying Start* show them at their commercial peak. The rhythmic bottom was irresistibly solid and danceable, the vocals were appropriately sparse and the instrumentation—particularly the horn charts—was melodically adventurous and fulfilling. After the success of *Flying Start,* the Blackbyrds began to view themselves as a disco attraction rather than a progressive, jazz-trained R&B act. *City Life* exhibited a dispiriting reliance on recycled riff-hooks and an embarrassing bent for hollow social and psychocybernetic commentary. The one instrumental track was a dud, and the vocals were depressingly imitative. Any traces of the Blackbyrds' Howard University jazz training had been erased by the time of *Unfinished Business.* The horn arrangements were inaudible, the rhythm tracks commensurate with the slavish vocals, and synthesizer bromides reigned to the point of nausea. — M.G.

ED BLACKWELL
★ ★ ★ El Corazon (with Don Cherry) / ECM/War.

★ ★ ★ **Mu, Part One / Aff.**
★ ★ ★ **Mu, Part Two / Aff.**
A native of New Orleans, drummer Ed
Blackwell (b. 1927) has built a creative style
on adapting that city's unique R&B and
street rhythms to contemporary jazz. His
work with Ornette Coleman and Old and
New Dreams lent both outfits an individual
rhythmic foundation through his engaging
use of cross-rhythms.

Blackwell's three albums as a leader were
all undertaken with longtime bandmate,
trumpeter Don Cherry. Both *Mu* discs were
originally recorded for BYG Records, and
the Affinity versions are reissues. Despite the
ten-plus years between *Mu* and *El Corazon,*
there is a striking similarity in their use of
small hand instruments, folk melodies and
sympathetic execution. — F.G.

EUBIE BLAKE
★ ★ ★ **Eighty-Six Years of Eubie Blake /
Col.**
★ ★ ★ **Eubie Blake Vol. 1 / RCA (France)**
★ ★ ★ ★ **Marches I Played . . . Vol. 2 /
RCA (France)**
This is a fairly comprehensive representation
of Blake's output. A better-than-average rag-
time pianist, Eubie Blake (1883–1983) wrote
several classic ragtime compositions and cov-
ered standards like "Maple Leaf Rag" before
making it big in the Twenties as a nightclub
performer, then later as a vaudeville act with
Noble Sissle. He and Sissle cowrote a number of popular songs, including "Memories
of You" and "I'm Just Wild about Harry."
The French Black and White LPs present
Blake at his best. — J.S.

ART BLAKEY
★ ★ ★ ★ ★ **A Night at Birdland with the Art
Blakey Quintet, Vol. 1 / Blue N.**
★ ★ ★ ★ ★ **A Night at Birdland with the Art
Blakey Quintet, Vol. 2 / Blue N.**
Abdullah Ibn Buhaina, better known as Art
Blakey (b. 1919), has two claims on jazz im-
mortality: as one of the most incendiary
drummers in history, the man who reawak-
ened interest in the most basic African
sources of jazz percussion; and as the leader
of the Jazz Messengers, a band that, at its
inception in 1954, ushered in the hard-bop
era, and to this day continues to provide an
uncompromising forum for new talent.

The *Night at Birdland* albums, from 1954,
have the seeds of the first Jazz Messenger
band (Horace Silver is on piano and the
chief composer), plus the lucid horns of Lou
Donaldson (alto) and Clifford Brown (trumpet). The first volume, with Brown's classic
"Once in a While," has the slight edge. Both

volumes can now be heard in their entirety
on the Mosaic Clifford Brown anthology.
★ ★ ★ ★ **The Jazz Messengers at the Cafe
Bohemia, Vol. 1 / Blue N.**
★ ★ ★ ★ ★ **The Jazz Messengers at the Cafe
Bohemia, Vol. 1 / Blue N.**
The first classic Jazz Messenger band con-
tained Blakey, Silver, trumpeter Kenny
Dorham, tenor saxophonist Hank Mobley
and bassist Doug Watkins. Their trend-
setting studio work is now available under
Horace Silver's name (on *Horace Silver and
the Jazz Messengers*); these live 1955 record-
ings are almost as good. Volume 2 contains
"Like Someone in Love," a hard-bop arche-
type pop-song transformation.
★ ★ ★ **Art Blakey Big Band / Beth.**
★ ★ ★ ★ ★ **Art Blakey's Jazz Messengers
with Thelonious Monk / Atl.**
★ ★ ★ **At the Jazz Corner of the World,
Vol. 1 / Blue N.**
★ ★ ★ ★ ★ **At the Jazz Corner of the
World, Vol. 2 / Blue N.**
★ ★ ★ **Messages / Rou.**
★ ★ ★ ★ **Moanin' / Blue N.**
★ ★ ★ **Paris Concert / CSP**
★ ★ ★ **Percussion Discussion / Chess**
Between 1956 and 1959, many fine soloists
(Jackie McLean, Hank Mobley, Johnny Grif-
fin, Lee Morgan) passed through the Mes-
sengers, but the records often descended into
a blowing session rut. The meeting with
Monk is notable for the sublime interaction
between drums and piano, and some good
Griffin tenor. *Moanin'* has the original of pi-
anist Bobby Timmons' title hit (one of the
first "soul-jazz" pieces along with Silver's
work) and the first flowering of Lee Morgan's brilliant trumpet.
★ ★ ★ ★ **The Big Beat / Blue N.**
★ ★ ★ ★ **The Freedom Rider / Blue N.**
★ ★ ★ ★ **Like Someone in Love / Blue N.**
★ ★ ★ ★ **Meet You at the Jazz Corner of
the World (2 vols.) / Blue N.**
★ ★ ★ ★ ★ **A Night in Tunisia / Blue N.**
★ ★ ★ ★ **Roots and Herbs / Blue N.**
Blakey's 1959–61 quintet was one of his best,
with a maturing Morgan and Timmons and
the then-raucous tenor sax of Wayne
Shorter. All of the soloists composed and all
played their tails off. *Night in Tunisia* gets
highest marks for the most bacchanalian ver-
sion of the title piece ever recorded, as well
as "So Tired," one of Timmons' best soul
pieces; but this group never made a bad rec-
ord.
★ ★ ★ **The African Beat / Blue N.**
★ ★ ★ **Jazz Message / Imp.**
★ ★ ★ ★ ★ **Jazz Messengers! / Imp.**
Jazz Messengers! is a transition album, with
Curtis Fuller's trombone making the band a

sextet. The group's reading of "Invitation" is a ballad classic. *Jazz Message,* a quartet with Sonny Stitt and McCoy Tyner, is surprisingly routine, while *African Beat* is a drum ensemble workout for percussion fanatics only.

★ ★ ★ ★ **Buhaina's Delight / Blue N.**
★ ★ ★ ★ **Caravan / Fan./OJC**
★ ★ ★ ★ ★ **Free for All / Blue N.**
★ ★ ★ ★ **Kyoto / Fan./OJC**
★ ★ ★ ★ **Mosaic / Blue N.**
★ ★ ★ ★ ★ **Thermo / Mile.**
★ ★ ★ ★ **Ugetsu / Fan./OJC**

The last great Blakey group is a sextet with Freddie Hubbard, Shorter and Fuller in the front line and pianist Cedar Walton and bassist Jymie Merritt, or Reggie Workman, joining Blakey in the rhythm section. The band, which stayed together from 1961 to 1964, may have been Blakey's most consistent. While all of the above are recommended, *Thermo* contains a particularly fired-up live Birdland set where Walton cuts the excellent horns.

★ ★ ★ **Anthenagin / Prest.**
★ ★ **Backgammon / Rou.**
★ ★ ★ **Buhaina / Prest.**
★ ★ ★ **Buttercorn Lady / Trip**
★ ★ **Child's Dance / Prest.**
★ ★ **Gypsy Folk Tales / Rou.**
★ ★ ★ **Jazz Messengers '70 / Cata.**
★ ★ **Live! / Trip**

The last twenty years have seen a decline in Blakey's personnel, and a formularization that has led him to place undue emphasis on repeating old hits. Still, for fans of blowing sessions there is always some strong soloing. *Buttercorn Lady,* from 1966, has special interest, for the Messengers of the time contained Chuck Mangione on trumpet and Keith Jarrett (heard here in his recording debut). Woody Shaw, Cedar Walton and Stanley Clarke participated in the early-Seventies Prestige sessions, and longtime Blakey associate Bill Hardman displays growing trumpet prowess on a couple of the others.

Blakey can be heard with countless other jazz leaders, including most of the people who have recorded for Blue Note, but special attention should be paid to his work with Silver, Monk and Miles Davis.

★ ★ ★ **Africaine / Blue N.**
★ ★ ★ ★ ★ **Hard Bop / Odys.**
★ ★ ★ **In My Prime, Vol. 1 / Timel.**
★ ★ ★ ★ **In This Korner / Conc. J.**
★ ★ ★ ★ ★ **Live Messengers / Blue N.**
★ ★ ★ **Mirage / Savoy**
★ ★ ★ ★ ★ **Original Messengers / Odys.**
★ ★ ★ **Reflections in Blue / Timel.**
★ ★ ★ **Straight Ahead / Conc. J.**

You say there weren't enough Jazz Messengers albums in the catalogue? The past few years have seen welcome reissues of important early work (especially the two Odysseys), and a continuing stream of new productions. And this list doesn't even include the recent material available only as imports from the Dutch Timeless label (which had a brief American distribution deal with Muse).

Blakey's bands are not the most consistent—the stunning *Hard Bop* and ordinary *Mirage* are from the same mid-Fifties edition—and the blowing session format can grow tedious over several albums in any case. So concentrate on the Odysseys, with Horace Silver, Donald Byrd and Hank Mobley on *Original* and the Bill Hardman/Jackie McLean front line on *Hard Bop*; *Live,* with a side of Clifford Brown and three from the Hubbard/Shorter edition; and *In This Korner,* the best by the recent Messengers. *Straight Ahead,* recorded in June '81, offers a glimpse of Blakey's most important recent discovery, trumpeter Wynton Marsalis.

★ ★ ★ ★ ★ **Album of the Year / Timel.**
★ ★ ★ **Jazz Messenger Big Band at Montreux / North Sea/Timel.**
★ ★ ★ **Killer Joe (with George Kawaguchi) / Story.**
★ ★ ★ ★ **Originally / Col.**
★ ★ ★ ★ **Straight Ahead / Conc. J.**

Over a quarter of a century after a liner-note writer called him ubiquitous, Blakey remains so. Albums listed above represent only part of early-Eighties Blakey (*Originally* contains rare performances from 1956). Particularly noteworthy is *Album of the Year,* recorded by the Wynton Marsalis/James Williams edition of the band. *Killer Joe,* with Japanese drummer Kawaguchi added, introduces a later and quite promising edition of the Messengers. — B.B.

CARLA BLEY
★ ★ ★ **Dinner Music / Watt**
★ ★ ★ ★ ★ **Escalator over the Hill / JCOA**
★ ★ ★ **Social Studies / ECM**
★ ★ ★ ★ **13 and 3/4 / Watt**
★ ★ ★ **Tropic Appetites / Watt**

This co-founder, sustainer and confounder of the Jazz Composers Orchestra is known almost exclusively for her infrequent recordings. And so each album appears by surprise, like a flash flood or a train wreck. They can seem just as momentous; each is a complete work, another strong offering on her own independently financed and distributed label, with each part carefully integrated. But she composes from a musical background so diverse and with a musical community so close to lunacy that her music remains tousled and untamed.

Her most accomplished talent may be her mixology—she has combined opera singers with singing tuba players, Linda Ronstadt with a singing string bassist, members of Ornette Coleman's band with Jack Bruce and John McLaughlin, English rock stars with Gato Barbieri, and everybody with her kid. Most of the above happens on *Escalator,* a massive, durable three-record set. *Tropic Appetites* is a similar dish (words again by Paul Haines, whose images are as brittle and jagged as Carla's attack) in a scaled-down version, featuring Julie Tippetts (née Julie Driscoll) as vocalist.

Her half of *13 and 3/4* (husband Mike Mantler wrote "13") is an orchestral piece in which musicians are added and subtracted like swirls in a runaway spiral. *Dinner Music* is some shoutin' in the woods with the funk section known as Stuff.

Carla Bley is a composer and a pianist. She loves the sound of low brasses and buzzy reeds. NRBQ, Robert Wyatt and others have recorded her music, but the influence rock has had on her is more important. She is a musician who likes to have fun, and takes her humor seriously.   — A.E.G.

PAUL BLEY
★ ★ ★ ★ ★ **Alone, Again** / IAI
★ ★ ★ ★ **Axis** / IAI
★ ★ ★ **Barrage** / Base
★ ★ ★ ★ ★ **Closer** / Base
★ ★ ★ **Japan Suite** / IAI
★ ★ ★ ★ **Live at Hillcrest** / Inner
★ ★ ★ ★ **New Music: Second Wave** / Savoy
★ ★ ★ ★ ★ **Open, to Love** / ECM/War.
★ ★ ★ **Quiet Song** / IAI
★ ★ ★ ★ **Scorpio** / Mile.
★ ★ ★ ★ **Solemn Meditation** / GNP
★ ★ ★ **Synthesizer Show** / Mile.
★ ★ ★ ★ ★ **Turning Point** / IAI
★ ★ ★ ★ ★ **Virtuosi** / IAI

Paul Bley (b. 1932) was an iconoclastic pianist with a strong rhythmic and harmonic stamp when he met Ornette Coleman in Los Angeles during 1958. *Solemn Meditation* captures his personal modernisms from the time; *Live at Hillcrest* (a poor recording released without Coleman's permission) suggests something more as Bley ostensibly leads the first Coleman quartet.

In a few years, Bley would be in the middle of the free jazz/energy music movement that assaulted chord changes and straight-ahead time. At this point he often worked in a trio similar in surface sound, though far more abstract, than that of Bill Evans. A key 1964 Bley session actually features Gary

Peacock and Paul Motian, a "liberated" Evans rhythm section, plus Sun Ra tenor saxophonist John Gilmore; the quartet's bold work on Carla Bley tunes was only released a dozen years later, and can be heard on *Turning Point* and the Savoy anthology. Most of Bley's work during this period, however, was in a trio context, with Barry Altshul's drumming and several fine bassists. *Closer* has Steve Swallow and several good tunes by Carla; *Virtuosi* and *Japan* offer longer blowing, from the Sixties and Seventies respectively, with Peacock.

The Seventies saw Bley turn to synthesizers (on the Milestone albums), then gravitate to more solo and chamber-style groupings as a greater spareness entered his music. *Open, to Love* and *Alone, Again* are both model unaccompanied recitals, with a lucidity of touch and dramatically restrained development that casts new light on Bley's now-standard repertoire of songs by ex-wives Carla and Annette Peacock. Both were recorded at Norway's Arne Bendiksen studio, on the legendary "ECM solo piano," and the results are a model of the efforts that the German label soon rode into a mood-jazz trend. *Axis* is newer, live, and a more playful solo recital.   — B.B.

ARTHUR BLYTHE
★ ★ ★ **Blythe Spirit** / Col.
★ ★ ★ ★ ★ **Bush Baby** / Adel.
★ ★ ★ ★ **Elaborations** / Col.
★ ★ ★ ★ ★ **The Grip** / In. Nav.
★ ★ ★ ★ ★ **Illusions** / Col.
★ ★ ★ **In the Tradition** / Col.
★ ★ ★ ★ **Lenox Avenue Breakdown** / Col.
★ ★ ★ ★ **Light Blue** / Col.
★ ★ ★ ★ **Metamorphosis** / In. Nav.

Alto saxophonist Blythe began recording under his own name in 1977 at the relatively advanced age of thirty-six (the India Navigation albums, both from a live concert), and quickly made good on the underground reputation he had cultivated in Los Angeles and New York for over a decade. While the blues inflection and rhythmic infectiousness of his playing are timeless, Blythe's vivid expressionism and frequent use of advanced textures in his bands place him clearly within the post-Ornette Coleman period. Blythe's explorations never go so far afield as to lose the listener, however, and he continues to use a standard rhythm section—and the standard repertoire—at least part of the time. He is a model of the outside-in/inside-out player that has recently gained favor.

Blythe's 1977 work on India Navigation and Adelphi is among his best on record. *The Grip* introduces his preference for tuba and cello in a small-group context (a sextet here); and with its programing of solo, trio and full-band pieces gives a nicely balanced view of his work. (*Metamorphosis* has fewer variations, due to its longer tracks.) *Bush Baby,* where Blythe is joined only by congas and the stunning tuba of Bob Stewart, is the place to hear him blow at greatest length and inspiration.

A Columbia recording contract turned Blythe into a force to be reckoned with on the international jazz scene, though the quality of the resulting sessions vary. The first, *Lenox Avenue,* adds "Blood" Ulmer's guitar and flute from James Newton to the tuba/cello band for a spirited if casually presented jam (too many fades, not enough sense of Blythe as focal point). *In the Tradition* is "inside" Blythe, playing Coltrane, Ellington and Waller with the fine Stanley Cowell/Fred Hopkins/Steve McCall rhythm section, but the results radiate surface heat without giving off any exceptional sparks. *Illusions,* equal parts traditional quartet and guitar/cello/tuba band in a program of Blythe originals, is a far more riveting set and perhaps the best introduction to Blythe's recent directions. *Blythe Spirit* strives for a different kind of balance, with the tuba band featured and originals programmed against "Strike Up the Band," "Misty" and "Just a Closer Walk with Thee"; unfortunately, the replacement of Ulmer by Kelvin Bell drops the intensity a notch, and the new material can't provide sufficient compensatory heat.

Recently Blythe has concentrated on his "tuba band" with the more introspective Bell having permanently taken over for Ulmer on guitar. Musicians are added and subtracted on *Elaborations,* a good sampling of Blythe originals. *Light Blue,* an all-Monk session, features several of that composer's neglected gems ("Coming On the Hudson," "Nutty").

For an indication of Blythe's power as a sideman, hear him with Lester Bowie and Jack DeJohnette. — B.B.

LESTER BOWIE
★ ★ ★ ★ **All the Magic** / ECM/War.
★ ★ ★ **Duet** (with Phillip Wilson) / IAI
★ ★ ★ ★ **Fast Last!** / Muse
★ ★ ★ ★ ★ **The Fifth Power** / Black S.
★ ★ **The Great Pretender** / ECM/War.
★ ★ ★ ★ ★ **Numbers 1 & 2** / Nessa
★ ★ ★ **Rope-a-Dope** / Muse

Like the other members of the Art Ensemble of Chicago, trumpeter Lester Bowie (b. 1941) occasionally conducts independent projects under his own name. *Numbers 1 & 2,* however, is really an early Art Ensemble

recording from 1967, at a point when Bowie, Roscoe Mitchell and Malachi Favors worked as the Roscoe Mitchell Art Ensemble. (They are under Bowie's name here for contractual reasons. Art Ensemble member-of-the-future Joseph Jarman is added for "Number 2.") This is one of the first, and best, Art Ensemble sets.

Recording away from Mitchell in the Seventies, Bowie tended more toward free blowing on structures, with greater humor and appreciation for the lyrical tradition (however transmogrified) than many of his contemporaries. *Fast Last!,* despite ragged passages, is recommended for the participation of Julius Hemphill (who arranged two tracks) and the inclusion of Bowie's Armstrong homage, "Hello Dolly." Both Muse sessions feature Lester's trombonist brother Joseph, who later attained New York newwave fame in Defunkt. 1978 found Bowie and drummer Phillip Wilson (an associate from early AACM days, before Wilson went on the road with Paul Butterfield) toying with "Three Blind Mice" to little consequence on *Duet,* then teaming in a first-rate quintet (with Arthur Blythe on alto, Art Ensemble bassist Favors and Amina Myers' piano and vocals) that ran the gamut from beautiful ballads to gospel extravaganzas. *The Fifth Power,* the better of two albums done on an Italian tour and the only one still available, suggests that this was one of the late-Seventies best groups.

Sometimes, Bowie's retrieval of Fifties material and broad humor seems indulgent (*The Great Pretender*); elsewhere, most notably on the band album sides of the *All the Magic* twofer, the references and moods flow and the music soars. Even with the less powerful second disc of idiosyncratic solo trumpet, *All the Magic* is still pushing a five-star rating.

Bowie can also be heard with the Jack DeJohnette New Directions band and, of course, the Art Ensemble of Chicago.
— B.B.

JOANNE BRACKEEN
★ ★ ★ **Aft** / Timel.
★ ★ ★ ★ **Ancient Dynasty** / Col.
★ ★ ★ **Mythical Magic** / Pausa
★ ★ ★ ★ **Prism** / Choice
★ ★ ★ ★ **Snooze** / Choice
★ ★ ★ ★ **Special Identity** / Ant.
★ ★ ★ **Tring-a-Ling** / Choice

Joanne Brackeen (b. 1938) is one of the most lauded pianists on the scene, and rightly so. Brackeen first gained noticed in the Seventies as a member of saxophonist Teddy Edwards' band, going on to stints with Art Blakey and

Stan Getz. As a soloist, she demonstrates a myriad of influences, the most pronounced of which are McCoy Tyner, from whom Brackeen seems to have gained her approach to comping, and Chick Corea, with whom she shares a penchant for a sprightly single-note right-hand approach.

As a leader, Brackeen appears most comfortable in the trio setting, and her recordings utilizing bassist Eddie Gomez tend to be her most successful. Brackeen's solo outing, *Mythical Magic,* is her least engaging, while the quartet date, *Ancient Dynasty,* featuring tenorman Joe Henderson, proves the most dynamic. — F.G.

RUBY BRAFF
★ ★ **America the Beautiful / Conc. J.**
★ ★ ★ **Grand Reunion (with Ellis Larkins) / Chi.**
★ ★ ★ **International Quartet Plus Three / Chi.**
★ ★ ★ **Live at the New School / Chi.**
★ ★ **Quartet Plays Gershwin / Conc. J.**
★ ★ **Quartet Salutes Rodgers and Hart / Conc. J.**
★ ★ ★ **Ruby Braff with the Ed Bickert Trio / Sack.**

Ruby Braff (b. 1927) is an excellent traditional trumpet/cornet player who suffered when he came up in the Fifties with Vic Dickenson because his kind of playing was considered out of date. Despite such obvious influences as Louis Armstrong and Bobby Hackett, Braff's style has always remained personal and full of conviction. His best moments were the duets with pianist Ellis Larkins which are now, like all of his early work, out of print. The recent records, represented above, are still quite listenable if not his best work. — J.S.

BRAND, DOLLAR
See IBRAHIM, ABDULLAH

ANTHONY BRAXTON
★ ★ ★ ★ **For Alto / Del.**
★ ★ ★ ★ ★ **3 Compositions of New Jazz / Del.**

Braxton (b. 1945) is one of the most interesting and certainly the most publicized musician to come out of Chicago's Association for the Advancement of Creative Musicians. His compositions create a diverse series of unique improvisational situations for a wide range of ensembles, and draw on contemporary European techniques as well as the Afro-American tradition. As a player, Braxton has led the way in making the unaccompanied saxophone recital an accepted form.

The above Delmark albums were made in Chicago before Braxton left for Europe in 1969. *3 Compositions* introduced four of the finest AACM players—Braxton, trumpeter Leo Smith, violinist Leroy Jenkins and pianist Richard Abrams. *For Alto,* two albums of unaccompanied sax, is historically important, although several of the solos sound like exercises in the more extreme avant-garde techniques.
★ ★ ★ ★ **Duo 1 (with Derek Bailey) / Eman.**
★ ★ ★ ★ **Duo 2 (with Derek Bailey) / Eman.**
★ ★ ★ **In the Tradition / Inner**
★ ★ ★ **In the Tradition, Vol. 2 / Inner**
★ ★ ★ ★ **Saxophone Improvisations/Series F / Inner**
★ ★ ★ **Together Alone / Del.**
★ ★ ★ ★ ★ **Trio and Duet / Sack.**

Braxton recorded prolifically during his European sojourn (1969–74), a period that found him hustling chess in order to make ends meet and pay for occasional concerts of his own work. His best recording of the period were made with the collectives Creative Construction Company and Circle, though the solo *Saxophone Improvisations* album and duo concerts with innovative British guitarist Bailey are interesting. *In the Tradition* is Braxton with a post-bop rhythm section playing jazz standards, which works pretty well when Braxton is not playing his contrabass clarinet. The Sackville album, a Canadian import, features his best work with synthesizer (played by frequent collaborator Richard Teitelbaum; Leo Smith is also present), plus three duets with bassist David Holland on Tin Pan Alley material.
★ ★ ★ ★ ★ **Creative Orchestra Music 1976 / Ari.**
★ ★ ★ ★ **Duets 1976 (with Muhal Richard Abrams) / Ari.**
★ ★ ★ ★ **Five Pieces 1975 / Ari.**
★ ★ ★ ★ ★ **New York, Fall 1974 / Ari.**
★ ★ ★ ★ **The Montreux/Berlin Concerts / Ari.**

After singing with Arista, which provided him with a commendable range of performing situations, Braxton came to stand for the contemporary jazz vanguard during the Seventies. While all of his Arista recordings are worthwhile, *Creative Orchestra Music* is his masterpiece, a vibrant blending of open-ended structures, swinging extensions of big-band tradition and even an abstract march; among the impressive personnel can be found Abrams, Holland, Leo Smith, Roscoe Mitchell and George Lewis. The *New York* album is also singled out because it is the most varied of Braxton's small-group works, with a clarinet/synthesizer duet and a com-

position for four saxophones. *Five Pieces* and
the concert album have Braxton's excellent
quartets with Holland, drummer Barry Altschul and either trumpeter Kenny Wheeler
or trombonist George Lewis.

Braxton also recorded in the Seventies
with Abrams, Holland, Marion Brown and
Teitelbaum and on the *Wildflowers* anthology.

★ ★ ★ ★ **The Complete Braxton 1971 / Ari.
/Free.**
★ ★ ★ ★ ★ **Composition 98 / Hat Hut**
★ ★ **For Two Pianos / Ari.**
★ ★ ★ **Open Aspects '82 (with Richard
Teitelbaum) / Hat Hut**
★ ★ ★ ★ ★ **Performance 9/1/79 / Hat Hut**
★ ★ ★ ★ **Seven Compositions 1978 / Moers**
★ ★ ★ ★ **Six Compositions: Quartet / Ant.**
Braxton continued releasing albums on
Arista through the close of 1979, but most—
including a composition for four orchestras
that spanned three records, and a 1979 solo
recital that revealed substantial growth—
were quickly deleted once the label lost in-
terest in new music. All that remains is the
Complete set, from the period when Braxton,
Chick Corea, David Holland and Barry Altschul comprised Circle. Besides these musicians and trumpeter Kenny Wheeler, the
double album has pieces for four overdubbed
sopranino saxes and five tubas.

As interest declined on the American
front, Braxton turned to European labels,
where he also recorded two impressive duet
sessions with drummer Max Roach. Both
Seven Compositions and *Performance* were
produced during a 1979 tour by a fine Braxton quartet including longtime AACM associate Thurman Barker on drums and two
strong younger players, trombonist Ray Anderson and bassist John Lindberg. While
each album contains fine music, *Performance*
offers the added delight of hearing the quartet build over a full concert program.

The four latest Braxton albums place his
music in four different settings. Most successful is *Composition 98,* a long and dense
blend of compositions and improvisations for
trumpet, trombone, saxes and piano, heard
in both studio and live performances. *Six
Compositions* is also notable for its "straight-
ahead" Braxton and rhythm section, and *Aspects* has surprisingly gentle duets with Teitelbaum's synthesizer, but the two-piano
piece on Arista (performed by Ursula Op-
pens and Frederick Rzewski) is slow going
for this listener. — B.B.

LENNY BREAU
★ ★ ★ ★ ★ **Five O'Clock Bells / Adel.**
★ ★ ★ ★ ★ **Mo' Breau / Adel.**

These remarkable solo guitar improvisations
show why Lenny Breau (1941–1984) was an
underground legend among other musicians
even before he'd documented his genius on
record. His technique is so lightning fast that
he often sounds like two guitarists playing at
once, yet his speed never sacrifices emotion
or feel. Breau's interpretive ability is magnificent as he recasts "Days of Wine and
Roses" and "My Funny Valentine" on *Bells*
and "Autumn Leaves" on *Mo' Breau.*
— J.S.

TERESA BREWER
★ **I Dig Big Band Singers / Doctor J.**
★ **In London / Doctor J.**
★ **Live at Carnegie Hall & Montreux,
Switzerland / Doctor J.**
★ ★ **Theresa Brewer/Stephane Grappelli /
Doctor J.**
★ ★ ★ **We Love You Fats (with Earl Hines)
/ Doctor J.**
Teresa Brewer (b. 1931) is a pop singer who
dabbles as a jazz vocalist, sometimes with
odious results as on *Live* and *Big Band,*
sometimes fairly gracefully, as on the Fats
Waller tribute record. Waller's material is al-
ways good to hear, and Earl Hines pays the
real tribute to Waller here with his warm,
intelligent piano structures. — J.S.

BRECKER BROTHERS
★ ★ **Back to Back / Ari.**
★ ★ ★ **Brecker Brothers / Ari.**
★ ★ **Detente / Ari.**
★ ★ ★ ★ **Heavy Metal Be-Bop / Ari.**
★ ★ **Straphanging / Ari.**
The Breckers were the most ubiquitous New
York session players during the heyday of
the Seventies' fusion era: Randy (b. 1945)
was Miles Davis' peer on electronic trumpet;
Michael (b. 1949) recognized as being among
the best of countless young tenor saxophonists. They formed their band with other New
York sessioneers and proceeded to track a
first album (*Brecker Brothers*) calculated to
appeal to the disco market, giving themselves
a commercial leg up when "Sneaking Up behind You" became a minor hit. Their formula took over as the group went on, and
by *Back to Back,* the playing is pure funk
process. They remained vital in live performance, as *Heavy Metal Be-Bop* indicates, but
they failed to carry their popularity through
to the Eighties. — J.S.

STAN BRONSTEIN
★ ★ **Living on the Avenue / Muse**
★ ★ **Our Island Music / Muse**

Elephant's Memory saxophonist tries his hand at leading conventional jazz sessions. — J.S.

BOB BROOKMEYER

★ ★ ★ **Back Again** / Sonet
★ ★ ★ ★ **Bob Brookmeyer and Friends** / Odys.
★ ★ ★ **In Concert Montreux '79** / Gry.
★ ★ ★ **Live at the Village Vanguard** / Gry.
★ ★ ★ **Small Band** / Gry.
★ ★ ★ **Through a Looking Glass** / Fine.
★ ★ ★ **With Mel Lewis and the Jazz Orchestra** / Gry.

Though he began his musical career in the Fifties as a pianist, Bob Brookmeyer (b. 1929) eventually became known for his sleek, mellifluous valve trombone playing with Gerry Mulligan later in the decade. The gem here is *And Friends,* a beautiful 1964 session with Stan Getz playing tenor sax, Herbie Hancock on piano, Gary Burton on vibes, Elvin Jones on drums and Ron Carter on bass. The recent Gryphon and Sonet LPs are good; *Live* also features drummer Mel Lewis, whose big band has spotlighted Brookmeyer's most recent substantial work as a composer and arranger. — J.S.

CLIFFORD BROWN

★ ★ ★ ★ **Big Band in Paris/1953** / Prest.
★ ★ ★ ★ **Brownie Eyes** / Blue N.
★ ★ ★ ★ ★ **Clifford Brown in Paris** / Prest.
★ ★ ★ ★ ★ **The Complete Blue Note and Pacific Jazz Recordings of Clifford Brown** / Mosaic, 197 Strawberry Hill Avenue, Stamford, CT 06902
★ ★ ★ ★ **The Paris Collection** / Inner
★ ★ ★ ★ **The Paris Collection, Vol. 2** / Inner
★ ★ ★ ★ ★ **Quartet in Paris/1953** / Prest.
★ ★ ★ ★ **Sextet in Paris/1953** / Prest.

Trumpeter Clifford Brown (1930–1956) could improvise with the flowing equilibrium of Fats Navarro, the crackling excitement of Dizzy Gillespie and more than enough potent ideas of his own. Had he not been killed in an auto accident, he undoubtedly would have grown even further; as it is, he left a modest number of recordings and never sounded less than very good.

In 1953 Brown made his first impression on the jazz world, first in some studio sessions collected on the Blue Note album, then on some European albums made while he toured with Lionel Hampton's band. *Clifford Brown in Paris* is a twofer that contains the master takes found on the three other more exhaustive Prestige volumes (masters plus all alternate takes). The Inner City albums are yet another packaging of the 1953 Paris ma-

terial, drawn from several sessions originally on the French Vogue label.

★ ★ ★ ★ ★ **The Quintet, Vol. 1** / Em.
★ ★ ★ ★ ★ **The Quintet, Vol. 2** / Em.

From 1954 until his death, Brown coled a band with drummer Max Roach, which also contained George Morrow on bass, Bud Powell's brother Richie on piano and either Harold Land or Sonny Rollins on tenor sax. The spectacular solo work of Brown, Roach and (later) Rollins, Powell's imaginative arrangements and the introduction of several classic compositions (Brown's own "Joy Spring" and "Daahoud" among them) made this one of the decade's premier groups. Both of the above double albums are excellent, with better tunes on Volume 1 and Rollins on Volume 2.

★ ★ ★ ★ ★ **The Beginning and the End** / Col.
★ ★ ★ **Best Coast Jazz** / Trip
★ ★ ★ **Clifford Brown All-Stars** / Trip
★ ★ ★ **Clifford Brown with Strings** / Trip

All-Stars and *Best Coast* are from a 1954 jam session by Brown, Roach and five others; the tracks are long and typical of the era's loose blowing encounters. Neal Hefti wrote some economical string arrangements to showcase Brown's strong tone and the results are pretty, though low on improvisation. *Beginning and End,* on the other hand, is essential Brown: two 1952 R&B tracks by Chris Powell's Blue Flames which contain the trumpeter's first recorded solos, and three lengthy jams taped in a Philadelphia music store the night before his death. Brown's passionate, life-affirming spirit overcomes any potential irony the performances might carry.

★ ★ ★ ★ ★ **Brown and Roach at Basin Street** / Em.
★ ★ ★ ★ ★ **Brown and Roach Inc.** / Em.
★ ★ ★ ★ ★ **Pure Genius** / Elek./Mus.
★ ★ ★ ★ ★ **More Study in Brown** / Em.

The Brown/Roach recordings have returned, in their original LP form, via Japanese reissue and PolyGram imports. The newly discovered *Pure Genius,* which is live, and *More Study in Brown,* which is not, have the added bonus of Sonny Rollins. — B.B.

RAY BROWN

★ ★ ★ ★ ★ **As Good As It Gets** / Conc. J.
★ ★ **Brown's Bag** / Conc. J.
★ ★ ★ **A Ray Brown 3** / Conc. J.
★ ★ ★ ★ **Something for Lester** / Contem.
★ ★ ★ ★ ★ **Tasty (with Jimmy Rowles)** / Conc. J.
★ ★ ★ **This Is Ray Brown** / Verve
★ ★ ★ **Trio, Live at the Concord Jazz Festival** / Conc. J.

No other bassist in the world sounds like Ray Brown. With his cavernous, richly acoustic tone and his immaculate accompaniment and soloing, Brown (b. 1926) has been the consummate musician for nearly forty years. Listeners raised on the speed-demon machinations of Eddie Gomez or Stanley Clarke will be astonished by the sheer musicality of Brown's *thinking* approach to the instrument.

All this brilliance is best heard on *Tasty* and *As Good,* two 1979 duet LPs he cut with pianist Jimmy Rowles. These two men really listen to each other, and their intimate ineraction is both exciting and deeply moving. In their own way these albums are the equal of the majestic Duke Ellington–Jimmy Blanton duets of the Forties.

Brown's small-group work does not approach the personal heights of the duets, but they all feature fine instrumentalists, Monty Alexander, Cedar Walton and Sam Most among them, and lots of miniature masterpiece solos from the leader. Only *Brown's Bag,* which is ruined by studio effects, is to be avoided.   — S.F.

TOM BROWNE
★ ★ **Browne Sugar / Ari.**
★ ★ **Love Approach / Ari.**
★ ★ **Magic / Ari.**
★ ★ **Yours Truly / Ari.**

Perhaps because he didn't even start listening to jazz until a friend played him an Ornette Coleman record at college, trumpeter Tom Browne (b. 1954) has had little difficulty sacrificing musicianship to commerciality. After building his reputation as a sideman with Sonny Fortune and Lonnie Liston Smith he made a pop-jazz debut with *Browne Sugar,* which covered familiar material like "What's Goin' On" and "The Closer I Get to You." A second album, *Love Approach,* included the hit "Funkin' for Jamaica" and earned Browne numerous awards in 1980. *Magic* and *Yours Truly* are more of the same.   — J.S.

DAVE BRUBECK
★ ★ ★ ★ **All the Things We Are / Atl.**
★ ★ ★ **The Art of Dave Brubeck / Atl.**
★ ★ ★ **Brother, The Great Spirit Made Us All / Atl.**
★ ★ ★ **Brubeck and Desmond—1975: The Duets / Hori.**
★ ★ ★ ★ **The Dave Brubeck Quartet at Carnegie Hall / Col.**
★ ★ ★ ★ **The Dave Brubeck Octet / Fan./ OJC**
★ ★ ★ ★ **Reunion / Fan./OJC**

★ ★ ★ ★ **Stardust / Fan.**
★ ★ **Time In / Col.**
★ ★ ★ ★ **Time Out / Col.**
★ ★ ★ **Two Generations of Brubeck / Atl.**

In Dave Brubeck's early-Fifties recordings, when he was still playing jazz and Broadway standards, he was generally overshadowed by his masterly alto saxophonist, Paul Desmond. Brubeck (b. 1920), who was classically trained under the tutelage of Darius Milhaud, has often been criticized for his approach to improvisation from a theoretical rather than swinging basis. Some of his earliest work can be heard on the 1946 *Octet.* Most of *Stardust* was recorded in '51 and '52. *The Art of* is a collection of two 1953 concerts, remarkable mostly for Desmond's contribution. *Reunion,* a '57 recording, combines Brubeck and Desmond with tenor saxophonist Dave Van Kriedt, who was part of the Octet.

Time Out is Brubeck's most popular and durable album, and ample evidence of his poignant maturity as a composer. Released in 1960, it has acquired an undeserved reputation as the first jazz work to explore "compound time," something Max Roach and others had long pursued. *Carnegie Hall* is probably the best Brubeck quartet sampler from the mid-Sixties, with sterling performances of standards like "Take Five," "Blue Rondo à la Turk" and "For All We Know." Their rapport was telepathic by this time, particularly Brubeck's coy piano forays and Desmond's sly alto counterpoint. *Time In* is more memorable for its reflective ballads than its halfhearted uptempo efforts. *Time In* was the last significant statement from the original Brubeck quartet, and even a cursory listen will reveal that all was not well—the offhand performance, sloppy endings and Desmond's reticence all smack of hurried first takes.

Nowhere is Brubeck's vitality more apparent than on the recordings with his sons, Chris, Darius and Danny. Occasionally their attempts to update a standard like "Blue Rondo à la Turk," from *Two Generations,* with its Ponty-esque violin, extraneous blues guitar and harp, and electric bop piano, falter embarrassingly. On balance, their exuberance and integrative excellence make up for the blind spots.

The Duets merely affirmed something most critics had been saying all along: the best part of the old Brubeck quartet was Paul Desmond. A few moments connect, but it's mostly one-dimensional, calculatedly saccharine stuff. Dave, especially, needs the accompaniment of a rhythm section. *Brother* presents more of Brubeck's familial flirtations with jazz rock, enhanced by spacious, thoughtful improvisations and hard-bop harmonic complexities, something Dad never accomplished with any group before. If *All the Things We Are* isn't the best Brubeck recording, it's certainly his bravest. One side features Dave trading ideas with Anthony Braxton, Lee Konitz and Roy Haynes, while the other is devoted largely to a stirring Jimmy Van Heusen medley, with perennial comrades Jack Six and Alan Dawson. Brubeck shines on both counts. — M.G.

RUSTY BRYANT
★ ★ ★ ★ **Fire Eater** / Prest.
★ ★ ★ ★ **Night Train Now!** / Prest.
★ ★ ★ ★ **Rusty Bryant Returns** / Prest.
★ ★ ★ ★ **Rusty Rides Again** / Phoen.
★ ★ ★ ★ **Soul Liberation** / Prest.
Soul tenor greatly influenced by Gene Ammons. Although Rusty Bryant (b. 1929) has been well recorded during his thirty-plus years as a group leader (including sixteen albums for Prestige), only a few are still available. *Rides Again* was made for a small New Jersey label. Samples of Bryant's work for Prestige are available via two tracks on that label's *Giants of the Funk Tenor Sax* collection. — F.G.

CARL BURNETT
★ ★ ★ **Carl Burnett Quintet Plays Richard Rodgers** / Discov.
This LP is the California drummer Carl Burnett's only date as a leader. Very competent performances all around on pleasant if predictable arrangements by Llew Mathews. The only surprise is saxophonist Eddie Harris, who cuts the fat out of his playing for several lean, straight-ahead solos. — F.G.

KENNY BURRELL
★ ★ ★ **Both Feet** / Fan.
★ ★ ★ ★ **Bluesin' Around** / Col.
★ ★ ★ **Crash!** / Prest.
★ ★ ★ ★ **Ellington Is Forever** / Fan.
★ ★ ★ ★ **Ellington Is Forever, Vol. 2** / Fan.
★ ★ ★ **For Duke** / Fan.
★ ★ ★ ★ ★ **Guitar Forms** / Verve
★ ★ ★ **Handcrafted** / Muse
★ ★ ★ **In New York** / Muse
★ ★ ★ ★ **Kenny Burrell** / Prest.
★ ★ ★ **Live at the Village Vanguard** / Muse
★ ★ **Moon and Sand** / Conc. J.
★ ★ ★ ★ **Moonglow** / Prest.
★ ★ ★ ★ **Out of This World** / Prest.
★ ★ ★ ★ **Quintet** / Prest.
★ ★ ★ **'Round Midnight** / Fan.
★ ★ ★ **Sky Street** / Fan.
★ ★ ★ **Soul Call** / Pres.
★ ★ **Stormy Monday** / Fan.
★ ★ ★ **Tin Tin Deo** / Conc. J.
★ ★ ★ **Up the Street** / Fan.
★ ★ ★ **When Lights Are Low** / Conc. J.
Kenny Burrell (b. 1931) hails from Detroit, where he built a solid reputation backing Candy Johnson, Count Belcher, Tommy Barnett and Dizzy Gillespie as well as leading his own groups. A facile, bluesy guitarist, Burrell owes the obvious debt to Django Reinhardt and Charlie Christian, but his soulful, easy-swinging playing style has carved its own mark. After moving to New York in the mid-Fifties Burrell led a number of hot improvisational "blowing" sessions with a variety of groups from quintets to larger units. These sets are for the most part excellent examples of this popular though occasionally boring genre. *Quintet,* a date from 1957, features outstanding saxophone soloing from John Coltrane, while *Kenny Burrell* uses the all-Detroit rhythm section of Tommy Flanagan on piano, Doug Watkins on bass and Elvin Jones on drums. *Crash!* teams Burrell up with jazz/blues organist Jack McDuff, while *Moonglow* and *Out of This World* are bolstered by the presence of the masterful tenor saxophonist Coleman Hawkins. *Bluesin' Around* presents hot early-Sixties sessions with several fine lineups. Burrell's most uncharacteristic album during this era is the beautiful *Guitar Forms,* which is built around exquisite Gil Evans charts rather than the usual head arrangements.

Burrell worked with smaller groups during the Seventies, relying on Jerome Richardson's sax and flute work as the other solo voice for most of the Fantasy sets (*Both Feet, Up the Street, Sky Street*). His best work during this period is the two-volume Duke Ellington tribute, *Ellington Is Forever,* which used Ellington sidemen along with musicians like Jimmy Smith and Nat Adderley in paying homage to the great composer's influence. *For Duke* compiles some of this material on a single album, but the full sets are recommended.

Most recently Burrell has been working with different trios to achieve some warm, open-ended results, which can be found on the Concord Jazz and Muse sets. *Tin Tin Deo,* with bassist Reggie Johnson and drummer Carl Burnett, is an especially good session. — J.S.

GARY BURTON
★ ★ ★ **Alone at Last** / Atl.
★ ★ ★ ★ **Gary Burton and Keith Jarrett** / Atl.

★ ★ ★ **Good Vibes / Atl.**
★ ★ ★ ★ **Paris Encounter / Atl.**
★ ★ **Throb / Atl.**
★ ★ ★ ★ **Turn of the Century / Atl.**
This conservatory-trained (Berklee College of Music) vibraphonist emerged in the Sixties as an accomplished soloist, bandleader and composer. As a soloist he perfected the technique of playing vibraphone with four mallets, and his classical training gave his ensemble work an understated, richly melodic chamber-music quality that was unusual amid the strident freneticism of most experimental music of the time.

Even though he was understated, Burton (b. 1943) was an experimentalist himself. His landmark quartet albums for RCA featuring electric guitarist Larry Coryell explored the melodic possibilities of a musical fusion between jazz, rock and country in delightfully subtle ways. (Unfortunately all the work of this period is out of print.)

The next phase of Burton's career, represented by the five albums recorded for Atlantic between 1969 and 1972, remains in print. During this time Burton worked in a variety of contexts, keeping only bassist Steve Swallow from his previous lineup. *Throb,* which features guitarist Jerry Hahn and violinist Richard Greene, shows a country-music influence. *Good Vibes,* which adds guitarists Sam Brown and Eric Gale, drummer Bernard Purdie, keyboardist Richard Tee and bassist Chuck Rainey, is an out-and-out R&B record. Burton is at his best in collaboration with another gifted improvisationalist or as a soloist, where his pristine melodicism is shown off to best effect, so *Gary Burton and Keith Jarrett, Paris Encounter* (with the legendary French violinist Stephane Grappelli) and *Alone at Last* (a solo album featuring Burton's set from the 1971 Montreux Jazz Festival) are among his finest albums. *Turn of the Century,* a compilation of several tracks from each of the five Atlantic albums, is a serviceable recap of this period.
★ ★ ★ **Colours of Chloë / ECM/War.**
★ ★ ★ ★ ★ **Crystal Silence / ECM/War.**
★ ★ ★ **Dreams So Real / ECM/War.**
★ ★ ★ **Duet / ECM/War.**
★ ★ ★ ★ **Easy as Pie / ECM/War.**
★ ★ ★ **Hotel Hello / ECM/War.**
★ ★ ★ ★ **In Concert (with Chick Corea) / ECM/War.**
★ ★ ★ **In the Public Interest / ECM/War.**
★ ★ ★ ★ **Matchbook / ECM/War.**
★ ★ ★ ★ **The New Quartet / ECM/War.**
★ ★ ★ ★ **Passengers / ECM/War.**
★ ★ ★ **Picture This / ECM/War.**

★ ★ ★ ★ **Ring / ECM/War.**
★ ★ ★ ★ **Times Square / ECM/War.**
At ECM, Burton found in Manfred Eicher a producer whose attitude toward music and recording fit perfectly with the vibraphonist's sensibility. Burton's sense of classical form and chamber-music delicacy has enabled him to benefit tremendously from Eicher's meticulous recording technique. Burton's ECM debut, *Crystal Silence,* a series of magnificent duets with pianist Chick Corea, picks up where his best work on Atlantic left off and is arguably a recording high point for both musicians, whose deft touch and lyricism complement each other perfectly. *The New Quartet* introduces guitarist Michael Goodrick, bassist Abraham Laboriel and drummer Harry Blazer on a number of compositions by Corea, Steve Swallow, Carla Bley and longtime Burton songwriter Michael Gibbs.

Burton's most prolific year was 1974. In May he reunited with Swallow from his old quartet for a duet album, *Hotel Hello.* He collaborated with Gibbs on *In the Public Interest,* a project of Gibbs compositions scored for a large (twenty-two musicians) ensemble. Then, in a four-day period that July, Burton recorded two albums for Eicher, the first—*Ring*—with a group made up of Goodrick, new guitarist Pat Metheny, percussionist Bob Moses and two bassists, Steve Swallow and Eicher's star instrumentalist, Eberhard Weber. After recording that set he went back into the studio with guitarist Ralph Towner to make a duet record, *Matchbook,* mostly of Towner's compositions (including the Winter Consort standard "Icarus"). The album closes with a stately reading of the Charles Mingus elegy for Lester Young, "Goodbye Pork Pie Hat."

Dreams So Real uses the Moses/Swallow rhythm section and both Goodrick and Metheny on guitars on a selection of Carla Bley material. *Passengers* combines drummer Dan Gottlieb with bassists Weber and Swallow and guitarist Metheny. Metheny contributes three songs and Swallow and Weber one each, but the high point of the record is Chick Corea's "Sea Journey." Burton has a special affinity for Corea's light-spirited melodicism and turns in a beautiful performance on this song. *Times Square* benefits from some strong Steve Swallow songwriting. *In Concert* reunites Burton with Corea in a sublime exchange.   — J.S.

JAKI BYARD
★ ★ ★ ★ **Experience / Prest.**
★ ★ ★ ★ **Family Man / Muse**

★ ★ ★ **Freedom Together** / Prest.
★ ★ ★ ★ **Giant Steps** / Prest.
★ ★ **Live! Vol. 1** / Prest.
★ ★ **Live! Vol. 2** / Prest.
★ ★ ★ ★ **On the Spot!** / Prest.
★ ★ ★ **Out Front** / Prest.
★ ★ ★ ★ ★ **Solo Piano** / Prest.
★ ★ ★ **Sunshine of My Soul** / Prest.
★ ★ ★ ★ ★ **There'll Be Some Changes Made** / Muse
★ ★ ★ ★ **To Them—To Us** / Soul N.
★ ★ **With Strings!** / Prest.

Jaki Byard (b. 1922) is the most complete pianist on the scene today. Not merely skilled in every style of jazz piano, his best playing creates a seamless continuum of the music itself. He freely mixes stride, gospel, bop, modal and avant-garde elements throughout his work with a technical aplomb and intuitive ease that bridges stylistic eras with unself-conscious elegance.

Like his former employer Charles Mingus, Byard is blessed with a sly sense of humor; his albums are equally inventive and entertaining. This playful and slightly irreverent quality is best found on the solo albums: *Solo, There'll Be, To Them.* Wildly imaginative and stunningly performed, these LPs feature a diverse set of show tunes, jazz standards, gospel songs and even transformed pop numbers ("I Know A Place" on *Solo,* Stevie Wonder's "Send One Your Love" on *To Them*).

Trio sessions include *Giant Steps,* a double-album reissue of early work with Ron Carter and Roy Haynes; *Sunshine* with Elvin Jones; *Freedom* uniting Bayard with Richard Davis and Alan Dawson, a marvelous rhythm section that also backed Booker Ervin, Eric Kloss and Phil Woods; and *Family* with Byard doubling sax and containing an ambitious side-long suite.

Out Front and *On the Spot!* use extra horns to good effect, but the gem is *Experience* with that other great musical eccentric, Roland Kirk. All these LPs reflect Byard's idiosyncratic spirit; only the two-volume *Live!* and the *With Strings* sets are to be approached with trepidation.   — S.F.

DON BYAS

★ ★ ★ **Don Byas** / Inner
★ ★ ★ **In Paris** / Prest.
★ ★ ★ ★ **Jam Party** / Savoy
★ ★ ★ ★ **Tribute To Cannonball** / Col.

Don Byas' ferocious tenor work is one of the key links between the swing and bop eras. His advanced harmonic knowledge and awesome command of his instrument make for some of the most stimulating listening from that transitional period.

After an impressive stint with Count Basie as Lester Young's replacement, Byas (1912–1972) hit 52nd Street just when the bop movement was taking off. He was in the "first" bop band with Dizzy Gillespie and Oscar Pettiford and participated in some important recording dates of the time. Byas' own work is documented on *Jam Party,* with able support from the humming bassist Slam Stewart and such early bop legends as "Little" Benny Harris on trumpet and pianist Clyde Hart.

Byas spent the next twenty years in Europe; the Prestige and Inner City LPs catch him during his stay. The Inner City release is notable for its two female pianists, Mary Lou Williams and Beryl Booker.

The Columbia LP was a summing-up date for the aging musician. Less a tribute to its producer Cannonball Adderley than a fond remembrance of glory days, it features a still explosive Bud Powell and expatriate drummer Kenny Clarke on some familiar bop blowouts and two poignant ballads.   — S.F.

CHARLIE BYRD

★ ★ ★ **Bluebyrd** / Conc. J.
★ ★ ★ ★ **Bossa Nova Pelos Pássaros** / Fan./ OJC
★ ★ ★ **Brazilian Soul (with Laurindo Almeida)** / Conc. J.
★ ★ ★ **Brazilville** / Conc. P.
★ ★ ★ **Byrd by the Sea** / Fan.
★ ★ ★ **Crystal Silence** / Fan.
★ ★ ★ ★ **Latin Byrd** / Mile.
★ ★ ★ **Tambu** / Fan.
★ ★ ★ **Top Hat** / Fan.

Ironically, Virginia-born guitarist Charlie Byrd (b. 1925) is known mostly for his pioneering influence on and promotion of Brazilian jazz. Impressed by this music while on a Latin American concert tour in the early Sixties, Byrd helped popularize bossa nova in the United States via recordings with Stan Getz as well as on his own. *Bossa Nova* features the hit "Meditation." *Latin Byrd* collects some historic 1962 sessions (including *Bossa Nova*) that cover many of the standard bossa nova titles like "One-Note Samba," "Desafinado" and "Carnaval."

An accomplished classical guitarist, whose purity of technique is widely acclaimed, Byrd studied under Segovia, owes a stylistic debt to Charlie Christian, and played in Woody Herman's orchestra before adopting Brazilian music. Yet, despite such a varied background, the Brazilian trademark has stuck with him. *Crystal Silence,* a 1973 trio with Byrd's brother Joe on bass, includes several effective Chick Corea tracks including the title cut. *Tambu,* an electric-band project released in '74, features Cal Tjader on vibes. *Byrd by the Sea* is trio concert material from '74, *Top Hat* a '75 quintet with Nat Adderley on cornet, *Brazilville* and *Bluebyrd* are sets from '79 and '81 respectively, with Bud Shank's alto saxophone playing on the former. *Brazilian Soul* adds guitarist Laurindo Almeida.　— J.S.

DONALD BYRD
★ ★ ★ **And 125th St. N.Y.C. / Elek.**
★ ★ ★ **Black Byrd / Blue N.**
★ ★ ★ **Cat Walk / Blue N.**
★ ★ ★ **Creeper / Blue N.**
★ ★ ★ **Fuego / Blue N.**
★ ★ ★ ★ **I'm Tryin' to Get Home / Blue N.**
★ ★ ★ ★ **Long Green / Savoy**
★ ★ ★ **Love Byrd / Elek.**
★ ★ ★ **Places and Spaces / Blue N.**
★ ★ **Street Lady / Blue N.**

★ ★ ★ **Thank You for F.U.M.L. / Elek.**
★ ★ ★ ★ **Young Byrd / Mile.**
Donald Byrd (b. 1932) was one of the group of promising young jazz musicians who came from Detroit to New York City in the mid-Fifties. His hot, full-toned trumpet playing with George Wallington and then Art Blakey's Jazz Messengers in '55 and '56 made him a sought-after session player. On his own he recorded with Gigi Gryce in the Jazz Lab Quintet, with Art Farmer and with Pepper Adams as well as a prolific session leader. (*Two Trumpets* is with Farmer; *Young Byrd* with Adams and Gryce). Byrd became one of the more successful crossover jazz artists in the Seventies, playing hard funk epitomized on the later Blue Note records and featuring the Blackbyrds group, which later recorded on its own. His Blue Note funk approach began to wear thin after a while, but the more recent records, made for Elektra, show Byrd continuing on in this genre in fairly good, if predictable, form.
　—J.S.

GEORGE CABLES
★ ★ ★ ★ **Cables' Vision / Contem.**
★ ★ ★ **Goin' Home (with Art Pepper) / Gal.**
★ ★ ★ *Tête-á-Tête* **(with Art Pepper) / Gal.**
One of the outstanding pianists on the West
Coast, George Cables (b. 1944) is best
known for his work with Art Pepper. The
duet album, *Goin' Home,* is a relaxed date,
demonstrating the musical sympathy the pair
developed. Pepper fans will also find a lot
more clarinet than they're accustomed to on
this one. *Tête* is more from that session.

Cables' Vision features the pianist in front
of a very strong outfit including Bobby Hutcherson, Erie Watts, Peter Erskine, Tony
Dumas and Freddie Hubbard, the latter
turning in one of his finest performances of
the Seventies. The compositions are varied in
mood and tempo, and Cables gets a chance
to show his versatility. — F.G.

CAB CALLOWAY
★ ★ ★ ★ **16 Cab Calloway Classics / CBS**
   (France)
Bandleader/singer Cab Calloway (b. 1907) is
well known as a jazz novelty figure from
cartoon soundtracks, a composer of marijuana tributes or as the goggle-eyed, high-
stepping "hi-de-ho" man. Although these
caricatures helped build a popular legend for
Calloway, they obscured the fact that he was
a terrific bandleader whose organizations always played the hottest material and featured some of the brightest instrumental
lights of the era, including saxophonists Chu
Berry and Hilton Jefferson, trumpeters Dizzy
Gillespie and Jonah Jones and drummer
Cozy Cole. — J.S.

GUS CANNON
★ ★ ★ ★ ★ **Cannon's Jug Stompers/Gus**
   Cannon as Banjo Joe 1927–1930 / Her.
This record, extremely important in the his-
tory of twentieth-century music, collects all

of Gus Cannon's recordings made in the period when he codified a jug-band tradition
that thirty-five years later would have extensive repercussions on rock & roll. Cannon
played banjo like a woodchopper, hitting the
strings with a fierce rhythmic intensity that
matched the ribald enthusiasm of his singing,
whistling, jug blowing and kazoo playing.
Cannon exuded an energy and love of playing on these sides that is incredibly infectious. His 1927 duets (as Banjo Joe) with
guitarist Blind Blake include such classics as
"Poor Boy, Long Ways from Home," the
great story-song "Madison Street Rag" and
the hilarious "My Money Never Runs Out."

The Stompers were a trio with Cannon,
the brilliant harmonica player Noah Lewis,
and Ashley Thompson on guitar. — J.S.

BARBARA CARROLL
★ ★ ★ **At the Piano / Discov.**
A veteran of 52nd Street and one of the first
female bop pianists, Barbara Carroll (b.
1925) spends most of her time these days
playing hotel-lounge gigs. Perhaps that's why
she has developed such an affinity for show
tunes and standards, and although one might
prefer to hear her tackle something with a
little more grit and a bit less glitz, she still
plays very well. — F.G.

BENNY CARTER
★ ★ ★ **Additions to Further Definitions /**
   MCA
★ ★ ★ **Alto Artistry / Trip**
★ ★ ★ ★ ★ **Benny Carter / Time-Life**
★ ★ ★ ★ **Benny Carter—1933 / Prest.**
★ ★ ★ ★ ★ **Benny Carter's Orchestra / RCA**
   (France)
★ ★ ★ ★ **Best of / Pablo**
★ ★ ★ ★ **Carter, Gillespie, Inc. / Pablo**
★ ★ ★ ★ **Early Benny Carter / Ev.**
★ ★ ★ ★ ★ **Further Definitions / MCA**
★ ★ ★ ★ **Jazz Giant / Contem.**

★ ★ ★ ★ **King / Pablo**
★ ★ ★ **Live and Well in Japan / Pablo L.**
★ ★ ★ ★ **Montreux '77 / Pablo L.**
★ ★ ★ **Opening Blues / Prest.**
★ ★ ★ **Summer Serenade / Story.**
★ ★ ★ **Swingin' the '20s / Contem.**
★ ★ ★ ★ **Swing 1946 / Prest.**

Composer/arranger/bandleader/alto saxophonist/trumpeter Benny Carter (b. 1907) is a figure of such brilliance in jazz history that his reputation has been obscured somewhat by the number of different directions he's gone in. This is why he's less known to the general public than he is to his legions of musician admirers. Throughout his career Carter has gone an unorthodox route that has often seen him using his musical abilities in the service of others rather than enhancing his own name. The self-taught, New York born musician was influenced in his youth by trumpeter Bubber Miley and played with Fletcher Henderson, Chick Webb and McKinney's Cotton Pickers. Though Carter is known as one of the finest alto saxophonists in jazz history, his trumpet playing is also influential; he's recorded on clarinet and trombone and he's also played piano.

Carter's 1933 group, which can be heard on the Prestige reissue, featured pianist Teddy Wilson, tenor saxophonist Chu Berry, trombonist Wilbur DeParis and drummer Sid Catlett. He spent a lot of time in Europe during the rest of the Thirties, doing a lot of arrangements for the BBC radio in England. His recorded work from this period can be heard on *The Early Benny Carter.* During the Forties he was back in the U.S. leading bands which included Dizzy Gillespie, Buddy Rich, Max Roach, J. J. Johnson and Joe Albany.

From the mid-Forties until the end of the Fifties Carter was a much-in-demand Hollywood arranger and composer for film and television soundtracks. He recorded with small bands occasionally during this time, to best effect on the Contemporary sides. *Swinging the '20s,* a 1959 session, is a quartet with the great Earl Hines on piano, Leroy Vinnegar's bass and Shelley Manne on drums. *Jazz Giant* was recorded in 1958 with a group including Ben Webster on tenor sax and Barney Kessell on guitar.

Perhaps Carter's most important album is the classic 1961 set *Further Definitions,* sublime music from a lineup of Coleman Hawkins and Charlie Rouse on tenor saxophones, Phil Woods and Carter on altos, Jo Jones on drums, Jimmy Garrison on bass, Dick Katz on piano and John Collins on guitar. Car-

ter's playing has remained fresh into the Seventies and Eighties on a number of fine albums for Pablo records, including the red hot live 1977 session from Montreux. The Time-Life anthology and the RCA Black and White set *Benny Carter's Orchestra* are the best representations of Carter's work.

— J.S.

BETTY CARTER

★ ★ ★ ★ ★ **Betty Carter / Bet-Car**
★ ★ ★ ★ ★ **Betty Carter Album / Bet-Car**
★ ★ ★ ★ **What a Little Moonlight Can Do / Imp.**

Betty Carter (b. 1930) is, in the words of Carmen McRae, "the only real jazz singer," an incredible interpreter of ballads and a fierce swinger who takes daring tonal and rhythmic liberties but never loses the musical thread. She came to popular notoriety with the 1976 reissue of *What a Little Moonlight Can Do,* a double album from the late Fifties that reveals her already formed style over a medium-sized combo and overblown big band.

Carter has owned her own Bet-Car label since 1971 and during the Seventies produced two albums of her own songs and uncommon standards. *Betty Carter,* with Betty and trio live at the Village Vanguard, contains her Charlie Parker medley, a spellbinding "Body and Soul" and two extended bouts of scatting. *Betty Carter Album* gathers many of her best originals ("I Can't Help It," "Happy," "Tight") plus more slow singing that approaches free-form.

★ ★ ★ ★ ★ **The Audience with Betty Carter / Bet-Car**
★ ★ ★ ★ ★ **Finally / Rou.**
★ ★ ★ ★ **Now It's My Turn / Rou.**
★ ★ ★ ★ **'Round Midnight / Rou.**
★ ★ ★ ★ **Social Call / Col.**
★ ★ ★ ★ **Whatever Happened to Love? / Bet-Car**

Social Call contains the first two sessions recorded under Carter's name—one of which was only issued in 1980, twenty-four years after it was made. Excellent supporting players and material, and some superb early Carter (particularly on the earlier session, with Quincy Jones arrangements and a Ray Bryant quartet), but not quite as bold as Carter would become in a few short years.

The Roulette discs are late-Sixties/early-Seventies live material, overlapping with the first Bet-Car *Betty Carter* LP. *Finally,* which previously appeared on two other small labels, was Carter's first all-out "blowing" album, and remains especially powerful. *The Audience* shows where Carter's club performances have arrived at as of 1979; these two records contain a stunning summation of the extended scatting, excellent taste in choice of standards, cryptically inspiring original notions, and daring harmonic/rhythmic predilections of a singer who creates on the level of jazz's finest instrumentalists. John Hicks, Curtis Lundy and Kenny Washington, Carter's rhythm section, had gigged themselves into an incredibly strong unit, and deserve full shares in the credit for these Carter triumphs. *Whatever Happened* is another live performance with strings added for four selections. — B.B.

RON CARTER
★ ★ ★ ★ **All Blues / CTI**
★ ★ ★ **Alone Together (with Jim Hall) / Mile.**
★ ★ ★ **Anything Goes / Kudu**
★ ★ ★ ★ **Blues Farm / CTI**
★ ★ ★ ★ **Etudes / Elek./Mus.**
★ ★ ★ ★ **Live at Village West (with Jim Hall) / Conc.**
★ ★ ★ **New York Slick / Mile.**
★ ★ ★ ★ **Patrão / Mile.**
★ ★ ★ **Parade / Mile.**
★ ★ ★ **Parfait / Mile.**
★ ★ ★ **Pastels / Mile.**
★ ★ ★ **Piccolo / Mile.**
★ ★ ★ **Pick 'Em / Mile.**
★ ★ ★ **Song for You / Mile.**
★ ★ ★ **Spanish Blue / CTI**
★ ★ **Super Strings / Mile.**
★ ★ ★ ★ **Uptown Conversation / Embryo**
★ ★ ★ **Where? / Prest.**
★ ★ ★ **Yellow and Green / CTI**
Ron Carter (b. 1937) became known as one of the finest acoustic bassists in the Sixties, after his work with the legendary Miles Davis band that also included Wayne Shorter, Herbie Hancock and Tony Williams. He has appeared as a session player on numerous records, and his taste, lyricism and rhythmic inventiveness have made him very influential. Carter's solo albums are examples of how vital small-ensemble jazz can sound without pandering to commercial tastes or avant-garde experimentation, just concentrating on superb playing, arrangements and song selection. *Uptown Conversation,* which features some electric bass playing by Carter and accompaniment from Herbie Hancock and Billy Cobham, is among his best work. His CTI albums are especially noteworthy for avoiding the overarranged style of music that serves as the label's trademark.

Carter went on to make a series of modestly excellent records for Milestone in the Seventies and Eighties. He refuses to be accepted on grounds other than his playing, a stance of integrity that may have cost him some popularity but ensures a loyal following that can depend on his records not being clinkers. The beautiful 1983 *Etudes* set is a quartet date with drummer Tony Williams, Art Farmer on fluegelhorn and young saxophonist Bill Evans. — J.S.

GEORGE CARTWRIGHT
★ ★ ★ **Bright Bank Elewhale (with Michael Lytle) / Corn P.**
★ ★ ★ ★ **Curlew / Landsl.**
★ ★ ★ **Meltable Snaps It (with Lytle and David Moss) / Corn P.**
George Cartwright (b. 1950) is an energetic saxophonist in the land of growls and squeaks. The two albums with Lytle are improvised cacophony, sounding for all the world like steam coming up through an old building with bad plumbing. *Curlew* was one of the first and most successful early-Eighties bands to attempt the jazz/new wave/dance synthesis that later got dubbed "punk jazz." The group had trouble surviving the loss of bassist Bill Laswell and appears as of this printing to have gone to an unmarked and undeserved grave. — F.G.

PHILIP CATHERINE
★ ★ ★ ★ **Nairam / War.**
★ ★ ★ **Splendid / Elek.**
★ ★ ★ ★ **Twin House (with Larry Coryell) / Elek.**
★ ★ ★ ★ **Trio '84 / Gram.**
★ ★ ★ ★ **The Viking (with N.H.O.P.) / Pablo**
An accomplished instrumentalist in a number of different contexts, guitarist Philip Catherine (b. 1942) has worked with jazz saxophonist Dexter Gordon as well as fusion bands like Passport. He was also prominent in French violinist Jean-Luc Ponty's late-Sixties European band and played with the Dutch-based fusion group Focus. Catherine's first U.S. solo album, *Nairam,* which is compiled from his two European solo ventures, *September Man* and *Guitars,* is a stunning presentation of his compositional, soloing and accompaniment capabilities in a modified fusion context. The backup instrumentation, built around the Gerry Brown (drums)/ John Lee (bass) rhythm section with which Catherine has done a number of sessions, is superb, and while there are occasional echoes of John McLaughlin's work with Miles Davis circa *Jack Johnson* and *Bitches Brew,* Catherine is obviously an original talent.

Twin House is a series of excellent duets

with Larry Coryell. *Trio '84* is a beautiful exchange with guitarist Christian Escoude and violinist Didier Lockwood. On *The Viking* Catherine and bassist Niels-Henning Orsted Pedersen combine on a series of inspired duets. — J.S.

SERGE CHALOFF
★ ★ ★ ★ ★ Blue Serge / Cap.
The ability of Serge Chaloff (1923–1957) to evoke emotions was as amazing as the ease with which he exploited the entire range of the baritone saxophone. His abilities as an improviser are unforgettable; Chaloff's death at the age of thirty-three left memories and the frustration of what could have been.

Charlie Parker's bop innovations had a large influence on Chaloff's conception. But his style also echoed the luxuriant, "big toned" tenors of the swing era, as witness his treatment of the ballad, "Thanks for the Memory," here on *Blue Serge. Blue Serge*'s stellar lineup features Sonny Clark, Leroy Vinnegar and Philly Joe Jones.

Some of Chaloff's better solos were with Woody Herman's Second Herd (his was the gorgeous "bottom" to the Four Brothers sound) and the Basie octet (1950–51). On the bandstand and in the recording studios, he conversed with Tommy Dorsey, Red Rodney, Al Haig, Denzil Best, Dick Twardik, Clifford Brown and Max Roach. If you can locate them, see *Brothers and Other Mothers* (Savoy); also *The Fable of Mable* (Storyville) for "Easy Street" and *Boston Blow-Up!* (Capitol) for his masterpiece "Body and Soul." — A.R.

JOE CHAMBERS
★ ★ ★ Double Exposure (with Larry Young) / Muse
Known primarily as an important session drummer for Blue Note in the Sixties, Joe Chambers (b. 1942) has recorded as a pianist on his own LPs, including an out-of-print solo disc for Japan's Denon label. *Double Exposure* is a series of duets between Chambers and the late Larry Young on organ. As a pianist, Chambers demonstrates a surprising melodic sensibility rather than a percussive approach. — F.G.

DOC CHEATHAM
★ ★ ★ Black Beauty (with Sammy Price) / Sack.
★ ★ ★ Doc and Sammy / Sack.
★ ★ Good for What Ails Ya / Class.
Trumpeter Adolphus Anthony "Doc" Cheatham (b. 1905) made his mark in the big-band sections of Cab Calloway, Teddy Wilson and Benny Carter during the Thirties and early Forties, then later in Latin bands led by Perez Prado and Machito. Cheatham remains a very listenable stylist, as the two Sackville duet albums with Sammy Price demonstrate, but the 1977 *Good for What Ails Ya* sextet set does not show him in a particularly good light. — J.S.

DON CHERRY
★ ★ ★ ★ ★ Complete Communion / Blue N.
★ ★ Don Cherry / Hori.
★ ★ ★ ★ Gato Barbieri and Don Cherry / Inner
★ ★ Hear and Now / Atl.
★ ★ ★ ★ Relativity Suite / JCOA
★ ★ ★ ★ Where Is Brooklyn? / Blue N.
To a great extent, cornetist/pocket trumpeter Don Cherry (b. 1931) is important because of his work with all of the Sixties' important saxophonists—Ornette Coleman, Sonny Rollins, Albert Ayler, Archie Shepp, John Coltrane—though his own bands have reinforced the spectrum of emotion contained within new music and the felicity of international influences.

While in Europe in 1965, Cherry assembled his best group—a quintet featuring Germany's Karl Berger on vibes and piano and a then-unknown Argentinean, Leandro "Gato" Barbieri, on tenor sax. Their recordings string playful themes together with solos that are free yet convey joy instead of the then prevalent anger. *Gato Barbieri and Don Cherry* is their first effort, a confident recital surpassed on *Complete Communion* through the use of Americans Henry Grimes and Ed Blackwell in the rhythm section. *Where Is Brooklyn?*, from 1966, is Cherry, Grimes and Blackwell with Pharoah Sanders in more discrete tracks and more biting performances.

Cherry's next American album, *Relativity Suite,* was made in 1973, after the trumpeter had traveled and studied in Africa, Asia and the more remote corners of Northern Europe. The piece is almost like an international travelogue, with lots of atmosphere and a few solo spots for Cherry, Carla Bley, Charlie Haden and Carlos Ward.

Later efforts by Cherry are a mixed bag of exotica, fusion and new-thing nostalgia. Both *Don Cherry* and *Hear and Now* attempt to cross over unsuccessfully; the former is defeated by electronic indulgence and poor playing on Cherry's part (except on "Malkauns"), while the latter sports poor material and the gloss one associates with producer Narada Michael Walden.
★ ★ ★ Codona / ECM/War.
★ ★ ★ Codona 2 / ECM/War.

★ ★ ★ **Codona 3 / ECM/War.**
★ ★ ★ ★ **El Corazon (with Ed Blackwell) /
ECM/War.**
★ ★ **Music/Sangam (with Latif Khan) / Eur.**
In recent years, Cherry has not produced
projects under his own name on records,
choosing instead to work in continuing cooperative affiliations, particularly Old and New
Dreams, the quartet of former associates
from Ornette Coleman bands. Codona, the
global-melting-pot trio with Oregon's Collin
Walcott and Brazilian percussionist Nana
Vasconcelos, has made less impact as a recording and touring band. With all of the
room for sitar, berimbau, tabla,
doussn'gouni, etc., things get a bit atmospheric in what has come to be known as
the ECM mold. Of the three LPs thus far,
Codona 2 has perhaps the best mix of material, though there's a rare (the only ?) Ornette Coleman/Stevie Wonder medley on the
first album.

More of Cherry's collaborative efforts appeared during 1982 and '83. *El Corazon* is
typically international in flavor, although
strongly centered on Cherry's native roots
thanks to the presence of Old and New
Dreams colleague Blackwell. *Music,* with the
Indian tabla player Latif Khan, is more
schematic and less successful.   — B.B.

CHARLIE CHRISTIAN
★ ★ ★ ★ **Charley [sic] Christian—Charley
Christian at Minton's / Saga**
★ ★ ★ ★ ★ **Solo Flight—The Genius of
Charlie Christian / Col.**
His recording career lasted only three years,
but Charlie Christian (1919–1942) continues
to be revered as the fountainhead of modern
jazz guitar for first harnessing the newly
electrified guitar to extended single-note
solos characteristic for their melodic freshness and novel rhythmic ideas—ideas credited as a key element in the stylistic transition from swing to the bop movement of the
postwar years.

Benny Goodman brought Christian from
Oklahoma to New York in 1939, and virtually all of their recorded music—
both with the Goodman Sextet and Orchestra—are preserved on *Solo Flight.* Only two
tracks—"Honeysuckle Rose" and the title
tune—featuring Christian and the full orchestra exist, and both show his compact
phrasing while confirming the definitive
emergence of the guitar from the rhythm
section. Christian was playing single-note
lines as early as 1938, voicing them as a
third part with trumpet and saxophone, and
this ability was an integral part of his work
with the sextet—which comprises most of

the selections on this LP. A more forceful,
experimental style can be found on three
tracks credited to the "Charlie Christian
Quintet," recorded live at a Minneapolis
nightclub in 1940.

Charley Christian at Minton's comes from
amateur recordist Jerry Newman's tapes of
the legendary jams at Minton's and Monroe's in Harlem with Christian, Monk, Gillespie and Kenny Clarke. The recording
quality is rough and the crowd boisterous,
but these bop workshops, often guided by
Christian's dramatic experiments in time, are
of significant value.   — J.C.C.

JUNE CHRISTY
★ ★ ★ **Best of June Christy / Cap.**
★ ★ **Impromptu / Discovery**
★ ★ ★ **Something Cool / Cap.**
Singer June Christy (b. 1925) was heavily influenced by Anita O'Day, whom she replaced in Stan Kenton's band in 1945. She
emulated O'Day's belting trombone-voiced
style effectively enough to bring her to national prominence. Her Capitol solo albums
trade off her Kenton reputation via "Something Cool," which is on both records.
Christy's most recent album, the 1977 *Impromptu,* is notable mainly for the playing of
the band, particularly Lou Levy's piano
work and arrangements and Frank Rosolino's trombone.   — A.R.

JOHN CLARK
★ ★ **Faces / ECM/War.**
★ ★ **Song of Light / Hidden M.**
The French horn has never been prominent
in jazz, and these two albums won't do
much to change that. John Clark (b. 1944) is
a facile soloist, but uninventive as a composer. Although he does select colorful
chords frequently passed over by others,
both albums meander in predictable directions.   — F.G.

SONNY CLARK
★ ★ ★ **Cool Struttin' / Blue N.**
★ ★ ★ **Leapin' and Lopin' / Blue N.**
★ ★ ★ **Sonny Clark, Max Roach and George
Duvivier / Bain.**
Pianist Sonny Clark (1932–1963) was one of
the most popular sidemen of the mid- to late
Fifties, performing on LPs by Serge Chaloff,
Curtis Fuller, Johnny Griffin and notably
Dexter Gordon who considered Clark his fa-
vorite accompanist. Unfortunately, drug
problems sidetracked Clark's burgeoning ca-
reer as a leader, and he only made a handful
of titles under his own name before his death
at the age of thirty-one.

Clark's Blue Note recordings stand out among the innumerable blowing sessions of the time due to his relaxed Bud Powell-influenced playing and contributions from such future stars as Jackie McLean and Art Farmer on *Struttin'*. Stoking the engine are bassist Paul Chambers and his Miles Davis quintet teammate Philly Joe Jones for the later LP. The Bainbridge set is hornless, but with those names in the rhythm section there is little to complain about. —S.F.

STANLEY CLARKE
★ ★ ★ ★ **Children of Forever / Poly.**
★ ★ ★ ★ **Clarke/Duke Project / Epic**
★ ★ ★ **Clarke/Duke Project II / Epic**
★ ★ ★ ★ **I Wanna Play for You / Nemp.**
★ ★ ★ **Journey to Love / Col.**
★ ★ ★ **Let Me Know You / Epic**
★ ★ ★ **Rocks, Pebbles and Sand / Epic**
★ ★ ★ **School Days / Col.**
★ ★ ★ ★ **Stanley Clarke / Col.**
★ ★ ★ **Time Exposure / Epic**
Stanley Clarke (b. 1951), the prodigiously talented bassist who coled Return to Forever along with Chick Corea in addition to fronting his own band, plays a pure hybrid of jazz rock because he is equally at home in either genre. His fuzz bass intro to "School Days" is a classic rock bass riff, and he pairs himself with guitarists Jeff Beck and John McLaughlin on *Journey to Love*. Yet his finest solo album is the more jazz-oriented *Children of Forever*, a Polydor outing recorded with the original Latin-style Return to Forever. *Stanley Clarke* is an all-star fusion session with vital contributions from ex-Lifetime drummer Tony Williams, ex-Mahavishnu keyboardist Jan Hammer and ex-Return to Forever guitarist Bill Conners.

Other Clarke solo efforts have suffered from an identity crisis since the bassist seems unsure whether to cast himself as pop star or musician. He settles the problem with the *Clarke/Duke Project* LPs by casting himself as both, which is a perfectly reasonable solution. It seems clear that Clarke works best in an organized group context, whether he's leading the lineup or not (see also Echoes of an Era entry and the *Griffith Park Collection* on Elektra/Musician), than as a freelance solo artist. — J.S.

JAY CLAYTON
★ ★ ★ ★ **All Out / Anima**
Jay Clayton's sound, style, technique and soul should admit her to the upper echelon of jazz singers, although she has not yet achieved due recognition. Among her greatest skills are her innate sense of melody and

rhythm, which enable her to improvise freely, as on the darkly passionate "Lonely Woman," included on *All Out*. This collaboration with soprano saxophonist Jane Ira Bloom and bassist Harvie Swartz introduces an otherworldly singer whose cool, post-bop sound is as spiritual and agile as that of her mentors Betty Carter and Abbey Lincoln. — A.R.

ARNETT COBB
★ ★ ★ **Funky Butt / Prog.**
★ ★ ★ ★ ★ **Go Power! / Prest.**
★ ★ ★ **Is Back / Prog.**
★ ★ ★ **Live at Sandy's / Muse**
★ ★ ★ **More Arnett Cobb and the Muse All Stars Live at Sandy's / Muse**
★ ★ ★ **Wild Man from Texas / Class.**
The "Wild Man of the Tenor Sax" was born in Houston, Texas, in 1918 and came up during the Thirties, closing out the decade as the featured saxophonist in Milton Larkins' band before replacing Illinois Jacquet in Lionel Hampton's organization during 1942. His five years with Hampton earned Arnett Cobb the "Wild Man" nickname and he has recorded sporadically in between illnesses since '47. Most of this material is out of print, but the Fifties tenor battle with Eddie "Lockjaw" Davis preserved as *Go Power!* is all the testimony to Cobb's playing ability you need. Cobb and Davis muscle their way through this record with Wild Bill Davis refereeing on Hammond organ and with George Duvivier (bass)/Arthur Edgehill (drums) pushing the tenor battle to its limits. There is no finer example of a shouting-blues blowing session than *Go Power!* The other records listed are more recent sessions that show Cobb can still lead a date even if he can't always summon up the force of his earlier, classic playing. — J.S.

BILLY COBHAM
★ ★ ★ **B.C. / Col.**
★ ★ ★ ★ **Best of / Atl.**
★ ★ ★ **Best of / Col.**
★ ★ ★ **Crosswinds / Atl.**
★ ★ **Funky Thide of Sings / Atl.**
★ ★ **Life and Times / Atl.**
★ **Live on Tour in Europe / Atl.**
★ ★ ★ **Magic / Col.**
★ ★ ★ **Observations & / Elek./Mus.**
★ ★ ★ **Shabbazz / Atl.**
★ ★ ★ ★ **Smokin' / Elek./Mus.**
★ ★ ★ ★ **Spectrum / Atl.**
★ ★ **Total Eclipse / Atl.**
After serving a decade-long apprenticeship backing R&B bands and playing with

Dreams and Miles Davis, drummer Billy Cobham's (b. 1944) powerful early-Seventies propulsion of the Mahavishnu Orchestra enabled him to leave that band with superstar credentials, which were immediately justified by his first solo album, *Spectrum. Spectrum* eschewed Mahavishnu's cerebrations for a gut punch, and Cobham pushed late rock guitarist Tommy Bolin to his finest moments as a soloist, getting a hit single, "Stratus," in the process.

Cobham then formed a band around soloists John Abercrombie (guitar), Randy Brecker (trumpet) and Michael Brecker (saxophone). Their three albums, *Crosswinds, Total Eclipse* and *Shabazz,* present them in top form, playing strong material with sublime fervor.

Cobham's next band, covering *Funky Thide, Life and Times* and *Live in Europe,* was an attempt at mid-Seventies disco funk that disappointed expectations generated by its stellar lineup (bassist Doug Rauch, keyboardist George Duke and guitarist John Scofield) and some inspired but all-too-brief moments of hot playing. As evidenced on its live album, the band's collective energy just didn't sustain each musician's chops, and Cobham's soloing, while still impressive, couldn't be as inventive as it once was.

Cobham retrenched for *Magic,* a shrewd move that speaks well of his judgment as a bandleader, and came up with an understated yet commercial session featuring instrumental support from keyboardist Joachim Kuhn, guitarist Pete Maunu, bassist Randy Jackson, percussionists Pete and Sheila Escovedo and clarinetist Alvin Batiste.

The Elektra/Musician records introduce Cobham's Glass Menagerie band, an outstanding post-fusion unit comprised of guitarist Dean Brown, bassist Tim Landers and keyboardist Gil Goldstein. The aptly titled *Smokin'* was recorded live at the 1982 Montreux Festival. — J.S.

AL COHN
★ ★ ★ ★ ★ America / Xan.
★ ★ ★ Be Loose / Bio.
★ ★ ★ ★ ★ Body and Soul (with Zoot Sims) / Muse
★ ★ ★ ★ Heavy Love (with Jimmy Rowles) / Xan.
★ ★ ★ Motoring Along (with Zoot Sims) / Sonet
★ ★ ★ Non Pareil / Conc. J.
★ ★ ★ ★ No Problem / Xan.
★ ★ ★ Overtones / Conc. J.
★ ★ ★ ★ ★ Play It Now / Xan.
★ ★ ★ The Progressive—Al Cohn / Savoy

★ ★ ★ ★ Standards of Excellence / Conc.
★ ★ ★ You 'n Me (with Zoot Sims) / Em.
Al Cohn (b. 1925) is always lumped with "the Brothers," the clique of white tenor sax players of the Forties who emulated the legato swing of Lester Young. But Cohn's sound has always been tougher and his ideas more adventurous than those of his fanatical compatriots. Along with Stan Getz and Cohn's occasional partner Zoot Sims, he remains the only survivor to rise above that era's tepid environment and to continue to make great music.

Cohn's early individuality can be found on *The Progressive,* a bop-oriented set that includes a side with the kicking rhythm section of Max Roach, Horace Silver and Curley Russell, and *Be Loose* with some excellent examples of his balladic mastery.

In the late Fifties Cohn hooked up with fellow tenorist and ex-Woody Herman bigband mate Zoot Sims, a union that continues to this day. Sims, with his milder tone and laid-back approach, is the perfect alter ego for Cohn. Theirs was never a "tenor madness" blowing battle. Cohn wrote and arranged intricate charts highlighting their faultless unison playing, interspersed with concise solo spots.

An early collaboration, *You 'n Me,* is a driving set with Mose Allison on piano. Their next recorded encounter took place thirteen years later, but the wait was well worth it. *Body and Soul* is a masterpiece. Backed by a superlative unit, Mel Lewis, George Duvivier and Jaki Byard, and with Sims doubling on soprano, they turn in an exceptional performance of everything from blues to bossa nova. *Motoring Along,* made with a Scandinavian rhythm section, also features some fluent blowing, but doesn't reach its predecessor's high points.

Cohn continued to lead sessions during this peak period, and the finest moments of his career are contained on *Play It Now* and *America.* This is mainstream tenor playing at its very best. *Heavy Love,* a delightful duet with pianist Jimmy Rowles, is a marvel of empathy. The Concord LPs are also exciting, but noninitiates are advised to pick up the Xanadus. — S.F.

NAT "KING" COLE
★ A Blossom Fell / Cap.
★ A Mis Amigos / Cap.
★ ★ The Best of Nat "King" Cole / Cap.
★ ★ Capitol Jazz Classics, Vol. 8 / Cap.
★ The Christmas Song / Cap.
★ Cole Español / Cap.
★ ★ Love Is Here to Stay / Cap.

★ ★ ★ ★ Love Is the Thing / Cap.
★ More Cole Español / Cap.
★ My Fair Lady / Cap.
★ Nat "King" Cole Live at the Sands / Cap.
★ ★ Nat "King" Cole Sings George Shearing
Plays / Cap.
★ ★ ★ The Nat "King" Cole Story, Vol. 1 /
Cap.
★ ★ The Nat "King" Cole Story, Vol. 2 /
Cap.
★ Ramblin' Rose / Cap.
★ ★ ★ ★ Trio Days / Cap.
★ ★ Unforgettable / Cap.
★ Walkin' My Baby Back Home / Cap.
This Earl Hines-influenced pianist-turned-crooner became the first black male singer to gain total pop mainstream acceptance and his own TV show in the early Fifties. Nat "King" Cole (1917–1965) specialized in romantic ballads; his most consistent album, *Love Is the Thing* (1957), with luscious Gordon Jenkins arrangements, is still a delightful dream and smooch record. An excellent technician but a bland interpreter, Cole was always indiscriminate in his choice of material. About half of the Cole in print is singles anthologies, and many of the songs are laughably trite. In the Sixties, Cole made the mistake of rerecording his early hits—"Nature Boy," "Mona Lisa," "Too Young" et al.—with arrangements that duplicated the originals. But these remakes, which comprise the bulk of the anthologies, capture little of the magic of the originals. For by the Sixties, Cole's voice had lost its smoothness and could evoke no longer these songs' innocent romanticism.

Cole's immense popularity as a singer obscured the fact that he was a brilliant and innovative pianist. His drummerless trio was a watershed jazz concept that is best heard on the recently reissued *Trio Days.* — S.H.

EARL COLEMAN
★ ★ A Song for You / Xan.
★ ★ ★ There's Something About an Old
Love / Xan.
Earl Coleman's (b. 1925) grand baritone voice has made him the choice of an impressive array of collaborators, among them Charlie Parker, on the 1947 tracks "Dark Shadows" and "This Is Always." His other associations include Jay McShann, Earl Hines, Billy Taylor and Fats Navarro. The Earl Coleman style owes much to Billy Eckstine, but is still his own. *A Song for You* is perhaps too low-key to inspire repeated listenings (the out-of-print *Love Songs* flows better). However, "The Very Thought of You," "All In Love Is Fair" and "Dark

Shadows" (especially for Al Cohn's moaning, sighing solo on the latter) are appropriate vehicles for Coleman's heartfelt singing.
 — A.R.

GEORGE COLEMAN
★ ★ ★ ★ Amsterdam After Dark / Timel.
★ ★ ★ ★ Big George / Aff.
Saxophonist George Coleman (b. 1935), part of the Miles Davis Quintet in 1963 and 1964, can be heard on the Davis albums *Seven Steps to Heaven, Four & More, My Funny Valentine* and *In Concert.* A soulful, aggressive yet beautifully swinging improviser, Coleman has also played with Max Roach, Elvin Jones (as part of a fantastic front line with Frank Foster, as on *Coalition*), Herbie Hancock, Horace Silver, Lee Morgan, Jimmy Smith and others. *Big George* is an octet session; *Amsterdam After Dark* a quartet. As good as both albums are, they still fall short of capturing Coleman at his absolute best. — J.S.

RICHIE COLE
★ ★ ★ Alto Madness / Muse
★ ★ ★ Battle of the Saxes (with Eric Kloss)
/ Muse
★ ★ ★ Cool "C" / Muse
★ ★ ★ New York Afternoon / Muse
★ ★ ★ ★ Richie Cole and . . . (with Art
Pepper) / Palo Alto
★ ★ ★ Side by Side (with Phil Woods) /
Muse
★ ★ ★ ★ Starburst (with the Reuben Brown
Trio) / Adel.
★ ★ ★ ★ Yakety Madness! (with Boots
Randolph) / Palo Alto
A former student of Phil Woods, bebop alto saxophonist Richie Cole (b. 1948) first came to the public's attention in the mid-Seventies on his self-pressed debut album, *Trenton Makes, The World Takes,* on the now defunct Philadelphia Richie Cole label. Since then Cole has had no trouble finding people to record him, and has established himself as a leading disciple of the Charlie Parker school of alto.

Aside from a slew of strong though similar saxophone battle LPs, Cole worked extensively with vocalist Eddie Jefferson during the Seventies, and the singer's presence on both *New York Afternoon* and *Alto Madness* are big pluses.

If the battle albums have a fault, it's that the competitive spirit has a way of substituting flash for substance. However, the disc with Art Pepper is a good deal more thoughtful than the others, although Pepper isn't at the top of his form here. The country/bop fusion idea of *Yakety Madness!* actually works quite well, and it's a very enjoyable LP if you can stand hearing "Yakety Sax."

Of the other discs, *Cool "C"* represents something of a departure by employing a big band, but *Starburst* remains Cole's most effective and unaffected album. — F.G.

ORNETTE COLEMAN
★ ★ ★ **Coleman Classics, Vol. 1 / IAI**
★ ★ ★ ★ **Something Else! / Contem.**
★ ★ ★ ★ **Tomorrow Is the Question! /**
  Contem.
The particular genius of Ornette Coleman (b. 1930), so centrally rooted to the blues continuum in one respect and yet so singularly eccentric, is really beyond a rating system. Perhaps two stars should be added to each of his albums as a mark of his consistent eloquence and undiminished importance.

The above albums are from his 1958–early 1959 Los Angeles period, when the alto saxophonist's conception of "free" jazz was still presented in group situations that stressed familiar chordal and structural formats. *Something Else!* is by a Coleman quintet including trumpeter Don Cherry and drummer Billy Higgins; the presence of a pianist (Walter Norris) ties the pieces further to the bop tradition. *Tomorrow,* without a keyboard, is closer to the breakthrough, and it's interesting to hear veteran rhythm players Percy Heath, Red Mitchell and Shelly Manne respond to the aharmonic flights of Coleman and Cherry. The IAI is from a 1958 club gig where pianist Paul Bley led Coleman's quartet.

★ ★ ★ ★ ★ **The Best of Ornette Coleman /**
  Atl.
★ ★ ★ ★ ★ **Change of the Century / Atl.**
★ ★ ★ ★ ★ **Free Jazz / Atl.**
★ ★ ★ ★ ★ **The Shape of Jazz to Come /**
  Atl.
★ ★ ★ ★ **This Is Our Music / Atl.**
★ ★ ★ ★ ★ **To Whom Who Keeps a Record**
  / Atl. (Japan)
Coleman's quartet ventures on Atlantic, recorded between 1959 and 1961, are not compared lightly to Armstrong's Hot Fives and Sevens and Parker's Savoy and Dial quintets; their innovations in improvisation without chord changes, variable pitch, asymmetrical phrases and ensemble voicings achieved a freer and more natural jazz form that influenced several established masters (Rollins, Coltrane, McLean, to name three) as well as the generation that followed.

Atlantic's *Best of* anthology is a fine introduction to Coleman, since it collects his most accessible compositions: "Lonely Woman" (from *Shape of Jazz*), "Una Muy Bonita" and "Ramblin' " (from *Change of the Century*), "Blues Connotation" (from *This Is Our Music*), plus the excellent "C and D," currently unavailable elsewhere. Joining the leader's plastic alto are Cherry on pocket trumpet; Charlie Haden or Scott LaFaro on bass; Higgins or Ed Blackwell on drums.

These six musicians, plus Freddie Hubbard and Eric Dolphy, collectively improvised *Free Jazz,* a 36-minute performance with tremendous vitality and uncanny coherence. All play superbly, but Coleman's alto solo and the passage shared by the bassists are some of the avant-garde's most sublime moments.

★ ★ ★ ★ ★ **At the "Golden Circle"**
  Stockholm, Vol. 1 / Blue N.
★ ★ ★ ★ **At the "Golden Circle" Stockholm,**
  Vol. 2 / Blue N.
★ ★ ★ ★ **Crisis / Imp.**
★ ★ ★ **The Empty Foxhole / Blue N.**
Coleman's Blue Note albums from 1965 to 1966 reveal an even more directed lyricism and, in the case of the *"Golden Circle"* volumes, the spunky rhythm section of David Izenson (bass) and Charles Moffett (drums). On the minus side is Coleman's self-taught trumpet and violin work, which is moving in its ragged expressionism but hardly on the level of his alto playing, and (on *Foxhole*) the untutored drumming of Coleman's ten-year-old son, Denardo.

The live *Crisis* is a 1969 quintet date with Cherry, Haden, Denardo and Dewey Redman that includes the first recording of Haden's "Song for Che."

★ ★ ★ **Friends and Neighbors / Fly. D.**
★ ★ ★ ★ ★ **Science Fiction / Col.**
★ ★ ★ ★ **Skies of America / Col.**
The early Seventies found Coleman leading one of his best groups, a quartet with Haden, Blackwell and Coleman's old Fort Worth high school friend Dewey Redman on tenor sax. The group made the informal *Friends* at Coleman's Artists' House studio, and participated in the fascinating retrospective *Science Fiction,* where they were joined by early Coleman associates Cherry, Higgins and Bobby Bradford (trumpet) plus the Indian vocalist Asha Puthli, for a multifaceted program of new Coleman compositions.

Skies of America, performed by Coleman with the London Symphony Orchestra, is an extended composition based on Coleman's "harmelodic theory" of writing unison passages that do not transpose (i.e., instruments play the same pitch in different keys). The writing is fairly conventional by contemporary European standards, and there is unfortunately little room for the composer's alto. (The two Columbia albums are available as a double-record set.)

★ ★ ★ ★ **Dancing in Your Head** / Hori.
After a four-year recording hiatus, Coleman released his free-fusion album, a ragged street jam congealed somewhere between Kingston and New Orleans (the Bermuda Triangle?) with a backup quartet of guitars, bass, drums and percussion sounding like Denardo times five. The alto playing, however, is still phenomenal, and there is a brief trance piece taped with the Master Musicians of Joujouka, Morocco.

★ ★ ★ ★ **Body Meta** / Artists H.
★ ★ ★ ★ ★ **Broken Shadows** / Col.
★ ★ ★ ★ ★ **The Great London Concert** / Ari./Free.
★ ★ ★ ★ **Of Human Feelings** / Ant.
★ ★ ★ ★ ★ **Soapsuds, Soapsuds** / Artists H.
★ ★ ★ ★ **Twins** / Atl.
Coleman did little recording in the late Seventies. Besides the Artists House albums listed above and James "Blood" Ulmer's debut as a leader on the same label, there are still a few tapes of that period that remain unreleased. *Body Meta,* produced at the *Dancing in Your Head* sessions, offers a better separation on Prime Time, Coleman's electric band, and a variety of moods and tempos, but Coleman's alto solos cover familiar territory. *Soapsuds* is a duet album with bassist Haden that finds Coleman returning to tenor sax on most tracks. All of the playing is superb from both men, and Coleman outdoes himself on, of all things, "Mary Hartman, Mary Hartman."

Vintage examples of Coleman's bands also appeared and reappeared. The Arista/ Freedom two-record set features the trio heard on the Golden Circle sessions recorded a few months earlier, plus an example of Coleman's chamber composition, in this case for a woodwind quintet. *Twins,* first issued in 1971, collects tracks from the 1959–61 Atlantic sessions, including a first take of "Free Jazz."

The best of the "old Coleman" to appear was *Broken Shadows,* a collection of unissued material from the early Seventies that features a miniature double-quartet performance along the lines of *Free Jazz* ("Happy House"), a rough draft of "Theme from a Symphony" ("Schoolwork") and a re-creation of Coleman's dues-paying days in Texas, complete with blues singer ("Good Girl Blues"). — B.B.

CAL COLLINS

★ ★ ★ **Blues on My Mind** / Conc. J.
★ ★ ★ **Cal Collins in San Francisco** / Conc. J.
★ ★ ★ ★ **Cincinnati to L.A.** / Conc. J.
★ ★ ★ **Cross Country** / Conc. J.
★ ★ ★ **Interplay (with Herb Ellis)** / Conc. J.
★ ★ ★ **Ohio Boss Guitar** / Fam. D.
Cal Collins (b. 1953) is a guitarist with chops galore. His playing has a strong country component, placing him somewhere between Chet Atkins and Johnny Smith. Although Collins tends to stick to the middle-of-the-road, his wit and a sprightly attack keep his style from becoming cumbersome, even though there's scant difference between his group recordings. *Cross Country* is a solo date and the live *Interplay* matches him with Herb Ellis. — F.G.

JOHN COLTRANE / 1956–60

★ ★ ★ ★ ★ **The Art of John Coltrane** / Atl.
★ ★ ★ **Bahia** / Prest.
★ ★ ★ ★ ★ **The Best of John Coltrane** / Atl.
★ ★ ★ **Black Pearls** / Prest. (includes The Believer and The Black Pearls)
★ ★ ★ ★ ★ **Blue Train** / Blue N.
★ ★ ★ ★ ★ **Coltrane Jazz** / Atl.
★ ★ ★ **The Coltrane Legacy** / Atl.
★ ★ ★ ★ **Countdown (with Wilbur Harden)** / Savoy
★ ★ ★ **Dial Africa (with Wilbur Harden)** / Savoy
★ ★ ★ ★ ★ **First Trane** / Prest.
★ ★ ★ ★ ★ **Giant Steps** / Atl.
★ ★ ★ ★ ★ **John Coltrane** / Prest.
★ ★ ★ **John Coltrane Plays for Lovers** / Prest.
★ ★ ★ **Kenny Burrell/John Coltrane** / Prest.
★ ★ ★ **The Last Trane** / Prest.
★ ★ ★ ★ ★ **Lush Life** / Prest.
★ ★ ★ ★ **More Lasting than Bronze** / Prest.
★ ★ ★ **The Stardust Session** / Prest. (includes Stardust and The Master)
★ ★ ★ ★ ★ **Trane's Reign** / Prest.
★ ★ ★ ★ **Trane Tracks** / Trip
★ ★ ★ **Turning Point** / Beth.
★ ★ ★ **Two Tenors** / Prest. (also on Elmo Hope, All-Star Sessions / Mile.)
★ ★ ★ **Wheelin' and Dealin'** / Prest.

JOHN COLTRANE / 1960–65

★ ★ ★ **Africa /Brass** / Imp.
★ ★ ★ ★ **Africa/Brass, Vol. 2** / Imp.
★ ★ ★ ★ ★ **Afro-Blue Impressions** / Pablo
★ ★ ★ **Ballads** / Imp.
★ ★ ★ ★ **Coltrane** / Imp.
★ ★ ★ ★ **Coltrane Plays the Blues** / Atl.
★ ★ ★ ★ **Coltrane's Sound** / Atl.
★ ★ ★ ★ **Crescent** / Imp.

★ ★ ★ Feelin' Good / Imp.
★ ★ ★ ★ First Meditations (For Quartet) / Imp.
★ ★ ★ ★ The Gentle Side of John Coltrane / Imp.
★ ★ ★ ★ ★ His Greatest Years, Vol. 1 / Imp.
★ ★ ★ ★ ★ His Greatest Years, Vol. 2 / Imp.
★ ★ ★ ★ His Greatest Years, Vol. 3 / Imp.
★ ★ ★ ★ ★ Impressions / Imp.
★ ★ ★ ★ The John Coltrane Quartet Plays / Imp.
★ ★ ★ John Coltrane with Johnny Hartman / Imp.
★ ★ ★ ★ ★ Live at Birdland / Imp.
★ ★ ★ ★ ★ Live at the Village Vanguard / Imp.
★ ★ ★ ★ ★ A Love Supreme / Imp.
★ ★ ★ ★ ★ My Favorite Things / Atl.
★ ★ ★ ★ Olé Coltrane / Atl.
★ ★ ★ ★ The Other Village Vanguard Tapes / Imp.
★ ★ ★ Selflessness / Imp.
★ ★ ★ ★ Sun Ship / Imp.
★ ★ ★ ★ To the Beat of a Different Drummer / Imp.
★ ★ ★ ★ ★ Transition / Imp.

JOHN COLTRANE / 1965–67
★ ★ ★ ★ Ascension / Imp.
★ ★ ★ ★ Concert in Japan / Imp.
★ ★ ★ Cosmic Music (with Alice Coltrane) / Imp.
★ ★ ★ ★ ★ Expression / Imp.
★ ★ ★ ★ Interstellar Space / Imp.
★ ★ ★ ★ Kulu Sé Mama / Imp.
★ ★ ★ ★ ★ Live at the Village Vanguard Again / Imp.
★ ★ ★ ★ ★ Meditations / Imp.
★ ★ ★ Om / Imp.

John Coltrane's (1926–1967) extensive catalogue has been listed above in roughly chronological order. The three groupings represent albums under Coltrane's name made while he worked for Miles Davis and Thelonious Monk (1956–60); the era of the classic Coltrane quartet with McCoy Tyner, piano, Elvin Jones, drums, and eventually Jimmy Garrison, bass (1960–65); and the final "free" period with Garrison, Pharoah Sanders, tenor sax, Alice Coltrane, piano, and Rashied Ali, drums (1965–67). Records are ranked against each other internally, to emphasize the best records of each period (a *** Coltrane album thus may be worth **** or ***** generally); and the Atlantic and Impulse samplers are ranked for how well they represent the period covered.

For most of the first period covered above,

Coltrane was under contract to Prestige Records, a label that (like several others at the time) recorded a fixed group of its artists in blowing sessions under rotating leadership. Some of the albums that now appear under Coltrane's name were actually jams loosely organized by one member of the band (often pianist Mal Waldron). Among the participants in these sessions were Donald Byrd, Jackie McLean, Freddie Hubbard, Red Garland and Paul Chambers. Among the best:

John Coltrane—two quartet sessions from 1957–58 with Garland, Chambers and drummer Art Taylor, all of whom had worked with Coltrane in the Miles Davis quintet. It was in this period that Coltrane developed what critic Ira Gitler called his "sheets of sound" approach—a harmonically intricate, oddly accented torrent of arpeggios delivered with superhuman intensity. Coltrane's starkly lyrical ballad approach also began to gain notice at this time.

Trane's Reign—the same quartet in a lesser-known but equally tight set.

Blue Train—a sextet album, celebrated for Coltrane's stirring tenor on two blues pieces, the presence of drummer Philly Joe Jones (a rare collaboration with Coltrane outside the Davis quintet) and "Moment's Notice," Coltrane's most challenging early composition. Lee Morgan is also present.

After moving to Atlantic in 1960, Coltrane summed up this era with two classic quartet albums. *Giant Steps,* the more celebrated, finds harmonic virtuosity at a peak on the title track, "Cousin Mary," "Spiral" and "Mr. P.C.," plus the first appearance of the beautiful "Naima." *Coltrane Jazz* features more standards and finds Coltrane experimenting with saxophone harmonics (producing several notes at once on the horn). Tommy Flanagan and Wynton Kelly sparkle on piano on each album.

In the second period, Coltrane's working quartet (with Steve Davis on bass) and the soprano sax were introduced on *My Favorite Things.* While the popularity of the title tune got the band off to a good start, equally impressive were the tenor solos on "Summertime" and "But Not for Me." This same version of the quartet is heard on *Plays the Blues* and the well-programed *Coltrane's Sound.* Both volumes of *Africa/Brass, Olé Coltrane, Live at the Village Vanguard, The Other Village Vanguard Tapes* and *Impressions* document the period between May and November 1961 when Eric Dolphy often collaborated with Coltrane (on *Olé,* Dolphy uses the pseudonym George Lane). This is also the time when Coltrane shifted to an emphasis on modal improvisation (a single scale or mode is used in place of chord sequences) and triple meter. On the *Africa/ Brass* albums, Dolphy wrote background orchestrations for Coltrane's band, a project that sounds magnificent but never rises to its own potential. The best record of the Coltrane/Dolphy partnership is contained on the three collections from the Village Vanguard, particularly in the various takes of "Spiritual" and "India." Even more valuable from these live dates are two exhaustive tours de force for Coltrane's tenor and Elvin Jones, "Chasin' the Trane" (on *Live at the Village Vanguard*) and the title track on *Impressions.*

Over the next three years the quartet established itself as one of the premier groups in jazz history, becoming a major influence through its hypnotic modal ensemble style and the individual conceptions of the four individuals (Garrison joined in late 1961). *Afro-Blue Impressions,* a European concert recording from the period, is one of the finest summaries of the group's repertoire and fever-pitch emotionalism.

Live at Birdland, similarly heated, contains such important performances as "Afro-Blue," "I Want to Talk about You" and the deeply moving "Alabama." *To the Beat of a Different Drummer* shows what happened when Jones was temporarily replaced in 1963 by Roy Haynes.

The masterpiece from the quartet's studio work is *A Love Supreme,* the first comprehensive statement of Coltrane's spiritual concerns, recorded in late 1964. Each man performs with eloquence and economy, and the album (along with *Giant Steps*) has formed the cornerstone of many Coltrane collections.

The remaining quartet albums, made in 1965, have a great deal of excellent music (the appropriately named *Transition* in particular), but by the time of *Sun Ship* and *First Meditations,* Coltrane was pushing toward greater harmonic and rhythmic freedom, a move which Tyner and Jones made reluctantly. The music is harsher, more unsettled, with hints that agreement is occasionally lacking in the rhythm section.

The final period produced the most tumultuous, unfettered music from a man never known for calm or restraint in his playing. Rashied Ali's loose, irregular percussion work was the key to this effort, while the railing presence of Pharoah Sanders allowed Coltrane to keep the energy constantly high at a time when his physical endurance began to fail.

The first four albums in this group (*Ascen-* *sion, Kulu, Om, Meditations*) were actually recorded while Tyner and Jones were still in the band, but the presence of Sanders and other guests clearly puts them in the later period. *Ascension* was an avant-garde conclave for seven horns (including Marion Brown, Freddie Hubbard, Archie Shepp and John Tchicai); hailed as a landmark of energy music, it quickly evolves into a simple series of solos and is best appreciated for the writing ensembles and the exposure it offered several young players. *Kulu Sé Mama* and *Om* are heavily spiritual and cacophonous, and strike this listener as Coltrane's least convincing efforts in the free genre.

Meditations, with Sanders, Tyner, Garrison, and Jones *and* Ali on drums, is a far more lasting realization of energy music, tempered as it is with a deep and accessible melodic strength. The same balance makes *Live at the Village Vanguard Again* such a coherent example of what many listeners dismiss as noise; both Coltrane and Sanders give a lesson in new-wave eloquence on "Naima" and "My Favorite Things." The band sounds strong on *Concert in Japan,* but (perhaps out of necessity) Sanders takes most of the solo space.

Coltrane's last recordings were made in February and March of 1967. *Interstellar Space,* four duets with Ali, are high-energy efforts in the style of the 1966 band, but *Expression* suggests something different. Aside from a negligible debut recording for Coltrane on flute, there are three brilliant free recitations for a quartet of Coltrane on tenor, Alice, Garrison and Ali. The sound of the tenor seems to have widened and deepened, and the melodic sweep subsumes the more abrasive aspects of the free style. Undoubtedly Coltrane was preparing to move on to yet another stage in his endless development, and the generous portion of music he left behind can only suggest what he took with him.

★ ★ ★ ★ **Bye, Bye Blackbird / Pablo**
★ ★ ★ **Cattin' / Prest.**
★ ★ ★ ★ **Coltrane / Prest.**
★ ★ ★ ★ **Dakar / Prest.**
★ ★ ★ **European Tour / Pablo**
★ ★ ★ ★ **Gold Coast (with Wilbur Harden) / Savoy**
★ ★ ★ **John Coltrane and Ray Draper / Prest.**
★ ★ ★ **Jupiter Variations / Imp.**
★ ★ ★ **On a Misty Night / Prest.**
★ ★ ★ **The Paris Concert / Pablo**
★ ★ ★ ★ **Rain or Shine / Prest.**
★ ★ ★ ★ ★ **Soultrane / Prest.**
★ ★ ★ ★ ★ **Trane's Modes / Imp.**

Recent reissues: the Prestige twofers tend to pair very good Coltrane sessions with ordinary efforts. *Dakar,* for example, contains an excellent session organized by pianist Mal Waldron for two trumpets and two tenors, plus a lesser date where Coltrane is joined by two baritone saxes. The excellent *Trane's Reign* material is now also on *Rain or Shine;* *Misty Night* has a quartet led by Tadd Dameron, who contributed good compositions, plus a four-tenor battle.

Of the Sixties material that has appeared in the Eighties, *Trane's Modes* completes the 1961 *Africa/Brass* and *Village Vanguard* collaborations of Coltrane and Dolphy, and contains a nice liner summary of the important Vanguard recordings. All the Pablos date from a European tour made about a year later; *Bye, Bye Blackbird,* with an intense version of the blues "Tranein' In," is the most interesting. *Jupiter Variations* has a side of alternate duets from the Interstellar Spaces dates, plus two band tracks with Alice Coltrane on piano. Coltrane releases of 1982–83 have, for the most part, repackaged single albums as twofers and vice versa. Back in circulation, however, are Coltrane's blowing session with fellow tenor player Paul Quinichette (*Cattin'*) and a dispensable meeting with Ray Draper's tuba. *Lush Life* has been reissued with original cover art as part of Fantasy's Original Jazz Classics series. — B.B.

EDDIE CONDON
★ ★ ★ **Jammin' at Condon's / CSP**
★ ★ **Jam Session / Jazzo.**
★ ★ **Japan / Chi.**
★ ★ **The Spirit of Condon / Jazzo.**
Eddie Condon (1905–1973) was a rhythm guitarist and raconteur who did much to popularize New Orleans-style jazz in Chicago during the Twenties as part of the McKenzie-Condon Chicagoans, then in New York as part of the Mound City Blue Blowers. Condon arranged countless jam sessions, wrote extensively about jazz (he's as well known for his outrageous quotes as for his playing) and ran the important New York jazz club that bore his name. *Jammin' at Condon's* documents the kind of free-form sessions he would organize and features some of his most frequent cronies—tenor saxophonist Bud Freeman, cornetist Wild Bill Davison, and clarinetists Ed Hall and Peanuts Hucko, among others. Condon's best work, however, is unavailable—it's worth searching for the Condon/Freeman collaboration titles, *The Commodore Years.* — J.S.

CHRIS CONNOR
★ ★ **Sketches / Bain.**
★ ★ **Sweet and Singing / Prog.**
Chris Connor (b. 1927) is a somewhat popular cult figure but critically unheralded recording artist. Her husky female vocals were once featured in Stan Kenton's orchestra. — J.S.

BILL CONNORS
★ ★ ★ **Of Mist and Melting / ECM/War.**
★ ★ ★ **Swimming With / ECM/War.**
★ ★ ★ **Theme to the Guardian / ECM/War.**
The searing pinpoint guitar playing of Bill Connors (b. 1949) in the original, heavily arranged, electric version of Return to Forever helped define a jazz/rock/fusion guitar style. Fans of his intense delivery will be surprised at these subdued, classically influenced records of guitar solos. Connors' compositional sense and shrewdly calculated, multiple-overdub technique suits the pristine recording style employed by ECM's Manfred Eicher. — J.S.

JUNIOR COOK
★ ★ ★ ★ **Good Cookin' / Muse**
★ ★ ★ ★ **Somethin's Cookin' / Muse**
A vastly underrated tenor saxophonist, Junior Cook (b. 1934) is best known for his playing in Horace Silver's popular soul-jazz quintet from 1958 to 1964. His full, deep tone and infectious rhythmic feel highlight both of these records—the 1980 septet *Good Cookin',* with his frequent partner Bill Hardman's trumpet and fluegelhorn, Mario Rivera's baritone saxophone and Slide Hampton's trombone sharing the front line with Cook; and the '82 quartet with Cedar Walton on piano, Buster Williams on bass and Billy Higgins on drums. — J.S.

JEROME COOPER
★ ★ ★ **For the People / Hat Hut**
★ ★ ★ **Root Assumptions / Anima**
★ ★ **The Unpredictability of Predictability / About T.**
Best known for his work with the Revolutionary Ensemble, drummer Jerome Cooper (b. 1946) has channeled his energies toward solo recordings since the dissolution of the Ensemble. Both the About Time and Anima recordings are solo ventures, and the Hat Hut album features duets with reedman Oliver Lake. Cooper's work tends to rely heavily on extended repetitive rhythmic patterns overlaid with folk counterpoints on flutes, whistles and balaphone. Just okay. — F.G.

CHICK COREA

★ ★ ★ **Inner Space / Atl.**
A two-record collection of everything pianist Chick Corea (b. 1941) recorded for the Atlantic and Vortex labels in the late Sixties, with Joe Farrell, Woody Shaw, Steve Swallow, Hubert Laws, Ron Carter and others. This is a robust, aggressive Corea, still caught between the shadows of McCoy Tyner, Bill Evans and Horace Silver. While he was then prone to more complex harmonic pursuits, the Latin and classical impulses were also evident.

★ ★ ★ **Circle Paris—Concert / ECM/War.**
A collaborative effort with Anthony Braxton, David Holland and Barry Altschul (who went by the group name Circle), and as far into the free-jazz arena as Corea ever ventured. Some moments are impenetrably dense, others inexplicably evocative. This is music with teeth, but that doesn't mean it'll bite if you try to get close to it.

★ ★ ★ ★ **Circling In / Blue N.**
The definitive late-Sixties Corea collection, comprised of sessions United Artists saw unfit to release until 1975. Again, much of it is in the Circle spirit—breakneck, free-form excursions—while some tracks favor an intimate, abstract chamber-bop style.

★ ★ ★ ★ ★ **Piano Improvisations, Vols. 1 and 2 / ECM/War.**
Of all of Corea's albums, these wear the best with time, from the oblique cuts to the serene ones. One can hear intimations of major themes in his Return to Forever period. With the exception of two tracks, all selections are first take, flawless and spontaneously composed.

★ ★ ★ ★ ★ **Return to Forever / ECM/War.**
The title, before it was a group. Although not released in the U.S. until 1975, this album was recorded three years earlier and marked Corea's first use of electric instruments since his tenure with Miles Davis and his first recorded attempts at songwriting, for Brazilian vocalist Flora Purim. Also Chick's first full-fledged flirtation with Latin music and sonata structures.

★ ★ ★ ★ **Light as a Feather, with Return to Forever / Poly.**
Here, Corea blended the Latin flavor of the first Return to Forever with a curious blend of ballad sensitivities and rock dynamics. Several modern jazz classics reside within, including "You're Everything," "500 Miles High" and "Spain." Flora was given more room to scat and soar. Essential for its joyousness, flawed for its lengthy noodling.

★ ★ ★ ★ ★ **Hymn of the Seventh Galaxy, with Return to Forever / Poly.**
With this 1973 outing, Chick forfeited Flora and Latin fantasies, and instead plugged in, turned up and joined the jazz-rock race. Not surprisingly, the results echoed the path previously charted by former Miles cohort John McLaughlin, with searing cross-levels of voracious synthesizers, lethal guitars and ear-numbing rhythm and tone clusters. Derivative but essential, a last bold lunge before fusion got funked.

★ ★ ★ **Where Have I Known You Before, with Return to Forever / Poly.**
Amazing how subtle the shades are between novelty and cliché. *Where Have I Known You Before* reintroduced Corea's classical leanings, but neither he nor the band were sure how to offer them. Overweight with tiresome, aimless riffing, but noteworthy for sporadic glimpses of an exquisite acoustic leitmotif. Al DiMeola's first appearance.

★ ★ **No Mystery, with Return to Forever / Poly.**
An apt title. No pleasure either. By this point (1975) the whole Return to Forever schtick seemed like a shuck. Gone were the graceful arching lines and fiery crossfire, and in their place resided a clobbery funk rhythm and fragmented riff phrasing.

★ ★ ★ ★ **The Leprechaun / Poly.**
1976 was a banner year for Corea and his cohorts, and his own *The Leprechaun* was the most prodigious achievement of their combined efforts. For the first time, Chick touched all of his bases, from classical suites to rock grooves, from free-form improvisation to gentle vocalizations, and all with equal conviction and competence. A much needed reminder of Corea's all-encompassing composing and arranging abilities.

★ ★ ★ ★ **Romantic Warrior, with Return to Forever / Col.**
The band's first for a new label, first without Corea's name in the forefront and their last as a quartet (unless a live album follows). Musically, it was a completely revivified, expanded approach. In place of improvisation, which translated to noodling before, Corea imposed a classical structure, complete with medieval motifs. A surprising milestone in a tired genre.   — M.G.

★ ★ **A.R.C. / ECM/War.**
★ ★ **Again and Again / Elek./Mus.**
★ ★ ★ **Children's Songs / ECM**
★ ★ ★ ★ **Chick Corea / Blue N.**
★ ★ ★ ★ **Chick Corea and Gary Burton / ECM/War.**
★ ★ ★ ★ **Circulus / Blue N.**
★ ★ ★ ★ **Evening with Chick Corea and Herbie Hancock / Col.**
★ ★ **Friends / Poly.**

★ ★ **Mad Hatter** / **Poly.**
★ ★ ★ **My Spanish Heart** / **Poly.**
★ ★ ★ ★ **Now He Sings, Now He Sobs** /
 Pac. J.
★ ★ **Secret Agent** / **Poly.**
★ ★ ★ ★ **Song of Singing** / **Blue N.**
★ ★ ★ **Tap Step** / **War.**
★ ★ ★ **Three Quartets** / **War.**
★ ★ ★ ★ **Trio Music** / **ECM/War.**

Chick Corea's continued success as one of the most popular jazz crossover artists during the Seventies has prompted the release of some obscure sessions that are, ironically, more important than the music he's best known for. Corea's first significant musical contributions came during and immediately after his late-Sixties stint in Miles Davis' historic *Bitches Brew* group. Davis challenged Corea's imagination to the fullest and the talented keyboardist went on to form one of the finest experimental groups of the time, Circle, with bassist Dave Holland, drummer Barry Altschul and later saxophonist Anthony Braxton.

Circle was ahead of its time and little of the group's music was released when it was made. *Circulus* completes the belated release of this unit's great 1970 recordings, more of which were assembled on *Circling In. Song of Singing,* the most accessible recording of the group (Holland and Altschul) from that time, presages the lighter, lyrical touch Corea would later use, as does the earlier *Now He Sings, Now He Sobs,* on which Corea is supported by drummer Roy Haynes and bassist Miroslav Vitous. *Chick Corea* is an excellent sampler of his United Artists material recorded between 1968 and 1970.

Unfortunately, Corea's post-Return To Forever records, which are the basis of his current popularity, sound like timid, emotionally bereft hack work next to his great recordings. When his simple, lyrical spirit shines through, as it does on the beautifully sparse duets with Gary Burton and Herbie Hancock and at moments on some of the other LPs like *My Spanish Heart,* Corea can still be considered an important contributor to the current music scene. Through most of the late Seventies, however, one could only lament the senseless waste of his great talent.

The spectacular 1982 record, *Trio Music,* was a dramatic return to form. With the virtuoso accompaniment of bassist Miroslav Vitous and drummer Roy Haynes, and a program that featured one disc of improvised trios and duets and a companion disc of Thelonious Monk compositions, Corea recapitulated his finest moments as a player. Corea, Vitous and Haynes first played together on the wonderful *Now He Sings, Now He Sobs.* — J.S.

LARRY CORYELL
★ ★ ★ ★ **Coryell** / **Van.**
★ ★ ★ **Lady Coryell** / **Van.**
★ ★ ★ **Larry Coryell at the Village Gate** /
 Van.

Though Larry Coryell (b. 1943) is one of the most creative and accomplished modern electric guitarists, he has never been as popular as many less capable but better promoted musicians. Coryell came to New York in 1965 to play jazz and ended up as second string to legendary guitarist Gabor Szabo in Chico Hamilton's band. In less than a year Coryell began his recording career with Hamilton as Szabo's replacement, and by 1968 Coryell had a formidable reputation as a jazz soloist. Part of that reputation came from the influential records he made with the Gary Burton quartet (including *Duster, Lofty Fake Anagram, In Concert*).

Lady Coryell is a tour-de-force debut with Coryell doing virtually all the playing, pinning high velocity runs with heavy-metal chord patterns. What the album loses through its psychedelic programing and Coryell's toneless singing is more than made up for by the freshness of the musical approach. *Coryell* is a better balanced effort where the guitarist is clearly a bandleader in firm control of his ideas. *Larry Coryell at the Village Gate* features Coryell live at the top of his rock form carrying a power trio.

★ ★ ★ **Barefoot Boy** / **RCA**
★ ★ ★ **Offering** / **Van.**
★ ★ ★ ★ **The Real Great Escape** / **Van.**

These albums, recorded between 1971 and 1973 with a band built around Coryell's old keyboard sidekick from high school rock bands, Mike Mandel, and saxophonist Steve Marcus, show a maturing Coryell less interested in soloing for its own sake than in a complete group sound with more harmonic variation. *Barefoot Boy* and *Offering* are almost traditional post-bop jazz albums until Coryell and Marcus duel with frenetic solos. This band reached its peak with *The Real Great Escape,* where Coryell comes closest to linking rock song structure and vocal dynamics with jazz execution.

★ ★ ★ **Aspects** / **Ari.**
★ ★ **Basics** / **Van.**
★ ★ ★ **The Essential Larry Coryell** / **Van.**
★ ★ ★ ★ ★ **Introducing the Eleventh House**
 / **Van.**
★ ★ ★ **Planet End** / **Van.**
★ ★ ★ ★ **The Restful Mind** / **Van.**
★ ★ ★ **Return** / **Van.**

★ ★ ★ ★ **Spaces** / Van.
★ ★ ★ **Splendid**
★ ★ ★ ★ **Twin House (with Philip Catherine)**
／ **Elek.**

Spaces, recorded with guitarist John McLaughlin, keyboardist Chick Corea, bassist Miroslav Vitous and drummer Billy Cobham, features Coryell's most tasteful and subdued playing since his days with Chico Hamilton and Gary Burton. His next band was an electric music powerhouse. *Introducing the Eleventh House* is beautiful, intelligent music with guts and urgency. *The Restful Mind,* a mostly acoustic album recorded with Oregon, presents a dialogue between Coryell and Ralph Towner's brilliant guitar work that surpasses even the Coryell/McLaughlin duets on *Spaces. Essential Coryell* is a good best-of compilation from the Vanguard catalogue. *Planet End* consists of outtakes from the *Spaces* and *Eleventh House* sessions, while *Basics* are Vanguard's crudest and earliest outtakes, from around the time of the second album. *Aspects* traces Coryell's decline with the Eleventh House into well-performed but directionless music. *Twin House* is an excellent album of acoustic duets between Coryell and Philip Catherine. — J.S.

TOM COSTER
★ ★ **Ivory Expedition** / Fan.
★ ★ **T.C.** / Fan.

During his long-running Seventies collaboration with Santana, keyboardist Tom Coster (b. 1941) established himself as one of the most imaginative fusion conceptualists, a master of a variety of keyboards. His own solo records are far more oriented toward synthesizers and suffer from over-conceptualization. Coster needs either to break through to the other side of the all-too-gimmicky sounds that dominate these records or else scale down to the simpler approach he used so effectively as part of the Santana band. — J.S.

CURTIS COUNCE
★ ★ ★ **Carl's Blues** / Contem.
★ ★ ★ **Counceltation** / Contem.
★ ★ ★ ★ **Exploring the Future** / Doo.
★ ★ ★ **Landslide** / Contem.
★ ★ ★ ★ **You Get More Bounce with Curtis Counce!** / Contem./OJC

The career of Curtis Counce (1926–1963), one of California's premier bassists in the Fifties, was cut short by his death at the age of thirty-seven. A popular sessionman, Counce also proved himself a very capable leader in these quintet dates, all recorded during the latter half of the Fifties. Tenorman Harold Land and drummer Frank Butler are constants on all the sessions, with either Elmo Hope or Carl Perkins on piano. A modern group with a strong drive, the Counce sessions are typical of the type of recordings the Contemporary label was making during this period. Very solid dates, but hardly remarkable, they're most interesting as an indication of the hard-bop blowing that was going on in California during that era. — F.G.

STANLEY COWELL
★ ★ ★ ★ **Equipoise** / Gal.
★ ★ ★ ★ **Illusion Suite** / ECM/War.
★ ★ ★ ★ **Musa-Ancestral Streams** / Strata-East
★ ★ ★ **New World** / Gal.
★ ★ ★ ★ **Regeneration** / Strata-East
★ ★ ★ **Talkin' Bout Love** / Gal.
★ ★ ★ **Waiting For** / Gal.

Stanley Cowell (b. 1931) is an imposing composer and pianist who recorded in the late Sixties with Marion Brown, Max Roach and Charles Tolliver before experimenting with his own albums, some of which have been released on the label he set up with Tolliver, Strata-East. He has worked in a variety of contexts, from the insightful solo piano record *Musa-Ancestral Streams* to such varied trio records as one with Stanley Clarke and Jimmy Hopps (*Illusion Suite*) and another with Cecil McBee and Roy Haynes (*Equipoise*). Cowell is currently a member of the Heath Brothers Band. — J.S.

HANK CRAWFORD
★ ★ ★ **Down On the Deuce** / Mile.
★ ★ ★ **Indigo Blue** / Mile.
★ ★ ★ **Midnight Ramble** / Mile.

Alto saxophonist Hank Crawford (b. 1934) worked with a number of blues bands and as baritone saxophonist and arranger of the Ray Charles band before making a series of albums under his own name in the Sixties for Atlantic and in the Seventies for CTI. The Milestone albums, recorded in the Eighties, represent a return to Crawford's blues roots for a pleasing soul jazz groove with Dr. John (*Indigo, Ramble*) and Cedar Walton (*Deuce*) on piano. — J.S.

CREATIVE CONSTRUCTION COMPANY
★ ★ ★ **Creative Construction Company** / Muse
★ ★ ★ **Creative Construction Company, Vol. 2** / Muse

A brief-lived sextet featuring violinist Leroy Jenkins (b. 1932), reedman Anthony Braxton, trumpeter Leo Smith, pianist Muhal Richard Abrams, drummer Steve McCall and bassist Richard Davis. The latter is the only group member who did not come out of Chicago's Association for the Advancement of Creative Musicians (AACM), an organization that has concentrated its efforts on the development of collective improvisation. This is a good example of the kind of music the AACM was making in the late Sixties and early Seventies, although less sympathetic than that of the AACM's best-known band, the Art Ensemble of Chicago. Both LPs are culled from a single concert at Greenwich Village's Peace Church in 1970, and each features one extended composition by Jenkins. The emphasis is on flow and texture rather than melody, although the first volume's vehicle, "Muhal," is somewhat more grounded in traditional melodic reference points. Not the best solo work available by any of these artists, but hardly without merits. It's really out there, too. — F.G.

THE CRUSADERS
★ ★ ★ Best of / MCA
★ ★ ★ Chain Reaction / MCA
★ ★ Free as the Wind / MCA
★ ★ Ghetto Blaster / MCA
★ ★ Images / MCA
★ ★ ★ Live Sides / Blue N.
★ ★ ★ ★ One / MCA
★ ★ ★ Ongaku-Kai: Live in Japan / Crus.
★ ★ Rhapsody and Blues / MCA
★ ★ Royal Jam / MCA
★ ★ ★ ★ Scratch / MCA
★ ★ ★ ★ Second Crusade / MCA
★ ★ ★ Southern Comfort / MCA
★ ★ Standing Tall / MCA
★ ★ Street Life / Crus.
★ ★ Those Southern Knights / MCA
★ ★ ★ ★ Young Rabbits / Blue N.
The Crusaders—drummer Stix Hooper (b. 1938), keyboardist Joe Sample (b. 1939), saxophonist/bassist Wilton Felder (b. 1940) and trombonist Wayne Henderson (b. 1939)—grew up listening to and playing jazz and R&B in their native Texas before moving to California in the late Fifties, where they dubbed themselves the Jazz Crusaders and made a number of excellent records. The *Young Rabbits* set collects some of their best moments from the Sixties. In the early Seventies the group dropped the word *Jazz* from its name, hired guitarist Larry Carlton and proceeded to record a series of highly successful pop/jazz LPs, even scoring a sizable hit single with the instrumental "Put It

Where You Want It" from *One. One, Second Crusade, Scratch* and *Southern Comfort* represent the group's creative high point—they played commercial, accessible music without compromising their ideals as players. Subsequently the band's sound became more formulaic and less convincing, and by the late Seventies, when they also began to make the inevitable solo records and produce other artists, the Crusaders seemed to lose not only their direction, but their purpose as well. In 1983 Stix Hooper left and was replaced by top session drummer Ndugu (Leon Chancler). — J.S.

TED CURSON
★ ★ ★ ★ Flip Top / Ari./Free.
★ ★ ★ Jubilant Power / Inner
★ ★ Snake Johnson / Chi.
★ ★ ★ ★ Tears for Dolphy / Ari./Free.
★ ★ ★ Ted Curson & Co. / In. Nav.
★ ★ ★ ★ The Trio / Interp.
The roughly spoken and smoothly executed trumpet playing of Ted Curson (b. 1935) can and does draw on a rich and widely learned vocabulary, including blues, Afro-Cuban, cool and free. More influenced than influential, his blowing—often within the same piece—refuses to be confined to any one style and will travel the distance from Clifford Brown fire to Miles Davis ice and hit most points in between.

Graduating from the same Philadelphia high school that Coltrane attended, Curson was encouraged to come to New York by Miles Davis, who had heard him perform live. Three years later in 1955, Curson made the jump and first landed with a Latin band, then with pianist Mal Waldron and finally with Cecil Taylor whom he recorded with in 1959 ("one concert, one record date, and a whole year of rehearsing"). The next year Curson had moved on to Mingus' Jazz Workshop, contributing to his Candid albums (now out on Jazz Man) and journeyed to Europe as the fifth member of the legendary Mingus/Richmond/Ervin/Dolphy team. Atlantic's *Mingus At Antibes* best captures Curson's "free" awakenings.

Upon returning to New York, Curson began to develop a group of his own. His first records as leader—particularly the rare 1961 *Plenty Of Horn* on Old Town—proved him not only an inspired cool-blowing composer (tunes like "Flatted Fifth" and "Nosruc" are exceptional) but also a varied stylist who introduced the four-valve piccolo trumpet to the jazz idiom. Also from this period and equally hard to find is the mellow, ballad-laden *Fire Down Below* on Prestige.

In 1964 Curson relocated to France, and recorded almost exclusively for European labels. Except for a fine set recorded for Atlantic in 1965 (*Quicksand* with tenor saxophonist Bill Barron), Curson's best from the late Sixties and early Seventies is limited to two albums, arguably his finest and most original ever. Both were rereleased on Arista/Freedom; *Flip Top* presents Curson as a matured master of cool sonorities, again with Barron (on side B he is accompanied by the Zagreb Radio Orchestra), and *Tears for Dolphy* reveals him just as assured and skilled handling the hurtling rhythms typical of Mingus.

Curson remained in Europe until the mid-Seventies, when the *Tears* reissue revitalized his reputation in America. Returning to the States, he recorded the rollicking *Jubilant Power* and the easy-rolling *Blue Piccolo* for the Japanese Whynot label (since released here as *& Co.* on India Navigation).

Recently, Curson's output has varied greatly in style and mood, ranging from 1979's excellent and exciting *Trio* (with bassist Ray Drummond and drummer Roy Haynes) to *Typical Ted,* a halfway convincing updating of a few early-Sixties compositions (with a French group), to the labored funk of *Snake Johnson* (with a large ensemble and Bill Barron). Almost as a rule, Curson's best comes in a small-group, pared-down package. — A.K.

KING CURTIS
★ ★ ★ **The Best of King Curtis / Prest.**
★ ★ ★ **The Best of King Curtis/One More Time / Prest.**
In the Fifties, King Curtis (1935–1971) was an emerging star as a session saxophonist. His honking, dirty solo on the Coasters' "Yakety Yak" was the trademark of his early style, as well as providing a definitive rock & roll performance. These two albums mark the best of his early sessions as a featured soloist. At the time, Curtis' tone, a lowdown, guttural growl, was very much in the mold of the then-popular Willis "Gatortail" Jackson. With sidemen like Brother Jack McDuff, Billy Butler and Eric Gale, King Curtis works his way through R&B standards like "Honky Tonk," "Fever" and "The Hucklebuck." The twist novelties are cloying, but a smoky reading of "Harlem Nocturne" is a stand-out.
★ ★ ★ **Jazz Groove / Prest.**
★ ★ ★ **King Soul / Prest.**
★ ★ ★ **Soul Meeting / Prest.**
As leader of a session that included jazz notables like Nat Adderley, Wynton Kelly and Paul Chambers, King Curtis didn't venture far from the brawling saxophone style he brought to R&B sessions. *Soul Meeting* and *King Soul* were combined in the reissue, *Jazz Groove.* And though King was not out of his league playing blues and bop with such a formidable lineup, he proves to be a jazz frontman of only marginal interest.
★ ★ ★ ★ **The Best of King Curtis / Atco**
★ ★ ★ ★ **Live at the Fillmore West / Atco**
But if King Curtis was merely a competent jazz musician, he was a master at a simpler form. By the mid-Sixties, Curtis had few peers as a soul saxophonist and bandleader. His tone had broadened, and though the rough, muscular edges were still very much in evidence, he displayed an increased lyrical sense that sparkled on the wafting, self-composed "Soul Serenade" and ballads like "Something On Your Mind" and "You've Lost That Lovin' Feelin'."

The *Fillmore* album shows King Curtis as a fully matured R&B master, fronting an awesome, powerhouse band that included stalwarts Cornell Dupree, Bernard Purdy and Gerald Jemmott. Though at times one wishes for more judicious material ("Mr. Bojangles"?), there's no arguing with the performance. Curtis and the band simply erupt on potboilers "Memphis Soul Stew" and "Them Changes." It was the supreme soul band of its time. — J.MC.

ANDREW CYRILLE
★ ★ ★ **Celebration / IPS**
★ ★ ★ **Dialogue of the Drums / IPS**
★ ★ ★ ★ **The Loop / Ictus**
★ ★ ★ ★ **Metamusician's Stomp / Black S.**
★ ★ ★ **The Navigator / Soul N.**
★ ★ ★ ★ **Pieces of Time / Soul N.**
★ ★ ★ **Special People / Soul N.**
"The new, free, creative, black drumming definitely has a beginning and that was it!" drummer/percussionist Andrew Cyrille (b. 1939) proudly declared after a live duo with Milford Graves recorded in 1974 and released as *Dialogue.* And since that time, Cyrille has spearheaded an experimental approach to solo and collective improvisation that draws as much from his many years accompanying Cecil Taylor's free explorations as from the timeless African tradition of drummer-as-leader. As such, multi-instrumentalist Cyrille prefers the label of "metamusician," emphasizing his intention to carry jazz drumming far beyond a simple accompanying role.

Cyrille has since the early Sixties worked with a wide range of fine musicians, including Illinois Jacquet, Coleman Hawkins, Mary

Lou Williams and Olatunji, but is best known for his fifteen-year association with Cecil Taylor, contributing to many of his most heralded mid-Sixties recordings, adding many extended, gear-shifting solos.

In the early Seventies, Cyrille struck out on his own, initially performing with other drummers, including Rashied Ali, Milford Graves and Don Moye, and establishing his own educational foundation and label—The Institute of Percussive Studies.

Throughout the Seventies, Cyrille continued to lead his own ensembles and explore the percussive possibilities of his art in varied contexts. *Celebration* (1975) saw him working with vocalist Jeanne Lee, poet Elouise Loftin, tenorman David Ware and trumpeter Ted Daniel among others. The collective was called Maono (May-oh-no)—Swahili for "feeling"—which produced an improvised collage that swung in its experimental mayhem, spiced with revolutionary lyrics. *Loop* (1978) presented Cyrille solo and at his exploratory best, successfully employing a multitude of approaches to his battery of instruments: accompanying his drumming with a police whistle, drumming with his hands, scratching and even barking through the skin of his snare.

By 1978 Maono had been distilled to its strongest elements, a quartet featuring Daniel, Ware and bassist Nick DeGronimo, with Cyrille as leader and primary composer. *Metamusician's Stomp* developed a slightly more accessible jazz style, and revealed Cyrille's excellent compositional abilities, particularly on the title track, and the explosive bop-bordering-on-anarchy of "5-4-3-2."

In the Eighties, Cyrille has been recording almost exclusively for the Italian Black Saint/Soul Note label family. *Special People* (1980) featured the same lineup as *Metamusician's* but lacked the drive and focus of that record. *The Navigator* was recorded in 1982 with the addition of pianist Sonelius Smith and without Ware, resulting in a much more straight-ahead set, with Cyrille withdrawing to a more accompanying stance. Currently performing much less in the experimental boundaries he helped pioneer, Cyrille responds to those who would ask, "Wherefore free?" with "I *love* doing that. But I feel there's nothing wrong with being comprehensive *and* being a virtuoso too."

Pieces of Time presents what is Cyrille's most enterprising project to date, a drummers-only quartet in an orgy of jazz and African rhythms. Recorded in late '83, *Pieces* features the collective efforts of Cyrille, Graves, Famoudou Don Moye of the Art Ensemble, and bebop veteran Kenny Clarke (liner notes by Max Roach). —A.K.

TONY DAGRADI
★ ★ ★ **Lunar Eclipse / Gram.**
★ ★ ★ **Oasis / Gram.**
Alto/tenor saxophonist and clarinetist Tony
Dagradi (b. 1953) got his start playing in
R&B horn sections for the likes of Marvin
Gaye, Ike and Tina Turner, and Archie Bell
and the Drells before moving to New Orleans to pursue his own musical course in
the late Seventies. His Astral Project group,
heard in two different lineups on each of
these albums, features Dagradi's tuneful
compositions and intelligent yet accessible
playing. Dagradi has also played with Professor Longhair and the Carla Bley band.
— J.S.

TADD DAMERON
★ ★ ★ ★ **The Arrangers' Touch / Prest.**
★ ★ ★ ★ **Strictly Bebop / Cap.**
Much of the modest recorded legacy of Tadd
Dameron (1917–1965) is currently available
under Fats Navarro's name, but the first
great modern jazz arranger does get half of
The Arrangers' Touch to display his 1953
and 1956 writing, with Clifford Brown and
Philly Joe Jones featured on the earlier date.
Strictly Bebop, a more representative sam-
pler, has six 1949 orchestra tracks and the
likes of Miles Davis, Dexter Gordon and
Navarro to play the lean and lyrical charts.
★ ★ ★ ★ **Fontainebleau / Fan./OJC**
★ ★ ★ ★ **The Magic Touch / Fan./OJC**
★ ★ ★ ★ **Mating Call (with John Coltrane) /**
   Prest.
★ ★ ★ ★ **Tadd Dameron Memorial Album /**
   Prest.
The two Prestige volumes listed above remain available singly in the old Prestige Historical Series. The *Memorial Album* contains
the 1956 band tracks heard on *The Arrangers' Touch,* plus one extended blues. (It is
also available, titled *Fontainebleau* and with
its original art and liner notes, on the Fanta-
sy/Original Jazz Classics label.) *Mating Call,*
a quartet session for which Dameron wrote
some striking lines for the then up-and-
coming tenor soloist John Coltrane, is also
currently half of a Coltrane twofer, *On a
Misty Night* (Prestige). *The Magic Touch* is
a 1962 set performed by large groups featuring Johnny Griffin, Bill Evans, George Duvivier, Philly Joe Jones and Charlie Shavers
among others.
   A minor Dameron comeback, launched
sixteen years after his death, has been generated by Dameronia, a nine-piece band playing original Dameron arrangements under
the direction of drummer Philly Joe Jones.
— B.B.

COW COW DAVENPORT
★ ★ ★ ★ **Cow Cow Blues / Oldie B.**
★ ★ ★ ★ **Cow Cow Davenport / Mag.**
Singer/piano player is generally described as
one of the first practitioners of boogie-
woogie. But his style is radically different
from the Albert Ammons/Meade Lux Lewis
school that has come to define the genre.
Davenport was closer to a style that predates
the New Orleans piano playing of Smiley
Lewis and Professor Longhair, although
ironically Davenport was from Alabama and
rarely worked in New Orleans. — J.S.

ANTHONY DAVIS
★ ★ ★ ★ **Crystal Texts (with James Newton)**
   / Moers
★ ★ ★ ★ ★ **Episteme / Gram.**
★ ★ ★ ★ ★ **Hemispheres / Gram.**
★ ★ ★ ★ ★ **Hidden Voices (with James**
   Newton) / In. Nav.
★ ★ ★ ★ **I've Known Rivers (with James**
   Newton and Abdul Wadud) / Gram.
★ ★ ★ ★ **Lady of the Mirrors / In. Nav.**
★ ★ ★ ★ **Of Blues and Dreams / Sack.**
★ ★ ★ ★ **Past Lives / Red R.**
★ ★ ★ ★ **Song for the Old World / In. Nav.**

★ ★ ★ ★ **Under the Double Moon (with Jay Hoggard) / Pausa**
★ ★ ★ ★ **Variations in Dream Time / In. Nav.**

Pianist Anthony Davis (b. 1951) came to be regarded as a major new voice on his instrument during the late Seventies, after his work with such important new musicians as Leo Smith, Oliver Lake, Leroy Jenkins and Barry Altschul. As the new decade began, he also rose to the forefront of those young black musicians placing increasing emphasis on compositional (as opposed to improvisational) elements in their music.

A sense of Davis' pianistic roots in Duke Ellington, Thelonious Monk and Cecil Taylor, as well as his ingenuity in the jazz combo format, can be gleaned from his earlier band albums. *Song for the Old World*—with Jay Hoggard (vibes), Mark Helias (bass) and Ed Blackwell (drums)—was a strong debut, introducing a craggy postmodernism that suggested Andrew Hill's Blue Note work (Hill is the subject of one piece). *Hidden Voices,* with stunning writing and a consistently high level of solos, features the quartet Davis coled with flutist James Newton; trombonist George Lewis appears as "special guest." After the solo title performance, *Of Blues and Dreams* presents yet another quartet, this one setting the leader's piano against the stark string sonorities of Leroy Jenkins and Abdul Wadud on violin and cello.

By 1980, Davis was stressing predetermined compositional devices that channel the performer's creative impulses, trying to move from predominantly improvised music to a greater compositional/improvisational balance. *Lady of the Mirrors,* an album of piano solos, is thus an extremely contained recital, with the strongly melodic written themes encouraging nuances as much as outright variations. (Compare the earlier *Past Lives,* an equally impressive solo set that feels more loose. Each album has a piece dedicated to Ellington; *Past Lives* also contains a suite of Monk material.) *Episteme* achieves what may come to be viewed as an early pinnacle of this approach in an octet that develops sonorities heard earlier on *Hidden Voices* and *Of Blues and Dreams* within a context that also suggests turn of the century Impressionism and contemporary minimalism.

Davis' recording career remained prolific through 1983, as duet albums with Hoggard and Newton, previously available only in Europe, appeared in America; newer work was released by American labels. Particularly enlightening are *Under the Double Moon,* a sublimely balanced piano/vibes encounter, and *I've Known Rivers,* a "chamber" trio with compositions by all three (Davis, Newton, Wadud) participants. *Variations* is a larger ensemble album, less compelling than *Episteme. Hemispheres* is another large-group format conceptualized in collaboration with choreographer Molissa Fenley and featuring beautiful playing.   — B.B.

EDDIE "LOCKJAW" DAVIS
★ ★ ★ ★ **The Cookbook / Prest.**
★ ★ ★ **The Heavy Hitter / Muse**
★ ★ ★ **Jaw's Blues / Enja**
★ ★ ★ **Jazz at the Philharmonic, 1983 / Pablo**
★ ★ ★ ★ ★ **Live at Minton's (with Johnny Griffin) / Prest.**
★ ★ ★ ★ **Montreux '77 / Pablo**
★ ★ ★ **Straight Ahead / Pablo**
★ ★ ★ **Swingin' Till the Girls Come Home / Steep.**

Truly tough tenor player with a husky, hard-hitting sound. The recent recordings of Eddie "Lockjaw" Davis (b. 1921) for Pablo show that neither time nor age have diminished the bite in his playing.

Davis' career, while always outstanding, has been marked by several extremely fruitful periods. He first made his mark in the big bands of the Forties, working with Andy Kirk, Cootie Williams and most notably Count Basie, a relationship he resumed in the Seventies. During the Fifties his work in a small group with Shirley Scott helped define the organ/tenor combos of the period (documented on *The Cookbook*). His two-tenor band of the Sixties with Johnny Griffin (*Live at Minton's*) was an incendiary pairing that measured up to the Wardell Gray/ Dexter Gordon yardstick of the Forties.

Now in his sixties, Davis is one of the strongest surviving links to the Coleman Hawkins/Ben Webster school of playing. An early-Eighties club tour of the U.S. reunited him with alter-ego Griffin and gave ample proof that "Jaws" can still muster more vigor and emotion than most name tenor players half his age.   — F.G.

MILES DAVIS
★ ★ ★ **Agharta / Col.**
★ ★ ★ ★ **Big Fun / Col.**
★ ★ ★ ★ ★ **Bitches Brew / Col.**
★ ★ ★ **Blue Haze / Fan./OJC**
★ ★ ★ **Blue Moods / Fan./OJC**
★ ★ ★ **Collector's Items / Fan./OJC**
★ ★ ★ ★ **Cookin' / Fan./OJC**
★ ★ ★ **Decoy / Col.**

★ ★ ★ ★ ★ Dig / Fan./OJC
★ ★ ★ Directions / Col.
★ ★ ★ ★ ★ ESP / Col.
★ ★ ★ ★ ★ ★ Filles de Kilimanjaro / Col.
★ ★ ★ ★ "Four" and More / Col.
★ ★ ★ Get Up with It / Col.
★ ★ ★ ★ Heard 'Round the World / Col.
★ ★ ★ ★ ★ In a Silent Way / Col.
★ ★ ★ ★ Jack Johnson / Col.
★ ★ ★ ★ ★ Kind of Blue / CBS
★ ★ ★ Live-Evil / Col.
★ ★ ★ Man with the Horn / Col.
★ ★ ★ ★ Miles Davis / Prest.
★ ★ ★ ★ Miles Davis/Milt Jackson / Fan./
OJC
★ ★ ★ ★ Miles in the Sky / Col.
★ ★ ★ ★ ★ Miles Smiles / Col.
★ ★ ★ ★ The Musings of Miles / Fan./OJC
★ ★ ★ ★ ★ Nefertiti / Col.
★ ★ ★ ★ The New Miles Davis Quintet /
Fan./OJC
★ ★ ★ On the Corner / Col.
★ ★ ★ ★ ★ Sorcerer / Col.
★ ★ ★ ★ Star People / Col.
★ ★ ★ Water Babies / Col.
★ ★ ★ ★ We Want Miles / Col.
★ ★ ★ ★ Workin' and Steamin'! / Prest.

Miles Davis (b. 1926) is widely conceded to
be the father of modern jazz, not because he
founded every major school of thought in
the field since Charlie Parker—although his
explorations as far back as the late Fifties set
the stage for the Sixties' avant-garde explosion—but because he has attracted, tutored
and spawned an unprecedented number of
this last generation's jazz cognoscenti.

With his historic Newport appearance in
1955, and the formation of one of the most
definitive quintets of all time (John Coltrane,
Red Garland, Paul Chambers and Philly Joe
Jones), Miles started to ride a crest of popularity that only showed some signs of dissi-
pation in the late Seventies, when he stopped
recording and performing for several years
due to reasons of health. For anyone interested in learning of Davis' or Coltrane's ger-
mination, the Prestige twofers listed above
are not only essential, but great fun. In either package, one will find the roots of three
elements which were to characterize the
Davis Sound for a generation and more: the
lonely, muted, introspective trumpet tone
(present here in the array of showtune ballads); the fast and furious neo-bop style; and
a gradual movement away from traditional
chord progressions and harmonics to a more
spacious modal sound. Fantasy's OJC series
has also reissued a number of LPs, most of
which predate the Coltrane quintet. *Cookin'*
marks the debut of that classic unit.

By the late Fifties the personnel of the
quintet/sextet was in constant flux, and
Miles fancied experimental settings. *Kind of
Blue* (with Coltrane, Adderley, Chambers,
James Cobb, Wynton Kelly and Bill Evans)
was pivotal, the first jazz album to utilize
modal principles in a wide-open improvisational framework. In 1964 Miles formed his
second quintet of any significant duration,
comprised of Ron Carter (bass), Tony Williams (drums), Herbie Hancock (piano) and
Wayne Shorter (tenor and soprano saxophone). With *"Four" and More*—the best
live album of Miles' career—*ESP* and *Miles
Smiles,* Miles forged a unique (albeit conservative) break from the modal freedom of
Kind of Blue with the hard blues undercurrent of the mid-Fifties quintet with Coltrane
et al. Twenty years later Columbia reissued a
two-record set of this group in concert,
Heard 'Round the World. Sorcerer and *Nefertiti* inched closer to a new vision, a me-
thodical mixture of elongated phrasing,
cross-rhythms and a strange conception of
still space.

Miles in the Sky (1968) introduced a
heavy-handed, rock-derived emphasis on
drums, which Williams was more than capable of exploiting to the hilt. It was also the
first time Miles made use of electric instruments: piano and guitar (the latter played by
George Benson). Though it's not until
Bitches Brew that the new style which eventually became known as jazz-rock fusion was
identified with Miles Davis, the seeds of that
change can be heard in the loose-jointed
rhythms and long solos that dominated
Miles' late-Sixties music, particularly the
masterful *Filles de Kilimanjaro.*

Like *Kind of Blue* eleven years before, *In
a Silent Way* (1969) changed the whole spectrum of modern jazz. With its sparse instrumentation, metronomically even pulse,
oblique solos and delicate rainfall motifs, it
left the listener feeling suspended in space.
The celebratory *Bitches Brew* followed, the
definitive vision of jazz rock and Miles'
greatest commercial success. *Jack Johnson,*
the soundtrack for a movie documentary,
was close to straight-ahead rock, with Miles'
piercing horn nailed on top of Billy Cobham's explosive drums and John
McLaughlin's roaring guitar. Where *Bitches
Brew* seemed to have a new, inconceivable
surprise at every turn, *Live-Evil* is an album
of brilliant moments, linked together with
aimless, soporific noodling. But its emphasis
on a single-minded rhythm, predominant in
places over the soloists, predated the current
funk obsession in jazz.

On the Corner was a hard-funk polyrhythmic excursion. *Big Fun,* which includes a session from the same period, is the ideal sampler of "turning point" Miles material, from *Bitches Brew* to *On the Corner. Get Up with It,* released in 1974, was Miles' first studio release in three years, following a car accident and chronic physical problems that at times threatened to derail his career. A vastly underrated album, it is a strange pastiche of mournful movements, razor-sharp electric blues and the most joyfully lyrical playing Miles has tendered in a decade. *Agharta,* recorded live in Japan with Sonny Fortune on saxophones, is Davis' power-amp dream come true, perhaps a little too bombastic and jerky for most listeners. *Water Babies*—the first in an "archive" series of unreleased sessions—offers some brilliant outtakes from *Nefertiti* and a questionable side of pre–*Silent Way* work tracks, enlightening and welcome stuff, nevertheless, to anyone who has loved Miles in that decade. *Directions* completed the release of Seventies outtakes.

Man with the Horn marked Miles' 1981 comeback attempt. The fact that he hadn't recorded in six years showed less in his playing than in the aimlessness of the accompanying band. Bassist Marcus Miller and drummer Al Foster were the standouts but it wasn't until Miles added the solo voices of guitarist Mike Stern and saxophonist Bill Evans on the live *We Want Miles* that the new lineup began to click. By the time of the exciting, lyrical *Star People,* it was apparent that Davis was in the middle of a full-fledged renaissance. Here guitarist John Scofield alternated with Stern with fantastic results.

Decoy, a 1984 set, continued Davis' renaissance. Scofield, Foster and saxophonist Branford Marsalis all contributed superb playing but the highlight of the set is Davis' own soloing, which has regained all the nuance and surprise of his heyday. — M.G./J.S.

RICHARD DAVIS
★ ★ ★ **As One (with Jill McManus) / Muse**
★ ★ ★ **Epistrophy and Now's the Time /
    Muse**
★ ★ **Fancy Free / Gal.**
★ ★ ★ **Harvest / Muse**
★ ★ ★ ★ **Heavy Sounds (with Elvin Jones) /
    Imp.**
★ ★ ★ ★ **Musings of Richard Davis / Muse**
★ ★ **Way Out West / Muse**
★ ★ ★ **With Understanding / Muse**
After Scott LaFaro, Richard Davis (b. 1930) is the most important of the young bassists

who helped extend the role of their instrument during the early Sixties. Davis' Blue Note work with Andrew Hill, Bobby Hutcherson and Joe Henderson is simply breathtaking. Breaking up time, commenting on the soloist's line, making use of double stops and daring runs across the body of his instrument, all while retaining an authentic grainy tone, Davis influenced every important bassist of his generation.

Like many brilliant sidemen, Davis doesn't score so well as a leader. There is a general lack of focus that few of his LPs have overcome. *Musings,* also released as *Jazz Wave* (Pausa), uses shifting settings and important guests—Freddie Hubbard, Jimmy Knepper, Pepper Adams—as its spice. *Epistrophy and Now's the Time* is exactly that; two side-length performances with extended blowing by Clifford Jordan and Hannibal Peterson.

As One, a live duet with pianist Jill McManus, is a showcase for Davis, while *With Understanding* uses second bassist Bill Lee for pizzicato playing to allow Davis to concentrate on arco bowing.

All the rest of the LPs suffer from a lack of imagination, and the avoidance of all the risks that made Davis famous in the first place. Despite their big names (Billy Cobham, Joe Henderson, etc.), these are pretty lifeless sessions. *Harvest* is better than most, but that's not saying all that much.

Those interested in hearing Davis reach his full potential should turn to *Heavy Sounds,* an Impulse date he shared with drummer Elvin Jones. — S.F.

BLOSSOM DEARIE
★ ★ ★ ★ **Blossom Dearie / Verve**
★ ★ ★ **Blossom Dearie 1975 (Vol. II) / Daf.**
★ ★ ★ **Blossom Dearie Sings (Vol. I) / Daf.**
★ ★ ★ **Blossoms on Broadway / DRG**
★ ★ ★ **My New Celebrity Is You (Vol. III)
    / Daf.**
★ ★ ★ **Needlepoint Magic (Vol. V) / Daf.**
★ ★ ★ ★ **Winchester in Apple Blossom Time
    (Vol. IV) / Daf.**
Blossom Dearie (b. 1926) creates and maintains her own sound-world. Her career spans genres—jazz, pop and supper club. Heedless of the various jazz movements and pop trends, Dearie writes songs (and selects others) that are light and, often, whimsical. She sings them in her baby-doll voice while accompanying herself at the piano. She even makes songs of deep regret bearable. To top it off, Daffodil Records is her own company. As Gerry Mulligan has said, "Blossom is blossom."

Although some may find Blossom Dearie's

style an acquired taste, she has many fans who find her kind of song-making delectable. *Blossom Dearie* and *Winchester in Apple Blossom Time* are special for their ballads ("It Amazes Me" on *Winchester* is a classic) that linger in the mind long after the music has stopped. — A.R.

ALEX DeGRASSI

★ ★ ★ **Clockwork / Wind. H.**
★ ★ ★ **Slow Circle / Wind. H.**
★ ★ ★ **Southern Exposure / Wind. H.**
★ ★ ★ **Turning: Turning Back / Wind. H.**

Alex DeGrassi (b. 1952) is a talented acoustic guitarist who combines jazz theory and composition with folk and classical playing techniques for a smooth, fluid sound that is characteristic of the Windham Hill penchant for creamy, atmospheric productions.
— J.S.

JACK DeJOHNETTE

★ ★ ★ ★ ★ **Album Album / ECM/War.**
★ ★ **Complex / Mile.**
★ ★ ★ **Cosmic Chicken / Prest.**
★ ★ ★ **Have You Heard? / Mile.**
★ ★ ★ **In Europe / ECM/War.**
★ ★ ★ **Inflation Blues / ECM/War.**
★ ★ ★ ★ **New Directions / ECM/War.**
★ ★ ★ ★ **New Rags / ECM/War.**
★ ★ ★ **Pictures / ECM/War.**
★ ★ ★ ★ **Ruta & Daitya (with Keith Jarrett) / ECM/War.**
★ ★ ★ **Sorcery / Prest.**
★ ★ ★ ★ **Special Edition / ECM/War.**
★ ★ ★ **Tin Can Alley / ECM/War.**
★ ★ ★ **Untitled / ECM/War.**

Drummer Jack DeJohnette (b. 1942) first came to public attention as part of Miles Davis' groundbreaking early-Seventies band. His eclectic style was perfectly suited to the myriad turns that characterized jazz-rock fusion, and his earliest solo albums (the Milestone and Prestige sides) show off his forceful, R&B-influenced side. Guitarist John Abercrombie's big-voiced, propulsive playing provides an exciting counterpoint to DeJohnette's fast-handed attack.

The ECM albums show DeJohnette moving away from the power style and overkill that characterized virtually all fusion drumming as the Seventies progressed; instead, DeJohnette explored increasingly subtle textures, while never quite neglecting that love for hypnotic propulsion one suspects he learned from Tony Williams' playing in the Miles Davis band of the Sixties. Abercrombie is a constant through *Untitled, New Rags,* the brilliant *New Directions* and *In Europe* (with trumpeter Lester Bowie and

bassist Eddie Gomez). Then, in the early Eighties, DeJohnette formed the spectacular Special Edition band to play acoustic jazz. The sublime *Special Edition* quartet pits David Murray's tenor saxophone and bass clarinet against Arthur Blythe's alto, with DeJohnette and bassist Peter Warren offering inspired accompaniment. *Tin Can Alley* repeats the format with Chico Freeman's flute and tenor and John Purcell on flute, baritone and alto sax in the front line. *Tin Can Alley* and its followup, *Inflation Blues,* couldn't match *Special Edition*'s intensity, but the 1984 *Album Album* surpassed it. The front line of David Murray, John Purcell and Howard Johnson makes *Album Album* the finest unit DeJohnette's ever led. — J.S.

EUMIR DEODATO

★ **Artistry / MCA**
★ ★ ★ **The First Cuckoo / MCA**
★ **Happy Hour / War.**
★ **In Concert / CTI**
★ **Knights of Fantasy / War.**
★ **Love Island / War.**
★ ★ **Motion / War.**
★ **Night Cruisin' / War.**
★ **Prelude / CTI**
★ ★ **2001: Also Sprach Zarathustra / CTI**
★ **Very Together / MCA**
★ **Whirlwinds / MCA**

Although wholly obedient to the laws of homogeneity, arranger/keyboardist/composer Eumir Deodato (b. 1942) has written a new chapter in the history of elevator music. His albums consist of disco-charged orchestral pop/rock/jazz/TV theme/classical swirling. Deodato has drawn melodic structures from Ravel, Page, Marley and Mancini on which to hang striding and rather chichi production formulas.

Because they are so environmental in strategy, Deodato's records are particularly hard to distinguish one from another. His version of Richard Strauss' "Zarathustra" was a hit, but the best-defined LP is *The First Cuckoo,* which contains a pair of lesser pop successes, "Black Dog" and "Caravan/Watusi Strut." The 1984 outing *Motion* yielded the minor hit "S.O.S., Fire in the Sky." — B.T.

PAUL DESMOND

★ ★ ★ ★ **East of the Sun / Discov.**
★ ★ ★ ★ ★ **Live / Hori.**
★ ★ ★ **The Only Recorded Performance (with the Modern Jazz Quartet) / Fine.**
★ ★ ★ ★ **The Paul Desmond Quartet / Fan. /OJC**
★ ★ ★ ★ **Pure Gold / RCA**

Best known for his work in the Dave Brubeck Quartet, alto saxophonist Paul Desmond (1924–1977) employed a crisp, airy tone and a direct, melodic approach to soloing, a combination that made him the most urbane sounding altoist of the post-bop era. His numerous LPs with Brubeck clearly demonstrate his cool, Lee Konitz-inspired approach to tonality; but it is on his own looser recordings that Desmond can best be appreciated for his undying sensitivity to melody.

Quartet is a pianoless session from 1956 with Brubeck's rhythm section of Norman Bates (bass) and Joe Dodge (drums). The reissued *East of the Sun* is a 1959 session featuring delicately understated support from Percy Heath, Jim Hall and Connie Kay, while *Pure Gold* matches Desmond with a string section. The two-record *Live*, recorded in Toronto during 1975, is Desmond's masterwork, featuring a sparkling version of the saxophonist's signature piece, "Take Five."

Although presently out of print, several albums recorded for A&M in the Sixties are frequently available as cutouts. Even suffering from the heavy hand of producer Creed Taylor, Desmond's playing on these LPs is—as it always was—flawless. — F.G.

MANU DiBANGO
★ ★ ★ **Afrovision** / Is.
Manu DiBango is a soprano saxophonist who scored a hit in 1973 with the catchy instrumental "Soul Makossa" but failed to reproduce the hit formula on subsequent releases. This side is one of his more recent attempts, a pleasant synthesis of African rhythms and jazz-rock instrumental stylings. — J.S.

VIC DICKENSON
★ ★ **Trombone Cholly** / Sonet
★ ★ ★ ★ **Vic Dickinson's Quintet** / Story.
A distinctive big-band session trombonist, Vic Dickenson (1906–1984) worked with the Benny Moten, Benny Carter and Count Basie bands. After World War II he concentrated on playing in small Dixieland combos, which is what you'll find on *Trombone Cholly*, but Dickenson could also play excellent small-band swing as on *Quintet*, supported by Buddy Tate on tenor saxophone and George Duvivier on bass. — J.S.

WALT DICKERSON
★ ★ ★ **Lifelines** / Soul N.
★ ★ ★ **To My Queen Revisited** / Steep.
★ ★ ★ **Visions (with Sun Ra)** / Steep.

The most daring vibraphonist around, Walt Dickerson (b. 1931) suffers from a lack of recognition, even by jazz standards. The natural tendency among vibraphonists has been to exploit the pretty, fluid and ringing tone of the instrument, but Dickerson takes a more percussive approach while remaining faithful to the vibraphone's sound. Along with fellow vibes player Jay Hoggard, Dickerson has been most concerned with the instrument's use in contemporary jazz, and his decision to work with Sun Ra on *Visions* and with bassist Sirone and drummer Andrew Cyrille on *Lifelines* reflects that.
— F.G.

AL DiMEOLA
★ ★ ★ **Casino** / Col.
★ ★ ★ ★ **Electric Rendezvous** / Col.
★ ★ ★ **Elegant Gypsy** / Col.
★ ★ ★ ★ **Friday Night in San Francisco** / Col.
★ ★ ★ **Land of the Midnight Sun** / Col.
★ ★ ★ ★ **Scenario** / Col.
★ ★ ★ ★ **Splendido Hotel** / Col.
★ ★ ★ **Tour de Force** / Col.
After serving a celebrated apprenticeship with Chick Corea and Stanley Clarke in Return to Forever, Al DiMeola (b. 1954) went on to a solo career that earned him virtually unparalleled acclaim. As *Land of the Midnight Sun, Elegant Gypsy* and *Casino* showed off DiMeola's unique guitar-playing skills and commercial application of jazz, Latin and fusion ideas, he won a staggering series of awards, including *Guitar Player* magazine's "Best Jazz Guitar" prize for five consecutive years (1977–81). His best records are *Splendido Hotel*, which reunited him with Chick Corea; *Electric Rendezvous*, featuring bassist Anthony Jackson and drummer Steve Gadd as well as one of Jan Hammer's better post-Mahavishnu keyboard sessions; and the live acoustic *Friday Night*, with guitarist John McLaughlin. A subsequent live electric *Tour de Force* was not as good. *Scenario* is a vital fusion session featuring keyboardist Jan Hammer, drummers Phil Collins and Bill Bruford and bassist Tony Levin. — J.S.

DIRTY DOZEN BRASS BAND
★ ★ ★ ★ **My Feet Can't Fail Me Now** / Conc. J.
This amazing amalgam of New Orleans street-marching music and R&B/bop/pop/rock/everything-but-the-kitchen-sink is a tribute to the adaptability and the resilience of the New Orleans tradition. It's music you want to listen to but have to dance to at the

same time. If you're lucky, it may even make you laugh.   — J.S.

DIXIE DREGS

★ ★ ★ **Dregs of the Earth / Ari.**
★ ★ ★ **Free Fall / Capri.**
★ ★ ★ ★ **Industry Standard / Ari.**
★ ★ ★ **Night of the Living Dregs / Capri.**
★ ★ ★ **Unsung Heroes / Ari.**
★ ★ ★ **What If / Capri.**

Formed by guitarist Steve Morse and bassist Andy West as a rock band called the Dixie Grits, what eventually became the Dixie Dregs materialized after both musicians attended the University of Miami music school. Using schoolmates Rod Morgenstern on drums and Allen Sloan on violin along with ex-Grits keyboardist Steve Davidowski, the Dregs made several albums for Capricorn that were heavily influenced by the Mahavishnu Orchestra and Jeff Beck. T. Lavitz replaced Davidowski on keyboards for the Arista albums, and by the 1982 *Industry Standard* LP virtuoso violinist Mark O'Connor had replaced Sloan. The Arista albums show the group evolving beyond their early influences into a distinct style centered around Morse's guitar playing, arrangements and production strategies. After Morse's departure to pursue a solo career the band's future seems uncertain at best.   — J.S.

BILL DIXON

★ ★ ★ **Bill Dixon in Italy, Vol. 1 / Soul N.**
★ ★ ★ **Bill Dixon in Italy, Vol. 2 / Soul N.**
★ ★ ★ **November, 1981 / Soul N.**

The music of composer/bandleader/trumpeter/pianist Bill Dixon (b. 1925) is both agitated and introspective. One of the earliest of the Sixties New York loft musicians, Dixon worked and recorded with both Archie Shepp and Cecil Taylor before leaving New York to teach in New England. His insulation from the later developments of the Seventies loft movement have helped keep his voice individual, although the earlier work with Shepp and Taylor has had a lasting effect on his present direction.

Both volumes of *In Italy* feature a unique three-trumpet front line, while *November, 1981* finds Dixon working with a two-bass quartet. The latter lineup affords the musicians greater freedom of movement, although the arrangements on the *In Italy* recordings result in more concise moods, especially on the first volume.   — F.G.

DNA

★ **A Taste of DNA / Amer. C.**

DNA was a brief-lived New York art trio. There's nothing new about noise, but the ballyhoo that surrounded DNA was a high-water mark for pretension. The problem with this record isn't so much that it's unmusical as that it's uninteresting.   — F.G.

JOHNNY DODDS

★ ★ ★ ★ ★ **The Complete Johnny Dodds / RCA (France)**
★ ★ ★ ★ **Johnny Dodds on Paramount, Vol. 1 / Her.**

Along with Jimmy Noone, Johnny Dodds (1892–1940) pioneered the early role of the clarinet in small jazz groups. Born in New Orleans, Dodds was in Kid Ory's legendary New Orleans band by 1911, and played with the Chicago groups of King Oliver in the Twenties, including the historic 1923 dates that featured Oliver and Louis Armstrong on cornets, trombonist Honore Dutrey, Dodds' brother Baby on drums, Lil Hardin on piano and Bill Johnson on banjo. *Complete* covers material Dodds recorded under his own name in the Twenties. The Herwin album collects a number of sessions featuring Dodds in the late Twenties, including Blythe's Washboard Band (we hear washboard player W. E. Burton lamenting the fact that Blythe's piano is out of tune, then they proceed to rip off at a blistering pace); spectacular clarinet interchanges with Junie Cobb in Junie Cobb's Home Town Band; warm clarinet/piano duets with Tiny Parham; and raucous sides from the Dixieland Thumpers—Dodds on clarinet, Natty Dominique on cornet, Jimmy Blythe on piano and Baby Dodds on drums.   — J.S.

ERIC DOLPHY

★ ★ ★ **Copenhagen Concert / Prest.**
★ ★ ★ **Dolphy in Europe, Vol. 2 / Prest.**
★ ★ ★ ★ ★ **Eric Dolphy / Prest.**
★ ★ ★ ★ ★ **Eric Dolphy at the Five Spot / Fan./OJC**
★ ★ ★ ★ ★ **Far Cry / Prest.**
★ ★ ★ ★ **The Great Concert of Eric Dolphy / Prest.**
★ ★ ★ ★ **Here and There / Prest.**
★ ★ ★ ★ ★ **Jitterbug Waltz / Doug.**
★ ★ ★ ★ **Last Date / Lime.**
★ ★ ★ ★ ★ **Magic / Prest.**
★ ★ ★ ★ ★ **Out There / Fan./OJC**
★ ★ ★ ★ ★ **Out to Lunch / Blue N.**
★ ★ ★ ★ ★ **Outward Bound / Fan./OJC**
★ ★ ★ **Status / Prest.**
★ ★ ★ ★ **Where? / Prest.**

Thanks to reissues, there is a healthy amount of Eric Dolphy (1928–1964) available—some of it in single and double album versions.

Outward Bound, a quintet with Freddie Hubbard and Jaki Byard, and *Out There,* an unusual quartet with Ron Carter's cello instead of the usual piano, are on *Eric Dolphy.* The first session, Dolphy's first as leader, thrust the alto saxophonist/bass clarinetist/flutist into the "new thing" controversy Ornette Coleman had created at the time (1960), but the conventional hard-bop format underlines that Dolphy could also be viewed as the most highly evolved sensibility still dealing with bebop techniques.

From the same period come *Far Cry,* another quintet with trumpeter Booker Little and pianist Byard, and *Where?,* which is actually Ron Carter's debut as a leader. With Carter and drummer Roy Haynes in the rhythm section, *Far Cry* features one of Dolphy's best bands, plus such originals as "Miss Ann" and "Ode to Charlie Parker."

In July 1961 Dolphy played the Five Spot in New York with a cooperative quintet including Little, pianist Mal Waldron, bassist Richard Davis and drummer Ed Blackwell. The three single volumes from that gig are now collected on *The Great Concert of Eric Dolphy,* which, given its long tracks, is uneven, but remains invaluable for the Dolphy and Little solos. Volume 1, *Eric Dolphy at the Five Spot,* if you just want a sample.

Two extra tracks from the Five Spot, plus other outtakes from the *Outward Bound* session and Dolphy's Copenhagen concerts of September 1961, are on *Here and There,* which contains the best bass-clarinet solo version of "God Bless the Child." The second volume of *Dolphy in Europe* is added to *Here and There* on the twofer *Status,* while Volumes 1 and 3 of *In Europe* comprise *Copenhagen Concert.* All of the European recordings present some very impressive Dolphy, but suffer from an unimaginative rhythm section.

Jitterbug Waltz, from 1963, is Dolphy's most varied twofer: one unaccompanied alto solo, three emotional duets with Richard Davis, three quintet tracks featuring Woody Shaw and Bobby Hutcherson, and two large ensemble pieces including the avant-garde mariachi of "Music Matador." A summation of Dolphy's roots.

Out to Lunch is well into the next phase and Dolphy's most impressive achievement. His compositions are now freer, the better to serve his always unfettered emotions, and they are performed by a dream group of Hubbard, Hutcherson, Davis and Tony Williams. From early 1964.

Shortly thereafter Dolphy went to Europe with a Charles Mingus band, where he died of natural but still clouded causes. *Last Date,* made in Holland with local players a month before his death, contains his flute tour de force on "You Don't Know What Love Is." Dolphy, like Coltrane, played with a passionate involvement that transcends his innovations and makes his music spellbinding for even the sometime jazz listener. Also hear him with Mingus, Coltrane, Coleman, Gunther Schuller, Andrew Hill, Oliver Nelson, Max Roach.

★ ★ ★ ★ **The Berlin Concerts / Inner**
★ ★ ★ **Caribe (with the Latin Jazz Quintet) / Prest.**
★ ★ ★ ★ **Fire Waltz / Prest.**
★ ★ ★ **−1 / Prest.**
★ ★ ★ **Stockholm Sessions / Inner**

The Inner Citys present still more material from Dolphy's 1961 European tour, with particularly heated solos on the two-record *Berlin* volume. *Fire Waltz* contains two sessions from the previous twelve months in which Dolphy was a featured sideman: one under the leadership of Ken McIntyre, a reedman who attacks his alto sax and flute with an intensity akin to Dolphy's; and a five-star sextet date, originally titled *The Quest,* with seven excellent and challenging tunes from pianist Mal Waldron, Booker Ervin's tenor sax and Ron Carter on cello.

"New" Dolphy can be found in the previously unreleased takes on *−1.* Once-rare Dolphy surfaced on *Caribe,* one of two inconsequential collaborations with a Latin jazz band. *Out There* and *Outward Bound* are especially worth acquiring in their old/new guise (as Fantasy/Original Jazz Classics reissues) with the surreal cover art of Prophet (Richard Jennings) restored.
— B.B.

LOU DONALDSON
★ ★ ★ **Sweet Poppa Lou / Muse**

Alto saxophonist Lou Donaldson (b. 1926) shared a debt to Charlie Parker in common with virtually all of his contemporaries on that instrument, but his sweet, self-assured style is a strong signature. He worked with hard-bop bands including Art Blakey and Horace Silver sessions before leading his own groups, which were always soulful, swinging outfits with an organist matching strides with Donaldson's alto. *Sweet Poppa Lou,* the only Donaldson in print, is a 1981 set that switches organ for Herman Foster's piano along with Idris Muhammad (drums) and Calvin Hill (bass). — J.S.

DOROTHY DONEGAN
★ ★ ★ **The Explosive Dorothy Donegan / Prog.**

Although Dorothy Donegan (b. 1924) is a technically prodigious pianist (the peer of Oscar Peterson and Phineas Newborn, Jr.), she remains a shadowy figure to the jazz audience at large. Even critics have dismissed her as strictly an entertainer, led astray by her "jazzing" of the classics and her sometimes eccentric dress and stage mannerisms. Despite these criticisms—and the verbosity that sometimes flaws her style—Dorothy Donegan is one hell of a pianist. At her best, she can be intense and earthy ("Donegan's Blues") or atmospheric (the Garnerish "I Like the Likes of You").   — A.R.

KENNY DORHAM

★ ★ ★ Blue Spring / Fan./OJC
★ ★ ★ ★ But Beautiful / Mile.
★ ★ ★ Ease It / Muse
★ ★ ★ ★ Jazz Contrasts / Prest.
★ ★ ★ ★ Kenny Dorham / Bain.
★ ★ ★ ★ Kenny Dorham Quintet / Fan./ OJC
★ ★ ★ Memorial Album / Xan.
★ ★ ★ ★ 1959 / Prest.
★ ★ ★ Scandia Skies / Steep.
★ ★ ★ Short Story / Steep.
★ ★ ★ Show Boat / Bain.
★ ★ Una Mas / Blue N.
★ ★ ★ ★ Whistle Stop / Blue N.

Overshadowed in the Fifties by Miles Davis and Clifford Brown and by Freddie Hubbard and Lee Morgan in the Sixties, trumpeter Kenny Dorham (1924–1972) is now recognized as a major bop stylist. Never a great innovator, nor an important bandleader, Dorham nonetheless helped transform the turbulent language of hard bop into a more free-flowing, lyrical expression through the exquisitely controlled eloquence of his solos.

Having played with Charlie Parker, Thelonious Monk and Bud Powell by the late Forties, Dorham was acknowledged as a talented and valuable sideman until his big break came when he replaced Clifford Brown in the Art Blakey band that would soon coalesce into the Jazz Messengers. Columbia and Blue Note recordings of those groups reveal Dorham as a sharp soloist with a superior melodic sense that separated him from the many Clifford Brown imitators popping up (see also Quintet). Little wonder that he was again asked to replace Brown, this time under less fortunate circumstances, in the Max Roach group that included Sonny Rollins.

This unnerving experience must have done Dorham much good, for he emerged as a distinct horn voice. While he could still handle rapid-fire bop tempos with ease, a confident, rounder tone, coupled with a gentle command of ballads, lent a cerebral rather than feverish edge to his late-Fifties playing.

Dorham-led dates from that time are among his best work; Jazz Contrasts uses Rollins and Roach and a featured harpist, and But Beautiful, a twofer that collects most of Contrasts, also has tastes from other important sessions, including one with Cannonball Adderley and a pianoless quartet date with Ernie Henry. Showboat uses material from the Broadway classic, while Blue Spring also features Adderley. 1959 is a lowkeyed collection of ballads and blues that captures the trumpeter at his most poised and emotive heights. A definitive hard-bop outfit, Philly Joe Jones, Paul Chambers, Kenny Drew and Hank Mobley kick 1961's Whistle Stop into overdrive.

A died-in-the-wool bopman, Dorham came to the musical advances of the Sixties slowly, and while never embracing "free" playing, he warmed to modal structures. His supporting work on Blue Note for frequent partner Joe Henderson shows him to be a compelling post-bop soloist; Dorham's most famous composition, "Blue Bossa," gets its debut on Henderson's Page One from 1963.

The rest of Dorham's Sixties dates are always proficient if not earthshakingly original. Ease It is a very solid set with fine contributions from the obscure tenorist Rocky Boyd, and a stellar rhythm section headed by Ron Carter. The eponymous Bainbridge LP is a standout from this period.   — S.F.

THE DORSEY BROTHERS

★ ★ ★ ★ The Dorsey Brothers Orchestra / MCA

This album collects the 1934–35 Decca sessions of the band that included Tommy Dorsey and Glenn Miller on trombones, Jimmy Dorsey on clarinet, alto sax and trumpet, and a pretty hot band that shows its debt to the Louis Armstrong orchestra of a few years before, particularly on "Dipper Mouth Blues" and "St. Louis Blues." Bob Crosby's characteristically hokey vocal on "Basin Street Blues" drags things down, but the verve and conviction of the players on this set makes it a classic.   — J.S.

TOMMY DORSEY

★ ★ ★ The Best of Tommy Dorsey / RCA
★ ★ The Complete Tommy Dorsey, Vol. 1 / RCA
★ ★ ★ The Complete Tommy Dorsey, Vol. 3 / RCA
★ ★ ★ ★ The Complete Tommy Dorsey, Vol. 4 / RCA
★ ★ ★ The Complete Tommy Dorsey, Vol. 5 / RCA

★ ★ ★ ★ The Carnegie Hall Concerts: January 1946 / Prest.
★ ★ ★ ★ The Carnegie Hall Concerts: December 1947 / Prest.
★ ★ ★ A Drum Is a Woman / CSP
★ ★ ★ ★ Duke Ellington 1938 / Smithsonian (Available by mail only from Smithsonian Recordings, P.O. Box 10230, Des Moines, Iowa 50336)
★ ★ ★ ★ Duke Ellington 1939 / Smithsonian
★ ★ ★ ★ Duke Ellington 1940 / Smithsonian
★ ★ ★ ★ Duke Ellington 1941 / Smithsonian
★ ★ ★ Duke Ellington Plays Duke Ellington / Quin.
★ ★ ★ Duke on the Air 1952 / Air.
★ ★ ★ ★ The Ellington Era, Vol. 1 (1927–40) / Col.
★ ★ Ellington '55 / Cap.
★ ★ ★ ★ The Golden Duke / Prest.
★ ★ ★ Greatest Hits / Col.
★ ★ ★ ★ Hi-Fi Ellington Uptown / CSP
★ ★ ★ ★ Hot in Harlem, Vol. 2 (1928–29) / MCA
★ ★ ★ The Many Moods of Duke Ellington / Quin.
★ ★ ★ ★ Masterpieces / CSP
★ ★ ★ ★ ★ Mood Indigo / Camd.
★ ★ ★ ★ ★ Music of Ellington / CSP
★ ★ ★ ★ Original Movie Soundtracks (1929–35) / Bio.
★ ★ ★ ★ ★ Piano Reflections / Cap.
★ ★ ★ ★ Presents Ivie Anderson / Col.
★ ★ ★ ★ ★ Rockin' in Rhythm, Vol. 3 (1929–31) / MCA
★ ★ ★ Sophisticated Ellington / RCA
★ ★ ★ ★ ★ Such Sweet Thunder / CSP
★ ★ ★ ★ ★ Suite Thursday/Controversial Suite/Harlem Suite / CSP
★ ★ ★ ★ ★ Take the "A" Train / Quin.
★ ★ ★ ★ ★ This Is Duke Ellington / RCA
★ ★ ★ ★ ★ The Works of Duke / RCA (France)
★ ★ ★ ★ The World of Duke Ellington, Vol. 1 / Col.
★ ★ ★ The World of Duke Ellington, Vol. 2 / Col.
★ ★ The World of Duke Ellington, Vol. 3 / Col.

EDWARD KENNEDY ("DUKE") ELLINGTON / Stereo Recordings
★ ★ ★ ★ Afro-Eurasian Eclipse / Fan.
★ ★ ★ ★ Anatomy of a Murder / Col.
★ ★ ★ Best of Duke Ellington / Cap.
★ ★ ★ Black, Brown and Beige (with Mahalia Jackson) / CPS

★ ★ ★ ★ Duke Ellington's Jazz Violin Session / Atl.
★ ★ ★ ★ Duke's Big 4 / Pablo
★ ★ Eastbourne / RCA
★ ★ ★ Ellingtonia Reevaluations: The Impulse Years, Vol. 1 / Imp.
★ ★ ★ Ellingtonia Reevaluations: The Impulse Years, Vol. 2 / Imp.
★ ★ ★ Ellington Indigos / Col.
★ ★ ★ ★ ★ Festival Session / Odys.
★ ★ ★ For Always / Star.
★ ★ ★ ★ The Ellington Suites / Pablo
★ ★ ★ The Girl's Suite/Perfume Suite / Col.
★ ★ ★ Greatest Hits / Rep.
★ ★ ★ The Great Paris Concert / Atl.
★ ★ ★ The Intimate Ellington / Pablo
★ ★ ★ Jazz at the Plaza, Vol. 2 / Col.
★ ★ ★ ★ Jazz Party / CSP
★ ★ ★ Latin American Suite / Fan.
★ ★ ★ ★ New Orleans Suite / Atl.
★ ★ ★ ★ ★ Newport 1956 / Col.
★ ★ ★ ★ Nutcracker Suite / Odys.
★ ★ ★ The Pianist / Fan.
★ ★ ★ ★ ★ Pure Gold / RCA
★ ★ ★ ★ Second Sacred Concert / Prest.
★ ★ ★ Unknown Session / Col.
★ ★ ★ Up in Duke's Workshop / Pablo
★ ★ ★ Violin Session / Atl.
★ ★ ★ Yale Concert / Fan.

EDWARD KENNEDY ("DUKE") ELLINGTON / With Other Artists Cofeatured
★ ★ At Tanglewood (with Boston Pops) / Camd.
★ ★ ★ ★ Duke Ellington and John Coltrane / Imp.
★ ★ ★ ★ Duke Ellington Meets Coleman Hawkins / Imp.
★ ★ ★ ★ ★ Echoes of an Era (with Louis Armstrong) / Rou.
★ ★ ★ ★ ★ Ella Fitzgerald Sings the Duke Ellington Songbook / Verve
★ ★ ★ ★ Ella Fitzgerald Sings the Duke Ellington Songbook, Vol. 2 / Verve
★ ★ ★ ★ ★ The First Time! (with Count Basie) / Col.
★ ★ ★ ★ The Great Tenor Encounters (with Coleman Hawkins and John Coltrane) / Imp.
★ ★ ★ ★ This One's for Blanton (with Ray Brown) / Pablo

Reviewing the recording career of Duke Ellington (1899–1974) in this limited space is a task comparable to reviewing similarly the complete works of Shakespeare—any attempt will hardly begin to convey the range of form, subject matter and emotion of such an invaluable treasury. Let me simply note that the rating system here might be called an "internal" one; that is, taking Ellington's greatest achievements as the (*****) standard, the total works are ranked accordingly.

The Twenties and Thirties: During the years between 1923 (when Ellington moved to New York from his native Washington) and 1940, Duke Ellington built the most magnificent orchestra dedicated to the expression of one man's mind and soul in jazz history. Much of the secret was in the sidemen Duke attracted and used so very personally: Bubber Miley (1925–29), Cootie Williams (1929–40), Rex Stewart (1934–44), trumpets; Tricky Sam Nanton (1926–48) and Lawrence Brown (1932–51), trombones; Barney Bigard (1928–42), Johnny Hodges (1928–51), Ben Webster (1939–43), Harry Carney (1926–74), reeds; Jimmy Blanton (1939–41), bass; Sonny Greer (1923–51), drums; Ivie Anderson (1931–42), vocals; and Billy Strayhorn (1939–67), compositional collaborator. After citing the numerous key contributors, however, Ellington must be acknowledged for his ability to get so much out of performers (who almost never sounded so commanding on their own) and for his ability to draw the most direct yet strikingly original colors from standard big-band instrumentation.

Ellington recorded for several small and large labels before World War II; the results are now scattered among Columbia, MCA and RCA and in various states of availability. MCA's material ends in 1931; of its three volumes, *Rockin' in Rhythm, Volume 3,* with some early classics and Ellington's first extended work ("Creole Rhapsody"), is the best. Columbia's three-album box *The Ellington Era, Volume 1* is an excellent overview of the period but hard to find, while the four Smithsonian albums, which focus on individual years and use Columbia-owned material exclusively and are available by mail only.

RCA owns some of the best Ellington from the early Thirties, plus *the best* Ellington by the best Ellington band (1940–42, after Webster, Blanton and Strayhorn had joined and before the wartime recording ban). Unfortunately RCA has not seen fit to reissue this material in any but the most cursory fashion, and it can only be sampled in bits and pieces on the Camden *Mood Indigo* and on *This Is Duke Ellington.* The bits and pieces are great, but just whet the appetite. The French Black and White imports thus take on additional importance. *The Works of Duke,* a twenty-five-LP package available in

five multirecord sets, is the most complete representation of Ellington's RCA output.

The Forties: The war took its toll on all big bands, though Ellington also had to fight a war of attrition that would have occurred anyway as sidemen left the band. Several key newcomers were attracted (Ray Nance, cornet and violin; Russell Procope and Jimmy Hamilton, reeds; Oscar Pettiford, bass), but generally the Forties were a period of difficulty.

Few of these problems were evident when Ellington made his annual visit to Carnegie Hall, an opportunity to unveil new extended pieces as well as review old masters. Four Prestige collections from four of the concerts are, again, fine samplings of the band; especially recommended are the concerts from 1943 (with the complete *Black, Brown and Beige,* Ellington's magnum opus, and Ben Webster still around on tenor) and 1947 (*The Liberian Suite* and new compositions featuring piano). *The Golden Duke* has solid 1946 band performances, plus some Ellington-Strayhorn piano tracks from 1950, while the first two volumes of Columbia's *World of Duke Ellington* finds the band sliding its way into the Fifties.

The Fifties: Ellington absorbed what might have been a fatal blow in 1951, when Hodges, Brown and Greer left, and muddled on through a few years of indifferent performances. The best band work from the period is *Hi-Fi Ellington Uptown,* with good signs given by new tenor player Paul Gonsalves (1950–74). The 1953 *Piano Reflections* remains the best of Duke's rare keyboard albums.

By 1956 things began to turn around; there were fine new soloists (Clark Terry, trumpet; Britt Woodman, Quentin Jackson, trombones), the great Hodges had rejoined, and Ellington's compositional juices began flowing anew. *The Bethlehem Years* is an excellent survey of earlier Ellingtonia, but it was the *Newport 1956* album from that summer, capped by Gonsalves' marathon tenor celebration on "Diminuendo and Crescendo in Blue," that put the band back on top with the public.

Of the work from the end of the decade, most of which has reappeared on Columbia Special Products, Ellington's Shakespearean suite *Such Sweet Thunder* is the finest example of his and the band's renewed capacities. *Jazz Party,* with folks like Jimmy Rushing and Dizzy Gillespie sitting in, is a lot of fun, and for the curious, the 1958 *Jazz at the Plaza* has Billie Holiday singing two tunes with the band.

The Sixties: At the top of the decade Ellington "met" several of his peers in the recording studio. The results were uniformly fascinating. Duke did some adventurous quartet blowing with Coltrane and featured Coleman Hawkins' tenor in front of a more Ducal ensemble (tracks from both of these albums are also available on Impulse's *Ellingtonia* sets, which collect Ellington compositions played by Duke and others). The Ellington/Armstrong encounter put Duke in the piano seat in Louis' sextet for an all-Ellington program (with alumnus Barney Bigard on clarinet)—an inspired approach that brings Ellington the small-band pianist to the fore. *First Time!* is a real powerhouse, with both Ellington's and Basie's full bands (one on each channel) wailing away.

The decade was also one of the orchestra's best, with old faces Cootie Williams and Lawrence Brown returning to the sections and several good albums of old and new material. *The Great Paris Concert,* from 1963, is the band's most inspired live work since Newport, while *Pure Gold* is another retrospective of similar quality done in a studio three years later. The best writing from the period (RCA's *Far East Suite*) is out of print, but the *Latin American* and *New Orleans* albums have exemplary music, and the latter features Hodges' final recordings. Pablo's *Ellington Suites* sandwiches the period (1969, 1971–72) with three lesser-known extended works. Atypical but fun is the *Violin Session,* a jam for Svend Asmussen, Stephane Grappelli and Ray Nance.

Ellington was often quoted to the effect that his *Sacred Concert* music was his greatest work, an opinion that at least this writer takes strong issue with. Currently only the second of three, which did have the most lasting music, is available.

The Seventies: musical and physical decline set in, beginning with the indifferent *Afro-Eurasian Eclipse* of 1971 and ending with the dreadful *Eastbourne* concert from shortly before Ellington's hospitalization (he died in 1974). There was also some small-band work on Pablo, of which *This One's for Blanton* stands out due to the bass work of Ray Brown. Yet even with this weak ending, and even with much of his work momentarily deleted, there is still more than enough magnificence left behind by the greatest composer America has produced.

The Eighties: You might think that various record companies would have put their Ellington catalogues in order by now, but in general the effort has been less than impressive. True, the three MCA volumes are available again in new layouts, and the Smithsonian project has hit the greatest RCA years. Still, listeners looking for RCA Ellington in record stores confront yet another hodgepodge sampler, sans personnel or liner notes (*Sophisticated Ellington*), plus material RCA has leased to Quintessence that (with the exception of the 1940–42 survey "*A" Train*) is packaged with little rhyme or reason. Retrieval efforts at CBS are confined to the Odyssey and Special Products lines, and there are some welcome returns here—especially the spirited 1959 *Festival Session*—though hardly enough, considering the wealth of material at CBS's disposal. Aircheck material has not been particularly enlightening, especially when the fabled Fargo, North Dakota concert by the early-Forties band is not in the catalogue, though the soundtrack collection culled from early shorts is worth having. Similarly, three previously unreleased sessions originally cut at various times in the Sixties (*Unknown, Workshop, Violin Session*) apparently sat on the shelf because Ellington was turning out more interesting material at the time.

Along with the Smithsonians, *Festival Session* and the anthology of suites, a sampling of recently rereleased Ellington should include Ella Fitzgerald's *Songbook,* in which the singer is enhanced by Ellington's arrangements and orchestra. Tenor-sax fans will appreciate Impulse's combination of the Hawkins and Coltrane albums into a two-record set.

Ellington releases slowed down a bit after early excitement engendered by the Broadway show *Sophisticated Ladies.* We did get *Anatomy of a Murder,* Ellington's spunkiest soundtrack, back in circulation, plus the combo items, featuring Ben Webster and Stuff Smith, from Fitzgerald's *Ellington Songbook. The Girl's Suite/Perfume Suite* are previously unreleased performances of lesser Ellington material now combined on a single LP. — B.B.

DON ELLIS
★ ★ ★ ★ Autumn / Col.
★ Connection / Col.
★ ★ Don Ellis at Fillmore / Col.
★ ★ ★ ★ Electric Bath / Col.
★ ★ ★ Music from Other Galaxies and Planets / Atco
★ ★ ★ The New Don Ellis Band / Col.
★ ★ ★ New Ideas / Prest.
★ ★ ★ Shock Treatment / Col.
★ ★ ★ ★ Tears of Joy / Col.

In his own way the innovative orchestra leader Don Ellis (1934–1979) probably did as much to advance the conceptual possibilities of jazz rock as did John Coltrane or Miles Davis. Ellis, a fair trumpet player, wrote spectacular, challenging arrangements that incorporated rock rhythmic and dynamic elements, and his charts on the landmark album *Electric Bath* undoubtedly influenced jazz-rock ensembles of the late Sixties such as Blood, Sweat and Tears, Chicago and Frank Zappa's various groups.

Blood, Sweat and Tears founder Al Kooper went on to produce *Autumn* for Ellis, which includes a live version of one of the more powerful tracks from *Electric Bath,* "Indian Lady."

Not all of Ellis' albums work, though. The live set from the Fillmore tries too hard to be space music and ends up stuck on Jupiter while *Connection* suffers from just the opposite impulse, an attempt to do an album of big-band versions of current hits like "Jesus Christ Superstar," "Alone Again (Naturally)" and "Lean on Me." — J.S.

HERB ELLIS
★ ★ ★ **After You've Been Gone (with Ray Brown) / Conc. J.**
★ ★ **At Montreux Summer '79 / Conc. J.**
★ ★ ★ **Herb Mix / Conc. J.**
★ ★ ★ ★ **Hot Tracks (with Ray Brown and Harry Edison) / Conc. J.**
★ ★ ★ **Jazz (with Joe Pass) / Conc. J.**
★ ★ **Pair to Draw To (with Ross Tomkins) / Conc. J.**
★ ★ **Rhythm Willie (with Freddie Green) / Conc. J.**
★ ★ ★ **Seven Come Eleven (with Joe Pass) / Conc. J.**
★ ★ ★ **Soft and Mellow / Conc. J.**
★ ★ ★ **Softly, but with That Feeling / Verve**
★ ★ ★ **Soft Shoe (with Ray Brown) / Conc. J.**
★ ★ ★ **Two for the Road (with Joe Pass) / Pablo**
★ ★ **Windflower (with Remo Palmier) / Conc. J.**

Texas-born guitarist Herb Ellis (b. 1921) emerged from Forties big-band jazz as a leading exponent of Charlie Christian's style of electric guitar playing and grew to be one of the main shapers of that style in the Fifties. Ellis did a long stint in Oscar Peterson's drummerless trio during that decade along with bassist Ray Brown.

Softly, but with That Feeling is an elegant record made in '61 that dates from Ellis' first period as a leader before he dropped from sight to do TV session work for almost two decades. The many Concord LPs he has done since returning to jazz on a regular

basis pretty much continue the light, fast and deft style that is Ellis' trademark. The several records he's made with Brown since their reunion and the three with Joe Pass are especially outstanding. — B.T.

PETER ERSKINE
★ ★ ★ ★ **Peter Erskine / Contem.**
Drummer Peter Erskine (b. 1954) is best known for his recent five-year stint with Weather Report, but this, his first album as a leader, presents him in a more versatile light. The outstanding session band used here includes Michael Brecker on tenor sax, Randy Brecker on trumpet and fluegelhorn, Mike Manieri on vibes and Eddie Gomez on bass. Erskine is also part of the Steps band along with Manieri, Gomez and Michael Brecker, which partially accounts for their wonderfully relaxed interchange here. — J.S.

BOOKER ERVIN
★ ★ ★ ★ **Blues Book / Prest.**
★ ★ ★ **Down in the Dumps / Savoy**
★ ★ ★ **Exultation (with Frank Strozier) / Prest.**
★ ★ ★ ★ ★ **Freedom and Space Books Sessions / Prest.**
★ ★ ★ **Groovin' High / Prest.**
★ ★ ★ ★ **Heavy! / Prest.**
★ ★ ★ **Settin' the Pace / Prest.**
★ ★ ★ ★ **Song Book / Prest.**
★ ★ ★ **The Trance / Prest.**

Next to John Coltrane, Booker Ervin (1930–1970) had the biggest tenor sound of the Sixties. Ervin was never the formalist innovator that Coltrane was; his specialty was a relentlessly driving, earthy blues-drenched sound that made him popular with some of the most advanced bandleaders of the day— Charles Mingus and Andrew Hill among them.

Everything that Ervin recorded has healthy doses of his super-charged horn, but his "book" series remain the classics. Starting in 1963 with his "freedom" book, Ervin began collaborating with one of the great rhythm sections in jazz history: Jaki Byard on piano, Richard Davis on bass and Alan Dawson on drums. On the two-record *Freedom and Space* set these men attack standards and blues with an intensity and cohesiveness that is remarkable for a group that existed only in the studio. While never as adventurous as some of the heady experiments of the time, these straightforward sessions are often twice as exciting.

Extra horns are added on *Heavy!,* and Byard is replaced on both *Blues* and *Song,* but the results are still fine. While the "books" will serve as his legacy, Ervin's other dates are recommended when appreciation of this overlooked musician starts to grow. *Down in the Dumps* is the earliest work available, but *That's It,* Ervin's second LP, should be picked up if found in cutout bins. This Candid/Barnaby release is a seminal example of Coltrane's influence on tenorists at the start of the Sixties. Another cutout, *Lament,* is a live recording from 1965 that has a 28-minute blues solo from the Texas fireblower. — S.F.

KEVIN EUBANKS
★ ★ ★ ★ **Kevin Eubanks—Guitarist / Elek./ Mus.**

So-called jazz/rock/fusion music had reached a stylistic dead end by the end of the Seventies, but that didn't prevent young musicians from exploring the possibilities of combining older forms of jazz with the electric concepts of rock music. If all the ersatz rock and semi-disco sessions gave such experimentation a bad name, records like Kevin Eubanks' 1983 debut show that there's plenty of reason to keep trying to synthesize seemingly disparate styles. Eubanks handles, with equal facility, solo acoustic pieces, "The Novice Bounce" and the Miles Davis/Bill Evans classic "Blue in Green"; standards ("Yesterdays"); and foot-to-the-floor band arrangements like "Inner-Vision." — J.S.

BILL EVANS
★ ★ ★ ★ **New Jazz Conceptions / Riv.**
★ ★ ★ ★ ★ **Peace Piece and Other Pieces / Mile. (contains all material on Everybody Digs Bill Evans / Riv.)**

New Jazz Conceptions, the first album from Bill Evans (1929–1980), revealed a pianist with a uniquely introspective harmonic approach, a fine compositional sense (particularly on "Waltz for Debby"), and at the time, an attractively brittle feel for bop rhythm. The *Peace Piece* collection was made in 1958 and '59 when Evans was the pianist in Miles Davis' sextet, and benefits from the propulsive drumming of Philly Joe Jones.

★ ★ ★ ★ ★ **Spring Leaves / Mile. (contains all material on Explorations / Riv.)**
★ ★ ★ ★ ★ **The Village Vanguard Sessions / Mile. (contains all material on Waltz for Debby / Riv.)**

The trio Evans formed with bassist Scott LaFaro and drummer Paul Motian in 1959 is one of the most influential groups in jazz history; they both not only redefined the in-terrelationship among the members of a piano trio, thanks to the free-ranging lines of LaFaro and the subtle patterns of Motian, but also helped to spread the use of scalar rather than chordal improvisation (something Evans had tried in collaboration with George Russell as well as Miles Davis). Milestone's two twofers represent the trio's total recorded output before LaFaro was killed in a highway accident in 1961. Evans became less rhythmically aggressive and more quietly beautiful at this point.

★ ★ ★ ★ **Alone / Verve**
★ ★ ★ **Trio (Motian, Peacock), Duo (Hall) / Verve**

Most of Evans' work in the Sixties was done for Verve and is currently out of print, though we can hear him in solo, duo and trio settings from the period. By this time Evans had become a stylist and, while the music is always well crafted and romantically engaging, there is a sameness (albeit a very pretty sameness) that creates predictability, even when such talented players as guitarist Jim Hall and bassist Gary Peacock are involved.

★ ★ ★ ★ **The Bill Evans Album / Col.**
★ ★ ★ ★ **Living Time (with George Russell) / Col.**
★ ★ ★ **Montreux II / CTI**

Evans entered the Seventies with bassist Eddie Gomez and drummer Marty Morrell in his trio, and the same old problem of finding new things to do within his well-established style. The Columbia albums are among the more notable of such efforts, especially *The Bill Evans Album* with its program of all-Evans compositions and mix of acoustic and Fender-Rhodes electric piano. *Living Time* is really George Russell's album, an exciting and radical use of a jazz orchestra that might hold together better if mounted around a more unfettered pianist.

★ ★ ★ ★ **Intuition / Fan.**
★ ★ ★ ★ ★ **Montreux III / Fan.**
★ ★ ★ ★ **Quintessence / Fan.**
★ ★ ★ **Since We Met / Fan.**
★ ★ ★ ★ ★ **The Tokyo Concert / Fan.**

There were few lapses in Evans' career— even the less interesting albums suffer from familiarity more than from any performance deficiencies—and his final work is still rewarding if somewhat predictable. Both *Intuition* and *Montreux III* are duets with bassist Gomez, one of the most technically astounding bassists in the LaFaro tradition, and *Quintessence* gathers a blue-ribbon quintet (Harold Land, Kenny Burrell, Ray Brown, Philly Joe Jones) for some mellow jamming.

★ ★ ★ ★ Affinity / War.
★ ★ ★ Alone (Again) / Fan.
★ ★ ★ ★ As Time Goes By (with Bob
   Brookmeyer) / Blue N.
★ ★ ★ ★ Conception / Mile.
★ ★ ★ Crosscurrents / Fan.
★ ★ ★ ★ Intermodulation / Verve
★ ★ ★ ★ I Will Say Goodbye / Fan.
★ ★ ★ New Conversations / War.
★ ★ ★ ★ The Paris Concert / Elek./Mus.
★ ★ ★ RE: Person I Knew / Fan.
★ ★ ★ ★ Second Trio / Mile.
★ ★ ★ ★ Symbiosis / Pausa
★ ★ ★ ★ We Will Meet Again / War.
★ ★ ★ You Must Believe in Spring / War.
Evans remained popular, and was thus extensively recorded, up to the time of his death in 1980. His last recordings (the Fantasys and Warners) displayed highly consistent musicianship and tune choices, yet little of this music stands up to the pianist's trailblazing early sessions. Part of the problem was the loss of whatever magic makes a trio of musicians something special, although the last working Evans band (with bassist Marc Johnson and drummer Joe LaBarbera— heard on *The Paris Concert, You Must Believe* and, with horns added, on the 1979 *We Will Meet Again*) gave signs in performance of capturing the missing spark. Of the later trio dates, *I Will Say Goodbye,* from '77 and one of Eddie Gomez' last efforts, is the pick.

Never unwilling to attempt projects in other formats, Evans tried other concepts also—they just didn't always work that well. The all-solo *Alone (Again)* is sabotaged by an endless version of "People," while the mix of electric keyboards and overdubs on *New Conversations* only creates an air of diffuseness. *Crosscurrents,* with Lennie Tristano's saxophone stalwarts Lee Konitz and Warne Marsh added, is another good idea that never turns great. Toots Thielemans proves to be the most winning added voice, and his harmonica blends gently with the pianist on *Affinity; We Will Meet Again,* where two horns are added for a program of Evans originals, is also a refreshing change. *Symbiosis* is Clause Ogerman's well-sculpted 1974 composition for the Evans trio and orchestra.

Reissued Evans has been more worthwhile, especially the *Second Trio* twofer by the underrated Evans/Chuck Israels/Motian edition of the trio formed shortly after LaFaro's death. *Conception* fleshes out the *New Jazz Conceptions* album with two sides of previously unissued solo work, which makes for telling comparison (again, though, there is a lengthy and maudlin entry to spoil

things). *As Time Goes By* finds Bob Brookmeyer setting his valve trombone aside in favor of a second piano, and the four-handed interplay anticipates later Evans adventures in multitracking. (*Intermodulation* is the better, Jim Hall half of *Trio, Duo.*)

★ ★ ★ ★ At Shelly's Manne-Hole / Riv.
★ ★ ★ ★ ★ California Here I Come / Verve
★ ★ ★ ★ ★ The Complete Riverside
   Recordings / Riv.
★ ★ ★ Eloquence / Fan.
★ ★ ★ ★ Everybody Digs Bill Evans / Fan./
   OJC
★ ★ ★ ★ ★ Explorations / Fan./OJC
★ ★ ★ From the 70s / Fan.
★ ★ ★ ★ ★ The Interplay Sessions / Mile.
★ ★ ★ Moonbeams / Riv.
★ ★ ★ ★ New Jazz Conceptions / Fan./OJC
★ ★ ★ ★ A Simple Matter of Conviction /
   Verve
★ ★ ★ ★ Sunday at the Village Vanguard
   / Fan./OJC
★ ★ ★ ★ ★ Trio at Town Hall / Verve
The Evans catalogue grows more voluminous and confusing as facsimile reissues appear in Japan and this country together with unreleased material. Most of the Riversides can now be had with original covers or as two-record sets on Fantasy/Original Jazz Classics. All of them are collected in the formidable eighteen-record package, *The Complete Riverside Recordings.* *More from the Vanguard* is previously unissued material from the 1961 trio date with LaFaro and Motian. The best of the "new" Evans is from the Sixties: half of the *Interplay* twofer, with Zoot Sims and Jim Hall in a quintet performance of Evans originals; and *California Here I Come,* a 1967 live trio recording with Eddie Gomez and Philly Joe Jones.   — B.B.

GIL EVANS
★ ★ ★ The Arrangers' Touch / Prest.
★ ★ ★ Big Stuff / Prest.
★ ★ ★ Blues in Orbit / Inner
★ ★ ★ The Gil Evans Orchestra Plays the
   Music of Jimi Hendrix / RCA
★ ★ ★ ★ Out of the Cool / MCA
★ ★ ★ ★ Pacific Standard Time / Blue N.
★ ★ ★ ★ Priestess / Ant.
★ ★ ★ ★ Svengali / Atl.
★ ★ ★ ★ There Comes a Time / RCA
Although Gil Evans (b. 1912) had been arranging for Claude Thornhill and Miles Davis for nearly a decade, the 1957 recording *Big Stuff* was the first under his own name. Another '57 session, *Gil Evans Plus Ten,* is available as half of *The Arrangers' Touch* twofer, which also includes a 1953

Tadd Dameron session. Evans utilized his signature, unswerving lines for trumpet and sax sections, but granted soloists and percussionists a free rein. *Pacific Standard Time* is a valuable reissue of Evans' two late-Fifties albums, both attempts to orchestrate a bible of jazz standards. Evans' basic formula was to promote a soloist (Cannonball Adderley or Johnny Coles in most cases) over a tightly checked orchestra, with the same style of seamless, lush undergrowth that characterized his haunting work with Miles. Shades of *Sketches of Spain* can be heard throughout *Out of the Cool,* the finest Evans album, although there's a quality of tension here missing from the Miles Davis classic. With its oddly punctuated counter-rhythm and lengthy Lydian chromatic blues statements, this album was ten years ahead of its time.

With *Svengali,* Gil Evans meets the rock age, which is much more interesting in concept than practice. Evans does nothing particularly innovative with the rock idiom, but rather transposes its dynamics and instrumentation—often embarrassingly—to the same concept at work in *Pacific Standard Time*: protruding solos with lush backgrounds. Evans was to have arranged for Jimi Hendrix, but the guitarist's sudden death iced the project. *Music of Jimi Hendrix* is a glimpse at that project, but it's not fully developed enough to give a real sense of what it should have been. The readings are perfunctory, lacking the sensuous, assaultive experience that Hendrix created. Evans only arranged two of the eight tracks. Japanese guitarist Ryo Kawasaki does provide some good moments, however.

There Comes a Time is Evans' first significant statement from the Seventies. Its scope ranges from tense, abstract blues and Evans' familiar Moorish obsessions to an elongated Tony Williams song and a swinging, revivified Jelly Roll Morton standard. Evans arranged and conducted the entire affair, and he gets the most from an impressive assembly of young musicians, including Tony Williams, David Sanborn, George Adams, Howard Johnson, Kawasaki, Hannibal Marvin Peterson and Lew Soloff.

Priestess is a wonderful live recording from 1977 that assembled a powerhouse band including George Adams on tenor sax, Arthur Blythe and David Sanborne on altos, Jimmy Knepper on trombone, Howard Johnson on tuba, Lew Soloff, Ernie Royal and Marvin "Hannibal" Peterson on trumpets and Pete Levin on synthesizer. — M.G./J.S.

ART FARMER

★ ★ ★ **Another Git Together (with Benny Golson)** / Mer.
★ ★ ★ **At the Half Note** / Atl.
★ ★ **Big Blues** / CTI
★ ★ **Crawl Space** / CTI
★ ★ ★ ★ **Early Art** / Prest.
★ ★ ★ **The Art Farmer Quintet Plays the Jazz Hits** / Odys.
★ ★ ★ ★ **Farmer's Market** / Prest.
★ ★ ★ **From Vienna with Art** / Pausa
★ ★ ★ **I'll Take Manhattan** / Soul N.
★ ★ ★ ★ **Interaction** / Atl.
★ ★ ★ **Listen to Art Farmer and the Orchestra** / Mer.
★ ★ ★ **Live at Boomer's** / Inner
★ ★ ★ **Mirage** / Soul N.
★ ★ ★ ★ ★ **Moment to Moment** / Soul N.
★ ★ ★ **On the Road** / Contem.
★ ★ ★ ★ **Portrait of Art** / Contem.
★ ★ ★ ★ **Sing Me Softly of the Blues** / Atl.
★ ★ **Something You Got** / CTI
★ ★ ★ ★ **The Summer Knows** / Inner
★ ★ ★ ★ **To Duke with Love** / Inner
★ ★ ★ ★ **To Sweden with Love** / Atl.
★ ★ ★ ★ **The Time and Place** / Col.
★ ★ ★ ★ **Trumpets All Out (with Donald Byrd)** / Prest.
★ ★ ★ **Warm Valley** / Conc. J.
★ ★ ★ **A Work of Art** / Conc. J.
★ ★ ★ **Yama (with Joe Henderson)** / CTI

Lyricism is Art Farmer's raison d'être. Although he can swing with the best of them, this trumpeter/fluegelhornist's real contribution is to the art of the ballad. His gorgeous tone, impeccable taste and incredible control make him one of the great storytellers in jazz history.

Trumpeters in the Fifties had two stylistic role models: the introspective musings of Miles Davis and the fiery flash of Clifford Brown. *Farmer's Market,* a double-set collection of early-Fifties Prestige sessions, finds Farmer (b. 1928) working on a synthesis that eventually leans toward Davis. Sonny Rollins and the brilliant unsung house rhythm section of Kenny Clarke, Percy Heath and Horace Silver make some terrific contributions; a highlight is the classic uptempo title piece.

For the next five years Farmer used Davis' example to develop his own form of finely honed lyricism and laconic swing. While never capturing the poetic depths of deep-blues feeling of Davis' style, Farmer worked out a personal means of expression that is always involving and never overly derivative. *Portrait* (1958) is Farmer in a still-favorite surrounding, his horn-plus-rhythm section, a grouping that gave him plenty of space while avoiding the familiar two-horned unit sound of the time.

In 1960, after having worked for both Horace Silver and Gerry Mulligan and becoming one of the most adaptable sidemen on the New York scene, Farmer organized the Jazztet with the talented saxist/composer Benny Golson. Only *Another Git Together,* with Harold Mabern replacing their original pianist McCoy Tyner, documents this productive but short-lived tenure; Farmer and Golson would reunite on *Moment to Moment* in the early Eighties. The next band Farmer put together featured a more unique lineup; the brilliant and wholly sympathetic guitarist Jim Hall replaced both the pianist and the second horn. The tonal color was as arresting as the setting, for Farmer in his quest for an ever-lyrical quality was now using the darker-toned fluegelhorn exclusively. The Atlantic recordings of this swinging chamber-jazz group, which also included Steve Swallow on bass, have recently been reissued on Japanese pressings. And together with *Sing Me* (featuring Steve Kuhn on piano) they are the best places to start for contemporary Farmer.

Before leaving for an extended stay in Europe, Farmer formed one other important group, a more typical bop-oriented quintet with piano and two horns. What made it exceptional was the still-undervalued saxist Jimmy Heath. *Time and Place,* a live set from 1967, is a testament to this band's range; they could ease heartbreak from "The Shadow of Your Smile" and then rage into a heated workout on "Blue Bossa."

Except for the occasional dates that pair him with a second horn (*Road, Yama, Mirage, Vienna*) and the misguided CTI recordings, Farmer sticks to the minimal horn-plus-rhythm setting, usually using the exceptionally tight backing of Cedar Walton, Sam Jones and Billy Higgins. While they are all consistently fine—as any LP containing a Farmer ballad would have to be—*To Duke* and *Summer Knows* might be the masterpieces. The only major disappointment in the Farmer canon is *Big Blues,* a reunion date with Hall that lacks the warmth and spirit of their original union. — S.F.

SHAMEK FARRAH
★ ★ La Dee La La / Ra

Saxophonist Shamek Farrah and friends (trumpeters Malachi Thompson and Abdullah Khalid, drummer Ron Rahsaan, and pianists Saeed Amir and Sonelius Smith) play it pretty conservatively here, sounding strikingly similar to the recordings made by Brooklyn musicians for the Strata-East label during the Seventies. Not bad, but Sonny Fortune topped it with *Long before Our Mothers Cried.* — F.G.

JOE FARRELL
★ ★ ★ Benson and Farrell / CTI
★ Canned Funk / CTI
★ ★ Farrell's Inferno / Jazz à la Carte
★ ★ ★ ★ Moon Germs / CTI
★ ★ ★ Outback / CTI
★ ★ ★ Penny Arcade / CTI
★ ★ ★ Skateboard Park / Xan.
★ ★ ★ Someday / Real.
★ ★ ★ Song of the Wind / CTI
★ ★ ★ Sonic Text / Contem.
★ ★ ★ Upon This Rock / CTI

In the late Sixties, reedman Joe Farrell (b. 1937) played on small-group record dates led by Chick Corea and Elvin Jones. Their agenda was solid modal jazz: either lyrical, straight-ahead or nearly "free." Their LPs strongly influenced Farrell's first records as a leader; *Song of the Wind, Outback* and *Moon Germs* are just as modal and they're also meatily composed and improvised. In addition they feature impressive personnel: pianists Corea and Herbie Hancock; bassists

Stanley Clarke, David Holland and Buster Williams; drummers Jack DeJohnette and Airto; and guitarist John McLaughlin. Their only fault, in fact, is their politeness; they lack the incisive ambiguities of a truly original product.

Such "politeness" is much more inappropriate when fused with a broader rock style. As a result, *Penny Arcade* is clumsily forced, and erratic; *Upon This Rock,* though more integrated, is not very distinctive; and *Canned Funk* is crude, even silly.

Benson and Farrell breaks back to the past a bit, featuring more lyrical, swinging Farrell soloing. (It even overshadows George Benson's usually contagious playing, which here seems obviously, lifelessly overdubbed.) However, the album makes too many commercial concessions to equal Farrell's best work.

Farrell moved away from a dependence on fusion in the Eighties. *Skateboard Park* features Chick Corea on piano. *Sonic Text* is an engaging quintet session with Freddie Hubbard adding fine trumpet and fluegelhorn to Farrell's playing. The '82 *Someday* set uses a quartet with George Cables on piano, John Dentz on drums and Tony Dumas on bass. — M.R./J.S.

LORRAINE FEATHER
★ ★ Sweet Lorraine / Conc. J.

Standard tunes receive the standard treatment from a sub-standard vocalist. — F.G.

WILTON FELDER
★ ★ Inherit the Wind / MCA
★ ★ We All Have a Star / MCA

As a member of the Crusaders, saxophonist/bassist Wilton Felder (b. 1940) developed the distinctive R&B instrumental groove that made the band famous. His solo albums, like the later Crusaders LPs, suffer from lack of both musical conviction and strong direction as Felder searches for a commercial sound that can satisfy his musical ambitions. — J.S.

ELLA FITZGERALD
★ ★ ★ Best Is Yet to Come / Pablo
★ ★ ★ ★ The Best of Ella / MCA
★ ★ ★ The Best of Ella Fitzgerald / Verve
★ ★ ★ The Best of Ella Fitzgerald, Vol. 2 / MCA
★ ★ ★ Brighten the Corner / Cap.
★ ★ ★ Carnegie Hall / Col.
★ ★ ★ ★ The Cole Porter Songbook / Verve
★ ★ Dream Dancing / Pablo
★ ★ ★ Ella and Duke on the Côte D'Azur / Verve

★ ★ ★ ★ **Ella and Louis** / Verve
★ **Ella Fitzgerald with Gordon Jenkins'
Orchestra and Chorus** / Voc.
★ ★ ★ **Ella in Berlin: Mack the Knife** /
Verve
★ ★ ★ **Ella Sings Gershwin** / MCA
★ ★ ★ ★ **Ellington Songbook** / Verve
★ ★ ★ **Embraces Jobim** / Pablo
★ ★ ★ **Fine and Mellow** / Pablo
★ ★ ★ **Gershwin Songbook** / Verve
★ ★ ★ **The History of Ella Fitzgerald** /
Verve
★ ★ ★ **In Hollywood** / Verve
★ ★ ★ **In London** / Pablo
★ ★ ★ **Lady Time** / Pablo
★ ★ **Memories** / MCA
★ ★ ★ **Things Ain't What They Used to Be**
/ Bain.
★ ★ ★ **Thirty by Ella** / Cap.
★ ★ **Whisper Not** / Verve

Ella Fitzgerald (b. 1918) has the most perfect pop-jazz voice on record, and her technique is matched by her serene impassivity. Guided by musical form instead of by lyrics, she brings an unparalleled sense of classicism to everything she does—from scat to pop ballads. Blessed with perfect pitch and perfect diction, she is mistress of the long-lined narrative phrase. But if for some, Fitzgerald is peerless, others find her coolness boring.

The MCA albums catalogue her long career with Decca (from the late Thirties to the mid-Fifties). But on Verve, the label started by her manager, Norman Granz, Fitzgerald hit her peak. The consistency of the material was much higher, for her records here were conceived for history. On *Ella and Louis,* she and Louis Armstrong displayed an extraordinary yin/yang vocal chemistry as they dueted on standard after standard. Though Fitzgerald's graciousness forbade wryness, *The Cole Porter Songbook* remains a monument of sedate pop-jazz that does the tunes proud. Fitzgerald's Seventies and Eighties records on Granz' RCA custom label, Pablo, show the voice in good repair and the styling intact, in mostly small jazz settings. — S.H.

TOMMY FLANAGAN
★ ★ ★ ★ **Ballads and Blues** / Enja
★ ★ ★ ★ **Confirmation** / Enja
★ ★ ★ ★ **A Dream Comes True (with Lilian
Terry)** / Soul N.
★ ★ ★ ★ **Eclypso** / Enja
★ ★ ★ ★ **Giant Steps** / Enja
★ ★ ★ ★ **Good Girl (with Kim Parker)** /
Soul N.
★ ★ ★ ★ **The Magnificent Tommy Flanagan**
/ Prog.

★ ★ ★ ★ **Something Borrowed, Something
Blue** / Gal.
★ ★ ★ ★ **Super-Session** / Enja
★ ★ ★ ★ ★ **Thelonica** / Enja
★ ★ ★ ★ **Three for All** / (with Phil Woods
and Red Mitchell) Enja

Pianist Tommy Flanagan (b. 1930) should be forced to will his body to science so we might discover how he always gets the things that are in his heart out through his hands. A superb accompanist, Flanagan has worked extensively with Ella Fitzgerald. Barry Harris, Hank Jones and Flanagan form a triumvirate of great bop pianists from Detroit, and Flanagan's incredible grace and taste make virtually anything he's played on well worth hearing.

As a sideman, Flanagan has worked in every setting. As a leader, he seems most comfortable in the trio. Able to spin the most delicate webs, Flanagan also has the power and personality to record in a small group with powerhouse drummers like Elvin Jones and Al Foster. There's scant difference in quality between the trio recordings, although *Giant Steps* is the most interesting from a conceptual standpoint; it allows listeners to compare Flanagan's trio treatments with the way he handled these tunes on the original historic Coltrane session. Incidentally, the record with Lilian Terry is a real find: she is an outstanding singer. Flanagan's tribute to Thelonious Monk, the 1984 release *Thelonica,* is a stunning trio set with bassist George Mraz and drummer Art Taylor.
— F.G.

RICKY FORD
★ ★ ★ ★ ★ **Flying Colors** / Muse
★ ★ ★ ★ **Interpretations** / Muse
★ ★ ★ ★ ★ **Loxodonta Africana** / New W.
★ ★ ★ ★ **Manhattan Plaza** / Muse
★ ★ ★ **Tenor for the Times** / Muse

Ricky Ford (b. 1954) is one of the most substantial players to attain prominence in recent years. Where other tenor saxophonists drew acclaim by absorbing avant-garde lessons (Chico Freeman, David Murray) or reverting to pre-bop models (Scott Hamilton), and where the rule for lesser lights became mere imitation of middle-period Coltrane (fill in any of dozens of names), Ford established an approach all his own, rooted to be sure (primarily in boppers Dexter Gordon and Sonny Rollins) but fresh enough to function in the most contemporary of contexts. In addition, Ford is an exceptional composer of structurally distinctive yet melodically straightforward material.

Loxodonta Africana, which includes writing for six- and nine-piece bands, is one of the most stunning debut albums of the period, filled with striking lines and pungent blowing; the long tenor solo on "My Romance" is particularly outstanding. *Manhattan Plaza,* a quintet session, features the strong Jaki Byard/David Friesen/Dannie Richmond rhythm section plus three of pianist Byard's tunes. Perhaps the best view of Ford the improviser is afforded on *Flying Colors,* a first-class program of music by Strayhorn, Ellington and Monk. *Tenor for the Times,* its sequel, disappoints due to less intriguing writing and the substitution of Albert Dailey for John Hicks in the piano chair. *Interpretations* is better, employing the same rhythm section but including two additional horn players for half of the performances.

Ford is also prominently featured on albums by Mercer Ellington, Mingus Dynasty, Red Rodney, Jack Walrath, Charles Mingus and Dannie Richmond. — B.B.

BRUCE FORMAN
★ ★ ★ Coast to Coast / Choice
★ ★ ★ ★ Full Circle / Conc.
★ ★ ★ In Transit / Muse
★ ★ ★ River Journey / Muse
★ ★ ★ ★ 20/20 / Muse
San Francisco guitarist Bruce Forman (b. 1956) was a sideman with Richie Cole. Forman's style is more traditional than might be expected from a young player, and his sense of swing and phrasing show absolutely no rock influences. A bit predictable but quite facile, and his 1981 album, *20/20,* found Forman taking more chances.

Full Circle, his most recent LP, is a good collaboration with pianist George Cables, vibraphonist Bobby Hutcherson, bassist Jeff Carney and drummer Eddie Marshall.
— F.G.

JIMMY FORREST
★ ★ ★ ★ Heart of the Forrest / Palo Alto
★ ★ ★ Live at the Barrel (with Miles Davis) / Prest.
★ ★ ★ ★ Out of the Forrest / Fan./OJC
A strong-blowing, hard-swinging tenor player, Jimmy Forrest (1920–1980) was a veteran of numerous big bands and one of the few musicians to play in both the Ellington and Basie units. Forrest's curse is that he will always be remembered for just one tune, "Night Train."

Although Forrest recorded albums as a leader for Prestige, Time and Delmark, little is presently available. The OJC title, from 1961, is a quartet date with Joe Zawinul on piano. The date for Palo Alto Jazz is a live recording with organist Shirley Scott and drummer Randy Marsh, and a fine example of his work. The album with Miles Davis is also live, but the quality of this 1952 recording is poor. — F.G.

SONNY FORTUNE
★ ★ ★ ★ Awakening / A&M
★ ★ ★ Serengeti Minstrel / Atco
★ ★ ★ ★ Waves of Dreams / A&M
★ ★ ★ With Sound Reason / Atl.
Sonny Fortune (b. 1939) is a virtuoso saxophonist who also plays flute and made quite a reputation for himself as a sideman with McCoy Tyner and Miles Davis before recording on his own. His two A&M albums are magnificently conceived and recorded works in a more traditional setting, with *Awakening* earning a slight edge for the beautiful ballad elegy to Duke Ellington and Cannonball Adderley, "For Duke and Cannon." — J.S.

RODNEY FRANKLIN
★ ★ Endless Flight / Col.
★ ★ Rodney Franklin / Col.
★ ★ You'll Never Know / Col.
The new Ramsey Lewis? Franklin is essentially a pop/jazz pianist with fair chops and an ear for black contemporary crossover ditties. — F.G.

MICHAEL FRANKS
★ ★ ★ The Art of Tea / Rep.
★ ★ ★ Burchfield Nines / War.
★ ★ ★ Objects of Desire / War.
★ ★ ★ One Bad Habit / War.
★ ★ ★ Sleeping Gypsy / War.
★ ★ ★ Tiger in the Rain / War.
Affectingly light, jazzy pop—smooth but not slick. Michael Franks (b. 1944) possesses a casual, slow, almost talking style of singing; his melodies and tempos are leisurely without dragging. The albums center on Joe Sample's relaxed electric piano, with generally only guitar, bass and drums accompanying. Occasional sax and string arrangements are handled judiciously. *Sleeping Gypsy* is slightly more spacious and less restricted, though many of the same musicians appear on all of the records. — C.W.

CHICO FREEMAN
★ ★ ★ ★ Beyond the Rain / Contem.
★ ★ ★ ★ Chico / In. Nav.
★ ★ ★ ★ Destiny's Dance / Contem.
★ ★ ★ Father and Sons (with Von Freeman) / Col.

★ ★ ★ ★ ★ **Kings of Mali** / **In. Nav.**
★ ★ ★ **No Time Left** / **Black S.**
★ ★ ★ ★ **The Outside Within** / **In. Nav.**
★ ★ ★ ★ ★ **Peaceful Heart, Gentle Spirit** /
Contem.
★ ★ ★ **The Search** / **In. Nav.**
★ ★ ★ ★ ★ **Spirit Sensitive** / **In. Nav.**
★ ★ ★ **Tangents** / **Elek./Mus.**
★ ★ ★ ★ **Tradition in Transition** / **Elek./
Mus.**

Many Chico Freeman albums appeared in a short period of time for good reason—he is perhaps the most flexible of the new tenor stars, and he always records with superb musicians. Chico (b. 1949) is the son of Chicago tenor legend Von Freeman, a member of the influential AACM, and a player for whom going outside *and* inside is second nature.

Sidemen like Muhal Richard Abrams, Elvin Jones, Cecil McBee and Jack DeJohnette are featured throughout Freeman's discography, which accounts in some measure for the consistent value of his sessions. Freeman's own playing, however, remains the primary focus. He can explore new music with a personal and identifiable sound and set of ideas, yet always manages to include at least some material of a more traditional bent for the less intrepid members of his audience.

Standouts among the albums listed above are *Kings of Mali,* with material drawn from African sources, a strong band featuring vibist Jay Hoggard and pianist Anthony Davis, and a chance to hear Freeman on soprano sax and flutes; *Peaceful Heart,* perhaps the best opportunity to sample Freeman's writing and instrumental arsenal (which includes clarinet and bass clarinet here); and the exquisite ballad album, *Spirit Sensitive,* where Freeman blows standards with more invention and conviction than most old-timers.

Recent Freeman albums have varied substantially in approach and quality. The winner is *Destiny's Dance,* with a superlative sextet including Wynton Marsalis and Bobby Hutcherson and an expert blend of material. *Tradition in Transition,* by Freeman's working group (which includes McBee and Billy Hart—Jack DeJohnette alternates with Hart on some tracks), is another strong program, if a bit too consciously designed as a sampler. *The Search* has more talented sidemen (including Kenny Barron and Jay Hoggard) but dwells on uninspired vocals. *Tangents* features vocalist Bobby McFerrin. Freeman and his father share half of a Columbia album with the Marsalis family and demonstrate in the process that Freeman *père* may be the more iconoclastic saxophonist.

Freeman is also well featured on albums by Cecil McBee, Jack DeJohnette, Don Pullen and Jay Hoggard, among others. — B.B.

DAVID FRIESEN
★ ★ ★ **StoryTeller** / **Muse**
David Friesen (b. 1943) is a strong bassist who also has a gentle touch as a composer. The quintet's lineup, which includes guitar, drums, fluegelhorn, and oboe/English horn, has a decidedly ECM-ish sound. Friesen has also made interesting duet LPs with guitarist John Stowell. — F.G.

DAVE FRISHBERG
★ ★ ★ **Dave Frishberg Songbook** / **Omni.**
★ ★ ★ **Dave Frishberg Songbook, Vol. 2** /
Omni.
★ ★ ★ **Getting Some Fun out of Life** /
Conc. J.
★ ★ ★ **You're a Lucky Guy** / **Conc. J.**
A devotee of Hoagie Carmichael, pianist/singer/songwriter Dave Frishberg (b. 1933) clearly sees himself as an entertainer first and foremost. Clever enough to keep his tunes from slipping into cocktail-lounge prattle, Frishberg also steers clear of any formularized approach, the result being wry, hip and off-beat. Had he been around at the height of Tin Pan Alley, Frishberg would have made a killing. As it is, he's developed a core of diehard fans. — F.G.

GALLERY
★ ★ ★ **Gallery / ECM/War.**
Formed around ex-Double Image vibist
Dave Samuels (b. 1948) and drummer Mi-
chael DiPasqua (b. 1953), Gallery moved
away from the percussion-oriented sound of
Double Image by adding Paul McCandless'
eerie oboe sonorities and fellow Paul Winter
Consort alumnus, David Darling. The resul-
tant sound is unique if not groundbreaking.
— J.S.

JAN GARBAREK
★ ★ ★ **Aftenland (with Kjell Johnsen) /
ECM/War.**
★ ★ ★ ★ **Belonging (with Keith Jarrett) /
ECM/War.**
★ ★ ★ **Dansere (with Bobo Stenson) /
ECM/War.**
★ ★ ★ **Dis / ECM/War.**
★ ★ ★ ★ **Esoteric Circle (with Terje Rypdal)
/ Ari./Free.**
★ ★ ★ **Eventyr / ECM/War.**
★ ★ ★ **Luminescence (with Keith Jarrett) /
ECM/War.**
★ ★ ★ **Magico / ECM/War.**
★ ★ ★ **Paths, Prints / ECM/War.**
★ ★ ★ **Photo with Blue Sky / ECM/War.**
★ ★ ★ **Places / ECM/War.**
★ ★ ★ ★ **Red Lanta / ECM/War.**
★ ★ ★ **Start / ECM/War.**
★ ★ ★ **Triptykon / ECM/War.**
★ ★ ★ ★ **Witchi-Tai-To (with Bobo Stenson)
/ ECM/War.**
Jan Garbarek (b. 1947) is a Norwegian saxo-
phone theorist who studied the Lydian Chro-
matic Concept with theorist/bandleader
George Russell, under whose auspices the
challenging *Esoteric Circle* was made. Gar-
barek's ECM work is among the best of the
rigorous, classically disciplined style carved
out by producer Manfred Eicher, and occasionally he can sound a little too icy in this
context, but his collaborations with pianists

Keith Jarrett on *Belonging* and *Luminescence* and Bobo Stenson on the beautiful
Witchi-Tai-To and *Dansere* show that he can
be accessible as well as experimental. The
other titles are repetitious. — J.S.

HANK GARLAND
★ ★ ★ ★ **New Direction / CSP**
This 1961 release not only represents the
first session of guitarist Hank Garland (b.
1930) as a jazz leader after a career of Nash-
ville country session work, it also introduces
the prodigious talent of vibraphonist Gary
Burton, then only seventeen. With Brubeck
drummer Joe Morello, and Joe Benjamin on
bass along for the ride, Burton and Garland
engage in an ecstatic dialogue throughout
the record. — J.S.

RED GARLAND
★ ★ ★ **A Garland of Red / Fan./OJC**
★ ★ ★ **Feelin' Red / Muse**
★ ★ ★ ★ **Jazz Junction / Prest.**
Pianist Red Garland (1923–1984) was a lyrical and passionate player who excelled as an
accompanist and improvisor. He came to
prominence as part of Miles Davis' late-Fifties quintet. *A Garland of Red,* a reissue of
his first album for Prestige, uses bassist Paul
Chambers and drummer Art Taylor from
the Davis band. Garland's compositional
strength and harmonic flow enabled him to
handle this kind of trio format, which he
went on to work in extensively, although he
became a bit repetitious at times. The 1979
set *Feelin' Red* is another trio with bassist
Sam Jones and drummer Al Foster. The
Prestige twofer *Jazz Junction* is a 1957 quintet date with John Coltrane and Donald
Byrd. — J.S.

ERROLL GARNER
★ ★ ★ ★ **Best of / Mer.**
★ ★ ★ ★ ★ **Concert by the Sea / Col.**

★ ★ ★ ★ The Elf / Savoy
★ ★ ★ ★ Feeling Is Believing / Mer.
★ ★ ★ ★ The Greatest Garner / Atl.
★ ★ ★ ★ Misty / Mer.
★ Other Voices / Col.
★ ★ ★ ★ Paris Impressions / Col.
★ ★ ★ ★ Play It Again, Erroll / Col.

In the Forties, pianist Erroll Garner (1921–1977) moved from his Pittsburgh home to New York where he was featured in bassist Slam Stewart's band before embarking on his own recording career toward the end of that decade. A self-taught musician, Garner has a unique style firmly rooted in the strong harmonic foundation of his greatest influence, Earl Hines. He alternates a pulsing change between softly stated figures and pounding arpeggios so forceful that the piano often sounds distorted in recordings. His right-hand flourishes are extremely decorative as he rolls through each chord, while his left turns steady, stabbing punctuation. His composition, "Misty," is one of the most famous jazz pieces ever written and has become a hit single for a number of other musicians besides Garner.

Garner recorded prolifically during the Fifties, and this material comprises the bulk of his currently available albums. The classic is *Concert by the Sea,* a 1956 West Coast live date with regular accompanists Denzil Best on drums and Eddie Calhoun on bass. The sparse settings of Garner's trio set his virtuosic playing off forcefully on trademark pieces such as "I'll Remember April," "Autumn Leaves" and "They Can't Take That Away from Me." The other records are consistently good except for the gruesome pairing with Mitch Miller's orchestra on *Other Voices.* Of the collections, *Paris Impressions,* '58 trio sessions featuring Garner on both piano and harpsichord, is particularly interesting, while *The Elf* collects some of his earliest sides from the Forties. — J.S.

CARLOS GARNETT

★ ★ ★ Black Love / Muse
★ ★ ★ ★ Cosmos Nucleus / Muse
★ ★ ★ Journey to Enlightenment / Muse
★ ★ Let This Melody Ring On / Muse
★ ★ ★ The New Love / Muse

Panamanian saxophonist Carlos Garnett (b. 1938) played in a variety of late-Sixties and early-Seventies jazz and fusion bands—Freddie Hubbard, Art Blakey, Miles Davis, Pharoah Sanders, Robin Kenyatta, Norman Connors—and his 1974 debut, *Black Love,* comes closest in spirit to the music he made with Connors. But Garnett's fusion is not the prefab process so much of that music be-

came—instead it's a real exploration of the overlapping elements in a variety of different North and Central American musics. The results are often engaging and even emotionally challenging. Garnett's own playing is tough and direct and most of these records feature outstanding vocal performances, from Dee Dee Bridgewater (*Black Love*), Ayodele Jenkins (*Black Love, Journey to Enlightenment*) and Cheryl Alexander (*Cosmos Nucleus*). *Cosmos Nucleus,* an expressive big-band record decidedly influenced by Sun Ra arrangements, is Garnett's finest work.
— J.S.

LUIS GASCA

★ ★ ★ Born to Love You / Fan.
★ ★ ★ Collage / Fan.

Veteran Bay Area trumpeter Luis Gasca (b. 1940), with some good sidemen in tow (Joe and Eddie Henderson, George Duke, Jack DeJohnette, Patrice Rushen, Bobby Hutcherson), presents two discs of modal and Latin-flavored tunes. The results are lyrical or loping music; nice enough, but with a relaxed sincerity that unfortunately borders on corn.
— M.R.

STAN GETZ

★ ★ ★ Another World / Col.
★ ★ ★ Best of / Col.
★ ★ ★ Best of—Two Worlds / Col.
★ ★ ★ ★ Captain Marvel / Col.
★ ★ ★ Captain of the World / Col.
★ ★ ★ ★ Diz and Getz / Verve
★ ★ ★ ★ The Dolphin / Conc. J.
★ ★ ★ Early Getz / Prest.
★ ★ ★ Echoes of an Era—Basie and Getz and Vaughan Live at Birdland / Rou.
★ ★ ★ Echoes of an Era—Best of Stan Getz / Rou.
★ ★ ★ Echoes of an Era—Stan Getz/Sonny Stitt / Rou.
★ ★ ★ ★ ★ Focus / Verve
★ ★ ★ Forest Eyes / Jazz M.
★ ★ ★ ★ ★ Girl from Ipanema: The Bossa Nova Years / Verve
★ ★ ★ In Stockholm / Verve
★ ★ ★ ★ Jazz Samba / Verve
★ ★ ★ Jazz Samba Encore / Verve
★ ★ ★ The Master / Col.
★ ★ ★ Mixes / Main.
★ ★ ★ Opus de Bop / Savoy
★ ★ ★ The Peacocks / Col.
★ ★ ★ Poetry (with Albert Dailey) / Elek./ Mus.
★ ★ ★ Pure Getz / Conc. J.
★ ★ ★ ★ Quartets / Fan./OJC
★ ★ ★ ★ Stan Getz / Prest.
★ ★ ★ ★ Stan Getz / Savoy

★ ★ ★ **Stan Getz and Oscar Peterson /
Verve**
★ ★ ★ **Stan Getz Au Go Go / Verve**
★ ★ **Stan Getz/Cal Tjader / Fan.**
★ ★ ★ **Stan Getz Gold / Inner**
★ ★ ★ **Stan Getz Greatest Hits / Prest.**
★ ★ ★ ★ **Stan Getz/João Gilberto, Vol. 1 /
Verve**
★ ★ ★ ★ ★ **Stan Getz: The Chick Corea/Bill
Evans Sessions / Verve**

Stan Getz (b. 1927) is one of the few modern saxophonists to carve out a strong reputation without resorting to iconoclasm or self-conscious avant-garde posturing. He has remained a warm, romantic player throughout his over forty years of recording. His first major recognition came as part of the Woody Herman band in the late Forties, when he and Zoot Sims, Al Cohn and Serge Chaloff were nicknamed the "Four Brothers." Getz was the best of those players and soon went out on his own. His cool, relaxed yet rhythmically interesting style is influenced heavily by Lester Young and Charlie Parker, and even though he is known for his understated, breathy tone, Getz can blow surprisingly hot when the mood strikes him, and his accessible style is echoed in a lot of today's West Coast R&B session reed players.

Opus de Bop features Getz in small-combo bop sessions from the mid- to late Forties and is a good representation of his early years. *Quartets* is another outstanding early set from 1949–1950. It wasn't until the Sixties, however, that he really began to take off. *Focus,* a brilliant 1962 collaboration with arranger Eddie Sauter, is an acknowledged classic and proof that plenty of experimentation was possible in a lyrical, understated context. Getz plays soaring, hypnotically rhythmic lines against the sweetly blocked-out string arrangements. A year later, Getz recorded an album of Brazilian tunes with guitarist Charlie Byrd. The record, *Jazz Samba,* started a bossa nova jazz craze when Antonio Carlos Jobim's "Desafinado" became a hit single. In the next few years Getz played with a variety of musicians. He produced the best samba records in the company of Jobim and guitarist João Gilberto, scoring a hit with "The Girl from Ipanema," for which he won four Grammy awards, and the *Getz/Gilberto* album in 1964. *Girl from Ipanema* is a fine collection of the Verve bossa nova albums. Rather than stay exclusively in that bag, Getz played with pianist Bill Evans, drummer Elvin Jones and bassists Ron Carter and Richard Davis (part of *Corea/Evans Sessions*); formed a touring

band with vibraphonist Gary Burton, bassist Steve Swallow and drummer Roy Haynes, a trio that went directly from playing with Getz to forming one of the first jazz-rock groups, the Gary Burton Quartet, with guitarist Larry Coryell; and recorded what may be his best album, *Sweet Rain,* with a quartet featuring the then-unknown pianist Chick Corea. (That album is now available as part of the two-record *Corea/Evans* set.)

Getz was still making good records into his fifties (*Pure Getz, Forest Eyes*) and reuniting with Corea for the fiery *Captain Marvel.* He also received a Grammy nomination for *Stan Getz Gold,* a live set recorded on his fiftieth birthday at a Copenhagen club he had opened twenty years before. *Poetry* is a 1983 duet session with pianist Albert Dailey. — J.S.

JOHN BIRKS "DIZZY" GILLESPIE

★ ★ ★ ★ **Afro-Cuban Jazz Moods (with
Machito) / Pablo**
★ ★ ★ ★ ★ **And His Big Band / GNP**
★ ★ ★ ★ **At the Salle Pleyel '48 / Prest.**
★ ★ ★ ★ ★ **Bahiana / Pablo**
★ ★ ★ ★ ★ **Big 4 / Pablo**
★ ★ ★ **Big 7 Montreux '75 / Pablo**
★ ★ ★ ★ **Carter, Gillespie, Inc. (with
Benny Carter) / Pablo**
★ ★ ★ ★ **Composer's Concepts / Em.**
★ ★ ★ ★ **Dee Gee Days / Savoy**
★ ★ ★ ★ ★ **The Development of an American
Artist / Smithsonian (available by mail
only from Smithsonian Recordings, P.O.
Box 10230, Des Moines, Iowa 50336)**
★ ★ ★ ★ **Diz and Getz (with Stan Getz) /
Verve**
★ ★ ★ ★ **Diz and Roy (with Roy Eldridge) /
Verve**
★ ★ ★ **Dizzy! / GNP**
★ **Free Ride (with Lalo Schifrin) / Pablo**
★ ★ ★ **The Giant / Prest.**
★ ★ ★ ★ ★ **In the Beginning / Prest.
(includes most of the selection on Big
Bands 1942–46 / Phoenix and Small
Groups 1945–46 / Phoenix)**
★ ★ **Jam Montreux '77 / Pablo L.**
★ ★ ★ ★ **Oscar Peterson and Dizzy Gillespie
/ Pablo**
★ ★ ★ **Paris Concert / GNP**
★ **Party / Pablo**
★ ★ ★ ★ **Something Old, Something New /
Trip**
★ ★ ★ ★ **The Sonny Rollins/Sonny Stitt
Sessions / Verve**
★ ★ ★ **Swing Low, Sweet Cadillac / MCA**
★ ★ ★ **With Mitchell–Ruff Duo / Main.**

John Birks "Dizzy" Gillespie (b. 1917), one of the founding fathers of the modern era, good-time showman, bebop personality, big-band and small-combo leader, Afro-Cuban jazz sessionist and as spectacular as any musician who ever improvised on a trumpet, is at this writing fortunately still with us and much (although by no means all) of his five-decade career is represented in the catalogue.

One of the best ways to study the evolution of swing into bebop is to study the Smithsonian album (which moves from 1940 sideman appearances with Cab Calloway through jam sessions at Harlem's Monroe's and 52nd Street combos to the classic 1946 recordings of "Confirmation" and "'Round Midnight"). Several rare tracks are included, and the double album has been programed (for the sake of focus) minus any Gillespie–Charlie Parker collaborations.

Diz and Bird can be heard on *In the Beginning* in 1945 combo cuts ("Salt Peanuts," "Groovin' High," "Shaw 'Nuff," etc.), which quickly became the manifesto of a new musical generation. Also included are "Things to Come," "Our Delight," "Emanon" and five other tracks by Gillespie's late-Forties big band (the GNP *Big Band* and *At the Salle Pleyel '48* have later live recordings by the band).

Gillespie was working with a combo and stressing novelty material by 1950 (*Dee Gee Days* exemplifies his music of the period); by 1953 he was affiliated with producer Norman Granz' Verve label, where he remained through 1961. The Verve years (a period that saw several interesting Gillespie projects, including a new orchestra that toured through 1956–57) are currently represented in reissue solely by encounters with other leaders. Recommended among these is the first session on *Diz and Getz* (a joyous date with Max Roach on drums) and the hard-blowing encounters, singly and together, with tenor giants Sonny Rollins and Sonny Stitt.

During the Sixties Gillespie led a strong quintet, featuring James Moody on reeds and pianist Kenny Barron, but his popularity waned as audiences turned their attention to more recent jazz and nonjazz styles. Few representations of the era remain available; of those (the EmArcy, Trip and MCA albums), *Something Old, Something New* is easily the best (and the hardest to find!)—the quintet does one side of bebop venerables and one side of originals by Tom McIntosh (three of the new items are also on *Composer's Concepts*).

Popular interest in Gillespie has grown once again in recent years, at a time when the trumpeter has made some of the best

music of his life and Norman Granz (who now owns Pablo) has returned to produce records at a ridiculously prolific rate. The nine items released under Gillespie's full or partial leadership since 1975 include some dogs (particularly two embarrassing attempts at disco), but there are also two certified masterpieces: *Big 4,* a super-mellow quartet with Joe Pass (guitar), Ray Brown (bass) and Mickey Roker (drums); and *Bahiana,* a double album of stunning trumpet against a two-guitar rhythm section. Also notable are the meeting with composer/alto-sax elder statesman Benny Carter, the Afro-Cuban reunion with Machito's band and Chico O'Farrill's writing, and the Oscar Peterson duo album, which—despite the pianist's usual overenthusiasms—is one hell of a trumpet record.

★ ★ ★ **Best of Dizzy Gillespie / Pablo**
★ ★ ★ **Digital at Montreux, 1980 / Pablo L.**
★ ★ ★ ★ ★ **Diz / Quin.**
★ ★ ★ ★ **Dizzy and the Double Six of Paris / Phi.**
★ ★ ★ ★ ★ **An Electrifying Evening with the Dizzy Gillespie Quintet / Verve**
★ ★ ★ ★ **The Gifted Ones (with Count Basie) / Pablo**
★ ★ ★ **The Giant / Jazz M.**
★ ★ ★ ★ **The Greatest Trumpet of Them All / Verve**
★ ★ ★ ★ **Have Trumpet Will Excite / Verve**
★ ★ ★ ★ **Havin' a Good Time in Paris / Inner**
★ ★ ★ **Jambo Caribe / Lime.**
★ ★ ★ ★ ★ **The King of Bop (with Charlie Parker, Miles Davis, etc.) / Arc. Folk.**
★ ★ **Musician-Composer-Raconteur / Pablo**
★ ★ ★ **The Source / Jazz M.**
★ ★ **Summertime / Pablo**
★ ★ ★ **To a Finland Station / Pablo**
★ ★ ★ ★ **The Trumpet Summit Meets the Oscar Peterson Big 4 (with Freddie Hubbard, Clark Terry) / Pablo**

Gillespie can still deliver in person, but the steam has temporarily gone out of his recording career. Best of the recent Pablos is *The Gifted Ones,* a relaxed 1977 session with Count Basie. *Trumpet Summit* is uneven but often fascinating for the manner in which the hornmen goad and respond to each other. *Montreux, 1980* is an unusual trio setting involving Toots Thielemans on guitar (no harmonica) and Pretty Purdie's drums, a fine idea but too cute in the execution.

Reissues have been the place to hear Gillespie on recent records. Both the Archive of Folk and the Quintessence albums are budget-priced samplers of the trail-blazing bebop recordings, with most of the era's greats on the former and Gillespie leading both combo and big band on the latter. *Havin' a Good Time,* from 1952, is meaty but heavy on alternate takes, while *Electrifying Evening* is one of the great Gillespie recitals by one of his best bands (Leo Wright, alto and flute; Lalo Schifrin, piano), in a 1961 Museum of Modern Art concert.

Gillespie albums both old and new continue to pour forth. From among the vintage material *The Greatest Trumpet* is a reflective 1957 octet session with writing by Gigi Gryce and Benny Golson. The trumpeter's encounter with the Parisian vocal group, the Double Six, dating from 1963, has the added bonus of Bud Powell on piano. The two Jazz Man albums were formerly joined as a Prestige twofer called *The Giant.*

In terms of new recordings, Gillespie is in a rut, leaning heavily on live performance and tired routines. *Finland Station,* his meeting with Cuban trumpeter Arturo Sandoval, an inspired pairing, is checked by the Finnish rhythm section and Gillespie's ever-increasing reliance on the jaw's-harp.
— B.B.

GIL GOLDSTEIN
★ ★ ★ **Pure as Rain / Chi.**
★ ★ ★ **Wrapped in a Cloud / Muse**
Pianist Gil Goldstein first gained notice for his work with guitarist Pat Martino, where he evinced a fluid bebop style and proved himself capable of keeping pace with a most frenetic and unpredictable soloist. On his own recordings he showcases a light but sure touch, although the melodies he frames for himself aren't the most challenging. — F.G.

BENNY GOLSON
★ ★ ★ **Another Git Together (with Art Farmer) / Mer.**
★ ★ ★ ★ **Blues on Down / Mile.**
★ ★ ★ ★ **New York Scene / Contem.**
★ ★ ★ ★ **Turning Point / Mer.**
Saxophonist/composer/bandleader Benny Golson's available catalogue does him a major injustice. As an instrumentalist, Golson (b. 1929) can be either a populist or a challenger, with a style equally suited to both hard bop and the rhythm & blues spheres. As a composer, he's inked such outstanding tunes as "Stablemates," "Killer Joe" and "I Remember Clifford," and as a bandleader, he coled the fine Jazztet with trumpeter Art Farmer.

In addition to his work with the Jazztet (*Another Git Together*), these records furnish fine examples of Golson at his best. *Turning Point* is a quartet date featuring both ballads

and hard-swinging arrangements, while *New York Scene* is split between quintet and nonet settings. Pianist Wynton Kelly and bassist Paul Chambers are featured on both albums, and the Contemporary date also boasts Farmer, Gigi Gryce, Sahib Shihab, James Cleveland and Julius Watkins. *Blues on Down* concentrates more on blowing than arrangements. — F.G.

BABS GONZALES
★ ★ ★ ★ **Babs / Chi.**
★ ★ ★ **Live at Small's Paradise / Chi.**
One of the first and finest practitioners of the vocalese style of singing, Babs Gonzales (1919–1980) was on a par with such great bebop vocalists as Eddie Jefferson and John Hendricks. Unfortunately, these are about all you can find at the moment, but at least on *Babs* the band—which features Johnny Griffin, Clark Terry, Melba Liston, Charlie Rouse, Horace Parlan, Ray Nance, Buddy Catlett and Roy Haynes—gives Gonzales a versatile session. — F.G.

JERRY GONZALEZ
★ ★ ★ **The River Is Deep (with the Fort Apache Band) / Enja**
★ ★ ★ ★ **Ya Yo Me Cure / Amer. C.**
Percussionist/trumpeter Jerry Gonzalez is part of an enclave of New York-based musicians continuing the Latin/jazz tradition begun during the bebop period. A veteran of both salsa and jazz bands, Gonzalez also has a complete command of Afro-Cuban and Yoruba rhythms, giving his recordings a distinctly historic continuum. Jerry and associates—including percussionists Gene Golden, Nicky Marrero, Steve Berrios and Flaco Hernandez, trombonist Steve Turre, pianist Jorge Dalto, saxophonists Mario Rivera and Wilfredo Velez, and brother Andy Gonzalez on bass—have a musical vocabulary that allows them to cover the traditional, rhythmic compositions of vocalist/percussionist Frankie Rodrigues, deliver strong covers of such disparate jazz classics as "Caravan," "Nefertiti" and "Evidence," and blow the doors off Dizzy Gillespie's "Bebop." More than historic travelogues, both albums are explorative, creative, and the work of musicians seeking to push a tradition-rooted and unjustly out-of-vogue music forward. — F.G.

BENNY GOODMAN
★ ★ ★ **All-Time Greatest Hits / Col.**
★ ★ ★ **Benny Goodman and the Giants of Swing / Prest.**
★ ★ **Benny Goodman Live at Carnegie Hall / Lon.**

★ ★ ★ Benny Goodman Performances / PSI
★ ★ ★ Benny Goodman Plays Solid Gold
Instrumental Hits / Col.
★ ★ ★ Benny Goodman Presents Eddie
Sauter Arrangements / CSP
★ ★ ★ Benny Goodman Presents Fletcher
Henderson Arrangements / CSP
★ ★ ★ Benny Goodman's Greatest Hits /
Col.
★ The Benny Goodman Story / MCA
★ ★ ★ The Best of Benny Goodman / RCA
★ ★ ★ ★ Carnegie Hall Jazz Concert /
Col.
★ ★ ★ ★ Complete Benny Goodman, Vol.
1 (1935) / Blueb.
★ ★ ★ ★ Complete Benny Goodman, Vol.
2 (1935–36) / Blueb.
★ ★ ★ ★ Complete Benny Goodman, Vol.
3 (1936) / Blueb.
★ ★ ★ ★ Complete Benny Goodman, Vol.
4 (1936–37) / Blueb.
★ ★ ★ ★ Complete Benny Goodman, Vol.
5 (1937–38) / Blueb.
★ ★ ★ Complete Benny Goodman, Vol. 6
(1938) / Blueb.
★ ★ ★ Complete Benny Goodman, Vol. 7
(1938–39) / Blueb.
★ ★ ★ ★ Complete Benny Goodman, Vol.
8 (1936–39) / Blueb.
★ ★ Great Benny Goodman / Col.
★ ★ Hits of Benny Goodman / Cap.
★ ★ ★ King of Swing / Col.
★ ★ ★ Legendary Performers—Goodman /
RCA
★ ★ ★ ★ Let's Dance / Sandy Hook
★ ★ On Stage (with Benny Goodman and
His Septet) / Lon.
★ ★ Pure Gold / RCA
★ ★ Seven Come Eleven / Col.
★ ★ ★ ★ This Is Benny Goodman / RCA
★ ★ ★ This Is Benny Goodman, Vol. 2 /
RCA

Clarinetist Benny Goodman (b. 1909) helped
popularize a hotter, rhythmically complex
jazz for white audiences who thought jazz
had to be "cleaned up" before they could listen to it. His Thirties big bands and smaller
groups featured such instrumental stars as
drummer Gene Krupa, trumpeter Bunny
Berigan, pianist Teddy Wilson, vibraphonist
Lionel Hampton and guitarist Charlie Christian. By featuring Wilson and Hampton
prominently in his live shows Goodman
helped break the color barrier in jazz.

Unlike other popular white organizations
of the period, such as the Paul Whiteman
and the Casa Loma orchestras and the
Tommy Dorsey and Glenn Miller big bands,
here a wild, dance-crazy version of swing
was part of the group's basic concept. Vocals

were not overused, and Goodman's penchant
for crisp, hard-driving arrangements (many
songs in the band's book boasted Fletcher
Henderson arrangements from Henderson's
earlier, all-black band) made his music less
suitable for B-movie soundtracks than for
quality listening.

Benny Goodman and the Giants of Swing
compiles early-Thirties recordings with
Goodman as leader and sideman in the company of several players who would become
stalwarts in his classic groups—Krupa, pianist Jess Stacy, tenor saxophonist Bud Freeman; trombonist Jack Teagarden and bassist
Israel Crosby.

Let's Dance and *Benny Goodman Performances,* 1934–35 and 1937–38 live shots respectively, document the band's impact during those radio broadcasts that earned
Goodman the justified nickname of "King of
Swing." The *Carnegie Hall Jazz Concert,*
possibly the most famous live show in jazz
history, is the triumphant 1938 performance
that caught Goodman at the height of his
popularity and included the crowd-pleasing
histrionics of Gene Krupa's influential drum
solo on "Sing Sing Sing."

The best Benny Goodman on records is
the Bluebird eight-volume set comprising
The Complete Benny Goodman, which collects all of Goodman's important studio
dates between 1935 and '39 and includes a
number of historic sessions during the same
period on which Goodman was a sideman.
Volume 1, from 1935, includes big-band
sides with Krupa, Berigan, Teagarden, Stacy
and trumpeter Pee Wee Erwin among others
as well as rhapsodic trio performances from
Goodman, Wilson and Krupa. Henderson
arrangements abound, including classics like
"Dear Old Southland" and "King Porter
Stomp." Volume 2 is devoted to big-band
sides from 1935 and '36, more great trio performances, and tracks recorded by a band
under Gene Krupa's name featuring Chu
Berry on tenor sax, Roy Eldridge on trumpet, Goodman, Krupa, Stacy, Crosby and
Allan Reuss on guitar.

Volume 3 collects more Henderson arrangements for 1936 big-band sessions and
sublime sides from the Benny Goodman
quartet, which added vibraphonist Lionel
Hampton to the trio. Volume 4 represents
the late 1936 and most of the 1937 output
from the big band and quartet. Volume 5
shows the Goodman band in transition, including the last sides made by the Carnegie
Hall Jazz Concert band and tracks done
with tenor-sax great Lester Young in the
lineup. Krupa left the band shortly after the

Carnegie Hall concert and was replaced on later cuts of this LP by Lionel Hampton or Dave Tough. Harry James and Ziggy Elman are the trumpet stars and Bud Freeman the main saxophone soloist on the 1938 tracks in Volume 6. The later 1938–39 band, quartet and quintet (with bassist John Kirby) sessions appear on Volume 7.

The last LP in the set, Volume 8, includes alternate takes and highlights ranging from 1936 to '39—more Lester Young and Metronome All-Star sessions with Charlie Spivak, Bunny Berigan and Sonny Dunham on trumpets, Tommy Dorsey and Jack Teagarden on trombones, Hymie Shertzer on alto sax, most of whom played in the Goodman band.

Goodman left Bluebird for Columbia at the end of the Thirties. The *Fletcher Henderson Arrangements* ranges from '39 to '43; *Solid Gold Instrumental* and *Eddie Sauter Arrangements* from '40 to '43.

Goodman's post-Forties efforts, despite his continued ability to play excellent clarinet, suffer from a nostalgic hero worship surrounding the "King of Swing." *The Benny Goodman Story* is the companion LP to the 1955 film in which Steve Allen played Goodman. *On Stage* is an early-Seventies live recording from Copenhagen with a small group including saxophonist Zoot Sims. *Seven Come Eleven* is a small-group studio recording from 1975. The London *Benny Goodman Live at Carnegie Hall* set is a recording of the 40th anniversary performance of the historic '38 Carnegie Hall show, and is not to be confused with the original as nostalgic remakes shoulder aside a Beatles tune.

The numerous Benny Goodman best-of collections tend to duplicate each other with the obvious tracks and are generally worth less than the classic Thirties sides in *The Complete.* The most useful of the best-of albums, though, are the two RCA volumes of *This Is Benny Goodman.* — J.S.

JERRY GOODMAN AND JAN HAMMER
★ ★ ★ **Like Children** / Nemp./Atl.
Violinist Jerry Goodman and keyboardist Jan Hammer recorded this engaging album fresh from their triumph as part of the Mahavishnu Orchestra. The atmosphere here is far more lighthearted than the intense pyrotechnics of their Mahavishnu work, and the fact that Hammer is a limited vocalist at best doesn't help things, but there are enough ideas at hand ("Country and Eastern Music" is a clever ploy) to make this a bet-

ter-than-average fusion record. Hammer later had better luck with Jeff Beck, but not for long.

See also separate entry for Jan Hammer.
— J.S.

DEXTER GORDON
★ ★ ★ ★ **The Bethlehem Years** / Beth.
★ ★ ★ ★ **Long Tall Dexter** / Savoy
Dexter Gordon (b. 1923) was not the only tenor saxophonist to reflect the dual influences of Lester Young and Charlie Parker in the Forties, but he was one of the first, and his mix (rhythmically charged and robustly inflected) became the primary influence on Sonny Rollins and John Coltrane.

Savoy's twofer has several of Gordon's influential 1945–47 sessions, with Bud Powell, Max Roach, Tadd Dameron, Art Blakey, J. J. Johnson and Fats Navarro among the personnel; there is also a touch of strident early R&B and a long jam from a California club. Drugs kept Gordon out of circulation for more than a decade, but he did make a couple of albums in the Fifties while he scuffled in Los Angeles. The Bethlehem set is a strong quartet outing.
★ ★ ★ ★ ★ **Dexter Calling** / Blue N.
★ ★ ★ **Dexter Gordon** / Blue N.
★ ★ ★ ★ **Doin' All Right** / Blue N.
★ ★ ★ ★ ★ **Go!** / Blue N.
★ ★ ★ ★ ★ **A Swingin' Affair** / Blue N.
In the span of one year (1961–62), Gordon returned to New York, signed with Blue Note, and reestablished himself as one of the crucial tenor stylists in jazz history. All of his work from the period is excellent, but the three quartet albums are the best—*Dexter Calling,* with Kenny Drew, Paul Chambers, Philly Joe Jones; *Go!* and *A Swingin' Affair,* with Sonny Clark, Butch Warren and Billy Higgins. *Go!* is his all-time masterpiece by consensus (Gordon included). The two-record reissue (*Dexter Gordon*) gets low marks for its mundane choice of tunes.
★ ★ ★ ★ **Blues Walk!** / Black L.
★ ★ ★ ★ ★ **The Montmartre Collection, Vol. 1** / Black L.
★ ★ ★ ★ **One Flight Up** / Blue N.
★ ★ ★ ★ ★ **Our Man in Paris** / Blue N.
These albums are from Europe in the Sixties, where Gordon worked and lived after his New York year. *Our Man* is a grand reunion with Bud Powell and Kenny Clarke, two other style-setting expatriates. Both Black Lions were made at Copenhagen's Montmartre, a club in Gordon's adopted hometown where he often played. *Volume 1* receives its high rating for the power-packed blues jam on "Sonnymoon for Two," one of

the best recorded examples of what excitement Gordon can generate in a club.

★ ★ ★ Ca'Purange / Prest.
★ ★ ★ Generation / Prest.
★ ★ ★ ★ The Jumpin' Blues / Prest.
★ ★ ★ ★ More Power! / Prest.
★ ★ ★ ★ ★ The Panther / Prest.
★ ★ ★ ★ Tangerine / Prest.
★ ★ ★ ★ The Tower of Power / Prest.

Prestige recorded Gordon whenever he visited New York between 1969 and '72, with a host of first-class companions such as James Moody, Thad Jones, Freddie Hubbard, Barry Harris and Stanley Clarke. The best record of the series is *The Panther*, which uses the familiar quartet format and has the benefit of Tommy Flanagan's eloquent piano. The rest are all good, but the excitement of the Blue Notes is often missing.

★ ★ ★ ★ The Apartment / Inner
★ ★ ★ Blues à la Suisse / Prest.
★ ★ ★ ★ More Than You Know / Inner
★ ★ ★ ★ Stable Mable / Inner
★ ★ ★ ★ Swiss Nights / Inner

Back to Europe for the early and mid-Seventies. *More Than You Know,* an orchestral session with occasionally overlush Palle Mikkelborg arrangements, has Gordon's debut on soprano and his freest playing on "Ernie's Tune." Otherwise these are quartet dates, good in and of themselves but not as good as *Go!.* I prefer *The Apartment,* which has the best rhythm section.

★ ★ ★ Homecoming / Col.
★ ★ ★ ★ Silver Blue / Xan.
★ ★ ★ Sophisticated Giant / Col.
★ ★ ★ True Blue / Xan.

Gordon made four heralded albums in this country right after his triumphal Bicentennial return—two jam sessions for Xanadu, the live twofer *Homecoming* with the Woody Shaw/Louis Hayes band and a small-orchestra album arranged by Slide Hampton. *Silver Blue* is the best, pitting Gordon in a side of tenor "battles" with Al Cohn that includes their unaccompanied duet "On the Trail." The Columbias were disappointing —*Homecoming* for giving too much space to Shaw and pianist Ronnie Mathews and for often inappropriate material, and *Sophisticated* for the ordinary writing and low-intensity tenor solos.

★ ★ ★ American Classic / Elek./Mus.
★ ★ ★ Best of Dexter Gordon / Col.
★ ★ ★ ★ Blows Hot & Cool / Doo.
★ ★ ★ ★ The Chase & the Steeple Chase (with Wardell Gray) / MCA
★ ★ ★ ★ Clubhouse / Blue N.
★ ★ ★ A Day in Copenhagen (with Slide Hampton) / Pausa

★ ★ ★ ★ Gotham City / Col.
★ ★ ★ Great Encounters / Col.
★ ★ ★ The Hunt (with Wardell Gray) / Savoy
★ ★ ★ Landslide / Blue N.
★ ★ ★ ★ ★ Lullaby for a Monster / Steep.
★ ★ ★ ★ Manhattan Symphonie / Col.
★ ★ ★ ★ Power / Prest. (includes The Tower of Power and More Power!)
★ ★ ★ Resurgence / Prest.
★ ★ ★ ★ ★ Something Different / Steep.

Gordon, building on the excitement generated by his 1976 homecoming, has become one of the two or three most popular tenor players around, and the subject of several new and reissued recordings. Unfortunately, his current work (on Columbia) lacks the overwhelming authority of his classic Blue Note sessions; even his tenor battles with Johnny Griffin on *Great Encounters* don't engender the expected fireworks. Still, *Manhattan Symphonie* is the best example of Gordon's recent quartet work, while *Gotham City* has superb playing from guests Art Blakey, Percy Heath, Cedar Walton and especially George Benson. Another less successful venture with guests is *American Classic,* where Gordon and Grover Washington collaborate over Shirley Scott's organ. Better than any of these, however, are two albums made shortly before Gordon's return to America: both *Something Different,* where Philip Catherine's guitar substitutes for the usual piano, and *Lullaby for a Monster,* with just bass and drums, contain some of Gordon's finest playing from any period.

From the reissues, search out the mid-Fifties *Blows Hot & Cool,* a taut set that has started to appear again in record stores. Both albums with fellow tenorman Wardell Gray capture the feel of the West Coast jam sessions of the late Forties and early Fifties, with a slight nod to the more compact performances on the MCA album. Of the previously unreleased Blue Notes, *Clubhouse* has Freddie Hubbard and Barry Harris along in a 1965 quintet that does one of the better long-metered funk tunes, "Devilette"; *Landslide* collects odds and ends. *Resurgence,* made in California shortly before Gordon's 1961 return to New York, is not up to the Blue Note sessions of the time.   — B.B.

JOE GORDON
★ ★ ★ Lookin' Good / Contem.

Bop trumpeter Joe Gordon (1928–1963) though never a barn burner or high-note artist, recorded a handful of better-than-average albums as a leader in the Fifties and Sixties. The 1961 *Lookin' Good* set is his only record currently available, and is well thought out and concisely executed. As a soloist, Gordon sounds relaxed and self-assured, drawing the same kind of performance out of his supporting musicians, saxophonist Jimmy Woods, pianist Dick Whittington, bassist Jimmy Bond and drummer Milt Turner. — F.G.

GRANT GREEN
★ ★ ★ Green Blues / Muse
★ ★ ★ ★ Iron City / Muse
★ ★ ★ ★ ★ Solid / Blue N.

St. Louis guitarist Grant Green (1931–1979) woodshedded in local jazz and R&B groups before coming to New York in the early Sixties, when his clean, driving rhythmic style made him a prized sideman on many of the soulful records being produced at the time on the Blue Note label. Green made a number of engaging records himself for Blue Note, none of which are currently in print except in Japanese facsimile import, but *Iron City* documents his Sixties style accurately. Try to find the exceptional *Solid*—it's worth the look. — J.S.

AL GREY
★ ★ ★ ★ Struttin' and Shoutin' / Col.

Trombonist par excellence, Al Grey (b. 1925) is a veteran of numerous big bands including those of Benny Carter, Count Basie, Lionel Hampton and Jimmie Lunceford. Entering his seventh decade, Grey is still capable of blowing the roof off any club.

Struttin' and Shoutin' is a nonet date with superior sidemen including Jimmy Forrest, Cecil Payne, Ray Bryant and Jack Jeffers. Although predominantly ballads and blues, the LP also includes a march, and the entire date has an energetic but familiar feel. Tenorman Forrest is particularly strong here. — F.G.

JOHNNY GRIFFIN
★ ★ ★ Big Soul / Mile.
★ ★ ★ Blowin' Sessions (with John Coltrane, Hank Mobley) / Blue N.
★ ★ ★ Bush Dance / Gal.
★ ★ ★ Call It Whachawana / Gal.
★ ★ ★ The Jamfs Are Coming (with Art Taylor) / Timel.
★ ★ ★ ★ ★ Little Giant / Mile.
★ ★ ★ ★ Little Giant / Fan./OJC
★ ★ ★ ★ Live! (with Eddie "Lockjaw" Davis) / Prest.
★ ★ ★ ★ Live, Vol. 2: The Late Show (with Davis) / Prest.
★ ★ ★ ★ Live at Minton's (with Davis) / Prest.
★ ★ ★ Live in Tokyo / Inner
★ ★ ★ ★ NYC Underground / Gal.
★ ★ ★ ★ ★ Return of the Griffin / Gal.
★ ★ ★ To the Ladies / Gal.
★ ★ ★ ★ The Toughest Tenors (with Davis) / Mile.
★ ★ ★ The Tough Tenors Again 'n' Again (with Davis) / Pausa
★ ★ ★ ★ ★ Way Out / Riv.

Johnny Griffin (b. 1928) is one of the classic hard-bop musicians. In the late Fifties, during his first period of prominence, he was considered the fastest tenor player around (this during the rise of John Coltrane), and his tone served as a definition of "wrenching." *Way Out,* one of his best sessions from this period, reveals Griffin in all his explosive glory. Some of these tracks are also available on the well-programed *Little Giant* survey. That anthology covers material released in OJC *Little Giant.* The first part of *Blowin' Sessions* is a bit long on sound and fury, as Griffin and Coltrane race while Mobley tries to keep up; the companion session with Clifford Jordan and John Gilmore is far better. *Big Soul* is an attempt at commercialism, with Griffin backed by big band and strings.

For three years, beginning in 1960, Griffin led a quintet with fellow tenor Eddie "Lockjaw" Davis, and the pair turned out consistently gritty battles. All of their recordings are exciting but plagued by watery piano solos from the likes of Junior Mance.

Like his friend Dexter Gordon, Griffin spent more than a decade in Europe before returning to a warm American welcome in the late Seventies. Unlike Gordon, however, the tempering effects of age have not always banked Griffin's fire. The frenzy of his past is clearly under control, but Griffin has learned to use it effectively as part of an expanded arsenal that has made him more commanding in other areas, such as ballad playing. *Return of the Griffin,* the first of his back-in-the-USA sessions, captures his current range best, although the exciting *NYC Underground,* taped at the Village Vanguard with Griffin's excellent quartet, is also highly recommended. *To the Ladies* attempts programmatic variety but several tracks are logy or overextended. *Call It Whachawana* is an '83 quartet session from Griffin's working group. Both *Jamfs* and *Live in Tokyo* are less impressive in-person efforts from the period before his return.

Griffin was also featured during the late Fifties on recordings by Art Blakey's Jazz Messengers and Thelonious Monk. — B.B.

STEVE GROSSMAN
★ ★ ★ **Perspective / Atl.**
★ ★ ★ **Some Shapes to Come / PM**
★ ★ ★ **Terra Firma / PM**

Tenor/soprano saxophonist Steve Grossman (b. 1952) came quickly to prominence in the early Seventies as a sideman in groups led by Miles Davis and Elvin Jones. His frenetic, high-energy style is well represented on these records. The PM sets include some fine keyboard work from ex-Mahavishnu Orchestra member Jan Hammer. — J.S.

GIGI GRYCE
★ ★ ★ ★ **The Gigi Gryce–Donald Byrd Jazz Laboratory and The Cecil Taylor Quartet at Newport (one side of an LP) / Verve**
★ ★ ★ ★ **The Rat Race Blues / Fan./OJC**
★ ★ ★ **When Farmer Met Gryce (with Art Farmer) / Fan./OJC**

Alto saxophonist, composer and bandleader, Gigi Gryce (1927–1983) was a subtle alto stylist and gifted arranger. On his instrument, he was one of the few players of his generation to absorb the impact of Charlie Parker without losing his own relaxed and blues-inflected style.

Rat Race Blues is composed entirely of poised blues compositions, and aside from Gryce's own contributions, it's further sparked by outstanding solos from trumpeter Richard Williams. Despite the presence of strong rhythm sections on *When Farmer Met Gryce*—Percy Heath, Horace Silver, Freddie Redd, Addison Farmer, Kenny Clarke and Arthur Taylor—the disc isn't quite as satisfying as *Rat Race Blues*. The coled date

with trumpeter Donald Byrd is the most adventuresome. — F.G.

VINCE GUARALDI
★ ★ ★ **At El Matador / Fan.**
★ ★ ★ **At Grace Cathedral / Fan.**
★ ★ ★ **Black Orpheus / Fan.**
★ ★ ★ **Bolo Sete and Friends / Fan.**
★ ★ ★ ★ **A Boy Named Charlie Brown / Fan.**
★ ★ ★ **From All Sides / Fan.**
★ ★ ★ **Good Grief / War.**
★ ★ ★ **Greatest Hits / Fan.**
★ ★ ★ **In Person / Fan.**
★ ★ ★ **Jazz Impressions / Fan.**
★ ★ ★ **Latin Side / Fan.**
★ ★ ★ **Vince Guaraldi Trio / Fan./OJC**

A bluesy and emotionally direct piano player, Vince Guaraldi (1928–1976) had an uncanny popular touch that distinguished him from many of his equally talented contemporaries. Guaraldi started out playing around his hometown of San Francisco in the Fifties with Cal Tjader, then later with Sonny Criss and Woody Herman. When he set out on his own as a leader, Guaraldi mastered a commercial touch with the hits "Jazz Impressions of Black Orpheus" and "Cast Your Fate to the Wind." One of the most intriguing aspects of his recording career is the fact that his finest work was the television soundtrack for the animated cartoon *A Boy Named Charlie Brown,* a series of beautifully programmatic portraits ranging from the Latin-jazz feel of the title theme to several Bill Evans-ish medium-tempo blues pieces. — J.S.

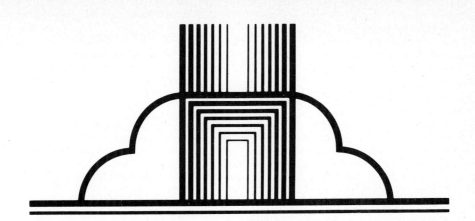

CHARLIE HADEN

★ ★ ★ ★ ★ **Closeness** / **Hori.**
★ ★ ★ ★ **The Golden Number** / **Hori.**
★ ★ ★ ★ ★ **Liberation Music Orchestra** /
  Imp.

Charlie Haden (b. 1937) established a role
for the bass in nonchordal improvised music
through his work with Ornette Coleman and
his startling plucking and strumming technique. Most of his career has been spent
with Coleman and Keith Jarrett, but he has
excellent recordings of his own. *Liberation
Music Orchestra* is a 1969 musical and political statement touching on the Spanish Civil
War, Vietnam and the Chicago convention,
with a railing orchestra containing Carla
Bley (who arranged), Don Cherry, Gato
Barbieri and others. *Closeness,* in contrast,
joins the bassist with Jarrett, Coleman, Alice
Coltrane and Paul Motian in four stunning
duets. *The Golden Number* also uses the
duet format, this time with Archie Shepp,
Hampton Hawes, Cherry and Coleman (on
trumpet).

★ ★ ★ ★ **As Long as There's Music (with
  Hampton Hawes)** / **Artists H.**
★ ★ ★ ★ **Ballad of the Fallen** / **ECM/War.**
★ ★ ★ **Folk Songs (as part of Magico, with
  Jan Garbarek and Egberto Gismonti)** /
  ECM/War.
★ ★ **Magico (with Garbarek and Gismonti)** /
  ECM/War.
★ ★ ★ ★ **Time Remembers One Time Once
  (with Denny Zeitlin)** / **ECM/PSI**

In addition to his work with the cooperative
quartet of Ornette Coleman alumni Old and
New Dreams, Haden continues to record in
more intimate settings. His duets with the
late pianist Hampton Hawes place the bassist
in a more traditional musical setting than
usual, and afford an uncommonly sensitive
glimpse of the sadly underrated Hawes.
Haden also records (and tours Europe) occasionally with Magico, a trio completed by

Norwegian saxophonist Jan Garbarek and
Brazilian guitarist/pianist Egberto Gismonti.
Unfortunately, Magico turns out some of the
most static and uninvolving music in the
ECM catalogue, a far cry from any of these
musicians' best work. *Folk Songs,* the
group's second album, is a better record than
Magico because the tracks are shorter.

Haden's duets with pianist Denny Zeitlin
provide one of the finest forums for his resonant, highly emotional conception. The intelligent program also underscores Zeitlin's
fondness for the late Bill Evans. Haden appeared as well on the all-star *Jazz at the
Opera House* (Columbia). He has also reorganized and recorded the Liberation Music
Orchestra on *Ballad of the Fallen.*

Soapsuds, Soapsuds, Haden's important
duet recording with Ornette Coleman, is discussed under Coleman's entry. — B.B.

JERRY HAHN

★ ★ ★ **Quintet** / **Arhoo.**

Jerry Hahn (b. 1940) is a jazz guitarist with
an ear for fusion playing who mixes styles
deftly. The Midwest native, who came to
recognition as part of the Gary Burton quintet, has recorded in a variety of contexts, but
this quintet setting is the only one remaining
in print. *Moses,* an out-of-print set on Fantasy, is worth looking for. — J.S.

JIM HALL

★ ★ ★ **Alone Together (with Ron Carter)** /
  Mile.
★ ★ ★ **Commitment** / **Hori.**
★ ★ ★ ★ **Concierto** / **CTI**
★ ★ ★ ★ **Jim Hall Live!** / **Hori.**
★ ★ ★ ★ **. . . Where Would I Be?** / **Mile.**

Lyrical invention, subtle swing and an uncompromising dedication to jazz mark the
understated guitar of Jim Hall (b. 1930), one
of the instrument's greatest stylists. The
above albums, all of which were recorded in

the Seventies, are consistent and never less than engaging.

. . . *Where Would I Be?* is a 1971 quartet with Airto Moreira on drums; Hall blows with calm assurance on a program heavily weighted with compositions by the guitarist and his wife. *Alone Together,* from the following year, is a live duo set with bassist Ron Carter. Both musicians are masters, but the consistently low-key mood detracts from the admittedly polished playing.

The year 1975 brought two Hall albums. *Concierto* has the distinction of being one of the most substantial records ever cut according to the CTI formula. A stellar band (Carter, Chet Baker, Paul Desmond, Roland Hanna, Steve Gadd) blow politely with Hall on a few tracks, then expand beneficially on arranger Don Sebesky's reworking of "Concierto de Aranjuez." *Jim Hall Live!* was done in Toronto with just bass and drums; despite the overextended ballad mood on side one, the record has some of Hall's best work, especially on the faster tracks. The mood might be called guitarish Bill Evans (with whom Hall has recorded several duets).

Commitment brought such simpatico players as Art Farmer and Tommy Flanagan into the studio with Hall, but a vocal track and another long Sebesky chart are unnecessary additions.

★ ★ ★ ★ **At the Village West (with Ron Carter)** / Conc.
★ ★ ★ **Circles** / Conc. J.
★ ★ ★ ★ **Jim Hall and Red Mitchell** / Artists H.

Circles is a typical Hall recital, a cut below the now out-of-print *Live!* album (which featured the same trio). On the Artists House disc, bassist Red Mitchell is a perfect partner for Hall, and their live duets take off—some of the time. The album is a slow starter, with most of the exceptional playing saved for side two, and the rating represents a compromise between excellent performances ("Fly Me to the Moon," "Blue Dove") and the merely workmanlike ("Big Blues," "Waltz New"). *At the Village West* is a 1984 live set with bassist Ron Carter. — B.B.

CHICO HAMILTON

★ ★ ★ ★ **Best** / MCA
★ ★ ★ **El Chico** / MCA
★ ★ ★ ★ **Gongs East** / Discov.
★ ★ ★ ★ **Man from Two Worlds** / MCA
★ ★ ★ ★ **Nomad** / Elek.
★ ★ ★ ★ **Passin' Through** / MCA
★ ★ ★ **Reaching for the Top** / Naut.

Drummer Foreststorn "Chico" Hamilton (b. 1921) played with Lionel Hampton, Lester Young, Gerry Mulligan's historic pianoless quartet and Count Basie and backed Lena Horne while taking part-time gigs dubbing movie soundtracks, such as the Hope/Crosby *Road to Bali.* In '54 Hamilton began leading his own band which appeared in films in 1957 (*Sweet Smell of Success*) and 1959 (*Jazz on a Summer's Day*). The latter group featured the then-unknown Eric Dolphy on alto sax/flute/bass clarinet. Dolphy, whose work with Hamilton soon made him one of the more respected musicians on the scene, enhanced Hamilton's reputation as a leader. Hamilton has made it a habit to introduce new talents ever since, providing a forum for guitarists Gabor Szabo and Larry Coryell, saxophonist/flutist Charles Lloyd and altoist Arthur Blythe. Much of Hamilton's recorded legacy is unavailable but *Gongs East* spotlights Dolphy, *Man from Two Worlds* and *Passin' Through* are with the Lloyd/Szabo group, and the Latin-based *El Chico* adds percussionists for an extra twist to Hamilton's delightfully mesmerizing rhythm patterns. — J.S.

JAN HAMMER

★ ★ ★ ★ **The First Seven Days** / Nemp.
★ ★ ★ **Melodies** / Nemp.
★ ★ ★ ★ **Oh, Yeah?** / Nemp.
★ ★ ★ **Timeless** / ECM/War.

Jan Hammer (b. 1948) became well known as John McLaughlin's multi-keyboardist in the Mahavishnu Orchestra. He plays adventurous space music with John Abercrombie and Jack DeJohnette on 1974's sinewy *Timeless.* But his latent love was R&B, and Hammer came out of the closet for his series on Nemperor; in 1975 his earth-hued *Seven Days* realized the sublimest meld of humanism with the new Electric Gestalt. For *Oh, Yeah?* (not to be confused with the 1962 Charlie Mingus album on Atlantic), he took along a talented young violinist named Steve Kindler (another ex-McLaughlin) plus drummer/lead singer Tony Smith (ex-Malo and Azteca) and bassist/vocalist Fernando Saunders in the rhythm battery. This has been his band ever since—it also backed up Jeff Beck on his 1976 tour. Trading concept for some mean blowing funk, *Oh, Yeah?* and *Melodies* leave behind the *musique-concrète,* digital sequencer, multitrack tape collage and sophistication of *Seven Days.* In fact, the sound has become closer to progressive R&B than Hammer's jazz roots over the years. — B.M.

GUNTER HAMPEL
★ ★ ★ ★ **All the Things You Could Be If Charles Mingus Was Your Daddy / Birth**
★ ★ ★ **Angel / Birth**
★ ★ ★ **Broadway / Birth**
★ ★ ★ **Cavana (Vol. 1) / Birth**
★ ★ ★ **Dances / Birth**
★ ★ ★ **The 8th of July 1969 / Birth**
★ ★ ★ **Enfant Terrible / Birth**
★ ★ ★ **Freedom of the Universe / Birth**
★ ★ ★ ★ **Journey to the Song Within / Birth**
★ ★ ★ ★ **That Came Down on Me / Birth**
Bandleader, composer and multi-instrumentalist (vibes, piano, reeds and percussion), Gunter Hampel (b. 1937) has been a dedicated workhorse among the experimentalists during the Sixties, Seventies and Eighties. With approximately forty albums on his own Birth label, Hampel's recorded work represents an encyclopedia of the avant-garde while closely describing the links between the jazz tradition and new compositional directions.

One of Hampel's major strengths has been his ability to recognize and attract first-rate sidemen for his Galaxie Dream Band, including reedmen Anthony Braxton, Mark Whitecage and Perry Robinson, as well as drummer Sunny Murray and vocalist Jeanne Lee.

The breadth of his catalogue also affords an opportunity to hear Hampel in nearly every conceivable setting: *Dances* is a solo performance; *Freedom of the Universe,* a duo with Lee; *Cavana,* a big-band date. The remaining recommended LPs feature small-to-medium-sized groups. The most recent dates, especially *All the Things* and *Cavana,* effect a link between Hampel's own freewheeling compositions and the big-band masters.
— F.G.

LIONEL HAMPTON
★ ★ ★ ★ ★ **Lionel Hampton / RCA (France)**
★ ★ ★ ★ ★ **Lionel Hampton Vols. 1 and 2 / RCA (France)**
★ ★ ★ ★ **Rarities / MCA**
Vibraphonist, drummer, pianist, vocalist, bandleader Lionel Hampton (b. 1913) was a sought-after player during the Thirties, working with the Les Hite orchestra and then in Benny Goodman's band during the late Thirties. Though he formed his own outfit in 1940, Hampton had already been leading pickup recording dates featuring some of the biggest names in jazz. These are the sides collected on the French Black and White LPs, with *Lionel Hampton,* a three-record set, offering the strongest coverage.

Rarities covers Hampton band recordings from 1946 and 1949. Hampton had one of the loudest and most popular swing bands of the era, and the group's performances hold up extremely well over the years. — J.S.

HERBIE HANCOCK
★ ★ ★ **The Best of Herbie Hancock / Blue N.**
★ ★ ★ **Herbie Hancock / Blue N.**
The career and music of Herbie Hancock (b. 1940) have gone through some significant changes that reflect trends occurring throughout the jazz world. The above albums are both anthologies from his Blue Note years (1962–69) that contain material available on albums still in print. Neither album is representative of Hancock's true range.
★ ★ ★ **My Point of View / Blue N.**
★ ★ ★ ★ **Takin' Off / Blue N.**
Donald Byrd introduced Hancock to New York, and the young pianist/composer quickly revealed himself as someone who could write and play with taste, soul, daring, romanticism—whatever the situation called for. His first album did indeed take off, after his "Watermelon Man" became a pop hit in Mongo Santamaria's cover version. Dexter Gordon and Freddie Hubbard contributed to that first effort. The sequel, despite a couple of interesting tunes and more good sidemen (Byrd, Hank Mobley, Tony Williams), suffered from an excess of material tailored to the soul trade.
★ ★ ★ ★ ★ **Empyrean Isles / Blue N.**
★ ★ ★ ★ ★ **Maiden Voyage / Blue N.**
★ ★ ★ **Succotash / Pausa**
Hancock's work took a more experimental tack after he worked with Eric Dolphy briefly in 1962, and the forms used in his compositions became more harmonically and structurally diverse. His lyricism remained, however, nurtured no doubt by his association with Miles Davis, which began in 1963. *Succotash* has no horns and very loose compositions that the supporting players, with their heads still in bop, fail to energize. The other two, *Empyrean* and *Maiden,* are masterpieces of the modal period. Both have Hubbard, Williams and Ron Carter (the latter two were Hancock's mates in Davis' rhythm section), and George Coleman's tenor is added on *Maiden.* The music is occasionally blue or unbounded but always lean, intelligent and beautiful.
★ ★ **Fat Albert Rotunda / War.**
★ ★ ★ ★ **The Prisoner / Blue N.**
★ ★ ★ **Speak Like a Child / Blue N.**
Speak, from 1968, finds Hancock employing

a sextet with a front line of fluegelhorn, bass trombone and alto flute that produced impressionistic textures in a Gil Evans style. The piano solos are more attuned to mood than before, and the album is a bit too concerned with prettiness. Shortly after this album, Hancock left Davis and formed his own sextet, which utilized the distinctive three-horn blend to more robust effect. Johnny Coles (fluegelhorn) and Joe Henderson (tenor) were the prime soloists besides Hancock. *The Prisoner* is the better of this band's two albums, and the first of Hancock's to feature electric piano. *Fat Albert,* with music from a cartoon special, is tedious funk showing little indication of Hancock's later success in the genre.

★ ★ ★ ★ **Crossings** / War.
★ ★ ★ **Mwandishi** / War.
★ ★ ★ **Sextant** / Col.

The 1970–73 Hancock band—with Eddie Henderson, trumpet; Julian Priester, trombones; Bennie Maupin, reeds; Buster Williams, basses; Billy Hart, drums; Patrick Gleeson, synthesizers—often tried to push in several directions at once. By turns free, jazz-rock, romantic and straight-ahead, it revealed and sometimes mastered a world of possibilities, but its recordings are often defeated by an excess of bass-line vamps or electronic overlays. *Crossings* is the best of the lot.

★ ★ **"Death Wish" Soundtrack** / Col.
★ ★ ★ **Head Hunters** / Col.
★ ★ **Man-Child** / Col.
★ **Secrets** / Col.
★ ★ ★ **Thrust** / Col.

Hancock moved to funk just in time to get in on the ground floor of disco, a trend his *Head Hunters* (and particularly the lead cut "Chameleon") was made for. The shift entailed Hancock's keeping Bennie Maupin as the only horn, doing all his own synthesizer work, hiring funk rhythm players like Paul Jackson, Harvey Mason and Bill Summers, and writing simpler compositions that stressed the beat instead of complex improvisations. *Head Hunters* was the first jazz album to be certified gold, so more of the same followed, and the formula quickly became stale.

★ ★ ★ ★ ★ **The Quintet** / Col.
★ ★ ★ ★ ★ **V.S.O.P.** / Col.

Just when most jazz listeners had written Hancock off, the pianist looked over his shoulder and returned to his real strength. *V.S.O.P.* was done at a 1976 Newport retrospective concert and features two sides of what quickly became the Quintet (Hubbard, Wayne Shorter, Hancock, Carter, Williams),

one side of the *Mwandishi* band and one side of the *Secrets* funk group. Hancock plays so much music on his electric grand piano he even salvages the tired licks of the final side.

The Quintet is more a collective effort than a Hancock album, with all five players contributing pieces and the pianist strictly acoustic (with one brief exception). Hancock's solos are much more reserved than on *V.S.O.P.,* but he comps marvelously and everyone else is very hot.

★ ★ **Best of Herbie Hancock** / Col.
★ ★ ★ ★ **Corea/Hancock (with Chick Corea)** / Poly.
★ ★ ★ ★ ★ **An Evening with Herbie Hancock & Chick Corea in Concert** / Col.
★ **Feets Don't Fail Me Now** / Col.
★ ★ **Future Shock** / Col.
★ ★ ★ ★ **Herbie Hancock Quartet** / Col.
★ **Lite Me Up** / Col.
★ ★ ★ ★ **Live under the Sky (with V.S.O.P.)** / Col.
★ **Magic Windows** / Col.
★ ★ ★ ★ **Mr. Hands** / Col.
★ **Monster** / Col.
★ ★ **Sound System** / Col.

Herbie Hancock has pursued three distinct directions in recent years. His Columbia albums continue to focus on fusion, and while *Feets, Lite, Magic* and *Monster* have virtually no interest from a jazz perspective, overladen as they are with vocoders and other gimmickry, *Mr. Hands* is actually a pretty good crossover sampler, as Hancock tries out various keyboards and rhythms against an ever-changing parade of his favorite bassists and drummers. (*Sunlight,* which also wasn't bad, has already been deleted.) *Future Shock* and *Sound System*, Hancock's most recent pop efforts, find him teaming with producer/players Material for extremely contemporary and extremely tedious dance mixes. "Rockit," the single from *Future Shock,* became a Grammy-award-winning hit.

During the winter of 1978, Hancock and Chick Corea did a series of acoustic piano duet concerts that featured some of the best playing from either man in recent years. Both Columbia and Polydor released two-record albums that capture representative concerts, with the nod going to Columbia for a better mix of standards and originals. The Polydor has a bit of Bartok, however. Both conclude with long, long medleys of "Maiden Voyage" and Corea's "La Fiesta."

The V.S.O.P. quintet has also been reorganized from time to time, and was most recently recorded digitally (*Under the Sky*) at a rain-soaked 1979 Tokyo concert that features particularly strong contributions from

Ron Carter. A later (1981) variation on V.S.
O.P.—with Hancock, Carter, Williams and
young trumpeter Wynton Marsalis—can be
heard on *Quartet,* evidence of the continuing
validity of mid-Sixties acoustic Miles Davis.
Minus Marsalis, this rhythm section becomes
a trio on Ron Carter's *Third Plane;* while
Hancock also appears on *Jazz at the Opera
House* (Columbia) and *Bill Evans—A Tribute* (Palo Alto Jazz). — B.B.

JOHN HANDY
★ Carnival / Imp.
★ Hard Work / Imp.
★ ★ ★ Live at the Monterey Jazz Festival /
   Col.
★ ★ ★ ★ New View! / Col.
Everything used to be high, loud and long
from this California alto sax player. John
Handy (b. 1933) was able to give his music a
pop orientation (with the help of, first, guitarist Jerry Hahn and then Pat Martino and
jazz violinist Mike White) without crass
commercialism, and what he lacked in importance, he made up for with sheer stam-
ina.

Then, after a nearly decade-long hiatus
during which he was teaching, Handy suddenly turned up on Impulse with a pair of
albums, proving that underneath that sometimes hot high register was a flaccid, sloppy,
lowest-common-denominator, lower register.
— A.E.G.

ROLAND HANNA
★ ★ Gershwin, Carmichael Cats / CTI
★ ★ ★ A Gift from the Magi / West 54
★ ★ ★ Perugia / Ari.
★ ★ ★ Plays the Music of Alec Wilder /
   Inner
★ ★ ★ Sir Elf / Choice
★ ★ ★ Sir Elf + 1 / Choice
★ ★ ★ Swing Me No Waltzes / Story.
★ ★ ★ Time for the Dancers / Prog.
Roland Hanna (b. 1932) is a pianist one has
to admire, but can't always enjoy. His florid,
highly romantic style is often marred by an
oppressively heavy touch. Hanna always
swings and never runs out of ideas, but even
his best work has an off-putting quality. This
classically trained musician rarely sounds as
if he *enjoys* playing jazz.

Because of his prodigious skills, Hanna
likes to record solo albums. With the aforementioned reservations, all those listed above
are impressive, but *+ 1* and *Time for the
Dancers,* with bassist George Mraz, display
more of Hanna's engagingly playful side.
The one large group date, *Gershwin,* doesn't
come off at all. — S.F.

KIP HANRAHAN
★ ★ ★ ★ Coup de Tête / Amer. C.
★ ★ ★ ★ Desire Develops an Edge / Amer.
   C.
A real anomaly, Kip Hanrahan (b. 1937) is
one of those rare people who knows precious
little about music, but has managed to make
a couple of very musical and timely albums.
A former clerk at New York experimental
music wholesaler New Music Distribution
Service, Hanrahan formed his own American
Clave label in 1980, recording and releasing
albums by Latin-jazz percussionist Jerry
Gonzalez and Soho art/noise boys DNA.

On his own first album, *Coup de Tête,*
Hanrahan's time at New Music proved well
spent; he employed the cream of New York's
underground, including Fred Frith, Arto
Lindsay, Bill Laswell, Anton Fier and Billy
Bang. Ted Macero, Carla Bley, Mike Mantler, Jamaaladeen Tacuma, Chico Freeman
and Carlos Ward also made cameo appearances, and the results were a not-so-small
victory for a fusion of seemingly disparate
musics. Hanrahan's lyrics were frequently
less than lucid, though, and his voice could
become tiresome. But those were mighty
small beefs when stacked against the album
as a whole.

Hanrahan recedes further into the background on his second album, *Desire Develops
an Edge,* handing vocal duties over to Jack
Bruce. The LP has a stronger Latin component than its predecessor, but its passion is
partly obscured by an inability to trim out
the fat. Released as an album-plus-EP, *Desire* would have been better as a single record. Still, Hanrahan has a fresh perspective
and should continue developing. — F.G.

BILL HARDMAN
★ ★ ★ ★ Focus / Muse
★ ★ ★ ★ Home / Muse
★ ★ ★ ★ Politely / Muse
Trumpeter Bill Hardman (b. 1933) and ten-
orman Junior Cook (b. 1934) occasionally
colead one of the finest hard-bop outfits
around. This isn't the Brownie/Roach band
but it is at least as good as most of the stuff
Blakey's been doing and there's nothing
wrong with that. Hardman also appears on
Cook's *Good Cookin'* album for Muse, where
the band is similar to the one on *Home.*
— F.G.

HAGOOD HARDY
★ Homecoming / Cap.
A mousy Canadian pianist and composer,
Hagood Hardy wrote ad music and still
scores the occasional movie. His one album

features Hardy's "stylings" in cushy arrangements favored on MOR radio. — B.T.

HARLEM HAMFATS
★ ★ ★ ★ **Hot Chicago Jazz, Blues and Jive 1936–37 / Arhoo.**
This engaging seven-piece group was led by New Orleans trumpeter Herb Morand, whose high-intensity playing derived from the fiery style of Louis Armstrong. The Hamfats' stomping attack, combined with Joe McCoy's guttural vocals over a simple, driving country-blues-style rhythm guitar accompaniment, eventually produced a new sound that anticipated the Chicago blues of the postwar era. The strange mixture of New Orleans jazz and blues is underscored here by the rest of the group's instrumentation— clarinet, piano, drums, string bass and mandolin. "Oh, Red," their first record, was an infectious hit that pretty much defined the Hamfats style and was a very obvious influence on, among others, Muddy Waters.
— J.S.

BARRY HARRIS
★ ★ **At the Jazz Workshop / Riv.**
★ ★ ★ ★ **Bull's Eye / Prest.**
★ ★ ★ ★ **In Tokyo: 1976 / Xan.**
★ ★ ★ **Live in Tokyo / Xan.**
★ ★ ★ **Luminescence! / Prest.**
★ ★ ★ ★ **The Magnificent! / Prest.**
★ ★ ★ **Plays Barry Harris / Xan.**
★ ★ **Plays Tadd Dameron / Xan.**
★ ★ ★ **Preminado / Riv.**
★ ★ **Stay Right with It / Mile.**
Because of his dedication, experience and undeniable technical skills there has been a tendency to overrate Barry Harris (b. 1929). A true second-generation bopman—he made his first records a year after Parker died— Harris immediately fell under the spell of pianist Bud Powell. While never a copyist, Harris' own playing was so reminiscent of the older pianist's, minus the manic intensity and creativity, that his early Riverside albums are marked by a disturbing sense of déjà vu.

The Prestige LPs show a marked growth; Harris began to let Monk and others seep into his playing. Still, compared to the expansive attitude of his contemporary Tommy Flanagan, Harris sounds mired in a period that has passed. He refines, but doesn't extend, the bop tradition.

The Magnificent!, with Ron Carter on bass, is the best of the trio dates, and *Bull's Eye,* with Kenny Dorham and Pepper Adams, clearly outshines *Luminescence!,* the other "plus horns" LP.

Harris' style, always precise if never really exciting, became more flexible and expressive during his Seventies stint for Xanadu, but the context of his work refused to change. Even on an LP of all-original material, *Plays Barry Harris,* the frameworks were inevitably "Cherokee" and "How High the Moon" variations.

In Tokyo: 1976 is a typically fine trio recording, but even here a nagging temptation to pull out the old Bud Powell Blue Notes and listen to the real thing still persists. Harris' true talent seems to be as a sideman; his sympathetic support and concise solo statements can be heard with Sonny Stitt, Charles McPherson, Al Cohn and many others on the Prestige, Riverside and Xanadu labels. — S.F.

BEAVER HARRIS
★ ★ ★ ★ ★ **From Rag Time to No Time / 360 Rec.**
★ ★ ★ ★ **In: Sanity / Black S.**
A sideman with Thelonious Monk, Archie Shepp, Sonny Rollins and Roswell Rudd before striking out on his own, drummer Beaver Harris (b. 1936) has focused on demonstrating the continuum between Third World musics and jazz's traditional and experimental forms with his own group, the 360 Degree Music Experience. While well schooled on his instrument, Harris is far more than a bright student; his versatility as both soloist and composer is everywhere in evidence on *From Rag Time to No Time,* a brilliant demonstration of the universality of rhythm and music. This first album has stronger roots in jazz and lacks the excesses found on *In: Sanity.* However, the latter's "Sahara" is an unequivocally exuberant offering, so charged with life by steel drummer Frances Haynes and his ensemble, that it makes one forgive the album's overly indulgent moments.
— F.G.

EDDIE HARRIS
★ ★ ★ ★ **Best of / Atl.**
★ ★ **Black Sax / GNP**
★ ★ **Cool Sax, Warm Heart / Col.**
★ ★ **E.H. in the U.K. / Atco**
★ ★ ★ **Exciting Eddie Harris / Kent**
★ ★ **Genius of Eddie Harris / Trad.**
★ ★ **How Can You Live Like That / Atco**
★ ★ ★ **Second Movement / Atl.**
★ ★ **Shades of Eddie Harris / Trad.**
★ ★ **Sounds Incredible / Angelaco**
★ ★ **Steps Up / Steep.**
★ ★ ★ ★ **Swiss Movement / Atco**
★ ★ **That Is Why You're Overweight / Atco**
★ ★ ★ **The Versatile Eddie Harris / Atl.**

Though tenor saxophonist Eddie Harris (b. 1936) first became known to the public through a 1960 ballad hit, a cover of the theme music for the film *Exodus,* his best work was recorded for Atlantic later in his career. Like many other important jazz musicians, Harris has since suffered from Atlantic's ruthless cutout policy, and much of his best work is now out of print.

Harris became one of the first jazz musicians to successfully adapt electronic effects to his horn with the 1968 album, *The Electrifying Eddie Harris,* which featured the space-funk classic "Listen Here." The album is now unavailable, but "Listen Here" is on the *Best of* collection.

Only the Atlantic/Atco records are truly representative of Harris, and aside from *Best of,* the only good ones left in print are the collaborations with keyboardist Les McCann, *Swiss Movement* and *Second Movement.* The later albums show Harris in search of another commercial formula, and to that end, reduced to singing, which usually spells disaster. Check for *Excursions, Compared to What* and the tremendous *Is It In* in cutout bins. — J.S.

JOHNNY HARTMAN

★ ★ ★ ★ **I Just Dropped by to Say Hello /
MCA**
★ ★ ★ ★ ★ **John Coltrane and Johnny
Hartman / MCA/Imp.**
★ ★ ★ ★ **Once in Every Lifetime / Bee**
★ ★ ★ ★ **The Voice that Is / MCA**

Johnny Hartman (1923–1983) was a velvet-rich Eckstine-influenced vocalist. Everybody has what they consider to be the definitive version of "Lush Life," and mine is on the Coltrane album. That disc is composed entirely of standards, and Coltrane's magnificent ballad work compliments Hartman's vocals so naturally that it's almost eerie. If *Once in Every Lifetime* falls short of the Coltrane collaboration, it's simply because the Impulse recording is as close to perfection as anyone is ever going to get. The Bee Hive date features a strong band with Frank Wess, Joe Wilder, Al Gafa and Billy Taylor, and the seventeen years between the two dates haven't hurt Hartman's voice a bit. — F.G.

HAMPTON HAWES

★ ★ ★ ★ **All Night Session, Vol. 1 /
Contem.**
★ ★ ★ **All Night Session, Vol. 2 / Contem.**
★ ★ ★ **All Night Session, Vol. 3 / Contem.**
★ ★ ★ ★ **For Real! / Contem.**
★ ★ ★ **Four! / Contem./OJC**
★ ★ ★ **The Green Leaves of Summer /
Contem.**
★ ★ ★ **Hampton Hawes at the Piano /
Contem.**
★ ★ ★ **Here and Now / Cont./OJC**
★ ★ ★ **I'm All Smiles / Contem.**
★ ★ ★ **Playin' in the Yard / Prest.**
★ ★ ★ **The Seance / Contem.**
★ ★ ★ **The Trio, Vol. 1 / Contem.**
★ ★ ★ **The Trio, Vol. 2 / Contem.**
★ ★ ★ **The Trio, Vol. 3 / Contem.**

Pianist Hampton Hawes (1928–1977) began his career in the late Forties gigging around his Los Angeles hometown with Big Jay McNeely. Hawes' bop-era keyboard style was influenced tremendously by Charlie Parker, whom Hawes played with in Howard McGee's band in 1947. Hawes worked with Wardell Grey, Red Norvo and Dexter Gordon before being drafted, and began recording in earnest when he returned to the scene in 1955.

The Trio LPs, with bassist Red Mitchell and drummer Chuck Thompson, date from 1955 and lead off with the jamming standard "I Got Rhythm" on Volume 1. The *All Night Session* sides, recorded in '56, also include Mitchell along with drummer Bruz Freeman, and add guitarist Jim Hall. Volumes 1 and 2 feature inspired takes of a number of Dizzy Gillespie tunes ("Groovin' High," "Two Bass Hit," "Blue 'n' Boogie," "Woody 'n' You"). *For Real!* is a hot '58 session with bassist Scott LaFaro, drummer Frank Butler and tenor saxophonist Harold Land.

Green Leaves of Summer, Here and Now I'm All Smiles and *The Seance* are trio LPs from the mid-Sixties. Hawes began playing electric as well as acoustic piano during the Seventies with very good results, as the live *Playin' in the Yard* indicates. On his last recording, *Hampton Hawes at the Piano,* he returned to Contemporary and the acoustic trio format he had become known for in the Fifties, accompanied by bassist Ray Brown and drummer Shelly Manne. Hawes was a gifted player who was never really given the credit he deserved. His soulful blues base always kept his music emotionally well grounded without being cliché-ridden. Hawes' moving autobiography, *Raise Up Off Me,* is well worth reading. — J.S.

COLEMAN HAWKINS

★ ★ ★ **Blues Groove / Prest.**
★ ★ ★ **Classic Tenors / Doctor J.**
★ ★ ★ ★ **Coleman Hawkins Vol. 1 / RCA
(France)**

★ ★ ★ ★ Coleman Hawkins at Newport / Verve
★ ★ ★ ★ Coleman Hawkins Encounters Ben Webster / Verve
★ ★ ★ Coleman Hawkins Meets the Big Sax Section / Savoy
★ ★ ★ ★ The Complete Coleman Hawkins / RCA (France)
★ ★ ★ Hawk Eyes! / Prest.
★ ★ ★ The Hawk Flies / Mile.
★ ★ ★ Jazz Reunion / Jazz M.
★ ★ ★ ★ Night Hawk / Prest.
★ ★ ★ Pioneers / Prest.
★ ★ ★ The Real Thing / Prest.
★ ★ ★ Sirius / Pablo
★ ★ ★ Tenor Tantrums / Acc.
★ ★ ★ ★ Thanks for the Memory / Xan.
★ ★ ★ Very Saxy / Prest.

A contemporary of Louis Armstrong, Coleman Hawkins (1904–1969) was influenced strongly by Armstrong's sharp, percussive style during his early days with the Fletcher Henderson band (1923), when Armstrong was also with that outfit. But Hawkins soon developed his own hard-hitting, full-throated tenor style, and is widely considered to be the first tenor saxophone soloist of note. He certainly had a lot to do with the tenor sax becoming as popular a jazz instrument as the trumpet. In fact, Hawkins influenced every tenor player after him and carved out a style for the instrument that was to dominate jazz for a decade until Lester Young popularized a cooler, more relaxed approach.

Hawkins became quickly acknowledged as the world's greatest tenor player during his stint with Henderson, which lasted until 1934. After a five-year stay in Europe, he recorded his most famous track, "Body and Soul," in 1939, setting an approach for reworking standard ballads that was to become the favorite format for the tenor saxophone showcase. A consummate musician with an open mind to experimentation, Hawkins embraced the small-combo bebop era of the Forties when many of his contemporaries from the big-band era disdained it. In almost every context he played, Hawkins managed to turn the convention into a statement of his playing's warm, rich personality.

Though Hawkins made many records, only a handful of his later LPs remain in print. Over half of the titles that were available as of 1980 have already disappeared. Of the still-remaining LPs, the live 1957 set from Newport and the meeting with one of Hawkins' protégés, Ben Webster, recorded in 1957, sound best. The recently deleted Impulse sides worth looking for in cutout bins are *Duke Ellington Meets Coleman Hawkins* and *Today and Now*. There is hardly a more moving record than *Sirius,* a disc made shortly before Hawkins' death in 1969. Even when ill health had enfeebled him, he still managed to express powerful emotion through his saxophone. The poor condition of the Hawkins catalogue is a sad commentary on the fickle nature of the recording industry. — J.S.

ROY HAYNES
★ ★ ★ ★ Bad News / Prest.
★ ★ ★ ★ Out of the Afternoon / MCA
★ ★ ★ Thank You / Gal.
★ ★ ★ Vistalite / Gal.

Roy Haynes (b. 1926) is a superb technician who was one of the most musically accomplished of all postwar drummers. Though his style was originally inspired by Jo Jones' playing with Count Basie, Haynes made a name for himself during the bop revolution via its headquarters on 52nd Street in New York. The list of musicians Haynes played with is a bop-era *Who's Who*: Charlie Parker, John Lewis, Lester Young, Sonny Rollins, Thelonious Monk, Kai Winding, Phineas Newborn, Miles Davis, Lennie Tristano, George Shearing, Lee Konitz, and Sarah Vaughan to name just a few. He replaced Elvin Jones for a year in the classic John Coltrane quartet and was part of the historic prefusion Gary Burton quartet with Larry Coryell. Partially because of his value as an ensemble player, Haynes has been a sought-after session star and is thus somewhat underrecorded as a leader.

As with so many of his contemporaries, what Haynes did record is not easy to come by, but of the available records, *Bad News,* with Booker Ervin, and *Out of the Afternoon,* with Roland Kirk, are highly recommended. — J.S.

ALBERT HEATH
★ ★ ★ ★ Kwanza (The First) / Muse

Long an outstanding sideman, drummer Albert "Tootie" Heath (b. 1935) has worked with brothers Jimmy (saxes) and Percy (bass) as the Heath Brothers, an outfit foreshadowed by 1973's *Kwanza,* Albert's only session as leader. A varied and strong LP, the album finds Heath experimenting with a variety of percussion instruments and writing rhythmically complex tunes. But it's not a drumming record. Brother Jimmy and guitarist Ted Dunbar hold down the frontmen duties. — B.T.

JIMMY HEATH
★ ★ ★ Fast Company / Mile.
★ ★ ★ ★ Jimmy / Muse
★ ★ ★ ★ Love and Understanding / Muse

★ ★ ★ Picture of Heath / Xan.
★ ★ ★ Swamp Seed / Riv.
The main writer and soloist of the Heath
Brothers (with brother Percy on bass), saxo-
phonist/flutist/composer Jimmy Heath (b.
1926) was long a respected young heir to the
tradition of Charlie Parker while working his
way up as sideman for established bop leaders like Dizzy Gillespie. A valued composer,
he has written for Miles Davis, Chet Baker
and Nat Adderley among others. Heath has
led his own sessions since 1959 but really hit
his stride during the late Sixties as a melodically rich and warm tenor player and moder-
ately experimental arranger (under the acknowledged tutelage of Yusef Lateef).

Heath's Seventies cycle of albums, especially *Jimmy* (1972), *Love and Understanding* (1973) and *Picture of Heath* (1975), provide an excellent portrait of his mature
authority as both writer and improviser.
— B.T.

HEATH BROTHERS
★ ★ ★ ★ ★ Brotherly Love / Ant.
★ ★ ★ ★ Brothers and Others / Ant.
★ ★ ★ Expressions of Life / Col.
★ ★ ★ In Motion / Col.
★ ★ ★ Live at the Public Theater / Col.
★ ★ ★ Marchin' On / Strata-East
★ ★ ★ Passing Thru / Col.
Here is a very talented family band—
featuring saxophonist/composer Jimmy (b.
1926), bassist Percy (b. 1923), and at times
drummer Albert (b. 1935)—that has simply
never been able to rise to the level of its potential. The ingredients are certainly in place:
Jimmy is one of modern jazz's best writers,
Percy a legendary bassist, Stanley Cowell
(another good composer) has filled the piano
chair from the outset, and the other sidemen
(guitarist Tony Purrone, drummers Keith
Copeland, then Akira Tana after Albert's departure) have never been less than first-rate.
But the Heath Brothers play it safe. They
don't take full advantage of Cowell's presence, and continually opt for Jimmy's most
commercial material. On *Live* and *Expressions* they have even allowed Jimmy's son
Mtume to insert some truly forgettable funk.
Yet even these last albums contain moments
of comfortable blowing, and Jimmy manages
to slip little twists into even his most innocu-
ous pieces. *Passing Thru* was the best of a
consistently okay lot until the band's recording career was substantially upgraded in
1982 with *Brotherly Love*, which eschews
gimmicks and allows the quintet to open up
for their strongest recital yet. *Brothers and
Others* continues that healthy trend. — B.B.

JULIUS HEMPHILL
★ ★ ★ Flat-Out Jump Suite / Black S.
★ ★ ★ ★ Raw Materials and Residuals /
Black S.
★ ★ Roy Boye and the Gotham Minstrels /
Sack.
Julius Hemphill (b. 1938) is another impor-
tant saxophonist out of the midwestern col-
lective movement. Born in Texas, he was a
founding member of St. Louis's Black Artists
Group and made some fine independent re-
cordings in the early Seventies. (*Dogon A.D.,*
a prophetic conjunction of new music and
funk, was reissued, then again deleted, on
Arista/Freedom.) In more recent years,
Hemphill has been the primary composi-
tional force behind the exceptional World
Saxophone Quartet (see separate entry).

The above albums were made in the late
Seventies for Canadian and Italian labels,
and show Hemphill to be a challenging
writer and conceptualizer even when his improvising falls short. *Raw Materials* is the
best place to hear his alto sax (his primary
horn), in an excellent trio completed by cellist Abdul Wadud and percussionist Don
Moye. On *Flat-Out* Hemphill plays tenor
and flute, and has another fine band with
trumpeter Olu Dara, Wadud and drummer
Warren Smith. The program is extremely
well plotted, but Hemphill's own playing is
not particularly inspired. *Roy Boye,* a solo
piece with prerecorded tape accompaniment,
stretches out over four sides and is simply
too much of a good idea that would have
functioned better if contrasted with some of
Hemphill's other pieces.

Hemphill can also be heard in duet with
Oliver Lake. — B.B.

EDDIE HENDERSON
★ ★ ★ Heritage / Blue N.
★ ★ ★ Inside Out / Capri.
★ ★ ★ Realization / Capri.
★ ★ ★ Sunburst / Blue N.
Trumpeter/fluegelhornist Eddie Henderson
(b. 1940) was first featured in Herbie Hancock's early-Seventies electric unit. Inspired
and guided by Miles Davis' *Bitches Brew,*
the band played angular riffs and solos over
shifting patterns of ostinato rhythms. The
experience also gave Henderson a conceptual
framework (plus most of the personnel) for
his first two Capricorn albums. Though a bit
impenetrable at times, both LPs still manage
to make the *Brew* formula, already incisive,
more accessible.

But in 1975, after moving to Blue Note,
Henderson rendered his music even more
communicable; he moved into funk, and tex-
tural emphasis gave way to simpler struc-

ture. Yet he didn't lose his cerebral stance completely; *Heritage,* his best record, mixes danceable grooves with minor-key cutting-edge lyricism, plus Henderson's uncompromisingly linear style on electric horns. It's a nice blend of two worlds. — M.R.

FLETCHER HENDERSON

★ ★ ★ ★ **The Complete Fletcher Henderson 1927–1936 / Blueb.**

★ ★ ★ ★ **Developing an American Orchestra 1923–1937 / Smithsonian (available by mail only from Smithsonian Recordings, P.O. Box 10230, Des Moines, Iowa 50336)**

★ ★ ★ ★ **The Immortal Fletcher Henderson / Mile.**

★ ★ ★ ★ **The Indispensable Fletcher Henderson / RCA (France)**

Fletcher Henderson (1897–1952) led the first important big band in jazz history, featured an array of great soloists (Louis Armstrong, Coleman Hawkins, Roy Eldridge and Benny Carter for openers) and provided for the evolution of an approach to arranging (with contributions by Don Redman, Carter, brother Horace and Fletcher himself) that became the foundation for the swing era. Redman's arrangements categorized the band's sound in the Twenties, and later Henderson wrote the arrangements himself. Many of these were used verbatim by Benny Goodman.

Most of the great Henderson records owned by Columbia are currently out of print. *The Immortal Fletcher Henderson* covers 1923–1931, with a stress on the band's earliest recordings, while *The Complete Fletcher Henderson 1927–1936* (recently deleted but worth searching for) works through the swing period and is burdened with some deadly novelty vocals. The material recorded for Bluebird can also be heard on the RCA French Black and White import *The Indispensable Fletcher Henderson.* The best of current Henderson collections is the Smithsonian's *Developing an American Orchestra 1923–1937,* a two-record summary of Henderson's musical and economic ups and downs.

★ ★ ★ ★ **The Black Swing Tradition / Savoy**

★ ★ ★ ★ ★ **First Impressions / MCA**

★ ★ ★ **Rarest Fletcher / MCA**

★ ★ ★ ★ **Swing's the Thing / MCA**

The reactivation of the old Decca Jazz Heritage series under the MCA logo offers a convenient survey of the Henderson band's work on two albums. *First Impressions,* covering 1924 through '31, contains two features for Louis Armstrong, early Don Redman ar-

rangements, and the evolving Coleman Hawkins, plus such other important players as Tommy Ladnier, Joe Smith and Jimmy Harrison. *Swing's the Thing* features music that directly led to the swing era (recorded 1931–34), with Henry "Red" Allen, Benny Carter and Ben Webster among the soloists. *Rarest Fletcher* finds the band in its earliest performances before the invigorating arrival of Armstrong.

Four other rare titles from Henderson's 1931 band can be found on the Savoy *Black Swing Tradition* anthology, which also offers samplings of the John Kirby and Stuff Smith small bands. — B.B.

JOE HENDERSON

★ ★ **Black Is the Color / Mile.**

★ ★ **Canyon Lady / Mile.**

★ ★ **The Elements / Mile.**

★ ★ ★ **Foresight / Mile.**

★ ★ **If You're Not Part of the Solution / Mile.**

★ ★ ★ **In Japan / Mile.**

★ ★ ★ ★ **In 'n Out / Blue N.**

★ ★ ★ ★ **Inner Urge / Blue N.**

★ ★ **In Pursuit of Blackness / Mile.**

★ ★ ★ **The Kicker / Mile.**

★ ★ ★ **Mirror, Mirror / Pausa**

★ ★ ★ ★ **Mode for Joe / Blue N.**

★ ★ **Multiple / Mile.**

★ ★ ★ ★ **Page One / Blue N.**

★ ★ ★ **Power to the People / Mile.**

★ ★ ★ **Relaxin' at Camarillo / Contem.**

★ ★ ★ **Tetragon / Mile.**

Joe Henderson (b. 1937) is representative of the first generation of jazzmen more influenced by Coltrane and Sonny Rollins than by Parker. As a young tenorist in the post–*Kind of Blue/Giant Steps* Sixties, Henderson was fully comfortable with modal forms and emulated the big "sheets of sound" blowing style that Coltrane had popularized.

The early Blue Notes, long-winded and often lacking in focus, are still impressive although much of this has to do with the extraordinary company Henderson was then keeping—Richard Davis, McCoy Tyner and Elvin Jones were frequent rhythm mates and Kenny Dorham often filled in as the extra horn.

Rather than solidifying his energies, the open-ended forms of the late Sixties and Seventies encouraged Henderson to squander them in excessive and ill-suited projects. The best LPs of this period are the most "traditional," Henderson being backed by a tight rhythm section working out on sharp, concisely organized material. The most worthy—*Tetragon, Power to the People, The*

Kicker—are all touched upon in the double-sampler, *Foresight.*

The Eighties show signs of rebirth for Henderson. Continuing in this more orderly vein and surrounding himself with seasoned players—Chick Corea, Ron Carter and Billy Higgins on *Mirror,* Richard Davis and Tony Williams on parts of *Relaxin'*—Henderson is regaining the power and clarity that had made him one of the most promising of the old new breed. — S.F.

WAYNE HENDERSON
★ ★ **Emphasized / Poly.**
Trombonist Wayne Henderson (b. 1939) recorded over fifty albums with his associates in the Crusaders before leaving that band in 1976 to produce records and develop a solo recording career. His biggest production credit has been the introduction of saxophonist Ronnie Laws, but Henderson's own disco-influenced outings have all been quickly forgotten. — J.S.

JON HENDRICKS
★ ★ ★ **Love / Muse**
Vocalese virtuoso Jon Hendricks (b. 1921) made his reputation with the vocal group Lambert, Hendricks and Ross. This album, recorded in the early Eighties, is not quite up to that group's brilliance, but is of interest nonetheless to fans of the genre. — J.S.

WOODY HERMAN
★ ★ ★ **All-Star Session / Acc.**
★ ★ ★ **Brand New / Fan.**
★ ★ **Chick, Donald, Walter and Woodrow / Cen.**
★ ★ **Children of Lima / Fan.**
★ ★ **Feelin' So Blue / Fan.**
★ ★ ★ **40th Anniversary Carnegie Hall / RCA**
★ ★ **Giant Steps / Fan.**
★ ★ ★ **Herd at Montreux / Fan.**
★ ★ **It's Coolin' Time / Picca.**
★ ★ **King Cobra / Fan.**
★ ★ **Lionel Hampton Presents / Who**
★ ★ **Live at the Concord Jazz Festival / Conc. J.**
★ ★ **The Raven Speaks / Fan.**
★ ★ ★ **Woody Herman, Vol. 2 / Arc. Folk**
★ ★ ★ **Woody Herman, Vol. 3 / Arc. Folk**
★ ★ ★ **Woody Herman and Friends at the Monterey Jazz Festival / Conc. J.**
Clarinetist and big-band leader Woody Herman (b. 1913) has been successfully running his mercurial "Herds" since the late Thirties. His early "Band That Plays the Blues" had a million-selling hit, "Woodchopper's Ball," in 1939. Although Herman's later work in-

spired Igor Stravinsky to pen Ebony Concerto (1945), Herman's successive "Herds" are mostly distinguished by the fact that they survived—and still do—well past the end of the swing era. Rare collector's albums can still be found to document the rambunctious early outfit, but the most interesting Herd of the late Forties and early Fifties is woefully underrepresented in extant LPs. *Woody Herman,* Volumes 2 and 3, sample some of the period, and it's worth seeking out the Capitol LP *Early Autumn.* This version of Herman's band was based on the "Four Brothers" sound of three tenors and a baritone sax, which included such Lester Young disciples as Zoot Sims, Stan Getz, Serge Chaloff and Al Cohn.

The later records, when Herman tries again and again to update the band, are uneven at best. *Live at the Concord Jazz Festival* and *40th Anniversary* partly portray the Herman band's best suit—as a caretaker's outfit. In the Sixties and Seventies, Herman also experimented with rock elements, without much success, on *The Raven Speaks* and *It's Coolin' Time* and arranger Alan Broadbent's *Children of Lima.* But *Chick, Donald Walter and Woodrow,* with its covers of Fagen/Becker tunes and an original side-long suite by Corea, stands up very well. — B.T.

BAIRD HERSEY
★ ★ ★ **Lookin' for That Groove (with Year of the Ear) / Ari./No.**
★ ★ ★ **ODO OP8 FX / Bent**
★ ★ ★ ★ **The Year of the Ear / Bent**
Guitarist/composer/bandleader Baird Hersey's large ensemble, The Year of the Ear, went virtually unnoticed in the late Seventies. But the group's two recordings have stood up very well. The session on Bent is less derivative in style, since Hersey's compositions on the Novus disk often sound too much like Gil Evans'.

As a guitarist, Hersey has a good command of both jazz and rock; his *ODO OP8 FX* is a solo guitar/electronics LP. Despite its strong lyrical sense, this solo disc is best left to guitar fanatics. — F.G.

BUCK HILL
★ ★ ★ ★ **Impressions / Steep.**
★ ★ ★ ★ **Scope / Steep.**
★ ★ ★ ★ **This Is Buck Hill / Steep.**
More heard about than heard until just a few years ago, Buck Hill (b. 1928) is a Washington, D.C.-based tenorman whose decision to support his family with a nine-to-five at the post office for a long time kept

him confined to his home area. During the Eighties he has recorded for the Danish SteepleChase label and journeyed beyond Washington with greater frequency. As a result, the rumors of his abilities have been substantiated; Hill is a bop player of considerable talents, and although he shows the influences of several of the instrument's modern giants, he can also stand on his own. *Impressions* is given marginal preference here because of the presence of bassist Wilbur Little and pianist Reuben Brown; the other albums also feature quality sidemen—Kenny Barron on piano, Buster Williams on bass and Billy Hart on drums. — F.G.

EARL "FATHA" HINES
★ ★ ★ ★ Another Monday Date / Prest.
★ ★ ★ At Home / Del.
★ ★ ★ At Sundown / Class.
★ ★ ★ ★ Boogie Woogie on St. Louis Blues / Prest.
★ ★ ★ ★ Comes in Handy / Audiop.
★ ★ ★ Earl Hines / GNP
★ ★ ★ Earl Hines All-Star Session / Hall
★ ★ ★ Earl Hines and His All-Stars / GNP
★ ★ ★ Earl Hines in New Orleans / Bio.
★ ★ ★ ★ Earl Hines Vol. 1 / RCA (France)
★ ★ ★ ★ Earl Hines Vol. 2 / RCA (France)
★ ★ ★ Evening with Hines / Chi.
★ ★ ★ Fatha / CSP
★ ★ ★ Fatha with Red Callender / Real.
★ ★ ★ Hines Does Hoagy / Audiop.
★ ★ ★ Incomparable Earl "Fatha" Hines / Fan.
★ ★ ★ In New Orleans / Bio.
★ ★ ★ Jazz Is His Old Lady and My Old Man / Cata.
★ ★ ★ Live Downtown / Improv
★ ★ ★ Live at the New School / Chi.
★ ★ ★ Live at the New School, Vol. 2 / Chi.
★ ★ ★ ★ Monday Date: 1928 / Mile.
★ ★ ★ My Tribute to Louis / Audiop.
★ ★ ★ Once upon a Time / Imp.
★ ★ ★ Paris Session / Inner
★ ★ ★ Plays Gershwin / Class.
★ ★ ★ Quintessential Continued / Chi.
★ ★ ★ Quintessential 1974 / Chi.
★ ★ ★ Quintessential Recording Session / Chi.
★ ★ ★ Solo Walk in Tokyo / Bio.
★ ★ ★ ★ ★ South Side Swing / MCA

They call him "Fatha" because Earl Hines (1905–1983) almost single-handedly carved out the standard vocabulary of jazz piano playing. After mastering the stride and ragtime piano techniques, Hines expanded the instrument's scope in a series of remarkable recordings with Louis Armstrong's Hot Five or Hot Seven in the late Twenties. Hines and Armstrong ran away from the other musicians who played with them—the rhythmic and melodic invention and their structural sense was too much for their fellow musicians to handle, so the two would end up accounting for most of the pyrotechnics on Armstrong's small-combo sessions. Hines' sound was often described as "hornlike" because of its staccato note clusters and piercing octave jumps—he and Armstrong obviously influenced each other as they played, and it took the rest of the jazz world ten years to catch up with them.

Hines went on to lead one of the hottest swing bands of the Thirties, based at Chicago's Grand Terrace Ballroom. This period is well represented on the outstanding *South Side Swing* LP. The Hines organization became a training ground for big-band jazz instrumentalists who then moved on to other groups. Still later, the organization became known for such featured vocalists as Billy Eckstine and Sarah Vaughan. Like Coleman Hawkins, Hines was not afraid of change, and the early-Forties band that featured Sarah Vaughan also included saxophonist Charlie Parker and trumpeter Dizzy Gillespie, two pioneers of the small-group bebop revolution that marked the end of the big-band era.

Hines remained a vibrant player on his numerous later recordings, which feature him in small combos and on delightful solo outings. *Another Monday Date* collects two fine Hines albums; one of Fats Waller tunes done with a quartet, the other a beautiful set of Hines solos. *Boogie Woogie on St. Louis Blues* features a remarkable interpretation of the W. C. Handy classic. — J.S.

CHRIS HINZE
★ ★ Bamboo / Atl.
European flutist Chris Hinze plays engaging if unassuming fusion jazz. — J.S.

ART HODES
★ ★ ★ Art Hodes with the All-Star Stompers / Jazzo.
★ ★ ★ Art of Hodes / Euphon.
★ ★ ★ Down Home Blues / Jazzo.
★ ★ ★ Echoes of Chicago / Jazzo.
★ ★ ★ Friar's Inn Revisited / Del.
★ ★ ★ Hodes' Art / Del.
★ ★ ★ Home Cookin' / Jazzo.
★ ★ ★ I Remember Bessie / Euphon.
★ ★ ★ ★ Just the Two of Us (with Milt Hinton) / Muse
★ ★ ★ Selections from the Gutter / Story.
★ ★ ★ Someone to Watch Over Me / Muse
★ ★ ★ When Music Was Music / Euphon.

Art Hodes (b. 1904) played piano in the Twenties and Thirties with a variety of groups led by Wingy Manone, Frank Teschemacher, Bud Freeman and others. In the Forties Hodes became a promoter of traditional jazz via radio shows and his own magazine, *The Jazz Record,* a move that hurt him musically since he was vehemently attacked by bop enthusiasts as a reactionary. Hodes was no "moldy fig," however, and his style shows it—he's a disciple of the austere, communicative playing logic of Jelly Roll Morton and James P. Johnson. His simple, direct manner is profoundly moving, and is best heard on solo piano or accompanied by a bassist, as he is on the magnificent collaboration with Milt Hinton, *Just the Two of Us.*
— J.S.

JOHNNY HODGES

★ ★ ★ ★ **The Big Sound** / Verve
★ ★ ★ **Caravan** / Prest.
★ ★ ★ ★ **Everybody Knows Johnny Hodges** / Imp.
★ ★ ★ ★ ★ **Hodge Podge** / CSP
★ ★ ★ **The Rabbit in Paris** / Inner
★ ★ ★ ★ **The Smooth One** / Verve
★ ★ ★ **Sportpalast, Berlin** / Pablo L.
★ ★ ★ ★ ★ **Things Ain't What They Used to Be** / Quin.

Johnny Hodges (1906–1970) was the first distinctive alto-saxophone soloist in jazz history and the primary influence on his instrument until the arrival of Charlie Parker. Equally important, Hodges was the definitive Duke Ellington sideman, and with the exception of four years in the early Fifties when he led his own medium-sized band, was featured in the Ellington Orchestra from 1928 until his death.

Always a masterful ballad and blues player, Hodges was also a convincing "hot" soloist who doubled on soprano saxophone at the start of his career. Most of his work, then and afterward, was done within the Ellington band, but Duke had a habit in the years before World War II of showcasing his featured players in small group sessions under their own name while he provided much of the material and the piano accompaniment. *Hodge Podge* and *Things Ain't* are stellar examples of small-band Ellingtonia, with the latter album (collecting the early Forties RCA sessions under Hodges' name) especially valuable. The two-record *Caravan,* an album's-worth of 1947 Hodges sessions plus another disc of 1950–51 small bands with Hodges' replacement Willie Smith, shows that the format did not prove so successful in later years.

The Hodges approach turned predictable and often listless as time passed, as the rehash of Ellington material from the 1961 Berlin concert demonstrates. There were moments, however, such as the sessions from 1959 and '60 that Verve finally released a few years back, and such other orchestral efforts as the late-Fifties *Big Sound* and the mid-Sixties *Everybody Knows.*

To really hear Hodges, of course, consult virtually any important Ellington album. He is also well served in the 1944 trio recordings contained on *Shelly Manne and His Friends* (Doctor Jazz). — B.B.

JAY HOGGARD

★ ★ **Love Survives** / Gram.
★ ★ ★ ★ **Mystic Winds, Tropic Breezes** / In. Nav.
★ ★ ★ **Rain Forest** / Contem.
★ ★ ★ ★ **Solo Vibes Concert** / In. Nav.
★ ★ ★ ★ **Under the Double Moon (with Anthony Davis)** / Pausa

Jay Hoggard (b. 1954) is the most impressive vibes player to surface in the last several years. He is also part of a truly new generation of musicians, one that sees no irreconcilable conflict in dividing their energies between totally uncompromising and blatantly commercial styles. This has led Hoggard to record music that is merely pleasant, as on *Days Like These* (a 1979 Arista/GRP album already out of print) and the better but still spotty *Rain Forest.*

So far, Hoggard has made his strongest impression in the intimate settings of duo and solo performance. He and pianist Anthony Davis share a true affinity and they interpret each other's music sensitively on the *Double Moon* album. The best introduction to Hoggard's talents, however, remains his first recording, a 1978 solo concert taped at New York's Public Theater. Here the church touches, the Latin and African influences, the social consciousness and romantic tenderness all come together in a stunning program where "May Those Who Love Apartheid Burn in Hell," a memorial to Steve Biko, coexists with music from *The Wiz.*

Recent releases show Hoggard continuing along his schizophrenic path. *Love Survives* is another forgettable effort at commercial music, but *Mystic Winds,* featuring Anthony Davis and other fine players, proves that Hoggard has the presence to lead a small, uncompromising combo. Hoggard also makes prominent contributions to *The Young Lions* (Elektra/Musician) and the eponymous *James Newton* album (Gramavision). — B.B.

BILLIE HOLIDAY

★ ★ ★ ★ ★ **The Billie Holiday Story, Vol. 1 / Col.**

★ ★ ★ ★ ★ **The Billie Holiday Story, Vol. 2 / Col.**

★ ★ ★ ★ ★ **The Billie Holiday Story, Vol. 3 / Col.**

★ ★ ★ ★ ★ **God Bless the Child / Col.**

★ ★ ★ ★ ★ **The Golden Years / Col.**

★ ★ ★ ★ ★ **Lady Day / Col.**

★ ★ ★ ★ **The Original Recordings / Col.**

From teenage vocalist to celebrated night-club attraction to ex-convict concert-hall amusement, Billie Holiday (1915–1959) was miscast throughout her life. During the early years of her career, a voice skillful enough to be featured on record with the most progressive jazz musicians of the day had no business residing in the body of so young a woman. Later, in her most fruitful years (the late Thirties), when club dates, concert tours and radio broadcasts attracted many, her records were restricted to the "race" labels, which distributed primarily to black neighborhoods. And although the hard drugs that put her in jail also took a toll on her voice, records from the years after her release from prison show there was still more reason to listen to her voice, midway between a moan and a sly reproach, than to gawk at this extremely beautiful, all-too-infamous woman of jazz.

Billie was blessed with an instinct for music as vigorous as it was untrained. She knew what she wanted to hear behind her and was fortunate to be teamed early in her career with pianist Teddy Wilson, with whom she recorded for Brunswick, Vocalion and Okeh from 1936 to 1942. All those Teddy Wilson dates are the bulk of Columbia's rereleases, and they are as much prized for the emboldening accompaniment as they are for Billie's tender nuances. Wilson's playing resembled Earl "Fatha" Hines' in its staccato riffs and lines suited more to a trumpet than to the piano; his style was the perfect match for Billie's blares, which were derived from Louis Armstrong's horn (the influence is most noticeable on the sessions from 1935 and 1936, Volumes 1 and 2 of the *Story* series).

Wilson hired men from Ellington's and Basie's bands, so he got the best: dozens of transitional musicians, including Roy Eldridge, Buster Bailey, Ben Webster and especially Lester Young on tenor sax, appearing again and again throughout the years to add one chorus or two of his taut tone and expansive ideas. Billie was often as unpredictable as the other musicians, and as continually rewarding.

The Columbia reissues exist in many overlapping forms. The two-volume, three-record sets called *The Golden Years* are the same as the three-volume, two-record sets dubbed *The Billie Holiday Story,* but neither compilation includes a number of important songs. *Lady Day* is a spirited supplement to the sets, a single-album feast of early recordings when Billie's voice was at its strongest—she sings from a point of wisdom, ripe with irony, turning Tin Pan Alley chestnuts into choice cuts.

The sides on *The Original Recordings* duplicate a few from *Lady Day*; most of the others can be found on the second volume of *The Billie Holiday Story.* The best two-record set is *God Bless the Child,* a collection that selects well from all three volumes of her recordings and adds about seven tunes, some of them gems not available on any other recording.

★ ★ ★ ★ **Strange Fruit / Atl.**

Billie recorded "Strange Fruit," a song about a black lynching in the South, for Commodore Records in 1939 when Vocalion wouldn't allow it. Her performance is surprisingly reserved, the music more consciously arranged to feature her than the songs recorded by Columbia (those were more like jam sessions), the lyrics all the more poignant for the straight rendition. "Fine and Mellow," the flip side of the original 78, was the big hit in Harlem. Most of the album was recorded five years later, when she had developed a dreamy delivery that reduced everything in range.

★ ★ ★ **The First Verve Sessions / Verve**

By 1952–54, Billie knew what went over. Her vocal characteristics, still appealing, were more automatic than organic; she'd sustain the end of a word like "river," so that it would float along, dropping off into a trickle of air, or close off a syllable or two of "memories" to make the word sound far away. "Sing" frequently takes up two or three notes. Since Norman Granz was the producer, Oscar Peterson was the piano player, and the settings are marked by his dry musicality.

★ ★ **Lady in Satin / Col.**

Lady in Satin presents the Lady overdressed. It's an album from the late Fifties, when most of Billie's punch was gone. She asked for the string arrangements, as Charlie Parker had also inadvisably done before her. At the time, jazz musicians thought strings brought them respectability.

★ **A Day in the Life of Billie Holiday / Dif. Drum.**

This tape was never intended to be a record, but some greedy human insisted. From a rehearsal very late in her career; not much left but the will to perform. — A.E.G.

DAVID HOLLAND

★ ★ ★ ★ ★ **Conference of the Birds** / ECM /War.

David Holland (b. 1946) came to America from his native England with Miles Davis in 1968, and has proceeded to prove himself one of jazz's supreme bass players. *Conference of the Birds* features three frequent collaborators (Anthony Braxton, Sam Rivers, Barry Altschul) in a definitive 1972 statement of swinging free expression.

★ ★ ★ **Emerald Tears** / ECM/War.
★ ★ ★ ★ ★ **Jumpin' In** / ECM
★ ★ ★ ★ **Life Cycle** / ECM/War.

Holland, who became seriously ill in 1981, spent most of the Seventies in the bands of Anthony Braxton and Sam Rivers, and in collaboration with a number of artists who frequented his record label (ECM) and his home environs (Woodstock, N.Y.). The two albums listed here are solo efforts for bass (*Emerald Tears*) and cello (*Life Cycle*). *Emerald* features several Holland originals plus one contribution each by former employers Braxton and Miles Davis. Not bad albums, by any means—his cello sound is as beautiful as expected—but not particularly exciting ones either; and hardly up to the elevated standards of *Conference of the Birds,* which only gets more impressive as time passes. Holland recovered his health and his abilities as a band leader on *Jumpin' In.* — B.B.

GROOVE HOLMES

★ ★ ★ **Best** / Prest.
★ ★ ★ **Best for Beautiful People** / Prest.
★ ★ ★ **Broadway** / Muse
★ ★ ★ **Good Vibrations** / Muse
★ ★ ★ ★ **Groovin' with Jug** / Pac. J.
★ ★ ★ **Misty** / Prest.
★ ★ ★ **Shippin' Out** / Muse
★ ★ ★ **Soul Message** / Prest.
★ ★ ★ **That Healin' Feelin'** / Prest.

Richard "Groove" Holmes (b. 1931) is one of the foremost disciples of the Jimmy Smith approach to Hammond B-3 organ playing. He moves from lounge jazz to high-intensity settings as if they were all of a piece (contrast "Ode to Larry Young" with "Moon River" from *Broadway*). He also recorded a hit version of Erroll Garner's "Misty." Most of all, he *burns,* especially on the great Gene Ammons collaborations on Prestige and Pacific Jazz. — J.S.

STIX HOOPER

★ ★ ★ **The World Within** / MCA

Percussionist Stix Hooper (b. 1938) made one of the better solo records produced by a member of the Crusaders when the band started to split into different directions toward the end of the Seventies. *The World Within* has an accessible contemporary sound without resorting to disco settings. At times the record is a bit ornate, but the strength of Hooper's rhythmic conception carries the album relentlessly forward and makes for interesting listening. Hooper left the Crusaders in 1984.
— J.S.

ELMO HOPE

★ ★ ★ ★ **All-Star Sessions** / Mile.
★ ★ ★ ★ ★ **Elmo Hope Trio** / Contem.

Underrated and underrecorded, pianist Elmo Hope (1923–1967) cut sides for numerous labels although these are all that remain in print. *All-Star Sessions* is just that—Hope is joined by John Coltrane, Donald Byrd, Jimmy Heath and Philly Joe Jones. *Trio* is a superb date with Jimmy Bond on bass and Frank Butler on drums, in which Hope manages to show both the influence of, and his independence from, Thelonious Monk and Bud Powell. Hope's selection of notes is impeccable throughout, and his feel is so sure that a listener feels familiar with Hope immediately. A beautiful player.
— F.G.

SHIRLEY HORN

★ ★ ★ ★ **A Lazy Afternoon** / Steep.
★ ★ ★ ★ **Live at the Northsea Jazz Festival** / Steep.
★ ★ ★ ★ ★ **Violets for Your Furs** / Steep.

Shirley Horn is a singer of hypnotic intensity, a pianist of both muscle and subtlety. She is a harmonic modernist with an old-fashioned, down-home feeling.

Foretelling the grace and seductiveness of the SteepleChases are the out-of-print early recordings (many can be found in collector's shops): of these, *Embers and Ashes/Songs of Lost Love Sung by Shirley Horn* (Bell, containing several of Curtis Lewis' blue ballads), *Travelin' Light* (ABC-Paramount) and *Where Are You Going* (Perception 31) stand out.

The three recordings made for the Danish SteepleChase label feature Shirley Horn's longtime associate and friend, drummer Billy Hart. Bassist Buster Williams performs splendidly on *Lazy Afternoon,* while Charles Abels (on electric bass) provides a harder, more blues-based foundation on the two live recordings (*Violets for Your Furs* was also recorded at the Northsea Jazz Festival in Holland). — A.R.

FREDDIE HUBBARD
★ Blue Spirit / Blue N.
★ ★ ★ ★ Breaking Point / Blue N.
★ ★ ★ ★ Freddie Hubbard / Blue N.
★ ★ ★ ★ Goin' Up / Blue N.
★ ★ ★ ★ Hub-Tones / Blue N.
★ ★ ★ ★ Ready for Freddie / Blue N.
★ ★ ★ ★ Takin' Off / Blue N.

Arriving on the scene in the late Fifties
Freddie Hubbard (b. 1938) provided with
regularity that component of Clifford
Brown's trumpet playing that Lee Morgan
sometimes disregarded: the fluency of motion, the agile gait. But then Lee developed
fires that were a lot hotter than Hubbard's.

The two-record reissue *Freddie Hubbard*
shows why he can be blamed for a lot of
younger musicians sounding the same. The
set contains selections from Hubbard's first
four albums for Blue Note, a few stray
tracks from *Breaking Point* and the only really transcendent tune from *Blue Spirit.*

Lots of short, often unison, themes, then
plenty of blowing in moody modes, makes
Goin' Up a classic hard-bop session. And
Hank Mobley, McCoy Tyner, Paul Chambers and Philly Joe Jones make it more than
an all-star cast. But Freddie always had his
choice of the Blue Note rotating roster;
Ready for Freddie puts the attractive front
line of Kiane Zawadi on euphonium and
Wayne Shorter on tenor up against Coltrane's rhythm section. On *Hub-Tones,* he
gets clear and courageous support from his
frequent sideman James Spaulding, added to
the shimmering chords of a fledgling Herbie
Hancock.

Breaking Point is one of the early high
points of Freddie's career, and still a plea-
sure because of the way each musician
speaks with an independent voice. All but
one composition are by the trumpeter, and
he plotted them well. Each song demands
something of the musicians in addition to
containing its own appeal.
★ ★ ★ A Little Night Music
★ ★ ★ Backlash / Atl.
★ Best of / Pablo
★ First Light / CTI
★ High Energy / Col.
★ ★ Keep Your Soul Together / CTI
★ Liquid Love / Col.
★ Love Connection / Col.
★ Midnight Matinee / Col.
★ Polar AC / CTI
★ ★ ★ Red Clay / CTI
★ Skagly / Col.
★ Sky Diver / CTI
★ Splash / Fan.

★ Straight Life / CTI
★ Windjammer / Col.

The one Atlantic record of Hubbard's still in
the catalogue uses a soul groove for a substantial part of the album. Aside from being
short on variety, Otis Ray Appleton, the
drummer, doesn't really swing and he sure
ain't funky. With him as guide, the jazz at
times passes through a choking fog.

Red Clay became a classic, and for good
reason: everybody plays great on it. Easily
appealing, it is one good example of a sound
very popular at CTI and with a lot of record
buyers, but it started Hubbard in a bad direction. *First Light,* for example, Hubbard's
Grammy-award-winning disc, contains a version of "Uncle Albert/Admiral Halsey"
(with Don Sebesky's string arrangement)
that manages to stay just this side of Muzak.
Most everything else, however, is just the
other side of real music. If only he didn't
blow ballads prettier than anyone, there
would be no reason to listen to this album
more than once. From *Polar AC* on, it was a
succession of fluegelhorn ballads, Hubbard's
characteristic, and safe, "tee-oo-whee!" in
full force and songs where Hubbard fluttered
for his supper—all on some of the day's pop
pablum and sophistifunk.
★ ★ ★ ★ Back to Birdland / Real.
★ ★ ★ Born to Be Blue / Pablo
★ ★ Intrepid Fox / Picca.
★ ★ ★ ★ Keystone Bop / Fan.
★ ★ Live at the Northsea Jazz Festival /
    Pablo
★ ★ ★ Mistral / Lib.
★ ★ ★ Outpost / Enja
★ ★ ★ ★ Ride Like the Wind / Elek./Mus.
★ ★ Rollin' / Pausa
★ ★ ★ ★ ★ Sweet Return / Atl.

Hubbard's Eighties recordings offer a dramatic return to his top form, often while
maintaining a somewhat commercial approach. The Pablo and Pausa sides document live European appearances with Hubbard giving a good account of himself in
energetic but uninspired contexts. *Back to
Birdland* pitches Hubbard against alto saxophonist Richie Cole and double trombonist
Ashley Alexander with spectacular results.
Outpost is a more introspective session with
Kenny Barron on piano, Buster Williams on
bass and Al Foster on drums. *Keystone Bop*
includes wonderful exchanges between Hubbard, tenor saxophonist Joe Henderson and
vibraphonist Bobby Hutcherson (they can
also be heard on *A Little Night Music*). *Ride
Like the Wind* is a monster session that
combines elements of big-band jazz, fusion
and Hubbard's distinctive ensemble style.

The basic sextet used here is augmented by a massive string section and a brass unit headed up by trombonist Bill Watrous and saxophonist Budd Shank. The high point of the set is a beautiful adaption of "Birdland," the Joe Zawinul fusion standard. *Sweet Return* features some of Hubbard's best playing in years on an acoustic session with drummer Roy Haynes, bassist Eddie Gomez, pianist Joanne Brackeen and saxophonist/flutist Lew Tabackin. — A.E.G./J.S.

BOBBI HUMPHREY
★ ★ Freestyle / Epic
★ ★ The Good Life / Epic
Texas-born flutist Bobbi Humphrey (b. 1950) came to prominence during the Seventies with a series of R&B/disco jazz albums on Blue Note that featured her aggressive soloing style in dance-music settings. The formula yielded crossover success on the pop charts and a subsequent recording contract with Epic. Her pop status led to sessions with Sly Stone and Stevie Wonder and encouraged Humphrey to start singing as well. — J.S.

ALBERTA HUNTER
★ ★ ★ ★ ★ Amtrack Blues / Col.
★ ★ ★ ★ The Classic / Stash
★ ★ ★ ★ The Glory of Alberta Hunter / Col.
★ ★ ★ ★ The Legendary Alberta Hunter / DRG
★ ★ ★ ★ Look for the Silver Lining / Col.
The venerable Alberta Hunter (1895–1984) retired from jazz when she was in her fifties to take up nursing after a long and successful career in Chicago and New York, documented on *The Classic* and *The Legendary*. She had played everything from "sporting houses" in her native Memphis in the Twenties to the Broadway stage in the Thirties. Her second retirement, from nursing this time, stretched on until she was over eighty. Coaxed back to performing for what was supposed to be a short stint at The Cookery in New York in the late Seventies, Hunter was a sensation and the gig led to her doing a 1978 movie soundtrack, *Remember My Name* (Columbia, deleted), regular concerts and LPs. Up until her death at the age of eighty-nine, Hunter remained a magical mixture of feisty and often risqué barroom singer, ethereal presence and historical reminder of the better jazz days of pop songwriting. All these records carry that magic, but *Amtrack Blues* is the one to have. — B.T.

IVORY JOE HUNTER
★ ★ ★ I've Always Been Country / Para.
★ ★ ★ Ivory Joe Hunter / Arc.
★ ★ ★ ★ ★ Jumping at the Dew Drop / Route 66, Swed. imp.
★ ★ ★ ★ Seventh Street Boogie / Route 66, Swed. imp.
Excellent stride piano player and smooth-voiced vocalist who grew up in Texas and played in a blues/jazz format, using saxophonists such as Illinois Jacquet and Arnett Cobb, who would later become jazz stars in their own right. Hunter moved to California in the Forties, where his compositions made him one of the most successful R&B writers and performers of the time, beginning with "Blues at Sunrise," on which he was accompanied by Johnny Moore's Three Blazers. Hunter's combination of jazz, blues, country and R&B styles was extremely influential, and his songs have been recorded by Elvis Presley, Nat King Cole, Pat Boone, Freddy Fender, Ruth Brown and Teresa Brewer. — J.S.

BOBBY HUTCHERSON
★ ★ Best of Bobby Hutcherson / Col.
★ ★ ★ ★ Medina / Blue N.
★ ★ Now! / Blue N.
★ ★ ★ Patterns / Blue N.
★ ★ ★ ★ Un Poco Loco / Col.
★ ★ ★ San Francisco / Blue N.
★ ★ ★ Solo Quartet / Contem.
★ ★ ★ ★ Spiral / Blue N.
★ ★ ★ View from Inside / Blue N.
Poll results to the contrary notwithstanding, Bobby Hutcherson (b. 1941) was the most important and influential vibraharpist to emerge since Milt Jackson. His brittle yet still fluid conception prepared him to operate in the advanced post-bop and free realms that his record label, Blue Note, specialized in during the Sixties, and bandleaders often chose to dispense with piano when Hutcherson was available. Some of his best work is to be heard on albums of the period by Eric Dolphy, Andrew Hill, Tony Williams, Jackie McLean and McCoy Tyner.

Most of Hutcherson's own superb Blue Note dates from that era are now out of print, although the recently uncovered *Medina, Spiral* and *Patterns* catch him at the end of this period. The first two, featuring the quintet he coled with tenor saxophonist Harold Land, are fine examples of what the music of that time was all about. Over the next decade commercial pressures often caught up with Hutcherson (see *Now!*, with voices, and the *Best of* sampler from his mostly deleted Columbia albums); but *Un*

Poco Loco finds him striking a successful balance in a quintet with George Cables, John Abercrombie and Peter Erskine.

Recently, Hutcherson has spent more time recording as guest star (with Freddie Hubbard, Harold Land, Sonny Collins, Woody Shaw, *Jazz at the Opera House*) than as a leader. His lone featured effort, *Solo Quartet*, is a mélange of formats with mixed results. The quartet side features McCoy Tyner and reflects the strength of earlier collaborations, while the overdubbed solo tracks are technically impeccable but surprisingly conservative. — B.B.

ABDULLAH IBRAHIM (DOLLAR BRAND)

★ ★ ★ African Piano / Plain.
★ ★ ★ African Portraits / Sack.
★ ★ ★ ★ Autobiography / NMDS
★ ★ ★ Black Lightning / Chi.
★ ★ ★ Echoes from Africa / PSI (Japanese)
★ ★ ★ Good News from Africa / Enja
★ ★ ★ ★ The Journey / Chi.
★ ★ ★ ★ Sangoma / Sack.
★ ★ ★ ★ Zimbabwe / Enja

Pianist Abdullah Ibrahim (b. 1934, a.k.a. Dollar Brand) is a South African expatriate who's had a subtle but profound influence on modern music. His knowledge of and sympathy for Africa make him a first-hand practitioner of styles and feelings many other musicians have adopted from afar, while his wide-ranging control of rhythmic dynamics and melodic improvisation marks him as a musical modernist. Ibrahim has recorded several fine solo piano records, including *Sangoma,* with a heartfelt tribute to Fats Waller, Duke Ellington and Thelonious Monk, *African Portraits, African Piano* and *Autobiography*; duets such as *Good News from Africa* and *Echoes from Africa*; and larger band recordings like *Black Lightning* and the fantastic *The Journey,* which features Hamiet Bluiett on baritone sax and clarinet, Don Cherry on trumpet, Talib Rhynie on alto sax and oboe, Carlos Ward on alto sax and a rhythm section augmented by two percussionists. — J.S.

JACKIE AND ROY
★ ★ **By the Sea** / Studio 7
★ ★ ★ **East of Suez** / Conc. J.
★ ★ ★ **High Standards** / Conc. J.
★ ★ **Jackie and Roy** / MCA
★ ★ ★ **Star Sounds** / Conc. J.
★ ★ ★ **A Stephen Sondheim Collection** /
    Fine.

Jackie and Roy's distinctive sound, a constant on the jazz scene since the late Forties, can be described as light and airy. Jackie Cain's (b. 1928) vocals and Roy Kral's (b. 1921) vocals and piano blend together quite well. They are fine musicians who know their ballads and their bebop. What is missing, though, is passion. — A.R.

MICHAEL GREGORY JACKSON
★ ★ ★ ★ **Clarity** / Bija
★ ★ **Cowboys, Cartoons and Assorted Candy**
    / Enja
★ ★ **Situation X** / Is.

Michael Gregory Jackson (b. 1953) is a strong guitarist originally linked to the loft scene via his association with artists like Oliver Lake, David Murray and Leo Smith, all of whom appear on the Bija recording. Out-of-print LPs on his own and with Lake for Arista indicated Jackson's willingness to play more commercial, electric music. *Cowboys* is a solo outing with vocals and an all-too-predictable ethereal sound. *Clarity* is still his best recording, demonstrating Jackson's versatility and chops.

Jackson's 1982 *Situation X* is a straightforward attempt by the guitarist to sever his identification with jazz. The rock album, produced by Nile Rodgers of the group Chic, features Jackson mostly as a vocalist. He also dropped his last name to avoid any confusion in the pop marketplace. — F.G.

RONALD SHANNON JACKSON
★ ★ ★ ★ **Barbecue Dog** / Ant.
★ ★ ★ ★ ★ **Eye on You** / About T.

★ ★ ★ ★ **Mandance** / Ant.
★ ★ ★ **Nasty** / Moers

Ronald Shannon Jackson is a veteran drummer who began attracting attention in the late Seventies for his work with Cecil Taylor and Ornette Coleman. He was particularly outstanding in the latter's Prime Time, where his ability to combine free percussion with basic New Orleans parade rhythms suggested a synthesis between new music and new wave. In 1980 he began working with his own band, the Decoding Society, an octet of varying instrumentation that performs Jackson's compositions exclusively.

Of the four Decoding Society albums to appear so far, *Eye on You* is a stunner. There is some marvelously quirky writing here and a fine ensemble balance (two saxes, two guitars, violin and Fender bass, drums and percussion), offering the most orchestral example of Coleman's "harmelodic" concepts to date, plus a selfless team spirit and some incredible drumming. *Nasty* works less well—the tracks are longer, vibes and a second electric bass are substituted to little effect, and the sound is less clean. *Mandance* and *Barbecue Dog* feature Jackson's working group. The ensemble has been scaled down (an economic necessity) since *Eye* and Jackson's writing is even more eclectic (touches of banjo for a country feeling on one *Mandance* track). While this material is slightly less bold than that on the first (*Eye*) album, it is executed with dash by Jackson and his young sidemen.

Other essential views of Jackson can be had on Coleman's *Body Meta*, Taylor's *3 Phasis* and "Blood" Ulmer's *No Wave*.
— B.B.

WILLIS JACKSON
★ ★ ★ **Bar Wars** / Muse
★ ★ ★ **Best** / Prest.
★ ★ ★ **Blue Gator** / Prest.
★ ★ ★ **Cool Guts** / Prest.

★ ★ ★ Gator's Groove / Prest.
★ ★ The Gator Horn / Muse
★ ★ ★ Gatorade / Prest.
★ ★ ★ Headed and Gutted / Muse
★ ★ ★ In the Valley / Muse
★ ★ ★ Live Action / Prest.
★ ★ ★ More Gravy / Prest.
★ ★ ★ Neapolitan Nights / Prest.
★ ★ ★ Single Action / Muse
★ ★ ★ Soul Night/Live! / Prest.
★ ★ ★ Together Again / Prest.
★ ★ ★ West Africa / Muse

Willis "Gatortail" Jackson (b. 1932) grew up in Miami, Florida, where his reputation as a hard-blowing local tenor saxophone player led to a tour with the Cootie Williams band. Jackson starred in that outfit, where he earned his nickname, and went on to front his own groups. His organ combos have consistently been among the most listenable groups working in that genre, and Jackson has, as a result, become an extremely durable recording artist over the years, making some soulful records in the Sixties for Prestige and featuring Jack McDuff's swinging organ accompaniment. By 1973 Jackson started recording for Muse, a series of sessions using organists Carl Wilson, Charles Earland and Mickey Tucker and some fine guitar playing from Pat Martino. These LPs contain few surprises—Jackson alternates between cooking uptempo tracks where he plays with a rhythmic dexterity inspired by Lester Young and Charlie Parker, and emotional ballads delivered with a deep, expressive Coleman Hawkins sound. *Gator Horn* includes a side of Jackson playing his unusual horn invention, the Gator horn, an extremely long reed instrument with qualities at times reminiscent of a French horn and both soprano and alto saxophones. — J.S.

ILLINOIS JACQUET
★ ★ ★ ★ The Blues Ain't News to Me / Verve
★ ★ ★ Blues: That's Me / Prest.
★ ★ ★ ★ Bottoms Up / Prest.
★ ★ ★ Genius at Work / Jazz M.
★ ★ How High the Moon / Prest.
★ ★ ★ Illinois Jacquet with Wild Bill Davis / Class.
★ ★ ★ Jacquet's Street / Class.
★ ★ ★ The King! / Prest.
★ ★ ★ Message / Cadet
★ ★ ★ Soul Explosion / Prest.

Illinois Jacquet (b. 1922) hails from Texas and cut his teeth playing in the hot combos of the Southwest in the Forties. He was featured tenor soloist in Lionel Hampton's band and later played with Count Basie before leading his own groups. Jacquet's solo on the Hampton band's 1943 side, "Flying Home," is regarded as a turning point between jazz and postwar R&B, characterized by honking volume and screeching high notes. Jacquet's sax style was highly influential on the early rock & rollers, who relied heavily on honking tenor solos before guitars took over.
— J.S.

AHMAD JAMAL
★ ★ ★ At Top—Poinciana Revisited / MCA
★ ★ ★ Awakening / MCA
★ ★ ★ Best of / Twentieth C.
★ ★ ★ Freeflight / MCA
★ ★ Genetic Walk / Twentieth C.
★ ★ ★ ★ In Concert / Pers.
★ ★ Intervals / Twentieth C.
★ ★ ★ Live at Oil Can Harry's / Cata.

Pittsburgh-born Ahmad Jamal (b. 1930) was a child prodigy, performing in concert by the age of eleven. A protégé of Art Tatum, Jamal played with a variety of jazz and pop groups before forming his famed trio, with bassist Israel Crosby and drummer Vernel Fournier, in the late Fifties. This group enjoyed unusual success with pristine chamber music pieces such as "Poinciana." The MCA/Impulse sides document this era, while the Twentieth Century-Fox sets show Jamal turning to electric piano and making overtures to Seventies pop-jazz and fusion styles. The 1981 *In Concert,* with vibraphonist Gary Burton, shows Jamal at his absolute peak in an extremely sympathetic setting.
— J.S.

BOB JAMES
★ All Around the Town / Col.
★ Bob James Four / Col.
★ Explosions / ESP
★ "H" / Tap.
★ Hands Down / Col.
★ Heads / Col.
★ Lucky Seven / Col.
★ ★ One / Col.
★ ★ One on One (with Earl Klugh) / Col.
★ ★ Rameau / CBS Masterworks
★ Sign of the Times / Col.
★ ★ Three / Col.
★ Touchdown / Col.
★ ★ 12 / Col.
★ ★ Two / Col.

Bob James (b. 1939) began his recording career in 1965 with an avant-garde trio effort for ESP Disk called *Explosions* that featured sound-effect explosions mixed in with the playing. A statement about war, no doubt. A few years later James became the architect for Seventies Muzak jazz, helping define the CTI easy-listening style and later bringing the same ideas to Columbia. His efforts to

commercialize jazz have been successful, but the records are unfortunately not much fun to listen to, although they always feature technically adept performances. Under his own name the James formula really suffers, although the results are remarkably similar to other albums he directs. Where the usual complaint is that James' style mutes the personality of the musician he's doctoring up, in his own case there's so little playing personality to begin with that the muting process is nowhere near as traumatic. Perhaps his most outlandish outing is the "switched on" versions of pieces written by the Baroque composer Jean Philippe Rameau. As Christmas party Muzak he can get away with it.
— J.S.

JOSEPH JARMAN
★ ★ ★ ★ As If It Were the Seasons / Del.
★ ★ ★ Earth Passage—Density (with Don Moye) / Black S.
★ ★ ★ ★ Song For / Del.

Joseph Jarman (b. 1937) is a seminal AACM member, one-fifth of the Art Ensemble of Chicago, and a reedman of broad capabilities. Jarman's recordings for Delmark are among the earliest of the AACM works and helped set the stage for the next decade of explorative music. These Delmarks evince a folklike simplicity that's somewhat misleading. The collective improvisation concept being spearheaded by Jarman, Muhal Richard Abrams, Anthony Braxton, and the Art Ensemble was a whole new ball game, and still a regional movement. The recordings Jarman was to make with the Art Ensemble became the measure for the new music, but these earlier Delmark LPs are much more than a group of musicians searching for something. The music is there. — F.G.

KEITH JARRETT
★ ★ ★ Arbour Zena / ECM/War.
★ ★ ★ Backhand / Imp.
★ ★ ★ Belonging / ECM/War.
★ ★ ★ ★ Best / Imp.
★ ★ ★ Birth / Atl.
★ ★ ★ Bob-Be / MCA
★ ★ ★ Byablue / MCA
★ ★ ★ Celestial Hawk / ECM/War.
★ ★ ★ Changes / ECM
★ ★ ★ ★ Death and the Flower / MCA
★ ★ ★ Expectations / Col.
★ ★ ★ Eyes of the Heart / ECM/War.
★ ★ ★ ★ Facing You / ECM/War.
★ ★ ★ ★ Forth Yawuh / MCA
★ ★ ★ Hymns/Spheres / ECM/War.
★ ★ ★ In the Light / ECM/War.
★ ★ ★ Invocations/The Moth and the Flame / ECM/War.
★ ★ ★ ★ Köln Concert / ECM/War.
★ ★ ★ Luminescence / ECM/War.
★ ★ Mourning of a Star / Atl.
★ ★ ★ My Song / ECM/War.
★ ★ ★ Mysteries / Imp.
★ ★ ★ Nude Ants / ECM/War.
★ ★ Ruta and Daitya (with Jack DeJohnette) / ECM/War.
★ ★ ★ Sacred Hymns / ECM/War.
★ ★ ★ Shades / Imp.
★ ★ ★ ★ ★ Solo Concerts / ECM/War.
★ ★ ★ ★ Somewhere Before / Atl.
★ ★ ★ ★ ★ Staircase / ECM/War.
★ ★ ★ ★ Standards, Vol. 1 / ECM/War.
★ ★ ★ Sun Bear Concerts / ECM/War.
★ ★ ★ ★ Survivors' Suite / ECM/War.
★ ★ Treasure Island / MCA

Keith Jarrett (b. 1945), prodigiously gifted young jazz pianist and composer, ex-sideman with Miles Davis and Charles Lloyd, plays in virtually every contemporary style. Jarrett's late-Sixties Atlantic and Seventies MCA/Impulse albums feature him in ensemble with the cream of New York's avant-garde; his group work encompasses styles as diverse as Bill Evans lyricism and furious Ornette Coleman dissonance. In *Mourning* (1971), Jarrett assembled a rhythm section of Charlie Haden (bass) and Paul Motian (drums), which, with the addition of saxophonist Dewey Redman on *Birth,* became the basic quartet on all the Impulse albums. The ensemble was augmented with guitarist Sam Brown for rock-oriented tunes and percussionist Guilherme Franco for Eastern exotica.

Jarrett's simultaneous career as an ECM "special projects" artist has been even more ambitious. *Facing You, Solo Concerts, Köln Concert* and *Staircase* feature extended freeform solo piano improvisations that blend European impressionism, gospel funk and LaMonte Young/Terry Riley–influenced trance music. *In the Light* collects eight orchestral and chamber works that favor an autumnal neoclassicism; *Hymns/Spheres* comprises pieces for organ. *Belonging, Luminescence* and *Arbour Zena* feature Norwegian saxophonist Jan Garbarek; the latter two have orchestral settings. Jarrett's expansiveness has been labeled self-indulgent, and it's true that his "conservatory" pieces lack structural definition. But especially in his solo piano works (*Solo Concerts, Sun Bear Concerts*), Jarrett's sheer outpouring of ideas, rendered with breathtaking physical resourcefulness, tends to override such criticisms. — S.H.

SCOTT JARRETT

★ **Without Rhyme or Reason / Ari.**
Guitarist Scott Jarrett is best known as
Keith Jarrett's younger brother, and this
album of pop/jazz tunes does little to change
that. — J.S.

EDDIE JEFFERSON

★ ★ ★ ★ **Body and Soul / Prest.**
★ ★ ★ ★ **Come Along with Me / Prest.**
★ ★ ★ ★ **Jazz Singer / Inner**
★ ★ ★ ★ **The Live-Liest / Muse**
★ ★ ★ **Main Man / Inner**
★ ★ ★ ★ **Still on the Planet / Muse**
★ ★ ★ ★ **There I Go Again / Prest.**
★ ★ ★ ★ **Things Are Getting Better / Muse**
Eddie Jefferson (1918–1979) pioneered the
technique of writing lyrics to famous instrumental jazz solos, an approach later popularized by King Pleasure and Lambert, Hendricks and Ross. He first made records in
the Fifties on his own and as part of saxophonist James Moody's group. The earliest
material here (*Jazz Singer*) was made between 1959 and 1961, while the rest dates
from the late Sixties and Seventies.

Jefferson's approach often adds surprising
illumination to the original performances on
which his songs are based. His adaption of a
James Moody solo, "Moody's Mood for
Love," derived in turn by Moody from the
standard "I'm in the Mood for Love," became a cult item in its King Pleasure version, and is one of the few jazz singles that
are now standard jukebox "oldies" around
the country. The Prestige sets show Jefferson's classic touch primarily on bop standards. This approach was continued on the
Seventies LPs made for Muse, but Jefferson
also updated his adaptations to contemporary material. On *Things Are Getting Better*
he handled Miles Davis' fusion classic,
"Bitches Brew," and Sly Stone's "Thank
You (Falletinme Be Mice Elf Agin)."
— J.S.

ANTONIO CARLOS JOBIM

★ ★ **A Certain Mr. Jobim / Discov.**
★ ★ **Plays / Verve**
★ **Terra Brasilis / War.**
A guitarist, singer and songwriter, Antonio
Carlos Jobim (b. 1927) is a delicate improviser and sophisticated melodist whose urbane compositions established the bossa nova
craze in the Sixties. His bossa nova standards include "One-Note Samba," "The Girl
from Ipanema," "Wave," "Corcovado,"
"Desafinado" and "Jazz Samba," several of
which were popularized by Stan Getz and
the Gilbertos, Astrud and João. These land-

mark works can be found on the Verve
package *Girl from Ipanema* under Getz'
name. Jobim's later work, the 1967 *A Certain Mr. Jobim* (arranged by a German,
Claus Ogerman) and the deleted *Tide* (arranged by Eumir Deodato), set out his songs
in opulent but elegant strings. *Terra Brasilis,*
which contains no actual songs, is an orchestral suite lacking any real distinction.
— B.T.

JAMES P. JOHNSON

★ ★ ★ ★ **Father of the Stride Piano / Col.**
★ ★ ★ ★ ★ **James P. Johnson / Time-Life**
★ ★ ★ ★ **James P. Johnson 1921–1926 /
Olym.**
★ ★ ★ ★ **James P. Johnson Piano Solos /
Folk.**
★ ★ ★ ★ **James P. Johnson Plays Fats
Waller / MCA**
★ ★ ★ ★ **New York Jazz / Stin.**
★ ★ ★ ★ ★ **Yamekraw / Folk.**
James P. Johnson (1891–1955) was one of
the foremost practitioners of the stride piano
style and a prolific composer of popular
tunes. Johnson influenced Fats Waller, who
in turn popularized many of Johnson's ideas.
Other pianists, including Duke Ellington,
learned a lot from Johnson. The albums
available show Johnson's technical fluency
and impeccable taste. He was also an experi-
menter, and his most ambitious work was
Yamekraw, a rhapsody used as the
soundtrack for a film short starring Bessie
Smith. — J.S.

ELVIN JONES

★ ★ ★ ★ **Brother John / Palo Alto**
★ ★ ★ ★ **Dear John C. / Imp.**
★ ★ ★ ★ **Elvin! / Riv.**
★ ★ ★ ★ **Heavy Sounds (with Richard Davis)
/ Imp.**
★ ★ ★ ★ **Illumination (with Jimmy Garrison)
/ Imp.**
★ ★ ★ **Jones Boys / Ev.**
★ ★ ★ ★ **Live at Town Hall / PM**
★ ★ **Main Force / Van.**
★ ★ ★ **New Agenda / Van.**
★ ★ ★ ★ **Night Dreamer / Blue N.**
★ ★ ★ ★ **On the Mountain / PM**
★ ★ ★ ★ **Oregon/Elvin Jones / Van.**
★ ★ ★ **Outback / CTI**
★ ★ ★ ★ **Puttin' It Together / Blue N.**
★ ★ ★ ★ ★ **Reevaluations: Impulse Years /
Imp.**
★ ★ ★ ★ **Remembrance / Pausa**
★ ★ ★ **Summit Meeting / Van.**
★ ★ ★ **Time Capsule / Van.**
★ ★ ★ ★ **Ultimate / Blue N.**

One of the most powerfully rhythmic drummers alive, Elvin Jones (b. 1927) is a jazz virtuoso who has influenced many modern percussionists. Jones played with Miles Davis and Sonny Rollins, but his work in the Sixties with John Coltrane earned him a secure place in music history, and his solo career, while not always consistent, features some fine moments. *Reevaluations* includes several outstanding tracks from the Coltrane days.

While Jones' great Blue Note quintet albums with saxophonists George Coleman and Frank Foster are out of print, the trio sides for that label with saxophonist Joe Farrell and bassist Jimmy Garrison are quite good. Jones' recordings for Vanguard are not up to his usual standard, although the collaboration with Oregon is interesting. The PM and Pausa sides reveal him in top form. *Brother John* shows Elvin rocking into the Eighties. — J.S.

JO JONES
★ ★ ★ ★ **The Essential Jo Jones / Van.**
Jo Jones (b. 1911) was the heartbeat of the Basie band and arguably the most influential drummer in the history of jazz. This collection spotlights him with a group composed largely of Basie alumni and is a fine representation of his work. However, his presence on the classic Basie recordings of the Thirties makes almost anything else superfluous. It's not that he was particularly highlighted on those discs—and techniques for recording drums were crude at the time—but rather that Jones was one of a handful of essential players without whom the Basie band wouldn't have been what it was. *Essential* is very good; but the Basie sides to be found on Columbia's *Super Chief* and MCA's *Best of Count Basie* are history. — F.G.

PHILLY JOE JONES
★ ★ ★ **Advance / Gal.**
★ ★ ★ **Blues for Dracula / Prest.**
★ ★ ★ ★ **Look, Stop and Listen / Uptown**
★ ★ ★ **Philly Mignon / Gal.**
★ ★ ★ ★ **Showcase / Riv.**
★ ★ ★ **To Tadd with Love / Uptown**
More controlled than Art Blakey, more dynamic than Roy Haynes and less rigid than Max Roach, Philly Joe Jones (b. 1923) was the quintessential hard-bop drummer. Constantly in demand, Jones was probably on more jazz records from 1955 to 1965 than any other major musician. His principal fame grew out of his membership in the classic (1955–58) Miles Davis quintet; alongside Paul Chambers on bass and Red Garland on drums, Jones helped comprise the greatest rhythm section of bop's second era.

Besides being a brilliant drummer, Jones is a highly skilled musician whose talents as a composer, arranger and occasional pianist are revealed to their best advantage on *Showcase.*

The Galaxy records from the late Seventies show a lot of care—the arrangements never let the performances degenerate into aimless jamming—but nothing earthshaking is taking place anyway. These are comfortable sessions between friends, some of whom (Dexter Gordon, Ira Sullivan) naturally stand out.

At the start of the Eighties, Jones organized Dameronia, a nonet dedicated to the preservation of bop-era arranger/composer Tadd Dameron's music. After a spotty first effort, *To Tadd with Love,* Dameronia, assisted by guest star Johnny Griffin on tenor saxophone, turned in a near-perfect tribute with *Look, Stop and Listen.* — S.F.

QUINCY JONES
★ ★ ★ **And Billy Eckstine / Mer.**
★ ★ **Best of / A&M**
★ ★ ★ **Body Heat / A&M**
★ ★ **I Heard That!! / A&M**
★ ★ **Mellow Madness / A&M**
★ ★ ★ **Quintessential Charts / MCA**
★ ★ **Sounds . . . and Stuff / A&M**
Composer/arranger Quincy Jones (b. 1933) played trumpet in Lionel Hampton's group during the early Fifties (alongside such greats as Clifford Brown and Art Farmer), but soon became more interested in writing and arranging. He worked in an A&R capacity at Mercury records for seven years, producing Sarah Vaughan and Dinah Washington as well as pop acts like Lesley Gore. His arrangements at Mercury, for his own big bands and for Dizzy Gillespie and Count Basie, concentrated on updating big-band swing rather than exploring dissonant tonalities and the experimental ideas that fascinated many of his contemporaries in the Fifties and Sixties. This led to more prestigious, if musically uneventful, freelance work with the likes of Sammy Davis, Jr., Frank Sinatra and Andy Williams. It also led to such film scores as *The Pawnbroker, Mirage, In Cold Blood, The Getaway* and *The New Centurions,* as well as various television themes (*Sanford and Son, Ironside, Roots*).

Jones' Seventies and Eighties work is as glib and successful as his film/TV approach. He moved effortlessly from MOR orchestrations to disco/funk in 1974 with the hit album *Body Heat* featuring the Brothers

Johnson as the rhythm section. Jones then went on to produce the Brothers Johnson's own highly commercial records, as well as subsequent chart-topping LPs by Donna Summer and Michael Jackson (including *Thriller,* the most popular album of the early Eighties). On his own Qwest label, Jones has produced both Lena Horne's *The Lady and Her Music* and Frank Sinatra's *L.A. Is My Lady.* — J.S.

CLIFFORD JORDAN

★ ★ ★ **The Adventurer / Muse**
★ ★ ★ ★ **Blowing in from Chicago / Blue N. /PSI**
★ ★ ★ ★ **Firm Roots / Steep.**
★ ★ ★ ★ **Hello, Hank Jones / East./PSI**
★ ★ ★ ★ **Inward Fire / Muse**
★ ★ ★ ★ **Cliff Jordan / Blue N./PSI**
★ ★ ★ ★ **Clifford Jordan and the Magic Triangle on Stage / Steep.**
★ ★ ★ ★ **Night of the Mark VII / Muse**
★ ★ ★ ★ **Remembering Me-Me / Muse**
★ ★ ★ ★ **Repetition / Soul N.**
★ ★ ★ ★ **Starting Time / Prest. OJC**

Tenor/alto saxophonist and flutist Clifford Jordan (b. 1931) grew up in Chicago playing with schoolmates Johnny Griffin and John Gilmore before gigging locally with bands led by Max Roach and Sonny Stitt. Jordan arrived in New York in the mid-Fifties as part of Horace Silver's band and became part of the thriving New York jazz scene (his first albums on Blue Note, *Blowing in from Chicago* with Gilmore, Silver and drummer Art Blakey and *Cliff Jordan,* date from this period). Jordan played with J. J. Johnson, Roach and Charles Mingus among other sessions during the Sixties (*Starting Time* is a '61 set with Kenny Dorham on trumpet, Cedar Walton on piano, Wilbur Ware on bass and Albert Heath on drums).

The other records listed above cover Jordan's career as a leader from 1975 on, presenting him in a variety of contexts, from the larger groups of *Inward Fire* and *Remembering Me-Me* to the excellent quartet records. *Night of the Mark VII, Firm Roots* and *On Stage* all use the same group— Walton, bassist Sam Jones and drummer Billy Higgins. *The Adventurer* has Tommy Flanagan on piano, Bill Lee on bass and Grady Tate on drums. The 1984 *Repetition* set uses Barry Harris on piano, Walter Booker on bass and Vernel Fournier on drums. — J.S.

DUKE JORDAN

★ ★ ★ **Change of Pace / Steep.**
★ ★ **Duke's Artistry / Steep.**
★ ★ ★ **Duke's Delight / Steep.**
★ ★ ★ **Flight to Denmark / Steep.**
★ ★ ★ **The Great Session / Steep.**
★ ★ ★ **Jordu / Prest.**
★ ★ ★ **Midnight Moonlight / Steep.**
★ ★ ★ **Thinking of You / Steep.**
★ ★ ★ **Tivoli One / Steep.**
★ ★ ★ **Truth / Steep.**
★ ★ ★ **Two Loves / Steep.**

It's easy to confuse Duke Jordan (b. 1922) with Kenny Drew these days. Both are bop-era pianists who since the early Seventies have done most of their recording for the Danish SteepleChase label, using many of the same sidemen associated with the company.

Jordan is a first-rate musician who had already immortalized himself through his supple work with Charlie Parker in the mid-Forties. His own work from the Fifties is available on but one LP, *Jordu,* a trio set whose title cut is his most enduring composition. Of the SteepleChase LPs, for which Jordan usually writes most of his own material, *Change of Pace,* with Niels-Henning Orsted Pedersen and Billy Hart, is typical of the pianist's attractive and surprisingly up-to-date style. *The Great Session* should have coleader credit for guest drummer Philly Joe Jones—his playing is that intense. *Duke's Artistry* with Art Farmer could have been terrific, but suffers from a monochromatic spirit. Jordan continues to experiment into the Eighties with guest artists and sidemen on his various SteepleChase dates. — S.F.

SHEILA JORDAN

★ ★ ★ ★ **Last Year's Waltz (with Steve Kuhn) / ECM/War.**
★ ★ ★ ★ ★ **Old Time Feeling (with Harvie Swartz) / Palo Alto**
★ ★ ★ **Playground (with Steve Kuhn) / ECM/War.**
★ ★ ★ ★ **Sheila (with Arild Andersen) / Steep.**

Sheila Jordan (b. 1929) combines an acute harmonic sensibility with the ability to project a wide range of emotions with neither guile nor pretense. In paying tribute to her harmonic sophistication, Charlie Parker spoke of her "million-dollar ears"; on *Old Time Feeling* she honors him with a heartfelt rendition of his line, "Quasimodo." Hers is a unique, searching style.

Jordan has spent much of her career working as a sideperson: with bassist Peter Ind (her first recording effort, "Yesterdays"); with George Russell on the classic "You Are My Sunshine" (*Outer Thoughts*); with trombonist Roswell Rudd on *The Flexible Flyer*

(Arista) and *The Jazz Composer's Orchestra Plays Numatik Swing Band* (JCOA); Carla Bley's *Escalator over the Hill* (JCOA); Marcello Melis' *Free to Dance* (Black Saint); Steve Swallow's luminescent *Home* (ECM); and Bob Moses' *When Elephants Dream of Music* (Gramavision).

Portrait of Sheila (1962), a five-star album, was Jordan's first as a leader. Unfortunately, today it is in print only in Japan, although it can sometimes be found in U.S. record shops. *Confirmation,* a 1975 date recorded by the Japanese East Wind label, has Bird's title tune and homages to another great influence, Billie Holiday. The versions of "God Bless the Child" and "Why Was I Born?" are among Jordan's finest ballad performances, and make this hard-to-find album also worth tracking down.

Sheila Jordan's association with pianist Steve Kuhn is documented on *Playground* and *Last Year's Waltz,* both on ECM. The latter gives Jordan a chance to sing both Kuhn's songs and standards and is a cut above *Playground.* Best of all her recent work are the two-voice/bass albums: the pickup date with Andersen and the masterful documentation of the Sheila Jordan/Harvie Swartz Duo, a working band, on *Old Time Feeling.* The interplay on the latter is at times astonishing. Sheila Jordan is, historically and emotionally, one of the finest jazz singers extant. — A.R.

VIC JURIS
★ ★ ★ ★ **Bleecker Street** / Muse
★ ★ ★ **Horizon Drive** / Muse
★ ★ ★ **Roadsong** / Muse

New Jersey guitarist Vic Juris (b. 1953) played on records by Barry Miles and Eric Kloss before making his 1978 debut album, *Roadsong.* His loping, bluesy fusion style is sometimes similar to that of Wes Montgomery and Larry Coryell, but his playing has its own character. Though he records in what is most easily described as fusion, Juris' reliance more on feel than on technical prowess sets him apart from many other contemporary guitarists. *Bleecker Street* features Kloss on alto sax. — J.S.

ED KELLY
★ ★ ★ ★ Ed Kelly and Friend / Ther.
★ ★ ★ ★ Music From the Black Museum /
  Ther.
Pianist Ed Kelly is one of a small group of
outstanding but unfortunately almost unknown improvisers based in the Bay Area.
Like his regional cohorts drummer Smiley
Winters, saxophonist Bert Wilson, trumpeter
Barbara Donald, and Kelly's own bassist,
Peter Barshay, the pianist has never gained
any kind of national attention despite some
very strong recordings. Kelly's greatest attri-
bute may be his ability to master virtually
every form of Afro-American folk music:
church music, blues, Afro-sambas, jazz standards and Sam Cooke tunes meld together
cohesively in his hands, yet Kelly is strong
enough as a soloist to leave his own imprint
on each. The friend on *Ed Kelly and Friend*
is Pharoah Sanders. — F.G.

WYNTON KELLY
★ ★ ★ ★ Blues on Purpose / Xan.
★ ★ ★ ★ Kelly Blue / Fan./OJC
Subtle, relaxed, and blues-inflected, pianist
Wynton Kelly (1931–1971) was an extremely
popular sideman in the Fifties and Sixties,
and these two remaining leader dates demonstrate cohesive and magnetic qualities. Both
LPs feature Kelly with bassist Paul Chambers and drummer Jimmy Cobb, thus reuniting the rhythm section of Miles Davis' classic early-Sixties band. On *Kelly Blue* the trio
is augmented by Nat Adderley, Bobby Jas-
par and Benny Golson on two tracks. The
Kelly trio recorded a number of other sessions, including the great Wes Montgomery
Verve set, *Smokin' at the Half-Note.*
  Kelly was a musician of consistent grace
and quality, and any subsequent reissues of
his work are sure to be on a par with these
available titles. — F.G.

STAN KENTON
★ ★ ★ The Comprehensive Kenton / Cap.
★ West Side Story / Cap.
From the Forties on, keyboardist Stan Kenton (1912–1979) led a controversial West
Coast big band known less for swing or
"sweet" music than for its eclecticism and
flair for the dramatic. The band's theme,
"Artistry in Rhythm," was also the title of
the 1943 album that brought it widespread
attention. Much of Kenton's Fifties output
featured overstuffed bands playing overblown
arrangements. When not too ponderous or
commercial, Kenton's music can prove surprisingly listenable. The Capitol two-record
sampler presents him well. Not long before
his death, Kenton reacquired the masters of
his recordings and released them on his own
Creative World label. — J.S.

ROBIN KENYATTA
★ ★ ★ ★ Beggars and Stealers / Muse
★ ★ ★ ★ Girl from Martinique / ECM/
  War.
★ ★ ★ ★ Nomusa / Muse
The strong vibrato, earthy tone and abstract
conception of Robin Kenyatta's saxophone
playing bridges styles from Coleman Hawkins to Charlie Parker. Kenyatta is a versatile artist who has worked in a number of
formats, playing with figures as varied as Archie Shepp, Barry Miles, Sonny Stitt and
Mongo Santamaria. *Beggars* documents a
1969 concert on which Kenyatta played
tenor sax, the only time he ever used that instrument on records. *Nomusa,* a '75 date,
presents Kenyatta on his regular alto saxophone, and features a good multitracked
duet with percussionist Dom Salvador, while
Girl from Martinique is a more abstract set
recorded with Wolfgang Dauner on keyboards, Arild Andersen on bass and Fred
Braceful on drums. — J.S.

B.B. KING

★ ★ ★ ★ **Anthology of the Blues—B. B. King 1949–50 / Kent**
★ ★ ★ ★ ★ **Back in the Alley / ABC**
★ ★ ★ ★ ★ **B. B. King Live / Kent**
★ ★ ★ ★ ★ **B. B. King Live at the Regal / ABC**
★ ★ ★ ★ ★ **B. B. King Live in Cook County Jail / ABC**
★ ★ ★ ★ **The Best of B. B. King / ABC**
★ ★ ★ ★ **Better Than Ever / Kent**
★ ★ ★ ★ **Blues and Jazz / MCA**
★ ★ ★ ★ **Blues Is King / ABC**
★ ★ ★ ★ **Blues on Top of Blues / ABC**
★ ★ ★ ★ **Boss of the Blues / Kent**
★ ★ ★ ★ **Confessin' the Blues / ABC**
★ ★ ★ ★ **Completely Well / ABC**
★ ★ ★ **Doing My Thing, Lord / Kent**
★ ★ ★ **Electric B. B. King / ABC**
★ ★ ★ **Friends / ABC**
★ ★ ★ ★ ★ **From the Beginning / Kent**
★ ★ ★ ★ **Greatest Hits of B. B. King / Kent**
★ ★ ★ ★ **Guess Who / ABC**
★ ★ ★ ★ **Incredible Soul of B. B. King / Kent**
★ ★ ★ ★ **Indianola Mississippi Seeds / ABC**
★ ★ ★ ★ ★ **The Jungle / Kent**
★ ★ ★ ★ **King Size / ABC**
★ ★ ★ ★ **L.A. Midnight / ABC**
★ ★ ★ ★ **Let Me Love You / Kent**
★ ★ ★ ★ **Live and Well / ABC**
★ ★ ★ ★ ★ **Live, B. B. King on Stage / Kent**
★ ★ ★ ★ **Lucille / ABC**
★ ★ ★ ★ **Lucille Talks Back / ABC**
★ ★ ★ ★ **Mr. Blues / ABC**
★ ★ ★ ★ **Original "Sweet Sixteen" / Kent**
★ ★ ★ ★ ★ **Pure Soul / Kent**
★ ★ ★ ★ **There Must Be a Better World Somewhere / MCA**
★ ★ ★ ★ **To Know You Is to Love You / ABC**
★ ★ ★ **Turn On with B. B. King / Kent**
★ ★ ★ ★ ★ **Underground Blues / Kent**

B. B. King is perhaps the greatest figure on the postwar urban blues scene, a powerful performer, a consolidator of blues styles, a great bandleader, an even greater singer and an innovative guitarist who's influenced virtually every blues guitarist to come after him. His clean, economical style can be heard quite clearly in the work of Eric Clapton and Michael Bloomfield, to use two stand-out examples among rock players.

King's intelligence and consummate professionalism have made him revered by a black audience that looks to his performance as the standard against which all else must be judged. Although King never made direct attempts to pander to a white audience, his reputation grew in the Sixties after his im-pact on rock players became obvious, and King played a series of enthusiastically received dates at the Fillmores East and West.

The key to King's success is the wide range of ideas he brings in very squarely under the umbrella of blues playing. As a child, he heard a great deal of gospel music and listened to recordings by Blind Lemon Jefferson; the Texas guitar style of Jefferson and T-Bone Walker became B.B.'s foundation. But King's musical exposure was extensive, and he appended many disparate elements to that base: Jimmy Rushing's singing with the Count Basie orchestra; Al Hibbler's singing with Duke Ellington; the guitar playing of jazz stars Django Reinhardt and Charlie Christian; other blues players like Bukka White, Lowell Fulsom, Elmore James and Johnny Moore and the Three Blazers.

In 1948 King became a Memphis disc jockey, quickly gained a reputation for playing great records that couldn't be heard elsewhere, and began to piece together ideas for his own recording career. King's ear for great material led him to cover a number of songs that did far better for him than for the original writers. His first hit, in 1950, was with Lowell Fulsom's "Three O'Clock Blues." Later in his career, he turned Memphis Slim's "Every Day I Have the Blues" and Robert Nighthawk's "Sweet Little Angel" into such personal statements that most people think King wrote them himself. King also successfully covered Arthur Crudup's "Rock Me Mama," Joe Turner's "Sweet Sixteen" and Roy Hawkins' "The Thrill Is Gone."

King's first Memphis band included vocalist Bobby Bland, who credits King as a major influence on his singing, pianist Johnny Ace and drummer Earl Forrest. Once King began touring behind the success of his first records, he developed a sophisticated band setup built around a solid rhythm backup and featuring tight horn sections to punctuate his highly emotional "crying" blues style and expressive guitar playing.

Over the years, King has recorded prolifically, yet he's kept his ideas varied and the emotional content well focused enough so that he never sounds stale. He has practically never cut a bad record.

His earliest available work is on the Fifties and Sixties Kent albums. Kent continued to release previously rejected material after King left for ABC (which later was taken over by MCA), but in general the Kent records are very good. The ABC material is more far-ranging, as King expanded into using session musicians and augmented line-ups. Some of these records, particularly several produced by Bill Szymczyk (*Completely Well, Indianola Mississippi Seeds*), show how many different things can be done within the seemingly tight restrictions of the blues.

In the Eighties King continued to make powerful records. *There Must Be a Better World Somewhere* is a moving set of contemporary blues, while the outstanding *Blues and Jazz* showcases some of King's finest vocal performances against exciting big-band arrangements.

King's best records, though, are the live sets, where the electricity of audience/performer interaction spurred King on to elaborate vocal and instrumental histrionics, and he demonstrated his total control over the concert experience. *Live at the Regal* is the generally acknowledged classic. — J.S.

MORGANA KING
★ ★ ★ **Everything Must Change** / **Muse**
★ ★ ★ **Higher Ground** / **Muse**
★ ★ **Looking through the Eyes of Love** / **Muse**
★ **Stretchin' Out** / **Muse**
Morgana King (b. 1930) is an enigma: a warm-voiced singer who can swing and scat and who knows good songs. But she drags in so much pop dross without transforming it that she dilutes her effectiveness. Also problematic are mannerisms that clutter rather than enliven her vocal lines. Some years ago, "A Taste of Honey" brought King to the attention of the record-buying public; her role as Mama Corleone in *The Godfather* claimed for her the attention of an even larger audience. The question now is whether she can bring herself back to warm, less affected singing. — A.R.

TEDDI KING
★ ★ ★ **Lovers and Losers** / **Audiop.**
★ ★ ★ **Marian Remembers Teddi (with Marian McPartland)** / **Hal.**
★ ★ **Someone to Light Up My Life** / **Audiop.**
★ ★ ★ ★ **. . . This Is New** / **Inner**
Although ignored by the jazz press and almost unknown to the larger jazz audience, Teddi King (1929–1977) was a knowledgeable, swinging singer with an ear for exceptional songs. Her early work, especially that with pianists Beryl Booker (herself an unsung giant) and Jimmy Jones on the out-of-print '*Round Midnight* and also with George Shearing, reveals her allegiance to jazz. Later dates with Marian McPartland and Dave McKenna (. . . *This Is New*) display fine

musicianship and great depth of expression. — A.R.

RAHSAAN ROLAND KIRK
★ ★ ★ ★ **The Best of Rahsaan Roland Kirk** / **Atl.**
★ ★ ★ **Boogie-Woogie String Along for Real** / **War.**
★ ★ ★ **The Case of the Three-Sided Dream in Audio Color** / **Atl.**
★ ★ ★ **Funk Underneath** / **Prest.**
★ ★ **Gifts and Messages** / **Trip**
★ ★ ★ ★ **Kirk's Works** / **Em.**
★ ★ ★ **Other Folk's Music** / **Atl.**
★ ★ ★ **Pre-Rahsaan (with Jack McDuff and Jaki Byard)** / **Prest.**
★ ★ ★ **The Return of the 5,000-Pound Man** / **War.**
★ ★ ★ **Rip, Rig and Panic** / **Trip**
★ ★ ★ **We Free Kings** / **Trip**
The most impressive characteristic of Rahsaan Roland Kirk (1936–1977) was his resilience. A continual innovator on reed instruments of every imaginable type (the "miscellaneous" category in jazz polls was his own before the synthesizers and percussionists took over), he developed ways to play three instruments at once; to blow flute and sing simultaneously (which gave Jethro Tull's Ian Anderson the idea for the two licks he uses); to play, without stopping, from now until Tuesday, by employing a circular breathing technique; and to shift effortlessly from his most political original compositions to standards, jingles and a variety of unidentifiable, but vaguely recognizable, worn-out phrases which he retreads with his own brand of steely spikes. Late in the Seventies he fought back from a crippling stroke, at first playing with one hand until he regained his strength. All this from a man who had seen only dim light since childhood.

Kirk was at the same time a prankster, a storyteller and a professor of dynamism. He would fly through chord changes, his soul ruffled by some personal demon, then sound off in a hard-edged, bluesy ballad. He led his own bands for over fifteen years—his energy, logic and balls always racing somewhere ahead of the rhythm.

The *Best of* and the *Kirk's Works* double album (recorded 1962–65) are the best place for neophytes to start. — A.E.G.

OSAMU KITAJIMA
★ ★ **Dragon King** / **Ari.**
★ ★ **Masterless Samurai** / **Head.**
Osamu Kitajima is a Japanese fusion guitarist with a twist—in addition to electric and

acoustic guitars he plays the koto and biwa, traditional Japanese string instruments. Unfortunately, his best album, *Benzaiten,* released on the Antilles label in 1976, is out of print. — J.S.

JOHN KLEMMER

★ ★ ★ **All the Children Cried** / Cadet
★ ★ **And We Were Lovers** / Cadet
★ ★ ★ **Arabesque** / MCA
★ ★ **Barefoot Ballet** / MCA
★ ★ ★ **Blowin' Gold** / Cadet
★ ★ ★ **Constant Throb** / MCA
★ ★ **Eruptions** / Cadet
★ ★ **Fresh Feathers** / MCA
★ ★ ★ **Intensity** / MCA
★ ★ **Involvement** / Cadet
★ **Lifestyle** / MCA
★ ★ **Magic and Movement** / MCA
★ ★ **Magic Moments** / Chess
★ ★ **Touch** / MCA
★ ★ ★ **Waterfall** / MCA

Chicago-based saxophonist/flutist John Klemmer (b. 1946) studied under Stan Kenton and was featured soloist in Don Ellis' band before forming his own combo in the Sixties. On his first albums, recorded for Chess and Cadet, Klemmer was obviously influenced by John Coltrane, and made several attempts to incorporate social-protest themes into the program of his music, all to little avail. Later, on his Impulse and ABC records (now rereleased on MCA), Klemmer went heavily into the use of Echoplex and other electronic effects on his saxophone. Some of these records sound interesting, but inevitably Klemmer's sound is just too gimmicky to hold up over repeated listenings. — J.S.

ERIC KLOSS

★ ★ **Bodies'** (with Barry Miles) / Muse
★ ★ **Celebration** / Muse
★ ★ ★ ★ **Consciousness!** / Prest.
★ ★ ★ **Essence** / Muse
★ ★ ★ **First Class Kloss** / Prest.
★ ★ ★ ★ **Grits and Gravy** / Prest.
★ ★ ★ ★ ★ **In the Land of the Giants** / Prest.
★ ★ ★ **Introducing** / Prest.
★ ★ ★ **Life Force** / Prest.
★ ★ **Now** (with Mike Nock) / Muse
★ ★ ★ ★ **One, Two, Free** / Muse
★ ★ **Sharing** (with Gil Goldstein) / Omni.
★ ★ ★ ★ **Sky Shadows** / Prest.
★ ★ **Together** (with Barry Miles) / Muse
★ ★ ★ ★ **To Hear Is to See!** / Prest.

When Eric Kloss (b. 1949) first hit the scene in the late Sixties, his youth and blindness were talked about as much as his prowess on the alto saxophone. The Prestige recordings from this period are still Kloss' best work. Teamed with some of the greatest rhythm sections of the day, he truly came alive. *Grits* and *Land of Giants* use the blockbuster force of Jaki Byard, Richard Davis and Alan Dawson with tenor titan Booker Ervin thrown in on the latter to stir things up even more. Kloss branched out even further on *Conciousness!* and *To Hear* by employing Miles Davis' adventurous rhythm section: Chick Corea, Dave Holland and Jack DeJohnette. *One, Two, Free,* as the title implies, is also in this advanced vein.

Unfortunately Kloss, who had recorded occasional pop numbers throughout his Prestige period, became increasingly interested in electric-fusion during the next decade and his work suffered. While he has retained his great command of the instrument, the music itself is shockingly lightweight. *Essence,* with Hannibal Peterson, is his last burst of inspired power. — S.F.

LEE KONITZ

★ ★ ★ ★ ★ **Duets** / Mile.
★ ★ ★ ★ **Ezz-thetic** / Prest.
★ ★ ★ **Figure and Spirit** / Prog.
★ ★ ★ ★ **Four Keys** (with Martial Solal) / Pausa
★ ★ ★ **Lee Konitz and Warne Marsh** / Atl.
★ ★ ★ ★ **Lee Konitz Meets Warne Marsh Again** / Pausa
★ ★ ★ ★ **Lee Konitz Quintet** / Chi.
★ ★ ★ ★ ★ **Motion** / Verve
★ ★ **Nonet** / Rou.
★ ★ ★ ★ **Nonet** / Chi.
★ ★ ★ ★ **Oleo** / Sonet
★ ★ ★ **Peacemeal** / Mile.
★ ★ ★ **Pyramid** (with Paul Bley and Bill Connors) / IAI
★ ★ ★ ★ ★ **Satori** / Mile.
★ ★ ★ ★ **Spirits** / Mile.
★ ★ ★ **Tenorlee** / Choice
★ ★ ★ ★ **Yes, Yes Nonet** / Steep.

Lee Konitz (b. 1927) has been among the purest jazz improvisers for thirty-five years. He emerged in the late Forties as a member of Claude Thornhill's band, where his alto-sax solos demonstrated how the instrument could be played in a modern style without mimicking Charlie Parker. Soon he was studying and working with Lennie Tristano (some of their important collaborations are on the Prestige anthology, *First Sessions 1949/50*), while becoming a featured soloist in Miles Davis' Birth of the Cool band and a leader in his own right. *Ezz-thetic,* with Davis as a sideman on four tracks, captures his early style, and the recently revised

Konitz/Warne Marsh meeting on Atlantic finds the saxophonist deeply enmeshed in the Tristano ethos.

Although Konitz played a critical role in defining the cool (and some would add Caucasian) alternative to hot bebop, this should not be taken to suggest that he lacked drive or passion. *Motion,* a 1961 trio session with the volcanic Elvin Jones on drums, shows just how intense Konitz can be. He retains, however, an identification with Tristano's highly intellectualized approach and has frequently brought the style to life, as on the 1971 retrospective *Spirits* (with Sal Mosca in the piano chair) and the 1976 in-person reunion with tenorman (and fellow Tristano student) Warne Marsh (*Again*).

Among the essential Konitz albums since his 1965 return after a brief performing hiatus are *Duets,* 1967 encounters with a diverse group of musicians (including Jim Hall, Ray Nance, Joe Henderson); *Satori,* explosive 1974 readings of standards with Dave Holland, Jack DeJohnette and pianist Martial Solal; *Oleo,* a drummerless trio venture from the same period; and *Quintet,* where he teams with the like-minded alto of Bob Mover.

In 1975 Konitz formed a nine-piece band for occasional club work in New York, and after a disappointing debut album on Roulette, it has turned out two well-written and -played efforts (*Nonet* on Chiaroscuro, *Yes, Yes*) that feature trombone great Jimmy Knepper in addition to the leader. — B.B.

IRENE KRAL
★ ★ ★ ★ Gentle Rain (with Alan Broadbent) / Choice
★ ★ ★ Irene Kral with the Junior Mance Trio / DRG
★ ★ ★ Kral Space (with Alan Broadbent) / Cata.
★ ★ ★ ★ ★ Where Is Love? (with Alan Broadbent) / Choice

Singer Irene Kral (1932–1978) reached the peak of her form in the two duet albums with pianist/arranger Alan Broadbent, *Where Is Love?* and *Gentle Rain.* She died after a long bout with cancer, leaving as her legacy jazz ballad-singing unlike any other singer's (her allegiance to Carmen McRae granted). — A.R.

KARIN KROG
★ ★ ★ ★ Some Other Spring (with Dexter Gordon) / Story.

Some Other Spring is the sole U.S. release by the powerful Norwegian singer Karin Krog (b. 1937). At times her Scandinavian accent gets in the way, but Krog is a passionate, skillful jazz improviser. Alongside the magisterial tenor of Dexter Gordon and Kenny Drew's blues-tinged piano (organ on Krog's incandescent "Blues Eyes"), she smokes "Jelly, Jelly" (Gordon joins in on vocals here), "I Wish I Knew" and "Everybody's Somebody's Fool." It can only be hoped that Krog's collaboration with Archie Shepp (*Hi-Fly*) and the gentle *As You Are* will be released here soon. — A.R.

GENE KRUPA
★ ★ ★ Original Battle / Verve

Drummer Gene Krupa (1909–1973) played in a number of Chicago bands during the Twenties before achieving fame as the powerful, showy drummer in Benny Goodman's organization during the mid-Thirties, when his drum solo was featured on the hit single "Sing, Sing, Sing." His popularity helped him to a successful run as a leader, but the only remaining in-print evidence of this period is the drum battle record with Buddy Rich listed above. — J.S.

PETER KUHN
★ ★ ★ ★ The Kill / Soul N.
★ ★ ★ ★ Livin' Right / Big City Records

Avant-garde clarinetist with a fine command of diverse tones. Peter Kuhn's recordings are in line with what was going on in the New York loft scene during the Seventies, and feature William Parker and Dennis Charles. *Livin' Right* is available only by mail from the Jazz Composers' Orchestra Association/New Music Distribution Service, 500 Broadway, New York, N.Y. 10012. — F.G.

STEVE LACY
★ ★ ★ ★ Ballets / Hat Hut
★ ★ ★ ★ ★ Capers / Hat Hut
★ ★ ★ ★ ★ Clinkers / Hat Hut
★ ★ ★ ★ ★ Evidence / Prest.
★ ★ ★ The Flame / Soul N.
★ ★ ★ ★ Prospectus / Hat Hut
★ ★ ★ ★ Raps / Adel.
★ ★ ★ ★ ★ Reflections / Fan./OJC
★ ★ ★ ★ Regeneration (with Roswell Rudd)
/ Soul N.
★ ★ ★ ★ ★ School Days / QED
★ ★ ★ ★ Sidelines (with Michael Smith) /
IAI
★ ★ ★ ★ Snake-Out (with Mal Waldron) /
Hat Hut
★ ★ ★ Songs (with Brion Gysin) / Hat Hut
★ ★ ★ ★ ★ Soprano Sax / Fan./OJC
★ ★ ★ Stamps / Hat Hut
★ ★ ★ Tips (with Steve Potts) / Hat Hut
★ ★ ★ Trickles (with Roswell Rudd) / Black
S.
★ ★ Troubles / Black S.
★ ★ ★ ★ ★ The Way / Hat Hut
Steve Lacy (b. 1934) was the first important
soprano saxophonist since Sidney Bechet. In
the Fifties, when no other modern player
was using the horn, he devoted himself to it
exclusively and made his mark with direct,
melodically coherent playing in the bands of
Cecil Taylor, Gil Evans and Thelonious
Monk. *Soprano Sax,* from '57, was his first
album as a leader. As the Sixties began, he
organized a quartet with trombonist Roswell
Rudd (heard on *School Days*) that devoted
itself exclusively to Monk's compositions.
Reflections, which predates the quartet, is an
excellent all-Monk recital that includes Mal
Waldron and Elvin Jones. *Evidence,* with
Don Cherry as the second horn and music
by Ellington and Strayhorn as well as Monk,
is another excellent album from this period.
Most of Lacy's time since 1965 has been
spent in Europe, and most of his available
albums were recorded there, often with his

quintet (Steve Potts, alto; Iréne Aebi, strings
and voice; Kent Carter, bass; Oliver Johnson, drums). The band's music, a mix of free
playing, Monkish angularity and repetition
akin to "process" composers Glass and
Reich, is best represented on *The Way,* a
complete performance of Lacy's "Tao" song
cycle, and *Prospectus,* with Lacy expanding
to a septet that includes trombonist George
Lewis.
Other examples of Lacy's highly consistent
playing can be found in his solo album
Clinkers, and *Capers,* a hard-blowing trio
performance made in New York with former
Cecil Taylor compatriot Dennis Charles on
drums and the late Ronnie Boykins (Sun
Ra's bassist). *Ballets,* a two-record set, allows listeners to experience Lacy both solo
and with his group.
Lacy is a loyal collaborator, and some of
his best recorded work has been done with
old friends. *Regeneration,* where he and
Rudd return to the music of Monk and Herbie Nichols in a quintet setting, stands out,
as do the knotty duets with Waldron on
Snake-Out. — B.B.

L.A.4
★ ★ Exec Suite / Conc. J.
★ ★ Just Friends / Conc. J.
★ ★ The L.A.4 / Conc. J.
★ ★ Montage / Conc. J.
★ ★ Scores / Conc. J.
★ ★ Watch What Happens / Conc. J.
★ ★ Zaca / Conc. J.
Four fine musicians—Ray Brown (b. 1926),
Laurindo Almeida (b. 1927), Bud Shank (b.
1926) and Jeff Hamilton—make seven anti-
septic and predictable albums. Party music
for retirement villages. — F.G.

BIRELI LAGRENE
★ ★ ★ 15 / Ant.
★ ★ ★ Routes to Django / Ant.

That Bireli Lagrene has captured the essence of Django Reinhardt's romantically expressive and technically awesome guitar style is remarkable; that he achieved this by the time he was thirteen is frightening. *Routes* documents this phenomenon with the gypsy prodigy ripping through Reinhardt-inspired material with verve and assurance. On *15,* the maturing whiz kid moves beyond re-creating the master's Thirties sound and begins to incorporate his massive acoustic chops into a more contemporary context. — S.F.

CLEO LAINE
★ ★ **Best Friends (with John Williams) / RCA**
★ ★ ★ **Live at the Wavendon Festival / Jazz M.**
Cleo Laine (b. 1927) is basically a pop singer whose choice of material runs the gamut from light opera to improvisational jazz vocals. She does some of her best things on the live *Wavendon* LP. Her reputation as a stylist of wide range and impeccable technique is more than a bit overblown; still, her theatrical sense and emotional dynamics can often astonish. — B.T.

OLIVER LAKE
★ ★ ★ **Bowie/Lake / Sack.**
★ ★ ★ ★ ★ **Heavy Spirits / Ari./Free.**
★ ★ ★ ★ ★ **Holding Together / Black S.**
★ ★ ★ **Ntu: Point from Which Creation Begins / Ari./Free.**
★ ★ ★ ★ **Passing Through / P.T.**
Oliver Lake (b. 1944) has proven in a short time to be the most interesting voice to emerge from the St. Louis music collective, Black Artists Group. A sample of BAG's scope can be detected on *Ntu: Point from Which Creation Begins,* a 1971 St. Louis production that manages to contain postbop, acid guitar, energy jazz and the adventures in spontaneous form that the closely aligned Association for the Advancement of Creative Musicians in Chicago first brought to national attention.

The best example of Lake the composer and soloist (primarily on alto sax, though he also uses soprano sax and flute) is the 1975 *Heavy Spirits.* His commanding expressionism works equally well in the standard jazz quintet instrumentation, which is enhanced by his irregular yet lyrical writing; a terse unaccompanied solo; and three unique pieces for alto and three violins. Trumpeter Olu Dara is impressive on the quintet tracks.

New music fans should take the time to seek out Lake's albums on foreign and private labels. *Passing Through,* his privately produced album from a 1974 Paris solo concert, has more variety and attention to nuance than most unaccompanied ventures. In 1976 Lake led a quartet with the innovative young guitarist Michael Gregory Jackson which tempered their wilder moments with complex structures and abstract balladry; bassist Fred Hopkins and drummer Paul Maddox complete the excellent group on the Italian *Holding Together.* A Canadian duet concert with trombonist Joseph Bowie has less shading but much playing at the edge of current horn technique.
★ ★ ★ **Buster Bee (with Julius Hemphill) / Sack.**
★ ★ ★ ★ **Clevant Fitzhubert (A Good Friend of Mine) / Black S.**
★ ★ **Jump Up / Gram.**
★ ★ **Plug It / Gram.**
★ ★ ★ ★ **Prophet / Black S.**
Arista has quickly retired its Freedom and Novus jazz series, and taken a lot of Oliver Lake out of the catalogue in the process (including the fine 1978 *Life Dance of Is*). Currently, Lake must be sought out on imports, where he records with the World Saxophone Quartet, various associates (Karl Berger, Michael Gregory Jackson, Jerome Cooper), and occasionally under his own name. *Buster Bee,* from Canada, is a duo album with Julius Hemphill, an associate from the St. Louis days who also works with Lake in the WSQ. An interesting record, but not the place for the uninitiated to begin. The 1980 *Prophet* employs almost conventional quintet instrumentation (too bad about the Fender bass, though) in a totally successful tribute to Eric Dolphy that includes three of Dolphy's fine compositions plus three Lake originals. One of the finest homages from a period when homage was becoming the norm. The Fender mistake is rectified on *Clevant Fitzhubert* by dropping bass entirely for a bassless quartet. The album is marked by Lake's varied compositions, and the impeccable percussion of Pheeroan ak Laff.

Since 1981, much of Lake's time has been devoted to Jump Up, his reggae band. Their debut record proves that Lake and company can handle the Jamaican idiom, but there is little room for the leader's saxophone and not much to suggest that the group is any more than merely competent. Lake is also a member of the World Saxophone Quintet. — B.B.

LAMBERT, HENDRICKS AND ROSS
★ ★ ★ ★ **Sing a Song of Basie / MCA**
★ ★ ★ **Sing Ellington / CSP**
★ ★ ★ **Way Out Voices / Odys.**
★ ★ ★ **With the Ike Isaacs Trio / Odys.**

Taking a cue from the popularity of vocalese as originated by Eddie Jefferson and King Pleasure, in 1958 Dave Lambert, Jon Hendricks and Annie Ross joined together for the recording project, *Sing a Song of Basie,* with Hendricks putting words to well-known Basie instrumental tracks. The project was so successful that the group went on to perform live and make a number of other records in the same style before breaking up in 1962. — J.S.

HAROLD LAND
★ ★ ★ ★ **The Fox / Contem.**
★ ★ ★ ★ **Grooveyard / Contem.**
★ ★ ★ ★ **West Coast Blues! / Fan./OJC**
★ ★ ★ ★ **Xocia's Dance / Muse**
Still best known for his recordings with Max Roach and Clifford Brown, Harold Land (b. 1928) is one of the finest of the hard-driving West Coast tenors to have emerged during the Fifties. His two albums for Contemporary are quintessential examples of the kind of music that label was recording in the late Fifties and early Sixties: vigorous hard bop with a twinge of modernism. *West Coast Blues!* was made in 1960 with a group including guitarist Wes Montgomery. His most recent album, for Muse in 1981, demonstrates that Land has continued to absorb changes, and one hears the influence of tenormen who came up after Land was already established. His approach is somewhat more romantic these days, and his tone is satisfyingly sweet and full, but without a hint of sugariness. A class player all the way. — F.G.

ART LANDE
★ ★ **Eccentricities of Earl Dant / 1750 Arch**
★ ★ ★ **Red Lanta / ECM/War.**
★ ★ **Rubisa Patrol / ECM/War.**
★ ★ **Story of Ba-Ku / 1750 Arch**
Keyboardist Art Lande (b. 1958) grew up in the United States but was discovered in Europe during the mid-Seventies by ECM producer Manfred Eicher, who teamed him with saxophonist/flutist Jan Garbarek on *Red Lanta.* Lande followed with his own group's debut, *Rubisa Patrol,* and has recorded sporadically since, including the solo piano set, *Eccentricities.* — J.S.

PRINCE LASHA
★ ★ **And Now Music (with Webster Armstrong) / Daagnim**
★ ★ ★ ★ **Firebirds (with Sonny Simmons) / Contem.**
★ ★ ★ **Firebirds Live at Berkeley Jazz Festival / Bird.**
★ ★ ★ **Inside Story / Enja**
Multi-reedman Prince Lasha (b. 1929) was among the handful of more experimental players in the Bay Area during the Sixties and Seventies. Like Sonny Simmons, with whom he worked and recorded, Lasha never really gained much attention outside his home area, despite the quality of his work, especially on the Contemporary *Firebirds.*

Lasha works best with a foil: on the *Live at Berkeley* album, the second reed player is Hadley Caliman, and on the Daagnim disc it's vocalist Webster Armstrong. The disorganization and lack of invention on that date, Lasha's most recent, suggests a decline in powers. — F.G.

AZAR LAWRENCE
★ ★ ★ **Bridge into the New Age / Prest.**
★ ★ ★ **Summer Solstice / Prest.**
A dead-earnest Coltrane disciple, Azar Lawrence (b. 1954) reached a career high point as sideman with both the Elvin Jones and the McCoy Tyner bands during the Seventies. Solo albums show him in the same light, but with less inspiring musical company. — J.S.

GARY LAWRENCE AND HIS SIZZLING SYNCOPATORS
★ ★ **Gary Lawrence and His Sizzling Syncopators / Blue G.**
Big-band posturing, somewhere in between nostalgia and camp. — J.S.

RONNIE LAWS
★ ★ **Fever / Blue N.**
★ ★ **Flame / Lib.**
★ ★ **Friends and Strangers / Blue N.**
★ ★ **Mr. Nice Guy / Cap.**
★ ★ ★ **Pressure Sensitive / Blue N.**
Ronnie Laws (b. 1950) came out of the Houston blues/jazz scene emulating "soul" saxophonists like David "Fathead" Newman while being influenced by other locals from his flutist brother Hubert to the Jazz Crusaders. Ronnie is equally at home playing blues, R&B, jazz and rock styles—he's performed as a sideman with both Hugh Masekela and Earth, Wind and Fire. His solo recordings all suffer to some extent from the fusion/disco formulae that have dominated Seventies and Eighties jazz albums under major label distribution, but the emotion and commitment of his hometown background animates most of his playing, particularly on *Pressure Sensitive.* — J.S.

JANET LAWSON
★ ★ ★ **Janet Lawson Quintet / Inner**
Janet Lawson has a sultry voice and a finely developed scat-singing technique rooted in the style of Ella Fitzgerald, Anita O'Day, Sarah Vaughan, Sheila Jordan and Betty Carter. Unlike those singers, though, Lawson neglects the lyric potential of the songs she covers. In her next outings, one hopes for greater parity between Janet Lawson the chord runner and Janet Lawson the storyteller. — A.R.

JOHN LEE AND GERRY BROWN
★ ★ **Mango Sunrise / Blue N.**
The native Philadelphia rhythm section of bassist John Lee (b. 1952) and percussionist Gerry Brown backed up Pharoah Sanders, Joe Henderson, Carlos Garnett and Lionel Hampton in the early Seventies before moving to Europe, where work with Joachim Kuhn and Philip Catherine led them in a fusion direction. Upon their return to the States they played in fusion bands led by Larry Coryell, Michal Urbaniak, Norman Connors and Lonnie Liston Smith. Their own music relies more on well-turned pop and R&B moves than on the hackneyed fusion jazz clichés they helped perpetuate as sidemen. — J.S.

GEORGE LEWIS
★ ★ ★ ★ **Chicago Slow Dance / Lovely M.**
★ ★ ★ ★ ★ **The George Lewis Solo Trombone Record / Sack.**
★ ★ ★ ★ ★ **Homage to Charles Parker / Black S.**
★ ★ ★ **The Imaginary Suite (duets by Lewis and Douglas Ewart) / Black S.**
★ ★ ★ ★ **Monads / Black S.**
George Lewis (b. 1952), trombonist and composer, is representative of a young generation of black musicians both prepared and determined to draw upon the most challenging aspects of all musical forms, including electronics and the European tradition. Lewis' own background includes early membership in Chicago's Association for the Advancement of Creative Musicians (AACM), a degree in philosophy from Yale, touring with diverse leaders (Count Basie, Carla Bley, Anthony Braxton, Gil Evans) and direction of the SoHo (N.Y.) experimental composers' forum The Kitchen.
The above albums represent Lewis' output between 1976 and 1978. With the exception of *Solo Trombone* (one of the finest solo-horn efforts on any wind instrument), all employ synthesizers, plus a kind of writing—extremely slow-moving textures and situa-

tions—in which the soloist is subordinated to the ensemble development. This does not necessarily sound like jazz as even avant-garde fans know it, but it results in stimulating and surprisingly warm contemporary music nonetheless.
Monads is perhaps the best introduction to Lewis' music, with two sextet pieces, a duet by the composer and reedman Douglas Ewart (the pair also have an entire album of duets), and one piece where Lewis is bracketed by two pianos. The *Chicago* disc, by a quartet including Richard Teitelbaum on synthesizer, finds Lewis expanding his techniques to an album-length piece—a convincing effort, but one bettered by the excellent *Homage to Charles Parker.* On this most recent of Lewis' works, another quartet (with Ewart, Teitelbaum and Anthony Davis) explores the blues and a more harmonically static form in music that points the way to the future. — B.B.

MEADE LUX LEWIS
★ ★ ★ **Barrelhouse Piano / Story.**
★ ★ ★ ★ ★ **The Complete Blue Note Recordings of Albert Ammons and Meade Lux Lewis / Mosaic**
★ ★ ★ **Meade Lux Lewis / Arc. Folk**
★ ★ ★ ★ **Tell Your Story / Oldie B.**
Lewis was one of the best-known practitioners of barrelhouse piano, which he learned in his native Chicago under the tutelage of Jimmy Yancey. He hit his high point in 1927 with the hard-driving "Honky-Tonk Train Blues," which became his trademark. Lewis and Albert Ammons were a powerful combination as the Mosaic collection demonstrates. — J.S.

MEL LEWIS
★ ★ ★ **Live in Montreux / Pausa**
★ ★ ★ **Make Me Smile / Fine.**
★ ★ ★ **Mellifluous / Gatem.**
★ ★ ★ **Naturally / Telarc**
★ ★ ★ **The New Mel Lewis Quintet Live / Sandra**
Drummer Mel Lewis (b. 1929) is an excellent big-band player whose work with co-leader Thad Jones has won much respect. The above sessions under his own name run along the same lines as those under Jones' name; both feature good players in spirited communion running through cleverly turned arrangements. — J.S.

RAMSEY LEWIS
★ ★ ★ **Best of / Col.**
★ ★ ★ **Blues for the Night Owl / Odys.**

★ ★ ★ Chance Encounter / Col.
★ ★ ★ Don't It Feel Good / Col.
★ ★ ★ Greatest Hits / Col.
★ ★ ★ Legacy / Col.
★ ★ ★ Live at the Savoy / Col.
★ ★ ★ Routes / Col.
★ ★ ★ Salongo / Col.
★ ★ ★ ★ Sun Goddess / Col.
★ ★ ★ Tequila Mockingbird / Col.
★ ★ ★ Three Piece Suite / Col.

Keyboardist Ramsey Lewis (b. 1935), a university-trained musician from Chicago, has been fronting his own groups since the late Fifties, concentrating on a very funky, blues-oriented approach to jazz improvisation. Lewis recorded a hit single, "Wade in the Water," for the Chicago-based Cadet Records in the mid-Sixties and then went on to make a series of similar discs for Columbia, earning instrumental hits with versions of "Hang On Sloopy" and "The In Crowd." His style is engaging, popular and extremely consistent from album to album, whether he's playing electric piano or synthesizers, the latter being featured to good effect on *Sun Goddess.*   — J.S.

DAVE LIEBMAN

★ ★ ★ Dave Liebman / West 54
★ ★ ★ ★ Drum Ode / ECM/War.
★ ★ ★ If They Only Knew / Timel.
★ ★ ★ ★ ★ Lookout Farm / ECM/War.
★ ★ ★ ★ Pendulum / Artists H.

Saxophonist/flutist Dave Liebman (b. 1946) worked in the horn section of the early-Seventies jazz/rock band Ten Wheel Drive before building his reputation as a jazz sideman with Elvin Jones, John McLaughlin, and the post-*Bitches Brew*-era Miles Davis. Liebman's first outings as a leader, Open Sky (see separate entry), with bassist Frank Tusa, drummer Bob Moses, pianist Richard Beirach and Liebman on space-age soprano sax, remain his best work along with the magnificent *Lookout Farm* here. *Pendulum* features Beirach and trumpeter Randy Brecker, another Davis disciple.

The 1980 *If They Only Knew* set includes Terumasa Hino on trumpet and fluegelhorn, John Scofield on guitar, Ron McLure on bass and Adam Nussbaum on drums. Liebman is also cofeatured on guitarist Steve Masakowski's album *Mars* (Prescription).
— J.S.

ABBEY LINCOLN

★ ★ ★ ★ ★ Abbey Is Blue / Fan./OJC
★ ★ ★ ★ ★ Golden Lady / Inner
★ ★ ★ ★ People in Me / Inner
★ ★ ★ Straight Ahead / Jazz

★ ★ ★ ★ Talking to the Sun / Enja
★ ★ That's Him! / Riv.

Abbey Lincoln (b. 1930, a.k.a. Aminata Moseka) began her career as a supper-club singer, but changed musical direction after becoming associated (professionally and personally) with drummer Max Roach. Their partnership attained its musical summit in 1960 with the release of Roach's *Freedom Now Suite* (Columbia), also featuring Coleman Hawkins.

Although Lincoln is an accomplished actress (*For Love of Ivy, The Girl Can't Help It* and the classic *Nothing But a Man*), it is jazz that has stirred her imagination and given her universalist visions their most effective expression ("People in Me" and "Kohjoh-No-Tsuki"). The sting of *Straight Ahead* has now been tempered by the more reflective mood of *Abbey Is Blue* to produce work that is both wry and probing yet hopeful and tender.

In the Fifties and Sixties luminaries such as Sonny Rollins, Kenny Dorham and Wynton Kelly (*That's Him!*) and Eric Dolphy, Coleman Hawkins and Booker Little (*Straight Ahead*) abetted Lincoln's presentations. The Seventies and Eighties have found her still in the company (on record, at least) of major improvisers: she appears on Cedar Walton's *The Maestro* (Muse); Al Foster and Dave Liebman enliven *People in Me* (devoted to Lincoln's own songs); and the 1981 release, *Golden Lady,* features Archie Shepp and Hilton Ruiz.

The songs Abbey Lincoln writes and sings (and the standards she chooses) are indicative of her character, determination and self-confidence. Her art represents the triumph of a strong, if slightly flat, voice and a big heart.   — A.R.

GARRETT LIST

★ ★ ★ ★ ★ Fire and Ice / Lovely M.

Trombonist/composer Garrett List (b. 1943) has a deep background in the avant-garde, having attended Juilliard school and played with John Cage, Karl Berger, Anthony Braxton and Musica Electronica Viva; he also served as musical director of The Kitchen in New York before forming the A1 band to make this record. The group consists of drummer Ronald Shannon Jackson, Byard Lancaster on reeds, Yusef Yancy on trumpet and theremin, and vocalist Eugenia Sherman. Their brilliantly conceptualized music is both challenging and entertaining, and one can only regret that they've made no more records together.   — J.S.

BOOKER LITTLE
★ ★ ★ ★ ★ Booker Little / Bain.
★ ★ ★ ★ ★ Out Front / Candid
★ ★ ★ ★ Victory and Sorrow / Beth.
★ ★ ★ ★ Waltz of the Demons / Aff.
Booker Little (1938–1961) was the Clifford
Brown of the Sixties. Before his untimely
death at twenty-three from uremia, Little
was already recognized among his peers as a
brilliant trumpeter, a daring and innovative
composer/arranger and a stimulating band-
leader.

Chiefly remembered today from his recordings with Max Roach, Eric Dolphy and
John Coltrane, Little has been too long overlooked and his work too little appreciated
despite its belated influence. On his last two
albums, particularly *Out Front,* Little began
to expand the tonal and metric boundaries of
jazz by experimenting with dissonance, orchestral coloration and structural tempo
changes. Unlike Ornette Coleman's groundbreaking work of the same time, Little employed written arrangements and ensemble
playing as well as solo improvisation. This
emphasis on tonal manipulation and the role
of composition would not surface in formal
jazz circles until the mid-Sixties; Little's
work thus predates both the advanced Blue
Note sessions and the structural innovations
of Chicago's AACM group that would so influence jazz in the Seventies.

As a trumpet soloist Little has not yet received his due either. While Freddie Hubbard, Lee Morgan and other up-and-comers
were still trying to assimilate Clifford
Brown's legacy, Little developed a style that
stepped beyond Brown and the hard-bop
idiom. (At times he sounds like Miles Davis,
Vintage 1968, though.) Still, Little could bop
with the best of them, as *Waltz* illustrates.
Originally released under altoist Frank Strozier's name, this cooking session is kicked off
by the Miles Davis rhythm section, Paul
Chambers, Wynton Kelly and Jimmy Cobb.

Little's original horn voice is heard more
fully on the Bainbridge LP, a more conventional date that teams him with another innovator who passed too quickly, bassist Scott
LaFaro.

Out Front, Little's most important date,
uses two men whose interaction was invaluable throughout Little's career—Max Roach
and Eric Dolphy. Although the written arrangements of Little's all-original material
are of extreme importance, the music never
sounds cold or studied. There actually is a
deep melancholy that pervades the session;
the off-kilter horn charts are moody and sor-
rowful. Little and Dolphy respond with

some of their most heartfelt solos. *Out Front*
is an extremely moving masterwork that
makes Little's demise all the more regrettable.

Victory and Sorrow is in no way the event
that *Out Front* was; it features less distinctive soloists and a less dynamic rhythm section, but remains a continuation of Little's
formal interests and on it he plays beautifully. Both it and *Out Front* are technically
out of print, but often pop up in cutout bins.

Little's first LP, *Plus Four* on United Artists, is very rare. His excellent work as a
sideman can be found on the Max Roach
LPs for Bainbridge and Columbia; his coled
group with Eric Dolphy appears under Dolphy's name on Milestone. Little can also be
heard in the horn ensemble on Coltrane's
Africa/Brass (MCA). — S.F.

CHARLES LLOYD
★ ★ ★ ★ ★ Forest Flower / Atl.
★ ★ ★ Montreux '82 / Elek./Mus.
In 1967 Charles Lloyd (b. 1938) was widely
heralded as the jazz musician most likely to
bridge the gap to younger, rock-oriented audiences. His beautiful, evocative tenor saxophone playing and fiery flute work had distinguished him in a number of sideman
situations, most notably in Chico Hamilton's
group. Lloyd's own quartet was magnificent,
featuring two of the most expansive, imaginative young players on the scene, drummer
Jack DeJohnette and pianist Keith Jarrett,
along with the mature, sure-handed accompaniment of bassist Cecil McBee. This group
left European audiences gasping in its wake
during the mid-Sixties and performed several
memorable West Coast concerts during the
same period in the U.S. Their brightest moment came at the 1966 Monterey Jazz Festival, the set recorded in *Forest Flower.*

Lloyd's popularity led to a number of
other records in the late Sixties and early
Seventies, all of which are presently unavailable. Despite its dated title, *Love-In,* another
live set, is particularly worthwhile, if you
can find it. Lloyd went into semiretirement
during the Seventies to devote his life to
spiritual pursuits, but he did not neglect his
music, as the solid *Montreux '82* set shows.
— J.S.

JEFF LORBER
★ ★ ★ Jeff Lorber Fusion / Inner
★ ★ Galaxian / Ari.
★ ★ In the Heat of the Night / Ari.
★ ★ It's a Fact / Ari.
★ ★ Soft Space / Inner

★ ★ ★ **Water Sign** / **Ari.**
★ ★ **Wizard Island** / **Ari.**
Berklee College of Music graduate Jeff Lorber (b. 1952) demonstrates on his records why conservatory training is not always a good way to learn to play jazz. Keyboardist Lorber shows dazzling technique and an eclectic bag of influences on these sets but rarely sounds emotionally convincing. His danceable blend of funk, Latin and jazz has proved commercial (*Wizard Island, Galaxian*) and sometimes even allows for inspired playing (*Water Sign,* featuring Freddie Hubbard on trumpet and Joe Farrell on sax).
— J.S.

JON LUCIEN
★ ★ ★ **I Am Now** / **RCA**
★ ★ ★ **Mind's Eye** / **RCA**
★ ★ ★ **Premonitions** / **Col.**
★ ★ **Rashida** / **RCA**
★ ★ ★ ★ **Song for My Lady** / **Col.**
Jon Lucien (b. 1942) is a baritone singer who croons his spirituals and love songs in fashionably glossy pop-jazz settings. He is also sometimes an instrumentalist and songwriter capable of writing unashamedly mushy music. Arrangements differ little from album to album, and their lushness often gives his work an unnecessary MOR bent. On romantic ballads, Lucien's phrasing is reminiscent of Johnny Hartman's, but he tends to be at his most imaginative on up-tempo songs. — J.MC.

BOBBY LYLE
★ ★ **The Genie** / **Cap.**
Ex–Young-Holt Unlimited keyboardist Bobby Lyle plays jazz/funk with lots of conviction but little subtlety. He has straddled genres and instrumentation, from George Benson to Sly Stone and from organ to synthesizer. His solo work is heavily influenced by the pop/funk vision of producer Wayne Henderson. — J.S.

JIMMY LYONS
★ ★ ★ **Other Afternoons** / **Picca.**
★ ★ ★ **Riffs (with Karen Borca)** / **Hat Hut**
As alto saxophonist for pianist Cecil Taylor's groups for nearly twenty years, Jimmy Lyons (b. 1916) has been the Ygor of the avant-garde to Taylor's Dr. Frankenstein. As a solo artist, Lyons makes scant changes in his approach, continuing to rely on long, long riff sections. His work with bassoonist Karen Borca has been well documented over the years, although the Hat Hut LP is presently the only one in print. *Other Afternoons* is a group date originally released on the French BYG label in the Sixties, and shows several influences other than Taylor, most notably Ornette Coleman.

These are good albums, but since Lyons' playing is well documented on numerous outstanding Cecil Taylor albums, you might as well hear him there. He's most prominent on Taylor's *Nefertiti, The Beautiful One Has Come.* — F.G.

JOHNNY LYTLE
★ ★ ★ **Everything Must Change** / **Muse**
★ ★ ★ **Fast Hands** / **Muse**
★ ★ ★ **Good Vibes** / **Muse**
★ ★ ★ ★ **The Village Caller** / **Prest. OJC**
The solid, blues-oriented instrumental grooves of vibraphonist Johnny Lytle (b. 1932) made him part of the soul/jazz movement of the Sixties via a hit single and album, *The Village Caller.* That LP has been reissued as part of the Original Jazz Classics series. His late-Seventies and early-Eighties sets for Muse present Lytle in good company (saxophonist Houston Person, keyboardist Mickey Tucker, drummer Idris Muhammad among others). — J.S.

GLORIA LYNNE
★ **Gloria Lynne** / **Ev.**
★ **I Don't Know How to Love Him** / **ABC**
Gloria Lynne is a relatively minor jazz singer with an unusually husky voice. She has seen better days. The production on both records is simultaneously garish and cloddish, and it brings out the worst in her—when she isn't drowned out by the wah-wah effects and violins. — R.G.

RALPH MACDONALD
★ ★ ★ **Sound of a Drum** / Mar.
★ ★ ★ **The Path** / Mar.
★ ★ ★ **Universal Rhythm** / Poly.
After a long apprenticeship with Harry Bela-
fonte in the Sixties and Roberta Flack in the
early Seventies, Ralph MacDonald (b. 1944)
became the Seventies' most prolific session
percussionist. His solo outings have demonstrated his shrewdness and taste as a leader
in assembling excellent studio bands and
providing commercial hooks for his records.
"Calypso Breakdown" and "Jam on the
Groove" from *Drum* have become popular
currency. *The Path* features MacDonald's
imaginative handling of synthesized drums
(syndrum), and that album's title track
traces a musicological evolution of disco
rhythms from African and Caribbean ori-
gins. *Universal Rhythm* is a 1984 session
musicians' clambake including a Bill
Withers vocal on "In the Name of Love."
— J.S.

JIMMY MADISON
★ ★ ★ **Bumps on a Smooth Surface** / Adel.
Drummer Jimmy Madison (b. 1947) has
played in a wide variety of contexts, working
in Lionel Hampton's band, then with Marian
McPartland, Roland Kirk, Lee Konitz, Chet
Baker and George Benson. He is also a
sought-after session player who was the
"house" drummer on a number of CTI sessions and toured with the James Brown band
for an extended engagement. For *Bumps on
a Smooth Surface,* his 1977 debut, Madison
assembled a very good band featuring pianist
Harold Danko, bassist Mike Richmond,
trumpeter/fluegelhornist Tom Harrell and
saxophonist Larry Schneider. Though well
played, the session lacks coherence, a common pitfall of sidemen turned leaders.
— J.S.

CHUCK MANGIONE
★ ★ ★ ★ **Alive!** / Mer.
★ ★ **Bellavia** / A&M
★ ★ ★ **Best of** / Mer.
★ ★ ★ **Chase the Clouds Away** / A&M
★ ★ ★ **Children of Sanchez** / A&M
★ ★ ★ **Encore** / Mer.
★ ★ ★ **Evening of Magic** / A&M
★ ★ **Feels So Good** / A&M
★ ★ ★ **Friends and Love** / Mer.
★ ★ ★ **Friends and Love (Highlights)** / Mer.
★ ★ ★ **Fun and Games** / A&M
★ ★ ★ **Jazz Brothers** / Mile.
★ ★ ★ **Land of Make Believe** / Mer.
★ ★ **Live at the Hollywood Bowl** / A&M
★ ★ **Love Notes** / Col.
★ ★ **Main Squeeze** / A&M
★ ★ ★ **Quartet** / Mer.
★ ★ **70 Miles Young** / A&M
★ ★ ★ **Tarantella** / A&M
★ ★ ★ **Together** / Mer.
Trumpeter/fluegelhornist Chuck Mangione
(b. 1940) played in Art Blakey's band in the
Sixties before leading his own group, the
Jazz Brothers, with his brother Gap Mang-
ione on keyboards. The *Friends and Love*
live concert recording from 1970, a fine piece
of multistylistic writing and direction in
which Mangione combined his own band
with the Rochester Philharmonic Orchestra,
established his solo career, and led to a few
similar projects. Mangione hit a commercial
high point during that era in collaboration
with vocalist Esther Satterfield on "Land of
Make Believe," which has since become a
standard.
   Mangione's quartet albums for Mercury
are quite good, and feature Gerry Niewood's
excellent soprano-saxophone work as well as
some fine playing by Mangione and consistently good session backing. *Alive!,* with
drummer Steve Gadd and bassist Tony
Levin, is the best of the quartet records. Unfortunately, Mangione's later albums for

A&M are exceedingly glib, so despite his musical taste and sense for commercial hooks ("Feels So Good"), the records remain unrewarding. — J.S.

HERBIE MANN
★ ★ ★ Best of / Atl.
★ ★ ★ Best of / Prest.
★ ★ Bird in a Silver Cage / Atl.
★ ★ ★ ★ The Common Ground / Atl.
★ ★ Discotheque / Atl.
★ ★ Et Tu Flute / Verve
★ ★ ★ Evolution of Mann / Atl.
★ ★ ★ First Light / Atl.
★ ★ Gagaku and Beyond / Fin.
★ ★ ★ Herbie Mann (with Gilberto & Jobim) / Atl.
★ ★ Latin Mann / CSP
★ ★ ★ Let Me Tell You / Mile.
★ ★ ★ London Underground / Atl.
★ ★ ★ ★ Mann at the Village Gate / Atl.
★ ★ Mann in Sweden / Prest.
★ ★ Mellow / Atl.
★ ★ ★ ★ Memphis Underground / Atl.
★ ★ ★ ★ Push Push / Embryo
★ ★ Reggae / Atl.
★ ★ Super Mann / Trip
★ ★ Surprises / Atl.
★ ★ ★ Turtle Bay / Atl.
★ ★ With Flute to Boot / Sp.
★ ★ Yellow Fever / Atl.
Herbie Mann (b. 1930) is a shrewd and accomplished bandleader who's been able to anticipate and cash in on musical fashions consistently for over two decades. His flute playing is almost always the least interesting aspect of his records, which are all carefully conceptualized around crack studio bands. During the Fifties and Sixties Mann organized an excellent Afro-Cuban combo and helped popularize that music by featuring top musicians in his group, especially great percussionists like Carlos "Potato" Valdes, Ray Barretto, Michael Olatunji, Ray Mantilla, Willie Bobo and Armando Peraza. Mann's records were always interesting during this period and a lot of people, including a number of rock musicians, were introduced to jazz through these records.

Unfortunately the only truly representative albums from Mann's classic period that remain in print are *Mann at the Village Gate* and *The Common Ground*. The rest of his older material is available only in compilations and shoddy repackagings. Check cutout bins for classics such as *Flautista, Brazil Blues* and *Standing Ovation at Newport*.

Mann's late-Sixties and Seventies attempts at contemporizing his material are less convincing, although at several points he locks into an exceptional R&B groove with the right supporting musicians. The best record from this period, *Memphis Underground,* is by far Mann's best-selling record and thus remains in print. Using guitarist Larry Coryell, vibraphonist Roy Ayers and a Memphis rhythm section, Mann put together a steamy groove that provided a link between jazz, R&B and some rock elements. The title track also became a hit single.

Mann's subsequent albums, often featuring the best studio musicians working out of New York, have been technically proficient and completely uninteresting. Titles like *Reggae* and *Discotheque* indicate the shallowness of Mann's attempts to stereotype these styles to his advantage, and it all ends up looking like he was casting around blindly, waiting for something to catch on. One of the more interesting Seventies albums, *Push Push,* features a guest appearance by Duane Allman on slide guitar. — J.S.

SHELLY MANNE
★ ★ Checkmate / Contem.
★ ★ ★ Double Piano Jazz Quartet / Trend
★ ★ ★ Double Piano Jazz Quartet, Vol. 2 / Trend
★ ★ ★ Essence / Gal.
★ ★ ★ French Concert / Gal.
★ ★ Interpretations / Trend
★ My Fair Lady / Contem.
★ ★ ★ Perk Up / Conc. J.
★ ★ ★ Rex / Discov.
★ ★ ★ ★ Shelly Manne and His Friends / Doctor J.
★ ★ ★ ★ ★ Shelly Manne and His Men at the Black Hawk, Vol. 1 / Contem.
★ ★ ★ Shelly Manne and His Men at the Black Hawk, Vol. 2 / Contem.
★ ★ ★ Shelly Manne and His Men at the Black Hawk, Vol. 3 / Contem.
★ ★ ★ ★ Shelly Manne and His Men at the Black Hawk, Vol. 4 / Contem.
Drummer Shelly Manne (1920–1984) had one of the most prolific recording careers of all jazz musicians. He is said to have played on well over a thousand jazz albums, a statistic that worked against him in that many of the sessions he appeared on were real turkeys. He was, however, a fresh, swinging and dedicated artist schooled in the big-band tradition but far more at home in bop-style small combos, where his interest in accents and more subtle playing could be fully expressed. Manne was a principal force in the various Stan Kenton bands of the Forties, an organization largely responsible for the West Coast cool-jazz trend that became a dominant style in the Fifties, but he also recorded

on adventurous small-group sets with Ornette Coleman (*Tomorrow Is the Question!*) and Sonny Rollins (*Way Out West*).

The earliest material here is on the Doctor Jazz set, a reissue of 1944 sides from sessions that were originally led by Barney Bigard and Eddie Heywood. Manne's advanced (for that time) drumming personality, especially his superior brushwork, make the reissue under his name logical, and the performances by Bigard on clarinet, Heywood on piano, Ray Nance on violin, Don Byas on tenor sax and Johnny Hodges on alto sax add up to tremendous listening.

Starting in 1956, Manne fronted his own groups after appearing in *The Man with the Golden Arm*, and wasted little time cashing in on what was a pretty commercial reputation. His capability for producing fast-selling junk was epitomized by the 1956 *My Fair Lady* set, where pianist André Previn and bassist Leroy Vinnegar joined him in Muzak-like run-through of "Get Me to the Church on Time," "With a Little Bit of Luck," etc. Naturally this became one of the biggest-selling jazz albums of the Fifties. Similar ideas, such as adaptations of the John Williams themes from the *Checkmate*, television series, were slightly less offensive.

Despite such commercial forays Manne led a very listenable small combo notable for its front line of tenor saxophonist Richie Kamuca and trumpeter Joe Gordon. This band is heard to beautiful effect on the live 1959 *Black Hawk* recordings that document three nights of performances at that San Francisco club. Bassist Monty Budwig and pianist Victor Feldman mesh neatly into Manne's bopish conception, especially on the exceptional Volume 1, which features a wonderful Kamuca solo on "Summertime."

The Trend, Galaxy, Concord Jazz and Discovery sets all date from the mid-Seventies to 1980 and showed him still performing in the style he'd perfected by 1960. — J.S.

MICHAEL MANTLER
★ ★ ★ ★ **Hapless Child / Watt**
★ ★ ★ **Movies / Watt**
★ ★ ★ **Silence / Watt**
★ ★ ★ ★ **Something There / Watt**
Trumpeter/composer Michael Mantler (b. 1943) writes fascinating experimental pieces that make creative use of electronics, jazz-rock fusion and serialism in a sometimes challenging sometimes jumbled marriage. His collaborations with his wife Carla Bley and percussionist Robert Wyatt beginning in the mid-Seventies produced the eccentric *Hapless Child,* a concept album of program music based on Edward Gorey tales, as well as *Silence.* Drummer Tony Williams and guitarist Larry Coryell join Mantler and Bley on the '77 *Movies.* On the 1983 *Something There* set Mantler, Bley, guitarist Mike Stern, bassist Steve Swallow and drummer Nick Mason are augmented by an evocative Michael Gibbs arrangement performed by the London Symphony Orchestra. Stern in particular is magnificent on this set. Try to find Mantler's wonderful *Jazz Composer's Orchestra* LP. — J.S.

WYNTON MARSALIS
★ ★ ★ **Hot House Flowers / Col.**
★ ★ ★ ★ **Think of One / Col.**
★ ★ ★ ★ **Wynton Marsalis / Col.**
Trumpeter Wynton Marsalis (b. 1961) is a prodigious new talent whose impact on the jazz world has been so great that he was accused in some circles of being a hype after releasing a single album. He and his brother, saxophonist Bradford Marsalis, were introduced to music in their native New Orleans by their father, pianist Ellis Marsalis.

Though Marsalis' greatest interest has always been jazz, his first recognition came as a classical musician performing works of Haydn and Bach. The young trumpeter later came to the attention of jazz followers through his stint with veteran drummer Art Blakey's Jazz Messengers. His virtuosic playing often recalled such great bop trumpeters as Dizzy Gillespie, Clifford Brown and Miles Davis. This similarity to Davis prompted pianist Herbie Hancock to hire Marsalis as trumpeter for his neoclassic quartet with bassist Ron Carter and Tony Williams, all alumni of the legendary Davis quintet of the Sixties.

Half of Marsalis' debut LP, *Wynton Marsalis,* was recorded with the same quartet, while the other half introduced Marsalis' own band. Later that year both Wynton and Bradford appeared with their father on the Columbia *Fathers and Sons* album.

Marsalis continued to demonstrate his reverence for bop-era jazz on his second LP, *Think of One,* released in '83. The title track is a great Thelonious Monk composition that Marsalis covers brilliantly, as he does Duke Ellington's "Melancholia," while introducing several of his own songs, the most impressive of which is "Later." At the same time that *Think Of One* was released CBS issued an album of Marsalis playing Haydn/Hummel/Leopold Mozart trumpet concertos. Marsalis took his reverence too far on *Hot House Flowers,* a "with-strings" project that suffers from what sounds like an overly cautious approach. — J.S.

WARNE MARSH
★ ★ ★ ★ **All Music / Nessa**
★ ★ ★ ★ **Apogee (with Pete Christlieb) / War.**
★ ★ ★ ★ **How Deep, How High / Discov.**
★ ★ ★ ★ **Lee Konitz with Warne Marsh / Atl.**
★ ★ ★ **Live at the Montmartre Club (with Lee Konitz) / Story.**

A student of pianist/theorist Lennie Tristano, tenorman Warne Marsh (b. 1927) championed a cool, lighter-toned approach to his instrument. Time has wrought changes on his style, though; his later recordings hint at a swagger positively anathematic to Tristano disciples. The evolution of Marsh's playing is best demonstrated by comparing the versions of "Donna Lee" available on the Atlantic LP with Konitz, and the Warner disc with Christlieb. The former, recorded in '55, is precise and somewhat stiff; the latter, cut twenty-five years later, is a pulsating chase spiced with bravado. *How Deep, How High* reunites Marsh with another Tristano student, pianist Sal Mosca for a re-examination of academic roots. The dedication to a fluid, melodic concept remains intact; but gone is the strict adherence to a lightly colored tone.

Comparatively, *All Music* is one of the best places to hear Marsh at work; the Atlantic recording with Konitz is preferred over the Storyville album because of the superior band featuring Mosca and bassist Oscar Pettiford. *How Deep, How High* is split between duets and quartet numbers, while *Apogee* is an unadulterated burner, guaranteed to work for tenor freaks.
— F.G.

PAT MARTINO
★ ★ ★ **Consciousness / Muse**
★ ★ **Exit / Muse**
★ ★ ★ **Footprints / Muse**
★ ★ **Joyous Lake / War.**
★ ★ ★ ★ **Live! / Muse**
★ ★ **Single Action / Muse**
★ ★ **Starbright / War.**
★ ★ ★ **We'll Be Together Again / Muse**

An excellent dark-toned jazz guitar player, Pat Martino (b. 1944) has also been a recording artist of such consistent quality it's hard for me to be critical. His five albums for Prestige (1967–72) start the skein; though all are out of print, they're worth looking for. On all those albums, Martino plays as much guitar—in long, supple, rich, lightning-fast lines—as is humanly possible. *Live!,* which is similar to the Prestige LPs, may be his best album in print. Its tunes are each over ten minutes long—giving the guitarist plenty of room to roll, regroup (usually by quoting from "The Flight of the Bumblebee"), and roll some more.

However, Martino's other Muse albums are really no less extensive, even though they show his slower, quieter and more conceptual side. *Consciousness* has a slight emphasis on Martino essaying solo ballads; *Footprints* is a varied tribute to Wes Montgomery's playing; and *Together Again* features soft duets with pianist Gil Goldstein.

After signing with Warner Bros. in 1976, Martino fit his oft-cooking, oft-somber nature into fusion. So even though *Starbright* is often as moody as *Baiyina* (out of print) and *Joyous Lake* sometimes soars like *Live!,* both newer albums use keyboard vamps aplenty, sometimes within a totally synthesized atmosphere. And both lose a star—because sometimes the bow to fusion seems too much like concession. — M.R.

HARVEY MASON
★ ★ **Earth Mover / Ari.**
★ ★ **Funk in a Mason Jar / Ari.**
★ ★ **Groovin' You / Ari.**
★ ★ **Marching in the Street / Ari.**
★ ★ **MVP / Ari.**

A top L.A. studio drummer, Harvey Mason (b. 1947) was Herbie Hancock's pulse for the hit LP, *Head Hunters*. His own albums are so-so. The first features many of Hancock's mid-Seventies bandmates playing Seventies mainstream, mildly electric jazz, instead of funk. Trouble is, they're joined by too many of Mason's studio buddies, who put an enervating gloss on everything. *Earth Mover*'s more commercial, eclectic (ranging from Blackbyrds-type stuff to a drum-keyboard duel with Jan Hammer) and energetic.
— M.R.

MATERIAL
★ ★ ★ **Busting Out / Ze/Island**
★ ★ ★ **Memory Serves / Elek./Mus.**
★ ★ **One Down / Elek.**

One of the most power-packed and promising outfits to emerge from New York thus far in the Eighties, Material has yet to make the record that delivers on that promise.

In its earlier incarnations, Material played both glass-shattering electric-jam music, spotlighting guitarists Ronnie Drayton and Sonny Sharrock, and slick funk rock when backing singer Nona Hendryx. The latter can be found on the Ze/Island disc, but unfortunately the former is only intimated on the band's first album, *Memory Serves.*

More recently, Material has opted to become a studio band built around the ideas of synthesizer player Michael Beinhorn, bassist Bill Laswell and engineer Martin Bisi. *One Down* was an attempt to make a commercial dance record, but suffers from an identity crisis. On one track the band sounds like Chic, on another Tower of Power, and on a third gives hip-hop a try. The results are far less satisfying than the chunky, funky *Memory Serves.*

Since then, Material has produced albums for Nona Hendryx and Herbie Hancock and begun its own experimental OAO label, giving every indication it might become a major production force in the Eighties. However, a spiritless solo album by bassist Laswell for Elektra/Musician (*Baselines*) leaves Material's future as a musical group very much in doubt. — F.G.

BENNIE MAUPIN
★ ★ ★ ★ The Jewel in the Lotus / ECM/ War.
★ ★ ★ Moonscapes / Mer.
★ ★ ★ Slow Traffic to the Right / Mer.
A sideman on many other LPs, including *Bitches Brew* and Herbie Hancock's early electric sides, reedman Bennie Maupin (b. 1946) has played ostinato funk and modal jazz with great emotion and facility. His *Jewel,* a 1974 release, is broodingly lyrical, an album of beautiful nuance; *Slow* is more commercial, but no less praiseworthy, setting steady grooves off against spacey soloing and melodies. All three albums feature Maupin's tunes and top sidemen. — M.R.

CECIL McBEE
★ ★ ★ ★ Alternate Spaces / In. Nav.
★ ★ ★ Compassion / Enja
★ ★ ★ ★ Flying Out / In. Nav.
★ ★ ★ Music From the Source / Enja
★ ★ ★ Mutima / Strata-East
Cecil McBee (b. 1935) is another awesomely talented bassist who came to prominence in the mid-Sixties. He played in the popular Charles Lloyd group and, after Richard Davis, was the most valuable bassist at Blue Note, performing on LPs by Jackie McLean, Grachan Moncur and Wayne Shorter.

Mutima, his debut LP as a leader, featured some of the most promising young players of the time, including George Adams and trumpeter Hannibal Peterson. McBee's albums of the Seventies also chronicle the

career of saxist Chico Freeman who makes guest appearances from *Alternate Spaces* on.

Apart from *Spaces,* with its more serene shorter pieces, a McBee LP invariably consists of some very long, very intense workouts on modal compositions. The soloing is always invigorating, particularly McBee's own work, but the overall effect can often prove numbing.

Flying Out counterbalances this with additional structure. Using violin, cello and trumpet as a front line and tighter arrangements, it is McBee's most provocative and interesting album. — S.F.

LES McCANN
★ ★ Another Beginning / Atl.
★ ★ ★ Change, Change, Change / Imp.
★ ★ Hustle to Survive / Atco
★ ★ In New York / Pac. J.
★ ★ In San Francisco / Pac. J.
★ ★ Invitation to Openness / Atl.
★ ★ Layers / Atl.
★ ★ ★ Live at Montreux / Atl.
★ ★ Live at Shelly's Manne Hole / Lime.
★ ★ ★ Live at the Bohemian Caverns, Washington, D.C. / Trip
★ ★ The Man / A&M
★ ★ Music Lets Me Be / Imp.
★ ★ Plays the Shout / Pac. J.
★ ★ ★ Second Movement / Atco
★ ★ Soul Hits / Pac. J.
★ ★ ★ Stormy Monday / Cap.
★ ★ ★ ★ Swiss Movement (with Eddie Harris) / Atl.
★ ★ Tall, Dark and Handsome / A&M
Simplicity is the key word used to describe Les McCann (b. 1935), and it's used equally by his supporters and his critics. The sparseness and clap-along features of his hit "Compared to What" have been reproduced numerous times, but never to the same effect. Almost his entire career can be seen as a footnote to that one cut and the album he recorded with saxophonist Eddie Harris, *Swiss Movement.*

Many of McCann's gospel and funk-based jazz ideas have been used far more successfully by Stanley Turrentine, Grover Washington, Donny Hathaway and Roberta Flack. On the now-deleted *Comment,* McCann's most interesting album, several luminaries-to-be cropped up—Flack (a discovery of his), Billy Cobham and Ashford and Simpson. Most of McCann's other albums tend to be either all instrumental or all vocal, but in both cases the result is awkward and uncomfortable. Individual cuts work—especially "Morning Song" on *Another Beginning* and "What's Goin' On" on

Invitation to Openness—but these are exceptions in an unending stream of mediocre material and arrangements. — R.G.

SUSANNAH McCORKLE
★ ★ ★ **The Music of Harry Warren / Inner**
★ ★ ★ ★ **Over the Rainbow: The Music of E. Y. "Yip" Harburg / Inner**
★ ★ ★ ★ **The People That You Never Get to Love / Inner**
★ ★ ★ **The Songs of Johnny Mercer / Inner**
Susannah McCorkle emerged in the late Seventies as a singer of great intelligence, projecting warmth and sincerity. She utilizes the grammar of jazz with a sense of personal involvement that is often lacking in singers of American popular songs. McCorkle is part of the Mabel Mercer tradition in the way she nurtures and continually expands her working repertoire. Stylistically, she descends directly from Billie Holiday.

The People That You Never Get to Love is the most varied recording in McCorkle's catalogue, encompassing songs by a number of disparate composers—Blossom Dearie, Duke Ellington, Dorothy Fields and Arthur Schwartz, Irene Kitchings, Oscar Brown, Jr. and Dave Frishberg, among others. This is state of the art in American popular song. — A.R.

JACK McDUFF
★ ★ ★ **At the Jazz Workshop / Prest.**
★ ★ ★ **Best of Big Soul Band / Prest.**
★ ★ ★ **Best Live / Prest.**
★ ★ ★ **Concert McDuff / Prest.**
★ ★ ★ **Cookin' Together / Prest.**
★ ★ ★ **George Benson/Jack McDuff / Prest.**
★ ★ ★ **Greatest Hits / Prest.**
★ ★ ★ **Hot Barbecue / Prest.**
★ ★ ★ **Live! / Prest.**
★ **Magnetic Feel / Cadet**
★ ★ **Natural Thing / Cadet**
★ ★ ★ **Prelude / Prest.**
★ ★ ★ ★ **Rock Candy / Prest.**
★ ★ ★ **Screamin' / Prest.**
★ ★ ★ **Steppin' Out / Prest.**
Like many of the big-name organists of the Sixties, Jack McDuff (b. 1926) took up the instrument after Jimmy Smith's explosive ascendance. While Smith wowed audiences with his machine-gun assaults, McDuff favored sparser blues and gospel lines, giving his music a real country-soul flavor. McDuff's best work was on Prestige, where his material centered around blues, ballads and shuffles. With the advent of the synthesizer, the B-3 organ has become an anachronism and like many of the instrument's players, Jack McDuff has switched to the synthesizer

on record, with predictably disastrous results. — J.MC.

BOBBY McFERRIN
★ ★ ★ ★ **Bobby McFerrin / Elek./Mus.**
★ ★ ★ ★ **The Voice / Elek./Mus.**
Vocalist Bobby McFerrin (b. 1950) brings a radical approach to vocalese based on a combination of jazz, classical and pop influences. Since his father sang with the Metropolitan Opera and his mother still teaches voice, McFerrin grew up with a strong inclination toward classical music. He claims that Miles Davis' *Bitches Brew* turned him into an avid jazz fan, which may account for the unusual character of his vocalizations. Traditional scat singers are often said to sound like saxophones or trumpets but McFerrin's voice is most often likened to electronic instruments. While the influence of the brilliant bop vocalist Betty Carter can be heard in McFerrin's rhythmic phrasing and the shape of his notes, the tones he emits are decidedly unique. On *Bobby McFerrin* he mixes pop tunes with jazz standards, engaging in a beautiful duet with Phoebe Snow on the R&B classic, "You've Really Got a Hold On Me." McFerrin is also influenced by the toe-tapping vocal approach invented by Sly and the Family Stone, which he adapts well on "All Feets Can Dance." *The Voice* is a live set recorded in Europe that also mixes pop tunes like "Blackbird" and "I Feel Good" with such jazz standards as "Take the 'A' Train." — J.S.

HOWARD McGHEE
★ ★ ★ **Cookin' Time / Zim**
★ ★ ★ **Jazzbrothers (with Teddy Edwards) / Story.**
★ ★ ★ **Live at Emerson's / Zim**
★ ★ ★ **Maggie's Back in Town / Contem.**
One of the leading trumpeters of the bebop period, but the Zim and Storyville recordings capture Howard McGhee (b. 1918) after his peak. The Contemporary disc features stronger playing, yet lacks imagination. Listeners seeking to hear McGhee's best work are advised to look for him as a sideman during the Forties and Fifties. Although these four albums are readily available, they don't do the trumpeter justice. If, however, you find the Savoy reissue, *Maggie,* get it. — F.G.

JIMMY McGRIFF
★ ★ ★ **Black and Blues / G.M.**
★ ★ ★ ★ **Countdown / Mile.**
★ ★ ★ ★ **Fly Dude / G.M.**
★ ★ ★ ★ **Flyin' Time / G.M.**

★ ★ ★ ★ Giants of the Organ in Concert
(with Richard "Groove" Holmes) / G.M.
★ ★ Groove Grease / G.M.
★ ★ ★ ★ The Groover / JAM
★ ★ ★ ★ Skywalk / Mile.
★ ★ ★ ★ Supa Cookin' / G.M.
To make good jazz on the Hammond B-3,
you play melody and improvisation on the
organ's top keyboard while riding a contrapuntal bass line on the bottom one. The result: either the punchy bass just hovers behind, and snaps at, the lighter melody, or
the upper-register, wailing melody contrasts
with the rock-solid bass line. The formula
may sound complex, but it's really classic in
its simplicity, and Jimmy McGriff (b. 1936)
and a handful of other organists have it
down.

A few of McGriff's records, in fact, are
among the finest jazz-organ LPs ever made.
Fly Dude, featuring George Freeman on guitar and Ronald Arnold on tenor, is simple
and cooking blues riffing off McGriff originals and a few jazz standards—an absolutely
tight example of the genre save for one
track, a commercialized atrocity called "Butterfly." McGriff's two collaborations with
Richard "Groove" Holmes are almost as
good; *In Concert,* recorded live at Boston's
Paul's Mall, is especially stretched out and
exciting. And *Black and Blues,* when it
sticks to what its title suggests, is also nice
'n' basic.

Otherwise, the organist has had to "funk
up" his art, ostensibly to avoid starving to
death. Thing is, McGriff isn't musically sophisticated enough to commercialize compel-
lingly. So the dismal cast of "Butterfly,"
something like a rabid Philly Dog, also
marks many of his LPs, like *Groove Grease.*

Fans of McGriff may also know his earlier
Solid State LPs. Though they contain a few
nice moments, they're mostly too orchestrated and dated.

McGriff's sound itself, however, manages
to avoid being stuck in a time as more recent records prove. The hard-edged set on
The Groover includes such jamming classics
as "Night Train," "Mercy, Mercy, Mercy"
and "Song for My Father." His Eighties
working bands set him off in classic style on
Countdown and *Skywalk,* the former featuring nice adaptions of some Frank Foster arrangements originally played by the Count
Basie band. — M.R./J.S.

JOHN McLAUGHLIN
★ ★ Apocalypse / Col.
★ ★ ★ Belo Horizonte / War.
★ ★ ★ Best of John McLaughlin / Col.

★ ★ ★ Best of the Mahavishnu Orchestra /
Col.
★ ★ ★ Between Nothingness and Eternity /
Col.
★ ★ ★ ★ ★ Birds of Fire / Col.
★ ★ ★ Devotion / Doug.
★ ★ Electric Dreams / Col.
★ ★ ★ ★ Electric Guitarist / Col.
★ ★ ★ Extrapolation / Poly.
★ ★ Friday Night in San Francisco / Col.
★ ★ ★ A Handful of Beauty / Col.
★ ★ ★ ★ ★ The Inner Mounting Flame /
Col.
★ ★ Inner Worlds / Col.
★ ★ Love, Devotion, Surrender (with Carlos
Santana) / Col.
★ ★ ★ ★ Mahavishnu / War.
★ ★ ★ Music Spoken Here / War.
★ ★ ★ ★ My Goal's Beyond / Elek./Mus.
★ ★ ★ ★ Natural Elements / Col.
★ ★ ★ ★ Shakti / Col.
★ ★ Visions of the Emerald Beyond / Col.
British guitarist John McLaughlin (b. 1942)
helped define the fusion-jazz style of the Sev-
enties and is unquestionably one of the most
influential musicians of his generation. His
first recorded work, the 1969 *Extrapolation*
album with British saxophonist John Surman, showed his interest in both acoustic
and electric playing, but his earliest impact
as part of the Tony Williams Lifetime and
Miles Davis bands came through his electric
guitar playing. The 1970 *Devotion* showcases
his fiery electric playing in a quartet with organist Larry Young and drummer Buddy
Miles. The brilliant 1972 LP, *My Goal's Beyond,* is the first full-scale exploration of his
fantastic acoustic playing. That album featured bassist Charlie Haden, saxophonist
Dave Liebman, percussionist Airto Moreira,
two Indian musicians and two members of
what would become McLaughlin's Mahavishnu Orchestra, drummer Billy Cobham
and violinist Jerry Goodman.

The Mahavishnu Orchestra, which also included bassist Rick Laird and keyboardist
Jan Hammer, established a high-water mark
for fusion with its first two albums, *The
Inner Mounting Flame* and *Birds of Fire.*
The band's swooping, vertiginous attack astonished the music world, but McLaughlin
soon lost his direction and the edge to his
playing. After the live *Between Nothingness
and Eternity,* subsequent Mahavishnu sets
(*Apocalypse, Visions of the Emerald Beyond*
and *Inner Worlds*) sound like parodies of the
band's original intent.

McLaughlin made an album with fellow
guitarist Carlos Santana (*Love, Devotion,
Surrender*) before settling into another cre-

ative groove with Shakti. Playing Indian music with a crack group of percussionists and with violinist L. Shankar sharing solo space, Shakti recorded three albums in the mid-Seventies, *Shakti, Natural Elements* and *A Handful of Beauty.* McLaughlin played superb acoustic guitar on all of these sets. Back on course, he followed with an excellent electric album, *Electric Guitarist. Electric Dreams* was less interesting, and McLaughlin entered the Eighties back on acoustic guitar with the beautiful *Belo Horizonte* and *Music Spoken Here* and the collaboration with Al DiMeola and Paco De Lucia, *Friday Night in San Francisco.* The 1984 *Mahavishnu* set reunites McLaughlin with drummer Billy Cobham and brings in saxophonist Bill Evans as the guitarist continued to excell in an electric format.

— J.S.

JACKIE McLEAN
★ ★ ★ **Lights Out** / Prest.
★ ★ **Strange Blues** / Prest.
★ ★ ★ **Two Sides of Jackie McLean** / Trip
Alto saxophonist Jackie McLean (b. 1932) recorded early and for a time quite often, thanks to encouragement from Bud Powell, Miles Davis and Charlie Parker; these albums (1955–57) reveal a clearly developed personality, particularly with the acid tone and vocalized inflections, often ignored amidst the tendency to label any alto player of the period a Parker imitator. The Trip album is notable for McLean's first session under his own name, with Donald Byrd and Mal Waldron, which contains his excellent composition "Little Melonae"; *Lights Out,* with Byrd again and the fine pianist Elmo Hope, is a typical blowing session of the era, built around "I Got Rhythm" chord changes and the blues; "Inding," however, has a more serpentine melodic line that would become known as "Quadrangle" during McLean's more adventurous period.
★ ★ ★ ★ **Bluesnik** / Blue N.
★ ★ ★ **'Bout Soul** / Blue N.
★ ★ ★ **Demon's Dance** / Blue N.
★ ★ ★ ★ ★ **Destination Out** / Blue N.
★ ★ ★ ★ **Jacknife** / Blue N.
★ ★ ★ ★ ★ **Let Freedom Ring** / Blue N.
★ ★ ★ ★ ★ **One Step Beyond** / Blue N.
Drug problems both active and passive (ex-offenders could not get a cabaret card, and thus could not work in New York nightclubs) limited McLean's activity in the Sixties. At decade's end he had stopped performing altogether, but his Blue Note albums (1962–67) contain his finest work. *Let Freedom Ring* is the breakthrough

album, where McLean reconciles his bop roots with the newer influence of Ornette Coleman and the rest of what at the time was called "the new thing." As an example of compositional solo and group achievement, the album is a masterpiece.

One Step Beyond and *Destination Out* are equally essential, for McLean moves beyond the alto-plus-piano-trio format with an inspired quintet blend of his sax plus trombone (Grachan Moncur III, who shared composing duties), vibes (Bobby Hutcherson), bass and drums. *One Step,* the more fiery of the pair, is also the recording debut of drummer Tony Williams, whom McLean brought to New York from Boston at the age of seventeen. The other albums from this period have more standard formats and feature the premier modern mainstream trumpets of the era—Freddie Hubbard, Lee Morgan, Charles Tolliver and Woody Shaw.
★ ★ ★ ★ **Antiquity (with Michael Carvin)** / Inner
★ ★ ★ **Ghetto Baby** / Inner
★ ★ ★ ★ **Live at Montmartre** / Inner
★ ★ ★ **The Meeting (with Dexter Gordon)** / Inner
★ ★ ★ **New York Calling** / Inner
★ ★ ★ **Ode Super (with Gary Bartz)** / Inner
★ ★ ★ ★ ★ **The Source (with Dexter Gordon)** / Inner
From 1972 to 1974, McLean renewed his recording career for the Danish SteepleChase label (the albums are now available on Inner City in the United States). The searing intensity and urgent rhythmic thrust are still present, particularly on side one of *Live at Montmartre* and *The Source,* with the altoist rising to the heady challenge of Dexter Gordon's tenor on the latter. *Antiquity,* a series of duets with percussionist Michael Carvin, is the imaginative album programmatically, while *New York Calling* documents the Cosmic Brotherhood, a young sextet McLean led that featured his son René on tenor and soprano sax and is particularly impressive on the title piece. McLean now lives in Hartford, Connecticut, where he teaches and is deeply involved in Afro-American cultural activities.
★ ★ ★ **Alto Madness (with John Jenkins)** / Prest.
★ ★ ★ ★ ★ **Consequence** / Blue N.
★ ★ ★ **Contour** / Prest.
★ ★ ★ ★ **4, 5 and 6** / Fan./OJC
★ ★ ★ **Hipnosis** / Blue N.
★ ★ ★ ★ **McLean's Scene** / Fan./OJC
★ ★ ★ **New Wine in Old Bottles (with the Great Jazz Trio)** / Inner
★ ★ ★ **Vertigo** / Blue N.

The above titles are the only McLean albums currently in Schwann, a shocking situation only slightly mitigated by the frequent reappearance of the old Blue Note and SteepleChase discs. *Contour* contains McLean's first two Prestige sessions from 1956, with strong signs of his growing mastery displayed in the second session.

All of the Blue Note titles were released years after their recording dates. The reasons vary, no doubt, for the delays. *Vertigo,* from 1963 and officially Tony Williams' first session, probably languished because the playing time was too short and had to be augmented by a 1959 title—and also perhaps because *One Step Beyond,* done shortly afterward, was so much better. *Hipnosis* contains lesser efforts by bands from '62 and '67, although the earlier session with trumpeter Kenny Dorham and pianist Sonny Clark offers quite a lineup. The delay of *Consequence,* a 1965 burner with soul mates Lee Morgan and Billy Higgins, remains inexplicable. It is a definitive McLean session.

New Wine, from 1978, is the lone example of recent McLean. The Great Jazz Trio is Hank Jones, Ron Carter and Tony Williams, and while the program is admirable (two great McLean tunes are included), one longs for the relentless intensity heard on albums like the deleted *Live at Montmartre.*

American McLean reissues have started to appear slowly now that Fantasy, Inc., has instituted its own facsimile reissue program. *McLean's Scene* is a late-Fifties quintet session with Bill Hardman on trumpet and Art Taylor on drums. Note that *4, 5 and 6* is the better half of the two-record *Contour* set, also still available. Superior Blue Note albums by McLean have been reissued in limited quantities in Japan. — B.B.

JIM McNEELY
★ ★ ★ The Plot Thickens / Gatem.
Jim McNeely is a New York-based pianist and probably best known for his work on trumpeter Ted Curson's outstanding *Jubilant Power* LP. *The Plot Thickens* is a quartet date featuring bassists Mike Richmond and Jon Burr, drummer Billy Hart and guitarist John Scofield, and its strongest point is the cohesive sympathy the players have for each other. As a pianist, McNeely relies here on single-note work, and his sound is sprightly. Nothing earth-shattering, but an honest date. — F.G.

MARIAN McPARTLAND
★ ★ ★ Ambiance / Hal.
★ ★ ★ At the Festival / Conc. J.
★ ★ ★ Delicate Balance / Hal.
★ ★ ★ Fine Romance / Improv
★ ★ ★ From This Moment On / Conc. J.
★ ★ ★ Interplay / Hal.
★ ★ ★ Live at the Carlyle / Hal.
★ ★ ★ Live at the Monticello / Hal.
★ ★ ★ Marian McPartland / Bain.
★ ★ ★ Now's the Time / Hal.
★ ★ ★ Plays Alec Wilder / Hal.
★ ★ ★ Portrait of / Conc. J.
★ ★ ★ Solo Concert at Haverford / Hal.
★ ★ ★ Swingin' / Hal.
★ ★ ★ Wanted! / Improv
British-born keyboardist Marian McPartland (b. 1920), known primarily these days for her atmospheric lounge-piano playing at chic watering places like the Carlyle, is actually a sturdy accompanist capable of marching through a series of blues changes as convincingly as she can caress a sentimental ballad. Her late husband, trumpeter Jimmy McPartland, was coleader on *Live at the Monticello, Swingin'* and *Wanted!* Most of these records were made during the Seventies, but *Marian McPartland,* an early-Sixties date, is interesting (despite sounding a bit dated) for its swinging Latin-jazz groove and the presence of bassist Ben Tucker's toe-tapping standard, "Coming Home Baby." — J.S.

CHARLES McPHERSON
★ ★ ★ ★ Beautiful / Xan.
★ ★ ★ Bebop Revisited / Prest.
★ ★ ★ Con Alma! / Prest.
★ ★ ★ Free Bop / Xan.
★ ★ ★ From This Moment On / Prest.
★ ★ ★ ★ Live in Tokyo / Xan.
★ ★ ★ ★ McPherson's Mood / Prest.
★ ★ ★ New Horizons / Xan.
★ ★ ★ ★ The Prophet / Disc.
★ ★ ★ Quintet/Live! / Prest.
The ghost of Charlie Parker hovers over every note that Charles McPherson plays. Like his mentor and fellow-Detroiter Barry Harris, alto saxophonist McPherson (b. 1939) has based his style on the Forties bebop era without actually having participated in it. Blessed with sharp ears, a pleasing tone and dangerous chops, McPherson is a notch above most of the practitioners of this demanding music. An original he is not, but his recordings are a perfect example of what it means to carry on a tradition.

Bebop Revisited, the title of his first LP, could sum up the entire Prestige period. This is straight-to-the-point bop, mainly distinguished by Harris' support and the surprising lack of growing pains in McPherson's exuberant blowing. *Mood,* with two post-bop sidemen, bassist Buster Williams and drummer Roy Brooks, is the least self-concious and therefore the best of the Prestige LPs. By this time McPherson's sound had grown more personal, and his confidence obviously proved infectious and inspiring.

From This Moment On (1968) finds the saxist flirting with soul and rock overtones. With the help of such able musicians as Cedar Walton and guitarist Pat Martino, McPherson successfully pulls off this updating with taste; still, this was a one-shot experiment. On his fine but unfortunately out-of-print Mainstream LPs, and then on his subsequent Xanadu discs, McPherson returned to more familiar bopish surroundings.

Back in his comfortable niche once again, McPherson recorded a series of highly accomplished sessions: *Beautiful,* with Duke Jordan on piano and devoted to mainstream standards, and *Tokyo,* highlighting a perfect team of bebop revivalists (Harris on piano, Sam Jones on bass, Leroy Williams on drums), are two of McPherson's most impressive displays of warm ballad playing and brisk uptempo cooking; *New Horizons* tried for just that with its modal pieces, but McPherson doesn't sound entirely convincing here. — S.F.

CARMEN McRAE

★ ★ ★ ★ As Time Goes By / Cata.
★ ★ ★ ★ Carmen McRae at the Great American Music Hall / Blue N.
★ ★ ★ ★ Carmen McRae Sings "Lover Man" and Other Billie Holiday Classics / Col.
★ ★ ★ Gold / MCA
★ ★ ★ ★ ★ The Great American Songbook / Atl.
★ ★ ★ The Greatest of Carmen McRae / MCA
★ ★ ★ Heat Wave (with Cal Tjader) / Conc. J.
★ ★ Love Songs / Acc.
★ ★ ★ November Girl (with Clarke/Boland Big Band) / Jazz M.
★ ★ ★ Recorded Live at Bubba's / Who
★ ★ ★ ★ Sound of Silence / Bain.
★ ★ ★ ★ Take Five (with Dave Brubeck) / CSP
★ ★ ★ ★ ★ Two for the Road (with George Shearing) / Conc. J.

When Carmen McRae (b. 1922) began her career, great singers were already established on all fronts: Ella Fitzgerald, Dinah Washington, Sarah Vaughan, Anita O'Day and McRae's idol, Billie Holiday. Instead of retiring in awe or becoming an imitator, she forged a distinctive approach to jazz singing. Today there is no doubt as to McRae's own identity or ability. She is unique and grand.

McRae's recordings are numerous. Unfortunately, most of her early sessions on Decca are out of print. The MCA set presents a good cross-section of this period, however. The Columbia recordings are from the early Sixties and they continue to impress, especially the tribute to Lady Day. The *Great American Songbook* and *Great American Music Hall* albums are stellar examples of how McRae cups an audience in the palms of her hands, making them believe virtually anything she wants. *It Takes a Whole Lot of Human Feeling* (Groove Merchant), dating from the late Sixties (like the aforementioned Atlantic and Blue Note discs), remains, regrettably, out of print.

The caliber of McRae's fellow participants should also be noted: the Dave Brubeck Quartet (on *Take Five*) and Nat Adderley, Norman Simmons, Eddie "Lockjaw" Davis, among others, on the *Holiday Classics* sessions. Jimmy Rowles and Joe Pass join the *American Songbook,* while Dizzy Gillespie guests on the *American Music Hall* set. Ben Webster makes a strong impression on *The Greatest of Carmen McRae.*

Of her most recent work, *Two for the Road* finds McRae at the height of her powers, aided in no small part by George Shearing's piano. While *As Time Goes By* is more personalized in that it features McRae solo on both vocals and piano, *Two for the Road* is the sum of two masterful, lyrical minds set loose on some choice songs.

Other singers speak with admiration of Carmen McRae's work. Since her early days with Benny Carter and Mercer Ellington, she chose to work with the finest musicians. A singer's singer and a musician's singer, McRae is in control and stronger than ever. — A.R.

HELEN MERRILL

★ ★ Autumn Love / Cata.
★ ★ ★ ★ Casa Forte / Inner
★ ★ ★ Chasin' the Bird / Inner
★ ★ ★ ★ Helen Merrill (with Clifford Brown) / Em.
★ ★ ★ Helen Merrill and John Lewis / Mer.
★ ★ ★ ★ Helen Sings, Teddy Swings! (with Teddy Wilson) / Cata.
★ ★ ★ Nearness of You / Em.
★ ★ ★ ★ Something Special / Inner

Possessing a whispery voice and a subdued sense of swing, Helen Merrill (b. 1930) moves adroitly through her own sound world, abetted by her finely crafted musicianship. She attracts jazz musicians of the highest order to work with her—Clifford Brown, Quincy Jones and the late, lamented Jimmy Jones (on her first date), Teddy Wilson, John Lewis, Gary Peacock, Oscar Pettiford and Gil Evans, among others.

The date with Clifford Brown is special for the trumpeter's responses to Merrill's moods. *Something Special* (originally on Milestone as *The Feeling is Mutual*), the first of two collaborations with pianist/arranger Dick Katz, remains a classic, but its out-of-print successor, *A Shade of Difference,* surpasses it. Thad and Elvin Jones, Ron Carter, Jim Hall and Hubert Laws are that difference.

Merrill has produced fine albums by Ann Burton, Tommy Flanagan, Roland Hanna and Al Haig. She brings to them her musical sensitivity and knowledge, thereby creating the proper circumstances for optimum performance. Her reading of "They Didn't Believe Me" with Haig (on his *Plays Jerome Kern,* Inner City) is a clear summation of all that is good in Helen Merrill's work: art that is sincere, warm and moving. — A.R.

PAT METHENY
★ ★ ★ ★ **Bright Size Life / ECM/War.**
★ ★ ★ **Watercolors / ECM/War.**
Pat Metheny (b. 1954) is the most refreshing guitarist to appear in recent years; with his full, warm tone, comprehensive yet unobtrusive technique and preference for direct melodicism and harmonic sophistication, he has returned to pre-jazz-rock verities in a contemporary context. His 1975 debut, *Bright Size Life,* benefits from the excellent support of Jaco Pastorius and Bob Moses, plus a well-balanced program. *Watercolors* was made shortly before Metheny left Gary Burton's quartet and covers much the same ground with less stimulating accompanists; the guitar playing remains convincing but doesn't deliver the expected step forward.
★ ★ **American Garage / ECM/War.**
★ ★ **As Falls Wichita, So Falls Wichita Falls / ECM/War.**
★ ★ ★ ★ **80/81 / ECM/War.**
★ ★ **First Circle / ECM/War.**
★ ★ **New Chautauqua / ECM/War.**
★ ★ ★ **Offramp / ECM/War.**
★ ★ **Pat Metheny Group / ECM/War.**
★ ★ ★ ★ **Rejoicing / ECM/War.**
★ ★ ★ **Travels / ECM/War.**
In 1977, Metheny and keyboard player Lyle Mays began developing a highly arranged and synthesized quartet sound. Their first recording, *Pat Metheny Group,* was made in early 1978, and the band's breezy, good-

natured manner immediately became a big success with the public. Later efforts, whether by the band (*American Garage, First Circle*), Metheny and Mayes (*As Falls Wichita*) or Metheny alone (*New Chautauqua*), have maintained the same tone and leave one with nothing but regret that Metheny didn't opt for a more spontaneous way of playing. In this respect, *Offramp* proves the most satisfying of his band's albums, with the greatest variety of material. *Travels,* a double live album, returns to the more homogenized approach.

80/81 is Metheny straight ahead, with a serious band (Michael Brecker, Jack De-Johnette, Charlie Haden, Dewey Redman) and a nice range of material, including the Ornette Coleman links (Keith Jarrett's quartet is part of that chain) inevitable with these players. More of Metheny in this vein can be heard on *Rejoicing,* a trio set with Haden and drummer Billy Higgins. — B.B.

MICROSCOPIC SEPTET
★ ★ ★ ★ **Take The Z Train / Prest.**
Four saxes (soprano to bari) and rhythm section make up this swing band with a twist. The "Micros" are a New York Lower East Side–spawned outfit with a truly distinctive sound that pumps Basie boogies, zestfully shifts from tangoed unison to Dixieland discordance with Mingus precision, and spins off sax solos that reach Eric Dolphy free *and* Earl Bostic blue within the same tune. With that much of the tradition mastered, this is one band that can afford to be seriously original and share a playful humor uncommon in New York jazz circles, especially where neotraditionalists saunter.

Filled with jerky Monkishness, fluid reed arrangements, false endings and titles like "Chinese Twilight Zone," *Z Train* is fueled by the compelling compositional talents of pianist Joel Forrester and saxman Philip Johnston. — A.K.

BUTCH MILES
★ ★ ★ **Butch Miles Salutes Chick Webb / Fam. D.**
★ ★ ★ **Butch Miles Salutes Gene Krupa / Fam. D.**
★ ★ ★ **Butch Miles Swings Some Standards / Fam. D.**
★ ★ ★ **Butch's Encore / Fam. D.**
★ ★ ★ **Miles and Miles of Swing / Fam. D.**
A neat, precise swing musician who knows all the licks, Butch Miles (b. 1944) was Count Basie's drummer in the Seventies. His

sextet is quite competent. The hitch is that they haven't found anything of their own.
— F.G.

GLENN MILLER

★ ★ ★ **The Complete Glenn Miller Vol. I /**
Bluebird
★ ★ ★ **The Complete Glenn Miller Vol. II /**
Bluebird
★ ★ ★ **The Complete Glenn Miller Vol. III**
/ Bluebird
★ ★ ★ **The Complete Glenn Miller Vol. IV /**
Bluebird
★ ★ ★ **The Complete Glenn Miller Vol. V /**
Bluebird
★ ★ ★ **The Complete Glenn Miller Vol. VI /**
Bluebird
★ ★ ★ **The Complete Glenn Miller Vol. VII**
/ Bluebird
★ ★ ★ **The Complete Glenn Miller Vol. VIII**
/ Bluebird
★ ★ ★ **The Complete Glenn Miller Vol. IX /**
Bluebird

Trombonist Glenn Miller (1904–1944) is one of the most popular figures in jazz history despite the fact that his musical importance is hardly significant. His creamy band sound and precise, disciplined arrangements were the essence of the "sweet" big-band style that was privately ridiculed by the era's top musicians. Miller's bands were notable for their lack of great soloists—his concept had little use for them—but he surrounded himself with superb technicians. The letter-perfect performances that ensued were appropriate to the kind of pop material Miller chose to cover, songs picked for their commercial potential rather than musical worth. All of this is not to say that Miller was a poor musician; on the contrary, he was a player and arranger of considerable talents, as his Thirties work as arranger for the Dorsey Brothers orchestra and as one of the top session players on radio broadcasts proved. Aside from his signature reed section of three saxophones and clarinet playing in unison, however, he left his most creative moments behind when he formed his own organization. His commercial efforts did much to popularize jazz to an audience less interested in playing than song selection.

Vol. I (1938–39) includes "Moonlight Serenade," which was the orchestra's theme, "Little Brown Jug," "Sunrise Serenade" and a version of "King Porter Stomp" that points out the band's emotional deficiencies. *Vol. II* (1939) showcases Miller's most popular performance, "In the Mood," and tunes from the *Wizard of Oz* film soundtrack. *Vol. III* (1939–40) includes "Indian Summer,"

"Star Dust" and "My Melancholy Baby." *Vol. IV* (1940) features "Tuxedo Junction" and "Pennsylvania 6-5000." *Vol. V* (also from '40) includes "Blueberry Hill" and "Beat Me Daddy, Eight to a Bar." *Vol. VI* (1940–41) covers ponderous classical pieces like "Anvil Chorus" and "Song of the Volga Boatmen" plus pop stuff like "Ida! Sweet As Apple Cider" and "Chattanooga Choo Choo." *Vol. VII* (1941) anticipates Miller's value as a cultural weapon in World War II with "The White Cliffs Of Dover," but also includes "Jingle Bells." *VIII* (1941–42) is pure war effort stuff ("Keep 'Em Flying," "On the Old Assembly Line," "Shh, It's a Military Secret," "When Johnny Comes Marching Home," "Soldier Let Me Read Your Letter," "That's Sabotage.") *IX* is a summation of Miller's recordings from '39 to '42. — J.S.

CHARLES MINGUS

Bassist, composer, arranger, leader, author, sometimes pianist and vocalist Charles Mingus (1922–1979) was one of the best-documented musicians in jazz with justification—he was one of the greatest. His relatively lesser known albums all bubbled over with intensity, his triumphs were sublime, and the following ratings are assigned with that in mind.

★ ★ ★ ★ **The Best of Charles Mingus / Atl.**
★ ★ ★ ★ **Charles Mingus / Prest.**
★ ★ ★ ★ **Trio and Sextet / Trip**

Mingus' first recordings as a leader show a rapid evolution toward greater power and cacophonous latitude for his sidemen with a constant personal stamp that uniquely drew on Ellington, black church music and modern European composers. The Trip album collects early (1954) compositions with great stress on the writing, European influences (the sextet features a cello) and early Thad Jones trumpet; the second half of this double album is a relaxed trio session from three years later with Hampton Hawes and Dannie Richmond. The Prestige twofer from 1955 is a looser though still carefully structured club recording with a quintet, revealing Mingus' sonic preference of the era (trombone and tenor sax, no trumpet). Max Roach drums on three of the tracks. *Best of* has the only available track by Mingus' excellent 1956 quintet with Jackie McLean on alto, J. R. Monterose on tenor and Mal Waldron on piano—the cataclysmic "Pithecanthropus Erectus."

★ ★ ★ ★ ★ **Better Git It in Your Soul / Col.**
★ ★ ★ ★ ★ **Tijuana Moods / RCA**
★ ★ ★ ★ ★ **Wonderland / UA**

In 1957, Mingus took a rhythm & blues tenor saxophonist named Dannie Richmond and, by his own account, taught him drums because he couldn't find another drummer besides Elvin Jones with whom he liked working. The Mingus/Richmond rhythm section, which has been intact with only occasional interruption ever since, ushered in the great Mingus era. Masterpieces from the 1957–59 period include "Haitian Fight Song" and "Wednesday Night Prayer Meeting," a bass and church-jazz tour de force respectively, on *Best of*; the whole of *Tijuana*, but especially "Ysabel's Table Dance"; the blowing tracks on *Wonderland* that pit John Handy's alto against Booker Ervin's tenor; and such varied gems from *Better Git It* as the title piece, the pensive Lester Young eulogy "Goodbye Pork Pie Hat," the pointedly evocative "Fables of Faubus," the abstract "Diane" and "Far Wells, Mill Valley," and such personal acknowledgements of sources as "Jelly Roll," "Open Letter to Duke," "Song with Orange" and "Self-Portrait in Three Colors." Ervin, Richmond and trombonist Jimmy Knepper are invaluable collaborators.

★ ★ ★ ★ ★ **The Great Concert of Charles Mingus / Prest.**
★ ★ ★ ★ **Mingus, Mingus, Mingus, Mingus, Mingus / Imp.**
★ ★ ★ ★ ★ **Mingus Revisited / Trip**
★ ★ ★ ★ ★ **Stormy Weather / Barn.**
★ ★ ★ ★ ★ **Town Hall Concert / Fan.**
★ ★ ★ **Town Hall Concert / Solid St.**

Eric Dolphy worked with Mingus frequently between 1960 and the reed giant's death in 1964, and sparks flew at every encounter. *Stormy Weather*, from early in the period and with the stunning quartet completed by Richmond and trumpeter Ted Curson, contains several of their masterpieces (the version of "Original Faubus Fables," with lyrics, makes an interesting comparison with the more picturesque one done for Columbia the previous year). *Great Concert*, a three-record set, and the Fantasy *Town Hall* album feature the group that traveled to Europe, where Dolphy died: Mingus, Dolphy, Richmond, Clifford Jordan on tenor, pianist Jaki Byard and trumpeter Johnny Coles. This is perhaps Mingus' best band.

Also, it was in this period Mingus began recording with expanded personnel: Dolphy is heard on *Revisited*, the *Town Hall Concert* and the Impulse *Mingus, Mingus*. The Trip album, from 1960, is the most fascinating, as it features early Mingus orchestrations such as the ambitious, quasi-classical "Half-Mast Inhibitions."

★ ★ ★ ★ ★ **The Black Saint and the Sinner Lady / Imp.**
★ ★ ★ ★ **Mingus at Monterey / Fan.**
★ ★ ★ **Mingus Plays Piano / Imp.**
★ ★ ★ **My Favorite Quintet / Fan.**
★ ★ ★ ★ ★ **Right Now / Fan.**

Mingus made equally important music without Dolphy during the Sixties, until his temporary withdrawal from the scene at the end of 1966. *Black Saint*, from 1962, is one of his most ambitious and best-realized works; an album-length exorcism of personal demons with a strong ten-piece band in which Charlie Mariano's alto stands out. While the 1965 Monterey Festival performance of "Meditations on Integrations" (also known as "Meditations on a Pair of Wire Cutters") has attained legendary status, I prefer the quartet version on *Right Now*, with tenor saxophonist Clifford Jordan outdoing himself.

★ ★ ★ ★ ★ **Changes One / Atl.**
★ ★ ★ ★ **Changes Two / Atl.**
★ ★ ★ ★ ★ **Charles Mingus and Friends in Concert / Col.**
★ ★ ★ ★ ★ **Let My Children Hear Music / Col.**
★ ★ ★ **Mingus at Carnegie Hall / Atl.**
★ ★ ★ **Mingus Moves / Atl.**
★ ★ ★ ★ **Reincarnation of a Lovebird / Prest.**
★ ★ ★ **Three or Four Shades of Blues / Atco**

While Mingus was inconsistent in the Seventies, his best music of the period clearly ranked with the best of his career. This would include *Let My Children*, a wide-ranging orchestral recital, and the fertile *Changes* albums by a working quintet which included George Adams on tenor, Don Pullen on piano and of course Richmond. The loose *And Friends* record is recommended for some of tenor saxophonist Gene Ammons' best recorded work.

★ ★ ★ ★ ★ **At Antibes / Atl.**
★ ★ ★ ★ **Cumbia and Jazz Fusion / Atl.**
★ ★ ★ ★ **Great Moments with Charles Mingus / MCA**
★ ★ ★ ★ **Jazz Workshop / Savoy**
★ ★ **Me, Myself an Eye / Atl.**
★ ★ ★ ★ **Mingus at Monterey / Prest. (same as earlier Fantasy record with same title)**
★ ★ ★ ★ **Mingus in Europe, Vols. 1 and 2 / Enja**
★ ★ ★ ★ ★ **Passions of a Man / Atl.**
★ ★ ★ ★ **Pithecanthropus Erectus / Atl.**
★ ★ ★ ★ **Portrait / Prest. (contains *My Favorite Quintet* and *Town Hall Concert*)**
★ ★ **Something like a Bird / Atl.**
★ ★ ★ **Soul Fusion / Quin.**

The prolific Mingus, who died at the start of 1979, had a catalogue that was always large and in flux. The growing appreciation of his music that (for once) preceded his death brought out some good new titles in the Seventies, although there was also a lot of familiar material among the Prestiges and the sampler versions of the long-deleted Impulse titles (check the Quintessence and the MCA sets—*Great Moments* does contain the complete *Black Saint*). Mingus' early burst to freedom can be traced on the Savoy and *Pithecanthropus* (the whole session is not as good as the title tune—Dannie Richmond's arrival the next year helped). *Antibes* is a real treat, though, from the 1960 Curson/Dolphy band with Booker Ervin and, on some tracks, Bud Powell. *Cumbia and Jazz Fusion,* easily the best of Mingus' last efforts, features two side-long soundtracks by an expanded version of the working band. Beware the overblown final orchestral effort, *Me, Myself* and its companion, *Something Like,* which is really just a long jam session. *Passions of a Man,* Atlantic's three-album retrospective, does a pretty good job of getting it all in, including some of the later lapses.

★ ★ ★ ★ ★ **Mingus / Jazz M.**
★ ★ ★ ★ **Mingus at the Bohemia / Fan./ OJC**
★ ★ ★ ★ ★ **Mingus Presents Mingus / Jazz M.**
★ ★ ★ ★ ★ **Music Written for Monterey, 1965 / East Coasting**
★ ★ ★ ★ ★ **Pre Bird / Lime.**
★ ★ ★ ★ ★ **Town Hall Concert / Fan./OJC**

Mingus recordings seem to be going round and round in the Eighties, with familiar titles reappearing, sometimes in new packages, sometimes not. The Jazz Man titles above are the famous sessions originally released on Candid. *Pre Bird* is a Japanese facsimile of Mingus' earliest full-orchestra album (from 1960); the *Mingus at the Bohemia* quintet album, from 1955, is also still available as half of the first Prestige twofer (*Charles Mingus*); and *Town Hall Concert* is the heated 1964 sextet with Dolphy, not the disorganized big band from the previous year. Some of the Jazz Workshop material from the 1984 *Music Written for Monterey* release has never been previously issued. — B.B.

RED MITCHELL

★ ★ ★ ★ **Jim Hall and Red Mitchell / Artists H.**
★ ★ ★ **Quartet / Contem.**
★ ★ ★ ★ **Three for All (with Phil Woods and Tommy Flanagan) / Enja**

Hidden in the studios during the Fifties, an expatriate to Scandinavia by the end of the Sixties, bassist Red Mitchell (b. 1927) has been unjustly overlooked. An exceptional timekeeper and a keenly inventive soloist, hence his studio popularity, Mitchell has a beautifully woody tone that gives him the sonority of a featured horn.

A veteran of the Forties Woody Herman big band and a sideman for virtually every artist who has recorded on the West Coast, Mitchell is the rare example of the consummate professional who has grown with the times. A great introduction to his artistry is his advanced playing on Ornette Coleman's second Contemporary LP, *Tommorrow Is the Question!*

Unfortunately, Mitchell has stepped out but a handful of times fronting an American band, and most of these dates are long out of print. *Quartet* is a bit of an oddity. A late-Fifties bop-oriented set, it features legendary saxman James Clay, pianist Lorraine Geller and drummer Billy Higgins before he joined Ornette on a regular basis.

Recent Mitchell work is usually under shared leadership. He has cut stunning duo work with guitarists Jim Hall and Joe Beck and trio dates with Tommy Flanagan.
— S.F.

ROSCOE MITCHELL

★ ★ ★ ★ **Congliptious / Nessa**
★ ★ ★ ★ ★ **Old/Quartet / Nessa**
★ ★ ★ **Roscoe Mitchell Quartet / Sack.**
★ ★ ★ ★ **The Roscoe Mitchell Solo Saxophone Concerts / Sack.**
★ ★ ★ ★ ★ **Sound / Del.**

Others will disagree, but I'd call Roscoe Mitchell (b. 1940) the most important voice to emerge from Chicago's Association for the Advancement of Creative Musicians (AACM). As a composer, he developed the spontaneous group form that his Art Ensemble (later called the Art Ensemble of Chicago) offered as an alternative to the endless blowout, and Mitchell's solo playing, primarily on alto sax, is among the most gripping experiences in the new music.

His 1966 debut, *Sound,* introduced the AACM to the world. Sololess performances, extended unaccompanied solos, sparing use of instruments and virtuoso performers (Lester Bowie, trumpet, and Malachi Favors, bass, would go on to collaborate with Mitchell in the Art Ensemble) abound.

Congliptious has a side of one solo piece each by Mitchell, Bowie and Favors, plus one of their best group performances, with drummer Robert Crowder added. Even better is *Old/Quartet,* recorded in 1967 before drummer Phillip Wilson left to join Paul Butterfield but only released in 1975. This is the best Mitchell sampler, with a solo, a free group form and homage to gutbucket funk.

Canada's Sackville label also has *The Roscoe Mitchell Solo Saxophone Concerts;* if you like such things, his tone and rhythm cut Braxton's. *Roscoe Mitchell Quartet* is only half quartet, and those pieces don't come off. Trombonist George Lewis duets with Mitchell and plays solo on the more interesting remainder of the album.

★ ★ ★ **Duets with Anthony Braxton** / Sack.

★ ★ ★ ★ **L-R-G/The Maze/S II Examples** / **Nessa**

★ ★ ★ ★ **Nonaah** / Nessa

★ ★ ★ ★ **Snurdy McGurdy and Her Dancin' Shoes** / Nessa

★ ★ ★ ★ **3 × 4 Eye** / Black S.

As Mitchell's music grows more involved with conceptual nuance and the gradation of individual sound, it risks overintellectualization and the trap of effects for their own sake. Thus the solo squawking on the two-record *Nonaah* detracts from such inspired moments as a version of the title piece by four alto saxophonists. Similarly, the complex extended trio piece, "L-R-G," with Leo Smith and George Lewis, and the surprisingly stately "The Maze" for eight percussionists, are grouped with the tedious soprano sax exercise of "S II Examples."

During 1980 and '81, Mitchell led a new quintet, the Sound Ensemble, when not touring with the Art Ensemble of Chicago. With guitarist A. Spencer Barefield and bassist Jaribu Shahid working on acoustic and electric instruments, some strong drumming by Tani Tabbal and a pungent second-lead voice in Hugh Ragin's trumpet, the quintet could move in many different directions, though some of the navel-gazing aspects remained. *Snurdy* and *3 × 4,* both by the Sound Ensemble, appeared early in 1982, but the Nessa contains the better program.

— B.B.

HANK MOBLEY

★ ★ ★ **Hard Bop** / Savoy

★ ★ ★ **Messages** / Prest.

★ ★ ★ **Roll Call** / Blue N.

★ ★ ★ ★ **A Slice of the Top** / Blue N.

★ ★ ★ ★ **Soul Station** / Blue N.

★ ★ ★ **Thinking of Home** / Blue N.

★ ★ ★ **Third Season** / Blue N.

Hank Mobley (b. 1930), a dependable but not always inspired tenorist, was a perennial sideman of the Fifties and Sixties. For a player who flourished during the hard-bop period, Mobley's playing could be flaccid and lazy rather than funky and biting. His greatest asset seems to have been an ability to adapt to different musical settings; he can be heard with such distinct leaders as Max Roach, Art Blakey and Miles Davis.

His own records are mostly solid but not indispensable blowing sessions with contributions from up-and-comers like Lee Morgan, Donald Byrd, Kenny Dorham and Jackie McLean. *Soul Station*, a quartet date with Blakely, is a stand-out.

Mobley always held his own in the fast company he kept, but the majority of his work is professional rather than memorable. The major exception is *Slice,* a great 1966 date with arrangements by Duke Pearson and support from Lee Morgan, McCoy Tyner and Billy Higgins. By this time Mobley had been touched, as had most tenorists, by the work of John Coltrane. This modernist bent adds verve and aggressiveness to Mobley's chops; he has never sounded better.

Third Season also finds Mobley surrounded by many of the same younger players who supply the needed sparks. — S.F.

MODERN JAZZ QUARTET

★ ★ ★ ★ ★ **The Art of the Modern Jazz Quartet** / Atl.

★ ★ ★ ★ ★ **Best of the Modern Jazz Quartet** / Atl.

★ ★ ★ ★ **Blues at Carnegie Hall** / Atl.

★ ★ ★ **Blues on Bach** / Atl.

★ ★ ★ **Collaboration (with Laurindo Almeida)** / Atl.

★ ★ ★ ★ ★ **European Concert** / Atl.

★ ★ ★ ★ ★ **Fontessa** / Atl.

★ ★ ★ **In Memoriam** / Li. Dav.

★ ★ ★ ★ **Last Concert** / Atl.

★ ★ ★ **The Legendary Profile** / Atl.

★ ★ ★ ★ ★ **Modern Jazz Quartet** / Atl.

★ ★ ★ ★ ★ **Modern Jazz Quartet** / Prest.

★ ★ ★ ★ ★ **One Never Knows** / Atl.

★ ★ ★ **Porgy and Bess** / Atl.

★ ★ ★ ★ ★ **Pyramid** / Atl.

★ ★ ★ ★ **Third Stream Music** / Atl.

The MJQ began its life as the rhythm section of Dizzy Gillespie's 1946 big band, with pianist/composer John Lewis (b. 1920), vibraharpist Milt Jackson (b. 1923), bassist Ray Brown (b. 1926) and drummer Kenny Clarke (b. 1914). The four worked and recorded together in various groups over the next five years; when they finally formed their cooperative band in 1952 under the musical direction of Lewis—and first used the name Modern Jazz Quartet—Brown had been replaced by another Gillespie alumnus, bassist Percy Heath (b. 1923).

The Prestige *Modern Jazz Quartet* twofer contains the band's 1952–55 work and highlights its most notable traits: the improvising prowess of Jackson on all types of material, but especially ballads ("Gershwin Medley,"

"Autumn in New York") and blues ("Ralph's New Blues"); Lewis' simple, optimistic piano, his conversational accompaniment, and compositions steeped in European counterpoint ("Concorde," "Vendome") as well as the blues, and such exquisite original forms as "Django"; and the superlative rhythm support of Heath, Clarke and drummer Connie Kay—the latter came on in 1955 to replace Clarke, who reportedly was uninterested in Lewis' baroque proclivities.

Kay's uncommonly subdued and sensitive drumming ushered in the MJQ's finest period, from 1956 to '60. Among the quartet's greatest achievements are *Fontessa,* a well-balanced program with a fugue, a bebop tune, three magnificent Jackson ballad solos, "Bluesology" and Lewis' lovely "Fontessa Suite"; *One Never Knows,* Lewis' film score for Roger Vadim's *No Sun in Venice,* with the joyous "Golden Striker"; and *Pyramid;* but it is the two-record near-perfect *European Concert* that best summarizes the quiet power of the MJQ in fifteen of their most representative pieces.

Third Stream Music, from 1960, finds Lewis in his most overt attempt to blend classical and jazz sources. Jimmy Giuffre's trio, a chamber quintet and a string quartet join the MJQ for five performances that, while modestly successful, serve as little more than an historic footnote to an unnaturally forced experiment. (Much of the great work from this period can be sampled in two Atlantic collections, *Best of* and the more comprehensive *Art of the MJQ.*)

After 1960, the MJQ became more and more predictable as Lewis produced fewer interesting compositions. The only albums from the decade still in print are the *Porgy and Bess* collection, a more spirited *Blues at Carnegie Hall* and some welcome variety in the form of *Collaboration* with acoustic guitarist Laurindo Almeida. This last has the best of three MJQ versions of the adagio from Rodrigo's *Concierto de Aranjuez* which Miles Davis recorded on *Sketches of Spain.*

Winding down to the disbanding of the group in late 1974 are albums where the strains of overfamiliarity become obvious. Lewis (as both writer and pianist) and Kay are both noticeably below their earlier peaks, and even the reliable Jackson can't shake the rut. A retreat to more classicism, in the form of Bach chorales and the orchestral *In Memoriam,* was a nonanswer to the problem of a group (and, more particularly, of a sensitivity embodied by John Lewis) that had outlived its time. But the MJQ went out wailing in a superb 1974 Avery Fisher Hall concert

that carried the bite of a quarter-century's music-making. Several critics called *Last Concert* the MJQ's finest album, and while I don't feel it comes up to their earlier Atlantics, it definitely deserves its reputation as the final achievement in a career filled with much great music.

★ ★ ★ ★ **At Music Inn, Vol. 1 (with Jimmy Guiffre) / Atl.**
★ ★ ★ ★ ★ **Concorde / Fan./OJC**
★ ★ ★ ★ ★ **MJQ / Fan./OJC**
★ ★ ★ ★ **More from the Last Concert / Atl.**

Although the MJQ was reunited for American and Japanese concerts, no recordings had appeared by the end of 1983. The lone new album (*More*) completes the program from the November 25, 1974 farewell at Avery Fisher Hall.

While the MJQ has not been reissued as extensively as their stature might suggest, Atlantic did put a very good 1956 album, with Jimmy Guiffre's clarinet added on three tracks, back into circulation. The excellent *Concorde,* which was Connie Kay's first recording session with the quartet, is also available as part of the Prestige two-record *Modern Jazz Quartet* set. *MJQ* is a combination of the first tracks recorded under the group name and several Milt Jackson quartet sides. — B.B.

THELONIOUS MONK

★ ★ ★ ★ ★ **The Complete Genius / Blue N.**
★ ★ ★ **Thelonious Monk / GNP**
★ ★ ★ ★ ★ **Thelonious Monk / Prest.**

That overworked term "genius" applies to pianist/composer Thelonious Monk (1917–1982), a modern pioneer whose iconoclastic approach to complex harmony, space, rhythmic irregularity, melodic angularity and thematically centered improvisation created a thoroughly personal musical universe that inspired all of the most daring post-Parker musicians. Many of his recordings are currently available in more than one issue; the present list attempts to avoid duplication.

Complete Genius is all of his 1947–52 Blue Note work, with several classic compositions ("'Round Midnight," "Criss Cross," "Misterioso," "Monk's Mood," etc.), and assists from Art Blakey, Milt Jackson, Max Roach, Kenny Dorham and Sahib Shibab. The Prestige twofer summarizes his period with that label (1952–54), where he worked with trios and quintets. Tenor players Sonny Rollins and Frank Foster are impressive, and the Monk/Percy Heath/Art Blakey threesome is his perfect trio. The GNP, which is also available on Trip, is a solid solo effort.

★ ★ ★ ★ ★ Brilliance / Mile.
★ ★ ★ ★ In Person / Mile.
★ ★ ★ ★ ★ Misterioso / Riv.
★ ★ ★ ★ ★ Pure Monk / Trip
★ ★ ★ ★ ★ Thelonious in Action / Riv.
★ ★ ★ ★ ★ Thelonious Monk and John
Coltrane / Mile.
★ ★ ★ ★ Thelonious Monk Meets Gerry
Mulligan / Riv.
★ ★ ★ Thelonious Monk Plays Duke
Ellington / Riv.
★ ★ ★ ★ The Unique Thelonious Monk /
Riv.

Monk's Riverside years, 1955–60, found the
jazz public slowly catching up to his music.
Of the top-rated albums above, *Pure Monk*
collects all of his solo work from the period,
easily his best unaccompanied performances;
Brilliance features his two best quintet dates,
one with Rollins and Roach featured, the
other containing the inspired front line of
Thad Jones' cornet and Charlie Rouse's
tenor; *Monk/Coltrane* has the only tracks by
the legendary 1957 Monk quartet with Coltrane, bassist Wilbur Ware and drummer
Shadow Wilson, plus a quirky septet from
the same year with Coltrane, Ware, Blakey
and Coleman Hawkins; and *In Person* and
Misterioso are live recordings by the underrated 1958 quartet of Johnny Griffin (tenor
sax), Ahmed Abdul Malik (bass) and Roy
Haynes (drums). *In Person* is also notable
for the 1959 Town Hall concert by a large
group playing Hall Overton arrangements of
Monk pieces.

★ ★ ★ ★ Criss-Cross / CSP
★ ★ ★ ★ It's Monk's Time / Col.
★ ★ ★ ★ Misterioso / Col.
★ ★ ★ Monk / Col.
★ ★ ★ ★ Monk's Dream / CSP
★ ★ ★ Solo / Col.
★ ★ ★ Straight No Chaser / Col.
★ ★ ★ ★ Underground / Col.
★ ★ ★ Who's Afraid of Big Bad Monk /
Col.

Monk's Columbia years, 1962–68, found him
primarily confined to the quartet format
(with Rouse as horn soloist) and reworking
his earlier triumphs in lesser versions. While
the playing is consistently good, the setting
is predictable and both Monk and especially
Rouse occasionally sound tired. *Who's Afraid*
combines Monk's two orchestral efforts of
the time, a brilliant Philharmonic Hall concert and a ludicrous studio date with Oliver
Nelson charts.

★ ★ ★ ★ The Man I Love / Black L.
★ ★ ★ ★ Something in Blue / Black L.
While hardly the best Monk, these 1971
trios are valuable for reuniting the pianist

with his perfect accompanist, Art Blakey,
and demonstrating that the genius can still
play.

★ ★ ★ ★ ★ Alone in San Francisco / Riv.
★ ★ ★ ★ April in Paris/Live / Mile.
★ ★ ★ ★ At the Black Hawk / Riv.
★ ★ ★ ★ ★ At the Five Spot / Mile.
★ ★ ★ ★ ★ At Town Hall / Riv./Fan./OJC
★ ★ ★ ★ Blues Five Spot / Mile.
★ ★ ★ ★ Brilliant Corners / Fan./OJC
★ ★ ★ ★ ★ The Complete Blue Note
Recordings / Mosaic (available by mail
only; see text below)
★ ★ ★ ★ Five by Monk by Five / Riv.
★ ★ ★ ★ ★ Live at the It Club / Col.
★ ★ ★ Live at the Jazz Workshop / Col.
★ ★ ★ ★ Live in Tokyo / Col.
★ ★ ★ ★ ★ Memorial Album / Mile.
★ ★ ★ ★ ★ Monk / Fan./OJC
★ Monk's Blues / Col.
★ ★ ★ ★ ★ Monk's Music / Riv.
★ ★ ★ ★ Monk Trio / Fan./OJC
★ ★ ★ Plays Duke Ellington / Fan./OJC
★ ★ ★ ★ The Riverside Trios / Mile.
★ ★ ★ ★ 'Round Midnight (with Gerry
Mulligan) / Mile.
★ ★ ★ ★ Something in Blue / Jazz M.
★ ★ ★ ★ ★ Thelonious Himself / Fan./OJC
★ ★ ★ ★ ★ Thelonious Monk with John
Coltrane / Fan./OJC
★ ★ ★ ★ ★ Thelonious Monk with Sonny
Rollins / Fan./OJC
★ ★ ★ ★ The Unique Thelonious Monk /
Fan./OJC

Monk, who never returned to performing,
died in February 1982. Many of the above
titles are reissues of Riverside or Prestige albums, either in Japanese facsimiles, budget-
priced American facsimiles or two-record
Milestone packages. *At the Five Spot* is an
essential set, comprising *Misterioso* and *In
Action,* but contains a serious flaw—the
track "Misterioso" has been inexplicably edited. Search out the Riverside singles. *Five by
Monk* is half of *Brilliance,* still available;
and *Himself* is the great first solo set. *Riverside Trios* has the *Ellington* and *Unique* albums paired, from the inception of Monk's
Riverside affiliation. *April in Paris* is 1961
concert material from the quartet with
Rouse. *Something* is the old Black Lion.
Some of the albums do contain new material. *Blues Five Spot* is new material from
the *Five Spot* set with some other live and
studio sides. All of the Columbia *Live* titles
are two-record sets from 1963 and 1964.
'Round Midnight also contains outtakes
from Monk's 1957 encounter with Mulligan,
plus a fascinating side-long series of solo versions of the title piece. A good collection of

previously unissued later work, *Always Know,* appeared on Columbia Contemporary Masters in 1979 but is no longer in the current catalogue.

The most important release in the current Monk deluge is a four-record set of complete recordings from his Blue Note years, including several new alternate takes and two brand-new titles not recorded by Monk anywhere else. The album is available by mail order only from Mosaic Records, 197 Strawberry Hill Avenue, Stamford, Connecticut 06902. — B.B.

J. R. MONTEROSE
★ ★ ★ ... And a Little Pleasure (with Tommy Flanagan) / Uptown
★ ★ ★ ★ J. R. Monterose / Blue N./PSI
★ ★ ★ Live in Albany / Uptown
★ ★ ★ ★ Straight Ahead / Xan.

Unsung tenorman from upstate New York. The Xanadu disc, cut in the Fifties, displays J. R. Monterose in all his power: quick-witted, muscular and in debt over his head to Sonny Rollins. That's not necessarily a knock, though, because Monterose does much more with it than most Newked-out players, using it as a tool rather than a get-over. The Blue Note facsimile import is his first album recorded with Ira Sullivan on trumpet, Horace Silver on piano, Wilbur Ware on bass and Philly Joe Jones on drums.

Although the Uptown discs are more recent, they suffer from a lack of polish. The tragedy is they fail to convey that this man can still blow up a storm. — F.G.

WES MONTGOMERY
★ ★ ★ ★ The Alternate Wes Montgomery / Mile.
★ ★ ★ ★ Beginnings / Blue N.
★ ★ ★ Best (with brothers Buddy and Monk Montgomery) / Fan.
★ ★ ★ Encores / Mile.
★ ★ ★ ★ Full House / Fan./OJC
★ ★ ★ Fusion / Riv.
★ ★ ★ Groove Bros. / Mile.
★ ★ ★ Guitar on the Go / Riv.
★ ★ ★ ★ Movin' / Mile.
★ ★ ★ Movin' Along / Riv.
★ ★ ★ Portrait of Wes / Riv./Fan./OJC
★ ★ ★ Pretty Blue / Mile.
★ ★ ★ ★ ★ Small Group Recordings / Verve
★ ★ ★ Wes Montgomery and Friends / Mile.

Belatedly discovered at the age of thirty-four by Cannonball Adderley, Wes Montgomery (1925–1968) left his hometown of Indianapolis for the West Coast and subsequently created a body of work that easily established him as the most influential jazz guitarist of the Fifties and Sixties. A thoroughly schooled player—he'd learned all of Charlie Christian's solos note for note—Montgomery immediately demonstrated a fluid single-note style brilliantly interfaced with a subtle use of chords. But Montgomery's signature sound was his phenomenal octave technique (presumably developed for a quieter sound so he wouldn't disturb the neighbors when practicing), a device first pioneered by Django Reinhardt. Montgomery took this difficult-to-control technique further than any other guitarist, with the possible exception of George Benson, a modern apostle of Montgomery.

Beginnings covers the late Indianapolis-early California period when Montgomery's style was rapidly solidifying. Although the Christian influence is still strong on seminal tracks like "Bock to Bock" and "Billie's Bounce," his dazzling technique emerges on the instrumental showpiece "Finger Pickin'," a recording credited as having totally intimidated many of Montgomery's contemporaries. Using the competent if unspectacular talents of his brothers Buddy (keyboards) and Monk (bass) on most of these L.A. sessions, Montgomery hits a high point in his collaboration with the underrated tenor sax player Harold Land on tunes like "Old Folks," "Leila," and "Wes' Tune." At this point, Montgomery was concentrating on his single note and chord work, and he used octaves sparingly. As his records became more and more overproduced in the latter part of his career, he would lean more heavily on this effect.

Small Group Recordings and *Movin'* preserve what is arguably Montgomery's most focused work. The former captures a series of stirring live performances at the old Half Note with Montgomery sympathetically backed by the Wynton Kelly Trio. His deep, warm tone—he played with his thumb, not a pick—graces stunning versions of "Misty," "Portrait of Jennie" and "Willow Weep for Me," songs that would be massacred by saccharine orchestrations on later Verve releases. His relaxed encounter with organist Jimmy Smith on side four shows why the organ-guitar combo was such a popular facet of the Fifties. *Movin'* recaps Californian sessions with producer Orrin Keepnews, in which Montgomery continues to refine his sound. *Full House* is the original live album that makes up one half of *Movin'*. *Encores* is alternate takes from Riverside sessions.

★ ★ ★ Best of, Vol. 1 / Verve
★ ★ ★ Bumpin' / Verve
★ ★ California Dreaming / Verve
★ ★ Day in the Life / A&M
★ ★ Down Here on the Ground
★ ★ Goin' Out of My Head / Verve
★ ★ Greatest Hits / A&M
★ ★ Jazz Guitar / Picca.
★ ★ Return Engagement / Verve
★ ★ Road Song / A&M
★ ★ Tequila / Verve
★ ★ While We're Young / Mile.
★ ★ Yesterdays / Mile.

In the waning stages of Montgomery's tenure with Verve, Creed Taylor took charge of his career and guided him in a pop MOR direction that brought Wes a lot of money and recognition while causing jazz guitar enthusiasts untold pain. These recordings are not so much grouped together for chronology as they are a representative sampling of a downward trend in Montgomery's musical contribution. The late Verve recordings and the A&M material are characterized by a predominance of cotton-soft octaves gently nudging up to generally abysmal arrangements of chart songs. The graphics of the A&M recordings are spectacular, but Montgomery sounds weary and resigned. His tragic death at the age of forty-three rendered the question of his return to "straight jazz" academic. — J.C.C.

TETE MONTOLIU
★ ★ ★ ★ Catalonian Folksongs / Timel.
★ ★ ★ ★ Catalonian Nights / Steep.
★ ★ ★ ★ I Wanna Talk about You / Steep.
★ ★ ★ ★ Lunch in L.A. (with Chick Corea) / Contem.
★ ★ ★ ★ Secret Love / Timel.
★ ★ ★ ★ Songs for Love / Enja
★ ★ ★ ★ Tête à Tête / Steep.

A Spanish pianist from Catalonia, Tete Montoliu (b. 1933) is an enigma: his playing is pure modern jazz, as if he had grown up in Philadelphia listening to Art Tatum, Erroll Garner and Bud Powell.

Montoliu's preferred setting is the trio, but he also records solo (*Catalonian Folksongs* and *Songs for Love*). Although he draws on folksongs from his native region, his repertoire is composed mainly of originals and American standards. A mature stylist, so there's scant difference between these albums. — F.G.

LEE MORGAN
★ ★ ★ A-1 (with Hank Mobley) / Savoy
★ ★ ★ ★ The Cooker / Blue N.

★ ★ ★ ★ LeeWay / Blue N.
★ ★ ★ Two Sides of Lee Morgan / Trip

By 1956, trumpeter Lee Morgan (1938–1972) was taking featured solos in Dizzy Gillespie's big band and participating actively in New York studio blowing sessions as leader and sideman. The albums above were made prior to 1961, when Morgan temporarily dropped out and returned to his native Philadelphia.

Even at this early stage, Morgan's brashly bright tone, crackling delivery, harmonic imagination and effective use of smears, half-valving and other expressive effects made him a major soloist. While his albums are dismissed by some as merely casual sessions, they are filled with swing and passion, especially *The Cooker* (with Pepper Adams, Bobby Timmons, Paul Chambers, Philly Joe Jones) and *LeeWay* (Jackie McLean, Timmons, Chambers, and Morgan's employer, Art Blakey).

★ ★ ★ ★ ★ Cornbread / Blue N.
★ ★ ★ ★ The Gigolo / Blue N.
★ ★ ★ ★ Lee Morgan / GNP
★ ★ ★ Lee Morgan Memorial Album / Blue N.
★ ★ ★ ★ Live at the Lighthouse / Blue N.
★ ★ ★ ★ The Rumproller / Blue N.
★ ★ ★ ★ ★ Search for the New Land / Blue N.
★ ★ ★ ★ The Sidewinder / Blue N.
★ ★ ★ The Sixth Sense / Blue N.

From his return in 1963 until the end of his life (he was shot on a New York club job by his long-time female companion), Morgan continued to champion the post-bop verities in work with all of the old excitement plus added depth and eloquence. Some of his albums may fail to reach their potential, but all are satisfying. I would single out *The Sidewinder,* Morgan's "comeback" album, with the title tune which was his only commercial success; *Search for the New Land,* with a sextet including Wayne Shorter, Herbie Hancock and Billy Higgins, for its dramatic and far more substantial title piece; *Cornbread,* a hard-bop delight featuring McLean, Mobley and Hancock, plus the exquisite "Ceora"; and the intense *Lighthouse* double album with Benny Maupin, Harold Mabern, Jymie Merritt and Mickey Roker. Other live albums, not listed, may be bootlegs.

★ ★ ★ ★ Infinity / Blue N.
★ ★ ★ ★ ★ The Procrastinator / Blue N.
★ ★ ★ Sonic Boom / Blue N.
★ ★ ★ ★ Take Twelve / Prest.
★ ★ ★ ★ Taru / Blue N.
★ ★ ★ ★ Tom Cat / Blue N.

A Morgan recording session from virtually every year between 1964 and 1969 has appeared in Blue Note's recent salvage effort on unreleased sessions. Easily the most intriguing is the 1967 half of *Procrastinator,* with three members of the then Miles Davis band (Herbie Hancock, Ron Carter, old friend and Messenger Wayne Shorter), plus Billy Higgins and Bobby Hutcherson. *Tom Cat* and *Infinity* are earlier sessions and both have Jackie McLean (*Tom Cat* also has McCoy Tyner and Art Blakey), but neither reaches the heights Morgan and McLean hit on the saxophonist's *Consequence* from the same period. The remaining sets have interesting personnel choices—David Newman's tenor on *Sonic Boom,* George Benson's guitar on *Taru.*

All of these titles, with the exclusion of *Infinity,* were quickly deleted by EMI, the current owner of the Blue Note catalogue. At the same time, EMI has restored *Sidewinder* to circulation.

Take Twelve was one of Morgan's rarest sessions, the only product of his brief 1961 affiliation with Jazzland. Clifford Jordan and Barry Harris are present in support, and Morgan contributes some of his best compositions. — B.B.

JELLY ROLL MORTON
★ ★ ★ ★ ★ **Jelly Roll Morton 1923–24 / Mile.**
★ ★ ★ ★ ★ **Jelly Roll Morton Vol. 1&2 / RCA (France)**
★ ★ ★ ★ ★ **Jelly Roll Morton Vol. 5&6 / RCA (France)**
★ ★ ★ ★ ★ **New Orleans Rhythm Kings / Mile.**
★ ★ ★ **Transcriptions for Orchestra / Col.**
One of the great disgraces in current jazz discography is the unavailability in the U.S. of the essential Red Hot Peppers recordings of Ferdinand Joseph La Menthe, a.k.a. Jelly Roll Morton (1885–1941). The virtual incarnation of New Orleans sporting life, and the subject of Alan Lomax's biography *Mister Jelly Roll,* Morton claimed to have invented jazz in 1902; without question he was a brilliant pianist, composer and arranger whose feeling for improvisation, blues tonality and a more relaxed, swinging sense of rhythm helped move black music from ragtime and other early sources to jazz.

The Seventies: The two-record *Jelly Roll Morton 1923–24,* with all of his early piano solos, is the best currently available set; he can also be heard with the *New Orleans Rhythm Kings,* the best white group from Morton's hometown. The out-of-print Red Hot Pepper material, a model of the traditional ensemble approach, is in the vaults of RCA, but can be obtained as an import on the Black and White label. The essential Vol. 1&2 as well as Vol. 5&6 of *Jelly Roll Morton* on French Black and White can be obtained, while Vol. 3&4 are currently unavailable in any form.

In *Transcriptions for Orchestra,* arranger/pianist Dick Hyman attempts to cash in on the Joplin craze by revamping Jelly for those who think any black composer who wrote before the Depression wrote only ragtime.
★ ★ ★ ★ ★ **Jelly Roll Morton / Arc. Folk**
★ ★ ★ ★ ★ **New Orleans Memories / Commo.**
★ ★ ★ ★ **1924–26 Rare Piano Rolls / Bio.**
The Eighties: Still no Morton reissues from RCA, but the important Commodore piano solos and vocals from the end of Morton's career have resurfaced, this time with two previously unissued tracks. All of the piano solos from the two-record Milestone (*1923–24*) set are now available on a single Archive of Folk album. The piano rolls on Biograph provide a nice supplement to the material on Milestone. — B.B.

SAL MOSCA
★ ★ ★ ★ **For You / Choice**
★ ★ ★ ★ **Sal Mosca Music / Interp.**
A musician's musician. Pianist Sal Mosca (b. 1927) has the rare ability to be unfailingly logical while retaining the power to surprise. One never knows exactly where Mosca is going, yet once he gets there it seems the only possible route.

Although he does perform now and again, Mosca is primarily a student of his instrument and spends a good deal of his time teaching. Good for him, bad for us: his recordings are outstanding but generally unacknowledged. — F.G.

PAUL MOTIAN
★ ★ ★ **Psalm / ECM/War.**
★ ★ ★ **Le Voyage / ECM/War.**
Percussionist Paul Motian (b. 1931) developed a subtle, polyrhythmic approach during the Fifties and earned his reputation for "touch" as the drummer with the Bill Evans trio of the early Sixties. Motian is indeed a master of coaxing unusual tonalities from percussion instruments, as both *Le Voyage* (1979) and *Psalm* (1982) demonstrate. Unfortunately Motian's approach tends toward overkill in the pristine settings characteristic of ECM productions. — J.S.

ALPHONSE MOUZON
★ ★ ★ **By All Means / Pausa**
★ ★ ★ **The Essence of Mystery / Blue N.**

★ Funky Snakefoot / Blue N.
★ ★ The Man Incognito / Blue N.
★ Mind Transplant / Blue N.
★ ★ ★ Morning Sun / Pausa
★ ★ ★ Virtue / Pausa

Alphonse Mouzon (b. 1948) built up a reputation as a creative musician when he was McCoy Tyner's drummer in the early Seventies; then he moved on to play powerhouse fusion with Larry Coryell. But so far, a comparably notable solo artist he ain't. His debut LP, *Essence,* was pretty promising; a distinctive agenda of modal-tinged easy-listening jazz and catchy R&B, it featured some nice soprano sax from Buddy Terry and some respectably commercial vocals from Mouzon. Then he began to slide (*Funky* and *Mind Transplant*). *Incognito,* his fourth album, at least had searing George Duke synthesizer work and a couple of lyrical Mouzon charts. The later Pausa sides are closer in sound and spirit to *Essence.*
— M.R.

IDRIS MUHAMMAD

★ ★ Black Rhythm Revolution / Prest.
★ ★ Foxhuntin' / Fan.
★ ★ Make It Count / Fan.
★ ★ One with a Star / Kudu
★ ★ ★ Peace and Rhythm / Prest.
★ ★ ★ Power of Soul / Kudu
★ ★ Turn This Mutha Out / Kudu
★ ★ You Ain't No Friend of Mine / Fan.

Versatile percussionist Idris Muhammad (b. 1939) is generally more accomplished as a sideman than as a leader (check out his long drum duet with Ralph MacDonald on *The Path*), but does not disgrace himself on these efforts. *Power of Soul* is his most accessible and coherent session.   — J.S.

GERRY MULLIGAN

★ ★ ★ ★ ★ The Complete Pacific Jazz and
  Capitol Recordings . . . (with Chet Baker)
  / Mosaic (available by mail only; see text
  below)
★ ★ ★ ★ A Concert in Jazz / Verve
★ ★ ★ ★ ★ Concert Jazz Band at the Village
  Vanguard / Verve
★ ★ ★ ★ ★ Freeway / Blue N.
★ ★ ★ ★ ★ Gerry Mulligan / Inner
★ ★ ★ Gerry Mulligan / Pausa
★ ★ ★ ★ ★ Gerry Mulligan and Chet Baker
  / Prest.
★ ★ Idol Gossip / Chi.
★ ★ ★ ★ ★ Jeru / CSP
★ ★ Little Big Horn / GNP
★ ★ ★ ★ Mulligan and Getz and Desmond /
  Verve
★ ★ ★ Mulligan Plays Mulligan / Fan./
  OJC

★ ★ ★ ★ Mulligan Quartet/Desmond
  Quintet / Fan.
★ ★ Night Lights / Phi.
★ ★ ★ ★ ★ Presenting the Gerry Mulligan
  Sextet / Em.
★ ★ ★ ★ Revelation (with Lee Konitz) /
  Blue N.
★ ★ ★ ★ Walk on the Water / DRG
★ ★ ★ ★ ★ What Is There to Say? / CSP

Gerry Mulligan (b. 1927) is an important baritone saxophonist, writer and leader. His work, much of which has long been out of print, is slowly being restored to the catalogue. Mulligan's innovative 1952–53 "pianoless" quartet with trumpeter Chet Baker can be heard in almost complete form via mail order from Mosaic Records (197 Strawberry Hill Avenue, Stamford, Connecticut 06902). An album-length sampling of the Mosaic material can be found on *Freeway* and a side of additional material not heard on the Mosaic is available both on the Prestige twofer (*Mulligan and Baker*) and the Fantasy *Quartet/Quintet.*

Mulligan Plays Mulligan features earlier work, including several titles for a medium-sized group and a long jam with tenor saxophonist Allen Eager. The Inner City is half of a superior 1954 concert, after valve trombonist Bob Brookmeyer had replaced Baker. Brookmeyer and Zoot Sims are present on the EmArcy *Sextet* recording, now available as a Japanese import. *Revelation* has Konitz as well as Baker (these titles are also all on the Mosaic), plus a later date for a sax section with other notables (Al Cohn, Eager, Sims). Mulligan's still elegant late-Fifties quartet work is featured on *Jeru* and *What Is There to Say?*

Mulligan the orchestra leader is available on two early-Sixties Verve *Concert* reissues, one a rousing live recording at the Village Vanguard, the other a more ambitious studio date with compositions by George Russell and Gary McFarland. *Walk on the Water* is a more tempered set by the revived 1980 band notable for its extensive sampling of Mulligan's writing. In this regard, also hear Miles Davis' *Birth of the Cool.*   — B.B.

MARK MURPHY

★ ★ The Artistry of Mark Murphy / Muse
★ ★ ★ Bop for Kerouac (with Richie Cole) /
  Muse
★ ★ ★ Bridging a Gap / Muse
★ ★ ★ Mark Murphy Sings / Muse
★ ★ ★ ★ Mark Murphy Sings Dorothy
  Fields and Cy Coleman / Audiop.
★ ★ Mark II / Muse
★ ★ ★ ★ Midnight Mood / Pausa
★ ★ ★ Rah / Riv./Fan. OJC

★ ★ ★ **Satisfaction Guaranteed** / **Muse**
★ ★ ★ **Stolen Moments** / **Muse**
★ ★ ★ **That's How I Love the Blues!** / **Riv.**
When Mark Murphy (b. 1932) plants his feet firmly and sings straight from the heart his greatness cannot be questioned. Unfortunately, too many of his recordings find him trying to be hip, diluting his natural gifts with artifice and affectation. This tendency toward the cute destroys the *Artistry* album and blunts the overall impact of *Bop for Kerouac.*

Midnight Mood, the Fields-Coleman date and two of the Muses, *Stolen Moments* and *Satisfaction Guaranteed,* boast inventive, full-bodied performances that create a feeling of cohesiveness. They, more than any of the others, prove that when the glitter is stripped away Mark Murphy is a singer of great power, depth and skill. — A.R.

DAVID MURRAY
★ ★ ★ **Flowers for Albert** / **In. Nav.**
★ ★ ★ ★ ★ **Home** / **Black S.**
★ ★ ★ ★ **Interboogieology** / **Black S.**
★ ★ ★ **Last of the Hipmen** / **Red R.**
★ ★ ★ ★ ★ **Live at the Lower Manhattan Ocean Club, Vol. 1** / **In. Nav.**
★ ★ ★ **Live, Vol. 2** / **In. Nav.**
★ ★ ★ **Low Class Conspiracy** / **Adel.**
★ ★ ★ ★ ★ **Ming** / **Black S.**
★ ★ ★ ★ ★ **Morning Song** / **Black S.**
★ ★ ★ ★ **Murray's Steps** / **Black S.**
★ ★ ★ **Sweet Lovely** / **Black S.**
★ ★ ★ **Third Family** / **Hat Hut**
David Murray (b. 1955) arrived in New York in 1975 from his native Berkeley, California, and quickly made an impact with his command of the lessons taught him by Archie Shepp and Albert Ayler. By tempering these influences with older shadings, and by employing varied formats while maintaining his hard-blowing ambiance, Murray has become one of the leading young tenors. Certainly he is the most recorded, and the above discography could be supplemented by several harder-to-find imports.

Standouts include *Low Class,* one of Murray's first sessions and still his best trio effort; the first volume of *Live at the Lower Manhattan Ocean Club,* an epoch-stretching quartet set (one piece has Murray on so-prano sax, recalling Bechet) with trumpeter Lester Bowie (*Interboogieology* and *Hipmen* employ Murray's more constant brass partner, fellow-Californian Butch Morris); and the rich octet albums Murray began recording in 1980. Of the latter, both *Ming* and *Home* display an excellent balance between written material and solos by a distinguished group of sidemen; *Murray's Steps* places greater emphasis on solos and is not as impressive. Murray should also be heard with Jack DeJohnette's Special Edition, "Blood" Ulmer and the World Saxophone Quartet. The 1984 *Morning Song,* a quartet date, is an inspired mixture of originals and standards with John Hicks on piano, Ed Blackwell on drums and Reggie Workman on bass. — B.B.

AMINA CLAUDINE MYERS
★ ★ ★ ★ **The Circle of Time** / **Black S.**
★ ★ ★ ★ **Jumping in the Sugar Bowl** / **Minor Music**
★ ★ ★ ★ ★ **Salutes Bessie Smith** / **E/Leo**
★ ★ ★ ★ **Song for Mother** / **E/Leo**
Amina Claudine Myers was active in the Association for the Advancement of Creative Musicians founded by pianist Muhal Richard Abrams and has been prominent in the cutting edge of the music since the mid-sixties, first in Chicago and then in New York. Still, she remains underrated and overlooked.

Of Myers' artistry, tenor saxophonist Frank Lowe stated, "She can play straight piano and bring out the right colors without sounding like some other personality. Yeah, and she's doused with gospel music and the blues . . . A premier talent, if you ask me." Her playing on Lowe's *Erotic Heartbreak* (Soul Note) justifies his praise, as does her work with such artists as Lester Bowie and gospel singers Martha and Fontella Bass.

Myers brings a keen understanding of tradition to all her work. Her keyboard playing (piano and organ), singing and composing reflect her Arkansas upbringing, for they remain close to the root musics even while keeping abreast of the more current jazz developments. Her readings of Bessie Smith classics like "Wasted Life Blues" and "Jailhouse Blues" also show her affinity for blues.
— A.R.

MILTON NASCIMENTO
★ ★ ★ **Journey to Dawn / A&M**
★ ★ ★ ★ **Milton / A&M**

Milton Nascimento is one of Brazil's most respected songwriters and vocalists. Though he'd made several outstanding Brazilian albums, his U.S. debut came on Wayne Shorter's *Native Dancer* album. On the 1977 *Milton* set Shorter returns the favor. *Journey to Dawn* continues Nascimento's penchant for strong commercial hooks but is less satisfying overall than *Milton.* — J.S.

THEODORE "FATS" NAVARRO
★ ★ ★ ★ **Fat Girl / Savoy**
★ ★ ★ ★ **Fats Navarro Featured with the Tadd Dameron Band / Mile**
★ ★ ★ ★ ★ **Prime Source / Blue N.**

Theodore "Fats" Navarro (1923–1950), whose long-lined and nearly impeccable middle-register approach offered the first successful modern trumpet alternative to Dizzy Gillespie, played some stunning music before heroin and tuberculosis took him out. His formative work (1946–47) is on *Fat Girl;* some of the earlier sessions, such as an all-star date with Kenny Dorham, Sonny Stitt, Bud Powell and Kenny Clarke, are ragged, but in the quintets with pianist/arranger Tadd Dameron, Navarro's poise and creativity are beyond reproach. *Fats Navarro Featured with the Tadd Dameron Band* contains the 1948 radio broadcast "air checks" from Manhattan's Royal Roost; besides Navarro, Dameron and Clarke there is the underrated early-bop tenor of Allen Eager. *Prime Source* is best overall, from 1947 to 1949, with more Dameron groups plus a Bud Powell quintet with young Sonny Rollins. — B.B.

BOB NELOMS
★ ★ ★ **Pretty Music / In. Nav.**

A popular New York sideman and with good reason. Pianist Bob Neloms (b. 1941)

can cut it at any tempo and convey all feels. Still, his frequent use of introspective and subtle shadings tends to make this a pianist's album rather than something for all jazz fans. — F.G.

OLIVER NELSON
★ ★ ★ ★ **Afro-American Sketches / Prest.**
★ ★ ★ ★ ★ **The Blues and the Abstract Truth / MCA**
★ ★ ★ ★ ★ **Images / Prest.**
★ ★ ★ **More Blues and Abstract Truth / MCA**
★ ★ ★ **Stolen Moments / Inner**
★ ★ ★ ★ **Straight Ahead / Fan./OJC**
★ ★ ★ ★ ★ **Three Dimensions / MCA**

Oliver Nelson (1932–1975) was a forceful, straightforward soloist on alto and tenor saxophones and flute; he was also an extremely skilled composer/arranger whose works still sound fresh and relevant twenty years later. Nelson's crowning achievements came during the early Sixties in small combos featuring the brilliant Eric Dolphy on flute, alto sax and bass clarinet. *Images* is a stunning twofer collecting sessions from 1960 and 1961 that match Nelson and Dolphy with drummer Roy Haynes, bassist George Duvivier, pianist Richard Wyands and, on the 1960 sides, trumpeter Richard Williams. Haynes and Duvivier are as sympathetic a team as you could want and the Nelson/Dolphy collaboration soars majestically through these tracks. It's hard to imagine a pair of soloists better suited to each other, as Dolphy's pulling angularity and Nelson's controlled, logical aggression create a fantastic ebb and flow of colors.

Dolphy also appears on the 1961 *Blues and the Abstract Truth* album, which is Nelson's most famous work. This all-star session also included Haynes on drums, Paul Chambers on bass, Bill Evans on piano, Freddie Hubbard on trumpet and George Barrow on baritone saxophone. The same performance, although without Nelson's liner notes for the original album, is also collected on the MCA twofer *Three Dimensions. Straight Ahead* is the original 1961 date collected on *Images.*

Nelson's later works gravitated more toward big-band arrangements and featured less and less of his own soloing, which makes them that much less interesting. He became a sought-after composer of film scores and television themes ("Ironside," "The Six Million Dollar Man") toward the end of his life.   — J.S.

PHINEAS NEWBORN, JR.
★ ★ ★ ★ ★ **The Great Jazz Piano of Phineas Newborn, Jr. / Contem.**
★ ★ ★ ★ **Harlem Blues / Contem.**
★ ★ ★ ★ **Please Send Me Someone to Love / Contem.**
★ ★ ★ ★ **A World of Piano! / Contem.**
★ ★ ★ ★ **Look Out, Phineas is Back / Pablo**
Widely and correctly heralded as a great pianist when he made his New York debut in the mid-Fifties, Phineas Newborn, Jr. (b. 1931), never really regained his public stature after being off the scene in the early Sixties. All of his earlier recordings for Atlantic, RCA, Roulette and United Artists are now out of print, but the four remaining titles on Contemporary are split between dates in 1961–62 and 1969, and they prove that Newborn never diminished as a pianist despite critical indifference.

Newborn's one-two punch is his ability to combine a relaxed lyricism with an outstanding set of chops. Although he is a masterful blues player, there seems little of any style he can't handle, and Newborn's LPs are sprinkled with bits of stride, Tatum and Powell, all held together by his own idiosyncratic blues sensibility.   — F.G.

JAMES NEWTON
★ ★ ★ ★ ★ **Axum / ECM/War.**
★ ★ ★ ★ ★ **I've Known Rivers (with Anthony Davis, Abdul Wadud) / Gram.**
★ ★ ★ ★ ★ **James Newton / Gram.**
★ ★ ★ ★ **Lyella / Gram.**
★ ★ ★ ★ ★ **The Mystery School / In. Nav.**
★ ★ ★ ★ **Paseo del Mar / In. Nav.**
★ ★ ★ ★ **Portraits / In. Nav.**
James Newton (b. 1953) is a virtuosic instrumentalist who has chosen to devote himself to the flute exclusively. In the process, he has become the most impressive new voice on the instrument in years. His talent for blowing, in the more or less standard small-band configuration, is well documented on both *Paseo del Mar,* featuring a strong

rhythm section with Abdul Wadud's cello in place of bass, and *Hidden Voices,* a cooperative band effort discussed under pianist Anthony Davis' listing. (Davis and Newton also appear on *Crystal Texts,* their duo album for the Moers Music label.)

In addition to his abilities as a soloist of fire and precision in the Eric Dolphy manner, Newton has also participated in current efforts to blend notated music with improvisation. *The Mystery School* features his writing for a woodwind quintet completed by clarinet, oboe or English horn, bassoon and tuba. All of the players are skilled Californians like Newton, and the program is one of the most convincing and warm in this budding genre. The equally impressive *I've Known Rivers* is contemporary chamber jazz at its finest, featuring the trio of Newton, Davis and Wadud.

Newton's recent and varied recordings continue to place him among the most consistent and fascinating musicians of the Eighties. For a suggestion of Newton's range, the solo recital *Axum,* and the more straight-ahead *James Newton,* and *Luella* taken together with *I've Known Rivers,* should make the point.   — B.B.

BIG NICK NICHOLAS
★ ★ ★ **Big and Warm / In. Nav.**
Tenor saxophonist Big Nick Nicholas (b. 1922) has been a minor jazz legend since his late-Forties stint with the Dizzy Gillespie band. Coltrane added to the legend by naming the tune "Big Nick" after him. *Big and Warm,* his 1983 debut as a bandleader, demonstrates Nicholas' instrumental ballad technique on the standard "Autumn in New York," includes an unspectacular vocal, presumably to give the album more varied commercial possibilities, and features a solid band highlighted by pianist John Miller.   — J.S.

HERBIE NICHOLS
★ ★ ★ ★ ★ **The Third World / Blue N.**
Herbie Nichols (1919–1963) is one of the supreme jazz tragedies: a thoroughly original composer and pianist who received virtually no recognition in his lifetime. Over half of his complete output is on *The Third World,* twenty-two trio tracks (1955–56) of stark yet fluent, rhythmically challenging music, with Max Roach and Art Blakey sharing percussion duty.
★ ★ ★ ★ **The Modern Jazz Piano Album / Savoy**
The last recordings under Nichols' name, a 1957 trio session, resurfaced then quickly

disappeared on *The Bethlehem Years* (Beth-lehem). Once again available, however, is the first Nichols session, made in 1952 and a bit frothier than his Blue Note efforts. This two-record anthology is also valuable for the Lennie Tristano and George Wallington items, some rare samples of Horace Silver, and Bud Powell alternate takes.
— B.B.

SAL NISTICO
★ ★ ★ ★ **NEO** / Bee
Sal Nistico (b. 1940), a former member of Woody Herman's Herd and a rough and ready tenorman, encounters equally hard-driving baritone saxomaniac Nick Brignola. Played at the proper volume, this record is guaranteed to destroy your speakers—and your mind. Blow, babe, blow!   — F.G.

ANITA O'DAY
★ ★ Angel Eyes / Emily
★ ★ Anita O'Day / Glen.
★ ★ ★ Anita Sings / Verve
★ ★ ★ Anita Sings the Winners / Verve
★ ★ ★ At Mister Kelley's / Verve
★ ★ ★ Big Band / Verve
★ ★ ★ ★ Hi Ho Trailus Boot Whip / Doctor J.
★ ★ In Berlin / Pausa
★ ★ Live at the City / Emily
★ ★ Live at Mingos / Emily
★ ★ Live in Tokyo / Emily
★ ★ Mello' Day / GNP
★ ★ My Ship / Emily
★ ★ Once upon a Summertime / Glen.

Vocalist Anita O'Day (b. 1919) began singing during the swing era, earning great popularity in the early Forties fronting Gene Krupa's powerful dance band. O'Day's full-bodied, husky voice and blues feeling stood in dramatic contrast to the standard white female vocalist sound of the time. In 1944 and '45 she further enhanced her reputation with a series of galvanic performances in front of Stan Kenton's experimental big band, the most famous of which was "And Her Tears Flowed Like Wine." *Hi Ho* is a collection of some of the first recordings O'Day made under her own name in the late Forties. The best of the others are the late-Fifties/early-Sixties sides for Verve, particularly *At Mister Kelley's* and *Anita Sings.*
— J.S.

OLD AND NEW DREAMS
★ ★ ★ ★ ★ Old and New Dreams / Black S.
★ ★ ★ Old and New Dreams / ECM/War.
★ ★ ★ ★ ★ Playing / ECM/War.

This cooperative quartet of former Ornette Coleman sidemen Don Cherry (b. 1936; pocket trumpet, piano), Dewey Redman (b. 1931; tenor sax, musette), Charlie Haden (b. 1937; bass) and Ed Blackwell (b. 1927;

drums) has continued to tour internationally since their debut Black Saint album of 1976, and thus rate a separate listing of their own.

Repertoire has remained strong over the life of the band, with a fairly even mix of music contributed by Coleman and originals from within the band. The first ECM album was a bit disappointing, however, with too much stress on ethnic re-creations, whale-song impressions and a version of "Lonely Woman" that suffered by comparison to the original. Things are back on track with *Playing,* a 1980 Austrian concert with the musicians concentrating once again on intense blowing. Redman is particularly impressive here, a forceful presence in a position that could have passed as a mere stand-in slot for Coleman.   — B.B.

JOSEPH "KING" OLIVER
★ ★ ★ ★ ★ Immortal King Oliver / Mile.
★ ★ ★ ★ King Oliver Creole Jazz Band 1923 / Olym.
★ ★ ★ ★ ★ King Oliver's Jazz Band—1923 / Smithsonian (album available by mail only from Smithsonian Recordings, P.O. Box 10230, Des Moines, Iowa 50336)

Louis Armstrong credits Joseph "King" Oliver (1885–1938) as his greatest (in fact, his only) influence. Oliver was recognized as the top cornet player of his era, which began before jazz groups started recording. He earned the nickname "King" from the great Dixieland bandleader Kid Ory, who used Oliver's piercing, emotive cornet as an integral part of his tight ensemble sound. Armstrong heard Oliver in New Orleans, but it wasn't until Oliver moved to Chicago in 1918 and called for Armstrong to join his Creole Jazz Band in 1922 that they began to work together.

From 1922 to 1924, Armstrong learned the ropes at Oliver's side and the two cornetists created the hottest sound of their time,

accompanied by clarinetists Johnny Dodds and Jimmie Noone (on separate dates), trombonist Honoré Dutrey, pianist Lil Hardin (who later married Armstrong), drummer Baby Dodds and several different bassists. The 1923 recordings of the Creole Jazz Band are considered one of the finest examples of small ensemble playing in jazz history. The Olympic set suffers from poor reproduction, while the Milestone and Smithsonian sets cover Oliver comprehensively and with better-than-average reproduction quality.
— J.S.

OPEN SKY
★ ★ ★ ★ Open Sky / PM
★ ★ ★ ★ Spirit in the Sky / PM

Two beautiful early-Seventies recordings by a trio comprised of Dave Liebman (b. 1946) on a variety of instruments including flutes and saxophones, bassist Frank Tusa and drummer Bob Moses (b. 1948). The rhythm section on both of these records is inspired and Liebman's stunningly virtuosic performances are among his finest recorded moments. Liebman's witty, mercurial soprano sax playing is his trademark, of course, but here his conception of flute playing adds an emotionally rich and original fillip. — J.S.

OREGON
★ ★ ★ Distant Hills / Van.
★ ★ ★ The Essential Oregon / Van.
★ ★ Friends / Van.
★ ★ ★ ★ In Concert / Van.
★ ★ ★ In Performance / Elek.
★ ★ ★ Moon & Mind / Van.
★ ★ Music Era / Van.
★ ★ ★ Music of Another Present Era / Van.
★ ★ ★ ★ Oregon / ECM/War.
★ ★ Oregon/Elvin Jones/Together / Van.
★ ★ ★ Out of the Woods / Elek.
★ ★ ★ Roots in the Sky / Elek.
★ ★ Violin / Van.
★ ★ ★ Winter Light / Van.

Oregon is not unlike its parent group, the Paul Winter Consort, in its use of Indian percussion and classical music compositional formalities to ground a jazzlike deployment of soloing. But Oregon differs from Winter and other transnationally utopian outfits in the group's refusal to explore the "cultural significance" of its musical ecumenism with lyrics or orchestral program music. And that refusal leaves lots of space on their records to pursue the fresh ideas each of the members brought to the band originally.

With the rise to prominence in the mid-Seventies of guitarist Ralph Towner (b.

1940), Oregon's reputation grew as its studio albums shifted colorations and compositional emphases from Indian/Western interplay back to jazz/modernist classical interface. The live *In Concert* (1975) and *In Performance* (1980) serve as a marvelous summary of their music. Their collaboration with Elvin Jones provides lots of space for the shifts, dives and bass-cymbal playoffs Jones is famous for, but there isn't much fire—just a lot of technique. The band revived itself on the 1983 set for ECM entitled *Oregon*. The 1984 death of percussionist Colin Walcott ended whatever immediate efforts the group had planned, however. — B.T.

EDWARD "KID" ORY
★ ★ ★ ★ ★ Kid Ory's Creole Jazz Band / Folklyric
★ ★ ★ ★ ★ Kid Ory's Creole Jazz Band 1944–45 / Good T.
★ ★ ★ ★ Kid Ory's Creole Jazz Band 1955 / Good T.
★ ★ ★ ★ Kid Ory's Creole Jazz Band 1956 / Good T.
★ ★ ★ ★ ★ The Legendary Kid / Good T.
★ ★ ★ ★ This Kid's the Greatest / Good T.

Trombonist Kid Ory (1886–1973) was one of the most important figures in jazz, a groundbreaking musical stylist, bandleader, and eventual musical historian whose importance still remains underrecognized. Ory is almost solely responsible for creating the trombone's crucial role in Dixieland ensemble playing, providing the deep, resonant foundation for the cornet/trumpet and clarinet interlace, gliding behind and through the chunking banjo/drums rhythm section to add that magical aspect of swing, and codifying the growling, impish sense of humor that not only Dixieland, but subsequent jazz played with lighthearted wit, is known for.

Ory's band was, along with Freddie Keppard's group, one of the first of the great Dixieland ensembles in New Orleans right after the turn of the century. With cornetist Joseph "King" Oliver as his featured soloist, Ory's band terrorized local groups who engaged in bandwagon "cutting sessions" on the streets of New Orleans to promote their gigs. Louis Armstrong recalled having his group embarrassed by Ory, and when Oliver moved to Chicago, Armstrong replaced him in the Creole Band. Ory's groups also included a series of great clarinetists—Johnny Dodds, Sidney Bechet, Jimmie Noone and George Lewis.

Despite Ory's tremendous reputation as a bandleader, the only material available from his heyday as the greatest trombonist of

Twenties jazz is as a sideman. But what a sideman! Ory appears on recordings with Oliver, Jelly Roll Morton's Red Hot Peppers and Louis Armstrong's Hot Five, including on his own song, "Muskrat Ramble."

Ory retired from performing in the Thirties, only to make a dramatic comeback in the mid-Forties, when he was one of the most influential figures spearheading the controversial Dixieland revival. The records listed above begin in that period, starting with the Folklyric set which documents an all-star band led by Ory in a series of 1944 performances on Orson Welles' Mercury Wonder radio show. The band on these tracks includes such venerable players as trumpeter Mutt Carey, drummer Zutty Singleton and clarinetist Jimmie Noone, who died during the series and was replaced by Barney Bigard. The record also includes five 1945 musical education broadcasts for schoolchildren.

The 1944–45 Good Time Jazz set was originally recorded by Neshui Ertegun for Crescent records and marks a milestone in jazz history, offering some of the first proof that jazz music was not just a passing fad linked to pop styles but was informed by a classical tradition of its own, worth not just preserving but reviving as well. Subsequent albums show that on both Dixieland and blues material Ory remained a vital player until at least the age of seventy (*The Legendary Kid*) and certainly one of the more brilliant lights in American music. — J.S.

DICK OXTOT'S GOLDEN AGE JAZZ BAND

★ ★ ★ **Down In Honky Tonk Town / Arhoo.** Banjo player Dick Oxtot has been organizing tributes to New Orleans jazz for several decades. The San Franciscan's approach avoids the drippy nostalgia that has marred so many similar attempts; nevertheless his conception is too reverential, his playing too committed to technique rather than emotional expression to truly capture the spirit of the music he so obviously loves. Marvelous individual performances make this a worthwhile record, though, with vocalists Terry Garthwaite and Willow Wray combining for the album's finest moments. — J.S.

CHARLES ("YARDBIRD") PARKER

★ ★ ★ ★ **Apartment Jam** / Zim
★ ★ ★ ★ ★ **Bird at the Roost** / Savoy
★ ★ ★ **Bird with Strings Live** / Col.
★ ★ ★ ★ **Charlie Parker** / Prest.
★ ★ ★ ★ ★ **Charlie Parker** / War. (6-record set) (also available as **Charlie Parker on British Spotlite** label in six individual volumes)
★ ★ ★ ★ **Charlie Parker, Vols. 1–5** / Arc. Folk
★ ★ ★ ★ **Echoes of an Era** (with Dizzy Gillespie) / Rou.
★ ★ ★ ★ ★ **Encores** / Savoy
★ ★ ★ ★ **First Recordings** / Onyx
★ ★ ★ ★ **Giants of Jazz** / Hall
★ ★ ★ ★ ★ **One Night in Birdland** / Col.
★ ★ ★ ★ **The Savoy Recordings (Master Takes)** / Savoy
★ ★ ★ ★ **Summit Meeting at Birdland** / Col.
★ ★ ★ ★ ★ **Takin' Off** / Hall
★ ★ ★ ★ **The Verve Years, 1948–50** / Verve
★ ★ ★ ★ **The Verve Years, 1950–51** / Verve
★ ★ ★ **The Verve Years, 1952–54** / Verve
★ ★ ★ ★ **The Very Best of Bird** / War.

Charlie Parker (1920–1955) was the leading figure of the bebop period, an unsurpassed alto saxophonist and one of the four or five greatest figures in jazz history; he was also a cult figure at a time when advances in recording and broadcast techniques allowed a lot of bootleg material to be captured and released. Thus ferreting out Parker's discography becomes akin to working out a crossword puzzle where some of the same clues apply to different boxes. This doesn't affect the music, of course, which is almost uniformly superb.

First Recordings has one side of Jay McShann's 1940 Kansas City band, with Parker's alto sax showing the unmistakable influence of Lester Young's tenor. There is also a 1942 Harlem jam tape on "Cherokee" that is like hearing the coming era in its embryo stage.

Between 1945 and 1948, Parker made most of his great recordings for Savoy and Dial. After Bird's death, both labels issued every available alternate take along with the originally issued master, and to compound the confusion the Dial material has also appeared on numerous other labels (of varying legality). The Savoy *Master Takes* twofer has the originals of "Now's the Time," "Ko-Do," "Donna Lee," "Parker's Mood" and others, with Miles Davis, Dizzy Gillespie, Bud Powell, John Lewis and Max Roach among the members of Parker's quintets. *Encores* samples the alternate takes, which besides having different alto solos often have better efforts by Miles Davis.

The Dial material is all over the place—it pops up on the Roulette and Hall of Fame albums as well as the Warner Bros. and the British Spotlites. The years of Parker's Dial affiliation, 1946 to 1947, were his most productive as far as recordings go, producing "Yardbird Suite," "Ornithology," "Night in Tunisia," "Bird of Paradise," "Relaxin' at Camarillo," "Klacto-veedseds-tene," "Out of Nowhere" and "Embraceable You," among other masterpieces. The Warner Bros. six-album set is complete but expensive and poorly annotated; their *Very Best* sampler also gives inadequate information and includes seven alternate takes. If you can find them, the British Spotlites are the best bet—start with Volumes 1, 4, and 5. (The Roulette double LP is valuable for four incendiary Parker/Gillespie items from a mid-Forties Carnegie Hall concert.)

The "air check" recordings (taped from radio broadcasts) begin around 1948 and run through 1953. Much of this material is on the Archive of Folk volumes; they give virtually no information and occasionally overlap with the Columbia *One Night in Bird-*

land, but have superb music nonetheless. *One Night* features a model quintet, with Fats Navarro on trumpet, Bud Powell's piano and a drummer listed as Art Blakey (my ears say it may be Roy Haynes); *Summit Meeting*, with Dizzy, Powell and Haynes on one incredible side, is even better. No better manifestation of the Parker cult can be found than the Prestige Parker twofer—tapes from live concerts where the machine was turned off when Parker was not soloing.

Parker concluded his life under contract to producer Norman Granz, and the two often labored to find more marketable settings for Parker. Their efforts are now on three twofers titled *The Verve Years,* which, if below the high standards of the Savoy and Dial recordings, have much great music anyway: the best "with strings" session and a reunion with Dizzy and Thelonious Monk on Volume 1; the last great quintet sessions (with Miles or Red Rodney on trumpet) on Volume 2; and two agile quartet dates on Volume 3. The best Parker from his final years, however, is found on *The Greatest Jazz Concert Ever* (Prestige), a 1953 Toronto meeting of Bird, Diz, Bud, Max Roach and Charles Mingus.

★ ★ ★ ★ **Bird at St. Nick's / Fan./OJC**
★ ★ ★ ★ **Bird on 52nd Street / Fan./OJC**
★ ★ ★ ★ **Charlie Parker with Strings / Verve**
★ ★ ★ ★ ★ **Complete Savoy Studio Sessions (1945–48) / Savoy (5-record set)**
★ ★ ★ ★ ★ **Encores, Vol. 2 / Savoy**
★ ★ ★ ★ **Every Bit of It / Spot.**
★ ★ ★ ★ **Jazz at Massey Hall / Fan./OJC**
★ ★ ★ **Jazz Perennial / Verve**
★ ★ ★ ★ ★ **Now's the Time / Verve**
★ ★ ★ ★ **One Night in Chicago / Savoy**
★ ★ ★ ★ ★ **One Night in Washington / Elek./Mus.**
★ ★ ★ **Pershing Ballroom Chicago, 1950 / Zim**
★ ★ ★ ★ ★ **Swedish Schnapps / Verve**

Savoy finally got around to assembling their complete Parker catalogue in a five-record boxed set with exemplary notes—but they omitted a couple of takes of "Marmaduke," which are picked up on the second volume of *Encores. One Night in Chicago* and *Pershing Ballroom* are tapes of different sets from a 1950 live date, with better sound on the Savoy.

Listeners who owned the old Savoy Parker Memorial albums and wonder what happened to the delightful Slim Gaillard session with Parker and Gillespie should consult *Every Bit of It,* a double album on the British Spotlite label that collects all of Parker's

1945 recordings currently unavailable elsewhere. There are a lot of vocals (Rubberlegs Williams, Trummy Young, Sarah Vaughan, Gaillard), Cootie Williams' band live at the Savoy Ballroom, and a hot session led by pianist sir Charles Thompson with Parker and Dexter Gordon.

All of the Verve and Fantasy titles listed above are also currently available in two-record reissues on Verve and Prestige respectively. The new Verve entries are superior Japanese import pressings.

One Night in Washington is an important and previously unreleased concert recording that finds Bird sitting in with a big band in 1955 and finding his way through some tricky orchestrations after apparently minimal rehearsal. — B.B.

TINY PARHAM
★ ★ ★ ★ **Hot Chicago Jazz / Folklyric**
Fine small-group performances from the late Twenties patterned after Louis Armstrong's small-group recordings of the time. Pianist Tiny Parham (1900–1943) had already played with Doc Cheatham and Kid Ory before making these sides and obviously knew his way around the New Orleans jazz style. These tracks feature excellent playing from Punch Miller or Ray Hobson on cornet, Charles Lawson on trombone and Charles Johnson on clarinet. — J.S.

HERMETO PASCOAL
★ ★ ★ **Hermeto / Muse**
★ ★ **Slaves Mass / War.**
I haven't heard his Brazilian recordings, but on his American LPs, composer/arranger/multi-instrumentalist Hermeto Pascoal (b. 1936) throws too many ingredients into his musical stew. He loves his roots, complicated composition, sound effects, and angular jazz solos and voicings. Nice, even majestic in spots, but still spotty. — M.R.

JOE PASS
★ ★ ★ **Checkmate / Pablo**
★ ★ ★ ★ **Chops / Pablo**
★ ★ ★ ★ **Complete "Catch Me!" Sessions / Blue N.**
★ ★ ★ **Eximious / Pablo**
★ ★ ★ **For Django / Pac. J.**
★ ★ **Guitar Interludes / Discov.**
★ ★ ★ **Intercontinental / Pausa**
★ ★ ★ ★ **I Remember Charlie Parker / Pablo T.**
★ ★ ★ **Joy Spring / Blue N.**
★ ★ ★ **Live at Long Beach City College / Pablo**
★ ★ **Live in the Netherlands / Pablo**
★ ★ ★ **Loves Gershwin / Pablo**

★ ★ ★ Montreux '75 / Pablo
★ ★ ★ Montreux '77 / Pablo L.
★ ★ ★ Northsea Nights / Pablo
★ ★ ★ ★ Portraits of Ellington / Pablo
★ ★ ★ Simplicity / Pac. J.
★ ★ ★ Tudo Bem! / Pablo
★ ★ ★ ★ ★ Virtuoso / Pablo
★ ★ ★ ★ Virtuoso #2 / Pablo
★ ★ ★ ★ Virtuoso #3 / Pablo
★ ★ ★ ★ Virtuoso #4 / Pablo

Joe Pass (b. 1929) is generally considered
one of the finest jazz guitarists in history.
His clean, melodic tone, understated dynamic sense, eschewal of gimmickry and formidable improvisational abilities were obvious to the jazz critics who voted him the top
"new star" in *Down Beat*'s 1963 poll despite
the fact that Pass still hadn't recorded as a
leader at that point. He'd been discovered by
Richard Bock, owner of Pacific Jazz Records, while a resident at California's Synanon drug rehabilitation center. Bock released Pass' jazz debut on a record called
Sounds of Synanon in 1962 and Pass then
went on to session on a number of Pacific
Jazz dates led by Gerald Wilson, Bud Shank,
Les McCann and Groove Holmes among
others.

The *Complete "Catch Me!" Sessions,* recorded in '63, mark Pass' debut as a leader
on beautiful quartet recordings featuring
Clare Fischer's sturdy and sympathetic piano
accompaniment. *For Django* is a moving
tribute to the Belgian guitarist who has had
the greatest influence on Pass.

The bulk of Pass material since the Seventies has been recorded for Pablo, where he
also appeared on numerous sessions headed
by Oscar Peterson, Duke Ellington, Dizzy
Gillespie and Ella Fitzgerald. He has, in
fact, suffered a bit in this context from being
overrecorded. Pass' debt to pianist Art
Tatum is well repaid on the *Virtuoso* solo
sets, the first of which, made in 1974, remains the most impressive (the latest set, the
1983 Volume 4 release, contains outtakes
from that first session). Pass has also varied
his solo outings on Pablo with a number of
duet and trio albums: with bassist Niels-
Henning Orsted Pedersen (*Chops* and *Northsea Nights*); harmonica player Toots Thielemans and Pedersen (*Live in the Netherlands*);
pianist Jimmy Rowles (*Checkmate*); and percussionist Paulinho da Costa (*Tudo Bem!*).
— J.S.

PASSPORT
★ ★ Blue Tattoo / Atl.
★ ★ Cross-Collateral / Atco
★ ★ Iguacu / Atco
★ ★ Infinity Machine / Atco

★ ★ ★ Looking Thru / Atco
★ ★ Man in the Mirror / Atl.
★ ★ Oceanliner / Atl.
★ ★ Sky Blue / Atl.

German saxophonist Klaus Doldinger (b.
1936) formed Passport in the early Seventies
and became a pioneer in the burgeoning European fusion movement, playing at numerous festivals and releasing several albums in
Germany before coming to the attention of
U.S. record companies. While Doldinger's
sparse, angular playing conception over am-
plified rhythm sections was novel at first, the
sound has lost its freshness over the years.
Nevertheless, Doldinger plugs on, working in
a grey area somewhere between jazz and
pop/rock. By the 1984 set *Man in the Mirror,* Passport could easily be mistaken for a
set of Steely Dan backing tracks.   — J.S.

JACO PASTORIUS
★ ★ ★ ★ Invitation / War.
★ ★ ★ Jaco Pastorius / Epic
★ ★ Word of Mouth / War.

Jaco Pastorius (b. 1951) emerged in the mid-
Seventies as the latest in a line of virtuoso
electric bassists whose specialty was a fusion
sound with tremendous high-frequency pop
washed over by a spacy sonority. He came
to prominence as a member of Weather Report and his debut, *Jaco Pastorius,* will
sound familiar to supporters of that band.
Word of Mouth was a troubled follow-up,
but Pastorius rebounded in the Eighties with
Invitation, a big-band outing that features
harmonica player Toots Thielemans, percussionist Don Alias, Randy Brecker and Jon
Faddis on trumpets, Peter Erskine on drums
and Bobby Mintzer on tenor and soprano
saxophone.   — J.S.

CECIL PAYNE
★ ★ ★ Bird Gets the Worm / Muse
★ ★ ★ Bright Moments / Spot.
★ ★ ★ Shaw Nuff / Charlie Parker Rec./
   Audio Fi.

Cecil Payne (b. 1922) is a bebop baritone
saxophonist who made his mark with the famous Dizzy Gillespie orchestra of the late
Forties. He has been very successful at trans-
ferring the approach of Gillespie and Parker
to the cumbersome baritone, handling the
horn with more than a modicum of dexterity.

Culled from '61 and '62 small-group dates,
Shaw Nuff features two strong quintets, with
either Clark Terry or Johnny Coles on trumpet acting as Payne's foil. *Bird Gets the
Worm,* from 1976, features Al Foster on
drums, Buster Williams on bass, Duke Jordan on piano and Tom Harrel on trumpet

and fluegelhorn. *Bright Moments,* a 1979 release, brings in Curtis Fuller on trombone, Mick Pyne on piano, Dave Green on bass and Alan Jackson on drums. — F.G.

GARY PEACOCK
★ ★ ★ December Poems /ECM/War.
★ ★ ★ Shift in Wind / ECM/War.
★ ★ ★ ★ Tales of Another / ECM/War.
★ ★ ★ Voice from the Past / ECM/War.
Bassist Gary Peacock (b. 1935) came up through the West Coast jazz scene in the late Fifties and early Sixties, playing with Barney Kessel, Hampton Hawes and Don Ellis. He moved into more experimental playing in New York during the Sixties, working with Bill Evans, Miles Davis, Archie Shepp, Don Cherry, Albert Ayler and Roswell Rudd. After a long sabbatical Peacock began his recording career as a leader with the excellent 1977 album, *Tales of Another,* a fast-flying collaboration with drummer Jack DeJohnette and keyboardist Keith Jarrett. *December Poems* is a solo bass recording. — J.S.

NIELS-HENNING ORSTED PEDERSEN (NHOP)
★ ★ ★ Dancing on the Tables / Steep.
★ ★ ★ ★ Double Bass (with Sam Jones) / Steep.
★ ★ ★ Jay Walking / Steep.
★ ★ ★ Just the Way You Are (with Rune Gustafsson) / Sonet
★ ★ ★ Pictures (with Keith Knudsen) / Steep.
★ ★ ★ ★ The Viking (with Philip Catherine) / Pablo
Europe has produced only a handful of important jazzmen, but Danish bassist Niels-Henning Orsted Pedersen (b. 1946), better known as NHOP, is surely one of them. Pedersen's technical skills are astonishing, and his sensitivity for accompaniment has made him popular with everyone from Ella Fitzgerald to Archie Shepp.

Between frequent sideman gigs NHOP cuts LPs that give him a chance to blow on his original tunes as well as some bop classics. Another European virtuoso, guitarist Philip Catherine, is the guest soloist on *Jay Walking* and *Viking,* while saxist Dave Liebman and guitarist John Scofield do the honors on *Dancing.* NHOP has also cut duets with Scandinavian talents Knudsen on piano and Gustafsson on guitar. *Double Bass* is an encounter with the great bass sideman, Sam Jones, whose funky, blues-based playing is the perfect complement to the flamboyant Dane.

NHOP can also be heard on duet recordings with Joe Pass, Archie Shepp, Paul Bley, Martial Solal and Kenny Drew. — S.F.

ART PEPPER
★ ★ ★ ★ Among Friends / Discov.
★ ★ ★ ★ Art Lives / Gal.
★ ★ ★ Art Pepper Quartet / Gal.
★ ★ ★ ★ Art Pepper Today / Gal.
★ ★ ★ Artworks / Gal.
★ ★ ★ ★ The Complete Pacific Jazz Small Group Recordings of Art Pepper / Mosaic
★ ★ ★ ★ Discoveries / Savoy
★ ★ ★ ★ Early Show / Xan.
★ ★ ★ Friday Night at the Village Vanguard / Contem.
★ ★ ★ ★ ★ Gettin' Together / Contem.
★ ★ ★ ★ ★ Goin' Home (with George Cables) / Gal.
★ ★ ★ ★ Intensity / Contem.
★ ★ ★ ★ Landscape / Gal.
★ ★ ★ ★ Late Show / Xan.
★ ★ ★ Living Legend / Contem.
★ ★ ★ ★ ★ Meets the Rhythm Section / Contem.
★ ★ No Limit / Contem.
★ ★ ★ ★ ★ Omega Alpha / Blue N.
★ ★ One September Afternoon / Gal.
★ ★ ★ Plays Shorty Rogers / Pac. J.
★ ★ ★ ★ ★ Plus Eleven / Contem.
★ ★ ★ ★ Road Game / Gal.
★ ★ ★ Saturday Night at the Village Vanguard / Contem.
★ ★ ★ ★ Smack Up / Contem.
★ ★ ★ ★ So in Love / Artists H.
★ ★ ★ Straight Life / Gal.
★ ★ ★ ★ Tête-À-Tête/(with George Cables) / Gal.
★ ★ ★ Thursday Night at the Village Vanguard / Contem.
★ ★ ★ The Trip / Contem.
★ ★ ★ ★ The Way It Was / Contem.
★ ★ ★ Winter Moon / Gal.
Art Pepper (1925–1982), the handsome and brilliant Los Angeles alto saxophonist who gained early acclaim as featured soloist with Stan Kenton's band, was perhaps as famous for his numerous heroin busts and decade in prison (described at length in his autobiography *Straight Life*) as for his music. He will be remembered, however, as being among the most impassioned and personal alto saxophonists to emerge in the period dominated by Charlie Parker.

Early Pepper recordings remain the best, and listeners should start with *Meets the Rhythm Section* and *Gettin' Together,* taped with Miles Davis' 1957 and 1960 accompanying trios respectively; *Omega Alpha,* a strong 1958 quartet with pianist Carl Perkins also well featured; and *Plus Eleven,* arranger Marty Paich's 1959 settings of classic jazz tunes. The Xanadu albums, taped live in 1952 with Hampton Hawes on piano, are also strong collections. The Mosaic set highlights Pepper's work with trumpeter Chet Baker.

Between 1960 and 1975, Pepper did time, lived at Synanon, scuffled and stayed out of the recording studio. After his return, he became prolific, generally with respected supporting players, but the results did not always come up to the level of his early work. The three *Village Vanguard* albums, with George Cables and Elvin Jones, are typical of promising sessions that don't live up to their billing. Among the last Pepper albums, the best are *Among Friends,* a boppish throwback made in 1978; *So in Love, Landscape* and *Road Game,* each of which contains fierce blowing and a good sense of Pepper's repertoire during his final period; *Art Pepper Today,* with its magnificent ballad "Patricia"; and the moving duets with pianist Cables on *Goin' Home,* Pepper's last recording session.

Pepper can also be heard on Savoy's *Black California* and *Cool California* anthologies, Galaxy samplers *Five Birds and a Monk* and *Ballads by Four,* and the Palo Alto blowing session *Richie Cole and . . . .* Pepper's solid reputation continues to grow with the posthumous release of *Quartet, Artworks* and *Tête.* — B.B.

CHARLI PERSIP

★ ★ ★ **Superband (with Gerry LaFurn) / Stash**

A popular New York drummer for groups of all sizes. Charli Persip (b. 1929) had his only date as a leader at the head of a big band with trumpeter Gerry LaFurn. Although Persip is extremely versatile as a percussionist, the album proves less imaginative than one would have hoped. The band's strong book is marred by an abundance of mediocre players. — F.G.

OSCAR PETERSON

★ ★ ★ **Action / Pausa**
★ ★ ★ **The Canadiana Suite / Lime.**
★ ★ ★ **Collection / Verve**
★ ★ **Digital at Montreux / Pablo**
★ ★ ★ **Girl Talk / Pausa**
★ ★ ★ **History of an Artist / Pablo**
★ ★ **Jam Montreux '77 / Pablo L.**
★ ★ **Jousts / Pablo**
★ ★ ★ **Live at the Northsea Jazz Festival / Pablo L.**

★ ★ ★ **The London Concert (with Louis Belson and John Heard) / Pablo**
★ ★ ★ **Mellow Mood / Pausa**
★ ★ ★ **Montreux '75 / Pablo**
★ ★ ★ **Motions and Emotions / Pausa**
★ ★ ★ **My Favorite Instrument / Pausa**
★ ★ **Nigerian Marketplace / Pablo**
★ ★ ★ **Night Child / Pablo T.**
★ ★ ★ **Night Train / Verve**
★ ★ **Oscar Peterson and Bassists at Montreux '77 (with Ray Brown) / Pablo**
★ ★ **Oscar Peterson in Russia / Pablo**
★ ★ **Oscar Peterson with Dizzy Gillespie / Pablo**
★ ★ ★ **Oscar Peterson with Harry Edison / Pablo**
★ ★ **Oscar Peterson with Herb Ellis / Pausa**
★ ★ ★ **Oscar Peterson with Joe Faddis / Pablo**
★ ★ ★ **Oscar Peterson with Roy Eldridge / Pablo**
★ ★ ★ **The Paris Concert / Pablo**
★ ★ ★ **The Personal Touch / Pablo T.**
★ ★ **Return Engagement / Verve**
★ ★ ★ **Reunion Blues / Pausa**
★ ★ ★ **The Silent Partner / Pablo T.**
★ ★ ★ **Something's Warm / Verve**
★ ★ **Soul Español / Lime.**
★ ★ ★ **Sound of the Trio / Verve**
★ ★ ★ ★ **Tracks / Pausa**
★ ★ ★ **Trio + 1 / Mer.**
★ ★ ★ **Trio Transition / Em.**
★ ★ ★ **Way I Really Play / Pausa**
★ ★ ★ **We Get Requests / Verve**
★ **West Side Story / Verve**
★ ★ **With Respects to Nat / Lime.**

An international jazz institution, Montreal-born pianist/composer Oscar Peterson (b. 1925) is an extremely forceful and expansive player in concert. Both in the studio and on stage, Peterson keeps pretty much to the mainstream and swing-era derivations and handles himself with great verve and taste. His live records (*The London Concert* especially), solo sides (in particular the earlier *Tracks*) and the many trio sessions offer a consistently clear portrait of Peterson.

Peterson's collaborations are a mixed bag (both the Edison and the Eldridge Pablo sessions come off well) and his experiments (like *The Canadiana Suite*) often prove uneven. Oddly enough, his film score for the 1978 thriller *The Silent Partner* (with Zoot Sims, Benny Carter and Milt Jackson, among others) turns out to be one of Peterson's best ensemble records to date. — B.T.

OSCAR PETTIFORD

★ ★ ★ **Blue Brothers / Jazz M.**
★ ★ ★ ★ **Bohemia after Dark / Beth.**

★ ★ ★ ★ ★ **My Little Cello** / Fan.
★ ★ ★ ★ ★ **The New Oscar Pettiford Sextet** / Fan./OJC

Oscar Pettiford (1922–1960) was one of the all-time greats and without doubt the most significant bassist to come along after Jimmy Blanton. Like Blanton, Pettiford helped to move the instrument out of its support role and transform it into a viable solo instrument.

Featured with Duke Ellington, Woody Herman and Charlie Barnet during the Forties, Pettiford became a regular on 52nd Street during the bebop era, fronting his own units and working as a sideman. He eventually settled in downtown at the Café Bohemia, where he led the house band.

Far from being relegated to the bebop era, Pettiford's career continued to blossom as modern jazz came on. Aside from recording with Miles Davis and Thelonious Monk, he also participated in Sonny Rollins' watershed trio date, "The Freedom Suite."

As a composer, Pettiford's work is outstanding, including such standards as "Bohemia after Dark" and "Tricrotism." In addition to his bass work, he introduced the cello as a solo instrument on the brilliant *My Little Cello*. On *Sextet* Pettiford plays cello while Charles Mingus is the bassist.

Toward the end of his life, Pettiford coled a group with trumpeter Howard McGhee that managed to cut a few sides for Savoy before an ill-fated tour of the Far East all but ended Pettiford's career. Resettling in Copenhagen in 1958, where he cut the sides heard on *Blue Brothers,* he died there two years later.

Aside from performing as a sideman in big bands, Pettiford also wrote, arranged and conducted his own big band, producing two albums for ABC-Paramount. Both are long out of print and extremely rare, a crime considering his stature and abilities.
— F.G.

BARRE PHILLIPS
★ ★ ★ **Call Me When You Get There** / ECM/War.
★ ★ ★ **For All It Is** / JAPO/PSI
★ ★ ★ **Journal Violone** / Op. One
★ ★ ★ ★ **Mountainscapes** / ECM/War.
★ ★ ★ **Three Day Moon** / ECM/War.
★ ★ ★ **II** / ECM/War.

Classically trained bassist Barre Phillips (b. 1934) has played extensively in both classical and jazz settings and was part of Gunther Schuller's Third Stream attempt to bridge the gap between the two musics in the Sixties. Since then he has worked extensively as a solo performer (*Journal, Call Me*), as part of the group Trio with saxophonist John Surman and drummer Stu Martin, in a fantastic duet session with bassist Dave Holland (*Music from Two Basses,* ECM) and with Norwegian guitarist Terje Rypdal (*What Comes After,* ECM). Phillips' conception, for all its pristine brilliance and rigorous experimentation, is a bit bloodless, though *Mountainscapes,* with guitarist John Abercrombie and synthesizer player Dieter Feichtner joining Trio, is a breathtaking set. — J.S.

FLIP PHILLIPS
★ ★ ★ **Flipenstein** / Prog.
★ ★ ★ ★ **A Melody from the Sky** / Doctor J.

A versatile swing tenor, Flip Phillips (b. 1915) is best known for his work with Woody Herman and as a featured soloist with Jazz at the Philharmonic.

Melody is a hot collection of Flip's first sides as a leader from 1944 and 1945.

Flipenstein is a superior quartet date cut in '81. Despite the ridiculous idea to give it a "horror show" concept (with song titles like "Vampire's Dream," "Dracula's Dance" and "Ghoul of My Dreams"), Phillips weathers the date with humor and taste.

The tenorman is also spotlighted on several Jazz at the Philharmonic recordings available on Verve and Pablo, where both his fine ballad abilities and raw power are demonstrated. — F.G.

DANIEL PONCE
★ ★ ★ **New York Now!** / Cell.

Cuban percussionist Ponce has worked with Paquito D'Rivera, Dizzy Gillespie, Tito Puente and Eddie Palmieri. *New York Now!,* his first solo outing, is a helter-skelter set highlighted by Ponce's lightning playing and guest saxophonist Paquito D'Rivera. — J.S.

JIMMY PONDER
★ ★ ★ ★ **Down Here on the Ground** / Mile.
★ ★ ★ **Illusions** / Imp.
★ ★ ★ **While My Guitar Gently Weeps** / Cadet
★ ★ ★ **White Room** / Imp.

Guitarist Jimmy Ponder (b. 1946) is a talented R&B-based player from Pittsburgh who started out playing with Charles Earland and went on to gigs with Lou Donaldson, Donald Byrd, Stanley Turrentine, Jimmy McGriff, Groove Holmes, Ron Carter and Roland Hanna. He tends to mix pop titles with jazz standards and the freewheeling 1984 *Down Here on the Ground* set is his

best work, contrasting versions of "Billie
Jean" and "Superstition" with "Epistrophy."
— J.S.

JEAN-LUC PONTY

★ ★ ★ **Aurora** / Atl.
★ ★ ★ ★ **Canteloupe Island** / Blue N.
★ ★ ★ **Civilized Evil** / Atl.
★ ★ ★ **Cosmic Messenger** / Atl.
★ ★ ★ ★ **Critics' Choice** / Prest.
★ ★ ★ **Enigmatic Ocean** / Atl.
★ ★ ★ **Imaginary Voyage** / Atl.
★ ★ ★ **Individual Choice** / Atl.
★ ★ ★ ★ **Live** / Atl.
★ ★ ★ ★ **Live At Dontes** / Blue N.
★ ★ ★ ★ **Live At Montreux** / Inner
★ ★ ★ **Meets Gaslini** / Pausa
★ ★ ★ **Mystical Adventures** / Atl.
★ ★ ★ **Open Mind** / Atl.
★ ★ ★ **Open Strings** / Pausa
★ ★ ★ **Sunday Walk** / Pausa
★ ★ ★ **A Taste for Passion** / Atl.
★ ★ ★ ★ **Upon the Wings of Music** / Atl.
Jean-Luc Ponty (b. 1942) is one of the jazz
world's most accomplished players on the vi-
olin. A child prodigy born into a family of
classical musicians and teachers, his goal was
to write symphonies until he heard New Or-
leans clarinetist Albert Nicholas' Paris-based
jazz group and asked to sit in. Ponty's impressive technique came to the attention of
the venerable French jazz violinist Stephane
Grappelli, who urged Ponty to continue in
the jazz idiom.

Ponty's introduction to the United States
came when he was invited to play the Monterey Jazz Festival in 1967 after having won
the Miscellaneous Instrument section of
Downbeat's '66 critic's poll. During that U.S.
stay Ponty began playing with keyboardist
George Duke, recording several excellent sessions in the process, the best material from
which is collected on *Cantaloupe Island.*
Ponty played with Frank Zappa on his *Hot
Rats* album, then joined Zappa's group on a
freelance basis. Before long he had brought
the electric violin to the point where it became one of the cornerstones of the jazz-
rock fusion sound.

In 1975 Ponty debuted his own fusion outfit with the excellent *Upon the Wings of
Music* LP and has continued to record
(mostly for Atlantic) in a similar vein ever
since. Though much of the sound's original
excitement has worn off through repetition,
Ponty's technique continues to be awesome
and his playing is still well worth hearing,
especially in the three *Live* settings. *Open
Mind* features some interesting work with
Chick Corea and George Benson. — J.S.

LENNY POPKIN

★ ★ ★ **Falling Free** / Choice
A student of Lennie Tristano, tenor saxophonist Lenny Popkin (b. 1941) concentrates
on the kind of long, snakelike melodic solos
that one associates with his mentor's piano
playing. Tonally, Popkin has also adapted
the thin, airy sound of Tristano's great alto
saxophonist, Lee Konitz, to his own tenor
instrument. This album is extremely well-
crafted, although not very exciting. Bassist
Eddie Gomez and drummer Peter Scattare-
tico lend support but are a shade too unobtrusive. — F.G.

EARL "BUD" POWELL

★ ★ ★ ★ ★ **The Amazing Bud Powell, Vol. 1**
/ Blue N.
★ ★ ★ ★ ★ **The Amazing Bud Powell, Vol. 2**
/ Blue N.
★ ★ ★ ★ **Bouncing with Bud** / Del.
★ ★ ★ ★ **Bud in Paris** / Xan.
★ ★ ★ ★ **Bud Powell Trio** / Fan.
★ ★ ★ ★ ★ **The Genius of Bud Powell** /
Verve
★ ★ ★ ★ ★ **Greatest Jazz Concert Ever** /
Prest.
★ ★ **Invisible Cage** / Black L.
★ ★ ★ ★ **Masters of the Modern Piano** /
Verve
★ ★ ★ **The Scene Changes** / Blue N.
★ ★ **Time Waits** / Blue N.
★ ★ **Ups 'n' Downs** / Main.
Earl "Bud" Powell (1924–1966) was the pre-
mier pianist of the bebop era, the most imi-
tated man on his instrument, as well as one
of the tragic casualties of an era overstocked
with disaster.

Powell's recordings from the late Forties,
after he had already been confined in a mental institution, are definitive bebop. *The
Amazing Bud Powell, Volume 1* features
three takes of his classic "Un Poco Loco," in
a trio that included drummer Max Roach,
plus other famous Powell tunes performed
by a quintet featuring Fats Navarro and the
young Sonny Rollins. *The Genius of Bud
Powell,* a double album of trios and unaccompanied solos, is also indispensable.

The first half of the Fifties saw Powell
begin his decline, though he is still strong on
The Amazing . . . Volume 2, much of which
was done in 1953 and consists entirely of
trios. *Bud Powell Trio,* with Mingus and
Roach, is uncommonly dissonant Powell
from the famous Massey Hall concert that
also featured Charlie Parker and Dizzy Gillespie (available as a twofer on the *Greatest
Jazz Concert Ever,* Prestige). The Powell selections on *Masters of the Modern Piano,*

from 1955, are his last consistently good American recordings.

Among his later work, *The Scene Changes,* made shortly before his 1959 departure for Paris, has some bright spots, but *Time Waits, Invisible Cage* and *Ups 'n' Downs* are more depressing than rewarding. His best later work is on the 1960 *Bud in Paris,* which has two duets with tenorman Johnny Griffin, and the 1962 *Bouncing with Bud,* which introduced the impressive Danish bassist Niels-Henning Orsted Pedersen, who was only fifteen at the time.

Powell played the piano with unmatched speed and intensity; his frenzied uptempo solos anticipate (emotionally if not through specific techniques) the avant-garde of the next decade. Besides his own best albums, Powell can be heard with Charlie Parker, Dexter Gordon, Fats Navarro and Sonny Stitt.

★ ★ ★ ★ **The Best Years** / **Vogue**
★ ★ ★ **Bud Powell** / **Quin.**
★ ★ ★ **Bud Powell '57** / **Verve**
★ ★ ★ ★ ★ **Inner Fires** / **Elek./Mus.**
★ ★ ★ ★ **In Paris** / **Discov.**
★ ★ ★ ★ ★ **Piano Interpretations** / **Verve**
★ ★ ★ **Portrait of Thelonious** / **Odys.**

The Quintessence album is taken from 1963 European concert performances and catches Powell in the lackluster form that was all too frequently the norm in his last years. *In Paris* and *Portrait of Thelonious,* recorded during the same period with trios, are better, especially the Discovery reissue of an album formerly on Reprise, one of the best late-period Powell recitals. By the way, the *Amazing* volumes, still listed in the catalogue, should be grabbed up quickly.

Powell's highly influential and long unavailable Roost trio sessions from '47 and '55 have appeared as half of a French Vogue reissue; unfortunately, the *Best Years* twofer also contains the desultory product of Powell's final recording session. Of the Verve Japanese imports, parts of the uneven *Bud Powell '57* and all of the excellent *Piano Interpretations* are also available on American Verve. *Inner Fires* contains tumultuous, previously unreleased live recordings from '53.
— B.B.

RUTH PRICE
★ ★ ★ **Lucky to Be Me** / **ITI**

In two cuts, "Little Jazz Bird" and "Irresistible You," Ruth Price (b. 1938) sets a standard for swinging, personalized expression and technical control that the rest of *Lucky to Be Me* fails to attain. Ms. Price's jazz connections—Charlie Ventura, Red Garland, Harry James, Shelly Manne—are impeccable. Still, her unyielding restraint leads to a lack of the kind of idiosyncratic expression that always informs a compelling jazz performance. — A.R.

SAMMY PRICE
★ ★ ★ **Fire** / **Class.**
★ ★ ★ **Sweet Substitute** / **Sack.**

Texas-born pianist Sammy Price (b. 1908) is best known for his blues and boogie-woogie and comp duties during a long tenure at Decca. His debut disc was in 1929 and he's still making fine records, particularly for Sackville. Though a noble traditionalist, Price is no folksy primitive. Both albums here typify his spry wit, sophistication and finish. — B.T.

BERNARD PURDIE
★ ★ **Delights of the Garden** / **Casa.**
★ ★ **Purdie Good** / **Prest.**
★ ★ **Shaft** / **Prest.**

Bernard Purdie (b. 1939) is an accomplished session drummer who apparently will never amount to much as a leader. His solo albums are banal and in desperate search of commercial hooks. — J.S.

FLORA PURIM
★ ★ **Butterfly Dreams** / **Mile.**
★ ★ **Carry On** / **War.**
★ ★ **Encounter** / **Mile.**
★ ★ **500 Miles High** / **Mile.**
★ ★ **Love Reborn** / **Mile.**
★ ★ **Open Your Eyes You Can Fly** / **Mile.**
★ ★ **Stories to Tell** / **Mile.**
★ ★ **That's What She Said** / **Mile.**

The flamboyant South American singer Flora Purim (b. 1942) came to prominence in the early seventies through her association with Chick Corea during his Return to Forever fusion period, as well as via work with her husband, percussionist Airto Moreira. She has built her sound on a highly rhythmic, usually quite exotic Latin hybrid. Sometimes she actually fronts the band vocally, articulating lyrics and soaring off on her own. Just as often, however, she fades into the post-fusion ensembles. While Purim has the expressive phrasing and occasionally suggests the taste of a good jazz singer, her propulsive settings and mannered monotony succeed or fail more on the strength of how well her rhythm section manages to make good dance music. Despite some too grandiose passages, they usually bring it off.
— B.T.

PAUL QUINICHETTE
★ ★ ★ ★ **The Kid from Denver / Bio.**
Paul Quinichette (1921–1983) was a former
Basie tenorman and Lester ("Pres") Young
devotee, so much so that he was nicknamed
"Vice Pres." This reissue of a '58 date for
the Dawn label is manned largely by Basie-
ites, and is as enjoyable for the work of such
sidemen as Thad Jones, Joe Newman, Nat
Pierce, Henry Coker and Freddie Green as it
is for the leader's performances. Less heralded these days than other Pres students
like Stan Getz and Zoot Sims, Quinichette
was nevertheless a master of the style.
—— F.G.

DEWEY REDMAN
★ ★ ★ ★ **Coincide** / Imp.
★ ★ ★ ★ **The Ear of the Behearer** / Imp.
★ ★ ★ **Look for the Black Star** / Ari./
Free.

His role of sideman with Ornette Coleman
and Keith Jarrett has led many listeners to
undervalue the strength of Dewey Redman
(b. 1931), one of the finest contemporary
tenor saxophonists. Limited recognition in
this case has translated to limited albums
under Redman's own name.

Look for the Black Star, from 1966, finds
Redman formulating his talking-horn technique and adding Latin rhythms as well as
more conventional free and modal touches.
The album's greatest significance is its picture of the San Francisco jazz underground
of the period.

Impulse recorded Redman to better effect
in 1973–74, on *The Ear of the Behearer* and
Coincide. Both use the same basic band
(trumpeter Ted Daniel, bassist Sirone, drummer Eddie Moore), with cellist Jane Robert-
son a particularly valuable addition to the
former. The weave of tenor and strings pro-
duces marvelous abstractions, while performances on Redman's secondary instruments
(musette and zither) tend to be less interesting. Both albums find Redman equally commanding when he returns to his hard-
cooking Texas roots, with "Qow" on *Coincide* a superior "inside" track.

★ ★ ★ **Musics** / Gal.
★ ★ ★ **Soundsigns** / Gal.
★ ★ ★ ★ **The Struggle Continues** / ECM/
War.

Both of the Galaxy albums were made in
1978 by Redman's quartet of the time, with
Charlie Haden added for two tracks on
Soundsigns. Redman gets the opportunity to
display his versatility with some limber
straight-ahead playing, and his musette work
has grown more interesting, but these remain

simply workmanlike sessions. The ECM
album, using the same instrumentation but
recorded four years later, affords a more
consistent and convincing sample of Redman's work. The best recent Redman can be
heard on the Old and New Dreams *Playing*
album. — B.B.

DON REDMAN
★ ★ ★ **Big Bands Uptown 1931–40** /
MCA (four tracks only)
★ ★ ★ ★ **For Europeans Only** / Steep.

Saxophonist/arranger/composer/bandleader
Don Redman (1900–1964) first made his
mark in the Twenties as arranger and soloist
for the early Fletcher Henderson orchestras
and later as musical director of McKinney's
Cotton Pickers. He formed his own big band
in the early Thirties, and the four tracks on
the MCA album demonstrate not only Redman's talents as a serious and prophetic arranger but his penchant for novelty tunes as
well. The results in both spheres are impressive: "Chant of the Weed" predates the mature Afro-American signature Duke Ellington would later fully develop by nearly a
decade, and "Shakin' the African" is as delightful and intelligent a commercial record
as the period has to offer.

Redman's 1946 Copenhagen concert captured on *For Europeans Only* is remarkable.
Not only are Redman's arrangements excellent, but he also includes charts by Tadd
Dameron and Mary Lou Williams. The band
is an absolute killer unit featuring Don Byas,
Tyree Glenn, Billy Taylor, Peanuts Holland
and Ray Abrams as the primary soloists.
Little was written about this album when it
was finally packaged and released in 1983,
but it deserves to be ranked with the great
Carnegie Hall Concerts Duke Ellington was
giving during the same period. Don't miss
this one. — F.G.

DIZZY REECE
★ ★ ★ **Blowin' Away (with Ted Curson)** /
Interp.
★ ★ ★ ★ **Manhattan Project** / **Bee**
Hip and underrated are the best ways to describe trumpeter Dizzy Reece (b. 1931).
Both of these albums were recorded in the
late Seventies when Reece was enjoying
something of a resurgence. Prior to that, he
had been up and down, shuttling between
relative renown and LP sessions for Blue
Note and Tempo Records that seemed to
end up in cutout bins the day after they
were released.

Both of these discs feature fine bands, with
tenormen Clifford Jordan and Charles Davis,
pianist Albert Dailey, bassist Art Davis and
drummer Roy Haynes on the Bee Hive session. Haynes is the only repeater on *Blowin'*
Away, where Reece shares trumpet duties
with Ted Curson.

As a player, Reece's work is marked by a
concise lyricism rarely captured on the trumpet, and his solos are always imaginative.
Both of these albums are well worth tracking
down. — F.G.

DIANNE REEVES
★ ★ ★ **Welcome to My Love** / **Palo Alto**
Clark Terry introduced Dianne Reeves (b.
1956) to the jazz audience some years ago at
the Wichita Jazz Festival. Subsequent gigs in
Wichita and at the 1980 Women's Jazz Festival in Kansas City revealed Reeves as an
exciting, warm-voiced jazz singer. Unfortunately, only her foxy, passionate reading of
"My Funny Valentine" in *Welcome to My*
Love fulfills that earlier promise. Although
some fairly hot dance tracks occur here,
Reeves would probably sound more distinctive and convincing in a strictly jazz format.
— A.R.

JACK REILLY
★ ★ ★ ★ **The Brinksman** / **Rev.**
★ ★ ★ ★ **Marco DiMarco and Jack Reilly** /
Mod. J.
★ ★ ★ ★ **November** / **Rev.**
★ ★ ★ ★ **Together (Again) . . . for the First**
Time / **Rev.**
★ ★ ★ ★ **Tributes** / **Car.**
Outstanding Brooklyn-based pianist capable
of combining a myriad of influences and traditions into an emotional yet highly intelligent personal style. Well versed in classical
and Eastern music, Jack Reilly (b. 1932) also
studied with both Bill Evans and Lennie Tristano. Although he spends most of his time
teaching, Reilly has begun releasing albums

annually, and they demonstrate that he is
neither academic nor allied with one particular tradition. Subtle and superior. — F.G.

DJANGO REINHARDT
★ ★ ★ ★ **Django 1935** / **GNP**
★ ★ ★ ★ **Django 1935–39** / **GNP**
★ ★ ★ **Django Reinhardt** / **Arc. Folk**
★ ★ ★ **Django Reinhardt, Vol. 2** / **Arc. Folk**
★ ★ ★ **Django Reinhardt, Vol. 3** / **Arc. Folk**
★ ★ ★ **Django Reinhardt, Vol. 4** / **Arc. Folk**
★ ★ ★ **First Recordings** / **Prest.**
★ ★ ★ ★ **Immortal Django Reinhardt** / **GNP**
★ ★ ★ ★ **Legendary Django Reinhardt** /
GNP
★ ★ ★ **Parisian Swing** / **GNP**
★ ★ ★ ★ **QHCF/Reinhardt/Grappelli** /
Angel
★ ★ ★ **Quintet of Hot Club of France** /
GNP
★ ★ **Swing It Lightly** / **Col.**
Jean-Baptiste (Django) Reinhardt (1910–
1953), a Belgian gypsy, developed the jazz
guitar as lead instrument out of the romantic
European tradition in the Thirties and Forties and continues to exert a powerful hold
on young improvisational guitarists, even
though many jazz critics—especially in
America where there is an understandable
bias for Charlie Christian—hotly contest his
credentials as a legitimate jazz musician.

Having lost the use of two fingers on his
left hand in a fire, he created a technique to
overcome this handicap, and in the process
pioneered a dazzling single-note style that
fairly shimmered with vibrato and a bright,
sparkling tone. Improvising on contemporary
standards with Stephane Grappelli (violin)
and the Hot Club of France, Django would
bring forth a flood of melodic ideas literally
jumping over one another to get out of his
guitar. Amid this torrent of notes, Reinhardt
would effortlessly drop in frantic octave passages and hard-edged chord vamps to push
the often-plodding Hot Club rhythm section
along. On slower tunes, like his classic "Nuages," his melodic improvisations were simply uncanny. The tone and phrasing positively throbbed with feeling.

Most critics object to the Hot Club's
"string heavy" sound and muddy rhythm
sections, and even the most dedicated Reinhardt fan will grow weary of the slightly
stodgy Hot Club style, but no one can deny
the sheer emotional impact when Reinhardt
digs into his Macaferri guitar to wrench out
another stunning solo. It is really as pointless to criticize Reinhardt for playing too
many notes as it would be to criticize Charlie Parker or John Coltrane for the same of-

fense, since he exercised such an effortless control over his prodigious technique.

Of the existing discography in America, the GNP Crescendo and Prestige LPs are probably the best available. Classic performances like "Mélodie du Crépuscule," "Minor Swing," "Place de Broukère," "Belleville," "Porto Cabello" and "September Song" can be found on a number of domestic and import albums. Hard-core Django aficionados favor the EMI-Pathé "Djangologies" import series—best for packaging and sound—but most of his work is readily available. — J.C.C.

EMILY REMLER
★ ★ ★ Firefly / Conc. J.
★ ★ ★ Take Two / Conc. J.
Women in jazz are still something of a rarity, and it's been both a blessing and a curse for guitarist Emily Remler (b. 1957). The good part is it got her noticed; the bad part is that's all anybody ever talks about. But Remler still sounds good even if you don't look at the cover. The discs for Concord are mainstream, her sound on them straight out of Wes Montgomery. She can swing.
— F.G.

REVOLUTIONARY ENSEMBLE
★ ★ ★ ★ Manhattan Cycles / In. Nav.
★ ★ ★ ★ ★ The People's Republic / Hori.
This trio, comprised of Leroy Jenkins (b. 1932) on violin, Sirone (b. 1940, a.k.a. Norris Jones) on bass and trombone and Jerome Cooper (b. 1946) on drums and piano, was the most exciting new music band of the Seventies. Their basic violin/bass/drums instrumentation is perfectly balanced and allows for maximum exploration without unnecessary assault. All three are demonic players, though each (especially the underrated Cooper) knew the value of restraint, and all three wrote intriguing material.

Manhattan Cycles, like two other discs no longer listed in the catalogue, is a poorly recorded concert. The single composition performed (by trumpeter Leo Smith) sets the trio against prerecorded tape. Their Horizon album is well produced and nicely programed, though it lacks a bit of the fire heard on the concert albums.

Jenkins can also be heard on his own albums and with Anthony Braxton, Richard Abrams, Alice Coltrane and others. Sirone has recorded with Jenkins, Marion Brown, Dewey Redman, Roswell Rudd and Cecil Taylor; Cooper with Braxton and on the *Wildflowers* anthology.
★ ★ ★ ★ ★ Revolutionary Ensemble / Inner
★ ★ ★ ★ ★ Vietnam 1 & 2 / Base

This trio disbanded in 1977, shortly after taping the concert performance on *Revolutionary Ensemble.* The album captures much of the range, intensity and complementary spirit that made the Revolutionary Ensemble special. *Vietnam 1 & 2* is the incendiary but poorly recorded ESP debut album from 1972, reissued in Italy. — B.B.

DOUG RILEY
★ ★ Dreams / PM
A serviceable sideman in the clubs, Toronto pianist Doug Riley (b. 1945) made one outing as a leader in the mid-Seventies, the pleasant, cottage-made *Dreams,* featuring his unambitious compositions. — B.T.

SAM RIVERS
★ ★ ★ ★ Contours / Blue N.
★ ★ ★ ★ Fuchsia Swing Song / Blue N.
★ ★ ★ Involution / Blue N.
Sam Rivers (b. 1930), who plays tenor sax, soprano sax and flute, finally got a recording contract in 1965 after years of gigs around Boston and the briefest of tours with Miles Davis. Of his Blue Note work, *Fuchsia,* with fellow Boston iconoclasts Jaki Byard and Tony Williams, is the most intriguing mix of post-bop and freer strains; *Contours,* with Freddie Hubbard and Herbie Hancock, comes closest to being a conventional quintet; and *Involution* shows his awareness of Ayler and the ESP bands in performances that perhaps try too hard to be "outside." Pianist Andrew Hill leads one of the bands on the last album.
★ ★ ★ ★ ★ Crystals / Imp.
★ ★ ★ ★ ★ Dave Holland/Sam Rivers / IAI
★ ★ ★ Hues / Imp.
★ ★ ★ ★ Sam Rivers/Dave Holland, Vol. 2 / IAI
★ ★ ★ Sizzle / Imp.
★ ★ ★ ★ Streams / Imp.
After several years of low-profile activity, Rivers returned in the Seventies with a fourth solo instrument (piano), an important New York music room of his own (Studio Rivbea), and an open-ended improvisational style that lets the ideas flow unfettered by rigid structure yet still finds many moments to swing straight out. Most notable among the above albums are *Streams,* from Montreux 1973, the only example of a complete standard Rivers performance (Cecil McBee, bass; Norman Connors, drums); *Crystals,* with his magnificent writing for a fourteen-piece band; and the first volume of his duets with bass master Holland, where Rivers plays tenor and soprano. *Sizzle,* sort of a free approach to crossover, is also special. At

The perfect place to start would be *The Peacocks,* a hard-to-find 1973 Columbia disc nominally led by Stan Getz. Rowles followed this revelatory date with a series of disappointing trio LPs for Choice and Xanadu, but his late-Seventies Progressive set is perfection itself. Working in a duet setting with the super-responsive bassist George Mraz, Rowles flaunts the economic delivery and all-encompassing harmonic knowledge that has kept him in such high regard and demand among his fellow musicians. His charmingly craggy singing, admittedly an acquired taste, is also featured. The Sonet captures more of the Rowles/Mraz stimulating interplay. The magnificent Concord Jazz records are discussed in Ray Brown's entry.

The Grammy-nominated Columbia LP is a solo recital and a loving tribute to two masters whose influence can be heard throughout Rowles' playing. Rowles can also be heard on Zoot Sims' recordings for Choice and Pablo.   — S.F.

HOWARD RUMSEY
★ ★ ★ **Music for Lighthouse Keeping / Contem.**
Bassist Howard Rumsey (b. 1917) was part of Stan Kenton's original 1941 band and then went on to form his own group. In 1949 Rumsey's band opened the legendary Lighthouse jazz club of Hermosa Beach, California, and soon became a fixture there. The "Lighthouse All-Stars" assembled on this 1956 set—tenor saxophonist Bob Cooper, trumpeter Conte Candoli, drummer Stan Levey, trombonist Frank Rosolino, pianist Sonny Clark—lay out a precise, understated appreciation of the "cool" aspects of bop that comes close to defining the "West Coast sound," as this kind of playing became known. Listen for the Monkish overtones of Clark's blues phrasing on "Topsy."   — J.S.

PATRICE RUSHEN
★ ★ **Before the Dawn / Prest.**
★ ★ **Let There Be Funk / Prest.**
★ ★ ★ **Now / Elek.**
★ ★ **Patrice / Elek.**
★ ★ **Pizzazz / Elek.**
★ ★ **Posh / Elek.**
★ ★ ★ **Prelusion / Prest.**
★ ★ ★ **Shout It Out / Prest.**
★ ★ **Straight from the Heart / Elek.**
Keyboardist Patrice Rushen (b. 1954) was a classically trained prodigy who recorded her first jazz album, *Preclusion,* before she was twenty. The all-instrumental set, with Joe Henderson's tenor saxophone as the other

voice, earned Rushen accolades, but she followed it up with a poor second album, *Before the Dawn,* that was marred by substandard material.

Rushen began to move away from jazz and toward R&B on her third try, *Shout It Out,* on which she also made her debut as a vocalist. Since moving to Elektra Rushen has gone so far into R&B territory that her latest records have outsold most jazz LPs and, in fact, resemble disco more than jazz. Rushen can play, but her best instincts often seem muffled by the airplay-conscious homogeneity of her style.   — J.S.

JIMMY RUSHING
★ ★ ★ ★ ★ **The Essential Jimmy Rushing / Van.**
★ ★ ★ ★ ★ **Every Day I Have the Blues / Blues.**
★ ★ ★ **Going to Chicago / Van.**
★ ★ ★ **If This Ain't the Blues / Van.**
★ ★ ★ ★ ★ **Mister Five by Five / Col.**
★ ★ ★ **Listen to the Blues / Van.**
Rushing is perhaps the greatest of the Kansas City blues shouters (who included Big Joe Turner and Walter Brown). Born in Oklahoma City, Rushing recalls hearing Bessie Smith as an early turning point in influencing his musical direction; in 1929 he made his first recording with Walter Page's Blue Devils (Count Basie playing piano). Rushing then fronted Benny Moten's band before joining Basie for his greatest years. For fifteen years Rushing was the mainstay of Basie's greatest organization, bellowing and crooning against that band's powerful horn section, until economic pressures in the Forties forced Basie to disband in favor of a smaller group.

The Vanguard sides were recorded by John Hammond with a small group of Basie sidemen. *Essential* collects the best moments of that era. Rushing recorded several good records for Bluesway, and *Every Day I Have the Blues* is a fine representation of that period. There's no question that Rushing is best served working with a full band rather than the small combos he recorded with on the Vanguard sides, and here the Oliver Nelson Orchestra is a great foil. *Mister Five by Five* collects Basie's late-Fifties work for Columbia, again some with a full orchestra, some with interesting small combos like the Brubeck/Desmond group. These sides feature incredible performances: Rushing fronting a band with Buck Clayton, Coleman Hawkins and Jo Jones; Rushing fronting Benny Goodman's band; Rushing in a vocal duet with Helen Humes.   — J.S.

GEORGE RUSSELL

★ ★ ★ ★ ★ **Ezz-thetics / Riv.**
★ ★ ★ ★ ★ **New York, N.Y. and Jazz in the Space Age / MCA**
★ ★ ★ ★ ★ **Outer Thoughts / Mile.**

George Russell (b. 1923) has played piano and percussion, but he is primarily important for his compositions and his *Lydian Chromatic Concept of Tonal Organization,* a theoretical study that predicted the shift from chord changes to scales or "modes" as the basis of jazz improvisation. His most influential recordings are from before his expatriation to Europe in 1964, especially in the years covered by the above albums (1958–61). MCA's double album joins two orchestral works, one a portrait of Manhattan, the other a more consciously far-out venture; soloists include John Coltrane, Art Farmer, Bill Evans and Paul Bley. *Outer Thoughts* samples the work of his various sextets, the best of which made *Ezz-thetics* and featured Don Ellis and Eric Dolphy.

★ ★ ★ ★ **Electronic Sonata for Souls Loved by Nature / Strata-East**
★ ★ ★ ★ ★ **The Essence of George Russell / Concept/Sonet**
★ ★ ★ ★ **Listen to the Silence / Concept**
★ ★ ★ ★ **Othello Ballet Suite/Electric Organ Sonata No. 1 / Concept/Sonet**

Currently Russell teaches at the New England Conservatory of Music in Boston and works on the second volume of his *Lydian Concept.* These recordings represent ambitious compositions from 1966 to 1971, recorded while he lived in Europe with responsive continental orchestras. *Essence* gives the best picture of his range, with a full band version of the Electronic Sonata (the album of that name is by a sextet). Also notable is the *Othello Ballet Suite,* with saxophonist Jan Garbarek as featured soloist, and *Listen to the Silence,* for electric/acoustic combo and chorus.

★ ★ ★ **Electronic Sonata for Souls Loved by Nature—1980 / Soul N.**
★ ★ ★ **Live in an American Time Spiral / Soul N.**
★ ★ ★ ★ **New York Big Band / Soul N.**
★ ★ ★ ★ **Trip to Prillarguri / Soul N.**
★ ★ ★ ★ ★ **Vertical Form VI / Soul N.**

Russell's recent contract with the Italian Soul Note label has produced both new recordings and the reissue of several earlier titles. From among the new works, the most valuable are *Trip to Prillarguri,* with the 1970 sextet including Garbarek and guitarist Terje Rypdal; the imposing *Vertical Form VI,* a 1977 live orchestral recording that captures Russell's innovative orchestration techniques in a stunning extended work; and *New York Big Band,* most of which was recorded in 1978. The *Time Spiral* album, from '82, pairs Russell's most recent recorded compositions with two long and surprisingly ordinary blowing tracks for the band. Russell has also given us yet another version of the *Electronic Sonata,* this time by a 1980 sextet. *Othello Ballet Suite* and *Essence* have also been reissued on Soul Note; while the Riverside *Ezz-thetics* album, for so long available only as a Japanese import, has now appeared on Fantasy/Original Jazz Classics in a less expensive American facsimile version. — B.B.

TERJE RYPDAL

★ ★ ★ **Afric Pepperbird / ECM/War.**
★ ★ ★ **After the Rain / ECM/War.**
★ ★ ★ **Descendre / ECM/War.**
★ ★ ★ **EOS / ECM/War.**
★ ★ ★ **Esoteric Circle (with Jan Garbarek) / Ari./Free.**
★ ★ ★ **Odyssey / ECM/War.**
★ ★ ★ **Sart / ECM/War.**
★ ★ ★ **To Be Continued / ECM/War.**
★ ★ **What Comes After / ECM/War.**
★ ★ ★ **Whenever I Seem to Be Far Away / ECM/War.**

For all his talent, Norwegian guitarist Terje Rypdal (b. 1947) veers dangerously close to sanctified cosmic trance music on some of his recorded work. His roots are rock & roll, but his rapid evolution into free jazz and studies of the Lydian Chromatic Concept of Tonal Organization with George Russell have led Rypdal into more abstract and reflective states, not readily accessible to most listeners.

Rypdal's ECM albums range from haunting melodic statements to long Mahavishnu-like passages over synthesizer textures (*Whenever I Seem to Be Far Away*), which a fan might call "stratosphere music." His most full-blooded work to date is on the hard-to-find *Esoteric Circle* where his shadowy guitar provides the perfect counterpoint to Jan Garbarek's impassioned saxophone. — J.C.C.

SAL SALVADOR
★ ★ ★ **In Our Own Sweet Way / Stash**
★ ★ ★ ★ **Juicy Lucy / Bee**
★ ★ ★ ★ **Starfingers / Bee**
Sal Salvador (b. 1925) is a Connecticut-based guitarist with loads of chops, plenty of ideas, and an unfailing sense of swing. The Bee Hive sessions are preferred for their superior bands, which include Joe Morello and Billy Taylor on *Juicy Lucy* and Nick Brignola on *Starfingers.* One track by Salvador's fine late-Fifties quintet with Sonny Stitt was made available in '83 on Columbia's *Newport Jazz Festival: Live* collection, the Salvador group more than holding its own in that all-star compendium. — F.G.

DAVID SANBORN
★ ★ ★ **As We Speak / War.**
★ ★ ★ **Beck & Sanborn / CTI**
★ ★ ★ **Heart to Heart / War.**
★ ★ ★ **Hideaway / War.**
★ ★ ★ **Promise Me the Moon / War.**
★ ★ ★ **Voyeur / War.**
On all six of these albums, oft-heard jazz-based studio altoist David Sanborn (b. 1945) tried very hard to make music that's both commercial and good. Mostly, he succeeds. The composing has hooks without being condescending, and Sanborn's blowing, rooted in the classic R&B tradition, is still enough his own to be original and incisive. — M.R.

SAHEB SARBIB
★ ★ ★ ★ **Aisha (with Multinational Big Band) / CJR**
★ ★ ★ **Quartet—Live on Tour / CJR**
★ ★ ★ ★ **Saheb Sarbib and His Multi-national Big Band Live at the Public Theater / CJR**
★ ★ ★ **Seasons / Soul N.**
New York bassist Saheb Sarbib (b. 1944) has been leading both small groups and his own Multinational Big Band for several years.

Seasons is a quartet date featuring West Coast reedman Mel Ellison and New York alto saxophonist Mark Whitecage in the front line, with drummer Paul Motian as Sarbib's partner in the rhythm section. The leader also doubles on piano on one track.

A strong group, and Sarbib has skillfully given them the proper compositions to showcase their skills, with Whitecage particularly impressive. *Seasons* is something of a poor man's *Conference of the Birds,* but quite capable of being taken on its own merits. Check out the big band for stronger stuff. — F.G.

CLIFF SARDE
★ ★ **Every Bit Better / MCA**
Tenor/alto/soprano saxophonist Cliff Sarde solos energetically over a slick, straitjacket studio funk backing, covering pop tunes like "Shotgun" and "Can't Find My Way Home." — J.S.

DAVE SCHNITTER
★ ★ ★ **Glowing / Muse**
★ ★ ★ **Goliath / Muse**
★ ★ ★ **Invitation / Muse**
★ ★ ★ **Thundering / Muse**
Dave Schnitter (b. 1948) is an accomplished if almost completely derivative tenor player of the Rollins school. His albums are all well made and he sounds good, but there's little here you haven't heard before. He takes the most chances on *Glowing,* and if you've only heard Schnitter in Art Blakey's late-Seventies Jazz Messengers, you'd be advised to listen here instead. — F.G.

GUNTHER SCHULLER
★ ★ **Country Dance / Col.**
★ ★ **Happy Feet: A Tribute to Paul Whiteman / Gold. C.**
★ ★ ★ ★ ★ **Jazz Abstractions / Atl.**
★ ★ **Road from Rags to Jazz / Gold. C.**

Besides his credits as a classical composer and conservatory president, Gunther Schuller (b. 1925) has been actively involved at both ends of jazz's historical spectrum. Projects such as *Road from Rags to Jazz, Happy Feet: A Tribute to Paul Whiteman* and *Country Dance* re-create earlier musical forms with scholarly rigor. Much more important is *Jazz Abstractions,* from 1960, perhaps the best example of the melding of jazz and classical composition that Schuller dubbed Third Stream music. The writing here, by Schuller and Jim Hall, is vibrant and challenging, particularly on the title piece and "Variations on a Theme by Thelonious Monk." Featured soloists Ornette Coleman, Eric Dolphy, Bill Evans, Scott LaFaro and Hall add immeasurably to the successful hybrid.

★ ★ ★ ★ **Symphony in Black (with the Smithsonian Repertory Jazz Ensemble) / Smithsonian**

Schuller's most recent jazz recording project stems from a 1980 Smithsonian concert in which an ensemble performed Schuller's transcription of Ellington music from film scores and other out-of-the-way sources. Along with coproducer Martin Williams, Schuller helped compile the Smithsonian's excellent six-record anthology, *Big Band Jazz.* These albums can be obtained by writing to Smithsonian Recordings, P.O. Box 10230, Des Moines, Iowa 50336. — B.B.

JOHN SCOFIELD
★ ★ ★ ★ **Electric Outlet / Gram.**
★ ★ ★ **Out like a Light / Enja**
★ ★ ★ **Shinola / Enja**

Of all the fusion guitarists to emerge in the Seventies and Eighties, John Scofield (b. 1951) seems the least tied to a trend. The buttery R&B, anonymous disco and technique-dominated heavy-metal fusion styles are noticeably absent from his approach, which is more in the Sixties "soul jazz" tradition of Wes Montgomery and Grant Green. Miles Davis chose Scofield for his Eighties band that recorded *Decoy.*

Shinola showcases Scofield's growing, rhythmic style in a trio setting with bassist Steve Swallow and drummer Adam Nussbaum. The '84 *Electric Outlet* set is a slick and hard-edged outing with Dave Sanborn on alto sax, Ray Anderson on trombone, Steve Jordan on drums and Peter Levin on synthesizer. — J.S.

TOM SCOTT
★ **Apple Juice / Col.**
★ **Best of / Col.**
★ **Blow It Out / Ode**
★ **Desire / Elek./Mus.**
★ **Great Scott! / A&M**
★ **Intimate Stranger / Col.**
★ **In L.A. / Fly. D.**
★ **New York Connection / Col.**
★ **Rural Still Life / MCA**
★ **Street Beat / Col.**
★ **Target / Atl.**
★ **Tom Cat / A&M**

Pop-jazz saxophonist Tom Scott (b. 1948) prefers playing lightweight money-making fusion and covering popular rock material to following his initial interests as an interpreter of the work of Charlie Parker and Oliver Nelson. He achieved fame when his band, the L.A. Express, backed up Joni Mitchell on several albums and recorded "Jazzman" with Carole King. Scott's done a lot of work since then in Hollywood backing rock stars and working on soundtracks. He will probably never live down his 1982 decision to work as Olivia Newton-John's musical director and flout the musicians' boycott of South Africa by playing ten days at South Africa's Sun City resort. — J.S.

DON SEBESKY
★ ★ **Giant Box / CTI**
★ **Rape of El Morro / CTI**
★ ★ ★ **Three Works for Jazz Soloists and Symphony Orchestra / Gry.**

As house arranger for CTI, Don Sebesky (b. 1937) is either the hero or villain of the slick, stylized Seventies jazz formularized by that label, depending on how you look at it. From this vantage point it looks pretty bad. His more recent *Three Works for Jazz Soloists and Symphony Orchestra* is a step in the right direction, at least. — J.S.

SHADOWFAX
★ ★ ★ **The Dreams of Children / Wind.**
★ ★ ★ **Shadowdance / Wind.**
★ ★ ★ **Shadowfax / Wind.**

This California-based sextet plays an eclectic amalgam of international styles they call "world music." With a nod to Oregon and more than a little inspiration from Shakti the group offers up a listenable pastiche highlighted by the interplay of guitarist G. E. Stinson and violinist Jamil Szmadzinski. — J.S.

SHAKTI
★ ★ ★ **Handful of Beauty / Col.**
★ ★ ★ **Natural Elements / Col.**
★ ★ ★ **Shakti (with John McLaughlin) / Col.**

After the electronic-blitz period of the Mahavishnu Orchestra died down, John McLaughlin gravitated to a collaboration with some of India's most gifted musicians during the latter half of the Seventies. His acoustic style, first evinced on *My Goals Beyond,* was already highly evolved before he further refined it for Shakti. Working with L. Shankar on violin and Zakir Hussain on tabla, McLaughlin uses an acoustic instrument redesigned to fit the needs of this music. The fretboard has been hollowed out like a sitar so that McLaughlin can bend notes and add vibrato in the Indian fashion, and the guitar has sympathetic strings across the soundboard.

Shakti, recorded live at Southampton College, introduces the group to an enthusiastic audience, and the long, ragalike compositions, both highly charged and softly reflective, serve as a contextual framework for McLaughlin, Shankar and Hussain to build their dizzying improvisations. One of the most heartfelt and intelligent syntheses of Eastern and Western music in many years.
— J.C.C.

L. SHANKAR
★ ★ ★ **Touch Me There / Zappa**
★ ★ ★ ★ **Who's To Know / ECM/War.**
Indian violinist L. Shankar (b. 1950) had made a number of recordings of Indian classical music before coming to the attention of Western listeners through his extraordinary work in Shakti, which he coled with John McLaughlin (b. 1942). After Shakti Shankar worked briefly with Frank Zappa, who produced *Touch Me There. Who's To Know* is closer in spirit to the Shakti material.
— J.S.

ARTIE SHAW
★ ★ ★ ★ **The Complete Artie Shaw, Vol. 1 / Blueb.**
★ ★ ★ **The Complete Artie Shaw, Vol. 3 / Blueb.**
★ ★ ★ **The Complete Artie Shaw, Vol. 4 / Blueb.**
★ ★ ★ ★ **The Complete Artie Shaw, Vol. 5 / Blueb.**
★ ★ ★ ★ **The Complete Artie Shaw, Vol. 6 / Blueb.**
★ ★ ★ ★ **The Complete Artie Shaw, Vol. 7 / Blueb.**
★ ★ ★ **This Is Artie Shaw / RCA**
★ ★ ★ **This Is Artie Shaw, Vol. 2 / RCA**
Clarinetist Artie Shaw (b. 1910) led one of the most innovative *and* popular big bands of the Thirties and Forties, but the two elements were constantly at war with each other in his music. He introduced the idea of using a string section in big-band swing in 1935, but when he began recording for Bluebird in 1938 he was using standard instrumentation. The success of that band's '38 recording of "Begin the Beguine" made Shaw an international star and a popular rival of Benny Goodman.

Volume I of the *Complete Artie Shaw* documents the recordings of Shaw's acclaimed 1938–39 organization. Tenor saxophonists Tony Pastor and George Auld, who were both aware of Lester Young's style, play beautifully, and sultry-voiced Helen Forrest does all the singing except for one exquisite Billie Holiday appearance on "Any Old Time." Shaw himself was the principal soloist and he played the clarinet with a soulful dedication that still sounds inspired. The precocious young drummer Buddy Rich joined up for the last ten tracks on the record. This group is also on the 1939 sides included on Volume 2.

At the end of 1939 Shaw made a celebrated and dramatic "retirement" at the height of his popularity, disbanded his group and went to Mexico. He returned to recording in 1940 with a ponderous band that played heavy-handed, orchestral-sounding pieces. One of them, "Frenesi," became a huge hit. This period is documented on the third volume of *Complete,* which has its moments but, like Volume 4, suffers from Shaw's smothering conception.

The quality of the music on Volume 5 (1941–42) is dramatically improved by the addition of such luminaries as trumpeters Henry "Red" Allen and Hot Lips Page, alto saxophonist Benny Carter, trombonist J. C. Higginbotham and drummer Dave Tough. The strings are still there, but the band isn't intimidated by them—the way Hot Lips Page cuts an Armstrong-inspired trumpet solo through the strings on "Blues in the Night" has to be heard to be believed.

Volume 6 spans 1942 through 1945 in an uneven but often spectacular fashion, including wonderful playing from Roy Eldridge on trumpet and Barney Kessel on guitar in both large group and quintet settings. The seventh volume is a retrospective beginning in 1939, but concentrates on 1945 sides with a few earlier tracks included. The RCA *This Is Artie Shaw* collections are not really the best way to hear his music since Shaw's most popular material was not necessarily his best.
— J.S.

WOODY SHAW
★ ★ ★ ★ **Blackstone Legacy / Contem.**
★ ★ ★ **Love Dance / Muse**
★ ★ ★ ★ **The Moontrane / Muse**
★ ★ ★ **Song of Songs / Contem.**
★ ★ ★ **The Woody Shaw Concert Ensemble at the Berliner Jazztage / Muse**

Trumpeter Woody Shaw (b. 1944) is the ideal leader for contemporary blowing sessions: he has good chops, can play outside without excess and inside without triviality, and he writes interesting tunes. The sessions made under his name vary according to the visiting roster.

Blackstone Legacy is a 1970 double album with Gary Bartz, Bennie Maupin, George Cables, Ron Carter, Clint Houston and Lenny White. Compositions by Shaw and Cables. The personnel tells the story.

Song of Songs (1972) features the same setup but some less interesting players on reeds (Emanuel Boyd, Ramon Morris) and drums (Woodrow Theus II). With so much solo room, the soloists make the difference.

The Moontrane is back on the track. Good young players like Azar Lawrence, Steve Turre, Onaje Allen Gumbs and Victor Lewis, plus master bassists Buster Williams and Cecil McBee. Good variety from track to track, with four of the musicians contributing pieces. A 1974 date.

The following year's *Love Dance* is off the mark slightly. There isn't enough room for the interesting soloists (Rene McLean, Billy Harper, McBee), while the below-par piano of Joe Bonner is heard on each track. Again there are several players and friends contributing tunes.

The Woody Shaw Concert Ensemble at the Berliner Jazztage takes the same approach with the quintet Shaw and drummer Louis Hayes colead swollen to septet size. An often bristling band, though below the level of Shaw's *Blackstone* and *Moontrane* groups.

★ ★ ★ **Best of Woody Shaw** / Col.
★ ★ ★ **For Sure** / Col.
★ ★ ★ ★ ★ **The Iron Men** / Muse
★ ★ ★ ★ **Little Red's Fantasy** / Muse
★ ★ ★ **Lotus Flower** / Enja
★ ★ ★ **Master of the Art** / Elek./Mus.
★ ★ ★ **United** / Col.
★ ★ ★ ★ **Woody III** / Col.

The Muse albums document Shaw's 1976–77 playing, with various guest stars mixed in with members of his combo from the period. *Iron Men,* perhaps Shaw's most satisfying pickup session, features Muhal Richard Abrams, Arthur Blythe and Anthony Braxton in music reflecting Shaw's apprentice years with the likes of Eric Dolphy, Andrew Hill and Jackie McLean.

In 1977 Shaw signed with Columbia, where his quintet (featuring Carter Jefferson on reeds, Onaje Allen Gumbs' piano and the consistently fiery young drummer Victor Lewis) quickly established itself among the most popular groups in the post-bop style.

For all the intense blowing on these albums, there is a certain anonymous quality to much of the soloing. By far the most impressive date is *Woody III,* with Shaw's three-part orchestral suite featured on one side. The *Best of* collection includes material from his first two Columbia albums (*Rosewood, Stepping Stones*), which have already been deleted. As a matter of fact, all of the Columbia albums are fast disappearing; check the cutout bins.

United features the realigned 1980 quintet, with trombonist Steve Turre as second horn, in a program reflective of such influences on Shaw as Clifford Brown, Miles Davis, and the Jazz Messenger heritage. Shaw's "trombone band" has continued working and recording into the Eighties and can be relied upon for a steady if not exceptional level of post-bop. Of the band's most recent work, *Lotus Flower* contains a lot of interesting original material, while *Master* benefits from the presence of guest artist Bobby Hutcherson. — B.B.

GEORGE SHEARING

★ ★ **Alone Together (with Marian McPartland)** / Conc. J.
★ ★ ★ **The Best of George Shearing** / Cap.
★ ★ **Black Satin** / Cap.
★ ★ ★ **Blues Alley Jazz** / Conc. J.
★ ★ ★ **An Evening with George Shearing and Mel Tormé** / Conc. J.
★ ★ **500 Miles High** / Pausa
★ ★ **George Shearing and Jim Hall—First Edition** / Conc. J.
★ ★ ★ **George Shearing and Stephane Grappelli—The Reunion** / Pausa
★ ★ **George Shearing and the Robert Farnon Orchestra—On Target** / Pausa
★ ★ **Getting in the Swing of Things** / Pausa
★ ★ **Light, Airy, and Swinging** / Pausa
★ ★ **On a Clear Day (with Brian Torff)** / Conc. J.
★ ★ ★ **The Shearing Touch** / Cap.
★ ★ **Swingin's Mutual** / Cap.

London-born pianist George Shearing (b. 1919) is a leading representative of the tradition of modern jazz piano that avoided the innovations associated with Powell, Tatum and Monk and the bop school they inspired. Shearing remained solidly within the swing manner and refined it in the direction of greater precision (sometimes pretentiously termed "Chopinesque"). He can be a bit rigid at times but then compensates, particularly on ballads, with a fine sense of tone and structure. Once past the Capitol catalogue, which goes up to the early Sixties, Shearing's most interesting pieces are on some of the duet sessions (especially with Grappelli and Tormé) and on the *Blues Alley Jazz* and *Getting in the Swing of Things* albums. The *Best of* compilation and *The Shearing Touch* are slightly preferable among the older LPs. — B.T.

ARCHIE SHEPP

★ ★ ★ ★ **Fire Music** / Imp.
★ ★ ★ ★ ★ **Four for Trane** / Imp.
★ ★ ★ **Kwanza** / Imp.
★ ★ ★ **The Magic of Ju-Ju** / Imp.
★ ★ ★ ★ ★ **Mama Too Tight** / Imp.
★ ★ ★ ★ **On This Night** / Imp.
★ ★ ★ **The Way Ahead** / Imp.

After being featured with Cecil Taylor in 1960 and John Coltrane in 1965, tenor saxophonist Archie Shepp (b. 1937) became a leading figure in the New York new-music scene of the mid-Sixties. Often lost amidst the musical, political and racial controversy surrounding Shepp is his superb playing, a mix of asymmetrical melodies and exaggerated tones that encompass much of the tenor's past, and much romanticism, together with the obvious avant-garde fury. As a composer/arranger, Shepp has also displayed a knack for utilizing small and large ensembles creatively in a loose style that suggests the influence of Charles Mingus. In the Seventies, Shepp began featuring soprano sax and teaching at the University of Massachusetts, played occasional piano, recited his own poetry and wrote plays.

Impulse recorded Shepp throughout the Sixties, with the earlier recordings making the greatest impression. *Four for Trane* gave important early exposure to trombonist Roswell Rudd and alto player John Tchicai as well as Shepp in performances of Coltrane tunes that now sound harmonically loose but rhythmically quite straightforward; still, the spirit and interaction of the band is marvelous. *Fire Music* has more interesting structures ("Hambone," "Los Olvidados") and more good players (Ted Curson, Marion Brown), plus the first of many Shepp readings of an Ellington song. On *Mama Too Tight,* from 1967, Shepp borrows from James Brown on one track and offers more shifting ensemble writing: there is also a side-long quintet performance that captures Shepp's open-ended railing combo style of the time. *The Magic of Ju-Ju,* with a large percussion section, begins Shepp's conscious incorporation of African devices.

★ ★ ★ **Archie Shepp and Philly Joe Jones** / Fan.
★ ★ ★ **Attica Blues** / Imp.
★ ★ ★ **Black Gypsy** / Prest.
★ ★ ★ **Coral Rock** / Prest.
★ ★ ★ **Doodlin'** / Inner

At the start of the Seventies Shepp was recording extensively for a variety of European labels. While the albums are often most interesting for their glimpse of the next generation of innovators (Roscoe Mitchell, Anthony Braxton), there is also a turn toward bop and affiliations with older musicians like Philly Joe Jones. *Coral Rock* and *Doodlin'* feature Shepp the pianist. His 1972 orchestral effort for Impulse is often a hodgepodge of jazz soul, subadolescent vocalists and political narrative, although there are moments of true power and brief but sparkling saxophone solos by the leader.

★ ★ ★ **A Sea of Faces** / Black S.
★ ★ ★ **Montreux One** / Ari./Free.
★ ★ ★ **Montreux Two** / Ari./Free.
★ ★ ★ ★ **Steam** / Inner
★ ★ ★ **There's a Trumpet in My Soul** / Ari. /Free.

Late-Seventies Shepp proved disappointing. *There's a Trumpet* is among his most unimaginative large-group efforts, the Montreux volumes offer a bop program by a band whose primary strength is not in the bop genre, and the Black Saint has an excessive amount of vamp pieces. Only on *Stream,* where Shepp enjoys the bare-bones support of bassist Cameron Brown and longtime associate Beaver Harris on drums, did his virile imagination cut through undimmed.

★ ★ ★ ★ ★ **Goin' Home (with Horace Parlan)** / Steep.
★ ★ ★ **I Know about the Life** / Sack.
★ ★ ★ ★ ★ **Looking at Bird (with Niels-Henning Orsted Pedersen)** / Steep.
★ ★ ★ **Mama Rose (with Jasper Van't Hof)** / Steep.
★ ★ ★ **Three for a Quarter, One For a Dime** / Jasmine
★ ★ ★ ★ **Trouble In Mind (with Horace Parlan)** / Steep.

The last few years have seen Shepp concentrating on traditional forms (including the earliest points in the traditional continuum), usually in a duo context. His albums with pianist Parlan explore spirituals (*Goin' Home*) and country blues (*Trouble*), with the former set particularly heartfelt. *Looking at Bird,* with Danish bass whiz Pedersen, is an equally successful (though more uptempo) reflection on Charlie Parker. All of these albums find Shepp proving his mettle "in the tradition," on both soprano and tenor sax. *I Know,* his 1981 quartet, is a more rough-hewn view of Coltrane, Monk and Shepp's own title ballad. One of Shepp's more unusual efforts, *Mama Rose,* finds him in duets with Jasper Van't Hof's synthesizers, a mellower setting than the saxophonist usually provides for himself. Shepp's recitation of the title poem is the highlight of the album.

Important examples of early Shepp can be found on *New Music: Second Wave* (Savoy). A number of the Impulse recordings have also begun to reappear as imports on the British Jasmine label. Among these are *Three for a Quarter,* an extended exercise in free blowing, and *On This Night.* — B.B.

BOBBY SHORT
Moments Like This / Elek.
Bobby Short (b. 1926) is a stylish piano-bar singer known mostly to habitués of upper-Manhattan's more exclusive watering holes. His latest (1982) LP is just too cozily arranged and the singing dull. Perhaps you just have to be there. — B.T.

WAYNE SHORTER
★ ★ ★ ★ **Adam's Apple / Blue N.**
★ ★ ★ ★ ★ **The All-Seeing Eye / Blue N.**
★ ★ ★ ★ **Juju / Blue N.**
★ ★ ★ ★ ★ **Native Dancer / Col.**
★ ★ ★ ★ **Night Dreamer / Blue N.**
★ ★ ★ ★ **Schizophrenia / Blue N.**
★ ★ ★ **Shorter Moments / Trip (same as Wayne Shorter / GNP)**
★ ★ ★ ★ ★ **Speak No Evil / Blue N.**
★ ★ ★ ★ ★ **Super Nova / Blue N.**
Wayne Shorter (b. 1933) is the most self-effacing great musician of the past twenty-five years. This stunning composer and saxophonist (first tenor, with soprano added in 1968) spent long stints as a sideman (with Art Blakey's Jazz Messengers, 1959–64, and Miles Davis, 1964–69) before forming the co-operative band Weather Report with Joe Zawinul and Miroslav Vitous (who was eventually replaced by Jaco Pastorius) in 1970. Albums under his own name are few and generally fine.

Shorter Moments, from the beginning of his Blakey tenure, features other good young players (Lee Morgan, Freddie Hubbard, Wynton Kelly, Paul Chambers) and nine Shorter originals, but is not up to his Jazz Messenger albums of the period. *Night Dreamer,* done four years later, gives a better picture of Shorter's personality; audible influences include the Blakey band (trumpeter Morgan is again present) and John Coltrane (in the McCoy Tyner/Reggie Workman/Elvin Jones rhythm section as much as in the tenor solos, which also show the effects of Sonny Rollins), as well as an airy, spacious feeling to the writing that is very much Shorter's own.

Juju, with the same rhythm section (all three had played together behind Coltrane) and no trumpet, almost seems like an attempt at minimalist Coltrane; even such scorchers as the title piece and "Yes or No" are marked by Shorter's characteristic economy. This leaner feeling is heightened in the excellent *Speak No Evil,* even with the presence of Hubbard's trumpet, by Miles Davis quintet colleagues Herbie Hancock and Ron Carter. Some of Shorter's finest writing is included—the ominous "Witch Hunt" and yearning "Infant Eyes" being most memorable.

While *The All-Seeing Eye,* an energy-laden septet session, hinted that Shorter was about to burst through to untempered avant-garde territory, the following *Adam's Apple* and *Schizophrenia* retreat to more tempered performances. On all three albums, Hancock and drummer Joe Chambers contribute greatly to Shorter's direct and meticulously conceived music. By 1968, when *Schizophrenia* was made, Shorter had developed a sensitivity on tenor that could only be matched by Stan Getz, one of his staunchest admirers.

The release of the 1969 *Super Nova,* which followed hard on the heels of Miles Davis' *In a Silent Way* and *Bitches Brew* (both feature Shorter), heralded the jazz-rock era. To this writer's taste, *Super Nova* is the most interesting album of the three, the one with the most complex horn soloing (Shorter plays soprano sax throughout) and energetic accompaniment (including John McLaughlin and Sonny Sharrock's guitars, bassist Miroslav Vitous, Airto Moreira's percussion, and Jack DeJohnette and Chick Corea (!) on drums). Two Blue Note albums from the period in a similar vein, *Moto Grosso Feio* and *Odyssey of Iska,* are unfortunately out of print but also highly recommended.

Nothing came under Shorter's name until 1975 and *Native Dancer,* which is one of the classic recordings of the decade. This perfect meeting of America and Brazil is jointly formed by Shorter and singer/guitarist Milton Nascimento, who performs on five of his own tunes. Among numerous highlights are "Tarde," where Shorter's tenor solo reaches a depth of feeling akin to Miles Davis at his most intense; "Beauty and the Beast," infectious acoustic funk; "From the Lonely Afternoons," a wordless tour de force for Nascimento (and Shorter's latest reflections on Coltrane); and the absolutely exquisite Shorter composition "Diana."
★ ★ ★ ★ ★ **Etcetera / Blue N.**
★ ★ ★ **The Soothsayer / Blue N.**

Soothsayer sports an all-star sextet (Freddie Hubbard, James Spaulding, McCoy Tyner, Ron Carter, Tony Williams), and contains the only meeting of Tyner and Williams prior to Tyner's 1977 *Supertrios* (Milestone), but the results are not exceptional given the talent involved. *Etcetera* is another matter, a bristling quartet album with a Herbie Hancock/Cecil McBee/Joe Chambers rhythm section and Shorter in intense transition from his multinoted early approach to his more spare and elusive later work. One of the best samples of Shorter's playing.

Shorter has also continued to record with Weather Report and V.S.O.P. — B.B.

DAN SIEGEL
★ ★ **The Hot Shot / Inner**
★ ★ **Reflections / Pausa**
Spyro Gyra goes to the Pacific Northwest. Okay if you like that stuff, otherwise forget it. As a keyboardist, Dan Siegel is nondescript and inoffensive; as a composer he favors clichés. Far from wretched, but why bother? — F.G.

HORACE SILVER
★ ★ ★ ★ **Best of Horace Silver / Blue N.**
★ ★ ★ ★ ★ **Blowin' the Blues Away / Blue N.**
★ ★ ★ ★ **Cape Verdean Blues / Blue N.**
★ ★ ★ ★ **Doin' the Thing / Blue N.**
★ ★ ★ ★ ★ **Finger Poppin' / Blue N.**
★ ★ ★ ★ **Horace Silver / Blue N.**
★ ★ ★ ★ ★ **Horace Silver and the Jazz Messengers / Blue N.**
★ ★ ★ **In Pursuit of the 27th Man / Blue N.**
★ ★ ★ **Serenade to a Soul Sister / Blue N.**
★ ★ ★ **Silver 'n' Percussion / Blue N.**
★ ★ **Silver 'n' Voices / Blue N.**
★ ★ **Silver 'n' Wood / Blue N.**
★ ★ ★ **Silver's Blue / CSP**
★ ★ ★ **Silver's Serenade / Blue N.**
★ ★ ★ ★ **Song for My Father / Blue N.**
★ **That Healin' Feelin' / Blue N.**
★ ★ ★ ★ ★ **The Stylings of Silver / Blue N.**
★ ★ ★ ★ **The Trio Sides / Blue N.**
In the course of over a quarter-century with Blue Note (broken by a single Columbia Special Products album) pianist/composer Silver (b. 1928) defined a quintet style that was the model of hard bop and funk (or what used to be known in the late Fifties as funk), perfected that style in a band that featured Blue Mitchell on trumpet and Junior Cook on tenor sax, then stuck with it while adding various accouterments with less than satisfying results.

Start with *The Trio Sides,* half of which were made in 1952–53, for a sense of Silver's brittle, bluesy, energetically personal amalgamation of Bud Powell, Thelonious Monk and earlier blues stylists. Then comes *Silver and the Messengers* in 1954–55, a cooperative band with Kenny Dorham, trumpet; Hank Mobley, tenor; Silver; Doug Watkins, bass; and Art Blakey, drums. In a program comprised mainly of Silver originals (including the popular "Doodlin' " and "The Preacher") the Messengers hit upon the kind of bracing, punching modern style which Silver would carry with him when he left to form his own quintet in 1956.

Some of Silver's finest work from the next decade is either out of print or only available on sampler collections ("Senor Blues," for example, appears on *Best of,* while "Strollin' " and "Nica's Dream" are in the *Horace Silver* double album). Of four albums by early editions of his band, only one is currently in print—*Silver's Blue,* a lesser effort. Check the cutout bins for *Stylings of Silver,* a typically varied program with the excellent front line of Mobley and trumpeter Art Farmer.

Finger Poppin', Blowin' the Blues Away, Doin' the Thing and *Silver's Serenade* are by the peerless 1959–63 quintet. Blue Mitchell and Junior Cook, though less famous than earlier Silver sidemen, shared a sense of lyrical economy perfectly suited to the often challenging compositions, bassist Gene Taylor was the soul of reliability, and drummer Louis Hayes (on the first two albums) never played with more taste (his replacement, Roy Brooks, is more of a basher). Silver was turning out memorable melodies that the ensemble delivered with audible joy, striking a spirit akin (as critic Martin Williams noted) to a later and smaller Basie band.

Of the four albums, *Finger Poppin'* and *Blowin' the Blues Away* are best; the latter has the rousing title tune and "Sister Sadie." *Doin' the Thing* was recorded at New York's Village Gate, and the title track on *Silver's Serenade* is perhaps Horace's most beautiful composition.

Mid-Sixties Silver quintets are heard on *Song for My Father, Cape Verdean Blues* (with J. J. Johnson making the band a sextet on some tracks) and *Serenade to a Soul Sister.* While the playing is generally good, and Silver had his biggest success with *Song for My Father,* the bands are not as tight and the writing begins to sound routine (Silver is also less successful with modal structures than the more boppish, heavily harmonic style of his earlier work). *Soul Sister* introduces electric piano to no particular effect, and features the horns of Stanley Turrentine and Charles Tolliver.

In 1970 Silver embarked on "The United States of Mind," a preachy, trendy series of vocal slogans; of three cloying albums that resulted from the project, only *That Healin' Feelin'* can sometimes be still found in remainder bins—but don't bother. *In Pursuit of the 27th Man* put Silver back in the instrumental business (with good help from the Brecker Brothers and vibist Dave Friedman); then another series began, the *Silver 'n'* sessions where his quintet is surrounded by various supporting ensembles (*Silver 'n' Brass,* the first and perhaps best in the series, has long been deleted). The writing is good if familiar, with nice arranging touches except where voices are heard, and in trumpeter Tom Harrell, Silver has a soloist in the true spirit of his music.

★ ★ ★ ★ **Guides to Growing Up** / Silveto
★ ★ ★ ★ **Silver 'n' Strings Play Music of the Spheres** / Blue N.
★ ★ ★ ★ ★ **Spiritualizing the Senses** / Silveto
★ ★ ★ **Sterling Silver** / U.A.

Sterling is for Silver completists—a collection of alternate takes and shortened versions made for 45-rpm release, all recorded between 1956 and '63 and previously unavailable in album format. *Silver 'n' Strings,* a double album, was Silver's swan song for Blue Note, a surprisingly solid set of 1978–79 compositions with the standard quintet augmented by strings and occasional voices. The Me Generation preaching is present, but can be ignored for the most part.

Silver launched his own Silveto label in the Eighties with two efforts featuring now typical but surprisingly innoffensive self-help themes. The latter album, *Spiritualizing the Senses,* with no vocals, gets the nod over *Guides to Growing Up,* which features lyrics by the duo Feather and inspirational commentary by Bill Cosby; all the same, both albums feature Silver's strongest music in years, plus stellar contributions by tenor saxophonist Eddie Harris on both and trumpeter Bobby Shew on *Spiritualizing.* Take away the words and it's not that far from "Song for My Father" to such new pieces as "Exercising Taste and Good Judgment."

— B.B.

ZOOT SIMS

★ ★ ★ **And Bucky Pizzarelli** / Class.
★ ★ ★ ★ **Basie and Zoot (with Count Basie)** / Pablo
★ ★ ★ **Blues for Two (with Joe Pass)** / Pablo
★ ★ ★ ★ ★ **Body and Soul (with Al Cohn)** / Muse
★ ★ ★ **Gershwin Bros.** / Pablo
★ ★ ★ **Hawthorne Nights** / Pablo
★ ★ ★ ★ ★ **If I'm Lucky** / Pablo
★ ★ ★ **"The Innocent Years"** / Pablo
★ ★ ★ **I Wish I Were Twins** / Pablo
★ ★ ★ **Just Friends** / Pablo
★ ★ ★ **Motoring Along (with Al Cohn)** / Sonet
★ ★ ★ **Otra Vez** / Main.
★ ★ ★ **Party** / Choice
★ ★ ★ ★ **Passion Flower** / Pablo T.
★ ★ ★ ★ **Plays Soprano Sax** / Pablo
★ ★ ★ ★ **Suddenly It's Spring** / Pablo
★ ★ ★ ★ **The Swinger** / Pablo
★ ★ ★ **You 'n Me (with Al Cohn)** / Em.
★ ★ ★ ★ ★ **Warm Tenor** / Pablo
★ ★ ★ **Zootcase** / Prest.

Zoot Sims (b. 1925) is the consummate swing-bop tenorist. His playing is a marvelous combination of restraint and virility; the emotional depth of his ballads is matched only by the intensity of his uptempo blowing.

One of the original Four Brothers in the Forties Woody Herman band, Sims' infatuation with Lester Young is evident throughout his Fifties sessions as a leader. *Zootcase,* a double-album reissue of this period, has appearances by Art Blakey, John Lewis and Sims' tenor cohort Al Cohn.

Sims' playing reached a new maturity in the Sixties; his tone deepens and his delivery takes on a profundity that had been formerly lacking. From this period, although it's no longer in Schwann, try to find *Otra Vez,* a bossa-nova date with both Jim Hall and Jim Raney on guitars.

The Seventies saw a 360-degree turn in Sims' public exposure. Norman Granz began exploiting him the way he had Oscar Peterson, glutting the market with new Pablo releases every few months. None of these albums are bad—Sims is too fine a musician—but their personnel will definetely determine their overall quality. When Sims gets to record with two men he often gigs with, pianist Jimmy Rowles and bassist George Mraz, the results are always exceptional. *Warm Tenor* and *If I'm Lucky* are filled with glorious moments from everyone involved, and even Sims outdoes himself here.

Other Pablo standouts are *Soprano,* a consistently swinging set that proves Sims is also a master of the straight horn; *Hawthorne Nights,* sporting an enlarged group; *Passion Flower,* an Ellington tribute with arrangements by Benny Carter and the inspired small-group meeting with Basie. All other Pablos depend on one's personal taste

regarding the surrounding musicians.
— S.F.

CAROL SLOANE
★ ★ ★ **Carol Sings / Prog.**
★ ★ ★ **Cottontail / Choice**
What a fine singer. Carol Sloane's musicianship and ability to project emotion exist together in sheer harmony. Her sidepersons are virtually beyond reproach, her repertoire is expansive—and she swings.

Cottontail, although not very well engineered, wears better than *Carol Sings* due to its more upbeat feeling and less esoteric material. On both dates, however, the performances flow warmly. Jimmy Rowles is a special presence on *Carol Sings,* Norris Turney wails on *Cottontail,* while George Mraz grooves on both sessions. — A.R.

BESSIE SMITH
★ ★ ★ ★ ★ **Any Woman's Blues / Col.**
★ ★ ★ ★ ★ **The Empress / Col.**
★ ★ ★ ★ ★ **Empty Bed Blues / Col.**
★ ★ ★ ★ ★ **Nobody's Blues but Mine / Col.**
★ ★ ★ ★ ★ **The World's Greatest Blues Singer / Col.**
These records are the crown jewels of Columbia's ambitious jazz repackaging program, the John Hammond collection. Five double sets cover virtually the entire recorded history of one of the greatest, most influential musicians of the twentieth century. Bessie Smith's impact is so widespread it's almost impossible to gauge. She turned the blues into a modern jazz form, outdistancing most of her accompanists with her uncanny sense of phrasing and clear, powerful tone. The young Louis Armstrong played with Smith and was undoubtedly affected. Billie Holiday brought Smith's style into a jazz vocal context and passed it on to all those who in turn followed her, while Smith's impact on straight blues comes down through Mahalia Jackson and Big Mama Thornton.

World's Greatest covers Smith's first and last sessions, in 1923 and 1933. The first recordings were extremely crude, but the 1933 set, produced by Hammond, combines Smith with a fine band composed of trumpeter Frankie Newton, trombonist Jack Teagarden, Benny Goodman on clarinet, tenor saxophonist Chu Berry, Buck Washington on piano, Bobby Johnson on guitar and Billy Taylor on bass.

The other records present Smith in a variety of contexts, often accompanied by the solo piano of James P. Johnson. Some of the collections' best moments, however, are the exchanges between Smith and Louis Armstrong, the only musician at the time who could nearly match Smith's uncanny ability to bend notes and completely personalize even the most trite material. The version of W. C. Handy's "St. Louis Blues," done in 1925, is an amazing recording. — J.S.

JIMMY SMITH
★ ★ ★ **Cool Blues / Blue N.**
★ ★ ★ **Greatest Hits / Blue N.**
★ ★ ★ **Keep On Comin' / Elek./Mus.**
★ ★ ★ **Midnight Special / Blue N.**
★ ★ ★ **Off the Top / Elek./Mus.**
★ ★ ★ **Organ Grinder Swing / Verve**
The master of the Hammond B-3 organ sound in jazz, keyboardist Jimmy Smith (b. 1925) exploded on the New York scene in the late Fifties. His soaring, hard-driving organ playing in a freewheeling trio format revolutionized that instrument's position in jazz. During the Fifties and Sixties he recorded scores of albums for Blue Note, most of which are unavailable but can occasionally be found in cutout bins. Some titles have started to appear in the Japanese facsimile Blue Note issues. *Midnight Special,* comparatively easy to find, is a good example of Smith's hardest-driving mid-Sixties form.

Smith is still working in the Eighties *Off the Top* is a live recording with Smith playing organ and synthesizer in an all-star lineup that includes guitarist George Benson, bassist Ron Carter, drummer Grady Tate and tenor saxophonist Stanley Turrentine. *Keep On Comin',* from '83, is a quartet date with guitarist Kenny Burrell, saxophonist Johnny Griffin and drummer Mike Baker. — J.S.

LEO SMITH
★ ★ ★ ★ **Divine Love / ECM/War.**
★ ★ ★ ★ **Go in Numbers / Black S.**
★ ★ ★ ★ **Mass on the World / Moers**
★ ★ ★ ★ **Rastafari / Sack.**
★ ★ ★ ★ **Spirit Catcher / Nessa**
★ ★ ★ ★ **Touch the Earth / FMP**
Trumpeter Leo Smith (b. 1941) has a startlingly original conception that expands on experiments made over the last fifteen years by Miles Davis and Lester Bowie. Using a personally devised notation system he calls "ahkreanvention," Smith tries to combine elements of composed music and improvisation simultaneously. One of his most impressive achievements in this style is *Divine Love,* recorded in 1978 and featuring the remarkable track "Tastalun," an ahkreanvention for three muted trumpets with Lester Bowie and Kenny Wheeler joining Smith. *Mass on the World* is a live 1978 set, *Spirit Catcher* a 1979 quintet recording (except for "Burning

of Stones" which also features a second
trumpet and strings), while *Go in Numbers*
is a 1980 live performance from The
Kitchen. His 1983 outing for Sackville,
Rastafari, proves to be a good drummerless
session.

Smith has also recorded several albums for
Kabell records, P. O. Box 102, New Haven,
Connecticut 06510, including the '71 solo
set, *Creative Music 1*; a '74 trio recording,
Reflectativity, with pianist Anthony Davis
and bassist Wes Brown; and a 1977 LP,
Kanto Pri Homaro (Song of Humanity), with
reedman Oliver Lake, Davis, Brown and
drummer Paul Maddox. All of these albums
are worth hearing. — J.S.

LONNIE LISTON SMITH AND THE COSMIC ECHOES
★ ★ ★ **Astral Traveling / Fly. D.**
★ ★ **Best of / Col.**
★ ★ **Best of / RCA**
★ ★ **Cosmic Funk / Fly D.**
★ ★ **Exotic Mysteries / Col.**
★ ★ **Expansions / Fly D.**
★ ★ **Love Is the Answer / Col.**
★ ★ ★ ★ **Reflections of a Golden Dream / Fly D.**
★ ★ ★ **Renaissance / RCA**
★ ★ ★ **Silhouettes / Doctor J.**
★ ★ **Song for the Children / Col.**
★ ★ ★ **Visions of a New World / Fly D.**
On his first LP, *Astral Traveling,* Lonnie
Liston Smith (b. 1940) made acoustic, chor-
dally limited, rhythmically ostinatoed, tex-
ture-laden music. But by Smith's fourth
record, he'd given his work a funkier background, through mild electrification and an
approach that owed more to R&B than to
Coltrane. *Cosmic Funk* and *Expansions*
evince this transition's growing pains, but
Smith's next three albums, culminating in
Renaissance, bring it to fruition. Currently,
the keyboardist has a unified, original approach to fusion. He writes tunes that rely
on the whimsical beauty of certain minor-
key chordal situations; beneath them chug
vaguely danceable beats. There's something
uniquely compelling about this juxtaposition,
and it's enhanced by Smith's brother Donald, who sings stylishly yet poignantly in a
cool, blissful near falsetto. Of all Smith's
output, though, the sadly out-of-print *Reflections of a Golden Dream* still remains his
high point. — M.R.

WILLIE "THE LION" SMITH
★ ★ ★ ★ **Harlem Piano (one side only) / Good T.**
★ ★ ★ ★ **The Original Fourteen Plus Two 1938–39 / Commo.**

One of the greatest of the Harlem stride pianists, The Lion (1897–1973) was a colorful
and popular figure in black New York during the Twenties and Thirties, perfecting his
straightforward, bouncy style at Harlem rent
parties.

Although somewhat less revered by jazz
historians than his two greatest party-circuit
rivals, Fats Waller and James P. Johnson,
Smith was consistently tagged by Duke Ellington as his greatest influence on piano.

The flip side of *Harlem Piano* features
Luckey Roberts. — F.G.

MARTIAL SOLAL
★ ★ ★ ★ **Bluesine / Soul N.**
★ ★ ★ **Four Keys (with Lee Konitz) / Pausa**
★ ★ ★ **On Homeground / Mile.**
★ ★ ★ ★ **Movability (with Niels-Henning Orsted Pedersen) / Pausa**
Algerian pianist Martial Solal (b. 1927) was
hailed as one of the greats by critics during
the early Sixties, but his low profile in this
country ensured his virtual anonymity
among record buyers. Although he can
adapt to earlier musical tradition—he is on
both Django Rheinhardt's final session and
Sidney Bechet's last great date (*When a Soprano Meets a Piano*)—Solal has a firm modernist perspective. Gifted with amazing technical dexterity and harmonic knowlege, Solal
is a highly cerebral player, which possibly
accounts for his occasional associations with
Lee Konitz (*Satori, Duo*). His scant U.S.
catalogue supplies a decent overview of this
stimulating and always challenging improviser. — S.F.

VICTORIA SPIVEY
★ **Blues Is Life / Folk.**
★ ★ **Queen and Her Nights / Spivey**
★ ★ **Recorded Legacy of the Blues / Spivey**
★ ★ **Victoria Spivey and Her Blues / Spivey**
★ **Victoria Spivey with the Easy Riders Jazz Band / GHB**
Spivey was a blues sex symbol of the Twen-
ties, but her records, even with the remark-
able guitarist Lonnie Johnson, were inconsis-
tent and mostly forgettable. The available
material is little more than historical nota-
tion. — J.S.

JEREMY STEIG
★ ★ **Energy / Cap.**
★ ★ **Firefly / CTI**
★ ★ **Monium / Col.**
★ ★ **Outlaws / Enja**
★ ★ **Temple of Birth / Col.**
★ ★ ★ **Wayfaring Stranger / Blue N.**
In the late Sixties Jeremy Steig (b. 1942)
formed one of the first jazz-rock outfits,

Jeremy and the Satyrs, and has gone on to make additional albums featuring his flute playing in Western and Eastern rhythmic contexts. *Outlaws* is a good set featuring bassist Eddie Gomez. — J.S.

SONNY STITT
★ ★ ★ Best / Prest.
★ ★ ★ Best for Lovers / Prest.
★ ★ ★ Blues for Duke / Muse
★ ★ ★ The Champ / Muse
★ ★ ★ ★ ★ Genesis / Prest.
★ ★ ★ In Style / Muse
★ ★ ★ ★ Kaleidoscope / Fan./OJC
★ ★ ★ The Last Session, Vol. 1 / Muse
★ ★ ★ The Last Session, Vol. 2 / Muse
★ ★ ★ Mellow / Muse
★ ★ ★ My Buddy / Muse
★ ★ ★ Night Letter / Prest.
★ ★ ★ 'Nuther Fu'thur / Prest.
★ ★ ★ Primitivo Soul / Prest.
★ ★ ★ Shangri-La / Prest.
★ ★ ★ Sonny's Back / Muse
★ ★ ★ Soul Electricity / Prest.
★ ★ Soul Girl / Paula
★ ★ ★ Soul People / Prest.
★ ★ ★ ★ Stitt's Bits, Vol. 1 / Prest.
★ ★ ★ ★ Stitt's Bits, Vol. 2 / Prest.
★ ★ ★ Turn It On / Prest.

Though alto/tenor saxophonist Sonny Stitt (1924–1982) was known as a disciple of Charlie Parker, it's reasonable to believe that Stitt had arrived at a proto-bop style similar to Parker's before he'd ever heard Bird play. The point is important because Stitt, though certainly overshadowed by Parker's genius, shouldn't be seen merely as an imitator of the great alto saxophonist. In fact, Stitt switched to tenor by the end of the Forties, perhaps to avoid comparisons with Parker, and went on to colead a historic two-tenor band with Gene Ammons during the early Fifties. He never completely stopped playing alto, however, and even dabbled in some baritone sax playing.

Stitt's superb Prestige recordings are the high point of his legacy. *Genesis* is a magnificent compilation sampling sides from '49 to '51 with Ammons, pianists John Lewis and Bud Powell, drummers Max Roach and Art Blakey and trombonist J. J. Johnson. The *Stitt's Bits* retrospective is fine material from the same era, as is *Kaleidoscope*—but there's enough duplication to make *Genesis* the one indispensable Stitt album.

During the Fifties Stitt played with the Jazz at the Philharmonic orchestras and with Dizzy Gillespie in addition to his own groups. During the Sixties he recorded organ combo albums, often featuring Jack McDuff, notable for their consistent if interchangeable

intensity. The other Prestige sets listed above date from the Sixties and show off that soulful style. The '65 *Soul People* session is notable for Stitt's interchange with the great saxophonist Booker Ervin. Stitt experimented quite a bit in the Sixties, often with unsatisfying results, as when he started to play the electric Varitone sax. The '73 *Soul Girl* pits Stitt against strings in an uncomfortable setting.

Stitt returned to form on the records for Muse he made toward the end of his life. *The Champ* is a listenable '74 quintet, as is *My Buddy,* a 1976 LP dedicated to the then recently deceased Gene Ammons. *Blues for Duke* is a '78 Ellington tribute with pianist Barry Harris, bassist Sam Jones and drummer Billy Higgins. *Sonny's Back,* from 1980, features second tenor Ricky Ford, Barry Harris, bassist George Duvivier and drummer Leroy Williams. *In Style* is a hot '82 quartet date with Harris, Duvivier and drummer Jimmy Cobb. Stitt died that same year and *The Last Session,* with Duvivier, Cobb, and Junior Mance on piano, was issued posthumously. — J.S.

CHARLES SULLIVAN
★ ★ ★ ★ Genesis / Inner
Fiery trumpeter leads a good band on a muscular date. Every track is a winner, with Charles Sullivan (b. 1944) proving himself an outstanding composer and small-group arranger. Featured soloists including altoman Sonny Fortune and pianists Stanley Cowell and Onaje Allen Gumbs put out some of their best work ever. — F.G.

MAXINE SULLIVAN
★ ★ ★ ★ ★ Close as Pages in a Book (with Bob Wilber) / Mon.-Ev.
★ ★ ★ ★ ★ Earl Hines and Maxine Sullivan / Chi.
★ ★ ★ ★ Maxine Sullivan and the Ike Isaacs Trio / Audiop.
★ ★ ★ Shakespeare and Hyman / Mon.-Ev.
★ ★ ★ We Just Couldn't Say Goodbye / Audiop.

Like Ivie Anderson, Helen Humes and Mildred Bailey before her, Maxine Sullivan (b. 1911) has never achieved much acceptance by the general public. This lack of recognition cannot be attributed to any lack of musical acumen, for her good taste and intelligence have kept Sullivan consistently true to her jazz muse.

Virtually all of Sullivan's extant recordings show her to be a model of phrasing, swing and feeling. Of those listed above, the collaborations with Earl "Fatha" Hines and Bob Wilber make the most long-lasting impression. The Shakespeare project is an interesting oddity; and other recordings, one with Wilber on Hoagy Carmichael songs (*The Music of Hoagy Carmichael,* Monmouth-Evergreen) and another with modernist Beaver Harris' 360 Degree Music Experience (*From Rag Time to No Time,* 360 Records), indicate both the breadth of her experience and the high regard in which she's held by her fellow musicians.   — A.R.

SUN RA
★ ★ ★ ★ **Sound of Joy** / Del.
★ ★ ★ ★ **Sun Song** / Del.
★ ★ ★ ★ **We Are in the Future** / Savoy
Most of the recorded work of composer/ arranger/multikeyboard artist Sun Ra (born Herman Blount in 1915 and nicknamed "Sonny") is currently only available on his own exclusive Saturn label; the two Delmark albums listed are from the 1956–57 period, when Sun Ra first organized the Arkestra that he continues to lead (with several original members, most notably tenor saxophonist John Gilmore) to this day. During this Chicago period Sun Ra had an intriguing boppish band that reflected such modern influences as Tadd Dameron and Charles Mingus as well as Sun Ra's former employer Fletcher Henderson; there are also a few visionary touches, particularly the leader's early use of electric keyboards.
★ ★ ★ **Cosmos** / Inner
★ ★ ★ **Pictures of Infinity** / Black L.
★ ★ ★ **Solo Piano, Vol. 1** / IAI
After leaving Chicago for New York and eventually Philadelphia, Sun Ra and his Arkestra defined the potential for free-jazz big bands, while retaining touches of bop and earlier influences and a comprehensive outer space cum black nationalism mythology. The Arkestra's masterpieces (*The Magic City; Heliocentric Worlds of Sun Ra, Volume 1; Nothing Is*) are officially out of print, so the uneven Black Lion set is the best indication of the Arkestra's breadth. *Cosmos* stresses their "inside" tendencies in a 1976 session from their European tour. The solo album, with Sun Ra exclusively on acoustic piano, is one of his warmest and most restrained performances.
★ ★ ★ ★ ★ **Heliocentric Worlds of Sun Ra, Vol. 1** / Base
★ ★ ★ ★ **Heliocentric Worlds of Sun Ra, Vol. 2** / Base
★ ★ ★ **Lanquidity** / Philly Jazz
★ ★ ★ ★ ★ **Live at Montreux** / Inner
★ ★ ★ ★ ★ **Nothing Is** / Base
★ ★ ★ ★ **The Other Side of the Sun** / Sweet Earth

★ ★ ★ **St. Louis Blues** / IAI
★ ★ ★ **Strange Celestial Road** / Roun.
★ ★ ★ ★ **Sunrise in Different Dimensions** / Hat Hut
In the Eighties, things have definitely improved on the Sun Ra front, with the great ESP albums available once again on Base as well as several more recent recordings. The first *Heliocentric* is a classic of free orchestral music, with instruments such as tympani and bass marimba playing central roles, while *Nothing Is* captures the live Sun Ra experience circa 1966 (particularly good John Gilmore here). From a decade later, the *Montreux* two-record set affords another stellar sampling of the Ra universe. *Sunrise,* again live, was made in 1980 and contains the definitive program of Sun Ra's reworked Fletcher Henderson, Ellington, Jelly Roll Morton, etc.

Both *Lanquidity* and *The Other Side of the Sun* provide samplers of Sun Ra's contemporary work, with the Sweet Earth album getting the nod for its updated version of "Space Is the Place."   — B.B.

HARVIE SWARTZ
★ ★ ★ ★ ★ **Old-Time Feeling (with Sheila Jordan)** / Palo Alto
★ ★ ★ ★ **Underneath It All** / Gram.
The brilliance of bassist Harvie Swartz (b. 1948) cannot be denied; his work with Sheila Jordan and his solo outing confirm this assertion. Swartz has lots of heart, a big warm sound, razor-sharp time and chops forevermore. Associations with Steve Kuhn, Double Image, Jim Hall, Sharon Freeman and Pat Metheney (among others), as well as with Jordan, demonstrate Swartz' sympathetic assistance to a highly idiosyncratic coterie of jazz musicians. Coupling his compositional skill (all of *Underneath It All* and the title tune, "I Miss That Old-Time Feeling") with his arranging acumen, one notes a well-rounded musician; in other words, Swartz emerges as a major player.   — A.R.

GABOR SZABO
★ ★ **The Drums** / Imp.
★ **Faces** / Mer.
★ ★ **Gabor Szabo: His Greatest Hits** / MCA
★ ★ **Mizrab** / CTI
★ **Nightflight** / Mer.
★ **Rambler** / CTI
★ ★ **Wind, Sky and Diamonds** / Imp.
Hungarian guitarist Gabor Szabo (1936–1982) emigrated to America in 1956. Studying at the Berklee College of Music and

playing with Chico Hamilton, he developed a thoughtful, supple style that reflected his background in Hungary. Playing with a variety of small groups, Szabo incorporated a ton of exotic musical influences (Middle Eastern, Indian, Oriental) to supplement his style.

But Szabo could also be described as an obsessive eclectic who never really defined his approach on the guitar. His albums are characteristically Sixties in that they experiment to the point of dilution. His tone is rather thin and some of his production ideas and instrumental collaborations are heart-stopping in their awkwardness. *His Greatest Hits* is the only possible selection here, and even that recommendation is offered with great trepidation. — J.C.C.

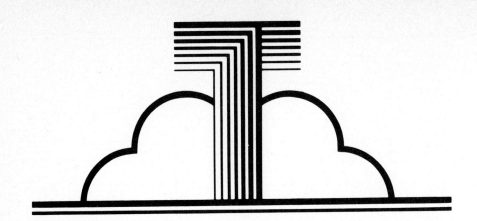

JAMAALADEEN TACUMA
★ ★ ★ ★ **Renaissance Man / Gram.**
★ ★ ★ ★ **Show Stopper / Gram.**
Bassist Jamaaladeen Tacuma (b. 1957) has
arrived at one of the most effective fusions of
new electric music on his dense, challenging
1983 debut, *Show Stopper*. The Philadelphia
native combines the heady pop funk of Sly
Stone, James Brown and Stevie Wonder with
a unique understanding of Ornette Coleman's "harmelodic" contemporary jazz conception. As part of Coleman's Prime Time
band Tacuma's playing rivaled Coleman for
center stage—he can be heard on the
groundbreaking *Dancing in Your Head, Body
Meta* and *Of Human Feelings*. He has also
played with James "Blood" Ulmer (*Tales of
Captain Black*), Walt Dickerson (*Serendip-
ity*), Kip Hanrahan, the Golden Palominos
and the Firespitters as well as leading Cos-
metic, his own band. *Show Stopper* features
one side with his own group Jamaal (Rick
Iannacone, guitar; Anthony McClary, drums;
Ron Howerton, percussion; James R. Watkins, alto saxophone and metal clarinet) and
one side with such luminaries as pianist Anthony Davis, Julius Hemphill on alto sax,
and James "Blood" Ulmer. *Renaissance Man*
uses the same Jamaal/guest star format for
consistent results.   — J.S.

HORACE TAPSCOTT
★ ★ ★ **At the Crossroads (with Everett
Brown, Jr.) / Nim.**
★ ★ ★ **The Call / Nim.**
★ ★ ★ **Flight 17 / Nim.**
★ ★ ★ **Live at I.U.C.C. / Nim.**
★ ★ ★ **Live at Lobero / Nim.**
Although he has never established himself as
a player of international repute, pianist Hor-
ace Tapscott (b. 1934) has exerted a major
influence on the Los Angeles jazz scene over
the years, serving as both teacher and musi-
cal guru. Among his protégés Tapscott can

number many of the finer young musicians
to come out of the area during the last fifteen years including Arthur Blythe, and his
Pan-African Peoples' Arkestra has served as
a finishing school for a lot of up-and-coming
players.
    Although the Arkestra does not have a
polished sound, the band's energy level is invariably high, and the music consistently
challenging. It can be heard on *Flight 17,
The Call* and *Live at I.U.C.C.* The other
two LPs feature Tapscott in duo and trio
dates, and demonstrate his ability to traverse
from delicate melodies to the most percussive effects.   — F.G.

ART TATUM
★ ★ ★ ★ ★ **Art Tatum / Cap.**
★ ★ ★ ★ ★ **God Is in the House / Onyx**
★ ★ ★ ★ ★ **Masterpieces / MCA**
★ ★ ★ ★ ★ **Masterpieces, Vol. 2 (plus James
P. Johnson) / MCA**
★ ★ ★ ★ **Piano Starts Here / Col.**
It is no exaggeration to label pianist Tatum
(1910–1956), who had only partial vision in
one eye, the greatest virtuoso ever to play
jazz on any instrument. Beyond his unbeliev-
able technique, Tatum had a supreme mastery of harmonic substitutions that inspired
the modernists who came to prominence in
the Forties.
    The ratings assigned to the above albums,
all made by Tatum in the Thirties and Forties, should be read as indicating the most
essential of his performances. Volume 1 of
Masterpieces is one of the essentials, covering
the Thirties and early Forties and featuring
Tatum solo, with his popular piano/guitar/
bass trio, and in a small band with the great
blues singer Joe Turner. Equally important is
the recently unearthed *God Is in the House*,
which contains privately made tapes of
Tatum jamming in 1941 Harlem clubs; the
closing tracks with trumpeter Frankie New-

ton achieve an amazing intensity. The Capitol album, perhaps the single best all-solo volume, is from the late Forties.

★ ★ ★ ★ **The Art Tatum Group
Masterpieces / Pablo (nine volumes)**
★ ★ ★ ★ **The Art Tatum Solo Masterpieces
/ Pablo (thirteen volumes)**

Between 1953 and the year of his death, producer Norman Granz involved Tatum in these two mammoth projects that have been reissued in boxed sets and singly (more solo albums are supposedly still to come). Perhaps five-star ratings should be awarded for sheer effort, but Tatum was never the most accommodating band player, and his solos reveal that he often hit upon a routine (compare earlier versions). Few listeners will want the entire solo box, and should choose individual volumes according to one's preference for the songs included in each. Among the nine combo records, the session with tenor saxophonist Ben Webster is a true masterpiece of heart-on-sleeve emoting, and trumpeter Roy Eldridge is in a jousting mood. Lionel Hampton, Benny Carter, Buddy Rich, Jo Jones and Buddy DeFranco also appear.

★ ★ ★ **The Genius / Jazz M.**
★ ★ ★ ★ **Get Happy / Jazz M.**
★ ★ ★ ★ ★ **Pieces of Eight / Smithsonian**
★ ★ ★ **Tatum-Hampton-Rich, Vol. 2 / Pablo**

The best of recent Tatum collections is *Pieces of Eight,* which surveys the pianist's career from 1939 to '55. All of the recordings are extremely rare; many were previously unissued or issued only in edited form. (It is available through mail order from Smithsonian Recordings, P. O. Box 10230, Des Moines, Iowa 50336.) Three tracks from *Pieces* also appear on *Get Happy,* a more extensive look at Tatum's solo work in 1938 and '39. Be leery, however, of *The Genius,* a repackaging of an earlier Black Lion LP. The album purports to contain solos from 1944 and 1945 but actually contains solos from '45 and '46 plus three 1946 solos by Frank Paparelli.

The entire thirteen-record *Solo Masterpieces* set is still available as single volumes from Pablo. The label also uncovered a second volume of 1955 trio performances with Lionel Hampton and Buddy Rich, which has been issued singly and also as the ninth record in the *Group Masterpieces* series.

— B.B.

BILLY TAYLOR

★ ★ ★ **Sleeping Bee / Pausa**
★ ★ ★ **Touch of Taylor / Prest.**
★ ★ ★ **Where've You Been / Conc. J.**

Pianist Billy Taylor (b. 1921) came up in the Forties playing with Ben Webster, Dizzy Gillespie, Stuff Smith, Slam Stewart and Don Redman, and formed his own quartet in 1949 which was converted into one of Artie Shaw's Gramercy Five lineups in '50. During the early Fifties Taylor was a fixture on the New York bop scene and a Birdland perennial. His tasteful, bop-derived style has continued to please listeners up to the present and his currently available records, from the late-Sixties *Sleeping Bee* to the 1980 *Where've You Been* set, provide quality listening. The urbane and well-spoken Taylor is also an effective promoter of jazz, having written several useful books and many perceptive critical articles on the subject.

— J.S.

CECIL TAYLOR

★ ★ ★ ★ **In Transition / Blue N.**
★ ★ ★ ★ **Looking Ahead! / Contem.**

Any understanding of post-Parker avant-garde jazz must be grounded in pianist/composer Cecil Taylor (b. 1933), the first player to successfully achieve a system of rhythmic energy, collectively shared by the others in his Units, which replaced the constant "time" (swing) common to all jazz through 1960.

In Transition, a double album, contains Taylor's first recordings (from 1956) with a quartet and a 1959 session for trio and quintet. Both dates suggest Monk in their percussiveness and angularity, though by the latter Taylor was giving clear indications of the rhythmic directions he would shortly pursue. "Carol/Three Points" is an early example of Taylor's declarative writing. *Looking Ahead!* is a 1958 quartet with a fine vibraphonist named Earl Griffith, and a particularly successful trio piece called "Of What."

(Other Taylor from this period, also highly recommended, is contained on the Verve anthology, *Masters of the Modern Piano,* which has Taylor's 1957 Newport performance, and half of the Impulse *Into the Hot,* three 1961 band tracks issued under Gil Evans' name.)

★ ★ ★ ★ **Cecil Taylor with the Jazz
Composer's Orchestra / JCOA**
★ ★ ★ ★ ★ **Conquistador / Blue N.**
★ ★ ★ ★ **The Great Concert of Cecil Taylor
/ Prest.**
★ ★ ★ ★ ★ **Nefertiti, the Beautiful One Has
Come / Ari./Free.**
★ ★ ★ ★ ★ **Unit Structures / Blue N.**

Nefertiti, made in a Copenhagen nightclub in 1962, is the breakthrough album, where the entire group feels Taylor's rhythmic passion for the first time. Jimmy Lyons on alto sax and Sunny Murray on drums complete the cataclysmic trio. Of the remaining Taylor recordings from the Sixties, *Unit Structures* is especially recommended for the variety of composition, the brilliant use Taylor makes of the septet (including three horns, two basses), and the inspired playing, especially from drummer Andrew Cyrille. *Conquistador,* by a sextet, is almost as good, though later performances fall into the trap of going on too long at one extreme dynamic level. The JCOA album is half of Michael Mantler's *Jazz Composer's Orchestra* box, available separately; here, an orchestra sets Taylor off on a railing solo. *Great Concert,* from Paris in 1969, is even more intense: three albums of high energy, with Lyons, Cyrille and Sam Rivers.

★ ★ ★ ★ **Dark to Themselves / Inner**
★ ★ ★ ★ **Indent / Ari./Free.**
★ ★ ★ ★ ★ **Silent Tongues / Ari./Free.**
★ ★ ★ ★ ★ **Spring of Two Blue-J's / Unit Core**

These albums, all from 1973 to 1976, are concert recordings, with the Arista/ Freedoms being solo recitals. *Two Blue-J's* is recommended as the best introduction to Taylor—one side solo, the other with Lyons, Cyrille and the Revolutionary Ensemble's marvelous bassist Sirone. *Silent Tongues,* from Montreux 1974, is Taylor's most sustained and diverse solo work on record. *Dark* is the most recent (1976) and features a new group, with Lyons (remaining from the old Unit) and three exciting additions (Raphe Malik, trumpet; David Ware, tenor; Marc Edwards, drums). Taylor's performances could still stand editing, but there is no denying their power or the technical and emotional skill of the players.

★ ★ ★ ★ **Air Above Mountains (Buildings Within) / Inner**
★ ★ ★ **Cecil Taylor / New W.**
★ ★ ★ **Embraced (with Mary Lou Williams) / Pablo**
★ ★ ★ ★ **It Is in the Brewing Luminous / Hat Hut**
★ ★ ★ **Live in the Black Forest / Pausa**
★ ★ ★ ★ **One Too Many Salty Swift and Not Goodbye / Hat Hut**
★ ★ ★ ★ ★ **3 Phasis / New W.**

The above titles were recorded between 1976 (the solo *Air Above*) and 1980 (*Brewing Luminous*), generally featuring various editions of the Unit. The best items are from 1978, when Lyons was joined in the front line by Raphe Malik (trumpet) and Ramsey Ameen (violin) and Sirone and Shannon Jackson

were in the rhythm section. *3 Phasis* is one of the essential Taylor albums, an hour-long composition with exceptional give-and-take between Taylor and the band and a climactic Lyons solo over Jackson's free-shuffle beat. *One Too Many* presents the same sextet in a three-record marathon taped in Stuttgart. *Brewing Luminous,* also live and not quite as long, reunites Taylor with two important early associates, Sunny Murray and bassist Alan Silva.

★ ★ ★ **Calling It the Eighth / Hat Hut**
★ ★ ★ ★ **Garden / Hat Hut**
★ ★ ★ ★ **The Gigi Gryce–Donald Byrd Jazz Laboratory and the Cecil Taylor Quartet at Newport / Verve**
★ ★ ★ ★ ★ **The World of Cecil Taylor / Jazz M.**

Taylor's most recent work is found on *Garden,* a digital double album of piano solos, and *Calling,* a typical quartet performance most notable for the presence of a new rhythm section (William Parker, bass, and Rashid Bakr, drums). Vintage Taylor has also become available again in reissue. The Verve album (with the Gryce-Byrd band on one side) is a Japanese facsimile import containing the performances available on the *Masters of the Modern Piano* anthology. *World of* is the classic Candid LP from 1960 that marked the recording debut of Archie Shepp. — B.B.

LILIAN TERRY

★ ★ ★ **Lilian Terry Meets Tommy Flanagan: A Dream Come True / Soul N.**

Lilian Terry is a proficient, warm-voiced singer who demonstrates good taste in her choice of repertoire and sidepersons. In this ballad set the jazz undercurrent comes from the typically elegant and incisive piano of Tommy Flanagan along with bassist Jesper Lundgaard and drummer Ed Thigpen.

— A.R.

TOOTS THIELEMANS

★ ★ ★ **Captured Live / Choice**

Toots Thielemans (b. 1922) has a harmonica sound institutionalized on sessions, soundtracks and numerous pop and jazz records. Personally expressive yet technically dazzling, his playing still manages to project a slick professionalism that made the sound of Thieleman's harmonica an essential element of many Quincy Jones productions. Despite his virtuosity, Thielemans is more effective as part of an arrangement than as the featured element, as *Captured Live* demonstrates. — J.S.

DON THOMPSON
★ ★ **A Beautiful Friendship** / Conc. J.
★ **Bells (with Rob Piltch)** / Umb.
★ **Country Place** / PM

Toronto bassist Don Thompson (b. 1940) is a valued accompanist to guitarists Don Bickert, Lenny Breau and Jim Hall. His own projects, however, find him playing stolid piano on his own mediocre tunes. Guitarist Rob Piltch's contributions to *Bells* are worth a listen, though, and on *Beautiful Friendship* Thompson is completely upstaged by John Abercrombie on guitar, Dave Holland on bass and Michael Smith on drums. — B.T.

LUCKY THOMPSON
★ ★ ★ ★ **Lullaby in Rhythm** / Bio.

A warm swing tenor, Lucky Thompson (b. 1924) effortlessly absorbed the changes brought by bebop. Thompson's catalogue has been decimated by time, and this LP is a reissue of a European date cut for Dawn Records in 1956. Fortunately, he remains front-and-center here, and his band features some of Europe's finest jazzmen, including pianist Martial Solal and bassist Pierre Michelot. That Thompson is so poorly represented on LPs these days is reason enough to hate the American record industry. — F.G.

CLIFFORD THORNTON
★ ★ ★ ★ **The Gardens of Harlem (with Jazz Composer's Orchestra)** / JCOA

At this point listeners will readily accept the strong link between jazz and the musics of Africa and the Caribbean. Recent recordings by the AACM and the New York Latin-jazz community have restated the case concisely. But this 1974 album by cornetist/composer/musicologist Clifford Thornton (b. 1936) still remains one of the more satisfying fusions of traditional Third World musics with the American jazz tradition.

Thornton's compositions get superb treatment here from the Jazz Composer's Orchestra, with especially fine solo work by Janice Robinson, Roland Alexander, Hannibal Marvin Peterson, Leo Smith, Dewey Redman and George Barrow.

Gardens of Harlem weaves together into one grand tapestry the many experimental directions being pursued on the New York scene during that period. — F.G.

HENRY THREADGILL
★ ★ ★ ★ ★ **Just the Facts and Pass the Bucket** / About T.
★ ★ ★ **When Was That?** / About T.

Henry Threadgill, the prime mover of Air, expanded his activities in 1982 with the creation of a seven-piece band that he insists upon calling his "sextet." The group has one of the most interesting instrumentations and strongest personnels of contemporary ensembles: trumpeter Olu Dara and trombonist Craig Harris flanking the leader's flutes and saxophones, a two-piece string section consisting of Airmate Fred Hopkins and (most recently) cellist Deidre Murray, and the tandem percussion of Pheeroan Aklaff and John Betsch. The sextet's debut, *When Was That?,* suffers from an excess of turgid tempos, despite the wild excitement of its title march. The follow-up, *Just the Facts,* has a far better balance of compositions and what amounts to Threadgill's death and resurrection suite on side two. A band to watch. — B.B.

STEVE TIBBETTS
★ ★ ★ **Bye Bye Safe Journey** / ECM/War.
★ ★ ★ **Northern Song** / ECM/War.

Guitarist Steve Tibbetts (b. 1954) is a self-taught virtuoso whose imaginative playing covers a wide stylistic range that seems more in the tradition of modal high energy saxophonists like John Coltrane than it does any guitarist's. Tibbetts came to public attention in the late Seventies via *Yr,* an exceptional homemade debut album. His 1981 *Northern Song* and the recent *Bye Bye,* though less impressive, still suggest the presence of considerable talent. — J.S.

BOBBY TIMMONS
★ ★ ★ **Little Barefoot Soul** / Prest.
★ ★ **Live at the Connecticut Jazz Party** / Chi.
★ ★ ★ ★ **Moanin'** / Mile.
★ ★ ★ **Soul Food** / Prest.
★ ★ ★ **Soulman** / Prest.
★ ★ ★ ★ **This Here Is Bobby Timmons** / Prest. OJC
★ ★ ★ **Workin' Out** / Prest.

Pianist Bobby Timmons (b. 1935–1974) was a valuable sideman on a number of sixties sessions (Cannonball Adderley, Kenny Dorham, Lee Morgan, Hank Mobley, Kenny Burrell) as well as a member of Art Blakey's Jazz Messengers. During the soul-piano boom of the late Fifties and Sixties, Timmons was one of the genre's best-known practitioners due to his work with Blakey, the Adderley quintet and in his own trios. He also authored several outstanding tunes, including "Moanin' " and "This Here." As a pianist, he had a light, accessible touch, and one suspects the funk style he eventually adapted came as easily to him as the bebop he first established himself with. Timmons' debut album, *This Here,* remains a great introduction to his work. — F.G.

CAL TJADER

★ ★ ★ Agua Dulce / Fan.
★ ★ ★ ★ Amazonas / Fan.
★ ★ ★ Breathe Easy / Gal.
★ ★ ★ ★ Concert by the Sea / Fan.
★ ★ ★ Demasiado Caliente / Fan.
★ ★ ★ A Fuego Vivo / Conc. P.
★ ★ ★ Goes Latin / Fan.
★ ★ ★ Gozamel! Pero Ya . . . / Conc. P.
★ ★ ★ Greatest Hits / Fan.
★ ★ ★ Greatest Hits, Vol. 2 / Fan.
★ ★ ★ Guarabe / Fan.
★ ★ ★ Here / Gal.
★ ★ ★ Huracán / Crys. C.
★ ★ ★ Jazz at the Black Hawk / Fan.
★ ★ ★ La Onda Va Bien / Conc. P.
★ ★ ★ Last Bolero in Berkeley / Fan.
★ ★ ★ Last Night When We Were Young / Fan.
★ ★ ★ Latin for Lovers / Fan.
★ ★ ★ Latino / Fan.
★ ★ ★ ★ Live and Direct / Fan.
★ ★ ★ ★ Live at Grace Cathedral / Fan.
★ ★ ★ ★ Live at the Funky Quarters / Fan.
★ ★ ★ Los Ritmos Caliente / Fan.
★ ★ ★ Mambo / Fan.
★ ★ ★ Mambo with Tjader / Fan.
★ ★ ★ ★ Monterey Concerts / Prest.
★ ★ ★ Night at the Black Hawk / Fan.
★ ★ ★ Primo / Fan.
★ ★ ★ Puttin It Together / Fan.
★ ★ ★ Quartet / Fan.
★ ★ ★ Quintet / Fan.
★ ★ ★ Quintet—Latin / Fan.
★ ★ ★ San Francisco Moods / Fan.
★ ★ ★ Shining Sea / Conc. J.
★ ★ ★ ★ ★ Tambu / Fan.
★ ★ ★ Tjader / Fan.
★ ★ West Side Story / Fan.

Vibraphonist Cal Tjader (1925–1982) was a vaudeville tap-dancer before becoming a drummer on the West Coast, where he joined Dave Brubeck's original group as percussionist before signing on as the vibraphonist in George Shearing's band. Neither Brubeck nor Shearing provided the right environment for the musical concept Tjader was developing, so in the early Fifties he formed his own group to play jazz and Latin-jazz with simple melodic purpose and delightfully relentless swing. Tjader soon became the standard-bearer for Latin-jazz in the U.S. as his graceful runs and smoking percussion sections influenced other popularizers of the music such as Herbie Mann and eventually players from the next generation like vibraphonist Gary Burton and pianist

Chick Corea. Tjader released over twenty well-received LPs for Fantasy between 1954 and 1962 featuring sidemen like tenor saxophonist Stan Getz, *congeros* Armando Peraza and Mongo Santamaria, multipercussionists Willie Bobo and Johnnie Rae and keyboardist Vince Guaraldi.

Tjader's mid-Sixties work with producer Creed Taylor at Verve produced the smash hit, "Soul Sauce (Guacha Guaro)," an adaptation of a Chano Pozo/Dizzy Gillespie composition. Tjader returned to Fantasy and recorded in a variety of settings until shortly before his death, although he made some of his final albums for Concord Picante. Highlights of Tjader's second stint with Fantasy include the fine collaboration with guitarist Charlie Byrd, *Tambu*; the Airto-produced *Amazonas*; and any number of hot live sets including *At Grace Cathedral.* — J.S.

CHARLES TOLLIVER

★ ★ ★ ★ Paper Man / Ari./Free.
★ ★ ★ The Ringer / Ari./Free.

Charles Tolliver (b. 1942) a strong trumpeter and composer in what is commonly called the post-bop style ("I feel, as Charlie Parker felt, that jazz is meant to swing and pretty notes are played" is the way he has put it), exemplifies the changes jazz recording has gone through in recent years. Had he arrived in New York in 1960, he would have cut several albums on one of the jazz labels; instead he arrived in the mid-Sixties, so his work was done for a European label and, eventually, his own Strata-East.

The Freedom albums are from 1968 and 1969, respectively. *Paper Man* is a true all-star quintet (Gary Bartz, Herbie Hancock, Ron Carter, Joe Chambers), but the leader's fine writing and the contained exuberance of his trumpet remain at the center of the session. *The Ringer* features the first edition of his Quartet Music Inc., with Stanley Cowell on piano.

★ ★ ★ ★ ★ Impact / Strata-East
★ ★ ★ ★ ★ Live at Slugs', Vol. 1 / Strata-East
★ ★ ★ ★ ★ Live at Slugs', Vol. 2 / Strata-East
★ ★ ★ Live at the Loosdrecht Jazz Festival / Strata-East
★ ★ ★ Live in Tokyo / Strata-East
★ ★ ★ ★ ★ Music Inc. / Strata-East

The best edition of the Music Inc. band, with Cowell, bassist Cecil McBee and drummer Jimmy Hopps, is heard on the two volumes recorded at Slugs' Saloon in 1970; the performances are lengthy, but the inspiration level remains generally high. *Loosdrecht* is a double album with the tight rhythm section of the infrequently heard John Hicks and Alvin Queen on piano and drums, plus bassist Reggie Workman.

The first and last Strata-East albums listed are orchestral versions of Tolliver's (and in the case of *Music Inc.,* Cowell's) music, and contain some of the most stirring large-ensemble work in the post-bop/modal idiom. *Music Inc.* is superior from the standpoint of compositional variety, while *Impact* makes room for neglected saxophone soloists Harold Vick, James Spaulding and George Coleman. — B.B.

MEL TORMÉ
★ ★ ★ **Mel Tormé and Friends Recorded at Marty's, N.Y.C. / Fine.**
Mel Tormé (b. 1925) is an extraordinarily gifted vocalist as well as a good songwriter and has even played a little drums. He's as much a pop performer as a jazz musician, however, and his talents have been somewhat obscured by that fact. This 1981 set includes some engaging music by Tormé fronting a piano/bass/drums trio augmented by other players and singers, including saxophonist Gerry Mulligan. — J.S.

RALPH TOWNER
★ ★ ★ ★ **Batik / ECM/War.**
★ ★ ★ **Blue Sun / ECM/War.**
★ ★ ★ ★ **Diary / ECM/War.**
★ ★ ★ ★ **Five Years Later (with John Abercrombie) / ECM/War.**
★ ★ ★ ★ **Matchbook / ECM/War.**
★ ★ ★ **Old Friends, New Friends / ECM/ War.**
★ ★ ★ ★ **Sargasso Sea (with John Abercrombie) / ECM/War.**
★ ★ ★ ★ **Solo Concert / ECM/War.**
★ ★ ★ **Towner/Solstice / ECM/War.**
★ ★ ★ ★ **Trios/Solos / ECM/War.**
Ralph Towner (b. 1940) plays twelve-string guitar, classical guitar and piano with equal brilliance. Generally, his music is quiet and introspective, with extraordinarily subtle shadings in terms of tone and dynamics. His technique is essentially classical but his background in jazz and his playing with Oregon have led him to a flexible compositional approach heightened by a startling sense of counterpoint and balance. He understands the use of space in improvisation and his compositions, although seemingly unstructured, are propelled by an inner logic.

Towner's ECM albums trace his already full solo career. *Diary,* aptly named, features Towner on all instruments and contains some of his best compositions, most notably the haunting "Icarus." "Images Unseen" recalls the Eastern influences that predominate in Oregon's music. *Matchbook* pairs Towner with the gifted Gary Burton on vibes, and their rapport is both instinctive and subtly complex. *Batik,* a 1978 date, uses bassist Eddie Gomez and drummer Jack DeJohnette to splendid effect.

One of Towner's most successful collaborations to date is with John Abercrombie on *Sargasso Sea,* where Towner's rich twelve-string chording envelops Abercrombie's dry, stinging electric lead lines, but both the *Trios/Solos* and the 1979 *Solo Concert* albums also contain much interesting writing and playing. — J.C.C.

LENNIE TRISTANO
★ ★ ★ **Descent into the Maelstrom / Inner**
★ ★ ★ ★ **A Guiding Light of the Forties / Mer. (Japanese)**
★ ★ ★ ★ ★ **Lennie Tristano Quartet / Atl.**
★ ★ ★ ★ **Live at Birdland 1949 / Jazz R.**
★ ★ ★ ★ ★ **Live in Toronto 1952 / Jazz R.**
★ ★ ★ **New York Improvisations / Elek./ Mus.**
★ ★ ★ ★ ★ **Requiem / Atl.**
Lennie Tristano (1919–1978), pianist, teacher, leader and theoretician, was a reclusive, opinionated man who spent the last quarter-century of his life teaching out of his Long Island home surrounded by an extremely devoted coterie of students. Since his death, Tristano's brilliance in the realm of sinuous, unclichéd improvisation in a less visceral bebop-derived style has gained wider appreciation, and much great music under his name has appeared.

By all means, begin with *Requiem,* an overdue pairing of two collector's items. Half of the album was made in 1955 and shows the pianist in early overdubbing experiments, plus live in a New York club with star-pupil Lee Konitz on alto. (Previously unreleased, and equally rewarding, examples of the club date, recorded in stereo to boot, are on the other Atlantic title; more unreleased trio titles from the period appear on *New York Improvisations.*) Completing the *Requiem* LP is a stunning 1961 solo recital in which Tristano achieves the complex contrapuntal effects he was aiming at in 1955—this time without overdubs. Don't take stories of Tristano as cool and antibop to heart; these performances prove that he is one of Bud Powell's most inventive followers. *Descent* contains outtakes from the 1961 session, plus odds and ends covering earlier and later periods. The recording quality is uneven, and tracks from 1965 and '66 don't add anything to what the 1961 solos tell us.

Earlier examples of Tristano's music have also surfaced recently. The material on Jazz Records, a label now owned by Tristano's estate, is especially enlightening. *Live at Birdland* contains quintet performances featuring tenor saxophonist Wayne Marsh, plus four 1945 piano solos that appear to be Tristano's first recordings. The Toronto concert contains classic early Tristano music played by a quintet featuring both Konitz and Marsh. Another valuable album, *A Guiding Light,* collects Tristano's 1946–47 trio sessions in a Japanese-import limited edition. Tristano's work from this era can also be sampled on Savoy's *Modern Jazz Piano* album and Prestige's *First Sessions 1949/50.*
    — B.B.

MICKEY TUCKER
★ ★ ★ ★ The Crawl / Muse
★ ★ ★ Mr. Mysterious / Muse
A veteran of several hard-hitting organizations including the Jazz Messengers, the Eddie Jefferson group, and a couple of Frank Foster's bands, pianist Mickey Tucker (b. 1941) leads his own outfits down a path that traverses both hard bop and well-orchestrated ballads. His recordings have a uniquely New York sound that compares favorably with bands like Blakey's and Bill Hardman/Junior Cook. *The Crawl* gets the extra star for its lineup which includes Cook, Slide Hampton, Marcus Belgrave and Billy Hart.   — F.G.

STANLEY TURRENTINE
★ ★ ★ Ain't No Way / Blue N.
★ ★ Betcha / Elek.
★ ★ ★ Come On Out / Fan.
★ ★ Don't Mess With Mr. T / CTI
★ ★ ★ Ever Seen Rain / Fan.
★ ★ Inflation / Elek.
★ ★ ★ In Memory of / Blue
★ ★ ★ In the Pocket / Fan.
★ ★ Man with the Sad Face / Fan.
★ ★ ★ Mr. Natural / Blue N.
★ ★ ★ Nightwings / Fan.
★ ★ ★ ★ Pieces of Dreams / Fan.
★ ★ ★ ★ Stan "The Man" / Bain.
★ ★ ★ Sugar / CTI
★ ★ Tender Togetherness / Elek.
★ ★ ★ ★ Use the Stairs / Fan.
★ ★ ★ West Side / Fan.
★ ★ ★ What about You / Fan.
The trademark of tenor saxophonist Stanley Turrentine (b. 1934) is a soulful, full-bodied tone that shakes the sweat off every note he hits. The technique was taught to him by his father, Thomas Turrentine, Sr., who played

saxophone for the Savoy Sultans in the late Thirties. In the early Fifties Stanley sat in with Lowell Fulson and Ray Charles before taking jazz gigs with Tadd Dameron and rocking R&B with Earl Bostic. By the end of the decade he'd made a name for himself with the Max Roach quintet. In 1960 he recorded his debut album, *Look Out,* with organist Shirley Scott. He and Scott later married, making a number of fine albums over an eleven-year period, including *Blue Flames* and *Soul Shoutin',* both of which are out of print but should be prime candidates for Prestige's ambitious Original Jazz Classics reissue series.

Turrentine went on to make some slick CTI albums in the Seventies, the best of which, *Sugar,* featured trumpeter Freddie Hubbard, guitarist George Benson and bassist Ron Carter. Carter also joins him on some of the Fantasy material. A hit LP, *Pieces of Dreams,* was released by Fantasy in 1974, and he went on to make eight more Fantasy albums by 1980. Turrentine has moved boldly into a disco/funk direction in the Eighties on Elektra, with mixed results.
    — J.S.

MCCOY TYNER
★ ★ ★ ★ Asante / Blue N.
★ ★ ★ ★ Atlantis / Mile.
★ ★ ★ Cosmos / Blue N.
★ ★ ★ The Early Trios / Imp.
★ ★ ★ ★ ★ Echoes of a Friend / Mile.
★ ★ ★ ★ ★ Enlightenment / Mile.
★ ★ ★ ★ ★ Expansions / Blue N.
★ ★ ★ ★ Extensions / Blue N.
★ ★ ★ Fly with the Wind / Mile.
★ ★ ★ Focal Point / Mile.
★ ★ ★ The Greeting / Mile.
★ ★ ★ Inception / Imp.
★ ★ ★ Inner Voices / Mile.
★ ★ ★ ★ "Live" at Newport / Imp.
★ ★ ★ Nights of Ballads and Blues / Imp.
★ ★ ★ Plays Ellington / Imp.
★ ★ ★ ★ Reaching 4th / Imp.
★ ★ ★ ★ The Real McCoy / Blue N.
★ ★ ★ ★ Reevaluation: The Impulse Years / MCA
★ ★ ★ ★ Sahara / Mile.
★ ★ ★ ★ Sama Layuca / Mile.
★ ★ ★ ★ Song for My Lady / Mile.
★ ★ ★ ★ Song of the New World / Mile.
★ ★ ★ ★ ★ Supertrios / Mile.
★ ★ ★ Tender Moments / Blue N.
★ ★ ★ ★ Time for Tyner / Blue N.
★ ★ ★ ★ Today and Tomorrow / Imp.
★ ★ ★ ★ ★ Trident / Mile.
Record-company affiliations divide McCoy Tyner's recording career as a leader into three distinct and instructive phases. From

1962 to 1965, while still the pianist in John Coltrane's immortal quartet (with bassist Jimmy Garrison and drummer Elvin Jones), Tyner (b. 1938) was under contract to Impulse, Coltrane's label. When he left the Coltrane group he also moved on to Blue Note, where he stayed for the next five years while his conception matured through several lean economic periods. By 1972, when he began his highly successful period with Milestone, his own playing had entered a new phase and he was leading the most powerful band working out of the middle-Coltrane tradition.

Tyner has stated that his Impulse albums were intended to present something different than what he did with Coltrane; that four of the six originally issued were trio albums liberally programed with pop standards suggests that the label was interested in developing its own more progressive entry for the piano-trio audience that supported Oscar Peterson, Erroll Garner, etc. The beneficial effect of horn players on Tyner's thick, darkly percussive style can be heard on *"Live" at Newport* and *Today and Tomorrow,* where trio tracks are mixed with larger combos (Clark Terry and Charlie Mariano are on the former, Thad Jones and John Gilmore on the latter).

Of the trio records, *Reaching 4th* has Tyner's strongest playing and the excellent support of Henry Grimes on bass and Roy Haynes' drums; *Inception,* however, also is notable for revealing that Tyner's now-familiar modal composition style was already taking shape on his debut album. All of his Impulse work emphasizes his roots in the music of Bud Powell, Thelonious Monk and of course Coltrane. *Reevaluation,* a good sampler of the period, contains four tracks by Trane's band.

The Blue Note albums are marked by some excellent sideman appearances and Tyner's growing fascination with Afro-Asian music, a concern reflected in both his playing and writing. *The Real McCoy* begins the series with an excellent quartet (Joe Henderson, Ron Carter, Elvin Jones) and five characteristic tunes; *Tender Moments* is Tyner's first writing for more than three horns and features Lee Morgan; *Time for Tyner* is by trio and quartet, with vibist Bobby Hutcherson a perfect partner (especially on "African Village"). *Expansions,* made in 1968, is a fantastic session by Tyner's working quintet (Gary Bartz on alto, Woody Shaw, trumpet) plus two added starters from Miles Davis' band, Wayne Shorter and Ron Carter (on cello). The variety in the writing, excellent solos by the horns and the feisty drums of

Freddie Waits make this album one of Tyner's best. The sequel *Extensions,* with Alice Coltrane's harp spelling Woody Shaw and Elvin Jones at the drums, isn't as strong, and the 1970 *Asante* is notable for the increased rhythmic interdependence in Tyner's two-handed solos and a rare glimpse of alto saxophonist Andrew White.

On *Sahara,* recorded slightly more than a year after *Asante* by Tyner's working quartet, everything finally falls together. Tyner now attacks the keyboard like a master African percussionist, building incredible solo swells and driving his Coltrane-derived horn soloists (Sonny Fortune here and on the next two albums) to unexpected heights. Alphonse Mouzon, who often deserves criticism for being too loud and unsympathetic, couldn't ask for a better setting to bash in.

A key to Tyner's success at Milestone is that he refuses to duplicate formats from one album to the next. Thus *Song for My Lady* has tracks by a septet (with Charles Tolliver, Michael White and Mtume added), *Echoes of a Friend* is a solo piano tour de force dedicated to Coltrane, and *Song of the New World* uses string or brass ensembles. By the time of Montreux 1973, where *Enlightenment* was recorded, Azar Lawrence was Tyner's saxophonist, and this two-record set remains the high-energy pinnacle of Tyner's working band recordings. (*Atlantis* was also done live the following year.)

If the limitations of Tyner's modal melodies become more apparent with the 1974 *Sama Layuca* (a nonet with Lawrence, Bartz, Hutcherson), there is still the invigorating strength of the music and the special delight of Tyner's piano. There is also an attempt to make Tyner's music more palatable to a nonjazz audience by adding strings (on the 1976 *Fly with the Wind*) and voices (*Inner Voices,* recorded in 1977); both albums are easy listening as far as Tyner goes, with a better rhythm section and horn soloists making *Inner Voices* preferable.

Tyner's real triumphs among his late-Seventies recordings are the trio albums *Trident* (with Ron Carter and Elvin Jones) and the two-record *Supertrios* (half Carter and Tony Williams, half Eddie Gomez and Jack DeJohnette). On these albums Tyner plays with masters on his own high level, a situation hard to sustain in his own working band. *The Greeting,* a live recording by his sextet from early 1978, is about what one would expect—hot, invigorating Afro-American music, but nothing that hasn't been done with more freshness and spirit on *Enlightenment* and *Sahara.* If Tyner has been in a holding pattern for the past few years, consolidating his ever-growing audience, we can at least take heart that his integrity is unsullied, his instrumental command and dedication to the improviser's art undimmed.

★ ★ ★ **The Early Trios** / **MCA**
★ ★ **4 × 4** / **Mile.**
★ ★ ★ **Great Moments with McCoy Tyner** / **MCA**
★ ★ ★ **Horizon** / **Mile.**
★ ★ ★ **La Leyenda de la Hora** / **Col.**
★ ★ **Looking Out** / **Col.**
★ ★ ★ ★ **Passion Dance** / **Mile.**
★ ★ ★ ★ **13th House** / **Mile.**
★ ★ ★ ★ ★ **Together** / **Mile.**

Little has changed for Tyner in the Eighties—his approach remains muscular but predictable, and he continues to seek modifications in instrumental format rather than in material. One exception, *Looking Out,* was a misguided attempt to attract a pop audience via the inclusion of forgettable lyrics sung by Phyllis Hyman and the occasional presence of guitarist Carlos Santana. *Together* is the most successful of his recent ventures, an all-star session with writing and playing contributed by Jack DeJohnette, Freddie Hubbard and Bobby Hutcherson; but the orchestral date *13th House* and the solo/trio (with Ron Carter and Tony Williams) *Passion Dance* also worked well. The others are just more of the same, with even *4 × 4* (Hubbard, Hutcherson, John Abercrombie and Arthur Blythe featured on a side each) sounding uninspired throughout most of its length.

Tyner can also be heard on the Columbia samplers, *God Rest Ye Merry, Jazzmen* and *The New York–Montreux Connection.* His 1962–65 Impulse recordings have begun appearing as imports on the Jazz Man label, but the two-record *Early Trios* and *Great Moments* sets from the Impulse years are now also available on domestic MCA repressings. — B.B.

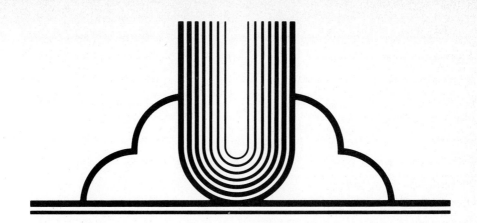

JAMES "BLOOD" ULMER
★ ★ ★ ★ **Are You Glad to Be in America? /
Artists H.**
★ ★ ★ **Black Rock / Col.**
★ ★ ★ ★ **Free Lancing / Col.**
★ ★ ★ ★ **No Wave / Moers**
★ ★ ★ ★ ★ **Odyssey / Col.**
★ ★ ★ **Tales of Captain Black / Artists H.**

James "Blood" Ulmer (b. 1942) was a journeyman rhythm & blues guitarist and vocalist when he met Ornette Coleman in 1972. The interaction of the two musicians, both of whom had an affinity for the country-blues tradition, led Coleman into his Prime Time phase and turned Ulmer into the most prominent exponent of Coleman's electric "harmelodic" approach. *Tales of Captain Black,* the pair's lone meeting on record, has raw vigor to spare and, in the presence of electric bassist Jamaaladeen Tacuma, an overpowering example of a style-spanning fusion sensibility. All the same, Ulmer's solos sound inconclusive, and although Ornette is always valuable he's often little more than a sideman on this program of eight Ulmer tunes. The drums are manned by Denardo Coleman.

In 1979 Ulmer began attracting attention as his band (often one or more new-music horn luminaries, plus the Blood-led rhythm section) worked New York's new-wave club circuit. The cataclysmic urgency of Ulmer live has always been hard to raise on vinyl, but was substantially improved when Artists House remixed *Are You Glad* (the LP had previously been available in an inferior mix on Rough Trade). On this exciting session Shannon Jackson and Calvin Weston, two fierce drummers, bring the intensity down a bit by deferring too much to each other. The horns appear on some tracks, again as secondary voices. "Are You Glad to Be in America?" may well by Ulmer's finest song, as heard here in its remarkable original version.

No Wave is admittedly a favorite for its more unreconstructed power, with Shannon Jackson unleashing tirades that set up a Sunny Murray/Albert Ayler atmosphere with tenor saxophonist David Murray. The cuts are long and loose barrages of sound. *Free Lancing,* Ulmer's debut record on Columbia, is more balanced, with Ulmer as power-trio leader (Amin Ali on bass and Weston on drums), as vocalist (female chorus added) and as small-band writer (Olu Dara, Oliver Lake and Murray are the horns) given equal prominence. Ulmer is a tauter soloist now, and his rhythm remains a marvel, with the curves displayed at their most dazzling on the trio pieces.

Black Rock, the second Columbia record, made a bid to expand Ulmer's audience by eliminating most of the horn parts and placing more stress on female vocalists. The result comes across as a compromise, which luckily cannot be said for the larger and far more successful change of direction heard on *Odyssey.* Here Ulmer has pared down to a trio, replaced electric bass with the impressive violin of newcomer Charles Birnham and reined in his own presence to create a more collective style that places greater emphasis on his country roots. No doubt the commercial chances of a music as quirky as Ulmer's remain unsettled even after hooking on with a major label, but the musical prospects are very encouraging, especially after *Odyssey.*

Ulmer has also recorded with Rashied Ali and Arthur Blythe. — B.B.

MICHAL URBANIAK
★ ★ ★ **Atma / Col.**
★ ★ ★ **Beginning / Cata.**
★ ★ **Body English / Ari.**
★ ★ ★ **Daybreak / Pausa**
★ ★ ★ **Ecstasy / Mar.**

★ ★ ★ ★ **Fusion** / **Col.**
★ ★ ★ **Fusion III** / **Col.**
★ ★ ★ **Heritage** / **Paula**
★ ★ ★ **Urbaniak** / **Inner**

Colorful, contagious albums. The music of Polish violinist Michal Urbaniak (b. 1943) sounds like Eastern European folk tunes gone sprightly fusion-funky. Full of rich synthesized touches and happy backbeat, his LPs also feature his wife, vocalist Urszula Dudziak; she sings as gutturally low as an electric bass, and as shriekingly high as Urbaniak's electric violin. It all adds up to persistently *musical* art. — M.R.

DAVE VALENTIN
★ ★ Hawk / Ari./GRP
★ ★ In Love's Time / Ari./GRP
★ ★ ★ Kalahari/GRP
★ ★ Pied Piper / Ari./GRP
Dave Valentin is an engaging flutist playing
fusion music with a decided Afro-Cuban/
salsa beat. All three of his records here are
danceable and somewhat listenable though
fairly anonymous.   — J.S.

SARAH VAUGHAN
★ ★ ★ After Hours / CSP
★ ★ ★ ★ Billie/Ella/Lena/Sarah / Col.
  (Jazz Odyssey Series)
★ ★ ★ ★ ★ Crazy and Mixed Up / Pablo
★ ★ ★ ★ Divine Sarah / Musicraft
★ ★ ★ Duke Ellington Songbook / Pablo T.
★ Feelin' Good / Main.
★ ★ ★ ★ The George Gershwin Songbook /
  Em.
★ ★ Gershwin Live! / CBS
★ ★ ★ Golden Hits / Mer.
★ ★ I Love Brazil / Pablo T.
★ ★ Linger Awhile / CSP
★ ★ ★ Live in Japan / Main.
★ ★ ★ Man I Love / Discov.
★ ★ ★ ★ ★ Recorded Live / Em.
★ ★ ★ ★ ★ Sarah Vaughan / Arc. Folk
  (three volumes)
★ ★ ★ ★ Sarah Vaughan / Em.
★ ★ ★ ★ Sassy Swings the Tivoli / Mer.
★ ★ ★ ★ Send in the Clowns / Pablo
★ Songs of the Beatles / Atl.
★ ★ A Time in My Life / Main.
★ ★ With Michel Legrand / Main.
Even at the age of nineteen when she first
began performing with Earl Hines' orchestra,
Sarah Vaughan (b. 1924) did not need to
mature musically. Rather, she arrived from a
Newark church choir with a voice operatic
in its pinpoint control and breathtaking
range (Marian Anderson was an early idol)
and totally unique in its jazzy, improvisatory

quirks. Like the risks that her bebop contemporaries Parker and Gillespie were taking in
the early Forties (all three ended up in Billy
Eckstine's band in 1944), "Sassy" interpreted
her way around and out of melodic convention—soaring effortlessly and dropping unex-
pectedly—and made it all sound right.

Vaughan has always inclined to the more
pop/sentimental side of jazz material, a penchant that led her in the early Fifties to the
saccharine settings of Percy Faith's strings,
and in 1982 to the even more regrettable
jazz/funk of the Beatles collection. Fortunately, much ground was crossed in between;
for the purists, small-group recordings are
still available in abundance but listeners at-
tached to her more orchestral achievements
are not denied either. No LP bearing
Vaughan's name is devoid of her incomparable talent; in the myriad of contexts in which
she has recorded, it is almost always over-
wrought production and pointless material to
blame for whatever's bad or insufferable.

The Discovery and Musicraft collections
cover Vaughan's earliest, mostly big-band efforts from 1946 to '48, after she had departed the Eckstine outfit and had met and
married her manager/trumpeter George
Treadwell. The offerings on both discs are
split between tunes with small jazz combos
(Treadwell, Stuff Smith Trio) and with large
orchestras ("The Lord's Prayer," for example, with an exceedingly ascendant string
section).

Conspicuously absent, however, is
Vaughan's 1945 classic "Lover Man" with
Gillespie's All-Star Quintet and that's the
reason why the Archive record is *the* one to
seek out from this period. It also features ap-
pearances by Bud Powell, Don Byas and
Teddy Wilson, and if all else fails, "Lover
Man" can still be found on the Dizzy *In
The Beginning* twofer on Prestige.

Columbia currently concentrates on

Vaughan's orchestrated work during her 1948–54 stint with that label. The Jazz Odyssey Series anthology, however, does capture an intriguing 1950 encounter with a young Miles Davis.

Linger unfortunately does just that: the second star earned primarily for a satisfyingly lighthearted "Nice Work" with Treadwell's unit. *After Hours* rates only slightly higher—sparser but still string-laden, a conceptually moody collection.

Vaughan moved over to the more jazz-directed Mercury in 1954, and for almost a decade that label recorded her in a variety of settings: small groups (including Jimmy Jones' piano, Joe Benjamin's bass and Roy Haynes' drums more often than not), small ensembles and full orchestras. In the early Seventies, many of these titles were reissued on the now-defunct Trip label; if found, definitely reel in 1954's Sarah-and-trio *Swingin' Easy.*

Most of the Mercury material still out is on EmArcy repackagings. *Sarah* is an unconditional must, pitting the vocalist in a deservedly tight and brilliantly matched group. The instrumental interplay between Vaughan and Clifford Brown, Herbie Mann and Paul Quinichette rewrote the standards that comprise this album.

The Gershwin double set cannot miss: one of America's greatest songwriters via one of his greatest interpreters. Largely culled from a 1957 session that kept the arrangements tastefully subdued and emphasizing Vaughan's sublime reading, it serves as a respectful primer on the composer's better known and more obscure songs.

Recorded Live, another double, and *Sassy* overlap plenty, capturing Vaughan's in-command and fun-loving onstage persona. For sheer quantity, the former is favored, featuring powerful sets from Chicago (1957 with trio), London (1958 with Thad Jones' trumpet and Frank Wess' tenor among others) and Copenhagen (1963 with trio again). *Golden Hits* consists of her crossover efforts: "Misty," "Moonlight In Vermont" and the 1958 charter "Broken-Hearted Melody."

Through the Sixties, Vaughan was signed with Roulette, which produced some excellent sides (one arranged by Benny Carter and a remarkable album with Count Basie that ended up on Emus Records). Sadly, the jazz racks have yet to see the return of these recordings.

The Mainstream titles date from the early Seventies. *Live* is enjoyable with solid accompaniment, including drummer Jimmy Cobb. Things took a turn for the commercial worse, however, as the remainder of her Mainstream output amounts to depressingly vapid Top Forty and movie themes.

The late-Seventies Pablo association slowly brought Vaughan back, and with Basie's Orchestra once again the magic was caught. Her energetic scatting flourishes on *Clowns* (easily her strongest of recent years) and the way in which her vocal acrobatics bring "If You Could See Me Now" to a close is itself a minor miracle.   — A.K.

JOE VENUTI

★ ★ ★ ★ ★ **Violin Jazz / Yazoo**
Violinist Joe Venuti (1898–1978) made a series of recordings in groups featuring guitarist Eddie Lang between 1925 and 1933. The technically virtuosic and relentlessly swinging music they made together was somewhere south of chamber music, yet Venuti's classical training was considered a novelty back in those days. *Violin Jazz* is all that's currently available of these classic performances.   — J.S.

LEROY VINNEGAR

★ ★ ★ **The Kid / PBR**
★ ★ ★ **The Leroy Vinnegar Sextet / Contem.**
★ ★ ★ **Leroy Walks! / Contem./OJC**
★ ★ ★ **Leroy Walks Again / Contem.**
Leroy Vinnegar (b. 1928) is known as "the walker" for his unerring "walking" time-keeping on the bass. A veteran of hundreds of West Coast jazz sessions, Vinnegar occasionally stepped into the spotlight to record some favorite standards and the infrequent original tune. Like the essence of Vinnegar's playing itself, these are workmanlike dates but they remain enjoyable in an easygoing and unpretentious manner.

West Coast favorite sons, tenorist Teddy Edwards and pianist/vibist Vic Feldman help out on the Contemporary LPs. *Walks Again* contains Vinnegar's lovely elegiac "For Carl," dedicated to the legendary pianist Carl Perkins who guests on *Walks!.*
— S.F.

MIROSLAV VITOUS

★ ★ ★ **First Meeting / ECM/War.**
★ ★ **Magical Shepherd / War.**
★ ★ ★ **Miroslav / Ari./Free.**
★ ★ ★ **Miroslav Vitous Group / ECM/War.**
★ ★ ★ ★ ★ **Mountain in the Clouds / Atl.**
★ ★ ★ **To Be Continued / ECM/War.**
Miroslav Vitous (b. 1947) arrived on the jazz scene from Czechoslovakia in the mid-Sixties and was immediately recognized as one of the best bass players available. After playing

around with various leaders and working with Miles Davis and Herbie Mann, Vitous recorded his first solo album, *Infinite Search.* It was later rereleased with an additional track and called *Mountain in the Clouds.* This record features Vitous' virtuoso bass playing, Joe Henderson on tenor saxophone, John McLaughlin on guitar, Herbie Hancock on electric piano and Jack DeJohnette and Joe Chambers on drums. Vitous went on to help form Weather Report, but his solo career since then has been spotty. Looking for direction, he even started to play guitar, which was a big mistake. On the ECM records he returns to playing acoustic bass with better results. — J.S.

ABDUL WADUD

★ ★ ★ ★ By Myself / Bisharra

Initially working out of St. Louis, cellist
Abdul Wadud made his first recordings for
that city's Black Artists Group (BAG), a
collective similar to Chicago's AACM. In
tandem with saxophonist Julius Hemphill,
Wadud appeared on several outstanding LPs
as a sideman, most notably *Dogon A.D.* and
Coon Bid'ness. He continued working with
Hemphill in New York during the late Seventies and into the Eighties, when he also
began recording and performing with alto
saxophonist Arthur Blythe.

A dynamic soloist, Wadud can cover a lot
of ground. By turns percussive, rhythmic
and melodic, he is a leader among the handful of cellists presently working in jazz. As
the title indicates, he goes it alone on his
own album, and as soon as Wadud picks up
his instrument, class is in session. — F.G.

COLLIN WALCOTT

★ ★ Codona 1 / ECM/War.
★ ★ ★ Codona 2 / ECM/War.
★ ★ ★ Codona 3 / ECM/War.
★ ★ Cloud / ECM/War.
★ ★ Grazing Dreams / ECM/War.

Collin Walcott (1945–1984) played a variety
of string and percussion instruments (sitar,
tabula, dulcimer, etc.) in several groups including the Paul Winter Consort and Oregon. His solo work is rather aimless but the
later three *Codona* ensemble efforts with
trumpeter Don Cherry and Nana Vasconcelos (on the berimbau and the talking
drum) display his subtle percussion work to
good advantage in an intimate setting.
— B.T.

FATS WALLER

★ ★ ★ Ain't Misbehavin' / Arc. Folk
★ ★ ★ ★ Ain't Misbehavin' / RCA
**★ ★ ★ ★ Complete Fats Waller, Vol. 1 /
RCA**
★ ★ ★ Fats Waller / Trip
★ ★ ★ Fats Waller Legacy / Olym.
★ ★ ★ Fats Waller on the Air / Trip
★ ★ ★ ★ Fats Waller Piano Solos / Blueb.
★ ★ ★ Fats Waller Plays Fats Waller / Ev.
★ ★ ★ ★ ★ Integrale / RCA (France)
★ ★ ★ Legendary Performer / RCA
★ ★ ★ Legend in His Lifetime / Trip

Waller (1904–1943) was a great stride piano
stylist and a very popular player, vocalist
and songwriter. He served as an accompanist
in the Twenties for Bessie Smith and other
blues singers, then established himself as a
composer and bandleader in the Thirties and
early Forties before dying in 1943 at the age
of thirty-nine. His score for the Broadway
show *Hot Chocolates* included his best-
known song, "Ain't Misbehavin'." He also
wrote "Honeysuckle Rose" and recorded
great versions of any number of pop standards, one of which, "I'm Gonna Sit Right
Down and Write Myself a Letter," became
his biggest hit. The RCA and Bluebird packages present Waller at his best. *Integrale,* the
10-LP set on French Black and White, is the
most complete. The Trip and Everest sides
are officially long out of print, but check the
cutout bins. *Ain't Misbehavin'* (RCA version)
has been in print for ages and holds up remarkably well. — J.S.

GEORGE WALLINGTON

★ ★ ★ Dance of the Infidels / Savoy
★ ★ ★ Live at the Café Bohemia / Prest.
★ ★ ★ ★ Our Delight / Prest.

George Wallington (b. 1924) was born to be
a footnote in the history of jazz. In 1943 and
'44 he was pianist for the first bop band on
52nd Street led by Dizzy Gillespie and Oscar
Pettiford; later in the decade he wrote
"Lemon Drop" for Woody Herman's classic
big band and "Godchild" for the historic
Birth of the Cool sessions.

Wallington's own recording career has had
its share of historical fascinations. *Our De-*

light, featuring Max Roach and either Charles Mingus or Curley Russell on bass, documents Wallington's complete absorption of Bud Powell's pianistic vocabulary by 1952. *Café Bohemia* from 1955 uses the cream of Detroit's jazz exports, Pepper Adams, Donald Byrd, and Paul Chambers *before* he joined Miles Davis. Byrd is again featured, this time with Phil Woods, two years later on *Infidels.* Little has been heard from Wallington since. — S.F.

JACK WALRATH

★ ★ ★ ★ **Demons in Pursuit / Gatem.**
★ ★ ★ **Montana, with special guest Jack Walrath / Labor**
★ ★ ★ **A Plea for Sanity / Stash**
★ ★ ★ **Revenge of the Fat People / Stash**

A native of Montana, trumpeter Jack Walrath (b. 1946) came up in the Seventies performing with Ray Charles and the rock group Cold Blood before settling in New York and landing a gig with bassist Charles Mingus. Walrath eventually became the orchestrator for the ailing Mingus, developing the charts for the bandleader's later dates including *Something like A Bird* and *Me, Myself an Eye.* Following the bassist's death, Walrath continued to work with Mingus cohorts Dannie Richmond and Ricky Ford, although the group's faithful treatment of Mingus' music was unfortunately eclipsed by the less accurate, Sue Mingus–backed Mingus Dynasty band.

Walrath's first solo album, *Demons in Pursuit,* demonstrated his sharp ear, keen wit, and no-nonsense ability as a player. A quintet featuring Richmond, bassist Ray Drummond, guitarist John Scofield and pianist Jim McNeely afforded Walrath plenty of solo space, while getting over such well-constructed and unlikely titled tunes as "Fungus" and "Ray Charles on Mars."

Walrath's second LP, *Revenge of the Fat People,* featured the trumpeter's working band of saxophonist Ford, pianist Michael Cochrane, bassist Cameron Brown and drummer and former Headhunter Mike Clark. The emphasis was a bit heavier on straight-ahead blowing vehicles, and the album included a sumptuous cover of Mingus's "Duke Ellington's Sound of Love." Something of a prankster, Walrath posed for the album's cover in clown's paint, only to become the brunt of the record company's last laugh when they spelled his name wrong on the jacket.

With *A Plea for Sanity,* Walrath attained the intensity of his earlier recordings, this time employing a drummerless trio. Joining pianist Cochrane was bassist Anthony Cox,

an immensely talented addition, and Walrath continued to make mirthful music while expanding his abilities in a more relaxed setting.

The material on *Montana* is less polished than on his own albums, but Walrath fits in well, performing on all tracks except one and contributing several tunes, including the surprisingly graceful "Wolfgang of Arabia." Probably the first—and last—jazz album to be recorded in Missoula. — A.E.G.

CEDAR WALTON

★ ★ ★ ★ **Cedar! / Prest.**
★ ★ ★ **The Electric Boogaloo Song / Prest.**
★ ★ ★ **Piano Solos / Clean Cuts**
★ ★ ★ ★ **Soul Cycle / Prest.**
★ ★ ★ ★ **Spectrum / Prest.**

Keyboardist Cedar Walton (b. 1934) came up with Art Blakey's Jazz Messengers in the Sixties before gigging with Freddie Hubbard, Kenny Dorham, Lee Morgan, Milt Jackson, Eddie Harris and others. Walton worked as a session pianist at Prestige and later made a number of records under his own name for the label. A smooth and rhythmically exciting stylist, Walton fit the blues-based blowing session concepts of most of the Prestige recordings. Walton tried his hand on electric keyboards during the Seventies, recording for several labels with little success, and that material is now unavailable. *Piano Solos* is a beautiful acoustic set from 1981. — J.S.

GROVER WASHINGTON, JR.

★ ★ **All King's / Kudu**
★ ★ **Anthology / Mo.**
★ ★ **Baddest / Mo.**
★ ★ **The Best Is Yet to Come / Elek.**
★ ★ **Come Morning / Elek.**
★ ★ **Feels So Good / Kudu**
★ ★ **Inner City Blues / Kudu**
★ ★ **Inside Moves / Elek.**
★ ★ ★ **Mister Magic / Kudu**
★ ★ **Paradise / Elek.**
★ ★ **Reed Seed / Mo.**
★ ★ **Secret Place / Kudu**
★ ★ **Skylarkin' / Mo.**
★ ★ **Soul Box / Kudu**
★ ★ **Winelight / Elek.**

Saxophonist Grover Washington, Jr. (b. 1943), started out playing blues and R&B with Philadelphia organ combos in the Sixties, eventually becoming a session player first for Fantasy records and then for Creed Taylor's CTI/Kudu organization. Taylor's Seventies jazz productions were mostly faceless settings that had little to do with any individual player's personality. When Washington was asked by Taylor to substitute for Hank Crawford on an album concept, the result proved successful enough to prompt Taylor to produce more records featuring Washington, including the enormous hit *Mister Magic*. Washington has little to offer, however, beyond the fact that he's a popularizer of jazz. The *Winelight* album proved Washington has carried that popularity into the Eighties with its hit single, "Just the Two of Us." — J.S.

CHUCK WAYNE
★ ★ ★ **Interactions (with Joe Puma) / Choice**
★ ★ ★ **Traveling / Prog.**
An original bebop guitarist, Chuck Wayne (b. 1923) is best known for his work with George Shearing. He's really a hard-swinging pro capable of a broad range of moods, but unfortunately his best albums are long out of print. The group on the Progressive LP doesn't do him justice, and *Interactions* is only recommended for guitar freaks. — F.G.

WEATHER REPORT
★ ★ ★ ★ ★ **I Sing the Body Electric / Col.**
★ ★ ★ **Weather Report / Col. (1971 recording, with M. Vitous)**
Joe Zawinul (b. 1932, keyboards) and Wayne Shorter (b. 1933, saxophones) were well-known sidemen with Cannonball Adderley and Miles Davis, respectively, who had been prime movers in Davis' popular *In a Silent Way* and *Bitches Brew* albums; they formed Weather Report in 1971, with bassist Miroslav Vitous (b. 1947) as original coleader, and have since released an album a year. The shifts in the band's music and personnel have charted both the pinnacles and pitfalls of jazz-rock "fusion" during the period.

The first album, *Weather Report,* with Alphonse Mouzon and Airto Moreira on drums and percussion, was an extension of the style first forged on *Silent Way*—lots of ensemble mood, few solos (except on Shorter's "Eurydice," the album's most substantial piece) and an overall feeling of incompleteness. "Orange Lady," a lovely Zawinul melody that never goes anywhere, typifies the problems of the album.

I Sing the Body Electric features the first permanent touring version of the band, with Eric Gravatt on drums and Dom Um Romao on percussion. One side, recorded live in Tokyo, plus Zawinul's "Unknown Soldier" from the studio sessions, is the best recorded example of the kind of intensity Weather Report still generates in concert.
★ ★ ★ ★ **Black Market / Col.**
★ ★ ★ ★ ★ **Mysterious Traveller / Col.**

★ ★ ★ **Sweetnighter / Col.**
★ ★ ★ ★ **Tale Spinnin' / Col.**
With *Sweetnighter* the band shows its intention to make a funkier music more directed to the rock audience, and while Zawinul's long pieces "Boogie Woogie Waltz" and "125th Street Congress" have the beat, they dissipate into a blue haze of electric jamming. From *Mysterious Traveller* forward there is a much keener awareness of studio technique, and a growing sense of how to integrate the various electronic keyboards on Zawinul's part; Vitous is replaced by the funkier electric bass of Alphonso Johnson and a string of players fill the percussion chairs. *Mysterious Traveller* is the most successful album of this period but, excellent improvisations like "Cucumber Slumber" and "Blackthorn Rose" notwithstanding, there is energy missing in all of these works due to the contained percussion work and the overall technological veneer of the music. Most troublesome of all is the minimal presence of Shorter, one of the great contemporary musical minds, who has tended to play less and take a less central role in the recorded ensembles as time passes (in-person performances are fortunately different).
★ ★ ★ ★ ★ **Heavy Weather / Col.**
Electric bassist Jaco Pastorius replaced Johnson in 1976 and quickly assumed coleader status with Shorter and Zawinul. Alejandro Acuna on drums and Manolo Badrena on percussion give the band a stable personnel, which recorded an album that manages to be both its most commercial and one of its most challenging. "Birdland," the hit from the record, shows the distance Zawinul has gone in his ability to use rock and studio techniques creatively, while "A Remark You Made" and "The Juggler" testify to his compositional range. Pastorius is simply the finest electric bassist around, and a multifaceted composer as well; and Shorter, ever pithier, contributes eloquent balladry on "Remark" and the infectious tune "Palladium." Like its namesake, Weather Report is always changing, occasionally frustrating and quite often right on target.
★ ★ ★ **Domino Theory / Col.**
★ ★ ★ **8:30 / Col.**
★ ★ ★ **Mr. Gone / Col.**
★ ★ ★ ★ **Night Passage / Col.**
★ ★ ★ **Procession / Col.**
★ ★ ★ **Weather Report / Col. (1981 recording, with J. Pastorius)**
After the overall success of *Heavy Weather,* which remains Weather Report's best-selling album, the end of the Seventies saw another change in the percussion section. *Mr. Gone*

was made with various drummers, including Peter Erskine, a young veteran of Stan Kenton and Maynard Ferguson. Erskine's bigband approach lent itself to the orchestral spreads of Zawinul's ensembles, and he joined the band permanently, the lone percussionist for a time, with hand drummer Robert Thomas, Jr., added in 1980. (By 1982 Pastorius, Erskine and Thomas had all departed, to be replaced on *Procession* by Victor Bailey, Omar Hakim and Jose Rossy.)

Weather Report remains something different live, where the various twists of the tunes have been absorbed over time and the rhythms are looser. Still, Zawinul's music seems to restrict the role of the others. Complaints about Shorter's underuse have grown tiresome, but as of *Weather Report* (late 1981 version) Pastorius didn't seem to be getting his due either. Zawinul is ever more sure of his various keyboards and synthesizers, and *Night Passage* affords a particularly good example of his feeling for the sounds of the other players. Recent compositions often visit familiar territory and (to judge by two nights of the concert tour summarized on *8:30* that I heard) so do the solos. Still, *8:30*'s format of three concert sides reprising earlier studio material, plus one new studio side, is a hard survey of recent Weather to beat. — B.B.

CHICK WEBB

★ ★ ★ ★ ★ Best / MCA
★ ★ ★ ★ Ella Swings the Band (with Ella Fitzgerald) / MCA
★ ★ ★ ★ ★ Legend / MCA
★ ★ ★ Princess of the Savoy / MCA
★ ★ ★ ★ Stompin' at the Savoy / CSP

Chick Webb (1902–1939), a short and physically deformed man who lived with all the other handicaps of black musicians in the Depression, spent the last decade of his life establishing himself as one of the premier drummers in jazz history and establishing his band as one of the prime attractions at Harlem's Savoy Ballroom. The MCA albums testify to the swing era's finer impulses, with *Legend* and *Ella Swings* bracketing the period and *Best* surveying the decade. *Best, Princess* and *Swings* all feature the young Ella Fitzgerald, who joined the band in 1934 at the age of sixteen.

In terms of soloists, the band is not without individual interest, but the opportunity to hear more of this orchestra only reinforces how completely Chick Webb understood rhythm and the various ways it could be unleashed by a large ensemble. — B.B.

EBERHARD WEBER

★ ★ ★ The Call / ECM/War.
★ ★ ★ ★ The Colours of Chloë / ECM/War.
★ ★ ★ Fluid Rustle / ECM/War.
★ ★ ★ ★ The Following Morning / ECM/War.
★ ★ ★ Little Movements / ECM/War.
★ ★ Passengers / ECM/War.
★ ★ ★ Ring / ECM/War.
★ ★ ★ Silent Feet / ECM/War.
★ ★ ★ ★ Yellow Fields / ECM/War.

Eberhard Weber (b. 1940) began playing the cello when he was seven. His bass playing has been heard alongside Chick Corea, Jean-Luc Ponty, Wolfgang Dauner and Volker Kriegel, among other free jazzers. Europeans have been listening to his stuff for a long time and finally America has begun to catch up, due to Manfred Eicher's decision to turn him into the Leland Sklar of ECM's session scene. Eicher has sponsored Weber further by releasing his solo work, some of it brilliant, as on his tensile *Colours of Chloë*, released in 1974. Eicher has also teamed him with other ECM artists, such as Gary Burton on *Ring* and *Passengers*. His bass playing is perhaps the most virtuosic in Germany, his cello is used with an expressionistic invention unrivaled in Europe and, though there is stiff competition from Martin Mull, Weber plays a mean ocarina. He brings out every drop of melancholy a cello can ring when he plays his fretless axe, creating the thousand spectacular voices of a singing-saw cello chorus (cello section shot through a Buchla synthesizer—along with heavy double-tracking, a trick he uses to great advantage). If America had more of Weber in its elevators, it'd be a better place to live. — B.M.

BEN WEBSTER

★ ★ ★ ★ ★ Tenor Giants (with Coleman Hawkins) / Verve

One of the greatest tenor saxophonists of the classic jazz era and the master of gruff, raspy blues and breathy sensuality. The important early work of Ben Webster (1909–1973) is scattered around; many of the most important performances, like the immortal Ellington band sides from 1940 to 1942, are now out of print, while Webster's mid-Forties combo work is spread over several Savoy and Onyx anthologies. *Tenor Giants* is from 1957 and 1959, to my mind his greatest period, and he can be heard outblowing his mentor Coleman Hawkins. Roy Eldridge, Budd Johnson (yes, a third tenor) and Oscar Peterson are among the other participants.

★ ★ ★ ★ ★ **Atmosphere for Lovers and Thieves** / Jazz M.
★ ★ ★ ★ **Duke's in Bed** / Black L.
★ ★ ★ ★ **Saturday Night at the Montmartre** / Black L.
★ ★ ★ ★ **See You at the Fair** / Imp.
Lack of interest in his work at home led Webster to Europe in 1964, though the Impulse disc shows he still was in noble form before he left. The out-of-print Black Lions are all from 1965 and all fine, but *Atmosphere* (once again available on the Jazz Man import label) contains probably the finest playing of Webster's European years.
★ ★ **At Work in Europe** / Prest.
★ ★ ★ **My Man** / Inner
Although *At Work* is marred by a disjointed session employing two pianos, Webster's last recordings were generally high-quality affairs. *My Man,* made live in Copenhagen months before his death in 1973, captures him in a typically mellow mood and reminds American listeners what joys we missed when Webster chose Europe for his final home.
★ ★ ★ **Ballads** / Verve
★ ★ ★ **Ben and Sweets (with Harry "Sweets" Edison)** / Odys.
★ ★ ★ ★ **Ben Webster and Associates** / Verve
★ ★ ★ ★ **Ben Webster/Joe Zawinul** / Fan./ OJC
★ ★ ★ ★ **Did You Call?** / Nessa
★ ★ ★ ★ ★ **Gerry Mulligan Meets Ben Webster** / Verve
★ ★ ★ ★ **King of the Tenors** / Verve
★ ★ ★ ★ **Kings of the Tenor Sax (with Don Byas)** / Commo.
★ ★ ★ ★ ★ **Soulville** / Verve
★ ★ ★ ★ **Travelin' Light (with Joe Zawinul)** / Mile.
★ ★ ★ ★ **The Warm Moods** / Discov.
Webster's popularity grows ever stronger, and valuable reissues of his work continued to appear throughout the Seventies and Eighties. Of the Verves, the double *Soulville* is a model of his blues-and-ballads mature Fifties perios, with Oscar Peterson's trios providing the basis of the accompaniment. The *And Associates* set, a Japanese import, is part of the earlier *Tenor Giants* package. Also available via Japan are *King of the Tenors,* a 1953 session that marked the beginning of Webster's fruitful affiliation with Verve, and the unbeatable 1960 conclave with Mulligan and pianist Jimmy Rowles, which features what may be Webster's supreme interpretation of "Chelsea Bridge." *The Warm Moods,* recorded around the same time, features Webster and strings.

The Odyssey and Milestone discs are slightly later, but before Webster left for Europe. Those who know Zawinul primarily for Weather Report should sample him in a mainstream setting. The Commodore package, in which Webster and Byas get a side each, features music recorded at the close of World War II, and is mainly valuable for the tour-de-force Byas/Slam Stewart duets.
Did You Call?, Webster's final studio session (from 1972), is one of the most gripping albums from his European period. Spanish piano whiz Tete Montoliu is in the rhythm section. — B.B.

DICKY WELLS
★ ★ ★ ★ ★ **In Paris, 1933** / Prest.
★ ★ ★ **Lonesome Road** / Uptown
A great trombonist from the classic Basie bands of the Thirties and Forties, Dicky Wells (b. 1909) has well passed his prime as a player on the Uptown LP. Still, the feeling for the music is intact, and it's a pleasure to hear him play plunger mute, even if it's for old-time's sake. The simple, craggy vocals are instructive: here's a man for whom playing music was as natural as speaking. Get the Prestige album to hear him at his peak. — F.G.

RANDY WESTON
★ ★ ★ ★ **African Nite** / Inner
★ ★ ★ **Berkshire Blues** / Ari./Free.
★ ★ ★ ★ **Blue Moses** / CTI
★ ★ ★ **Blues** / Trip
★ ★ ★ **Blues to Africa** / Ari./Free.
★ ★ ★ **Carnival** / Ari./Free.
★ ★ ★ **Get Happy** / Riv.
★ ★ ★ ★ ★ **Little Niles** / Blue N.
Randy Weston (b. 1926) has been an eloquent pianist and composer in the Duke Ellington-Thelonious Monk tradition for over two decades. His increasing interest in Africa led to his settling in Morocco for five years (1967–72). *Get Happy* has some of his first trio work, from 1955, with his strong touch and sense of dark harmonies and strategic silences already developed.
Little Niles is the finest Weston collection currently available. A 1958 sextet gives definitive readings of such memorable Weston compositions as the title track, "Pam's Waltz," and "Babe's Blues"; also included is a quintet with Kenny Dorham and Coleman Hawkins, adding such Weston staples as "High Fly" and "Where" in nightclub performances from 1959.
Weston spent the early Sixties with an ex-

cellent band that the record companies ignored. *Blues* represents a late addition of the group, after tenor saxophonist Booker Ervin had left. *Berkshire Blues,* produced in 1965 by Ellington, has one side of so-so trios by the band's rhythm section and a much more intriguing side of solo piano.

The early Seventies brought Weston home and stepped up his recording activity. *Blue Moses* marked his return; there are the usual CTI lapses (electric piano, overdubbed orchestrations), but the basic combo tracks—with Freddie Hubbard, Grover Washington, Ron Carter and Billy Cobham—are among the label's most substantial. Weston has done all of his post-1973 recording in Europe, where his 1974 Arista/Freedom sessions were made. *Carnival,* a Montreux performance, has overextended quintet tracks (with Billy Harper and Don Moye) plus a heartfelt solo tribute to Ellington; *Blues to Africa* shows the more dramatic traces of his African experiences in eight solo piano solos.

African Nite is another solo set from a year later. Weston is exploring the keyboard with greater rhythmic freedom, yet his feeling for melody remains and several good new tunes are introduced.

★ ★ ★ ★ **Randy Weston / Pausa**
★ ★ ★ ★ **Trio and Solo / Riv.**
★ ★ ★ ★ **Zulu / Mile.**

Zulu, a two-record set, reissues early-Weston (1954–56) Riverside sessions, in solo, trio or (with baritone saxophonist Cecil Payne) quartet format. The focus is on Weston's angular, Monk-inspired playing rather than on composing. (If you're seeking only one LP of the same material, the Japanese import *Trio and Solo* duplicates the *Zulu* set, but omits the quartet dates.) The Pausa is another good solo set from the Seventies.

All of the above are fine collections, if not the pianist's best.   — B.B.

ANDREW WHITE

★ ★ ★ ★ **Collage / Andr.**
★ ★ ★ ★ **Passion Flower / Andr.**
★ ★ ★ **Seven Giant Steps for Coltrane / Andr.**

Washington, D.C.-based Andrew White (b. 1942) is nothing if not unique. He has toured with Stevie Wonder and the Fifth Dimension on electric bass, recorded on that instrument plus English horn with Weather Report, transcribed 421 John Coltrane solos, arranged Coltrane's music for orchestra, and recorded as a saxophone soloist with McCoy Tyner (alto) and on more than forty albums (alto and tenor) for his own label, Andrew's Music. White's album covers are uniformly

gold print on white background, with, judging from those I have seen, a version of his composition "Theme" always included.

The White albums rated above are those which this writer has heard. Both *Passion Flower* and *Collage* are mid-Seventies quartets, with Steve Novosel on bass, and Blackbyrds Kevin Toney (piano) and Keith Killgo (drums) showing what they can do in a "straight-ahead" context. *Passion Flower* seems like a study of Coltrane's evolution, with White reflecting much of the spectrum in tenor solos on his own blues lines. *Collage* stresses some interesting arranging ideas and tune choices (Wayne Shorter's "Contemplation," Coltrane's "Just for the Love," Les Baxter's "Dock at Papeete" [!]). *Seven Giant Steps,* containing seven live, unaccompanied alto solos, supposedly based on Coltrane's "Giant Steps," is a bit indulgent even for White. The records are available from 4830 S. Dakota Ave., N.E., Washington, D.C. 20017.   — B.B.

LENNY WHITE

★ ★ ★ **Adventures of the Astral Pirates / Elek.**
★ ★ ★ **Big City / Nemp.**
★ ★ ★ **Streamline / Elek.**
★ ★ ★ **Venusian Summer / Nemp.**

Lenny White is one of the better fusion drummers, probably due to his work with more mainstream leaders like Joe Henderson, Stan Getz and Jackie McLean. His playing on the landmark *Hymn of the Seventh Galaxy* with Chick Corea's Return to Forever gives better-known names like Billy Cobham a run for their money. But White suffers from the problem that seems to plague all fusion drummers when they try to record on their own—his albums are badly unfocused, trying to do a million different things at once and accomplishing none of them. Each of White's solo albums have moments that make them worthwhile, but none of them hold together for a full listening. White is better as a producer as his Echoes of an Era projects (on which he also plays) prove.
   — J.S.

WIDESPREAD DEPRESSION ORCHESTRA

★ ★ **Boogie in the Barnyard / Stash**
★ ★ **Downtown Uproar / Stash**
★ ★ **It's Time to Jump and Shout / Stash**

Thirties swing revival band. Probably fun live, but why bother with their discs when you can buy records by Chick Webb?
   — F.G.

JACK WILKINS
★ ★ ★ ★ ★ Merge / Chi.

Why isn't Jack Wilkins (b. 1944) as well known as Pat Metheny? *Merge* is a virtual godsend for those who have lost hope for the future of jazz guitar. Warm-toned, limber, comfortable with bop, modality and everything in between, Wilkins is probably ignored by the public because he shuns effects for old-fashioned melodic picking, both electric and acoustic.

Besides being a showcase for the leader's inspiring playing, *Merge* features the dream band of Jack DeJohnette, Eddie Gomez and Randy Brecker. Among the revelations: Gomez' thrilling arco work and hard evidence that Brecker really can play. This album should have alerted everyone (but unfortunately didn't) to one of the very best young guitarists since Wes Montgomery.
— S.F.

BUSTER WILLIAMS
★ ★ ★ Crystal Reflections / Muse
★ ★ ★ Heartbeat / Muse
★ ★ ★ Pinnacle / Muse

Although he has been threatening to turn into a Ron Carter clone recently, bassist Buster Williams (b. 1942) established himself in the late Sixties and Seventies as one of the more distinctive sidemen on his instrument. Williams developed a modernist style that retained a solid, supportive feel which fit right into the niche left open when Richard Davis left the scene, and Carter became too busy. His willingness to restrain his obvious finger-flying skills has always set Williams apart from his flashy peers. Listen to his accompaniment on Herbie Hancock's *The Prisoner*; he is astute, alert, but also very funky.

Williams does not play shy on his own albums; he gives himself *lots* of solo space. He avoids ego-tripping and boredom by constantly shifting personnel and settings around. *Crystal* uses Kenny Barron and Jimmy Rowles in separate trio tracks, and a bass-vibes duet with Roy Ayers. *Heartbeat* has a sextet track with strings and voice and a bass solo. *Pinnacle* incorporates horns. Not all of this is successful, but at least Williams is in there trying. — S.F.

JESSICA WILLIAMS
★ ★ ★ ★ ★ Orgonomic Music / Clean Cuts
★ ★ ★ ★ The Portal of Antrim / Adel.
★ ★ ★ ★ Portraits / Adel.
★ ★ ★ ★ Rivers of Memory / Clean Cuts
★ ★ ★ ★ Update / Clean Cuts

Keyboardist Jessica Williams has a chameleonlike approach to playing that results in being compared at various times to Cecil Taylor, Keith Jarrett, McCoy Tyner, Chick Corea, Thelonious Monk, Herbie Hancock and Art Tatum. This sort of eclecticism is unusual and potentially too disjointed, but Williams animates her different moods with emotional conviction. *Rivers of Memory,* her debut, features her on seven different keyboard and percussion instruments and shows that Williams is able to use them all very well conceptually. *Portal* continues to feature her to good effect in a trio format, while *Portraits* is a dazzlingly virtuosic live acoustic piano solo performance. *Orgonomic Music,* her most acclaimed album, is a high-powered septet outing with trumpeter Eddie Henderson sharing the solo spotlight with Williams. *Update* is a more languid set in which Williams returns to a quartet with saxophonist Eddie Harris as the featured guest soloist. — J.S.

MARION WILLIAMS
★ ★ ★ ★ ★ Lord, You've Been Mighty Good to Me / JHR/Col.
★ ★ ★ ★ This Too Shall Pass / Nashb.

Marion Williams (b. 1927) remains one of the few gospel singers with a direct connection to jazz. She performed brilliantly in 1964 with Milt Jackson and Ray Brown on *Much in Common* (Verve, out of print). Junior Mance, Keith Jarrett, Ray Bryant, Hank Jones and Joe Zawinul were enlisted for two of her Atlantic releases in 1969 and '71. Jo Jones and Milt Hinton abetted her performance at the 1967 *Spirituals to Swing Concert* (Columbia). Williams has also had a long association with jazz impresario John Hammond, for whom she now records.

Despite these jazz affiliations, Williams remains a four-square gospel singer who's at her best in hymns and gospel songs. She injects each performance, however, with a dazzling array of jazz and blues devices—from shouts to moans to growls. Her gift for improvisation is legend among fellow performers.

An early association with the Clara Ward Singers (1947–58) during gospel's golden age established Williams' own credentials as well as aiding that group's artistic and commercial success. After an interim with her own group, the Stars of Faith, Williams began a solo career in 1965 with a concert at Yale University. Since then she has performed in colleges, churches and jazz festivals throughout the U.S., Europe and Africa.

Now in her mid-fifties, Williams is at the peak of her powers. *Prayer Changes Things* (Atlantic, unfortunately out of print) is perhaps the quintessential gospel recording, moving beyond words and accessible to believer and nonbeliever alike. Try to find it in cutout bins. As gospel scholar Tony Heilbut (also Williams' producer) noted in *The Gospel Sound: Good News and Bad Times,* "Marion is simply the most lyrical and imaginative singer gospel has produced . . . The actual lyrical procedure assumes a musical interest comparable to the most lustrous and coherent jazz improvisations."

Heilbut's praise seems not at all excessive after one listens to Williams perform the title song on *Precious Lord: New Recordings of the Great Gospel Songs of Thomas A. Dorsey* (Columbia). Professor Dorsey concluded his spoken introduction to this most famous of gospel songs by telling his singer to perform it with "the feeling and the fervor." Williams responded with a small masterpiece of seamlessly wedded feeling and technique.

Both albums listed in the discography are fine, with the edge given to Hammond's due to its better production values. Simply put, Marion Williams is a treasure. — A.R.

MARY LOU WILLIAMS
★ ★ ★ ★ ★ **The Asch Recordings, 1944–47 / Folk.**
★ ★ ★ **Embraced (with Cecil Taylor) / Pablo L.**
★ ★ ★ ★ **My Mama Pinned a Rose on Me / Pablo**
★ ★ ★ **Rehearsal, Vol. 1 / Folk.**
★ ★ ★ ★ **Solo Recital—Montreux Jazz Festival '78 / Pablo L.**
★ ★ ★ ★ ★ **Zodiac Suite / Folk.**
Pianist, composer and arranger Mary Lou Williams (1910–1981) accomplished the near impossible in her fifty-six-year career: as a pianist she was able to absorb and translate the entire history of jazz piano into a personal style; as an arranger and composer she contributed to the band books of Duke Ellington, Benny Goodman and others, and almost single-handedly ensured the success of Andy Kirk & His Clouds of Joy swing band with her compositions.

Williams' work with Kirk is documented on several of the bandleader's albums (now on MCA), especially *The Lady Who Swings the Band* and *Instrumentally Speaking,* the latter including the classic "Froggy Bottom," "Mary's Idea" and "Walkin' And Swingin'."

Zodiac Suite, a twelve-part interpretation of the zodiac scored for an eighteen-piece orchestra, is Williams' master work as a composer. *The Asch Recordings,* culled from the same period, show Williams working in a variety of settings on original material and standards, invariably with outstanding side-

men. *Rehearsal* is exactly that: ten minutes of partial takes.

The later recordings for Pablo are ample demonstration that even though Williams began her career as a disciple of the Earl Hines school of piano, she never retrogressed but continued to be intrigued by the ever-changing directions of jazz. Although her own albums are more successful than her meeting with Cecil Taylor, that she would consider such a challenge—let alone record it—is testament to her great exploratory spirit. — F.G.

TONY WILLIAMS
★ ★ ★ ★ **Believe It / Col.**
★ ★ ★ **Best of / Col.**
★ ★ **Joy of Flying / Col.**
★ ★ ★ **Million Dollar Legs / Col.**
★ ★ ★ ★ ★ **Once in a Lifetime / Verve**
One of the few genuinely innovative post-Art Blakey jazz drummers, Tony Williams (b. 1945) earned his reputation as the rhythmic mainspring for the mid-Sixties Miles Davis quintet that also included Herbie Hancock, Wayne Shorter and Ron Carter. Williams has been in the forefront of jazz-rock fusion since his collaboration with John McLaughlin in Lifetime. Some of their best work is collected on the Verve set. His in-print records include *Believe It* and *Million Dollar Legs,* both funk fusion delights featuring the guitar playing of ex-Soft Machine axeman Alan Holdsworth. Williams also plays with V.S.O.P., the acoustic band which reunites Miles Davis' great rhythm section. — J.S.

BERT WILSON
★ ★ ★ **Kaleidoscopic Visions/Bert Wilson and Rebirth / Au Roar**
A superior post-Coltrane saxophonist from the Bay Area, Bert Wilson has recorded intermittently as a sideman during the last fifteen years with regional compatriots Sonny Simmons, James Zitro and Smiley Winters, but *Kaleidoscopic Visions* is his only LP as a leader. Stricken with polio during his childhood, Wilson began playing reeds to clear his lungs of congestion. Subsequently, he developed into a player of enormous power, capable of explosive bursts of sound. His tone is thicker and sweeter than most progressive saxophonists', and his technical abilities are demonstrated in stunning, pyrotechnic lines that employ brains as well as brawn. Wilson has sounded better live and on other unreleased recordings than he does on *Kaleidoscopic Visions,* but that's not enough reason to pass on this album. — F.G.

PHIL WOODS
★ ★ ★ **At the Vanguard** / **Ant.**
★ ★ ★ ★ **Birds of a Feather** / **Ant.**
★ ★ ★ **More Live** / **Clean Cut**
★ ★ ★ ★ **Musique Du Bois** / **Muse**
★ ★ ★ ★ **Pairing Off** / **Fan./OJC**
★ ★ ★ ★ **Phil Woods Quartet Vol. 1** /
  Clean Cut
★ ★ ★ ★ **Round Trip** / **Verve**
★ ★ ★ ★ **Three for All (with Tommy**
  Flanagan and Red Mitchell) / **Enja**
★ ★ ★ ★ **Woodlore** / **Prest. OJC**

Alto saxophonist Phil Woods (b. 1931) established himself as a hot Charlie Parker-inspired bop player in stints with Dizzy Gillespie, Quincy Jones, Charlie Barnett and Benny Goodman in the Fifties and Sixties while leading his own groups. The OJC and Verve sides document some of his earlier work. *Pairing Off* is particularly interesting in that it's a septet date in which a second alto sax (Gene Quill) joins Woods against two trumpeters, Kenny Dorham and Donald Byrd. After moving to Europe at the end of the Sixties, Woods returned to the U.S. in the Seventies and has been extremely successful since. He is consistently voted top honors in critics' and readers' polls and has received a handful of Grammy nominations—two for *Quartet Vol. 1.* Check the cutout bins for his Grammy-award-winning albums *Images* (1975; coled by Michel Legrand) and *Live from the Showboat* (1977). Woods also won an award for the best instrumental performance by a jazz group at the twenty-fifth Grammy ceremony.
— J.S.

WORLD SAXOPHONE QUARTET
★ ★ ★ ★ **Live in Zurich** / **Black S.**
★ ★ ★ **Point of No Return** / **Moers**
★ ★ ★ ★ ★ **Revue** / **Black S.**
★ ★ ★ ★ **Steppin' with the World Saxophone**
  Quartet / **Black S.**
★ ★ ★ ★ ★ **W.S.Q.** / **Black S.**

Jazz's more daring players have been moving toward unconventional instrumentations since the AACM made its mark in the mid-Sixties, so an all-reed band like the World Saxophone Quartet was inevitable. As it happens, three of the players—Hamiet Bluiett, Julius Hemphill (b. 1940) and Oliver Lake (b. 1944)—are from St. Louis' Black Artists Group, a collective with strong ties to the AACM. David Murray (b. 1955), from California and a generation younger, completes the W.S.Q. Each player has also done extensive work under his own name: Bluiett, the leading new-music baritone player, recorded *Birthright* (India Navigation), one of the best solo-horn recitals, plus such good band records as *Dangerously Suite* (Soul Note); see separate entries for Hemphill, Lake and Murray.

Point of No Return, their debut album, is a monochromatically shrill live performance, without any of the attention to nuance the band would soon attain. *Steppin'* was recorded eighteen months later and reflects the care that the saxophonists, especially Hemphill (who did most of the writing here), began paying to ensemble possibilities. Funk and bop are touched upon as well as more abstract terrain. *W.S.Q.* has shorter pieces, writing duties spread more evenly among the members, and a growing richness in the section harmonies. *Revue* marks a further step in the band's evolution, with gentler ensemble textures and solo features for each of its members. A band that manages to entice both the mind and the feet, W.S.Q. is one of today's premier groups. — B.B.

JIMMY YANCEY

★ ★ ★ ★ ★ **Chicago Piano / Atl.**
★ ★ ★ ★ ★ **The Immortal Jimmy Yancey /**
  Oldie B.
★ ★ ★ ★ ★ **Jimmy Yancey / Oldie B.**

Possibly the best of all the barrelhouse piano practitioners, Yancey brought a quiet eloquence and nuance to the style that the rough-and-tumble barroom soundtrack genre lacked elsewhere. Yancey played for himself and did not actively pursue recording dates, so his output is limited but precious. By day he worked as a professional baseball player and later as a groundskeeper for the Chicago White Sox; at night he would play his piano. The Oldie Blues sides collect his earliest work, from 1939 on *Immortal* and from 1943 on the other, which also includes a rare and beautiful private party recording. The Atlantic sides are reissues of an eloquent session made just a few weeks before his death in 1951 with Jimmy's wife, Mama Yancey, singing on some tracks. — J.S.

LARRY YOUNG

★ ★ ★ **Groove Street / Prest.**
★ ★ ★ **Larry Young's Fuel / Ari.**
★ ★ ★ **Mother Ship / Blue N.**
★ ★ ★ **Spaceball / Ari.**

A wildly innovative keyboardist, Larry Young (1940–1978) was noted for his virtuoso organ playing with Tony Williams, Jimi Hendrix and Miles Davis. He recorded a series of solo albums in the Sixties on Blue Note and Prestige, most of which are unfortunately out of print. *Groove Street* is representative if not exemplary of this period. The two mid-Seventies recordings for Arista represent Young's attempt at a comeback in the disco-funk mold. The albums were neither commercial nor artistic successes, yet the force of Young's tremendous imagination keeps everything moving even at the worst

moments. *Spaceball* especially is a triumph of musicianship over terrible ideas. Young's multikeyboard pyrotechnics scale along interminable vamps with names like "Sticky Wicket." — J.S.

LESTER YOUNG

Lester Young (1909–1959), whom Billie Holiday dubbed the President (shortened to Pres or Prez), is one of the half-dozen greatest soloists in jazz history. He moved beyond Coleman Hawkins' domination of tenor sax style with his first recordings in 1936, producing a light tone and oblique melodic ideas that seemed to skim the music's harmonic surface. His swing, a strange blend of floating and stomping, was the most inexorable of the period, and nobody before or since has conveyed more soulful lyricism. Young's ideas led to bebop, cool jazz and rhythm & blues—in other words, to every black music trend of the following decade. Rating his albums should be unnecessary, although the attempt has been made.

★ ★ ★ ★ ★ **The Lester Young Story, Vol. 1**
  / Col.

First in CBS' chronological series of every Young performance they own. This 1936–37 material has his debut, with a quintet from Count Basie's band (where Young worked until 1940), and his first transcendent collaborations with Teddy Wilson and Billie Holiday (Jo Jones, Benny Goodman and Buck Clayton also participate).

★ ★ ★ ★ ★ **Pres at His Very Best / Trip**

From 1943 and 1944, before his emotionally damaging stay in the Army. His best quartet work, with Johnny Guarnieri, Slam Stewart and Sid Catlett; and a Basie septet featuring the Count, Clayton, Jones, Dicky Wells and Freddie Green.

★ ★ ★ ★ ★ **Classic Tenors / Fly. D.**

Four tracks by a similar septet, same vintage, with Young's relevance to the R&B

tenors especially evident. Also eight Coleman Hawkins titles from 1943.

★ ★ ★ ★ ★ **Pres/The Complete Savoy Recordings / Savoy**
Recorded just before entering the Army (with most of the Basie Band and combos featuring Cozy Cole and Basie), plus a side from 1949, less brilliant but still substantial Young.

★ ★ ★ ★ ★ **The Aladdin Sessions / Blue N.**
Quintets, sextets, septets from 1945 to 1948, with the scars of racial harassment and incarceration for possession of marijuana while in the service evident. The twenty-seven performances are still beautiful, in a kicking swing-to-bop style.

★ ★ ★ ★ **Lester Swings / Verve**
Young is clearly a changed man in the 1950–51 quartets here, although the eight 1945 performances by the odd trio of Young, pianist Nat "King" Cole and drummer Buddy Rich are among the best postwar Pres.

★ ★ ★ ★ ★ **Bird and Pres: The 1946 Concerts / Verve**
These Jazz at the Philharmonic tapes find Young lapsing into crowd-pleasing exhibitionism on the final side, but the company (Charlie Parker, Dizzy Gillespie, Coleman Hawkins) can't be beat.

★ ★ ★ ★ ★ **Pres Lives / Savoy**
Admittedly from 1950, but revealing for the aural picture of Young in a club blowing long and hard over his familiar mix of standards and blues.

★ ★ ★ ★ ★ **Pres and Teddy and Oscar / Verve**
Teddy is Wilson, Oscar is Peterson, the collaborations are from 1956 and 1952 respectively. Young is changed, more predictable and sometimes too languid, but even in decline he was a master. His best from the Fifties.

★ ★ ★ **Pres in Europe / Onyx**
Privately recorded performances from 1956 and 1957. This supposedly defeated giant could still move mountains—hear "Lester's European Blues." He died in 1959 at the age of fifty.

★ ★ ★ ★ ★ **In Washington D.C. at Olivia Davis' Patio Lounge, Vol. 1 / Pablo**
★ ★ ★ ★ ★ **In Washington D.C., Vol. 2 / Pablo L.**
★ ★ ★ ★ ★ **In Washington D.C., Vol. 3 / Pablo L.**

★ ★ ★ **Jazz Giants '56 (with Roy Eldridge, Teddy Wilson) / Verve**
★ ★ ★ ★ ★ **Kansas City Six and Five / Commo.**
★ ★ ★ ★ **Master Takes / Savoy**
★ ★ **Mean to Me / Verve**
★ ★ ★ ★ **The Lester Young Story, Vol. 2: A Musical Romance (with Billie Holiday) / Col.**
★ ★ ★ ★ ★ **The Lester Young Story, Vol. 3: Enter the Count (with Count Basie, Holiday) / Col.**
★ ★ ★ ★ ★ **The Lester Young Story, Vol. 4: Lester Leaps In (with Basie, Holiday) / Col.**
★ ★ ★ ★ ★ **The Lester Young Story, Vol. 5: Evening of a Basie-ite (with Basie) / Col.**
A lot of stars up there, but then some immortal Young records have been appearing. The Columbia project was completed with four more two-record sets, laying out every take and alternate in the label's catalogue on which Young soloed during the Thirties. This covers much of the great Young with Basie, and all of the great Young with Holiday. The Commodore album, from the same general period, is Kansas City chamber jazz with Buck Clayton, Basie's stunning "all-American" rhythm section (minus the Count), early electric guitar solos by Eddie Durham and rare samplings of Young on clarinet.

The later Verve and Pablo material should probably be awarded lower ratings than Young's vintage performances, but *Jazz Giants '56* catches several swing-era stars in their glowing maturity, and the taped performances that surfaced on Pablo find Young relaxed and luminous in 1956. These albums give the lie to Young's supposed artistic collapse. The *Master Takes* is *The Complete Savoy* without alternates.

★ ★ ★ **Laughin' to Keep from Cryin' (with Harry Edison, Roy Eldridge) / Verve**
★ ★ ★ ★ **Pres / Verve**
★ ★ ★ **Pres and Sweets (with Harry Edison) / Verve**
Young reissues in the Japanese Verve facsimile series tend to duplicate material already available on domestic two-record sets. An exception is *Laughin' to Keep from Cryin'*, one of Young's last recordings and notable primarily for his return to the clarinet on one side of the album. — B.B.

JOE ZAWINUL
★ ★ ★ ★ **Zawinul** / Atl.

This fine solo album by the master keyboardist who leads Weather Report includes an adaptation of "In a Silent Way," which Joe Zawinul (b. 1932) wrote for one of Miles Davis' most innovative groups, and pairs Zawinul with another virtuoso keyboardist, Herbie Hancock. With Weather Report, Zawinul expanded his keyboard arsenal to an astounding array of synthesizers and related equipment, but here he uses only electric piano, to sublime effect. — J.S.

Bibliography

Albertson, Chris. *Bessie.* New York: Stein and Day, 1972.

Allen, Walter C., and Brian Rust. *King Joe Oliver.* Belleville, NJ: Allen and Rust, 1955.

Armstrong, Louis. *Satchmo.* New York: Prentice-Hall, 1954.

———. *Swing That Music.* New York: Longmans, Green, 1936.

Baker, David. *Jazz Improvisation.* Chicago: Music Workshop Publication, 1969.

Balliett, Whitney. *American Singers.* New York: Oxford University Press, 1979.

———. *Dinosaurs in the Morning.* Philadelphia: Lippincott, 1962.

———. *Jelly Roll, Jabbo and Fats.* New York: Oxford University Press, 1983.

———. *New York Notes.* Boston: Houghton Mifflin, 1976.

———. *Night Creature.* New York: Oxford University Press, 1981.

———. *The Sound of Surprise.* New York: Dutton, 1959.

———. *Such Sweet Thunder.* New York: Bobbs-Merrill, 1966.

Bechet, Sidney. *Treat It Gentle.* New York: Da Capo, 1975.

Berendt, Joachim. *The Jazz Book.* New York: Lawrence Hill, 1975.

Berton, R. *Remembering Bix.* New York: Harper, 1974.

Blackstone, Orin. *Index to Jazz.* New Orleans: Gordon Gullickson, 1947.

Blesh, Rudi. *Combo: USA.* New York: Chilton, 1971.

———. *Eight Lives in Jazz.* New York: Hayden, 1971.

———. *Shining Trumpets.* New York: Da Capo, 1975.

———. *This Is Jazz.* San Francisco, 1943.

——— and Harriet Janis. *They All Played Ragtime.* New York: Oak Publications, 1971.

Boulton, David. *Jazz in Britain.* London: W.H. Allen, 1958.

Brunn, H.O. *The Story of the Original Dixieland Jazz Band.* Baton Rouge: Louisiana State University Press, 1960.

Buerkle, Jack V., and Danny Barker. *Bourbon Street Black.* New York: Oxford University Press, 1973.

Carey, Dave, and Albert McCarthy. *The Directory of Recorded Jazz and Swing Music.* Fordingsbridge, Hampshire, Eng.: Delphic Press, 1949.

Carmichael, Hoagy. *The Stardust Road.* New York: Rinehart, 1946.

Case, Brian, and Stan Britt. *The Illustrated Encyclopedia of Jazz.* New York: Harmony, 1978.

Cerulli, Dom, Burt Korall, and Mort Nasatir. *The Jazz World.* New York: Ballantine, 1960.

Charters, Samuel. *Jazz: New Orleans 1885–1963.* New York: Oak Publications, 1971.

——— and L. Kunstadt. *Jazz: A History of the New York Scene.* New York: Doubleday, 1962.

Chilton, John. *Billie's Blues.* New York: Stein and Day, 1975.

———. *Who's Who of Jazz.* New York: Chilton, 1972.

Coker, Jerry. *Improvising Jazz.* Englewood Cliffs, NJ: Prentice-Hall, 1964.

———. *The Jazz Idiom.* Englewood Cliffs, NJ: Prentice-Hall, 1975.

Cole, Bill. *John Coltrane.* New York: Schirmer, 1976.

———. *Miles Davis.* New York: Morrow, 1974.

Collier, Graham. *Jazz.* London: Cambridge University Press, 1975.

Collier, James Lincoln. *The Making of Jazz.* New York: Delta, 1978.

Condon, A.E., and H. O'Neal. *The Eddie Condon Scrapbook of Jazz.* New York: St. Martin's, 1973.

Condon, Eddie, and Richard Gehman, eds. *Eddie Condon's Treasury of Jazz.* New York: Dial, 1956.

Condon, Eddie, and Thomas Sugrue. *We Called It Music.* New York: Holt, 1947.

Connor, Donald Russell. *B.G.—Off the Record.* Fairless Hills, PA: Gaildonna Publishers, 1958.

Coryell, Julie, and Laura Friedman. *Jazz-Rock Fusion.* New York: Delta, 1978.

Courlander, Harold. *The World of Earl Hines.* New York: Charles Scribner's Sons, 1977.

Dance, Stanley. *The World of Count Basie.* New York: Charles Scribner's Sons, 1980.

———. *The World of Duke Ellington.* New York: Da Capo, 1970.

———. *The World of Swing.* New York: Charles Scribner's Sons, 1974.

Delaunay, Charles. *Django Reinhardt.* New York: Da Capo, 1961.

De Toledano, Ralph, ed. *Frontiers of Jazz.* New York: Ungar, 1962.

Dexter, Dave, Jr. *The Jazz Story.* Englewood Cliffs, NJ: Prentice-Hall, 1964.

Dodds, Warren, and Larry Gara. *The Baby Dodds Story.* Los Angeles: Contemporary Press, 1959.

Easton, Carol. *Straight Ahead: The Story of Stan Kenton.* New York: Da Capo, 1973.

Eaton, Jeanette. *Trumpeter's Tale: The Story of Young Louis Armstrong.* New York: Morrow, 1955.

Ellington, Duke. *Music Is My Mistress.* New York: Doubleday, 1973.

Feather, Leonard. *The Book of Jazz.* New York: Horizon Press, 1957.

———. *The Encyclopedia of Jazz.* New York: Horizon Press, 1955, 1960.

———. *The Encyclopedia of Jazz in the Sixties.* New York: Horizon Press, 1967.

———. *The Pleasures of Jazz.* New York: Horizon Press, 1976.

———. *From Satchmo to Miles.* New York: Stein and Day, 1972.

Feather, Leonard, and Ira Gitler. *The Encyclopedia of Jazz in the Seventies.* New York: Quartet, 1976.

Finkelstein, Sidney. *Jazz: A People's Music.* New York: Da Capo, 1975.

Fox, Charles. *Fats Waller.* New York: A.S. Barnes, 1961.

———. *Jazz in Perspective.* London: BBC, 1969.

Freeman, Budd. *You Don't Look Like a Musician.* Detroit: Balamp Publishing, 1974.

Gammond, Peter. *Scott Joplin and the Ragtime Era.* New York: St. Martin's, 1975.

Garfield, Jane. *Books and Periodicals on Jazz from 1926 to 1932.* New York: Columbia University School of Library Science, 1933.

Gelatt, Roland. *The Fabulous Phonograph.* New York: Appleton-Century, 1965.

Giddins, Gary. *Riding On a Blue Note.* New York: Oxford University Press, 1981.

Gitler, Ira. *Jazz Masters of the Forties.* New York: Collier Books, 1974.

Gleason, Ralph J. *Celebrating the Duke.* New York: Dell, 1975.

———, ed. *Jam Session: An Anthology of Jazz.* New York: Putnam, 1958.

Goffin, Robert. *Horn of Plenty: The Story of Louis Armstrong.* New York: Allen, Towne and Heath, 1947.

———. *Jazz: From the Congo to the Metropolitan.* New York: Da Capo, 1975.

Gold, Robert S. *Jazz Talk.* New York: Bobbs-Merrill, 1975.

Goldberg, Isaac. *Jazz Masters of the Fifties.* New York: Macmillan, 1965.

Goodman, Benny, and Irving Kolodin. *The Kingdom of Swing.* New York: Ungar, 1961.

Gordon, Max. *Live at the Village Vanguard.* New York: Da Capo, 1980.

Graham, Alberta. *Strike Up the Band! Bandleaders of Today.* New York: Nelson, 1949.

Green, Benny. *Drums in My Ears.* New York: Horizon Press, 1973.

———. *The Reluctant Art.* New York: Horizon Press, 1963.

Grossman, William, and Jack W. Farrell. *The Heart of Jazz.* New York: New York University Press, 1955.

Hadlock, Richard. *Jazz Masters of the Twenties.* New York: Collier, 1974.

Hammond, John. *John Hammond on Record.* New York: Summit, 1977.

Handy, W.C. *Father of the Blues.* New York: Collier Books, 1970.

Handy, W.C., and Abbe Niles. *A Treasury of the Blues.* New York: C. Boni, 1949.

Harris, Rex. *Jazz.* Harmondsworth, Middlesex: Penguin, 1952.

——— and Brian Rust. *Recorded Jazz: A Critical Guide.* Baltimore: Penguin, 1958.

Hawes, Hampton, and Don Asher. *Raise Up Off Me.* New York: Coward, McCann & Geoghegan, 1972.

Hentoff, Nat. *Jazz Country.* New York: Harper & Row, 1965.

———. *Jazz Is.* New York: Random House, 1976.

———. *The Jazz Life.* New York: Da Capo, 1975.

Hentoff, Nat, and Albert McCarthy, eds. *Jazz.* New York: Rinehart, 1959; Da Capo, 1974.

Hobson, Wilder. *American Jazz Music.* New York: W.W. Norton, 1939.

Hodier, Andre. *Jazz: Its Evolution and Essence.* New York: Grove Press, 1956.

Holiday, Billie, with William Dufty. *Lady Sings the Blues.* New York: Lancer Books, 1965.

Horne, Lena, with Helen Arstein and Carlton Moss. *In Person, Lena Horne.* New York: Greenberg, 1950.

Horricks, Raymond. *Count Basie and His Orchestra.* New York: Citadel Press, 1958.

——— and others. *These Jazzmen of Our Time.* London: Gollancz, 1959.

Hughes, Langston. *The Big Sea: An Autobiography.* New York: Knopf, 1945.

———. *Famous Negro Music Makers.* New York: Dodd, Mead, 1955.

———. *The First Book of Jazz.* New York: F. Watts, 1955.

Hughes, Patrick C. *Opening Bars, Beginning an Autobiography.* London: Pilot Press, 1946.

Hughes, Patrick C. *Second Movement.* London: Museum Press, 1951.

James, Burnett. *Bix Beiderbecke.* New York: A.S. Barnes, 1961.

James, Michael. *Dizzy Gillespie.* New York: A.S. Barnes, 1961.

———. *Miles Davis.* New York: A.S. Barnes, 1961.

Jewell, Derek. *Duke: A Portrait of Duke Ellington.* New York: W.W. Norton, 1977.

Jones, LeRoi. *Black Music.* New York: Morrow, 1967.

———. *Blues People.* New York: Morrow, 1963.

Jones, Max, and John Chilton. *Louis: The Louis Armstrong Story.* Boston: Little, Brown, 1971.

Kaminsky, Max, with V.E. Hughes. *My Life in Jazz.* London: Jazz Book Club, 1965.

Keepnews, Orin, and Bill Grauer, Jr. *A Pictorial History of Jazz.* New York: Crown, 1955.

Keil, Charles. *Urban Blues.* Chicago: University of Chicago Press, 1969.

Kennington, Donald. *The Literature of Jazz.* Chicago: American Library Association, 1971.

Kirkeby, Ed, with Duncan P. Schiedt and Sinclair Trail. *Ain't Misbehavin'.* New York: Da Capo, 1975.

Kmen, Henry A. *Music in New Orleans.* Baton Rouge: Louisiana State University Press, 1966.

Kofsky, Frank. *Black Nationalism and the Revolution in Music.* New York: Pathfinder Press, 1970.

Lambert, G.E. *Duke Ellington.* New York: A.S. Barnes, 1961.

———. *Johnny Dodds.* New York: A.S. Barnes, 1961.

Leonard, Neil. *Jazz and the White Americans.* Chicago: Chicago University Press, 1962.

Lomax, Alan. *Mister Jelly Roll.* Berkeley: University of California Press, 1950.

Longstreet, Stephen. *The Real Jazz Old and New.* Baton Rouge: Louisiana State University Press, 1956.

Manone, Wingy, and Paul Vandervoort. *Trumpet on the Wing.* Garden City, NY: Doubleday, 1948.

McCarthy, Albert. *Big Band Jazz.* New York: Putnam's, 1974.

———. *Coleman Hawkins.* London: Cassell, 1963.

———. *The Dance Band Era.* London: Spring Books, 1971.

———. *Louis Armstrong.* New York: A.S. Barnes, 1961.

———. *Piano Jazz No. 2.* London. 1945.

McCarthy, Albert, and others. *Jazz on Record: A Critical Guide to the First Fifty Years, 1917–1967.* London: Hanover Press, 1968.

Mehegan, John. *Jazz Improvisation,* 4 vols. New York: Watson-Guptill Publications, 1958–65.

Meryman, Richard. *Louis Armstrong—A Self-Portrait.* New York: Eakins Press, 1971.

Mellers, Wilfred. *Music in a Newfound Land.* New York: Knopf, 1965.

Merriam, Alan P., with Robert J. Banford. *A Bibliography of Jazz.* New York: Da Capo, 1970.

Mezzrow, Milton, and Wolfe, Bernard. *Really the Blues.* New York: Random House, 1946.

Mingus, Charles. *Beneath the Underdog.* New York: Knopf, 1971.

Morgan, Alun, and Raymond Horricks. *Modern Jazz.* London: Gollancz, 1956.

Murray, Albert. *Stomping the Blues.* New York: McGraw-Hill, 1976.

Nanry, Charles, ed. *American Music: From Storyville to Woodstock.* New Brunswick: Transaction Books, 1972.

Newton, Francis. *The Jazz Scene.* New York: Da Capo Press, 1975.

Nisenson, Eric. *Round About Midnight: A Portrait of Miles Davis.* New York: Dial, 1982.

Nketia, J.H. Kwabena. *The Music of Africa.* New York: W.W. Norton, 1974.

Oliver, Paul. *Bessie Smith.* New York: A.S. Barnes, 1961.

———. *The Meaning of the Blues.* New York: Collier Books, 1963.

————. *Savannah Syncopators.* New York: Stein and Day, 1970.

Osgood, Henry. *So This Is Jazz.* Boston: Little, Brown, 1926.

Ostransky, Leroy. *The Anatomy of Jazz.* Seattle: University of Washington Press, 1960.

————. *Understanding Jazz.* Englewood Cliffs, NJ: Prentice-Hall, 1977.

Panassie, Hughes. *Louis Armstrong.* New York: Charles Scribner's Sons, 1971.

————. *The Real Jazz.* New York: Smith and Durrell, 1942.

Paul, Elliott H. *That Crazy American Music.* New York: Bobbs-Merrill, 1957.

Pepper, Art, and Laurie Pepper. *Straight Life.* New York: Schirmer Books, 1979.

Preston, Denis. *Mood Indigo.* Egham, Surrey, Eng.: Citizen Press, 1946.

Priestley, Brian. *Mingus: A Critical Biography.* London: Quartet Books, 1982.

Ramsey, Frederick, Jr. *Been Here and Gone.* Brunswick, NJ: Rutgers University Press, 1960.

————. *A Guide to Longplay Jazz Records.* New York: Long Player Publications, 1954.

Ramsey, Frederick, Jr., and Charles Edward Smith, eds. *Jazzmen.* New York: Harcourt, Brace, 1939.

Reisner, Robert G. *Bird: The Legend of Charlie Parker.* New York: Da Capo Press, 1973.

————. *The Jazz Titans.* New York: Doubleday, 1960.

————. *The Literature of Jazz: A Preliminary Biography.* New York: New York Public Library, 1954.

Rivelli, Pauline, and Robert Levin. *Giants of Black Music.* New York: Da Capo Press, 1965.

————. *Black Giants.* New York: World Publishing, 1970.

Roach, Hildred. *Black American Music.* Boston: Crescendo Publishing, 1973.

Roberts, John Storm. *Black Music of Two Worlds.* New York: Praeger, 1972.

Robinson, Julien L. *Band Leaders.* London: Rockliff, 1950.

Rose, Al, and Edmond Souchon. *New Orleans Jazz: A Family Album.* Baton Rouge: Louisiana State University Press, 1967.

Rublowsky, John. *Black Music in America.* New York: Basic Books, 1971.

Russell, Ross. *Bird Lives!* New York: Charterhouse, 1973.

————. *Jazz Style in Kansas City and the Southwest.* Berkeley: University of California Press, 1971.

Sanford, Herb. *Tommy and Jimmy: The Dorsey Years.* New York: Da Capo Press, 1972.

Sargeant, Winthrop. *Jazz: Hot and Hybrid.* New York: Da Capo Press, 1975.

Schafer, William J. *Brass Bands and New Orleans Jazz.* Baton Rouge: Louisiana State University Press, 1977.

Schuller, Gunther. *Early Jazz.* New York: Oxford University Press, 1968.

Scott, Allen. *Jazz Educated, Man.* Washington, DC: American International Publishers, 1973.

Seldes, Gilbert V. *The Seven Lively Arts.* New York: Harper, 1924.

Shapiro, Nat, and Nat Hentoff, eds. *Hear Me Talkin' to Ya.* New York: Rinehart, 1955.

Shapiro, Nat. *The Jazz Makers.* New York: Rinehart, 1957.

Shaw, Arnold. *Honkers and Shouters: The Golden Years of Rhythm and Blues.* New York: Macmillan, 1978.

————. *52nd Street.* New York: Da Capo, 1971.

Shaw, Artie. *The Trouble with Cinderella.* New York: Farrar, Straus and Young, 1952.

Sidran, Ben. *Black Talk.* New York: Holt, Rinehart and Winston, 1971.

Simon, George T. *The Big Bands.* New York: Macmillan, 1967.

————. *The Feeling of Jazz.* New York: Simon & Schuster, 1961.

————. *Glenn Miller and His Orchestra.* New York: Crowell, 1964.

Simpkins, Cuthbert Ormond. *Coltrane.* New York: Herndon House, 1975.

Simosko, Vladimir, and Barry Tepperman. *Eric Dolphy.* New York: Da Capo, 1979.

Smith, Charles Edward, with Frederick Ramsey, Jr., Charles Payne Rogers, and William Russell. *The Jazz Record Book.* New York: Smith & Durrell, 1942.

Smith, Jay D., and Len Guttridge. *Jack Teagarden: The Story of a Jazz Maverick.* London: Cassell, 1960.

Smith, Willie the Lion, with George Hoefer. *Music on My Mind.* New York: Da Capo Press, 1975.

Southern, Eileen. *The Music of Black Americans.* New York: W.W. Norton, 1971.

————. *Readings in Black American Music.* New York: W.W. Norton, 1971.

Spaeth, Sigmund. *A History of Popular Music in America.* New York: Random House, 1948.

Spellman, A.B. *Black Music: Four Lives (Four Lives in the Bebop Business).* New York: Schocken, 1973.

Stearns, Marshall. *The Story of Jazz.* New York: Oxford University Press, 1956.

Stewart, Rex. *Jazz Masters of the Thirties.* New York: Macmillan, 1972.

Stoddard, T. *Pops Foster, the Autobiography of a New Orleans Jazzman.* Berkeley: University of California Press, 1971.

Sudhalter, Richard M., and Philip R. Evans with William Dean-Myatt. *Bix, Man and Legend.* New Rochelle: Arlington House, 1974.

Terkel, Studs. *Giants of Jazz.* New York: Crowell, 1957.

Thomas, J.C. *Chasin' the Trane.* New York: Doubleday, 1975.

Toll, Robert C. *Blacking Up.* New York: Oxford University Press, 1974.

Ulanov, Barry. *Duke Ellington.* New York: Creative Age, 1946.

———. *Handbook of Jazz.* New York: Viking Press, 1957.

———. *A History of Jazz in America.* New York: Viking Press, 1952.

———. *The Incredible Crosby.* New York: Whittlesey House, 1948.

Vance, Joel. *Fats Waller: His Life and Times.* Chicago: Contemporary Books, 1977.

Walton, Ortiz M. *Music: Black, White and Blue.* New York: William Morrow, 1972.

Wareing, Charles H., and George Barlick. *Bugles for Beiderbecke.* London: Sidgwick and Jackson, 1958.

Waters, Ethel, and Charles Samuels. *His Eye Is on the Sparrow.* New York: Doubleday, 1951.

Wells, Dickie, with Stanley Dance. *The Night People.* Boston: Crescendo Publishing, 1971.

Whiteman, Paul, and Mary Margaret McBride. *Jazz.* New York: J.H. Sears, 1926.

Williams, Martin, ed. *The Art of Jazz: Essays on the Nature and Development of Jazz.* New York: Oxford University Press, 1959.

Williams, Martin. *Jazz Masters in Transition, 1957–69.* New York: Macmillan, 1970.

———. *Jelly Roll Morton.* New York: A.S. Barnes, 1963.

———. *King Oliver.* New York: A.S. Barnes, 1961.

———. *Jazz Masters of New Orleans.* New York: Macmillan, 1967.

———. *The Jazz Tradition.* New York: Oxford University Press, 1970.

———, ed. *Jazz Panorama: From the Pages of Jazz Review.* New York: Crowell-Collier, 1962.

———. *Where's the Melody?* New York: Pantheon, 1966.

Wilmer, Valerie. *As Serious As Your Life.* Westport, CT: Lawrence Hill, 1980.

———. *Jazz People.* Indianapolis: Bobbs-Merrill, 1970.

Wilson, John S. *The Collector's Jazz: Traditional and Swing.* New York: Lippincott, 1958.

———. *The Collector's Jazz: Modern.* New York: Lippincott, 1959.

———. *Jazz: The Transition Years, 1940–1960.* New York: Appleton-Century-Crofts, 1966.